Economists have always recognized that human endeavors are constrained by our limited and uncertain knowledge, but only recently has an accepted theory of uncertainty and information evolved. This theory has turned out to have surprisingly practical applications: for example in analyzing stockmarket returns, in evaluating accident prevention measures, and in assessing patent and copyright laws. This book presents these intellectual advances in a readable form for the first time. It unifies many important but partial results into a satisfying single picture, making it clear how the economics of uncertainty and information generalizes and extends standard economic analysis.

Part I of the volume covers the economics of uncertainty: how each person adapts to a given fixed state of knowledge by making an optimal choice among the immediate "terminal" actions available. These choices in turn determine the overall market equilibrium reflecting the social distribution of risk bearing. In part II, covering the economics of information, the state of knowledge is no longer held fixed. Instead, individuals can to a greater or lesser extent overcome their ignorance by "informational" actions. The text also addresses at appropriate points many specific topics such as insurance, the Capital Asset Pricing Model, auctions, deterrence of entry, and research and invention.

# The analytics of uncertainty and information

# CAMBRIDGE SURVEYS OF ECONOMIC LITERATURE

*Editor*
Professor Mark Perlman, University of Pittsburgh

The literature of economics is expanding rapidly, and many subjects have changed out of recognition within the space of a few years. Perceiving the state of knowledge in fast-developing subjects is difficult for students and time-consuming for professional economists. This series of books is intended to help with this problem. Each book gives a clear structure to and balanced overview of the topic, and is written at a level intelligible to the senior undergraduate. They will therefore be useful for teaching but will also provide a mature yet compact presentation of the subject for economists wishing to update their knowledge outside their own specialism.

# The analytics of uncertainty and information

Jack Hirshleifer

*and*

John G. Riley

*University of California, Los Angeles*

CAMBRIDGE
UNIVERSITY PRESS

Published by the Press Syndicate of the University of Cambridge
The Pitt Building, Trumpington Street, Cambridge CB2 1RP
40 West 20th Street, New York, NY 10011-4211, USA
10 Stamford Road, Oakleigh, Melbourne 3166, Australia

© Cambridge University Press 1992

First published 1992
Reprinted 1993

Printed in Great Britain at the University Press, Cambridge

*A catalogue record for this book is available from the British Library*

*Library of Congress cataloguing in publication data applied for*

ISBN 0 521 23956 7 hardback
ISBN 0 521 28369 8 paperback

UP

# Contents

* Starred sections represent more difficult or specialized materials that can be omitted without significant loss of continuity.

# Acknowledgments

The number of people who have made helpful contributions is very great indeed. In particular we are indebted to the following current or former UCLA graduate students for their assistance: Svend Albaek, Nigel Chalk, Alex David, Maxim Engers, Deborah Frohman, Gerry Garvey, Geoffrey Hosta, Kwanho Kim, Son Ku Kim, Fernando Losada, Wai-Nang Po, and Eduardo Siandra.

# Introduction: The economics of uncertainty and information

All human endeavors are constrained by our limited and uncertain knowledge – about external events past, present, and future; about the laws of Nature, God, and man; about our own productive and exchange opportunities; about how other people and even we ourselves are likely to behave. Economists have of course always recognized the all-pervasive influence of inadequate information, and its correlate of risk, on human affairs. But only in the period after the Second World War did an accepted *theory of uncertainty and information* begin to evolve. This theory provides a rigorous foundation for the analysis of individual decision-making and of market equilibrium, under conditions where economic agents are unsure about their own situations and/or about the opportunities offered them by market dealings.

With recent explosive progress in the analysis of uncertainty, the topic can no longer be described as neglected. Nor have the advances been "merely academic." The economic theory of uncertainty and information now flourishes not only in departments of economics but in professional schools and programs oriented toward business, government and administration, and public policy. In the world of commerce, stockmarket analysts now regularly report measures of share-price uncertainty devised by economic theorists. Even in government and the law, formal analysis of uncertainty is beginning to play a role in dealing with issues like safety and health, allowable return on investment, and income distribution.

Unfortunately, these new advances have not taken a form comprehensible to the general economic reader. Brilliant intellectual progress often appears in erratic and idiosyncratic guise; novel terminologies, approaches, and modes of thought can easily hamper understanding. That has certainly been the case here. Even specialists in some areas of the economics of uncertainty and information often find it hard to grasp the import of closely related research originating from a slightly different angle. As a related point, early explorers may have mistaken the part for the whole – a foothill for the mountain, an outlying peninsula for the mainland. Specifically, some scientific contributions that have appeared under ambitious titles like "the economics of information" or the "economics of uncertainty" actually deal only with tiny portions of those large subjects.

We view our task mainly as one of integration: unifying these important though partial new results and concepts into a satisfying single picture. We would not want to claim that our own view of the whole is the only one logically possible or useful. But we believe that it is an outlook with many appealing and satisfying features: (1) it goes far in de-mystifying the topic; (2) with certain significant exceptions, it provides a natural taxonomy for essentially all the major problems that have been studied; and (3) most important of all, our approach makes it clear that the economics of uncertainty and information is not a totally new field utterly disconnected from previous economic reasoning, but is rather a natural generalization and extension of standard economic analysis.

A first fundamental distinction is between the *economics of uncertainty* and the *economics of information*. In the economics of uncertainty, each person adapts to his or her given state of limited information by choosing the best "terminal" action available. In the economics of information, in contrast, individuals can attempt to *overcome* their ignorance by "informational" actions designed to generate or otherwise acquire new knowledge before a final decision is made. Put another way, in the economics of uncertainty the individual is presumed to act on the basis of *current fixed beliefs* (e.g., deciding whether or not to carry an umbrella in accordance with one's present estimate of the chance of rain). In the economics of information, a person typically is trying to arrive at improved beliefs – for example, by studying a weather report or by looking at a barometer before deciding to take the umbrella.

A second crucial distinction is between *market uncertainty* and *event uncertainty*. Were there only market uncertainty, everyone would be fully certain about his or her own preferences, endowment, and productive opportunities. A person would be unsure only about the supply–demand offers of other economic agents. Under the heading of market uncertainty, the central topics are optimal search for trading partners on the individual level of analysis and, on the economy-wide level of analysis, disequilibrium processes and price dynamics. In a world subject only to *event* uncertainty, in contrast, all market prices would be fully known. Each individual would be uncertain only about exogenous occurrences as they affect his or her own personal circumstances or the market as a whole. These uncertain contingencies might concern resource endowments (will the wheat crop be large or small?), or productive opportunities (will fusion power be available in the near future?), or public policy (will taxes be cut?). Thus, market uncertainty concerns the *endogenous* variables of the economic system, event uncertainty the *exogenous* variables.

The present text is limited to the relatively more tractable topic of *event uncertainty*. This limitation permits us to employ the traditional model of perfect markets in which all dealings take place at equilibrium prices. While we have omitted market uncertainty with its attendant phenomena of search and dynamic convergence to equilibrium, that is not because we regard it as unimportant. On the contrary, market uncertainty has highly significant normative and positive implications, for microeconomics and macroeconomics both. But, we felt, market uncertainty is too big and too complex a topic to be integrated with event uncertainty within the space limits and for the analytical level of this volume.

The sequence of topics in this book is guided by the pedagogical principle of advancing from the easy to the difficult, from the familiar to the more strange and exotic. Part I deals with terminal actions only – the economics of uncertainty. The first three chapters analyze the optimal risk-involved decisions of the individual. Chapter 4 moves on to the market as a whole, showing how the overall equilibrium that determines the prices of risky assets also distributes social risks among all individuals in the economy.

Part II turns to the economics of information. Starting with a discussion of the value of better information in chapter 5, we then explore the effect of autonomously *emergent* information upon the market equilibrium solution (chapter 6). Chapter 7 examines the incentives for expenditures on information gathering (research and development). The issue of information leakage via changes in asset prices is also considered. Chapter 8 then analyzes contracting between two agents, one of whom has only imperfect information about the other's preferences (hidden knowledge) or is unable to observe the other's behavior (hidden actions). We show how the former condition leads to adverse selection in markets while the latter results in moral hazard.

With imperfect information about other agents' preferences, the standard Nash equilibrium concept often produces multiple equilibria, some of which seem intuitively implausible. Chapter 9 reviews various efforts to refine the notion of equilibrium. The following two chapters employ these refinements to examine individual behavior and market equilibrium in environments with hidden knowledge. Finally, in chapter 12 we consider additional issues that arise when interactions among agents are repeated over long or indefinite time periods.

Our mode of exposition will be highly eclectic. "Literary" reasoning, geometrical demonstration, and analytical proofs are all employed from time to time – as called for by the nature of the topic, by the psychological need for variety, and by our desire to illustrate all the major forms of economic argument arising in these contexts. In addition, certain more advanced topics are separated from the main text in specially marked starred sections which can be omitted with minimal loss of continuity. Finally, mixed with the more purely formal portions of our analysis will be applications to important real-world phenomena such as insurance, securities markets, corporate financial structures, the use of experts and agents, group decisions where returns and risks are shared, and the value of education.

# Part I

# 1    Elements of decision under uncertainty

Every individual must choose among *acts* – or synonymously, he or she must make *decisions*, or select among *actions*, *options*, or *moves*. And, where there is uncertainty, Nature may be said to "choose" the *state of the world* (or *state*, for short). You decide whether or not to carry an umbrella; Nature "decides" on rain or sunshine. Table 1.1 pictures an especially simple $2 \times 2$ situation. Your alternative acts $x = (1, 2)$ are shown along the left margin, and Nature's alternative states $s = (1, 2)$ across the top. The body of the table shows the *consequences* $c_{xs}$ resulting from your choice of act $x$ and Nature's choice of state $s$.

More generally the individual under uncertainty will, according to this analysis, specify the following elements of his decision problem:

(1) a *set of acts* $(1, \dots, x, \dots, X)$ available to him;
(2) a *set of states* $(1, \dots, s, \dots, S)$ available to Nature;
(3) a *consequence function* $c(x, s)$ showing outcomes under all combinations of acts and states.

And, in addition:

(4) a *probability function* $\pi(s)$ expressing his beliefs (as to the likelihood of Nature choosing each and every state);
(5) an *elementary-utility function* (or *preference-scaling function*) $v(c)$ measuring the desirability of the different possible consequences to him.

We will explain below how the "Expected-utility Rule" integrates all these elements so as to enable the individual to decide upon the most advantageous action. Put another way, we will show how the economic agent can derive a personal preference ordering of his possible *acts* from his given preference scaling over *consequences*.

COMMENT: The approach here does not allow for the psychological sensations of vagueness or confusion that people often suffer in facing situations with uncertain (risky) outcomes. In our model the individual is neither vague nor confused. While recognizing that his knowledge is imperfect, so that he cannot be sure which state of the world will occur, he

Table 1.1. *Consequences of alternative acts and states*

|      |       | States |        |
|------|-------|--------|--------|
|      |       | $s = 1$ | $s = 2$ |
| Acts | $x = 1$ | $c_{11}$ | $c_{12}$ |
|      | $x = 2$ | $c_{21}$ | $c_{22}$ |

nevertheless can assign exact numerical probabilities representing his degree of belief as to the likelihood of each possible state. Our excuse for not picturing vagueness or confusion is that we are trying to model economics, not psychology. Even the very simplest models in economic textbooks, for example indifference-curve diagrams, implicitly postulate a degree of precise self-knowledge that is descriptively unrealistic. The ultimate justification, for indifference-curve diagrams or for theories of decision under uncertainty, is the ability of such models to help us understand and predict behavior.

## 1.1     The menu of acts

There are two main classes of individual actions: *terminal* moves versus *informational* moves. Here in part I of the book we consider a simplified world where only terminal acts are available, so that the individual is limited to making the best of his or her existing combination of knowledge and ignorance. An example of terminal action under uncertainty is the statistical problem of coming to a decision on the basis of sample evidence now in hand: for instance, when a regulatory agency has to decide whether or not to approve a new drug on the basis of experimental test results. We will be considering terminal actions of this type, and especially the risk-involved decisions of *individuals in markets*: whether or not to purchase insurance, to buy or sell stocks and bonds, to participate in a partnership, etc. Anticipating a bit, a key theme of our analysis will be that markets allow decision-makers to share risks and returns in ways that accord with the particular preferences and opportunities of the different transactors.

Part II of the book will be covering *informational* actions – decisions concerning whether and how to improve upon one's state of knowledge before making a terminal move. In the class of informational actions would fall statistical choices such as how much additional evidence to collect before coming to a terminal decision, what sampling technique to employ, etc. Once again, our emphasis will be on ways of acquiring new information *through markets*. Knowledge can be acquired by direct market purchase – by buying newspapers for weather and stockmarket reports, by undergoing a course of training to gain "know-how" in a trade, or by employing an expert for private advice. Rather less obviously, markets open up an indirect means of acquiring information: for example, a person can observe the market choices of better-informed traders, or might draw inferences from people's reputations acquired in the course of their previous market dealings. Or, a producing firm might imitate other commercially successful firms. But these interesting phenomena involving information-involved actions will have to be set aside until part II.

## 1.2    The probability function

We assume that each person is able to represent his beliefs as to the likelihood of the different states of the world (e.g., as to whether Nature will choose rain or shine) by a "subjective" probability distribution (Irving Fisher, 1912, chapter 16; Leonard J. Savage, 1954). Assuming discrete states of the world, the individual is supposed to be able to assign to each state $s$ a degree of belief, in the form of numerical weights $\pi_s$ lying between zero and one inclusive, and summing to unity: $\Sigma_s \pi_s = 1$. In the extreme case, if the person were certain that some particular state $s$ would be occurring, the full probabilistic weight of unity would be assigned to that state. Then $\pi_s = 1$, so that zero probability is attached to every other state in the set $1, \ldots, s, \ldots, S$. More generally, a high degree of subjective assurance will be reflected by a relatively "tight" probability distribution over the range of possible states; a high degree of doubt would be reflected by a wide dispersion.

At times we shall find it will be more convenient to assume that the variable or variables defining the state of the world vary continuously (rather than discretely) so that the number of distinct states is uncountably infinite. Here the probability of any exact single state coming about is regarded as zero ("infinitesimal"), although the event is not *impossible*. Making use of a continuous state-defining variable $s$, where $s$ can be any real number between 0 and $S$, the individual's subjective probability beliefs would be represented by a probability density function $\pi(s)$ such that $\int_0^S \pi(s)\,ds = 1$.

### 1.2.1    *Risk versus uncertainty*

A number of economists have attempted to distinguish between risk and uncertainty, as originally proposed by Frank H. Knight (1921, pp. 20, 226). (1) "Risk," Knight said, refers to situations where an individual is able to calculate probabilities on the basis of an *objective* classification of instances. For example, in tossing a fair die the chance of any single one of the six faces showing is exactly one-sixth. (2) "Uncertainty," he contended, refers to situations where no objective classification is possible, for example in estimating whether or not a cure for cancer will be discovered in the next decade.

In this book we disregard Knight's distinction, which has proved to be a sterile one. For our purposes risk and uncertainty mean the same thing. It does not matter, we contend, whether an "objective" classification is or is not possible. For, we will be dealing throughout with a "subjective" probability concept (as developed especially by Savage, 1954): probability is simply *degree of belief*. In fact, even in cases like the toss of a die where assigning "objective" probabilities appears possible, such an appearance is really illusory. That the chance of any single face turning up is one-sixth is a valid inference *only if the die is a fair one* – a condition about which no one could ever be "objectively" certain. Decision-makers are therefore never in Knight's world of risk but instead always in his world of uncertainty. That the alternative approach, assigning probabilities on the basis of subjective degree of belief, is a workable and fruitful procedure will be shown constructively throughout the book.

### 1.2.2   "Hard" versus "soft" probabilities

While we have not been able to accept Knight's attempt to distinguish between risk and uncertainty, he was getting at – though imperfectly expressing – an important and valid point. In his discussion Knight suggested that a person's actions may well depend upon his "estimate of the chance that his estimates are correct," or, we shall say, upon his *confidence in his beliefs*. This brings us to a distinction between "hard" versus "soft" probability estimates.

Suppose that for purposes of an immediate bet you had to estimate the probability of heads coming up on the next toss of coin A – the coin having been previously tested many times by you and found to have historically come up heads and tails with just about equal frequency. If you are a reasonable person you would assign a degree of belief (subjective probability) of about 0·5 to heads, and you would be rather confident about that number. In contrast, imagine instead that you are dealing with coin B, about which you know absolutely nothing. You have not even been able to inspect it to verify whether it is possibly two-tailed or two-headed. Nevertheless, if you *had* to pick some single number you would be compelled again to assign 0·5 probability to heads coming up on the next toss, since as a reasonable person you lack any basis for a greater or lesser degree of belief in heads than tails. But, your *confidence* in the 0·5 figure for coin B would surely be much less.

It is not the psychological sensation of confidence or doubt that interests us, but the possible implications for decisions. If the same probability assignment of 0·5 will be made either way, as has just been argued, is there any action-relevant difference between the two cases? The answer is NO, if you are committed to *terminal* action. If you must bet now on the basis of your current information, 0·5 is the relevant probability for guiding your choice of heads or tails. In either situation, you have no grounds for thinking heads more likely or tails more likely. But the answer is YES, there is indeed a difference between the two situations if you have the option of *informational* action. When this option is available, you should be more willing to invest money or effort to obtain additional information about coin B than about coin A. In short, greater prior doubt (lesser degree of confidence) makes it more important to acquire additional evidence before making a terminal move. So we see that a person's *informational* actions, though not his *terminal* actions, do depend upon his confidence in his beliefs – in Knight's language, upon his "estimate of the chance that his estimates are correct." Confidence will be an important topic in part II of the book, where we cover the economics of information, but will not be involved in our more elementary treatment of the economics of uncertainty in part I.

EXERCISES AND EXCURSIONS 1.2

*1 Consistency of probability beliefs*

An individual believes that credible information will soon arrive in the form of news about the probability of rain. He believes there is a 50% chance that the news will be "rain certain," a 30% chance that the news will be "no rain," and a 20% chance that the news will be "rain with probability 0·5." Is this consistent with his currently believing that the odds in favor of rain are 2:1?

ANSWER: The last sentence implies an estimate of the probability of rain, prior to receiving the news, of $\frac{2}{3}$. For this to be consistent with his beliefs as to what he thinks the new information will reveal, it would have to be that:

$$50\%(1·0) + 30\%(0) + 20\%(0·5) = \tfrac{2}{3}$$

Since this is an *untrue* equation, his current beliefs about the chance of rain are not consistent with his beliefs about what the arriving information will reveal.

## 2 *Information and confidence*

In terms of the chances of a coin coming up heads, suppose there are three states of the world regarded as possible:

        State 1:  chance of heads is 100% [coin is 2-headed]

        State 2:  chance of heads is 50% [coin is fair]

        State 3:  chance of heads is 0% [coin is 2-tailed]

An individual initially assigns equal probabilities $(\pi_1, \pi_2, \pi_3) = (\frac{1}{3}, \frac{1}{3}, \frac{1}{3})$ to all three states.

(A)  For an immediate bet (terminal action), what is his best estimate for the probability $p$ of heads on the next toss?

(B)  Suppose new information were now to change his probability vector to $(\pi_1, \pi_2, \pi_3) = (0, 1, 0)$. What can you now say about his best estimate for $p$? What has happened to his *confidence* in that estimate?

(C)  Same question if, instead, the new information changed his probability vector to $(\frac{1}{2}, 0, \frac{1}{2})$.

ANSWER:

(A)  His best estimate is:

$$\tfrac{1}{3}(1) + \tfrac{1}{3}(0{\cdot}5) + \tfrac{1}{3}(0) = \tfrac{1}{2}$$

(B)  His best estimate obviously remains $\frac{1}{2}$. But his *confidence* that the true $p$ actually is $\frac{1}{2}$ has now increased, indeed that confidence is as high as it can possibly be.

(C)  Once again his best estimate, for the purposes of a bet on the next toss of the coin, is $p = \frac{1}{2}$. But he can have no confidence at all in that estimate. Indeed, since he has learned that the coin is either two-headed or two-tailed, he is absolutely sure that the true $p$ – i.e., the parameter of the process actually at work when the coin is tossed – *cannot* be $\frac{1}{2}$.

## 1.3      The consequence function

As shown in table 1.1, each *consequence* is the outcome of an economic agent's choice of action combined with Nature's "choice" of the state of the world. In principle, the consequence is a full description of all aspects of the individual's environment resulting from such an interaction. For example, if someone decides not to carry an umbrella and Nature chooses rain, the consequences might include getting wet, being late for work, and a variety of other discomforts. But we shall mainly be concerned with consequences describable in terms of alternative *baskets of consumption goods* that enter into individuals' preference functions. Very frequently we shall deal with an even more simple picture in which consequences take the form of entitlements to a single summary variable like monetary *income*.

Consequences might be quantities certain, or might themselves be probabilistic – depending upon how states of the world are described. If the states are defined deterministically, as in "Coin shows heads," and supposing the action chosen was "Bet \$1 at even money on heads," then the consequence would be "Win one dollar." But states of the world can sometimes be defined as probabilistic processes. The relevant states might be "Coin has 50% chance of coming up heads" versus "Coin is biased to have 75% chance of coming up heads." Here the act "Bet on heads" will be reflected, in either state of the world, by an uncertain consequence taking the form of a specified chance of winning the dollar.

## 1.4     The utility function and the Expected-utility Rule

Utility attaches directly to consequences, and only derivatively to actions. A surprising amount of intellectual turmoil has been caused by failure to appreciate this simple distinction. To minimize the chances for confusion we shall use the notation $v(c)$ to represent a person's *preference-scaling function* (or *elementary-utility function*) over the consequences $c$; the notation $U(x)$ will be used for his derived preference ordering over his actions $x$.

A CRUCIAL DISTINCTION

$v(c)$ is a preference-scaling function defined over consequences

$U(x)$ is the utility function defined over actions

The analytical problem is to explain and justify this derivation, that is, to show how, given his direct preferences over *consequences*, the individual can order the desirability of the *actions* available to him.

To choose an act is to choose one of the rows of a consequence matrix like table 1.1. Since the individual is also supposed to have attached a probability (degree of belief) to the occurrence of every state, each such row can be regarded as a probability distribution. We may therefore think of a person as choosing among probability distributions or "prospects." A convenient notation for the "prospect" associated with an act $x$, whose uncertain consequences $c_x = (c_{x1}, c_{x2}, ..., c_{xS})$ are to be received with respective state-probabilities $\pi = (\pi_1, \pi_2, ..., \pi_S)$ – the probabilities summing, of course, to unity – is:

$$x \equiv (c_{x1}, c_{x2}, ..., c_{xS}; \pi_1, \pi_2, ..., \pi_S)$$

The crucial step is to connect the $v(c)$ function for consequences with the utility ordering $U(x)$ of acts. We can take this step using the famous "Expected-utility Rule" of John von Neumann and Oskar Morgenstern (1944, pp. 15–31):

EXPECTED-UTILITY RULE

$$U(x) \equiv \pi_1 v(c_{x1}) + \pi_2 v(c_{x2}) + \ldots + \pi_S v(c_{xS}) \qquad (1.4.1)$$

$$\equiv \sum_{s=1}^{S} \pi_s v(c_{xs})$$

This says that the utility $U(x)$ of act $x$ is calculable in an especially simple way: to wit, as the mathematical expectation (the probability-weighted average) of the elementary utilities $v(c_{xs})$ of the associated consequences. Note that equation (1.4.1) is simply additive over states of the world, which means that the consequence $c_{xs}$ realized in any state $s$ in no way affects the preference scaling $v(c_{xs^o})$ of consequences in any other state $s^o$. Equation (1.4.1) is also linear in the probabilities, another very specific and special functional form. As the Neumann–Morgenstern Expected-utility Rule is absolutely crucial for our theory of decision under uncertainty, we shall be devoting considerable space to it.

It turns out that the Expected-utility rule is applicable *if and only if the $v(c)$ function has been determined in a particular way that has been termed the assignment of " cardinal" utilities to consequences.* More specifically, the proposition that we will be attempting to explain and justify (though not rigorously proving) can be stated as follows:

> Given certain "postulates of rational choice," there is a way of assigning a cardinal preference-scaling function $v(c)$ *over consequences* such that the Expected-utility Rule determines the individual's preference ranking $U(x)$ *over actions.*

A "cardinal" variable is one that can be measured quantitatively, like altitude, time, or temperature. While different measuring scales might be employed, such scales can diverge only in zero-point and unit-interval. Temperature, for example, can be measured according to the Celsius or the Fahrenheit scales; 32° Fahrenheit is 0° Celsius, and each degree up or down of Celsius is 1·8° up or down of Fahrenheit. Similarly, altitude could be measured from sea level or from the center of the Earth (shift of zero-point) and in feet or meters (shift of unit-interval). Cardinal variables have the following property: regardless of shift of zero-point and unit-interval, the relative magnitudes of *differences* remains unchanged. The altitude difference between the base and crest of Mount Everest exceeds the difference between the foundation and roof of even the tallest man-made building – whether we measure in feet above sea level or in meters from the center of the Earth.

In dealing with certainty choices, standard economic theory treats utility (intensity of preference) as an *ordinal* rather than a cardinal variable. The individual, it is postulated, can say "I prefer basket A to basket B." He is not required to quantify *how much* he prefers A to B. Put another way, if any given preference-scaling function in the form of an assignment of cardinal numbers to consequences (consumption baskets) correctly describes choices under certainty, so will any ordinal (positive monotonic) transformation of that function. Suppose that, for choices not involving risks, some scale $u$ of cardinal numbers was attached as preference labels to consequences – where of course higher $u$ indicates greater level of satisfaction. Then any positive monotonic transformation of those numbers would lead to the same decisions. For example, suppose an individual always prefers more consumption income $c$ to less. Then we might say, "He is trying to maximize the function $u = c$." But the income level that maximizes $u$ also maximizes log $u$ or $e^u$, both of which are positive monotonic transformations of $u$. So $u = e^c$ or $u = \log c$ could equally well have served to indicate the preference scaling. More formally, if $u$ is a satisfactory function for choices under certainty, then so is $\hat{u} \equiv F(u)$, provided only that the first derivative is positive – $F'(u) > 0$.

In contrast, when it comes to choices under *uncertainty*, the Expected-utility Rule is applicable only if the preference-scaling function $v(c)$ has been constructed in a particular way that provides fewer degrees of freedom. In fact, as will shortly be seen, given any initially satisfactory $v(c)$ function, only the *cardinal* (positive linear, rather than positive monotonic) transformations of $v(c)$ will leave preference rankings unchanged. Formally, if $v(c)$ satisfactorily describes the individual's choices under uncertainty, then so does $\hat{v} = \alpha + \beta v$, where $\alpha$ is any constant and $\beta$ is any positive constant.

Why are all the positive monotonic transformations of the preference-scaling function permissible in the riskless case, while only the positive *linear* transformations are allowed when it comes to risky choices? In the absence of uncertainty, deciding upon an action is immediately equivalent to selecting a single definite consequence. It follows that if someone can rank *consequences* in terms of preferences he has already determined the preference ordering of his *actions* – which is all that is needed for purposes of decision. But in dealing with risky choices it is not immediately evident how a ranking of consequences leads to an ordering of actions, since each action will in general imply a probabilistic mix of possible consequences. The great contribution of Neumann and Morgenstern was to show that, given plausible assumptions about individual preferences, it is possible to construct a $v(c)$ function – "cardinal" in that only positive linear transformations thereof are permissible – whose *joint* use with the Expected-utility Rule (1.4.1) will lead to the correct ordering of actions.

### 1.4.1    The Expected-utility Rule: informal presentation

To formally justify the joint use of a cardinal preference-scaling function and the Expected-utility Rule, for dealing with choices among risky prospects, involves a somewhat higher order of technical difficulty. What follows here is an informal presentation (based mainly upon Robert Schlaifer, 1959) illustrating, by direct construction, how the required type of preference-scaling function can be developed.

For the purpose of this discussion, assume that the consequences $c$ are simply amounts of income a person might receive. Let $m$ represent the worst possible consequence (the smallest amount of income) that can occur with positive probability, and $M$ the best possible consequence (the largest amount of income). More income is preferred to less – so the individual already has, to begin with, an *ordinal* utility scale. The problem is to "cardinalize" this scale, that is, to show that there is a way of assigning numerical values (arbitrary only with respect to zero-point and unit-interval) to the degrees of preference associated with all levels of income. These values must be rising with income, else they would not be consistent with the given ordinal preference ("more is preferred to less"). But the chosen scale must also lead to correct answers when used in conjunction with the Expected-utility Rule. The method we shall employ to establish such a cardinal scale is called "the reference-lottery technique."

Consider any level of income $c^*$ between $m$ and $M$. Imagine that the individual is faced with the choice between $c^*$ and some "reference lottery" having the form $(M, m; \pi, 1 - \pi)$ in prospect notation. That is, he has a choice between $c^*$ for certain versus a gamble yielding the best possible outcome $M$ with probability $\pi$ and the worst possible outcome $m$ with probability $1 - \pi$. We shall suppose that the individual can say to himself: "When $\pi$ becomes very close to unity, I surely will prefer the gamble; for lotteries with $\pi$ very close to zero, I surely prefer the certainty of $c^*$. Consequently, in between there must be some intermediate probability $\pi^*$ of success in the reference lottery, such that I am exactly indifferent between the certain income $c^*$ and the prospect $(M, m; \pi^*, 1 - \pi^*)$." After due introspection, we assume, the individual can in fact specify this $\pi^*$. The $\pi^*$ so derived is a cardinal measure of the utility of income level $c^*$ for him. That is: $v(c^*) = \pi^*$.[1] Or, more elaborately:

$$v(c^*) \equiv U(M, m; \pi^*, 1 - \pi^*) \equiv \pi^* \tag{1.4.2}$$

An individual proceeding to assign cardinal preference values to income in

[1] Because shifts of zero-point and unit-interval are permissible for cardinal scaling, more generally we can write $v(c^*) = \alpha + \beta\pi^*$, for arbitrary $\alpha$ and $\beta > 0$. We will henceforth ignore this uninteresting generalization.

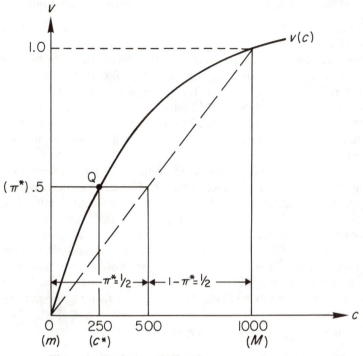

Figure 1.1 Preference-scaling function

this way will generate a $v(c)$ function over the range $m \leqslant c \leqslant M$, which can be employed with the Expected-utility Rule (1.4.1) to order his choices among actions.

Figure 1.1 illustrates a hypothetical individual situation. Let $m = 0$ and $M = 1,000$ (in dollars, we can suppose) be the extremes of income that need be considered. For the specific income $c^* = 250$, the person's success-in-equivalent-reference-lottery probability is assumed to be $\pi^* = 0.5$ – meaning that he finds himself indifferent between a sure income of \$250 and a 50% chance of winning in an income lottery whose alternative outcomes are \$1,000 or nothing. Then the utility assigned to the sure consequence \$250 is just $\frac{1}{2}$ – that is, $v(250) = 0.5$, determining the location of point Q on the $v(c)$ curve. Repeating this process, the reference-lottery technique generates the entire $v(c)$ curve between $m = 0$ and $M = 1,000$.

A full justification, showing why this particular procedure works to derive a suitable cardinal scale, requires a more formal analysis (to be touched on in section 1.4.2 below). But we can give the intuitive idea here. The essential point is that the $v(c)$ measure obtained via the reference-lottery technique is in the form of a *probability*, so that the Expected-utility

Rule (1.4.1) becomes equivalent to the standard formula for compounding probabilities.

### EXAMPLE 1.1

Imagine that the individual described in the text above finds that his reference-lottery utilities over the range $0 \leqslant c \leqslant 1,000$ satisfy the specific function $v(c) = (c/1,000)^{1/2}$. (This formula is consistent with the previously obtained point $v(250) = 0.5$.) Suppose he is now offered a choice between option A, representing \$250 for certain once again, and option B taking the form of a three-way prospect: $B = (810, 360, 160; 0.1, 0.5, 0.4)$. Which should he choose?

We already know that $v(250) = 0.5$: option A is equivalent to a reference lottery with 50 % chance of success. For the elements of option B, we can readily compute: $v(810) = 0.9$, $v(360) = 0.6$, and $v(160) = 0.4$. That is, in option B the high possible payoff of \$810 is equivalent in preference to a reference lottery with 90 % chance of success, the middling payoff \$360 is equivalent to a 60 % chance of success, and the poor payoff \$160 to a 40 % chance of success. Now we ask ourselves: What is the *overall* equivalent probability of success associated with option B? We can simply compute it by using the rule for compounding probabilities:

$$0.1(0.9) + 0.5(0.6) + 0.4(0.4) = 0.55$$

So prospect B offers, overall, the equivalent of a 0.55 chance of success in the reference lottery whereas option A was equivalent only to a 0.5 chance of success. Evidently, option B is better. The key point is that the equation leading to the 0.55 number, which we presented as the familiar formula for compounding probabilities, is also an instance of applying the Expected-utility Rule (1.4.1).

In short, the prescribed way of determining a cardinal $v(c)$ function for use with the Expected-utility Rule *makes it possible to interpret each $v(c)$ value as a probability* – to wit, the equivalent chance of success in a standardized reference lottery – and therefore to use the laws of compounding probabilities for determining the desirability of more complicated prospects.

A few additional comments:

1   We have been assuming here that consequences take the form of simple quantities of income. More generally, each consequence $c$ might be a basket (vector) of consumption goods. The same technique can be employed so long as the individual has an *ordinal* preference scaling of baskets (an indifference map) to begin with.

2   We have also assumed that the same $v(c)$ scale is applicable in each and every state of the world. But, if the states are defined as "rain versus shine," or "healthy versus sick," it might appear that attitudes toward

income and income risks, as reflected in the $v(c)$ function, could differ from state to state. We shall see in chapter 2, under the heading of "state-dependent utilities," how this difficulty can be handled.

3  Some people find it disturbing that the additive form of the Expected-utility Rule (1.4.1) excludes any "complementarities," positive or negative, between consequences in different states. For example, if consequences are simple incomes, a higher or lower income in any state $s^o$ is supposed in no way to affect the $v(c)$ number assigned to income received in any other state $s^*$. The reason is simple: incomes in the distinct states $s^o$ and $s^*$ can never be received *in combination* but only as *mutually exclusive alternatives*. There can be no complementarity where no possibility of jointness exists.

4  There has been some debate over whether or not the Neumann–Morgenstern analysis proves that utility is "really" cardinal rather than ordinal.[2] Some of the difficulty stems from confusion between the $v(c)$ and the $U(x)$ functions. The cardinality restriction applies to the $v(c)$ function – the preference scaling over *consequences*. But we are ultimately interested in the utility rankings of alternative *actions*, and when it comes to actions any ordinal transformation of an acceptable utility measure will always serve equally well. Suppose, for example, that use of the reference-lottery technique provides the needed preference-scaling function $v(c)$ such that an individual's *actions* (prospects) are correctly ordered by the expected-utility formula $U(x) = \Sigma_s \pi_s v(c_s)$. Then any positive monotonic transformation of $U(x)$, such as $\hat{U}(x) = e^{U(x)}$, would provide an equally correct ordering of the *actions*.

5  We have emphasized that the Neumann–Morgenstern analysis justifies this particular method of constructing a cardinal $v(c)$ scale only when jointly used with the Expected-utility Rule. Correspondingly, the Expected-utility Rule has not been "proved" to be true. All that has been shown is that there exists a way of constructing a $v(c)$ function that *makes* the Expected-utility Rule valid as a way of deriving preferences as to actions from given preferences as to consequences.

*1.4.2    The Expected-utility Rule: Axiom of complex gambles*
We are not providing here a formal proof of the Expected-utility Rule. Instead our objective is to clarify the crucial element in the proof, the principle of *non-complementarity of incomes in different states* (see comment 3 above). The formal postulate expressing this principle, the Axiom of complex gambles, is also sometimes known as the Independence axiom or the Substitution axiom.

---

[2]  See the argument put forward by William Baumol (1951) and the responses of Armen A. Alchian (1953) and Robert H. Strotz (1953).

*Axiom of complex gambles*: Suppose an individual is indifferent between two actions or prospects $x$ and $y$. Then, for any other prospect $z$ and any fixed probability $p$, he will be indifferent between a first complex lottery in which he receives $x$ with probability $p$ and $z$ otherwise, versus a second complex lottery yielding $y$ with probability $p$ and $z$ otherwise. Moreover, if he strictly prefers $x$ over $y$, he will strictly prefer the first complex lottery. Thus, using the symbol $\sim$ to indicate indifference and the symbol $\succ$ for strong preference:

$$\text{If } x \sim y, \quad \text{then: } (x, z; p, 1-p) \sim (y, z; p, 1-p)$$
$$\text{If } x \succ y, \quad \text{then: } (x, z; p, 1-p) \succ (y, z; p, 1-p)$$

This axiom would be violated if, in a complex prospect, the presence of $z$ differentially affected the attractiveness of $x$ relative to $y$ – i.e., if there were any complementarity effect. It might seem this could happen if, say, $x$ and $y$ were amounts of ordinary commodities like bread and margarine and $z$ were a commodity like butter (since butter is a consumption complement for bread but a substitute for margarine). However, in the complex prospects or lotteries dealt with here, positive or negative complementarity can never play a role – since the occurrence of $x$ in the one case or of $y$ in the other rules out $z$. An individual can never simultaneously enjoy both $x$ *and $z$* together, or both $y$ *and $z$.*

An immediate implication of this axiom is that, for two lotteries $x$ and $y$ such that $x \sim y$, we can *substitute* one for the other in any prospect in which either appears, without changing the relative preference ordering of prospects.

In the reference-lottery process, the $v(c)$ associated with any income level $c$ was determined by finding the probability of success in the reference lottery equally preferred to that income, i.e.:

$$\text{If } c \sim (M, m; \pi, 1-\pi), \quad \text{then } v(c) = \pi$$

Consider now two levels of income $c^o$ and $\hat{c}$ and their equivalent reference lotteries:

$$c^o \sim (M, m; \pi^o, 1-\pi^o) \quad \text{and} \quad \hat{c} \sim (M, m; \hat{\pi}, 1-\hat{\pi})$$

so that $v(c^o) = \pi^o$ and $v(\hat{c}) = \hat{\pi}$.

In what follows, it will be helpful to introduce the notation $l^*(\pi)$ to represent a reference lottery in which $M$ is the outcome with probability $\pi$ and $m$ is the outcome with probability $1-\pi$.

$$l^*(\pi) \equiv (M, m; \pi, 1-\pi)$$

Consider now two levels of income $c_1$ and $c_2$ and their equivalent reference lotteries $l^*(\pi_1)$ and $l^*(\pi_2)$. Then $v(c_1) = \pi_1$ and $v(c_2) = \pi_2$.

Suppose we wanted to find the preference equivalent of a lottery $(c_1, c_2; p, 1-p)$ involving consequences $c_1$ and $c_2$ with respective prob-

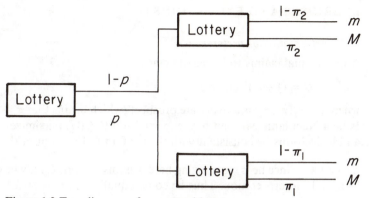

Figure 1.2 Tree diagram of compound lottery

abilities $p$ and $1-p$. Using the ability to *substitute* preference equivalent prospects:

$$c_1 \sim l^*(\pi_1) \Rightarrow (c_1, c_2; p, 1-p) \sim (l^*(\pi_1), c_2; p, 1-p)$$

Moreover:

$$c_2 \sim l^*(\pi_2) \Rightarrow (l^*(\pi_1), c_2; p, 1-p) \sim (l^*(\pi_1), l^*(\pi_2); p, 1-p)$$

Combining these implications:

$$(c_1, c_2; p, 1-p) \sim (l(\pi_1), l(\pi_2); p, 1-p) \tag{1.4.3}$$

The lottery on the right-hand side of (1.4.3) is depicted as a "tree diagram" in figure 1.2. Each box or "node" represents a point at which nature makes a move. Outcomes are indicated at the end of each branch of the tree.

At the initial node, nature "chooses" probabilistically between the two reference lotteries. Then, depending on this choice, one of the reference lotteries is played. Note that there are only two outcomes of this compound lottery, $M$ and $m$. Adding probabilities, outcome $M$ is reached with probability $p\pi_1 + (1-p)\pi_2$. Then the compound lottery is itself equivalent to a reference lottery:

$$(l^*(\pi_1), l^*(\pi_2); p, 1-p) = l^*(p\pi_1 + (1-p)\pi_2) \tag{1.4.4}$$

Combining (1.4.3) and (1.4.4) it follows that the individual is indifferent between $(c_1, c_2; p, 1-p)$ and a reference lottery in which the probability of success is $p\pi_1 + (1-p)\pi_2$. Since $\pi_1 \equiv v(c_1)$ and $\pi_2 \equiv v(c_2)$, it follows that:

$$U(c_1, c_2; p, 1-p) = p\pi_1 + (1-p)\pi_2$$
$$= pv(c_1) + (1-p)v(c_2)$$

Thus, the Axiom of complex gambles, which formalizes the principle of non-complementarity of income over states of the world, leads directly to the Neumann–Morgenstern Expected-utility Rule.

EXERCISES AND EXCURSIONS 1.4

*1 Transformation of preferences*

An individual claims to be maximizing:

$$U = (1 + c_1)^{\pi_1} (1 + c_2)^{\pi_2}$$

where $(c_1, c_2; \pi_1, \pi_2)$ is a two-state prospect (which means that $\pi_1 + \pi_2 = 1$). Is he a Neumann–Morgenstern expected-utility (EU) maximizer? Would all his decisions be consistent with those of an EU maximizer?

ANSWER: Since he is maximizing here over his *actions*, $U$ may be given an "ordinal" interpretation. Thus he could equally well maximize:

$$\hat{U} \equiv \ln U = \pi_1 \ln(1 + c_1) + \pi_2 \ln(1 + c_2)$$

This is the equivalent of maximizing expected utility if the "cardinal" preference-scaling function has the form:

$$v(c) = \ln(1 + c)$$

So in this case the individual's choices would indeed meet the Neumann–Morgenstern conditions.

*2 Indifference curves in consequence space*

(A) If the preference-scaling function is $v(c) = c^{\frac{1}{2}}$, where $c$ is income, suppose a person's preference ordering over actions or prospects in a 2-state world is given by:

$$U(c_1, c_2; \pi_1, \pi_2) = \pi_1 (c_1)^{\frac{1}{2}} + \pi_2 (c_2)^{\frac{1}{2}}$$

Depict the indifference curves in a diagram with $c_1$ on the horizontal axis and $c_2$ on the vertical axis (probabilities held constant). Show that each indifference curve touches the axes and is everywhere bowed toward the origin.

(B) If $U = \Sigma_1^2 \pi_2 v(c_s)$ and $v(\cdot)$ is a strictly concave function, show that if the individual is indifferent between $(c_1, c_2)$ and $(c_1', c_2')$ he will strictly prefer the convex combination $(\lambda c_1 + (1 - \lambda)c_1', \lambda c_2 + (1 - \lambda)c_2')$. Hence draw a conclusion about the shape of the indifference curves in the $(c_1, c_2)$ plane.

*3 The Expected-utility Rule*

Let $v(c)$ be the preference-scaling functions for certain outcomes. Then, for lotteries of the form $(c_1, c_2; \pi_1, \pi_2)$, we have seen that:

$$U(c_1, c_2; \pi_1, \pi_2) = \sum_{s=1}^{2} \pi_s v(c_s)$$

In this exercise you are asked to generalize this result to lotteries with three outcomes. An inductive argument can then be used to show that for any lottery $(c_1, c_2, \ldots, c_S; \pi_1, \pi_2, \ldots, \pi_S)$:

$$U(c_1, \ldots, c_s; \pi_1, \ldots, \pi_s) = \sum_{s=1}^{S} \pi_s v(c_s)$$

(A) Consider the lottery:

$$\hat{l} \equiv \left(c_1, c_2; \frac{\pi_1}{\pi_1 + \pi_2}, \frac{\pi_2}{\pi_1 + \pi_2}\right)$$

Explain why $\hat{l} \sim l^*(\bar{v})$ where:

$$\bar{v} \equiv \frac{\pi_1}{\pi_1 + \pi_2} v(c_1) + \frac{\pi_2}{\pi_1 + \pi_2} v(c_2)$$

(B) Appeal to the Axiom of complex gambles to establish that:

$$(\hat{l}, c_3; 1 - \pi_3, \pi_3) \sim (l^*(\bar{v}), c_3; 1 - \pi_3, \pi_3)$$

and

$$(l^*(\bar{v}), c_3; 1 - \pi_3, \pi_3) \sim (l^*(\bar{v}), l^*(v(c_3)); 1 - \pi_3, \pi_3)$$

(C) Depict the two lotteries $(\hat{l}, c_3; 1 - \pi_3, \pi_3)$ and $(l^*(\bar{v}), l^*(v(c_3)); 1 - \pi_3, \pi_3)$ in tree diagrams.

(D) Confirm that the first is equivalent to the lottery $(c_1, c_2, c_3; \pi_1, \pi_2, \pi_3)$. Confirm that the second is equivalent to the reference lottery with success probability $\Sigma_{s=1}^{3} \pi_s v(c_s)$.

(E) Suppose the Expected-utility Rule is true for prospects with $S$ outcomes. (We have seen that it is true for $S = 2$ and 3.) Show that the above argument can, with only slight modifications, be used to establish that the Expected-utility Rule must be true for prospects with $S + 1$ outcomes.

## 1.5    Risk-aversion

In figure 1.1 the individual pictured was indifferent between a certainty income of $250 and a prospect yielding equal chances of $1,000 or nothing. Such a person is termed *risk-averse*. More generally:

DEFINITION: A person is *risk-averse* (displays *risk-aversion*) if he strictly prefers a certainty consequence to any risky prospect whose mathematical expectation of consequences equals that certainty. If his preferences go the other way he is a *risk-preferrer* (displays *risk-preference*); if he is indifferent between the certainty consequence and such a risky prospect he is *risk-neutral* (displays *risk-neutrality*).

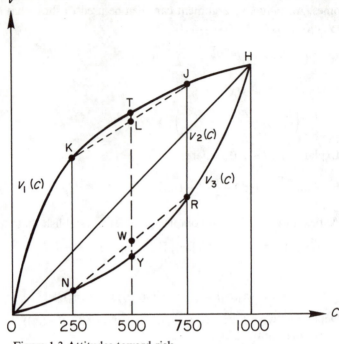

Figure 1.3 Attitudes toward risk

The risky prospect described above, equal chances of $1,000 or nothing, has a mathematical expectation of $500 of income. Since our individual was indifferent between the prospect and a mere $250 certain, for him $500 certain is surely preferable to the risky prospect, which verifies that he is indeed risk-averse.

The term "fair gamble" is used to describe an uncertain prospect whose mathematical expectation is zero. (A gamble with negative expectation is called "unfavorable"; one with positive expectation is called "favorable.") For example, odds of 5:1 on a roll of a fair die represent a fair gamble: since you lose (say) a dollar if the face you name does not come up, and win five dollars if it does come up, the expectation of gain is $(-1)\frac{5}{6} + 5(\frac{1}{6}) = 0$. Then a risk-averse person would refuse a fair gamble; a risk-preferrer would accept a fair gamble; and a risk-neutral person would be indifferent.[3]

Figure 1.3 displays three possible preference-scaling functions: $v_1(c)$ would apply to a risk-averse individual, $v_2(c)$ to someone who is risk-

---

[3] However, as we shall see below, a risk-averse individual would accept a fair gamble if it offset *other* risks to which he was exposed. To purchase insurance, for example, is to accept an offsetting (risk-reducing) gamble.

neutral, and $v_3(c)$ to a risk-preferrer. Consider the fair prospect or gamble $G = (750, 250; \frac{1}{2}, \frac{1}{2})$ whose mathematical expectation is \$500. For the first or risk-averse individual the utility of \$500 certain, $v_1(500)$, is indicated by the height of point T along the $v_1(c)$ curve. The utility he attaches to the risky prospect, choosing the gamble $G$, is indicated by point L – whose height is the probability-weighted average of the heights of points J and K. This is of course the geometrical equivalent of the Expected-utility Rule which tells us that $U_1(G) = \frac{1}{2} v_1(750) + \frac{1}{2} v_1(250)$. Evidently, whenever the preference-scaling function has the "concave" shape of $v_1(c)$, points associated with a certainty income (like T in the diagram) will be higher than points (like L) representing a fair gamble with the same expectation of income. By an analogous argument, for the risk-preferring individual, $v_3(500)$ at point Y will be less than at point W; such a person would choose the gamble $G$ rather than receive its mathematical expectation of income, \$500, as a certainty. Finally, the $v_2(c)$ curve indicates that the risk-neutral person would be indifferent between the gamble $G$ and the certainty of \$500.

We will often have occasion to make use of *Jensen's inequality*: If $\tilde{c}$ is a random variable (taking on at least two values with non-zero probability) and $v(c)$ is a twice-differentiable function:

If $v''(c) < 0$,   then $\mathrm{E}v(c) < v[\mathrm{E}(c)]$
If $v''(c) = 0$,   then $\mathrm{E}v(c) = v[\mathrm{E}(c)]$
If $v''(c) > 0$,   then $\mathrm{E}v(c) > v[\mathrm{E}(c)]$

Evidently, these conditions correspond immediately to the risk-averse, risk-neutral, and risk-preferring cases of figure 1.3.

We now want to consider what observation of the world tells us about the actual $v(c)$ curves entering into people's decisions. First of all, we have already postulated that *more income is preferred to less*, justified by the observation that only rarely do people throw away income. This implies a rising $v(c)$ function, with positive first derivative $v'(c)$, that is, positive marginal utility of income. The question of risk-aversion versus risk-preference concerns the second derivative $v''(c)$ – whether marginal utility of income falls or rises with income.

Risk-aversion – "concave" curves like $v_1(c)$ displaying diminishing marginal utility – is considered to be the normal case, based upon the observation that individuals typically hold *diversified portfolios*. Suppose someone were merely risk-neutral, so that for him $v''(c) = 0$. Then he would ignore the riskiness or variance of different investment options or assets (gambles), and take account only of the mathematical expectation of income associated with each. Such a person would plunge all his wealth into that single asset which, regardless of its riskiness, offered the highest mathematical expectation of income. But we scarcely ever see this behavior pattern, and more commonly observe individuals holding a variety of assets. Since the risks associated with different assets are generally partially offsetting, diversification reduces the chance of ending up with an extremely low level of income. This safety feature is achieved, however, only by accepting a lower overall mathematical expectation of income; some expected income has been sacrificed in order to reduce risk.[4]

What of the seemingly contrary evidence that "unfavorable" (negative mathematical expectation) gambles are cheerfully accepted by bettors at Las Vegas and elsewhere? Even more puzzling, why is it that the same person might behave quite conservatively (insure his house, diversify his asset holdings) in some circumstances, and in other circumstances accept fair or even unfavorable gambles? There have been attempts to construct preference-scaling functions $v(c)$ that would be consistent with avoiding gambles (insuring) over certain ranges of income *and* with seeking gambles over other ranges (Milton Friedman and Leonard J. Savage, 1948; Harry M. Markowitz, 1952). We will briefly discuss the Friedman–Savage version.

Consider the doubly inflected preference-scaling function in figure 1.4. The $v(c)$ curve is concave, reflecting normal risk-aversion, in the region OK and once again in the region LN. But it is convex, reflecting risk-preference, in the middle region KL. With this sort of $v(c)$ function, risk-taking behavior will vary with wealth. For those whose endowments fall in the first concave segment, the tendency is to insure against relatively small risks but to accept fair (or even mildly adverse) long-shot big-payoff gambles, offering a chance of landing somewhere toward the upper end of the curve. It can be verified that this pattern will particularly apply for those with incomes toward the upper edge of the bottom segment – the less indigent poor, and perhaps the lower-middle class. The *very* poor, in contrast, would be much less inclined to gamble. Looking now toward the top of the scale, those with incomes near the lower edge of the upper concave segment – the rich but not super-rich, and perhaps the upper middle class – would seem to have a taste for risks likely to have a favorable payoff but offering a long-shot chance of a really large loss. (But the super-rich, like the super-poor, are very disinclined to gamble at all.) The central group finally, would be happy to accept almost any fair or not-too-unfavorable gamble.

The doubly inflected preference-scaling function of figure 1.4 does then explain why a person might gamble in some circumstances and insure in others, or accept some fair gambles while rejecting other ones. But it also

---

[4] An individual characterized by *risk-preference* might also plunge all of his wealth into a single asset, but this need not be the asset with the highest mathematical expectation of income. He might choose an asset with greater riskiness over the asset with highest income yield (that is, he would sacrifice some expected income in order to *enlarge* his risk).

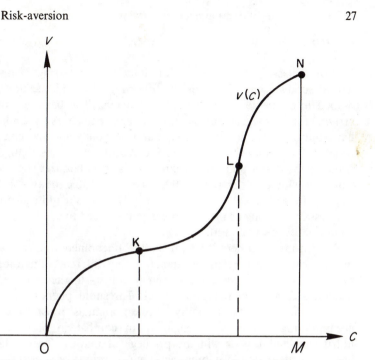

Figure 1.4 Gambling and insuring – doubly inflected preference-scaling function

implies other behavior that is quite inconsistent with common observation. It is hard to believe that people of middling incomes are always great gamblers. If the picture in figure 1.4 were correct, the middle group in the convex KL segment would be so anxious to gamble as to seek out enormous riches-or-ruin bets. These middle ranges of income would then rapidly be depopulated, which is surely not what is observed. And that the really solid risk-avoiders in our society are only the very poor and the super-rich is equally difficult to credit.

A more acceptable explanation, of why people simultaneously gamble and insure, is that most of us engage in gambling as a recreational rather than an income-determining activity. Put another way, gambling is normally more like a consumption good than an investment good. As it happens, it is quite possible operationally to distinguish recreational or pleasure-oriented from serious wealth-oriented gambling. The latter, if efficiently conducted, would take the form of once-and-for-all wagers at enormous stakes. Pleasure-oriented gambling, in contrast, being designed to yield enjoyment over some period of time, will be characterized by repetitive minuscule bets practically guaranteed *not* to change one's wealth status in any drastic way. What is observed at Las Vegas is very much more the repetitive small-stake than the riches-or-ruin huge-stake betting pattern.[5]

Nevertheless, in exceptional situations, risk-preferring behavior does indeed surely occur. Consider the following. As bank cashier you have dipped into the till to the extent of $30,000. The bank examiners are arriving tomorrow, so you have time to replace the missing funds, but you have only $10,000 left on hand. Suppose you value the consumption benefit of spending the remaining $10,000 today far less than you value avoiding the shame and pain of exposure as an embezzler. Then you surely would be willing to risk the $10,000 on a fair gamble today – say, with a $\frac{1}{3}$ chance of winning $20,000. You'd probably even take quite an adverse bet if necessary, so long as the possible payoff sufficed to cover the $20,000 of additional funds you need.

What is involved here is a "threshold" phenomenon, a critical level of income where a little bit more can make a big difference. Put another way, there is a range of *increasing* marginal utility – in the extreme, a single discrete step to a higher utility level. Threshold phenomena are quite common in Nature. In many species, animals must take risks in accumulating resources or engaging in combat in order to achieve nutritional viability or win the privilege of mating. These phenomena have evident analogs for humans living in primitive societies. To what extent they may explain risk-taking behavior under modern conditions may be left an open question.[6]

This discussion may possibly suggest, contrary to a point made earlier, that it is after all true that utility must "really" be cardinal. A viability threshold, for example, might seem to be a cardinal feature of preference

---

[5] No doubt a substantial amount of wealth-oriented gambling does take place, primarily *among the poor*. There seem to be both rational and irrational elements here. On the rational side, charity or government welfare relief might drastically modify an individual's perfectly sound calculations in the direction of heavy gambling. The availability of such a "safety net" means that, if you win you win, while if you lose someone else will help you out. Evidently, such considerations would operate mainly for people toward the lower end of the income scale, consistent with the observation that such wealth-oriented gambling as occurs is concentrated among the poor. On the irrational side, truly pathological gambling is indeed sometimes observed (see Dostoyevsky, *The Gambler*). Not perhaps quite falling under the heading of irrationality are mistaken beliefs in hunches or infallible systems. (*Given* the belief that one has the best of the deal, gambling could be quite rational. Even a risk-averse person might well accept a bet at odds he regards as favorable.) Of course, people with such mistaken beliefs are very likely to end up impoverished.

[6] See Rubin and Paul (1979). These authors suggest that the propensity of young males to engage in highly risky activities – as evidenced, for example, by their high automobile accident rates – may be the result of natural selection for risk-taking. The evolutionary history of the human species may have instilled risk-preferring attitudes among individuals in age and sex groups liable to encounter viability or mating thresholds. (Note that the threshold argument is also consistent with the observation that risk-taking behavior will be observed predominantly *among the poor*.)

that would apply to riskless as well as to risky decision-making. Nevertheless, our original point remains valid. For certainty choices, only ordinal comparisons of consequences are needed. For decisions under uncertainty we can derive, by the reference-lottery technique, a $v(c)$ function that may have convex or concave or mixed curvature, as the case may be. But the shape of this function for any individual is an inseparable blend of two elements: (i) the individual's valuations of the consequences, and (ii) his attitudes toward risk. We may therefore interpret a concave $v(c)$ function as reflecting *either* risk-aversion (attitude toward risk) or diminishing marginal utility (attitude toward income); similarly, a convex $v(c)$ function can be said to reflect *either* risk-preference or increasing marginal utility. Both terminologies are somewhat misleading, since what the curvature of $v(c)$ really represents is the *interaction* of the two factors working together.

Finally, another category of seeming risk-taking behavior may be explainable in terms of *state-dependent utility functions*. An example: suppose it is very important to me, as the psychological equivalent of having a large sum of money, that the home team wins the big game. Then I might plausibly bet *against* the home team, at fair or even adverse odds! (How this works out in detail will be left for the chapter following.)

EXERCISES AND EXCURSIONS 1.5

*1 Risk-aversion, risk-preference, risk-neutrality*
(A) Identify each of the following "cardinal" preference-scaling functions with risk-averse, risk-preferring, or risk-neutral behavior:
   (i) $v = \ln c$      (ii) $v = ac - bc^2$ ($a, b$ positive constants)
  (iii) $v = c^2$      (iv) $v = c^{\frac{1}{2}}$
   (v) $v = 100 + 6c$   (vi) $v = 1 - e^{-c}$
(B) The quadratic form (ii) above has an unsatisfactory feature for $c > a/2b$. Explain.

ANSWER:
(A) If $v = \ln c$:

$$v'(c) = 1/c > 0$$
$$v''(c) = -1/c^2 < 0$$

Since the first derivative is positive and the second derivative is negative, $v = \ln c$ is a preference-scaling function that corresponds to risk-averse behavior.
(B) For $c > a/2b$, the first derivative $v'(c)$ becomes negative for sufficiently large $c$.

## 2 Diversification

Three individuals have respective preference-scaling functions $v_1 = c$ (risk-neutral), $v_2 = c^{0.5}$ (risk-averse), and $v_3 = c^2$ (risk-preferrer). They each have the option of investing in *any one* of the three following prospects or gambles, with mathematical expectations of income as shown:

$$G1 = (480, 480; 0.5, 0.5) \qquad E1(c) = 480$$
$$G2 = (850, 200; 0.5, 0.5) \qquad E2(c) = 525$$
$$G3 = (1{,}000, 0; 0.5, 0.5) \qquad E3(c) = 500$$

Notice that, comparing the first two gambles, higher risk is associated with greater mathematical expectation of income. The third gamble has highest risk of all, but intermediate mathematical expectation.

(A) Show that risk-neutral individual 1 will prefer gamble G2 with the highest expectation, while risk-averse individual 2 will prefer gamble G1 with the lowest risk. Show that the risk-preferring individual 3 is willing to sacrifice some expectation to *increase* his risk, by choosing G3.

(B) If the individuals could "diversify" by choosing any desired mixture of these gambles, which of them would diversify? (Assume that the payoffs of gambles G2 and G3 are perfectly correlated.)

ANSWER: Risk-neutral individual 1 will continue to invest exclusively in G2, since his mathematical expectation of utility is identical with his mathematical expectation of income. The risk-averse individual 2 will avoid G3, but there are mixtures of G1 and G2, for example in the proportions (0.5, 0.5), that yield him higher utility than either G1 or G2 alone. (The solution for the risk-preferring individual 3 is left as a challenge for the reader.)

## 3 Doubly-inflected preference-scaling function

In the doubly inflected $v(c)$ curve shown in figure 1.4, suppose that the borders of the segments (inflection points) occur at $c = 250$ and at $c = 750$.

(A) Illustrate geometrically that an individual with initial income of $240 would be likely to accept a (fair) gamble offering a one-sixth chance of a $600 gain and a five-sixth chance of a $120 loss. Show that someone with initial income of $120 would be much less likely to accept the same gamble.

(B) Show that someone with initial endowed income of $760 would be likely to accept a fair gamble which is the reverse of the above: a five-sixth chance of a $120 gain and a one-sixth chance of a $600 loss. What about a person with initial wealth of $880?

(C) Show that someone with endowed wealth of exactly \$500 would surely accept *any* fair gamble with 50:50 odds – at least up to a scale of \$250 gain and \$250 loss. He might even accept much larger fair gambles of this type; indicate geometrically the limits of what he would accept.

## 4 Linear risk-tolerance

Risk-aversion is characterized by the condition $v''(c) < 0$. For some purposes, as we shall see below, the ratio $-v''/v'$ is a useful measure of risk-aversion. The reciprocal of this ratio, $-v'/v''$, is known as the *risk-tolerance*. An interesting class of $v(c)$ functions is defined by the condition of *linear* risk-tolerance: $-v'/v'' = \alpha + \beta c$.

(A) Show that, for arbitrary constants $M, N$ with $N > 0$:
  (i) $\beta = 0$ implies $v = M - Ne^{-c/\alpha}$
  (ii) $\alpha = 0, \beta \neq 1$ implies $v = M + Nc^{1-\gamma}/(1-\gamma)$   where   $\gamma = 1/\beta$
  (iii) $\alpha = 0, \beta = 1$ implies $v = M + N\ln c$
  (iv) $\alpha > 0, \beta = -1$ implies $v = M - N(\alpha - c)^2$

(B) Some of the above functions are valid only in restricted ranges of $c$. Indicate the restrictions, if any, that apply in each case. Also explain why $N$ must be positive if $v$ is to be a well-behaved preference-scaling function.

## 5 The bank examiner is coming

You have stolen \$30,000 from the bank but have the opportunity to replace it by winning a fair gamble. You have at your disposal just \$10,000. Your preference-scaling function is such that $v(c) = -B$, where $B$ is a very big number, when $c < 0$ (i.e., should you not replace *all* the missing funds), and otherwise $v(c) = c^{\frac{1}{2}}$. Assuming fair gambles are available at any terms you desire, solve *geometrically* for your optimal fair gamble. Will you surely stake all your \$10,000? Will you look only for a \$20,000 payoff, or would you prefer a bet with a smaller chance of a bigger payoff?

## 6 Preference-scaling functions with multiple goods

The argument in the text above, developing a cardinal preference-scaling function $v(c)$ for use with the Expected-utility Rule, ran in terms of a single desired good or commodity $c$. Extend the argument to cardinal preference-scaling functions of two goods, in the form $v(a, b)$. Show that, starting with an *ordinal* preference function defined over combinations of $a$ and $b$ (that is, starting with an ordinary indifference map on $a, b$ axes), the reference-lottery technique can be used to generate a cardinal scaling that amounts to giving a numerical utility value to each indifference curve.

### 7 Risk-aversion with multiple goods

An individual has a preference-scaling function $v(a, b) = a^{\frac{1}{2}}b^{\frac{1}{4}}$. He has income $I$ available for spending on $a$ and $b$, and faces fixed prices $P_a = P_b = 1$.

(A) Show that he would strictly prefer the certain income of 50 to an equal chance of his income rising or falling by 49 before he makes his consumption choices.

(B) Obtain an expression for the individual's "indirect" preference-scaling function. (That is, the maximized level of $v$ given income $I$ and prices $P_a$ and $P_b$.) Hence show that this individual exhibits aversion to income risks.

(C) Suppose $I = 50$ and $P_b = 16$. Would the individual prefer to face a certain $P_a = 64$ or a stochastically varying $P_a$ that might equal 1 or 81 with equal chances? Does your answer cast doubt upon whether the individual is really risk-averse? Explain.

ANSWER:

(B) The "indirect" preference-scaling function is:

$$v = (\tfrac{2}{3})^{\frac{1}{2}}(\tfrac{1}{3})^{\frac{1}{4}} I^{\frac{3}{4}}/(P_a^{\frac{1}{2}}P_b^{\frac{1}{4}})$$

Thus there is diminishing marginal utility with regard to income $I$.

### 8 Jensen's inequality $(I)$

(A) If the preference-scaling function $v(c)$ is twice continuously differentiable with $v''(c) \leqslant 0$, show that for any random variable $\tilde{c}$:

$$Ev(\tilde{c}) \leqslant v(E(\tilde{c}))$$

(B) If $v''(c) < 0$ and $\text{Prob}(\tilde{c} \neq Ec) > 0$, show that:

$$Ev(\tilde{c}) < v(E(\tilde{c}))$$

ANSWER:

(A) Define $\bar{c} = E(\tilde{c})$. By Taylor's expansion, for any $c \neq \bar{c}$ there exists a $c^*$ between $c$ and $\bar{c}$ such that:

$$v(c) = v(\bar{c}) + v'(\bar{c})(c - \bar{c}) + \tfrac{1}{2}v''(c^*)(c - \bar{c})^2$$

If $v''(c) \leqslant 0$ for all $c$ it follows that:

$$v(c) \leqslant v(\bar{c}) + v'(\bar{c})(c - \bar{c})$$

Thus $Ev(\tilde{c}) \leqslant v(\bar{c}) + v'(\bar{c})E(\tilde{c} - \bar{c}) = v(\bar{c})$.

(B) If $v''(c) < 0$ for all $c$ it follows that:

$$v(c) < v(\bar{c}) + v'(\bar{c})(c - \bar{c}), \quad \text{for} \quad c \neq \bar{c}$$

Then as long as $c \neq \bar{c}$ with positive probability:

$$Ev(c) < v(\bar{c})$$

*9 Jensen's inequality (II)*

Suppose $v(c)$ is a concave function (not necessarily differentiable or even continuous), that is, for any $c_1, c_2$:

$$v((1-\lambda)c_1 + \lambda c_2) \geqslant (1-\lambda)v(c_1) + \lambda v(c_2), \quad 0 \leqslant \lambda \leqslant 1$$

(A) Prove by induction that, for any $c_1, \ldots, c_n$:

$$v\left(\sum_{i=1}^{n} \mu_i c_i\right) \geqslant \sum_{i=1}^{n} \mu_i v(c_i), \text{ for } \mu_i \geqslant 0, \sum_{i=1}^{n} \mu_i = 1$$

(B) Hence derive Jensen's inequality once again.

## 1.6    Utility paradoxes and rationality

A very considerable "dissident" literature has appeared in recent years. Its main thrust has been that actual decision-makers do not behave rationally in the face of uncertainty, or at any rate do not consistently follow the Expected-utility Rule.[7] And to some extent, these complaints have been supported by experimental evidence.[8]

Three illustrations:

### 1 PROBABILITY MATCHING

You are paid $1 each time you guess correctly whether a red or a white light will flash. The lights flash randomly, but the red is set to turn on twice as often as the white.

It has been found that subjects tend to guess red about two-thirds of the time and white one-third. Yet, obviously, it would be more profitable always to guess red.

### 2 FRAMING THE QUESTION

Imagine that you have been given $200, and are asked to choose between (i) $50 additional, or (ii) a 25% chance of winning $200 additional (or else, gaining nothing). Alternatively, imagine that you have been given $400, but you must now choose between (i) giving up $150, or (ii) a 75% chance of losing $200 (or else, losing nothing).

Most experimental subjects choose option (i) in the first version of the question, but option (ii) in the second. Yet, obviously, option (i) generates the same income prospect whichever way the question is framed, and similarly for option (ii).

### 3 ELLSBERG PARADOX

Urn I has 50 red balls and 50 black balls. Urn II also has 100 red and

---

[7] Machina (1987) provides a very helpful and clear survey, sympathetic to the dissident viewpoint.

[8] See, for example, Paul Slovic and Sarah Lichtenstein (1983), Amos Tversky and Daniel Kahneman (1981), and Paul J. H. Schoemaker (1982).

black balls, but in unknown proportions. You will win $100 in the event of a correct choice. (A) Of the two red bets $R_I$ or $R_{II}$ (a bet on Red if the drawing is made from the first, or alternatively from the second urn), which do you prefer? (B) Same question, for the two black bets $B_I$ and $B_{II}$.

It has been found that most subjects prefer $R_I$ over $R_{II}$, and also prefer $B_I$ over $B_{II}$. But these preferences are inconsistent: to say that you prefer $R_I$ over $R_{II}$ is logically the same as saying that you prefer $B_{II}$ over $B_I$.

The dissident literature claims that the discrepancies revealed by these results refute the economist's standard assumption of rationality, or at least the expected-utility hypothesis as a specific implication of that assumption. We reject this interpretation. A much more parsimonious explanation, in our opinion, is that this evidence merely illustrates certain limitations of the human mind as a computer. It is possible to fool the brain by the way a question is posed, just as optical illusions may be arranged to fool the eye. Discovering and classifying such mental illusions are fruitful activities for psychologists, but these paradoxes are of relatively little significance for economics.

We would not go so far as to insist that rationality failures have *no* economic implications. If these shortcomings do indeed represent ways in which people could systematically be fooled, economists would predict that tricksters, confidence men, and assorted rogues would enter the "industry" offering such gambles to naive subjects. For example:

PROBABILITY MATCHING: The trickster could challenge the subject along the following line: "I have a secret method of guessing which light will flash. (His secret method, of course, is always to bet on red.) I will write my guess down on paper each time, and you will write yours down. At the end we will total up our successes. For each time I am right and you are wrong, you will pay me $1; in the reverse case, I will pay you $1.50."[9] If the subject really believes that his is the right method, he should surely accept so generous an offer.

And similarly, clever tricksters could win sure-thing income from the inconsistent answers offered by naive individuals in our other two illustrations. The confidence-man profession does obviously exist, and is unlikely (given the limitations of the human mind) ever to disappear.[10] But

[9] The maximum or breakeven payment that the trickster could offer is $2 exactly. Clearly, there will be no payment either way in the two-thirds of the cases where the naive subject bets on red. And when he bets on white, he will be wrong twice as often as he is right.

[10] An analogous example is the racetrack tout who offers to predict the winning horse for $20, telling you that he will refund your money unless his prediction is correct. His intention, of course, is to tout customers onto all the horses in the race.

the more important the decision, the more it is worth people's while to learn how not to be fooled.

It will be of interest to analyze some of the parallels and differences among these various rationality failures, and in particular to attempt to identify more precisely the source of the slippage in each case.

If the subjects in PROBABILITY MATCHING did mentally compare the matching rule with "Always bet on red" and chose the former, they committed a straightforward logical error.[11] We know that people do often commit such errors, even in contexts where no uncertainty is involved. Consider the following example from a psychological experiment (adapted from Cosmides, 1985):

> You are faced with a card-sorting task, in which each card has a number on one side and a letter on the other. There is only one rule: "Every card marked with an 'X' on one side should have a '1' on the other." Indicate whether you need to inspect the reverse side of the following cards to detect violation of the rule: (a) a card showing an 'X'; (b) a card showing a 'Y'; (c) a card showing a '1'; (d) a card showing a '2'.

In a large preponderance of cases, while the subjects correctly realized the need to inspect the reverse of card (a), they failed to notice that they should do the same for card (d).

What is instructive for our purposes, however, is that the experimenter went on to investigate a logically identical choice, presented to the subjects more or less as follows:

> You are the bouncer in a Boston bar, assigned to enforce the following rule: "Anyone who consumes alcohol on the premises must be at least twenty years old." To detect violation of the rule, indicate whether you need more information about any of the following individuals: (a) someone drinking whisky; (b) someone drinking soda; (c) an individual aged twenty-five; (d) an individual aged sixteen.

Here almost everyone perceived the need for more information about individual (d) as well as individual (a). Evidently, humans have trouble with purely abstract problems, but do a lot better when the logically equivalent choices are offered in a realistic context – particularly where possible cheating or violations of social norms may be involved. Returning

---

[11] Another possibility is that the correct rule never came to mind at all – in effect, the subjects did not think very hard about what was going on. This would not be too surprising if the stakes were trivial in magnitude.

to PROBABILITY MATCHING, in our opinion few individuals would be more than momentarily fooled by the trickster described above if some serious issue or some substantial amount of money were at stake.

The second example, FRAMING THE QUESTION, is rather like an optical illusion involving perspective, a nearby small object being made to seem larger than a far-off large object. In the first choice offered the subjects, the risk – the chance of losing $50 – is placed in the foreground, so to speak. From this viewpoint, the 25 % chance of gaining an extra $200 does not seem enough recompense. In the second version what is placed in the foreground is the unpleasant option of a $150 loss. Here the risk of losing an additional $50 fades into comparative insignificance, as compared with the 25 % hope of recouping the $150 and suffering no loss at all.

Notice that these experimental subjects proved to be highly risk-averse; they were fooled by a shift in the setting, the same risk being highlighted in the one choice and left in the shadows in the other case. The ELLSBERG PARADOX also plays on the subjects' risk-aversion, but in a somewhat different way. Recalling the discussion of " hard " versus " soft " probability estimates earlier in the chapter, the subjects appear to have been fooled into thinking that acting on the basis of a hard probability (the urn known to have fifty black and fifty red balls) is less risky than acting on the basis of a soft probability (the urn with an unknown mixture). But if only an immediate *terminal* action is called for, as postulated here, it makes no difference whether the probability is hard or soft. In the absence of any basis for one color being more likely than the other, the subjective probability of success has to be the same for the second as for the first urn – whether betting on black or on red. The subjects went wrong, it seems, in confusing *higher confidence* (which indeed holds with regard to the probability of success using the first urn) with *lesser risk* (which does not hold).[12]

## 4 ALLAIS PARADOX

We will provide a more extended discussion of a fourth example, the ALLAIS PARADOX, which illustrates the powerful effect of just how the choices are framed:[13]

You are offered the choice between prospects A and B:

A: with certainty, receive $1,000,000

---

[12] There is also an alternative, entirely rational explanation. In an actual experiment the first urn would presumably be transparent, to allow everyone to see that half the balls are red and half black. But of course the second urn could not be transparent, which makes trickery more possible. A subject attaching even a small likelihood to being cheated (by the experimenter shifting the proportions in the second urn after the bet is down) would definitely and quite rationally prefer drawing from the first urn.

[13] M. Allais (1953).

> B: with probability 0·10, receive $5,000,000
> with probability 0·89, receive $1,000,000
> with probability 0·01, receive zero.

Alternatively, you are offered the choice between C and D:

> C: with probability 0·11, receive $1,000,000
> with probability 0·89, receive zero
> D: with probability 0·10, receive $5,000,000
> with probability 0·90, receive zero.

It has been found that most people prefer A to B, but D to C. But it is easy to show that choosing A over B but D over C is inconsistent with the Expected-utility Rule. According to that theorem:

If  A ≻ B,  then  $v(\$1,000,000) > 0·10\,v(\$5,000,000)$
$+0·89\,v(\$1,000,000)+0·01\,v(\$0)$

Then, by elementary algebra:

$$0·11\,v(\$1,000,000)+0·89\,v(\$0) > 0·10\,v(\$5,000,000)+0·90\,v(\$0)$$

But the latter inequality is equivalent, according to the Expected-utility Rule, to C ≻ D.

The explanation, in perceptual terms, appears to be that the A versus B framing makes the 0·01 chance of receiving zero stand out as a very adverse feature in making option B undesired – but exactly the same chance fades into comparative insignificance, psychologically speaking, as an adverse feature of D in comparison with C.

The question is, does the observed failure of subjects to follow the dictates of the Expected-utility Rule represent only a logical lapse, akin to an optical illusion? Or is it perhaps that the rule is an incorrect, or at least an excessively narrow, specification of rational behavior? The latter was the position taken by Allais. He argued, essentially, that the utility of an action $x$ need not rationally follow from the utility of consequences by the simple expected-utility formula $U(x) = Ev(c_{xs})$. Instead, he proposed allowing some more general formula like:

$$U(x) = F(E[v(c_{xs})], \sigma^2[v(c_{xs})])$$

Notice that Allais would have the individual take into account not only the expectation but also the variance of his consequence utilities $v(c_{xs})$, in accordance with some function $F$ representing his personal degree of risk-tolerance. The Neumann–Morgenstern rule is evidently a limiting special case of Allais' formula.

However, a very convincing argument exists for showing that the more narrow, and therefore far more powerful, Neumann–Morgenstern rule is the correct one. For our purposes it will suffice to refute Allais' example, i.e., to show that a rational person, upon realizing that he has been tricked by the "framing" of Allais' question, would revise his answers to make them correspond with the Expected-utility Rule (i.e., if he has chosen A over B then he will prefer C to D, and vice versa). Put another way, if he does not revise his choices, you can become a confidence-man and extract money from him![14]

Consider the following prospect:

> Y: with probability 10/11, receive $5,000,000
> with probability 1/11, receive zero.

Most people seem to prefer A (the certainty of $1,000,000) to Y, but it would not be a violation of logic for even a risk-averse person to choose Y over A – it is simply a matter of the degree of one's personal risk-tolerance.

Now define the more complex prospect M as follows:

> M: with probability 0·89, receive A
> with probability 0·11, receive *your choice* of A or Y.

Evidently, if your preference was for A over Y as a simple choice, then if you are at all a reasonable person you should also choose A over Y if the 0·11 chance of doing so arises under prospect M. Then, M would reduce to A – receiving $1,000,000 with certainty. On the other hand, if you chose Y over A initially and are consistent in doing the same if the chance arises under prospect M, then M would reduce to B. Thus, using the symbols $\succ$ and $\prec$ for directions of preference:

> If A $\succ$ Y,   then A $\succ$ B.
> If A $\prec$ Y,   then A $\prec$ B.

Now consider a different complex prospect *N*:

> *N*: with probability 0·89, receive zero
> with probability 0·11, receive *your choice of* A or Y.

Here, if you prefer A to Y, then prospect N would reduce to C. But if you prefer Y to A, then N would reduce to D. And so:

> If A $\succ$ Y,   then C $\succ$ D
> If A $\prec$ Y,   then C $\prec$ D.

Thus, someone who chooses A over B (thereby revealing a preference for A over Y) should, consistently with that same underlying preference,

---

[14] This development is due to Harry Markowitz (1959).

choose C over D. There does not seem to be any way for a rational person to escape this conclusion, unless special features of the situation are considered: for example, if the individual does not value a one-stage lottery as highly as a two-stage lottery with the same ultimate outcomes (perhaps because he gets more of a thrill to see a roulette wheel spin twice). Apart from such uninteresting qualifications, Allais' objection has been refuted.

We do not want to be excessively dismissive of what is, on a number of grounds, an intellectually significant literature.[15] As an empirical matter, such important phenomena as advertising and political persuasion depend very importantly upon clever use of fallacious analogy, irrelevant associations, and other confidence-man tricks. But the analysis of error is only a footnote to the analysis of valid inference. It is only because people have a well-justified confidence in reason that deception, whether artful or unintended, can sometimes occur. Especially when it comes to subtle matters and small differences, it is easy for people to fool themselves, or to be fooled. But less so when the issues are really important, for the economically sound reason that correct analysis is more profitable than error.

EXERCISES AND EXCURSIONS 1.6

*1 Framing the question*

Could a confidence-man or trickster exploit individuals whose choices are as described in the *framing the question* example above?

ANSWER: A trickster could not profit if he had to offer them and pay off on gambles with positive returns, like those hypothetically presented in that example. However, he might be able to exploit their inconsistent choices if the funds backing the gambles come from some exogenous source, supposing that the trickster is in a position to direct who initially gets which.

Specifically, let there be two individuals A and B (Alex and Bev) with identical endowments and preferences. The two exogenously supplied gambles, after stripping away the confusing framing of the question, amount to (i) \$250 certain, versus (ii) the prospect (\$400, \$200; 0·25, 0·75). Suppose that Alex had indicated a preference for option (i) in the first version of the question and Bev a preference for (ii) in the second version. Then the trickster need only arrange matters so that Alex and Bev each

---

[15] But, we would like to add, while economists' attention has been drawn almost exclusively to those psychological studies illustrating real or supposed failures of rationality, there is another stream of psychological research emphasizing the strengths rather than the failures of popular reasoning. See, for example, Kelley (1973), Cosmides and Tooby (1987), Shepard (1987).

initially receives his/her non-preferred option. Having done this he can say:

> (To Alex): You had indicated a preference for $200 + $50 with certainty (call it option 1a) over $200 plus a 25% chance of winning an extra $200 (call it option 1b). You now have option 1b. I will take that off your hands and give you 1a instead, except that since you definitely prefer 1a you should be willing to sweeten the deal a little for me and give me just $1.

> (To Bev): You had indicated that receiving $400 − $150 with certainty (call it option 2a) is less desired than receiving $400 subject to a 75% chance of losing $200 (call it option 2b). You now have option 2a. I will take that off your hands and give you 2b instead, except that since you definitely prefer 2b you should be willing to sweeten the deal a little for me and give me just $1.

Given that 1a and 2a are identical, as are 1b and 2b, by "re-framing" the two gambles the trickster has been able to make a middleman's profit.

*Note*: If Alex and Bev are both risk-averse, each of them actually should prefer the certainty option (i) to the fair gamble (ii). Thus, in the described exchange Alex really gains; it is Bev who loses out, owing to the confusing framing of the question.

## 2 A second Ellsberg paradox

An urn contains thirty red balls and sixty other balls, some yellow and some black. One ball is to be drawn at random from the urn.

(A) You are offered the opportunity to choose either red or black. If you pick the color of the ball drawn you win $100. Which color do you choose?

(B) Alternatively suppose you are offered once again the opportunity to choose either red or black. However, now you win $100 as long as the ball drawn is *not* the color picked. Which color do you choose?

(C) Show that only two of the four possible combinations of choices (for questions A and B respectively) – red-red, red-black, black-red, and black-black – are consistent with the Axiom of complex gambles.

(D) If your choices were inconsistent with the Axiom, do you wish to change either of them?

## 3 The Allais paradox

(A) Does Allais' paradox violate the Axiom of complex gambles? If so, how?

(B)  As a confidence-man, how would you exploit an individual whose choices were consistent with Allais' paradox?

## 4  Risk-aversion – price or quantity?

This exercise illustrates a different kind of utility "paradox." Suppose an individual with given wealth $W$ can purchase commodities $x$ and $y$. Let his preference-scaling function be:

$$v(x,y) = x + \alpha \ln y$$

Note that, in terms of our definitions above, for variations in $x$ alone the individual is risk-neutral ($\partial^2 v / \partial x^2 = 0$), while for variations in $y$ alone he is risk-averse ($\partial^2 v / \partial y^2 < 0$).

(A)  Let the price of $x$ be fixed at unity, and let $p$ be the price of $y$. Show that his "indirect" utility, that is, elementary utility as a function of $p$, is given by:

$$\hat{v}(p) = \underset{x,y}{\text{Max}}\,\{v(x,y)|x+py = W\} = \underset{y}{\text{Max}}\,(W + \alpha \ln y - py)$$

(B)  Letting $y^*$ denote his optimal consumption of good $y$, show that:

$$y^*(p) = \alpha/p$$
$$\hat{v}(p) = W - \alpha + \alpha \ln \alpha - \alpha \ln p$$

(C)  Show that $\hat{v}(p)$ is a *convex* function of $p$, that is, $d^2\hat{v}/dp^2 > 0$.

(D)  Explain the paradox that, while the $v(x,y)$ function displays risk-aversion with respect to quantities of $y$, the $\hat{v}(p)$ function seems to display risk-preference with respect to the price of $y$.

ANSWER: The situations leading respectively to the $v(x,y)$ and $\hat{v}(p)$ functions vary with regard to: (i) the source of uncertainty and, more importantly, (ii) the scope of allowable action once the uncertainty is resolved. In speaking of the $v(x,y)$ function as representing risk-aversion with respect to good $y$, the source of uncertainty was possible variation in the person's endowment of good $y$ alone, the other good $x$ being held constant. And implicit in the definition of $v(x,y)$ is that the individual can take *no* further action once endowed with smaller or larger amounts of good $y$. The $\hat{v}(p)$ function contemplates quite a different situation. Here the source of uncertainty for the individual is not his endowment (which is held fixed at $W$) but rather possible variations in price $p$. And, what is crucial, implicit in the $\hat{v}(p)$ function is that the individual is allowed now to respond to variations in $p$ by *optimally adjusting his $x, y$ consumption pattern after the uncertainty has been resolved.* The more extreme the price variation, the greater the gain from such ex-post optimal adjustments. Hence, unless an individual is highly risk-averse with respect to uncertainty about $x$ and $y$, he is likely to prefer price variability.

REFERENCES AND SELECTED READINGS

Alchian, Armen A., "The Meaning of Utility Measurement," *American Economic Review*, 43 (March 1953), 26–50.

Allais, M., "Le Comportement de l'homme rationnel devant le risque," *Econometrica*, 21 (October 1953).

Baumol, William, "The Neumann–Morgenstern Utility Index: An Ordinalist View," *Journal of Political Economy*, 59 (February 1951), 61–6.

Cosmides, Leda, "Deduction or Darwinian Algorithms: An Explanation of the Elusive Content Effect on the Wason Selection Task," unpublished Harvard University Ph.D. thesis (1985).

Cosmides, Leda and Tooby, John, "From Evolution to Behavior: Evolutionary Psychology as the Missing Link," chapter 13 in John Dupré (ed.), *The Latest on the Best: Essays on Evolution and Optimality*, Cambridge, MA: MIT Press, 1987.

Fisher, Irving, *The Nature of Capital and Income*, New York: Macmillan, 1912.

Friedman, Milton and Savage, Leonard J., "The Utility Analysis of Choices Involving Risks," *Journal of Political Economy*, 56 (August 1948), 279–304.

Kelley, Harold, "The Processes of Casual Attribution," *American Psychologist*, 28 (February 1973), 107–28.

Knight, Frank H., *Risk, Uncertainty and Profit*, New York: Houghton Mifflin, 1921.

Machina, Mark J., "Choice under Uncertainty: Problems Solved and Unsolved," *Economic Perspectives*, 1 (Summer 1987), 121–54.

———, *The Economic Theory of Individual Behaviour Towards Risk: Theory, Evidence and New Directions*, Cambridge University Press, forthcoming.

Markowitz, Harry, "The Utility of Wealth," *Journal of Political Economy*, 60 (April 1952), 151–8.

———, *Portfolio Selection*, New York: Wiley, 1959.

Neumann, John von and Morgenstern, Oskar, *Theory of Games and Economic Behavior*, Princeton, NJ: Princeton University Press, 1944.

Rubin, Paul H., and Paul, C. W., "An Evolutionary Model of the Taste for Risk," *Economic Inquiry*, 17 (October 1979).

Savage, Leonard J., *The Foundations of Statistics*, New York: Wiley, 1954.

Schlaifer, Robert, *Probability and Statistics for Business Decisions*, New York: McGraw-Hill, 1959.

Schoemaker, Paul J. H., "The Expected Utility Model," *Journal of Economic Literature*, 20 (June 1982).

Shepard, Roger N., "Evolution of a Mesh Between Principles of the Mind and Regularities of the World," chapter 12 in John Dupré (ed.), *The Latest on the Best: Essays on Evolution and Optimality*, Cambridge, MA: MIT Press, 1987.

Slovic, Paul and Lichtenstein, Sarah, "Preference Reversals: A Broader Perspective," *American Economic Review*, 83 (September 1983).

Strotz, Robert H., "Cardinal Utility," *American Economic Review*, 43 (May 1953), 384–97.

Tversky, Amos and Kahneman, Daniel, "The Framing of Decisions and the Psychology of Choice," *Science*, 211 (January 1981), 453–8.

# 2 Risk-bearing: the optimum of the individual

The individual's best action under uncertainty – the "risk-bearing optimum" – involves choosing among prospects $x \equiv (c;\pi) \equiv (c_1, \ldots, c_S; \pi_1, \ldots, \pi_S)$ where the $c_s$ are the state-distributed consequences and the $\pi_s$ are the state probabilities. In the realm of the economics of *uncertainty* proper, before turning to the economics of *information*, the individual's probability beliefs $\pi$ remain constant and so the $c_1, \ldots, c_S$ are the only decision variables. In general, each $c_s$ represents the multi-good basket that the individual is entitled to consume if state $s$ occurs. For simplicity, however, we will often think in terms of a single generalized consumption good ("corn"). Then $c_s$ would simply be the individual's state-$s$ entitlement to corn if state $s$ occurs, and the risk-bearing problem is how to choose among alternative vectors $(c_1, \ldots, c_S)$ of "corn incomes" distributed over states of the world. Unless otherwise indicated, when the symbol $c_s$ is described as representing "income" the implication is that we are using the simplified model of a single consumption good.[1]

## 2.1 The risk-bearing optimum: basic analysis

Suppose there are only two states of the world $s = 1, 2$. The two states might represent war versus peace, or prosperity versus depression. In the state-claim space of figure 2.1 the axes indicate amounts of the contingent income claims $c_1$ and $c_2$.

To represent preferences in this space we can start with equation (1.4.1), the Expected-utility Rule. In a simplified two-state world this reduces to:

$$U \equiv \pi_1 v(c_1) + \pi_2 v(c_2), \text{ where } \pi_1 + \pi_2 = 1 \tag{2.1.1}$$

For a given level of $U$, equation (2.1.1) describes an entire set of $c_1, c_2$

---

[1] With multiple consumption goods, only if the price ratios among them were *independent of state* could there be an unambiguous interpretation of "income." Consider an individual whose multi-commodity physical endowment is distributed over two states $s^0$ and $s^*$. When price ratios vary over states it might be that, valued in terms of good $g$ as numeraire, his endowed "income" is higher in state $s^0$ – while in terms of good $h$ as numeraire instead, the value of endowed "income" in state $s^*$ is higher.

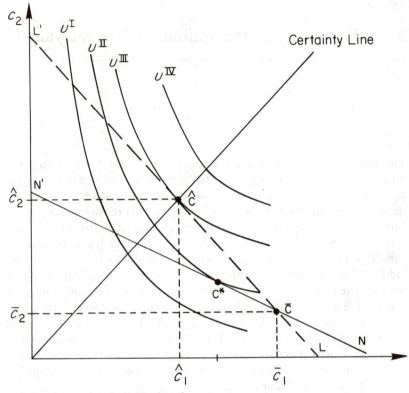

Figure 2.1 Individual optimum

combinations that are equally preferred, so this is the equation of an indifference curve. As $U$ varies, the whole family of indifference curves implied by the individual's preference-scaling function $v(c)$ and probability beliefs $\pi_1, \pi_2$ is traced out – as indicated by the various curves $U^{\text{I}}, U^{\text{II}}, \ldots$, shown in the diagram.

It is elementary to verify that the absolute indifference-curve slope $M(c_1, c_2)$ in figure 2.1, the Marginal Rate of Substitution in Consumption, is related to the marginal utilities $v'(c_1)$ and $v'(c_2)$ via:[2]

$$M(c_1, c_2) \equiv -\frac{dc_2}{dc_1}\bigg|_{U=\text{constant}} \equiv \frac{\pi_1 v'(c_1)}{\pi_2 v'(c_2)} \tag{2.1.2}$$

---

[2] Along an iso-utility curve, $0 = dU \equiv \pi_1 v'(c_1)\,dc_1 + \pi_2 v'(c_2)\,dc_2$. Then, $-dc_2/dc_1 = [\pi_1 v'(c_1)]/[\pi_2 v'(c_2)]$.

The 45° "certainty line" in the diagram connects all the points such that $c_1 = c_2$. Note that any indifference curve, as it crosses the certainty line, has absolute slope equal simply to $\pi_1/\pi_2$ – the ratio of the state probabilities.

Intuitively, risk-aversion in state-claim space corresponds to convex ("bowed toward the origin") indifference curves as shown in figure 2.1. Risk-aversion, we know, leads to diversification. Non-convex indifference curves, when juxtaposed against the individual's opportunity set, would lead to a corner optimum – to choice of an all-$c_1$ or an all-$c_2$ state-claim holding, a non-diversified portfolio. More specifically, a risk-averse preference-scaling function $v(c)$, one with positive first derivative $v'(c)$ and negative second derivative $v''(c)$, does indeed imply that indifference curves in state-claim space will be bowed toward the origin. That is, $v'(c) > 0$, $v''(c) < 0$ imply that along any indifference curve, the absolute indifference curve slope diminishes moving to the right – $dM(c_1, c_2)/dc_1$ will be negative.[3]

It will also be of interest to translate into state-claim space the proposition that a risk-averse individual would never accept a fair gamble in "corn" income (would always prefer a sure consequence to any probabilistic mixture of consequences having the same mathematical expectation). In figure 2.1 the dashed line LL' through the point $C \equiv (\bar{c}_1, \bar{c}_2)$ shows all the $c_1, c_2$ combinations having the same mathematical expectation of income $Ec = \hat{c}$ as the combination $(\bar{c}_1, \bar{c}_2)$. The equation for LL' is:

$$\pi_1 c_1 + \pi_2 c_2 = \pi_1 \bar{c}_1 + \pi_2 \bar{c}_2 = \hat{c} \qquad (2.1.3)$$

Along LL' the most preferred point must be where the line is just tangent to an indifference curve of expected utility. The slope of LL' is $dc_2/dc_1 = -\pi_1/\pi_2$, which (we know from 2.1.2) is the same as the slope along any indifference curve where it crosses the 45° line. Hence the tangency must be on the 45° line, to wit, at point $\hat{C}$ where $c_1 = c_2 = \hat{c}$. Thus, the certainty of having income $\hat{c}$ is preferred to any other $c_1, c_2$ combination whose mathematical expectation is $\hat{c}$.

---

[3] The sign of $dM(c_1, c_2)/dc_1$ will be the same as that of $d\ln M(c_1, c_2)/dc_1$ where:

$$\frac{d}{dc_1} \ln M(c_1, c_2) = \frac{d}{dc_1}[\ln \pi_1 + \ln v'(c_1) - \ln \pi_2 - \ln v'(c_2)]$$

$$= \frac{v''(c_1)}{v'(c_1)} - \frac{v''(c_2)}{v'(c_2)} \frac{dc_2}{dc_1}$$

$$= \frac{v''(c_1)}{v'(c_1)} + \frac{v''(c_2)}{v'(c_2)} \frac{\pi_1 v'(c_1)}{\pi_2 v(c_2)}$$

Since the first derivatives are both positive, $v''(c_1)$ and $v''(c_2)$ both negative imply a diminishing Marginal Rate of Substitution.

### 2.1.1    Contingent-claims markets

As discussed in chapter 1, section 1.1, we are particularly interested in the risk-involved actions that economic agents can take through *market* dealings. Suppose the individual is a price-taker in a market where contingent income claims $c_1$ and $c_2$ – each of which offers a unit of "corn income" if and only if the corresponding state obtains – can be exchanged in accordance with the price ratio $P_1/P_2$. This is indicated in figure 2.1 by the budget line NN′ through the point $\bar{C} \equiv (\bar{c}_1, \bar{c}_2)$, now interpreted as the individual's endowment position. (The overbar will be used henceforth to represent endowed quantities.) The equation for the budget line NN′ is:

$$P_1 c_1 + P_2 c_2 = P_1 \bar{c}_1 + P_2 \bar{c}_2 \tag{2.1.4}$$

Maximizing expected utility from (2.1.1), subject to the budget constraint (2.1.4), leads (assuming an interior solution) to the indifference-curve tangency[4] condition:

$$\frac{\pi_1 v'(c_1)}{\pi_2 v'(c_2)} = \frac{P_1}{P_2} \tag{2.1.5}$$

Thus, at the individual's risk-bearing optimum, shown as point C* in figure 2.1 along indifference curve $U^{\text{II}}$, the quantities of state-claims held are such that the ratio of the probability-weighted marginal utilities equals the ratio of the state-claim prices.

Making the obvious generalization to $S$ states, we arrive at an equation which will be used repeatedly throughout the book: "The Fundamental Theorem of Risk-bearing":

FUNDAMENTAL THEOREM OF RISK-BEARING

$$\frac{\pi_1 v'(c_1)}{P_1} = \frac{\pi_2 v'(c_2)}{P_2} = \dots = \frac{\pi_S v'(c_S)}{P_S} \tag{2.1.6}$$

----

[4] The necessary conditions for maximizing expected utility are obtained from the usual Lagrangian expression:

$$\text{Max } L = U(c_1, c_2) - \lambda(P_1 c_1 + P_2 c_2 - P_1 \bar{c}_1 - P_2 \bar{c}_2)$$
$$(c_1, c_2)$$

Using the expected-utility formula (2.1.1), setting the partial derivatives equal to zero implies:

$$\pi_1 v'(c_1) = \lambda P_1 \quad \text{and} \quad \pi_2 v'(c_2) = \lambda P_2$$

Dividing the first equality by the second, we obtain (2.1.5). Conceivably, however, the tangency conditions cannot be met in the interior (i.e., for non-negative $c_1, c_2$) in which case the optimum would be at an intersection of the budget line with one of the axes. If such holds at the $c_1$-axis, (2.1.5) would be translated to an inequality:

$$\frac{\pi_1 v'(c_1)}{\pi_2 v'(c_2)} > \frac{P_1}{P_2}$$

where $c_2 = 0$, $c_1 = (P_1 \bar{c}_1 + P_2 \bar{c}_2)/P_1$.

In words: assuming an interior solution, at the individual's risk-bearing optimum the expected (probability-weighted) marginal utility per dollar of income will be equal in each and every state. (The interior-solution condition will henceforth be implicitly assumed, except where the contrary is indicated.)

In terms of the simplified two-state optimum condition (2.1.5), we can reconsider once again the acceptance or rejection of fair gambles. If a gamble is fair, then $\pi_1 \Delta c_1 + \pi_2 \Delta c_2 = 0$ – the mathematical expectation of the contingent net gains must be zero. But in market transactions $P_1 \Delta c_1 + P_2 \Delta c_2 = 0$ – the exchange value of what you give up equals the value of what you receive. So if the price ratio $P_1/P_2$ equals the probability ratio $\pi_1/\pi_2$, the market is offering an opportunity to transact fair gambles. Geometrically, the line NN' would coincide with LL' in figure 2.1. It follows immediately from equation (2.1.5) that the tangency optimum would be the certainty combination where $c_1 = c_2 = \hat{c}$.

Thus, confirming our earlier result, *starting from a certainty position* a risk-averse individual would never accept any gamble at fair odds. But, if his initial endowment were not a certainty position (if $\bar{c}_1 \neq \bar{c}_2$), when offered the opportunity to transact at a price ratio corresponding to fair odds he would want to "insure" by moving to a certainty position – as indicated by the solution $\hat{C}$ along the fair market line LL'. Thus an individual with an uncertain endowment might accept a "gamble" in the form of a risky contract offering contingent income in one state in exchange for income in another. But he would accept only very particular risky contracts, those that offset the riskiness of his endowed gamble. (Notice that mere acceptance of a risky contract therefore does not tell us whether the individual is augmenting or offsetting his endowed risk.) Finally, if the market price ratio did not represent fair odds, as in the case of market line NN' in figure 2.1, whether or not he starts from a certainty endowment the individual *would* accept some risk; his tangency optimum would lie off the 45° line at a point like C* in the direction of the favorable odds.

### 2.1.2    Regimes of asset markets – complete and incomplete
In their risk-bearing decisions individuals do not typically deal directly with elementary state-claims – entitlements to consumption income under different states of the world like war versus peace, prosperity versus depression, etc. Rather, a person is generally endowed with, and may be in a position to trade, *assets* like stocks, bonds, and real estate. An asset is a more or less complicated bundle of underlying pure state-claims. A share of stock in some corporation is desired by an individual because it promises

to yield him a particular amount of income if state 1 occurs, perhaps a different amount under state 2, and so on through the entire list of states of the world that he perceives. There must then be a relationship between the price of any such marketable asset and the underlying values that individuals place upon the contingent-claim elements of the bundle. This is the relationship we now proceed to analyze.

The income yielded by asset $a$ in state $s$ will be denoted $z_{as}$. Suppose there are only two states of the world $s = 1, 2$ and just two assets $a = 1, 2$ with prices $P_1^A$ and $P_2^A$.[5] Then the budget constraint in asset units can be written:

$$P_1^A q_1 + P_2^A q_2 = P_1^A \bar{q}_1 + P_2^A \bar{q}_2 \equiv \bar{W} \qquad (2.1.7)$$

Here $q_1$ and $q_2$ represent the numbers of units held of each asset, and as usual the overbar indicates endowed quantities. $\bar{W}$, which is the individual's endowed wealth, is defined as the market value of his asset endowment.

Someone might possibly hold an asset as a "non-diversified" (single-asset) portfolio, in which case $q_a = \bar{W}/P_a^A$ for the single asset held (while $q_{a^\circ} = 0$ for any other asset $a^\circ \neq a$). The vector of state-contingent incomes generated by such a single-asset portfolio would be:

$$\begin{pmatrix} c_1 \\ c_2 \end{pmatrix} = \begin{pmatrix} z_{a1} \\ z_{a2} \end{pmatrix} \bar{W}/P_a^A \qquad (2.1.8)$$

More generally, a person in a two-asset world will hold some fraction $\kappa_1$ of his wealth in asset 1 and $\kappa_2 \equiv 1 - \kappa_1$ in asset 2 – so that $q_1 \equiv \kappa_1 \bar{W}/P_1^A$ and $q_2 \equiv \kappa_2 \bar{W}/P_2^A$. Then the contingent incomes from the portfolio will be:

$$\begin{pmatrix} c_1 \\ c_2 \end{pmatrix} \equiv q_1 \begin{pmatrix} z_{11} \\ z_{12} \end{pmatrix} + q_2 \begin{pmatrix} z_{21} \\ z_{22} \end{pmatrix} \qquad (2.1.9)$$

$$\equiv \kappa_1 (\bar{W}/P_1^A) \begin{pmatrix} z_{11} \\ z_{12} \end{pmatrix} + \kappa_2 (\bar{W}/P_2^A) \begin{pmatrix} z_{21} \\ z_{22} \end{pmatrix}$$

The lower line of (2.1.9) expresses the vector of state-contingent portfolio incomes as the share-weighted average of the incomes generated by the two single-asset portfolios.

For concreteness, define a unit of a *certainty asset* (asset 1) so that the contingent returns are unity for each state: $(z_{11}, z_{12}) = (1, 1)$. Let its price be $P_1^A = 1$. Suppose there is also an asset 2 that pays off relatively more

[5] *Asset* prices will be written $P_1^A, P_2^A$, etc. to distinguish them from *state-claim* prices which have numerical subscripts only ($P_1, P_2$, etc.) Throughout this discussion we continue to assume that individuals are price-takers in all markets.

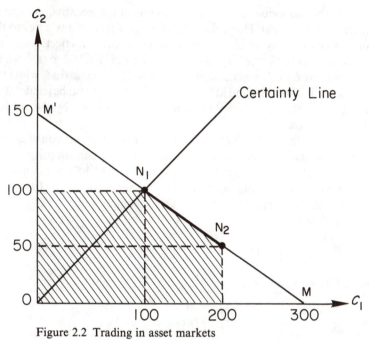

Figure 2.2 Trading in asset markets

heavily in state 1 than in state 2 – specifically, $(z_{21}, z_{22}) = (4, 1)$ – and that its price is $P_2^A = 2$. But imagine that the individual is initially endowed with nothing but 100 units of asset 1 ($\bar{q}_1 = 100$, $\bar{q}_2 = 0$). Then point $N_1$ in figure 2.2 pictures the implied endowed contingent incomes $(\bar{c}_1, \bar{c}_2) = (100, 100)$. Since the value of the individual's endowment is $\bar{W} = 100$, he could trade away his asset-1 holding for fifty units of asset 2 and attain the final consumptions $(c_1, c_2) = (200, 50)$ – point $N_2$ in the diagram. More generally, from equation (2.1.9) we see that the final consumption vector $(c_1, c_2)$ will lie along the line joining $N_1$ and $N_2$, at distances toward $N_1$ and $N_2$ in proportion to the relative wealth shares $\kappa_1$ and $\kappa_2$.

If the individual were constrained to hold non-negative amounts of assets, the opportunity boundary would be only the line-segment between $N_1$ and $N_2$ in the diagram. However, it is entirely permissible to let either $q_1$ or $q_2$ go negative. A negative $q_1$ (which implies, of course, a negative $\kappa_1 \equiv P_1^A q_1 / \bar{W}$) means that the individual holds *liabilities* rather than assets of type 1; he is, in effect committed to *deliver* the amount $|q_1 z_{11}|$ if state 1 occurs and the amount $|q_1 z_{12}|$ if state 2 occurs. (This is sometimes described as being in a "short" position with regard to asset 1.) We will, however, be imposing a *non-negativity constraint upon the ultimate $c_1, c_2$ combinations* *arrived at*; the individual cannot end up consuming negative income in either state of the world. He cannot therefore go short on any asset to the extent of violating any of his delivery commitments – in effect, he is not permitted to "go bankrupt" in any state of the world. (And, *a fortiori*, he cannot go short on *all* assets simultaneously!) This means that, while the trading possible along the line MM' in figure 2.2 may extend beyond points $N_1$ and $N_2$, the attainable combinations remain bounded by the vertical and horizontal axes.

Having described the feasible alternatives we now consider the individual's actual portfolio-choice decision. Since the consumption vector $(c_1, c_2)$ is generated by his asset holdings as shown in (2.1.9), the individual can be regarded as choosing his portfolio asset shares $(\kappa_1, \kappa_2) \equiv (q_1 P_1^A/\overline{W}, q_2 P_2^A/\overline{W})$ so as to maximize expected utility subject to his asset-holding constraint, that is:

$$\underset{(\kappa_1, \kappa_2)}{\text{Max}}\ U = \pi_1 v(c_1) + \pi_2 v(c_2) \text{ subject to } \kappa_1 + \kappa_2 = 1$$

From (2.1.9) we know that:

$$\frac{\partial c_s}{\partial \kappa_1} = \frac{\overline{W}}{P_1^A} z_{1s} \quad \text{and} \quad \frac{\partial c_s}{\partial \kappa_2} = \frac{\overline{W}}{P_2^A} z_{2s}$$

Then the endowed wealth cancels out of the first-order condition for an interior optimum, which can be written:[6]

$$\frac{\sum\limits_{s=1}^{2} \pi_s v'(c_s) z_{1s}}{P_1^A} = \frac{\sum\limits_{s=1}^{2} \pi_s v'(c_s) z_{2s}}{P_2^A}$$

This says that, at his risk-bearing optimum, the individual will have adjusted his holdings of the two assets until their given prices become proportional to the expected marginal utilities he derives from the contingent consumptions they generate. Or, we can say: at the optimum, he will derive the same *expected marginal utility per dollar* held in each asset.

[6] The Lagrangian expression is:

$$\underset{(\kappa_1, \kappa_2)}{\text{Max}}\ L = \pi_1 v(c_1) + \pi_2 v(c_2) - \lambda(\kappa_1 + \kappa_2 - 1)$$

Setting the partial derivatives equal to zero leads to:

$$\pi_1 v'(c_1)(\overline{W}/P_1^A) z_{11} + \pi_2 v'(c_2)(\overline{W}/P_1^A) z_{12} = \lambda$$
$$\pi_1 v'(c_1)(\overline{W}/P_2^A) z_{21} + \pi_2 v'(c_2)(\overline{W}/P_2^A) z_{22} = \lambda$$

(Henceforth, the maximization calculus will not be spelled out in detail except where points of special interest or difficulty arise.)

An obvious generalization to any number $A$ of assets and $S$ of states leads to an adaptation of (2.1.6), The Fundamental Theorem of Risk-bearing, for a regime of asset markets:

RISK-BEARING THEOREM FOR ASSET MARKETS

$$\frac{\sum_s \pi_s v'(c_s) z_{1s}}{P_1^A} = \frac{\sum_s \pi_s v'(c_s) z_{2s}}{P_2^A} = \dots = \frac{\sum_s \pi_s v'(c_s) z_{As}}{P_A^A} \qquad (2.1.10)$$

We have now described the individual's optimal risk-bearing decision (i) in a market of elementary state-claims and (ii) in a market of more generally defined assets. It is natural to ask if trading in asset markets can replicate the results of a regime in which all state-claims are explicitly traded. The answer turns out to depend upon whether the set of tradable assets constitutes a regime of *complete* or *incomplete* markets.

*Complete markets*

Returning to the numerical example depicted in figure 2.2, where $A$ (the number of distinct assets) and $S$ (the number of states) both equal 2, if the individual has endowment $N_1$ and can trade elementary state-claims at prices $P_1$ and $P_2$ his budget constraint (line MM' in the diagram) would be:

$$P_1 c_1 + P_2 c_2 = P_1(100) + P_2(100) = \bar{W}$$

A market regime allowing trading in all the elementary state-claims is obviously complete. We will call it a regime of Complete Contingent Markets (CCM). The CCM regime provides a benchmark for measuring the completeness of alternative asset-market regimes.

In any asset-trading regime, the prices of assets can be directly computed if the state-claim prices are known. Specifically in our example, since any asset $a$ has state-contingent yields $z_{a1}, z_{a2}$, the market values of assets 1 and 2 are:

$$P_1^A = z_{11} P_1 + z_{12} P_2 = P_1 + P_2$$
$$P_2^A = z_{21} P_1 + z_{22} P_2 = 4P_1 + P_2$$

In order to establish whether an asset-market regime is or is not complete we must invert this analysis. That is, for given asset prices $P_a^A$ $(a = 1, \dots, A)$, the question is whether or not it is possible to extract the implicit state-claim prices. In our example, knowing that $(z_{11}, z_{12}) = (1, 1)$ and $(z_{21}, z_{22}) = (4, 1)$, we can rewrite the above equations in matrix form:

$$\begin{bmatrix} P_1^A \\ P_2^A \end{bmatrix} = \begin{bmatrix} 1 & 1 \\ 4 & 1 \end{bmatrix} \begin{bmatrix} P_1 \\ P_2 \end{bmatrix}$$

As the two rows are not proportional, we can invert the matrix and obtain:

$$\begin{bmatrix} P_1 \\ P_2 \end{bmatrix} = \begin{bmatrix} 1 & 1 \\ 4 & 1 \end{bmatrix}^{-1} \begin{bmatrix} P_1^A \\ P_2^A \end{bmatrix} = \begin{bmatrix} -\frac{1}{3} & \frac{1}{3} \\ \frac{4}{3} & -\frac{1}{3} \end{bmatrix} \begin{bmatrix} P_1^A \\ P_2^A \end{bmatrix}$$

So in this case it *is* possible to compute "implicit" state-claim prices from given asset prices. In our example, if (say) $P_1^A = 1$ and $P_2^A = 2$, then $P_1 = 1/3$ and $P_2 = 2/3$. So the implicit budget constraint in state-claim units would be:

$$\tfrac{1}{3}c_1 + \tfrac{2}{3}c_2 = \tfrac{1}{3}(100) + \tfrac{2}{3}(100) = 100$$

Thus, on the assumption (as already discussed) that traders are allowed to "go short" on either asset so long as they can guarantee delivery, the asset-market equilibrium is the same as would be attained under CCM. We will call a set of asset markets meeting this condition a regime of Complete Asset Markets (CAM).

Generalizing this example, suppose there are $S$ states and $A$ assets, exactly $S$ of which have *linearly independent* yield vectors. That is, suppose it is impossible to express any one of these $S$ yield vectors as a linear sum of the other $S-1$ asset yields. In economic terms this means that it is not possible to duplicate any of these $S$ assets by buying a combination of the other $S-1$ assets – i.e., all of the $S$ assets are economically distinct.[7] (Of course, this case can only come about if $A \geqslant S$, although $A$ greater than or equal to $S$ does not *guarantee* the existence of $S$ linearly independent assets.) So a complete asset markets (CAM) regime exists, in a world of $S$ states, if among the $A$ assets there are $S$ with linearly independent yield vectors.

Summarizing in compact and general form, given a state-claim price vector $(P_1, \ldots, P_S)$ the market value of asset $a$ is:

$$P_a^A = \sum_s z_{as} P_s \tag{2.1.11}$$

Or, in matrix notation for the entire set of assets:

$$P^A = P[z_{as}] \equiv PZ \tag{2.1.12}$$

This permits us always to generate asset prices from a known state-claim price vector. But the reverse can only be done under linear independence

---

[7] In our simple example with $A = S = 2$, the two yield vectors $(z_{11}, z_{12})$ and $(z_{21}, z_{22})$ were linearly independent since otherwise one vector would have been a scalar multiple of the other. I.e., the two rows of the $z$-matrix were not proportional, which is what permitted inverting the matrix.

(so that the matrix $Z \equiv [z_{as}]$ can be inverted). If so, the asset-market regime is complete (CAM holds): for any prices $P_1^A, \dots, P_A^A$ of the $A$ assets there will be a unique implicit state-claim price vector $(P_1, \dots, P_S)$. It follows that under CAM the Fundamental Theorem of Risk-bearing (2.1.6) also holds, in addition to the weaker Risk-bearing Theorem for Asset Markets (2.1.10).

### Incomplete markets

Consider now a three-state world with asset trading. For this trading regime to be complete, there would have to be three assets with linearly independent return vectors. In figure 2.3 the points $N_1, N_2, N_3$ represent an individual's three attainable single-asset portfolios, for assets $1, 2, 3$ respectively, while E indicates his endowed mixed portfolio of these three assets. The interior of the shaded triangle $N_1 N_2 N_3$ represents the state-contingent consumption combinations attainable by holding non-negative amounts of all three assets. As in the previous two-asset case, however, there is no reason to exclude "going short" on any asset – so long as the individual ends up with non-negative *consumption* entitlements in all three states, i.e., in the positive octant. If going short to this extent is allowed, any point in the larger triangle MM′M″ is an income combination attainable by holding some diversified portfolio. The equation of the "budget plane" through MM′M″ is:

$$P_1 c_1 + P_2 c_2 + P_3 c_3 = \overline{W}$$

It will be evident that, if the asset-market budget constraint corresponds to the full triangle MM′M″, we have a CAM regime: the choice of an optimal asset portfolio at given asset prices $(P_1^A, P_2^A, P_3^A)$ is equivalent to choosing an optimal state-claim consumption vector given some endowment point and a full set of implicit state-claim prices $(P_1, P_2, P_3)$.

Markets in such a three-state world can be *incomplete* in several distinct ways. First, there might simply be fewer than three assets available. In figure 2.3, if only assets 1 and 2 exist the individual's market opportunities consist only of the state-claim combinations shown by a "degenerate" budget constraint – the market line KK′ through points $N_1$ and $N_2$. Second, it might be that there is a third asset, in addition to asset 1 and 2, but this third asset is linearly dependent[8] upon 1 and 2 – indicated geometrically by the collinearity of points $N_1$, $N_2$, and $N_3'$. The line KK′ through these three points remains degenerate; once again, not all the $c_1, c_2, c_3$ state-claim combinations are attainable by market trading. Third,

---

[8] That is, it is possible to find an $\alpha$ and $\beta$ such that $(z_{31}, z_{32}, z_{33}) = \alpha(z_{11}, z_{12}, z_{13}) + \beta(z_{21}, z_{22}, z_{23})$.

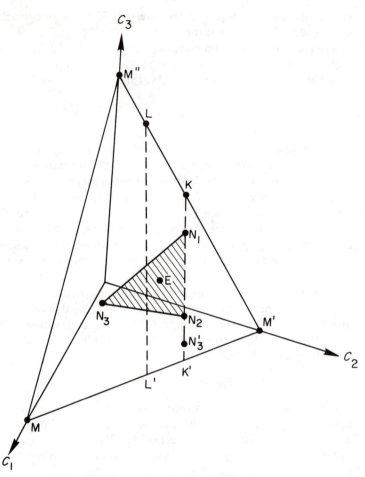

Figure 2.3  Alternative patterns of incomplete markets

it might be that the third asset, while present in an individual's endowment
and linearly independent of the other two, is *non-tradable*. (An example of
such a non-tradable asset might be one's "human capital.") Suppose now
that point E in figure 2.3 represents an endowment containing positive
amounts of a non-tradable asset 3 as well as of marketable assets 1 and 2.
Here the dotted line LL′ is the "degenerate" budget constraint for the
individual. Note that LL′ is parallel to the KK′ line that applied when there
was no third asset at all.

   In each of these cases there is no longer equivalence between trading in
asset markets and trading in Complete Contingent Markets (CCM). It

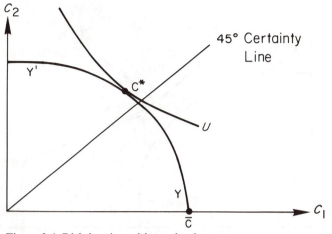

Figure 2.4 Risk-bearing with production

follows, and this is the crucial point, that, while the Risk-bearing Theorem for Asset Markets (2.1.10) will always hold, the Fundamental Theorem of Risk-bearing (2.1.6) does not.

When and why it is that *incomplete* trading regimes exist, despite the disadvantages just described, is a question we must leave to chapter 4.

### 2.1.3   Productive opportunities

So far in this section we have considered only the risk-bearing decisions of individuals in markets. But it is also possible to respond to risk by *productive* adjustments.

A Robinson Crusoe isolated from trading can adapt to risk solely by productive transformation. Before he takes productive action, suppose Robinson's corn crop is sure to be good if the weather is moist (state 1) but will fail entirely if the weather is dry (state 2). Thus, Robinson's endowment position $\bar{C}$ is along the $c_1$-axis of figure 2.4. However, by installing irrigation systems of greater or lesser extent, Robinson can improve his state-2 crop $y_2$. On the other hand, the effort required to do so will divert him from ordinary cultivation, and hence reduce his state-1 crop $y_1$. Then Robinson's feasible state-contingent outputs $(y_1, y_2)$ might lie in the convex set bounded by the axes and the curve YY'. This curve is "bowed away from the origin" reflecting the operation of diminishing returns. Robinson's productive-consumptive risk-bearing optimum will evidently be at point C\* (*not* in general on the 45° certainty line) where the production frontier YY' is tangent to his highest attainable indifference curve.

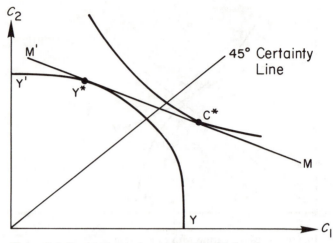

Figure 2.5 Productive and consumptive risk-bearing

Writing Robinson's productive opportunity constraint as $F(y_1, y_2) = 0$, his optimum (tangency) condition can be expressed as:

$$\frac{\partial F/\partial y_1}{\partial F/\partial y_2} \equiv -\left.\frac{dy_2}{dy_1}\right|_F = -\left.\frac{dc_2}{dc_1}\right|_U \equiv \frac{\pi_1 v'(c_1)}{\pi_2 v'(c_2)} \qquad (2.1.13)$$

By an obvious modification of our earlier argument, Robinson's optimum will lie on the 45° line only in the exceptional case where his Marginal Rate of Technical Substitution (the absolute slope $-dy_2/dy_1$ along YY′) happens to be exactly equal to the probability ratio $\pi_1/\pi_2$ at the point where YY′ cuts the certainty line. So, in his productive decisions, Robinson will not in general want to avoid all risk, even though it may be possible for him to do so. Some risks are profitable enough to be worth taking, i.e., they may represent sufficiently favorable productive gambles.

Now consider individuals who can combine both market opportunities and physical productive opportunities. In general, any such individual will have a productive optimum (indicated by Y* in figure 2.5) distinct from his consumptive optimum (indicated by C*). The availability of markets for trading contingent claims makes it possible to separate *productive* risk-bearing from *consumptive* risk-bearing. An example in everyday terms: a corporation may engage in risky productive activities, yet the shareholders may be able to largely eliminate personal risks by diversifying their individual portfolios.

Without going through the straightforward derivation, we will state the conditions for the individual's productive and consumptive optimum positions – assuming a regime of Complete Contingent Markets with explicit state-claim prices $P_1$ and $P_2$ (or an equivalent CAM regime for which the corresponding prices are implicitly calculable):

$$-\frac{dy_2}{dy_1}\bigg|_F \overset{\substack{\text{PRODUCTIVE} \\ \text{OPTIMUM} \\ \text{CONDITION}}}{=} \frac{P_1}{P_2} \overset{\substack{\text{CONSUMPTIVE} \\ \text{OPTIMUM} \\ \text{CONDITION}}}{=} -\frac{dc_2}{dc_1}\bigg|_U \qquad (2.1.14)$$

The price ratio here may be said to *mediate* between the individual's productive optimum and consumptive optimum. Whereas the Crusoe condition (2.1.13) required a direct equality of the YY' slope with an indifference curve at a single common productive-consumptive optimum, the availability of markets makes it possible for a person to separate his Y* and C* positions and thereby attain improved combinations of contingent consumptions.

As no essentially new ideas depend thereon, the generalized productive solutions for any number $S$ of states of the world and the complexities introduced by regimes of incomplete markets will not be detailed here.

EXERCISES AND EXCURSIONS 2.1

*1 Linear independence*

(A) With state-yields expressed in the form $(z_{a1}, z_{a2}, z_{a3})$, the rows below indicate different possible asset combinations (i) through (iv). Verify that only combinations (i) and (ii) are linearly independent.

|       | $a = 1$   | $a = 2$   | $a = 3$   |
|-------|-----------|-----------|-----------|
| (i)   | $(1,0,0)$ | $(0,1,0)$ | $(0,0,1)$ |
| (ii)  | $(1,1,1)$ | $(1,4,0)$ | $(0,7,1)$ |
| (iii) | $(0,2,3)$ | $(1,0,1)$ | $(0,4,6)$ |
| (iv)  | $(1,3,2)$ | $(4,0,5)$ | $(2,2,3)$ |

(B) For each of the combinations above, *if* it is possible to have $P_1^A = P_2^A = P_3^A = 1$ what can you say about the implied state-claim prices $P_1, P_2, P_3$? For given asset endowment holdings $\bar{q}_1 = \bar{q}_2 = \bar{q}_3 = 1$ solve for and picture the market plane $MM'M''$ in state-claim space, wherever it is possible to do so. (Where it is not possible to do so, picture the relevant trading opportunity constraint.)

ANSWER: In cases (i) and (ii) the three asset vectors are linearly independent.

(i)   From the symmetry of the problem, $(P_1, P_2, P_3) = (1, 1, 1)$.

(ii)  Equation (2.1.12), $PW = P^A$, becomes:

$$[P_1, P_2, P_3] \begin{bmatrix} 1 & 1 & 0 \\ 1 & 4 & 7 \\ 1 & 0 & 1 \end{bmatrix} = [1, 1, 1]$$

Inverting:

$$[P_1, P_2, P_3] = [1, 1, 1] \begin{bmatrix} 0.4 & -0.1 & 0.7 \\ 0.6 & 0.1 & -0.7 \\ -0.4 & 0.1 & 0.3 \end{bmatrix} = [0.6, 0.1, 0.3]$$

For the linearly independent cases, the market plane MM′M″ is determined by the price vector and the value of the endowment position ($\overline{W} = 3$):

(i)  $c_1 + c_2 + c_3 = 3$

(ii) $0 \cdot 75\, c_1 + 0 \cdot 0625\, c_2 + 0 \cdot 1875\, c_3 = 3$

For the linearly dependent case (iv), we must take account of the elements of the endowment position. Specifically, $\bar{q}_1 = \bar{q}_2 = \bar{q}_3 = 1$ translates into $(c_1, c_2, c_3) = (7, 5, 10)$. The trading opportunity constraint is a line in this space, cutting through the endowment position and all the single-asset portfolio points, for example, the point $(3, 9, 6)$ where only asset 1 is held. Then the equations of the line can be written:

$$\frac{c_1 - 7}{3 - 7} = \frac{c_2 - 5}{9 - 5} = \frac{c_3 - 10}{6 - 10}$$

which reduce to:

$$12 - c_1 = c_2 = 15 - c_3$$

(C)  For cases (i) and (ii) only of (A) above, assume instead that the endowment is given in state-claim units as $(\bar{c}_1, \bar{c}_2, \bar{c}_3) = (1, 1, 1)$, and that $P_2^A = P_3^A = 1$ while no trading is possible in asset 1. Picture the trading opportunity constraint in state-claim space.

## 2 Non-negativity

(A)  For each of the combinations in 1(A) above, would the asset-holding portfolio $q_1 = -1$, $q_2 = q_3 = 1$ violate the non-negativity constraint on state-incomes?

(B)  Suppose case (i) above were modified by replacing $a = 1$ with a new $a = 1'$ whose returns are $(-1, 2, 3)$. Would the combination $q_{1'} = q_2 = q_3 = 1$ be feasible? What if this new asset were instead to replace the first asset in case (ii) above?

## 3 Risk-bearing optimum

(A) In cases (i) and (ii) under 1(A), if explicit trading in state claims is ruled out, find the individual's risk-bearing optimum expressed as $(q_1^*, q_2^*, q_3^*)$ in asset units and as $(c_1^*, c_2^*, c_3^*)$ in state-claim units – if $\pi_1 = \pi_2 = \pi_3 = 1/3$, $P_1^A = P_2^A = P_3^A = 1$, $\bar{q}_1 = \bar{q}_2 = \bar{q}_3 = 1$, and $v(c) = \ln c$.

ANSWER: Since $v(c) = \ln c$, with state-claim prices $(P_1, P_2, P_3)$ the first-order conditions are:

$$\frac{\pi_1}{P_1 c_1} = \frac{\pi_2}{P_2 c_2} = \frac{\pi_3}{P_3 c_3} = \frac{1}{W}$$

where wealth $W$, value of the asset endowment, evidently equals 3. Since $\pi_1 = \pi_2 = \pi_3 = 1/3$, it follows that $c_s = 1/P_s$.

(i) $P = (1, 1, 1)$ implies $c^* = (1, 1, 1)$. Also, we can see that $q^* = (q_1^*, q_2^*, q_3^*) = (1, 1, 1)$.

(ii) $P = (0.6, 0.1, 0.3)$ implies $c^* = (10/6, 10, 10/3)$. And since $c^* = q^*[z_{as}]'$, $q^* = c^*[z_{as}]'^{-1} = (2, -1/3, 4/3)$.

(B) What can you say about cases (iii) and (iv)?

## 4 Consumer choice

An individual with preference-scaling function $v(c) = \ln c$ must choose a state-contingent consumption bundle $(c_1, \ldots, c_S)$. The price of a state-$s$ claim is $P_S$ and the consumer's initial endowment has a value of $\bar{W}$.

(A) Solve for the individual's optimum in each state.

(B) Hence show that for any pair of states $s$ and $s'$:

$$\frac{c_s}{c_{s'}} = \frac{\pi_s}{\pi_{s'}} \frac{P_{s'}}{P_s}$$

(C) What condition defines the state in which consumption is greatest? Least?

(D) Is the rule derived in (C) true for any concave preference-scaling function $v(c)$?

## 5 Portfolio choice

Asset 1 and asset 2 both cost \$150. Yields on asset 1 in states 1 and 2 are $(z_{11}, z_{12}) = (100, 200)$ and on asset 2 are $(z_{21}, z_{22}) = (200, 100)$. An individual with an initial wealth of \$150 has a preference-scaling function:

$$v(c) = -e^{-c}$$

(A) Show that the state-contingent budget constraint can be expressed as:

$$c_1 + c_2 = 300$$

(B) If the individual believes that state 1 will occur with probability $\pi$, show that his optimal consumption in state 1 is:

$$c_1^* = 150 + \tfrac{1}{2}\ln\left(\pi/(1-\pi)\right)$$

(C) If $q_1$ is the number of units of asset 1 purchased show that:

$$c_1^* = 200 - 100q_1^*$$

and hence obtain an expression for $q_1^*$ in terms of $\pi$, the probability of state 1.

(D) What values do $c_1^*$ and $q_1^*$ approach as the probability of state 1 becomes very small?

## 2.2    State-dependent utility

In risk-bearing decisions it sometimes appears that the individual's preference-scaling function $v(c)$ might itself depend upon the state of the world, contrary to our assumption in section 1.4 above. To take an extreme case, if the states under consideration were "being alive" versus "being dead" a typical individual would likely value rights to income in the former state more heavily! (Yet he might attach *some* "bequest utility" to income contingent upon his own death.) Similar considerations could apply if states of the world were defined in terms of one's sickness versus health, or life versus death of one's child, or success versus failure at love, or retention versus loss of a unique heirloom.[9]

For concreteness, think in terms of two states $s = \ell, \mathrm{d}$ corresponding to life versus death of one's child. Then we can imagine a *pair* of preference-scaling functions for consumption income, $v_\ell(c)$ and $v_\mathrm{d}(c)$ as in figure 2.6. For any given amount of income $c$, the former curve would definitely be the higher (an *ordinal* comparison). But the question is whether our analysis in section 1.4 can be extended so that, despite what appear to be two distinct $v(c)$ functions, a single cardinal scaling can be arrived at permitting use of the Expected-utility Rule.

This seemingly difficult problem resolves itself immediately, once it is realized that we are still really dealing with a *single* underlying preference-scaling function $v$. The only change is that $v$ is now to be regarded as a function of two "goods": $v \equiv v(c, h)$. The first argument $c$ still represents amounts of the consumption commodity, just as before. The second argument $h$ represents the amount of the state-determining or "heirloom" good; in our example, if the child lives (state $\ell$) then $h = 1$, if she dies (state $d$) then $h = 0$. The curves $v_\ell(c)$ and $v_\mathrm{d}(c)$ can therefore be more explicitly labelled $v(c, 1)$ and $v(c, 0)$; these two curves are not two separate preference-scaling functions for the parent, but two sections of his single overall

---

[9] Our discussion here follows Cook and Graham (1977) and Marshall (1984).

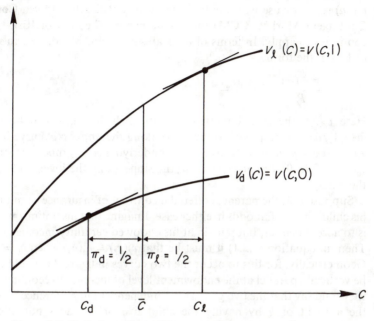

Figure 2.6 State-dependent utility – complementary preferences

$v(c, h)$ function. We already know, of course, that there is no difficulty deriving a cardinal preference-scaling function, where $v$ is a function of two or more goods (see Exercises and excursions 1.3).

We now turn to the risk-bearing decision under state-dependent utility. Suppose a risk-averse person is endowed with a given quantity $\bar{c}$ of income certain, but faces a gamble involving the heirloom commodity – his child might live or might die. Is it rational to insure one's child's life, at actuarial ("fair") odds? (Doing so means that the parent will end up with higher income if the child dies.) Or, should the parent do the opposite and buy an annuity upon his child's life, a contractual arrangement that provides more income so long as the child lives, but less if the child dies? Here is a less agitating example: if our college team is playing its traditional rivals in a crucial match, is it rational for us as loyal yet risk-averse fans to bet at fair odds *against* our team (equivalent to insuring our child's life), or to bet the other way (buy the annuity instead)? We can press matters further and ask: if it pays at fair odds to bet against the home team, might it ever be rational to bet so heavily as to end up preferring that the home team lose – or, as the disturbing equivalent, having optimally insured the child's life could loving parents ever prefer that the child die?

Since, as argued above, there is no difficulty in developing a cardinal $v(c, h)$ scale for use with the Expected-utility Rule, then (given Complete Contingent Markets CCM) the Fundamental Theorem of Risk-bearing continues to apply. In terms of the states $s = \ell$ and $s = $ d, we can rewrite (2.1.6) in the form:

$$\frac{\pi_1 v'_\ell(c_1)}{P_\ell} = \frac{\pi_d v'_d(c_d)}{P_d} \tag{2.2.1}$$

Here $v'_\ell(c_1)$, the state-1 marginal utility – which could also be written $\partial v(c, 1)/\partial c$ – corresponds to the slope along the upper $v(c)$ curve in figure 2.6, and is a *partial* derivative of the underlying $v(c, h)$ function. Similarly $v'_d(c_d) \equiv \partial v(c, 0)/\partial c$ corresponds to the slope along the lower $v(c)$ curve in the diagram.

Suppose that the parent is offered a contract of insurance or annuity on his child's life, at fair odds in either case. Imagine that his optimizing choice is to accept neither, but remain at his endowed certainty-income position. Then, in equation (2.2.1) it must be that $v'_\ell(c_\ell) = v'_d(c_d)$ when $\bar{c}_1 = \bar{c}_d = \bar{c}$. Geometrically, for this to occur the two curves in figure 2.6 would have to be vertically parallel at the endowment level of income. In economic terms we would say that the two goods are "independent in preference": varying the amount of $h$ by having the child live or die does not affect the *marginal* utility of the $c$ commodity (although it certainly affects the parent's *total* utility).

Suppose instead that the two goods are "complements in preference": an increase in $h$ raises $v'(c)$. Then at the endowment level of income the upper curve has steeper slope: $v'_\ell(\bar{c}) > v'_d(\bar{c})$; this is the situation pictured in figure 2.6. Because the slope along either curve diminishes as income increases (diminishing marginal utility, reflecting the risk-aversion property), it follows that the optimality equation (2.2.1) can be satisfied only by having $c_\ell > c_d$. (And specifically, if the probabilities are $\pi_\ell = \pi_d = \frac{1}{2}$, as in the diagram, then $c_\ell - \bar{c} = \bar{c} - c_d$.) To achieve this position the parent would purchase an annuity on his child's life. The economic interpretation is this: if having your child alive raises the marginal utility of income to you (perhaps because you mainly desire income only in order to meet her needs), then at fair odds you would not insure your child's life but would buy the annuity to generate more income while she lives.

Finally, if $c$ and $h$ are "substitutes in preference," i.e., if $v'_\ell(c) < v'_d(c)$, you would insure your child's life. This might correspond to a situation where your child, if she lives, would support you in your old age; not having that source of future support raises your marginal utility of income, since should the child die you will have to provide for your declining years yourself.

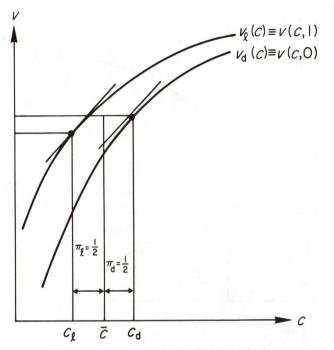

Figure 2.7 Insuring so that utility is higher in the loss state

Is it economically rational ever to insure so heavily as to actually end up preferring that the loss of $h$ occur? While an extreme case, it can happen! This is illustrated in figure 2.7, again with $\pi_d = \pi_\ell = \frac{1}{2}$ so that at fair odds $c_d - \bar{c} = \bar{c} - c_\ell$. The $v_d(c)$ curve lies entirely below the $v_\ell(c)$ curve, meaning that at any given level of income state $\ell$ is preferred over state d (the parent always prefers that his child lives). But, at the disparate contingent-income levels of the individual-optimum position after purchase of insurance, it is nevertheless the case that $v_d(c_d) > v_\ell(c_\ell)$. The interpretation is that the child's death raises the *marginal* utility of income to the parent so sharply that he optimally insures to the point of doing better should she die.

What about a parent insuring his *own* life on behalf of a child? Here the child's survival is not in question, so now we must let the states $s = \ell$ versus $s = d$ refer to the *parent's* life as the "heirloom" commodity. In such a situation the upper curve $v_\ell(c) \equiv v(c, 1)$ in figure 2.6 pictures the parent's "living utility" of consumption income while the lower curve $v_d(c) \equiv v(c, 0)$ shows the "bequest utility" he attaches to the child's income after his own death. There appears to be a puzzle here. It is reasonable to assume that $h$ and $c$ are complements in preference – in state $\ell$ there are

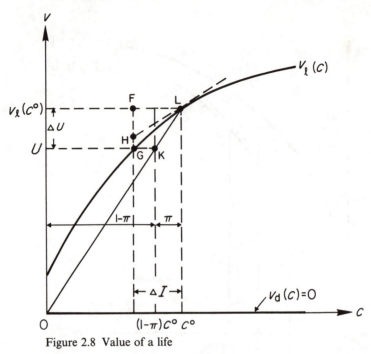

Figure 2.8  Value of a life

two persons, parent and child, who need income for purpose of consumption while in state d only the latter requires income. But whereas in our previous discussion complementary preferences led to purchase of an annuity rather than insuring, we know that parents do typically insure their lives on behalf of their children.

The puzzle is resolved when we realize that death of a parent will typically mean not only loss of the heirloom commodity (life), but *also* loss of income earnings that the parent would have generated. Consequently, the typical endowment position is not a life-risk plus a quantity of income certain ($\bar{c}_\ell = \bar{c}_d$), but rather involves a life-risk plus a correlated income-risk ($\bar{c}_\ell > \bar{c}_d$). In buying life insurance a risk-averse parent is purchasing an *offsetting gamble*, tending to reduce the overall riskiness of a situation in which both $c$ and $h$ take on low values should the state d occur.

### An application: the "Value of Life"

Figure 2.8 illustrates the situation of an individual choosing between higher income and higher survival probability, for example, working at a risky high-income profession versus a lower-paying but safer occupation.

As an analytical simplification, suppose that the individual has no dependents, so that his "bequest utility" function $v_d(c)$ can be assumed to be everywhere zero. Thus, the lower curve of our previous diagram now runs along the horizontal axis.[10] Let us suppose that he finds himself initially in the risky situation, with income $c^o$ if he survives. (His non-survival income, if any, is irrelevant since $v_d(c) = 0$ everywhere.) Denote the death probability as $\pi$, so the probability of survival is $1 - \pi$. Then the expected utility $U$ of this risky prospect is:

$$U \equiv (1 - \pi)v_\ell(c^o)$$

The expected utility of the endowed gamble is indicated in the diagram by the vertical height of point K, which is the probability-weighted average of point L where $(c, h) = (c^o, 1)$ and the origin 0 where $(c, h) = (0, 0)$. (Here as before, life is the "heirloom" commodity $h$.)

The *utility loss* due to the existence of the hazard (that is, in comparison with a situation with the same $c^o$ but where the death probability is $\pi = 0$) can be expressed as:

$$\Delta U = v_\ell(c^o) - U = \pi v_\ell(c^o)$$

This corresponds to the vertical distance between $v_\ell(c^o)$ and $U$ as marked off on the vertical axis of the diagram – the vertical distance between points F and G. Along the $v_\ell$ function, point G has the same utility as the endowed gamble (point K). So $\Delta I$, the income equivalent of the utility loss, is the horizontal difference between points G and L. $\Delta I$ may be termed the income-compensation differential: the remuneration reduction (viewed from point L) that this individual would be just willing to accept to be free of his endowed death risk.

We now seek a more general analytical expression for $\Delta I$. The line tangent to the $v_\ell(c)$ curve at L has slope $v'_\ell(c^o)$. Then the vertical distance between points F and H equals $\Delta I v'_\ell(c^o)$. As long as the death probability is fairly small[11] this distance is approximately equal to the vertical distance between the points F and G, which we have already seen is the utility loss $\pi v_1(c^o)$. So to a first approximation:

$$\Delta I v'_\ell(c^o) = \pi v_\ell(c^o)$$

or:

$$\Delta I = \frac{\pi v_\ell(c^o)}{v'_\ell(c^o)} = \frac{\pi c^o}{e}$$

---

[10] The $v_\ell(c)$ curve is shown as intersecting the vertical axis, which represents an arguable assumption that life (even at zero income) is preferable to death. However, only the local shape of $v_\ell(c)$ in the neighborhood of the endowment income plays any role in the analysis, so there is no need to insist upon this assumption.

[11] In occupational choices, $\pi$ is indeed quite low. The most hazardous industry grouping (logging, mining) had a reported fatality rate of $37 \cdot 6/10^8$ per hour, or approximately $0 \cdot 00075$ per year of 2,000 working hours. See Rappaport (1981).

where:

$$e = \frac{dU/dI}{U/I} = \frac{v_\ell'(c^o)}{v_\ell(c^o)/c^o}$$

Here $e$ signifies the income elasticity of utility, evaluated at the income level $c^o$. Since $\pi$ is the probability of loss, the other factor $v_\ell(c^o)/v_\ell'(c^o) = c^o/e$ then represents the *value of life*[12] implied by this analysis.

We must be careful not to misinterpret this value, however. It does not represent the amount that an individual would pay to "buy his life," for example if he were being held for ransom. It represents the exchange rate at which he would be willing to give up a *small* amount of income for a *small* reduction in the probability of death $\pi$ (when $\pi$ is close to zero). This can be shown more explicitly as follows. Since $U = (1-\pi)v_\ell(c^o)$, the Marginal Rate of Substitution $M(c, \pi)$ between income $c$ and death probability $\pi$ is:

$$M(c, \pi) \equiv \frac{dc}{d\pi}\bigg|_U \equiv \frac{-\partial U/\partial \pi}{\partial U/\partial c} = \frac{v_\ell(c^o)}{(1-\pi)v_\ell'(c^o)}$$

For $\pi$ close to zero the denominator is approximately $v_\ell'(c^o)$. Thus $v_\ell(c^o)/v_\ell'(c^o) = c^o/e$ does not represent the purchase price of a whole life, but the *Marginal Rate of Substitution* between small increments of income and survival probability.

Nevertheless, the interpretation in terms of "value of life" is not wholly unwarranted when we think in terms of society as a whole. Suppose that each member of a large population voluntarily accepts a 0.001 decrease in survival probability in order to earn $200 more income, implying a figure of $200,000 for the "value of life." Again this does not mean that any single individual would trade his whole life for $200,000; indeed, there might be no-one willing to make such a trade, for any amount of income whatsoever. But if everyone in a population of 1,000,000 accepts such a small per-capita hazard there will be about $200,000,000 more of income and about 1,000 additional deaths. So, in a sense $200,000 is indeed the "value of a life"!

---

[12] Of course, since death is ultimately certain, any increased chance of life can only be temporary. If we are dealing with *annual* death probability, we should really speak of the value of an *incremental year of life expectation*. But the dramatic, if misleading, term "value of life" is too firmly established to be displaced.

EXERCISES AND EXCURSIONS 2.2

*1 Betting for or against the home team?*

Your endowed income is $\bar{c} = 100$. There is a 50:50 chance that the home team will win the big game. You can bet at fair odds, picking either side to win and for any amount of money. Each of the utility functions (i) through (iv) below consists of a *pair* of preference-scaling functions, which differ depending upon whether the home team wins (W) or loses (L):

(i)  $v_W(c) = 2c^{0.5}$          and    $v_L(c) = c^{0.5}$
(ii) $v_W(c) = 2 - \exp(-c)$   and   $v_L(c) = 1 - \exp(-c)$
(iii) $v_W(c) = 1 - \exp(-2c)$   and   $v_L(c) = 1 - \exp(-c)$
(iv) $v_W(c) = \ln(50 + c)$    and   $v_L(c) = \ln(c)$

For each utility function:
(A) Verify that, at any level of income $c$, you prefer the home team to win.
(B) Find the optimal $b$, the amount of money bet on the home team (so that $b$ is negative if you bet *against* the home team).
(C) Having made the optimal bet, do you still want the home team to win? Explain the differences among the four cases.

ANSWER to (B) and (C): Since the odds are fair, in meeting the first-order conditions the individual in each case will set:

$$v'_W(\bar{c} + b) = v'_L(\bar{c} - b)$$

Straightforward computation then leads to:
(i) $b = 60$: You bet on the home team and so evidently continue to prefer that the home team win.
(ii) $b = 0$: You do not bet, so you still prefer that the home team win.
(iii) $b = -33.1$ (approximately): You bet *against* the home team, but nevertheless still prefer that the home team win.
(iv) $b = -25$: You bet *against* the home team, but now you are indifferent as to which team wins.

*Explanation*: (HINT) In (ii) the preference-scaling functions are vertically parallel; in (iv) they are horizontally parallel.

*2 Risk-preference under state-dependent utility?*

An individual can choose between two suburbs in which to live. The homes in the first suburb are small, while in the second they are large. Utility in the first suburb is:

$$v(c, h_1) = 8c^{\frac{1}{2}}$$

where $c$ is spending on goods other than housing (i.e., on "corn," whose price is unity). Utility in the second suburb is:

$$v(c, h_2) = 5c^{\frac{2}{3}}$$

Housing in the first suburb costs $20 per year and in the second costs $56.

(A) Sketch the two preference-scaling functions. Verify that the preference-scaling functions cross at $\bar{c} = 120$, and explain what this signifies.

(B) Suppose that before having invested in housing the individual's endowed income was $120. Consider the gamble corresponding to the prospect $(181, 56; 0.5, 0.5)$. Note that this is an adverse gamble; in comparison with the endowment income, the payoff is $61 and the possible loss is $64. Compute the individual's utility for each outcome and hence confirm that taking the gamble does raise expected utility.

(C) Indicate, geometrically, the optimal gamble for this individual. Explain why the individual wants to undertake such a gamble. [HINT: are $c$ and $h$ complements here?]

(D) Can this kind of argument explain why some people gamble regularly?

### 3 "Superstars" and the value of life

An individual with endowed income $\bar{c}$ has a concave preference-scaling function $v(c)$. He has contracted a disease which, if not treated, will be fatal with probability $1 - p_0$ and will spontaneously cure itself with probability $p_0$. His "bequest utility" in the event of death is zero everywhere.

(A) Suppose that, when treated by a physician who charges $z$, his probability of survival rises to $p$. If $z$ is his maximum willingness to pay for that treatment, show that:

$$pv(\bar{c} - z) = p_0 v(\bar{c})$$

(B) Hence show that:

$$\frac{dp}{dz} = \frac{p_0 v(\bar{c}) v'(\bar{c} - z)}{v(\bar{c} - z)^2}$$

Depict the relationship between $p$ and $z$ in a figure. Interpret its shape.

(C) Suppose a "superstar" physician can increase the individual's probability of survival by $1 - p_0$, so that he is sure to live, while another physician can increase this probability by only $(1 - p_0)/2$. Indicate in the figure the maximum amounts X and Y that the two physicians could charge.

(D) It has been asserted that "superstars" tend to receive disproportionally high incomes. In this context, this means that the ratio of physicians' fees would exceed the ratio of the survival rate increments that they provide. Assuming that both physicians can charge the maximum, is the assertion $X/Y > 2$ valid here?

(E) The maximum that the individual would be willing to pay a physician, who (in effect) provides him with "a fraction $p - p_o$ of his life," is $z(p)$ where this function is defined implicitly in part (A). Then it can be argued that his implied valuation of his own life is $z(p)/(p - p_o)$. For example, if $p_o = p - p_o = 0 \cdot 5$ and $X = \$100,000$, the value of his life would be \$200,000. Carry this argument to the limit in which $p$ is small and show that, at this limit, the value he places upon his life is $p_o v'(\bar{c})/v(\bar{c})$. Compare this conclusion with that reached at the end of the discussion in the text.

## 2.3    Choosing combinations of mean and standard deviation of income

### 2.3.1    $\mu, \sigma$ preferences

We have described decision-making under uncertainty as choice among actions or prospects $x = (c_1, \ldots, c_S; \pi_1, \ldots, \pi_S)$ – probability distributions that associate an amount of contingent consumption in each state of the world with the degree of belief attaching to that state. There is another approach to the risk-bearing decision that has proved to be very useful in modern finance theory and its applications. This alternative approach postulates that, for any individual, the probability distribution associated with any prospect is effectively represented by just two summary statistical measures: the *mean* and the *standard deviation* of income. Specifically, the individual is supposed always to prefer higher average income (measured by the expectation or mean $\mu(c)$ of the probability distribution achieved by holding any particular portfolio of assets) and lower variability of income (measured by the standard deviation $\sigma(c)$).[13] His preferences can therefore be represented by the indifference curves pictured on $\mu(c)$ and $\sigma(c)$ axes as in figure 2.9.

The approach in terms of preference for high $\mu(c)$ and low $\sigma(c)$ is broadly consistent with the previous analysis. In maximizing expected utility $Ev(c)$ under uncertainty, other things equal a higher average level of income is surely to be preferred. And, given risk-aversion, the theorem that fair gambles would not be accepted implies that distributions with low $\sigma(c)$ tend to be more desirable. Nevertheless, in moving from a probability

---

[13] Some analysts prefer to think in terms of the variance of income $\sigma^2(c)$. But for purposes of economic interpretation the standard deviation is more convenient, since $\sigma(c)$ has the same dimensionality as $\mu(c)$ and $c$ itself.

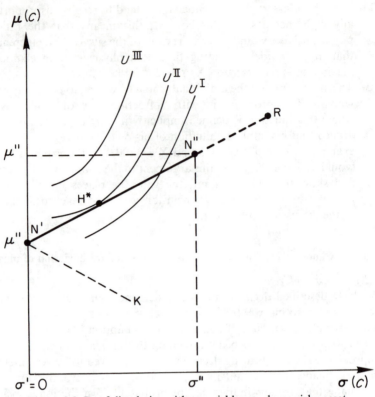

Figure 2.9 Portfolio choice with one riskless and one risky asset

distribution that was fully defined in terms of consequences in each and every state of the world to a mere statistical summary of that distribution – one that makes use only of the two parameters $\mu(c)$ and $\sigma(c)$ – some information has been lost. The question addressed here is: when, if ever, is such a reduction valid, exactly or at least approximately? That is, when can we justifiably convert $U = \mathrm{E}v(c)$ into a function only of $\mu(c)$ and $\sigma(c)$?

To indicate the nature of the approximation involved, $v(c)$ can be expanded in a Taylor's series about its expected value $\mathrm{E}\tilde{c} = \mu$:[14]

$$v(\tilde{c}) = v(\mu) + \frac{v'(\mu)}{1!}(\tilde{c}-\mu) + \frac{v''(\mu)}{2!}(\tilde{c}-\mu)^2 + \frac{v'''(\mu)}{3!}(\tilde{c}-\mu)^3 + \dots$$

$$(2.3.1)$$

Taking expectations, remembering that $U = \mathrm{E}v(\tilde{c})$ while noticing that the

[14] A tilde overlying any symbol indicates a random variable. We will use this notation only when it is desired to emphasize that feature.

expectation of $(\tilde{c}-\mu)$ is zero and that the expectation of $(\tilde{c}-\mu)^2$ is the variance $\sigma^2(\tilde{c})$, we have:

$$U = v(\mu) + \frac{v''(\mu)}{2!}\sigma^2 + \frac{v'''(\mu)}{3!}E(c-\mu)^3 + \dots \qquad (2.3.2)$$

The omitted terms suggested by the dots are functions of the fourth or higher powers of $(\tilde{c}-\mu)$ – higher moments about the mean, in statistical terminology.

Possible justifications for treating $U$ as a function only of the mean and standard deviation of income may be found (i) in the properties we are willing to assume for the preference-scaling function $v(c)$ or (ii) in the properties of the probability distribution of $\tilde{c}$.

(i) First of all, suppose that the $v(c)$ function is quadratic, so that it can be written (with $K_0, K_1$, and $K_2$ as constants):

$$v(c) = K_0 + K_1 c - \tfrac{1}{2}K_2 c^2 \quad (K_1, K_2 > 0) \qquad (2.3.3)$$

Then the third derivative $v'''(c)$ is always zero, as are all higher derivatives. So (2.3.2) can be expressed more specifically as:

$$U = K_0 + K_1 \mu - \tfrac{1}{2}K_2(\mu^2 + \sigma^2)$$

With $U$ as parameter, this equation represents a family of indifference curves on $\mu, \sigma$ axes in figure 2.9. By completing the square it may be verified that the curves constitute a set of concentric circles, the center being $\mu = K_1/K_2, \sigma = 0$.

However the preference-scaling function $v(c)$ given by (2.3.3) has an economically unacceptable implication – that the marginal utility of income, $v'(c) = K_1 - K_2 c$, eventually becomes negative. A quadratic $v(c)$ function thus leads to a highly special indifference-curve map, with acceptable properties only over a limited range.

(ii) Turning now to possible justifications that run in terms of probability distributions for $\tilde{c}$, the Central Limit Theorem of probability theory offers a lead. While a full discussion would be out of place here, the Central Limit Theorem essentially says that the distribution of the sum of any large number $N$ of random variables approaches the *normal distribution* as $N$ increases – provided only that the variables are not perfectly correlated. The point is that the overall or portfolio income $\tilde{c}$ yielded by an individual's holdings of assets can be regarded as the sum of underlying random variables, each summand representing the income generated by one of the assets entering into his portfolio. The normal distribution is fully specified by just two parameters, its mean and standard deviation. Then, in equation

(2.3.2), while the terms involving higher moments do not all disappear,[15] the higher moments remaining are functions of the mean and standard deviation.[16] It therefore follows that indifference curves for alternative normal distributions of consumption income $\tilde{c}$ can be drawn on $\mu(c)$, $\sigma(c)$ axes.[17]

The tendency toward normality under the Central Limit Theorem is the stronger, roughly speaking, the closer to normal are the underlying random variables, the more equal are their weights in the summation, and the less correlated they are with one another. Looking at portfolio income as the summation variable, income yields of the assets that comprise portfolios will rarely if ever have normal distributions themselves. In particular, the normal distribution extends out to negative infinity, whereas any "limited liability" asset cannot generate unlimited negative income. (And even without limited liability, personal bankruptcy establishes a lower limit on how large a negative yield the individual need consider.) Furthermore, asset weights in portfolios tend to be highly unequal: a person will likely have more than half his income associated with his wage earnings – the income generated by his single "human capital" asset. And, finally, there typically is considerable correlation among returns on the different assets comprising any portfolio. Portfolios for which the Central Limit Theorem justifies use of the normal distribution as approximation are called "well-diversified"; unfortunately, we have no handy rule for deciding when a portfolio may be considered well-diversified. For all the reasons given above, use of the normal distribution as approximation remains subject to considerable questions.

It is of interest to consider the effect upon utility of the third moment $E(\tilde{c} - \mu)^3$ – entering into the leading term dropped from (2.3.2) if the normal approximation is adopted. The third moment is a measure of *skewness*: skewness is zero if the two tails of a distribution are symmetrical, positive if the probability mass humps toward the left (so that the right tail is long and thin), and negative in the opposite case. To see the effect of skewness, consider an investor choosing between two gambles with the same means and standard deviations. Specifically, suppose gamble J offers 0.999 probability of losing \$1 and 0·001 probability of gaining \$999, while

---

[15] Since the normal distribution is symmetrical about its mean, all the higher *odd* moments are zero, but the even moments do not disappear.

[16] There are other families of statistical distributions, besides the normal, that are fully specified by the mean and standard deviation. However, as we have seen, the Central Limit Theorem leads specifically to the normal as the approximating distribution of portfolio income.

[17] We have not, however, justified the standard shape of the preference map pictured in figure 2.9. A proof that normally distributed returns imply positive indifference-curve slope and curvature, as shown in the diagram, is provided in Copeland and Weston (1983), pp. 82–4.

gamble K offers 0·999 probability of gaining $1 and 0·001 probability of losing $999. J and K have the same mean (zero) and the same standard deviation, but J is positively skewed while K is negatively skewed. Almost all commercial lotteries and games of chance are of form J, thus suggesting that individuals tend to prefer positive skewness. While the primary purpose of diversification is to reduce the standard deviation of income, diversification also tends to eliminate skewness – since the normal distribution that is approached has zero skewness. We would expect to see, therefore, lesser desire to diversify where skewness of the portfolio held is positive, greater desire to diversify where skewness is negative. But the main point is that the survival of preference for positive skewness suggests that individual real-world portfolios are typically not so well-diversified.

The upshot, then, is that the attempt to reduce preferences for income prospects to preferences in terms of $\mu(c)$ and $\sigma(c)$ falls short of being fully satisfying. But the approach remains an eminently manageable approximation, expressed as it is in terms of potentially measurable characteristics of individual portfolios and (as we shall see shortly) of the assets that comprise portfolios. The ultimate test of any such approximation is, of course, its value as a guide to understanding and prediction.

### 2.3.2   Opportunity set and risk-bearing optimum

In examining the individual's opportunities for achieving combinations of mean and standard deviation of portfolio income – $\mu(c)$ and $\sigma(c)$ – in his risk-bearing decisions, we need to show how these statistical properties of consumption income emerge from the yields generated by the separate assets held.

For any asset $a$, let $\mu_a$ represent the mean of the income yield $\tilde{z}_a$ per unit of $a$ held. Let $\sigma_a$ represent the standard deviation of $\tilde{z}_a$, and $\sigma_{ab}$ the covariance of $\tilde{z}_a$ and $\tilde{z}_b$. Then, following the usual statistical definitions:

$$\mu_a \equiv E(\tilde{z}_a) \tag{2.3.4}$$
$$\sigma_a \equiv [E(\tilde{z}_a - \mu_a)^2]^{\frac{1}{2}} \tag{2.3.5}$$
$$\sigma_{ab} \equiv E(\tilde{z}_a - \mu_a)(\tilde{z}_b - \mu_b) \tag{2.3.6}$$

And, of course, $\sigma_a \equiv (\sigma_{aa})^{\frac{1}{2}}$.

If the individual holds a portfolio consisting of $q_a$ units each of assets $a = 1, \ldots, A$ his portfolio income statistics are related to the asset return parameters above via:

$$\mu(c) \equiv \mu \equiv \sum_a q_a \mu_a \tag{2.3.7}$$

$$\sigma(c) \equiv \sigma \equiv \left( \sum_a \sum_b q_a \sigma_{ab} q_b \right)^{\frac{1}{2}} \equiv \left( \sum_a \sum_b \sigma_a q_a \rho_{ab} q_b \sigma_b \right)^{\frac{1}{2}} \tag{2.3.8}$$

Here $\rho_{ab}$ is the simple correlation coefficient between the distributions of $\tilde{z}_a$ and $\tilde{z}_b$, using the identity $\sigma_{ab} \equiv \sigma_a \rho_{ab} \sigma_b$ that relates covariance and the correlation coefficient.

The individual's budget constraint can be written in terms of his asset holdings (compare equation (2.1.7)) as:

$$\sum_a P_a^A q_a = \sum_a P_a^A \bar{q}_a \equiv \overline{W} \tag{2.3.9}$$

Drawn on $\mu(c)$, $\sigma(c)$ axes, this budget constraint bounds an opportunity set of feasible combinations of mean and standard deviation of portfolio income. We now need to determine the characteristic shape of this opportunity set. (But notice that, since the individual desires high $\mu$ and low $\sigma$, he will be interested only in the north-west boundary.)

To start with the simplest case, suppose there are just two assets, and that asset 1 is riskless ($\sigma_1 = 0$) while asset 2 is risky ($\sigma_2 > 0$). For this to be at all an interesting situation, it must of course also be true that $\mu_2/P_2^A > \mu_1/P_1^A$ – i.e., the risky asset has a higher mean yield per dollar. The portfolio income yield is a random variable given by:

$$\tilde{c} \equiv q_1 z_1 + q_2 \tilde{z}_2 \tag{2.3.10}$$

In this simplest case, with $q_2$ units of asset 2 purchased at a cost of $P_2^A q_2$ the individual has $\overline{W} - P_2^A q_2$ dollars to invest in the riskless asset 1. For any security $a$, we can define its rate of return $R_a$ in:

$$\frac{z_a}{P_a^A} \equiv 1 + R_a \tag{2.3.11}$$

Then $R_1 \equiv z_1/P_1^A - 1$ is the rate of return on the riskless asset.[18] Expression (2.3.10) can then be rewritten as:

$$\tilde{c} = (\overline{W} - P_2^A q_2)(1 + R_1) + q_2 \tilde{z}_2$$

And the parameters of the income distribution become:

$$\mu(c) = \overline{W}(1 + R_1) + [\mu_2 - (1 + R_1) P_2^A] q_2 \tag{2.3.12}$$
$$\sigma(c) = \sigma_2 q_2 \tag{2.3.13}$$

It then follows that the budget constraint on $\mu, \sigma$ axes is a straight line, shown as $N'N''$ in figure 2.9. (The opportunity set consists of the line and the area lying below it in the diagram.) Point $N'$ is the $\mu, \sigma$ combination

---

[18] This terminology would be appropriate if, as is usually assumed in the finance literature, the assets are purchased (the prices $P_a^A$ are paid out) one time-period earlier than the date of the income yields $\tilde{z}_a$. Strictly speaking, such a convention implies an *intertemporal* choice situation, where earlier consumption should be balanced against later consumption, over and above the a-temporal risk-bearing choices we have dealt with so far. However, we will follow the finance tradition in using "rate of interest" terminology without necessarily addressing the problem of intertemporal choice.

$\mu', \sigma'$ attainable by holding a single-asset portfolio consisting of the riskless asset (asset 1) exclusively. For this portfolio, $\mu'(\tilde{c}) = (\overline{W}/P_1^A)z_1 = \overline{W}(1 + R_1)$ while $\sigma'(\tilde{c}) = 0$. Point N″ is the $\mu, \sigma$ combination $\mu'', \sigma''$ generated by the single-asset portfolio consisting of the risky asset (asset 2). Here $\mu''(\tilde{c}) = (\overline{W}/P_2^A)\mu_2$ while $\sigma''(\tilde{c}) = (\overline{W}/P_2^A)\sigma_2$.

What about portfolios containing mixtures of the two assets? If the fractional shares of wealth devoted to the riskless and the risky assets are $\alpha = q_1 P_1^A / \overline{W}$ and $\kappa = q_2 P_2^A / \overline{W}$ respectively, where $\alpha + \kappa = 1$, the portfolio statistics $\mu$ and $\sigma$ can each be written in two useful ways:

$$\mu = \alpha\mu' + \kappa\mu'' = \overline{W}(1 + R_1) + [\mu_2 - (1 + R_1)P_2^A]q_2 \qquad (2.3.14)$$
$$\sigma = \kappa\sigma'' \qquad = \sigma_2 q_2$$

It follows that the budget constraint can also be written in two ways:

$$\mu = \frac{\mu'' - \mu'}{\sigma''}\sigma + \mu' \qquad (2.3.15)$$

$$\mu = \overline{W}(1 + R_1) + [\mu_2 - (1 + R_1)P_2^A]\sigma/\sigma_2$$

It is evident that all the $\mu, \sigma$ combinations satisfying these conditions (meeting the budget constraint) fall along the straight line N′N″ in the diagram. The constant slope $d\mu/d\sigma$ of this budget constraint line is known as "the price of risk reduction," which we will symbolize as $\Theta$:

### THE PRICE OF RISK REDUCTION

$$\Theta \equiv \frac{d\mu}{d\sigma} = \frac{\mu'' - \mu'}{\sigma''} = \frac{\mu_2 - (1 + R_1)P_2^A}{\sigma_2} \qquad (2.3.16)$$

Note that the steepness of the opportunity line reflects only the market or "objective" data.[19]

To find the individual optimum, the budget constraint must be juxtaposed against the "subjective" data of the individual's preference function. This solution is, of course, a familiar type of tangency: in figure 2.9, the point H* is the individual's risk-bearing optimum on $\mu, \sigma$ axes.

Could a portfolio be represented by a $\mu, \sigma$ combination along the (dashed) extension of N′N″ lying to the north-east of point N″, which would correspond to holding *negative amounts* of the riskless security? This is sometimes referred to as "selling short" the riskless security, which means incurring a liability requiring *delivery* of the promised amount of income certain. Incurring such a debt can also be thought of as "issuing"

---

[19] The parameters involved in the expression for $d\mu/d\sigma$ are "objective" in that they reflect the individual's market opportunities independent of what his personal *preferences* might be. However, a "subjective" element may still enter if *beliefs* about market parameters vary from person to person. While asset prices $P_a^A$ can usually be taken as interpersonally agreed data, there might well be disagreement about some or all of the security yield parameters $\mu_a, \sigma_a$. If there were such disagreement, the implicit "price of risk reduction" would vary from person to person.

units of the riskless security. As explained earlier, doing so would be perfectly reasonable provided that the issuer can really satisfy such an obligation with certainty. Clearly, the opportunity line N′N″ cannot be extended to the north-east without limit: someone with risky assets and riskless liabilities faces some likelihood of bankruptcy, owing to states of the world in which the risky earnings fail to cover the fixed obligation of repaying the debt.[20] In the literature of finance theory it is usually assumed that tangencies in the "short sales" region are possible, at least within the range of practical interest. In our diagram, the termination of the dashed extension of N′N″ at point R indicates the limit to which riskless debt can be issued by the investor in order to achieve a larger holding of risky assets.

What about "selling short" the *risky* security instead – i.e., incurring an obligation to meet varying payments over states of the world, while enlarging one's holding of riskless claims? By an analogous argument, this may also be feasible up to a point. It is not difficult to show that such portfolios lead to $\mu, \sigma$ combinations along a line like N′K in figure 2.9, which clearly cannot be a portion of the efficient opportunity boundary.

Figure 2.10 illustrates the efficient boundary for proper portfolio combinations of two *risky* securities. (We will not consider "short selling" in this discussion.) If asset 2, let us say, has a higher mean return per dollar than asset 3 ($\mu_2/P_2^A > \mu_3/P_3^A$), then for the situation to be interesting once again it must also be that asset 2 involves a greater risk per dollar as well ($\sigma_2/P_2^A > \sigma_3/P_3^A$). In the diagram, points N″ and N‴ represent the single-asset portfolios for securities 2 and 3, respectively, where $\mu'' > \mu'''$ and $\sigma'' > \sigma'''$.

The diagram illustrates how *diversification*, holding a mixture of assets, tends to reduce portfolio standard deviation $\sigma$. The power of diversification is a function of the size and sign of the correlation coefficient $\rho_{23} \equiv \sigma_{23}/\sigma_2\sigma_3$ (henceforth, $\rho$ for short) between the asset return distributions $\tilde{z}_2$ and $\tilde{z}_3$.

Consider first the limiting case of *perfect positive correlation* ($\rho = 1$). Here the $\mu, \sigma$ combinations associated with mixtures of assets 2 and 3 would lie along the straight line N″N‴ in figure 2.10, at distances proportionate to the relative budget shares.[21] If instead the yields on the

---

[20] If risky portfolio income were normally distributed, there would always be some non-zero probability of negative returns exceeding *any* preassigned limit. No holder of such a risky distribution could ever issue even the tiniest riskless security obligation, since he could not guarantee to repay a debt with certainty.

[21] If the budget shares are $\kappa = q_2 P_2^A/\overline{W}$ and $1 - \kappa = q_3 P_3^A/\overline{W}$ then $\mu = \kappa\mu'' + (1-\kappa)\mu'''$, where $\mu'' = \overline{W}\mu_2/P_2^A$ and $\mu''' = \overline{W}\mu_3/P_3^A$ are the mean yields on the respective single-asset portfolios. And $\sigma$, from (2.3.8), is:

$$\sigma = [(\kappa\sigma'')^2 + 2\rho\kappa(1-\kappa)\sigma''\sigma''' + ((1-\kappa)\sigma''')^2]^{\frac{1}{2}}$$

If $\rho = 1$, then $\sigma = \kappa\sigma'' + (1-\kappa)\sigma'''$. So $\mu$ and $\sigma$ both increase linearly with $\kappa$, proving the assertion in the text.

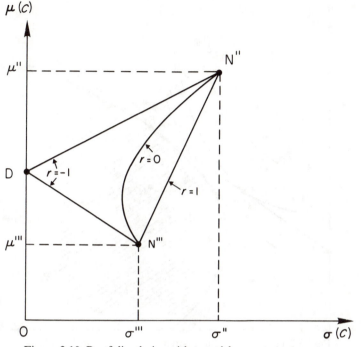

Figure 2.10 Portfolio choice with two risky assets

two assets were *uncorrelated* ($\rho = 0$), the attainable $\mu, \sigma$ combinations would fall on a boundary represented by the middle curve connecting N" and N''' in the diagram. It is important to notice that in the region of point N''' the slope $d\mu/d\sigma$ of this curve becomes actually negative, the implication being that the efficient opportunity boundary no longer includes point N''' itself.[22] Thus, for any portfolio of two uncorrelated risky assets, the single-asset portfolio consisting of the lower-$\mu$, lower-$\sigma$ (per dollar of cost) security is driven out of the efficient set. More generally, the slope $d\mu/d\sigma$ will be negative if $\sigma''' > \rho\sigma''$.[23] So, for any number of risky assets, if all yields are uncorrelated then only one single-asset portfolio would be located on the efficient boundary, to wit, the portfolio consisting of that

---

[22] As $\kappa$ increases, the slope along any of the curves connecting N" and N''' can be written:

$$\frac{d\mu}{d\sigma} = \frac{d\mu/d\kappa}{d\sigma/d\kappa} = \frac{\mu'' - \mu'''}{[\kappa(\sigma'')^2 + (1-2\kappa)\sigma''\rho\sigma''' - (1-\kappa)(\sigma''')^2]/\sigma}$$

If $\rho \leqslant 0$, at point N''' where $\kappa = 0$ the denominator will be negative, hence $d\mu/d\sigma$ will be negative. So there will exist a portfolio with $\kappa > 0$ having lower $\sigma$ and higher $\mu$ than the asset-3 single-asset portfolio.

[23] From the preceding footnote, the sign of $d\mu/d\sigma$ when $\kappa = 0$ will be the same as the sign of $\rho\sigma''\sigma''' - (\sigma''')^2$ or $\rho\sigma'' - \sigma'''$.

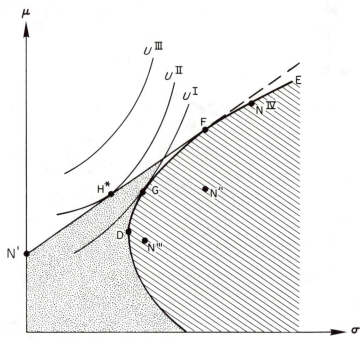

Figure 2.11 Mutual-fund theorem

asset $a^*$ which offers highest yield per dollar ($\mu_{a^*}/P_{a^*}^A > \mu_a/P_a^A$ for any $a \neq a^*$). But, if asset yields are correlated, any asset with sufficiently high positive correlation with $a^*$ might also be an efficient single-asset portfolio.

Finally, in the limiting case of *perfect negative correlation* ($\rho = -1$), the $\sigma$-reducing effect of diversification is so great that the curve N″N‴ breaks into two lines meeting at the vertical axis (at point D). Thus, with $\rho = -1$ it is possible to achieve a riskless combination of two risky assets.[24] Of course, here again point N‴ can no longer be in the efficient set.

Generalizing the previous diagram to any number of assets, figure 2.11 is intended to suggest the nature of the opportunity set and efficient (north-west) boundary. If there are only risky securities available, the opportunity set will be the shaded area whose north-west (efficient) boundary is the curve DE. Here points N″ and N‴ represent single-asset portfolios that are not efficient, whereas point N^{IV} represents an efficient single-asset portfolio. Owing to the power of diversification, almost all of the boundary DE would likely represent multiasset portfolio mixtures.

The introduction of a *riskless* asset, whose single-asset portfolio is represented by point N′, enlarges the opportunity set by the dotted area in

[24] If $\rho = -1$, then $\sigma = \kappa\sigma'' - (1-\kappa)\sigma'''$. Setting $\kappa = \sigma'''/(\sigma''+\sigma''')$, we have $\sigma = 0$.

the diagram. The efficient boundary now becomes the line from N' drawn tangent to the DE curve (at point F). In general, as just argued, F would represent a particular mixed portfolio of assets.

In the absence of the riskless asset the individual's risk-bearing optimum (indifference-curve tangency) would be at point G along the curve DE. But for the opportunity set enlarged by the presence of the riskless asset, the optimum is at point H* along the line N'F. As discussed earlier, we also admit the possibility that H* might fall in the dashed extension to the north-east of F along this line, representing an individual who issues riskless obligations in order to hold more than 100% of his endowed wealth in the form of the risky combination F.

### The Mutual-fund Theorem

An important result follows from our previous discussion:

> If individuals' preferences are summarized by desire for large $\mu$ and small $\sigma$, and if there exists a single riskless asset and a number of risky assets, in equilibrium the asset prices will be such that everyone will wish to purchase the *risky* assets in the same proportions.

Thus, if one individual holds risky assets 2 and 3 in the quantities $q_2 = 10$ and $q_3 = 9$, someone who is richer (or less risk-averse) might hold larger amounts of each risky asset – but still in the ratio 10:9! This remarkable "Mutual-fund Theorem" underlies all the main properties of the Capital Asset Pricing Model (CAPM), which constitutes the centerpiece of modern finance theory. (CAPM will be discussed further in chapter 4.)

Justification of the theorem requires no complicated analytical apparatus. All we need do is to re-interpret the opportunity set of figure 2.11 in per-dollar-of-wealth terms. Thus, for any individual the vertical axis would now be scaled in units of $\mu/\overline{W}$ and the horizontal axis in units of $\sigma/\overline{W}$. Since both axes are being divided by the same constant, the opportunity set would change only by a scale factor. For example, the single-asset portfolio corresponding to any asset $a$ that formerly was represented by the vector $(\mu^a, \sigma^a)$ – where $\mu^a = (\overline{W}/P_a^A)\mu_a$ and $\sigma^a = (\overline{W}/P_a^A)\sigma_a$ – would now have the coordinates $\mu^a/\overline{W} = \mu_a/P_a^A$ and $\sigma^a/\overline{W} = \sigma_a/P_a^A$. And, in particular, points N' and F would similarly maintain their positions, so that the efficient boundary N'F would have the same slope as before.

The significance of this conversion to per-dollar dimensions is that, in these per-dollar units, *every individual in the economy, regardless of wealth, faces exactly the same opportunities*! If asset $a$ offers a mean yield per dollar $\mu_a/P_a^A$ to one individual, it offers the same per-dollar mean yield to everyone. And similarly for the standard deviation per dollar $\sigma_a/P_a^A$ of asset $a$, and for all combinations of assets as well. Thus, every individual will hold, in whatever fraction of his wealth is devoted to risky securities, the same proportionate mixture of assets represented by point F in the diagram. So, we can say, a "mutual fund" of risky securities set up to meet the needs of any single investor will meet the needs of all.[25] What still does vary among individuals is the *fraction of wealth held in riskless versus risky form*, a decision that will depend upon individuals' varying personal preferences as to risk-bearing (the shapes of their indifference curves in the original diagram of figure 2.11).

In the economy as a whole, there is exactly one unit of this mutual fund $F$, corresponding to the economy-wide amounts $(q_2^F, ..., q_A^F)$ of the risky assets $a = 2, ..., A$. (So the typical individual will be holding a fractional unit of F.) Then the price $P_F^A$ of a unit of the fund is:

$$P_F^A = \sum_{a=2}^{A} q_a^F P_a^A \tag{2.3.17}$$

Writing the mean return and standard deviation of return for a unit of portfolio $F$ as $\mu_F$ and $\sigma_F$, we can obtain an expression for $\Theta \equiv d\mu/d\sigma$ – the price of risk reduction – in terms of the slope of the line N'F in figure 2.11. For any individual, point N' (the riskless single-asset portfolio) has $\mu$-coordinate $\mu' = (\overline{W}/P_1^A)\mu_1 = \overline{W}(1 + R_1)$ and $\sigma$-coordinate $\sigma' = 0$. Point F (the portfolio held entirely in the mutual fund) has $\mu$-coordinate $\mu^F = (\overline{W}/P_F^A)\mu_F$ and $\sigma$-coordinate $\sigma^F = (\overline{W}/P_F^A)\sigma_F$. So the steepness of the line is:

$$\frac{d\mu}{d\sigma} = \frac{\mu^F - \mu'}{\sigma^F - \sigma'} = \frac{(\overline{W}/P_F^A)\mu_F - \overline{W}(1 + R_1)}{(\overline{W}/P_F^A)\sigma_F} = \frac{\mu_F/P_F^A - (1 + R_1)}{\sigma_F/P_F^A}$$

$$\tag{2.3.18}$$

Note that, consistent with our previous discussion, the individual wealth parameter $\overline{W}$ has cancelled out. Thus, a corollary of the Mutual-fund Theorem is that *the price of risk reduction is the same for every individual.*

## EXERCISES AND EXCURSIONS 2.3

### 1 Ranking of alternative wealth prospects

An individual with preference-scaling function $v(c) = c^{0.5}$ has an initial wealth of zero. He must choose one of two jobs. In the first there is an equal probability of earning 1 or 3. In the second there is a probability of $\frac{1}{9}$ that

---

[25] If, however, individuals differed in their personal estimates of the asset characteristics $\mu_a$ and $\sigma_a$, their perceived opportunity sets would not be identical in per-dollar units and the Mutual-fund Theorem would not be valid.

he will earn zero, a probability of $\frac{7}{9}$ that he will earn 2, and a probability of $\frac{1}{9}$ that he will earn 4.

(A) Show that both jobs have the same mean income $\mu$, that the standard deviation of income $\sigma$ is lower in the second job, and that despite this the individual will choose the first job.

(B) Can you explain this result in terms of preferences for skewness? If not, what is the explanation?

## 2 Constant absolute risk-aversion and normally distributed asset returns

(A) Show that

$$Ac+\frac{1}{2}\left(\frac{c-\mu}{\sigma}\right)^2 = \frac{1}{2}\left(\frac{c-(\mu-A\sigma^2)}{\sigma}\right)^2 + A\left(\mu-\frac{1}{2}A\sigma^2\right)$$

where $A \equiv -v''(c)/v'(c)$ is known as the measure of "absolute risk-aversion." Hence, or otherwise, show that if $c$ is distributed normally with mean $\mu$ and variance $\sigma^2$ and if $v(c) = -e^{-Ac}$ then:

$$Ev(c) = -\int_{-\infty}^{\infty} e^{-Ac}\frac{1}{(2\pi)^{\frac{1}{2}}}\exp\left\{-\frac{1}{2}\left(\frac{c-\mu}{\sigma}\right)^2\right\}dc = -e^{-A(\mu-\frac{1}{2}A\sigma^2)}$$

(B) Under the above assumption it follows that preference can be represented by the indirect utility function:

$$U(\mu, \sigma) = \mu-\frac{1}{2}A\sigma^2$$

Suppose an individual with such preferences must choose between a riskless asset and a normally distributed risky asset. Show that the amount of the risky asset purchased is independent of initial wealth and decreasing in the degree of absolute risk-aversion $A$. What happens if the indicated expenditure on the risky asset exceeds the individual's endowed wealth $\bar{W}$?

## 3 The $\mu,\sigma$ opportunity locus

An individual spends a fraction $\kappa$ of his wealth $\bar{W}$ on asset $a$ and the remainder on asset $b$. Each asset has a price of unity and the yields $(\tilde{z}_a, \tilde{z}_b)$ have means $\mu_a$ and $\mu_b$ and covariance matrix $[\sigma_{ab}]$.

(A) Obtain expressions for the mean $\mu$ and standard deviation $\sigma$ of the portfolio as functions of $\kappa$.

(B) Hence show that the standard deviation can be expressed as:

$$\sigma = \{[(\mu-\bar{W}\mu_a)^2\sigma_{aa}-2(\mu-\bar{W}\mu_a)(\mu-\bar{W}\mu_b)\sigma_{ab}$$
$$+(\mu-\bar{W}\mu_b)^2\sigma_{bb}]/(\mu_a-\mu_b)^2\}^{\frac{1}{2}}$$

(C) Suppose $\mu_a > \mu_b$ and $\sigma_{aa} > \sigma_{bb} > 0 \geqslant \sigma_{ab}$. Obtain an expression for the rate of change of $\sigma$ with respect to $\mu$. Hence establish that if the individual begins with all his wealth in asset $b$ he can increase the mean yield and simultaneously reduce the standard deviation by trading some of asset $b$ for asset $a$. Illustrate the locus of feasible $\mu, \sigma$ combinations in a diagram.

(D) Assuming the individual's utility is a function only of the mean and standard deviation, can you draw any conclusions as to the composition of his optimal portfolio?

## 4 Investor's portfolio optimum in a $\mu, \sigma$ model

In a competitive economy there are $I$ investors, all having the same utility function $U = \mu^{10} e^{-\sigma}$. Each individual is endowed with exactly one unit each of assets 1, 2, and 3 with payoff statistics as shown in the table below, all the payoff distributions being uncorrelated ($\sigma_{ab} = 0$, for all $a \neq b$). Given asset prices are also shown:

|         | $\mu_a$ | $\sigma_a$ | $P_a^A$ |
|---------|---------|------------|---------|
| Asset 1 | 1       | 0          | 1.0     |
| Asset 2 | 1       | 3          | 0.46    |
| Asset 3 | 1       | 4          | 0.04    |

(A) Sketch the indifference curves on $\mu(c), \sigma(c)$ axes. Locate, for any single individual, the three single-asset portfolios he might hold.

(B) Under the assumptions here, each individual's optimum portfolio H* must evidently be the same as his endowed portfolio. Locate this portfolio, and also the mutual fund portfolio $F$. What fraction of his wealth does the individual hold in the mutual fund?

(C) Verify that the price of risk reduction is $\Theta = \frac{3}{10}$. What is the equation of the individual's budget line? What is his Marginal Rate of Substitution (the slope of the indifference curve) at H*?

REFERENCES AND SELECTED READINGS

Cook, P. J. and Graham, D. A., "The Demand for Insurance and Protection: The Case of Irreplaceable Commodities," *Quarterly Journal of Economics*, 91 (February 1977).

Copeland, Thomas E. and Weston, J. Fred, *Financial Theory and Corporate Policy*, 2nd edn, Reading, MA: Addison-Wesley, 1983.

Marshall, John M., "Gambles and the Shadow Price of Death," *American Economic Review*, 74 (March, 1984).

Rappaport, Edward, "The Demand for Improvements in Mortality Probabilities," unpublished UCLA Ph.D. thesis (1981).

# 3    Comparative statics of the risk-bearing optimum

The elements of the decision problem under uncertainty – the individual's preferences, opportunities, and beliefs – were surveyed in chapter 1. We distinguished between *terminal* choices, actions undertaken on the basis of given probability beliefs (covered in part I of this volume), and *informational* choices, actions designed to improve one's knowledge of the world before a terminal decision has to be made (to be covered in part II). Chapter 2 analyzed the individual's *risk-bearing optimum*, the best terminal action to take in the face of uncertainty.

We now want to explore how these optimizing decisions change in response to variations in the person's character or situation (his or her wealth, tastes for risk, the endowment of goods, the market prices faced, and so forth). Modeling the before-and-after effects of such "parametric" changes, without attending to the dynamics of the actual transition path from one solution to another, is called the *method of comparative statics*. This chapter is devoted to the comparative statics of the individual's risk-bearing optimum.

## 3.1    Measures of risk-aversion

The individual's risk-bearing optimum depends critically upon his attitudes towards risk. And, since parametric changes generally involve positive or negative wealth effects, it will often be crucial to take into account how attitudes toward risk vary as a function of wealth.

As discussed in chapter 2, in a regime of Complete Contingent Markets with two states of the world the individual's wealth constraint is:

$$P_1 c_1 + P_2 c_2 = P_1 \bar{c}_1 + P_2 \bar{c}_2 \equiv \overline{W} \qquad (3.1.1)$$

Endowed wealth, $\overline{W}$, represents the market value of the endowment vector $\bar{C} = (\bar{c}_1, \bar{c}_2)$. As shown in figure 3.1, expected utility is maximized at the indifference-curve tangency $C^*$ along the original budget line $LL'$ (assuming an interior solution). As endowed wealth increases, the optimum position moves outward from $C^*$ along some *wealth expansion path* like $C^*B$ or $C^*D$ in the diagram.

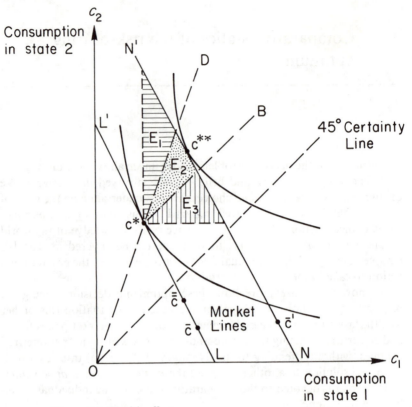

Figure 3.1 Wealth effects

Suppose that, after an increase in endowed wealth, the individual's new optimum lies north-east of the old optimum C* but below the line C*B (i.e., in region $E_3$). Since C*B is drawn parallel to the 45° line, all the points in $E_3$ lie closer to the 45° line than does C*. Thus, an individual whose wealth expansion path lies in this region reduces his *absolute consumption risk* (gap between $c_1$ and $c_2$) as his wealth increases. If instead (as shown in the diagram) his new optimum lies above the line C*B (in regions $E_1$ or $E_2$) his "tolerance" for absolute risk must be increasing with wealth. A solution along the dividing line C*B would represent constant tolerance for absolute risk. Or, putting it the other way, we can speak of increasing, decreasing, or constant *absolute risk-aversion* as wealth increases.

These alternative responses to changes in wealth imply restrictions upon the shape of the individual's preference-scaling function $v(c)$. We can use these restrictions to construct a measure of the individual's absolute risk-aversion. Consider a change in the absolute steepness of the indifference curve – the Marginal Rate of Substitution $M(c_1, c_2)$ – in moving from some arbitrary point $(c_1, c_2)$ to a nearby point $(c_1 + dc_1, c_2 + dc_2)$. From equation (2.1.2) the Marginal Rate of Substitution can be expressed as:

$$M(c_1, c_2) = \frac{\pi_1 v'(c_1)}{\pi_2 v'(c_2)} \tag{3.1.2}$$

Taking the logarithm of both sides:

$$\ln M = \ln \pi_1 + \ln v'(c_1) - \ln \pi_2 - \ln v'(c_2)$$

The total differential of the expression is then:

$$d \ln M = \frac{dM}{M} = \frac{v''(c_1)}{v'(c_1)} dc_1 - \frac{v''(c_2)}{v'(c_2)} dc_2 \tag{3.1.3}$$

If $c_1$ and $c_2$ increase by the same absolute amount $(dc_1 = dc_2 = dx)$, the $(c_1, c_2)$ vector moves outward parallel to the 45° line. Then the proportionate change in $M(c_1, c_2)$ is:

$$\frac{dM}{M} = \left[ \frac{v''(c_1)}{v'(c_1)} - \frac{v''(c_2)}{v'(c_2)} \right] dx \tag{3.1.4}$$

Suppose that, as depicted in figure 3.1, an increase in wealth leads to a new optimum C** that lies in region $E_2$ and therefore is further from the 45° line. Since the Marginal Rate of Substitution is the same at C* and C**, it follows that $M(c_1, c_2)$ is necessarily lower where the new budget line NN' intersects the line C*B parallel to the 45° line. If this holds everywhere then, from (3.1.4):

$$c_1 < c_2 \Rightarrow \frac{dM}{M} = \left[ \frac{v''(c_1)}{v'(c_1)} - \frac{v''(c_2)}{v'(c_2)} \right] dx < 0$$

Rearranging we obtain:

$$c_1 < c_2 \Rightarrow \frac{-v''(c_1)}{v'(c_1)} > \frac{-v''(c_2)}{v'(c_2)}$$

Of course, the condition is reversed below the 45° line where $c_1 > c_2$.

Thus an individual displays decreasing aversion to absolute wealth risks if and only if $A(c)$ is a decreasing function, where:

$$A(C) \equiv \frac{-v''(c)}{v'(c)} \tag{3.1.5}$$

The function $A(c)$, which is evidently a property of the individual's preference-scaling function $v(c)$, measures the individual's *absolute risk-aversion*.

Since the individual depicted in figure 3.1 moves farther from the 45° line as his wealth grows, he exhibits decreasing absolute risk-aversion (DARA). If instead he had constant absolute risk-aversion (CARA), $A(c)$ would remain unchanged as wealth rises. In that case the wealth expansion path would be parallel to the 45° line (line C\*B). Finally, if $A(c)$ rises with wealth, the individual exhibits increasing absolute risk-aversion (IARA); the wealth expansion path would then converge toward the 45° line, and the new optimum would lie in region $E_3$.

A second useful measure of attitude toward risk is obtained by considering *proportional* rather than absolute changes in an individual's consumption levels. If $c_1$ and $c_2$ increase proportionately, the consumption vector moves outward along a ray out of the origin. Along such a ray:

$$c_2 = kc_1 \quad \text{and} \quad dc_2 = kdc_1$$

Eliminating $k$ we obtain:

$$\frac{dc_2}{c_2} = \frac{dc_1}{c_1}$$

Rearranging terms in (3.1.3) and substituting, we can see that along the ray C\*D in figure 3-1 the Marginal Rate of Substitution changes in accordance with:

$$\frac{dM}{M} = \left[ \frac{c_1 v''(c_1)}{v'(c_1)} - \frac{c_2 v''(c_2)}{v'(c_2)} \right] \frac{dc_1}{c_1} \tag{3.1.6}$$

As depicted, C\*\*, the optimum at the higher wealth level, lies in region $E_2$ and so is closer to the 45° line than the ray C\*D. To be the same at C\* and C\*\*, the absolute indifference-curve slope $M(c_1, c_2)$ must be increasing along the ray C\*D. That is, from (3.1.6):

$$c_1 < c_2 \Rightarrow \frac{dM}{M} = \left[ \frac{c_1 v''(c_1)}{v'(c_1)} - \frac{c_2 v''(c_2)}{v'(c_2)} \right] \frac{dc_1}{c_1} > 0$$

Rearranging, we obtain:

$$c_1 < c_2 \Rightarrow \frac{-c_1 v''(c_1)}{v'(c_1)} < \frac{-c_2 v''(c_2)}{v'(c_2)}$$

Let us define as measure of *relative risk-aversion*:

$$R(c) \equiv \frac{-cv''(c)}{v'(c)} \tag{3.1.7}$$

Then an individual like the one depicted, who displays *increasing* aversion to proportional (or relative) risk as wealth grows, must be characterized by an $R(c)$ that is an increasing function. We say he displays increasing relative risk-aversion (IRRA).

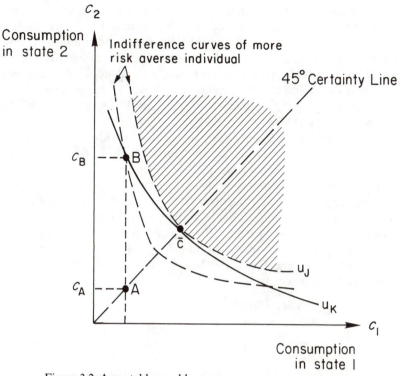

Figure 3.2 Acceptable gambles

If the wealth expansion path is a ray out of the origin, so that the individual prefers to accept risks that are exactly proportionally larger as his wealth rises, his $R(c)$ is constant – he displays *constant relative risk-aversion* (CRRA). Finally, if his tolerance for risk rises more than proportionally with wealth, then $R(c)$ declines with $c$ and the individual is said to exhibit decreasing relative risk-aversion (DRRA).

Both $A(c)$ and $R(c)$ are *local* measures. That is, they are defined in terms of small changes in wealth and consumption. In general, there is no reason why an individual should not exhibit increasing absolute or relative risk-aversion over some consumption levels and decreasing risk-aversion over others. However, in theoretical investigations it is common to make *global* assumptions about both measures of risk-aversion.

Pratt (1964) has argued, as an empirical generalization, that individuals will be willing to bear greater *absolute* risk as wealth rises. This is very plausible. Every unit purchased of a risky asset buys a given absolute risk. Assuming that the state-1 yield of asset $a$ is greater than its state-2 yield, the absolute risk per unit of $a$ held is $z_{a1} - z_{a2}$. A rich individual, other things equal, should be willing to hold more of every kind of asset; acquiring more units of risky assets, he would inevitably accumulate a larger absolute consumption risk. Empirically less obvious is the contention by Arrow (1965) that individuals, as they become richer, will buy relatively more safety so as to reduce their *proportionate* risk. If both arguments are accepted, the typical wealth expansion path will lie in the region $E_2$ as depicted in figure 3.1, rather than in $E_1$ or $E_3$. Individuals will be characterized by DARA and IRRA.

We now compare the preference maps of two individuals, one of whom is everywhere more risk-averse. In figure 3.2 the solid curve is an indifference curve for individual K. As depicted, this individual is indifferent between a certainty endowment point $\bar{C} = (\bar{c}, \bar{c})$ along the 45° line and the gamble B. Moving away from the certainty line to the north-west, i.e., to consumption vectors with $c_2 > c_1$, his Marginal Rate of Substitution (steepness of the indifference curve) must evidently increase. Since the Marginal Rate of Substitution $M(c_1, c_2)$ is the same everywhere along the certainty line, the change $M(c_1, c_2)$ in moving from $\bar{C}$ to B can be expressed logarithmically as:

$$\ln M_{\mathrm{B}} - \ln M_{\bar{\mathrm{C}}} = \ln M_{\mathrm{B}} - \ln M_{\mathrm{D}}$$

$$= \int_{c_{\mathrm{D}}}^{c_{\mathrm{B}}} -\frac{v''(c_2)}{v'(c_2)} dc_2$$

$$= \int_{c_{\mathrm{D}}}^{c_{\mathrm{B}}} A_{\mathrm{K}}(c_2) dc_2$$

The proportional decline in $M(c_1, c_2)$ around the indifference curve therefore varies with the degree of absolute risk-aversion. It follows immediately that if individual J has an everywhere greater degree of absolute risk-aversion than individual K, so that $A_{\mathrm{J}}(c) > A_{\mathrm{K}}(c)$, the proportional decline in J's $M(c_1, c_2)$ is greater. Yet, if both have the same beliefs, we know from section 2.1 and equation (2.1.2) that along the 45° line the Marginal Rates of Substitution are equal to one another. Therefore, at any point B above the 45° line, the more risk-averse individual has a steeper indifference curve. Exactly the same logic reveals that below the 45° line the more risk-averse individual has a flatter indifference curve.

It follows that individual J's indifference curves must be "curvier" than K's (compare the dotted and the solid indifference curves in figure 3.2). So, starting from the same endowment, the set of gambles acceptable to J is strictly smaller than the acceptable set for K.

We have shown that greater $A(c)$ implies a smaller set of acceptable gambles. It is easy to verify that the converse is also true. That is, if J has an everywhere smaller acceptance set, his degree of absolute risk-aversion $A_J(c)$ is greater.

## EXERCISES AND EXCURSIONS 3.1

### 1  Well-behaved preferences

(A) Does the quadratic preference-scaling function exhibit either DARA or IRRA?

(B) An individual with a preference-scaling function $v(c)$ such that $-v'(c)/v''(c) = \alpha + \beta c$ is said to exhibit linear risk-tolerance. For what parameter values does such an individual exhibit DARA and IRRA?

### 2  Preference for positive skewness

Suppose two prospects $\tilde{c}_1$ and $\tilde{c}_2$ have the same mean and variance but $\tilde{c}_1$ has negative and $\tilde{c}_2$ positive skewness, that is:

$$E(\tilde{c}_1 - \mu)^3 < 0 < E(\tilde{c}_2 - \mu)^3$$

(A) Does the typical lottery, offering just a few large prizes with a high probability of a small loss, exhibit positive skewness? Demonstrate.

(B) Ignoring moments higher than the third, use Taylor's expansion to show that, if $v'''(c)$ is positive, then positive skewness is indeed preferred.

(C) Show that decreasing absolute risk-aversion is a sufficient condition for $v'''(c)$ to be positive.

### 3  Absolute risk-aversion and concavity of the preference-scaling function

Let $A_i(c)$ be the degree of absolute risk-aversion corresponding to the twice differentiable increasing functions $v_i(c)$, $i = J, K$.

(A) If individual J's preference-scaling function $v_J(c)$ can be written as an increasing twice differentiable concave function of individual K's $v_K(c)$, that is:

$$v_J(c) = f(v_K(c)), \qquad f'(\cdot) > 0, \qquad f''(\cdot) < 0$$

show that $A_J(c) > A_K(c)$.

(B) Since $v_J(c)$ is an increasing function there is a one-to-one mapping $g: v \rightarrow v$ such that $g(v_K(c)) = v_J(c)$. Differentiate twice and rearrange to establish that:

$$g'(v_K(c)) = \frac{v_J'(c)}{v_K'(c)} \quad \text{and} \quad g''(v_K(c)) = \frac{-v_J'(c)}{v_K'(c)^2}[A_J(c) - A_K(c)]$$

Hence establish the converse of (A).

### 4 Small and large gambles

An individual exhibiting constant absolute risk-aversion of degree $A$ has an initial riskless endowment $\bar{c}$. He rejects (but only just) the small gamble $(x, -1; \pi, 1-\pi)$ but accepts the all-or-nothing gamble $(y, -\bar{c}; \pi, 1-\pi)$. A second individual with the same initial endowment has preference-scaling function $v(c) = \ln(c)$. If $A$ is sufficiently large, show that the second individual will be better off accepting the small gamble but will be worse off rejecting the large gamble. Is this still true if $v(c)$ exhibits constant relative risk-aversion of degree greater than unity?

### 5 The risk premium

Formally, the "risk premium" associated with a risky prospect $\tilde{c}$ is the amount of income $b$ that an individual is willing to give up in order to receive the expected value of $\tilde{c}$ with certainty. That is:

$$E\{v(\tilde{c})\} = v(\bar{c}-b), \quad \text{where} \quad \bar{c} = E\{\tilde{c}\}$$

(A)   If the risk is small so that third and higher-order terms can be neglected, apply Taylor's expansion to show that the risk premium is proportional to the degree of absolute risk-aversion.

(B)   Let $b_0$ be the initial risk premium and let $b_1$ be the risk premium when the individual's wealth rises by $w$. That is:

   (i)  $E\{v(\tilde{c})\} = v(\bar{c}-b_0)$
   (ii) $E\{v(w+\tilde{c})\} = v(w+\bar{c}-b_1)$

   If the risk is small, appeal to (A) to establish that, if absolute risk-aversion is decreasing with wealth, then $b_0 > b_1$.

(C)*  Show that this result holds for all risks as long as the degree of absolute risk-aversion is decreasing with wealth. HINT: Define the new preference-scaling function $\bar{v}(c) = v(w+c)$. That is, we can think of the wealth effect as changing the preference-scaling function. Given the assumptions, explain why the preference-scaling function $\bar{v}(c)$ exhibits a lower degree of risk-aversion than $v(c)$. Then appeal to exercise 3 to establish that $v(w+\tilde{c}) = f(v(\tilde{c}))$, where $f$ is a convex function.

### 6 Effect of an uncertain increase in wealth on the risk premium

Extending the analysis of exercise 5, suppose two individuals face the same income risk $\tilde{c}$ but one has an additional uncertain endowment $\tilde{w}$. Let $b_0$ be the amount the first individual is willing to pay to replace the income risk

---

* Starred questions or portions of questions may be somewhat more difficult.

with its expected value $\bar{c}$. Then $b_0$ satisfies (i) above. Similarly, let $b_2$ be the amount the second individual is willing to pay to replace the income risk with its expected value. That is:

(iii) $E\{v(\tilde{w}+\tilde{c})\} = E\{v(\tilde{w}+\bar{c}-b_2)\}$

Arguing by analogy with exercise 5, it is tempting to think that, with decreasing absolute risk-aversion, $b_0 > b_2$. However, consider the following example. There are three states and each is equally likely. The two risky prospects are:

$$\tilde{w} = (w,0,0) \quad \text{and} \quad \tilde{c} = (\bar{c}, \bar{c}+e, \bar{c}-e)$$

(A) Write out equations (i) and (iii) for this example and hence show that $b_2$ must satisfy:

$$[v(\bar{c}+w)-v(\bar{c}+w-b_2)] - [v(\bar{c})-v(\bar{c}-b_2)] = 3[v(\bar{c}-b_2)]-v(\bar{c}-b_0)]$$

(B) Explain why the left-hand side of this expression is negative and hence why $b_2 > b_0$. That is, the risk premium may *rise* as wealth increases stochastically regardless of whether or not absolute risk-aversion is decreasing (see Machina, 1982).

(C) What is the intuition behind this result?
   HINT: You can also show that $b_2$ is a strictly increasing function of $w$. Then compare the effect of paying a risk premium on state-1 utility (i) when $w = 0$ and (ii) when $w$ is large.

## 3.2   Endowment and price effects

This section analyzes the effects of parametric changes in endowments and in prices upon the individual's risk-bearing optimum. We first take up the case where Complete Contingent Markets (CCM) are provided by a full set of tradable state-claims (section 3.2.1). Equivalent results can of course be obtained under Complete Asset Markets (CAM) – i.e., where the number of tradable assets with linearly independent return vectors equals the number of states. Section 3.2.2 then covers *incomplete* market regimes.

### 3.2.1   Complete markets

In accordance with the analysis in chapter 2, section 1, under Complete Contingent Markets the individual chooses among state-claim bundles $(c_1, ..., c_S)$ so as to maximize expected utility $U = \Sigma_s \pi_s v(c_s)$ subject to the budget constraint:

$$\sum_{s=1}^{S} P_s c_s = \sum_{s=1}^{S} P_s \bar{c}_s \equiv \bar{W} \tag{3.2.1}$$

Ignoring for expositional ease the possibility of a corner solution, the preferred position C* is the one satisfying the budget constraint and the Fundamental Theorem of Risk-bearing:

$$\frac{\pi_1 v'(c_1)}{P_1} = \frac{\pi_2 v'(c_2)}{P_2} = \ldots = \frac{\pi_S v'(c_S)}{P_S} = \lambda \qquad (3.2.2)$$

where $\lambda$ can be interpreted as the expected marginal utility of income. This condition can only be an optimum, of course, if risk-aversion ($v''(c) < 0$) is postulated – else a corner solution would always be preferred.

In the two-state diagram of figure 3.1, consider exogenous shifts in the individual's endowment vector, state-claim prices being held constant. The effect upon the risk-bearing optimum depends only upon whether or not the change in endowment alters endowed wealth $\overline{W}$ in (3.2.1). An endowment variation leaving $\overline{W}$ unchanged is illustrated in figure 3.1 by a shift from $\overline{C}$ to $\overline{\overline{C}}$ along the same market line LL'. Such a change in the composition of the endowment does not in any way affect the position of the optimum vector C*. (On the other hand, this change will of necessity affect the scope of the *transactions* undertaken by the individual in order to attain the C* optimum.) The more interesting class of endowment shifts will be those in which $\overline{W}$ does change, so that the individual's optimum position must also be revised. (But, it is at least possible that the *transactions* he must undertake to attain his new optimum from his new endowment might remain unchanged.) For concreteness, we will speak in terms of *increases* in $\overline{W}$.

An increase in wealth at given prices must raise the optimum amount of contingent consumption claims held in at least one state $t$. Assuming risk-aversion, $\lambda$ must fall in (3.2.2). And, given the separable form of the expected-utility function, as in equation (1.4.1), when any $c_t$ rises in (3.2.2) then $c_s$ must increase in each and every other state as well. Thus, in risk-bearing theory under the Neumann–Morgenstern postulates, there are no "inferior-good" state-claims; all wealth effects are necessarily "normal." Then the analysis of wealth expansion paths in the previous section can be applied directly. For any pair of states $s$ and $t$ the impact of an increase in wealth can be depicted essentially as in figure 3.1. We need only let the axes be $c_s$ and $c_t$, and interpret the budget lines LL' and NN' as indicating those combinations of state-claims costing the same as the *optimal* purchase of state-claims at the two wealth levels. It follows directly that under the assumption of decreasing (increasing) *absolute* risk-aversion the absolute difference between any pair of state-claim holdings, $|c_t^* - c_s^*|$, rises (falls) with wealth. Similarly, under the assumption of decreasing (increasing) *relative* risk-aversion, if $c_t > c_s$ then the ratio of expenditures $P_t c_t / P_s c_s$ rises (falls) with wealth.

We next consider the "pure substitution effect," the impact upon $c_s$ of a *compensated* increase in the price $P_s$ of one of the state-claims. That is, we postulate an exogenous increase in $P_s$ together with a simultaneous change in endowment such that expected utility (after the individual revises his state-claim holdings in accordance with the new price vector) is the same as before.

Suppose for concreteness that it is $P_1$, the price of claims to consumption in state 1, that rises. Under our standard assumption of state-independence (so that $v'(c_s)$ is independent of consumption in any state $t \neq s$), and, since $P_2, ..., P_S$ are all unchanged, the Fundamental Theorem of Risk-bearing indicates that if $\lambda$ rises $c_2, ..., c_S$ must fall and vice versa. That is, claims in all states other than state 1 move together. Since expected utility is required to remain constant, either $c_1$ falls and $c_2, ..., c_S$ all rise or the reverse. But, if $c_1$ and $P_1$ both were to rise, the marginal utility of income $\lambda$ in equation (3.2.3) would fall. Then, to maintain the equality, holdings of all other state-claims would also rise. But this is inconsistent with constant utility. We have therefore established that the "pure substitution effect" of a price increase is negative and that all cross-effects are positive. In the language of traditional theory, state-claims must be *net substitutes* in demand.

To determine the *uncompensated* effect of an increase in $P_s$ on demand, note that, if $\bar{c}_s$ is the individual's state-$s$ endowment, the Slutsky equation is:

$$\frac{\partial c_s}{\partial P_s} = \frac{\partial c_s}{\partial P_s}\bigg|_{\text{comp}} - (c_s - \bar{c}_s)\frac{\partial c_s}{\partial W}$$

Since it has been shown that all wealth effects are normal, the two terms on the right-hand side of this expression are reinforcing as long as the individual is a net buyer of state-$s$ claims. Informally, the increase in $P_s$ makes a net buyer poorer and so the income effect is negative. However, when we consider the effect of a rise in $P_t$ upon the demand for state-$s$ claims $c_s$, the substitution effect tending to increase $c_s$ must be weighed against the income effect that tends to reduce $c_s$. So state-claims may be either *gross substitutes* or *gross complements* in demand.

## EXERCISES AND EXCURSIONS 3.2.1

### 1 The Law of Demand for state-claims

(A) Suppose an individual is a net buyer of consumption claims in state 1 ($c_1^* > \bar{c}_1$). If the price of state-1 claims rises, show directly that the quantity of state-1 claims demanded must fall.

HINT: Suppose the proposition is false. Then $c_1^*$ does not fall and spending on state-1 claims must rise. Apply the Fundamental Theorem of Risk-bearing to show that $c_2^*, \ldots, c_S^*$ must also rise. Hence obtain a contradiction.

(B) What if the individual is a net *seller* of state-1 claims?

## 2 Elastic own-demand curves and gross substitutes in demand

An individual begins with a fixed nominal wealth $\bar{W}$.

(A)    Show that if, for each state $s$, the own-price elasticity of demand exceeds unity so that total spending on state-$s$ claims falls with a rise in $P_s$, then all state-claims are gross substitutes in demand.

HINT: Use the Fundamental Theorem of Risk-bearing, and the fact that $P_s c_s$ declines as $P_s$ rises, to establish that $\lambda$ must decline.

(B)    If an individual is highly risk-averse (so that indifference curves are essentially L-shaped) explain graphically why consumption in each state declines as $P_s$ rises. In this case does the own-price elasticity of demand exceed unity?

(C)* Show that the own-price elasticity of demand exceeds unity if and only if relative risk-aversion is less than unity.

HINT: Show that consumption in state $s$ and state 1 must satisfy:

$$\pi_s c_s v'(c_s) = (P_s c_s)\pi_1 v'(c_1)/P_1$$

Use (A) to establish that, as $P_s$ rises, the right-hand side of this equation declines if and only if own-price elasticity exceeds unity. What happens to the left-hand side as $c_s$ declines?

### 3.2.2    Incomplete markets

To illustrate trading in a regime of incomplete markets, in a world of $S > 2$ states consider an individual who must balance his portfolio between a riskless asset and a single risky asset. As before, we want to examine the effect of changes in endowments or in prices upon the individual's risk-bearing optimum.

Let the first asset, with price $P_1^A$, have the certain return $z_1$ while the second asset, with price $P_2^A$, pays off $z_{2s}$ dollars in state $s$ ($s = 1, 2, \ldots, S$). Equivalently, the return on asset 2 is a random variable $\tilde{z}_2$ with realizations $z_{21}, \ldots, z_{2S}$. Then, if an individual with preference-scaling function $v(\cdot)$ holds $q_1$ units of asset 1 and $q_2$ units of asset 2, and if he has no source of income in any state other than returns from asset holdings, his expected utility is:

$$U(q_1, q_2) = E_s v(q_1 z_1 + q_2 \tilde{z}_2) = \sum_s \pi_s v(q_1 z_1 + q_2 z_{2s}) \qquad (3.2.3)$$

* Starred questions or portions of questions may be somewhat more difficult.

As long as the individual is risk-averse so that $v(c)$ is a concave function, it can be shown that his derived preferences *over assets* must be convex ("bowed toward the origin") as depicted in figure 3.3.[1]

Asset demands must satisfy the budget constraint:

$$P_1^A q_1 + P_2^A q_2 = P_1^A \bar{q}_1 + P_2^A \bar{q}_2 \equiv \bar{W} \tag{3.2.4}$$

Using the budget constraint, we can substitute for $q_1$ in (3.2.3) so as to express expected utility as a function $\bar{U}(q_2)$ of $q_2$ only:

$$
\begin{aligned}
\bar{U}(q_2) &= Ev\left(\left(\frac{\bar{W}}{P_1^A} - \frac{P_2^A}{P_1^A}q_2\right)z_1 + q_2 z_2\right) \\
&= Ev\left(\frac{\bar{W}z_1}{P_1^A} + P_2^A q_2\left(\frac{z_2}{P_2^A} - \frac{z_1}{P_1^A}\right)\right)
\end{aligned} \tag{3.2.5}
$$

For the analysis that follows, it is more convenient to work with net asset yields per dollar invested (or, for short, simply the *yields*) rather than with the asset payoffs or returns.

For any asset $a$, the yield distribution is definitionally related to the payoff distribution by:

$$1 + \tilde{R}_a \equiv \frac{\tilde{z}_a}{P_a^A} \tag{3.2.6}$$

Substituting into (3.2.5) we obtain:

$$\bar{U}(q_2) = Ev((1 + R_1)\bar{W} + (\tilde{R}_2 - R_1)P_2^A q_2)$$

where $R_1$ (like $z_1$) is non-stochastic. The marginal increase in expected utility associated with an increased demand for the risky asset is then:

$$\bar{U}'(q_2) = P_2^A E\{(\tilde{R}_2 - R_1)v'(\tilde{c})\} \tag{3.2.7}$$

The random variable $\tilde{c}$ represents contingent consumption over states:

$$\tilde{c} \equiv (1 + R_1)\bar{W} + (\tilde{R}_2 - R_1)P_2^A q_2 \tag{3.2.8}$$

In particular, at $q_2 = 0$ we have:

$$\bar{U}'(0) = P_2^A v'((1 + R_1)\bar{W})E\{\tilde{R}_2 - R_1\}$$

This is positive if and only if the expected yield on the risky asset exceeds the yield on the riskless asset.

Thus, no matter how risk-averse an individual is, he will always want to hold some amount of the risky asset if its expected yield is even slightly higher than the riskless yield. While this may at first seem puzzling, the explanation is simple. As long as the risk holding is sufficiently small, the

---

[1] See the first exercise at the end of this section.

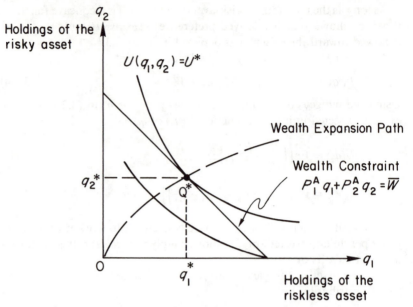

Figure 3.3 Optimal portfolio selection

individual's final consumption distribution is nearly riskless and so marginal utilities are almost the same across states. His behavior towards a very small favorable gamble is therefore essentially that of a risk-neutral agent.

We now suppose that $E\tilde{R}_2 > R_1$ so that the optimal asset holding, $q_2^*$, is strictly positive. From (3.2.7) and (3.2.8), $q_2^*$ satisfies the first-order condition:

$$\bar{U}'(q_2^*) = P_2^A \, E\{(\tilde{R}_2 - R_1)v'(\tilde{c}^*)\} = 0 \tag{3.2.9}$$

What happens to demand for the risky asset as wealth increases? From the previous section, we would anticipate that an individual characterized by decreasing absolute risk-aversion (DARA) should want to hold more of the risky asset. We now show that this intuition is correct.

The analysis proceeds by asking what happens to the marginal utility of $q_2$ as $\bar{W}$ increases. At the asset-holding optimum for the initial wealth level, we have seen, $U'(q_2^*) = 0$. If the effect of an increase in wealth is to raise this marginal utility, the new optimum will have to be at a higher level of $q_2$. Differentiating (3.2.9) by $\bar{W}$ and making use of (3.2.8) we obtain:

$$\frac{d}{d\bar{W}}\bar{U}'(q_2) = P_2^A(1+R_1)\,E\{(\tilde{R}_2-R_1)v''(\tilde{c}^*)\}$$

$$= -P_2^A(1+R_1)\,E\{(\tilde{R}_2-R_1)v'(\tilde{c}^*)A(\tilde{c}^*)\} \tag{3.2.10}$$

where $A(\tilde{c}) \equiv -v''(\tilde{c})/v'(\tilde{c})$ is the degree of absolute risk-aversion.

If $A(c)$ is constant this can be rewritten as:

$$\frac{d}{dW}\bar{U}'(q_2) = -P_2^A(1+R_1)\bar{A}\,\mathrm{E}\{(\tilde{R}_2-R_1)v'(\tilde{c}^*)\}$$

From (3.2.9) the expectation is zero. Therefore, under constant absolute risk-aversion (CARA), demand for the risky asset is independent of wealth.

Under the normal assumption of decreasing $A(c)$, the analysis is only a bit more complicated. If $R_2 = R_1$ then, from (3.2.8), $c = (1+R_1)\bar{W}$ and so $A(\tilde{c}) = A((1+R_1)\bar{W})$. If $R_2 > R_1$, $c$ is larger and so $A(c) < A((1+R_1)\bar{W})$. Then:

$$(R_2-R_1)A(c) < (R_2-R_1)A((1+R_1)\bar{W})$$

If $R_2 < R_1$, $c$ is smaller and so $A(c) > A((1+R_1)\bar{W})$. Then again:

$$(R_2-R_1)A(c) < (R_2-R_1)A((1+R_1)\bar{W})$$

Since this is true for all $c$ it follows from (3.2.10) that:

$$\frac{d}{d\bar{W}}\bar{U}'(q_2^*) > -P_2^A(1+R_1)\,\mathrm{E}\{(\tilde{R}_2-R_1)v'(\tilde{c}^*)A((1+R_1)\bar{W})\}$$

Again, from (3.2.9), the right-hand side of this inequality is zero. Therefore, at the initial optimum, an increase in wealth raises the expected marginal utility of investing in the risky asset and so raises demand for the asset.

Returning to figure 3.3, it follows that the wealth expansion path in asset space is upward sloping.[2] As depicted it bends forwards so that, as wealth increases, there is a less-than-proportional increase in demand for the risky asset. You are asked to confirm in an exercise at the end of this section that this will be the case under increasing relative risk-aversion (IARA).

CONCLUSION: In a regime of incomplete markets with a single risky asset, the wealth effect upon the demand for that asset will be positive, zero, or negative according as *absolute* risk-aversion $A(c)$ is decreasing (DARA), constant (CARA), or increasing (IARA). So the uncompensated demand for the risky asset, in the region where the individual is a net buyer, will surely have negative slope under DARA or CARA but not necessarily so under IARA. As for the *riskless* asset, its demand (once again, in the region

---

[2] It is tempting to generalize from this and conjecture that, with one riskless asset and several risky assets, total spending on the latter would rise with wealth. However, as Hart (1975) has shown, special cases can be constructed for which this is not the case. Despite this, there remains the presumption that wealth and total spending on risky assets will be positively related.

where the individual is a net buyer) must always have negative slope – since the wealth effect is surely positive. (A richer individual will always want to increase his contingent consumption in each and every state of the world.)

EXERCISES AND EXCURSIONS 3.2.2

*1 Concavity of the derived utility function*

Let $q = (q_1, \ldots, q_A)$ be an individual's holdings of $A$ assets. In state $s$ the return on each of these assets is $z_s = (z_{1s}, \ldots, z_{As})$ so that the total state-$s$ income is:

$$q \cdot z_s = \sum_{a=1}^{A} q_a z_{as}$$

Expected utility is then:

$$U(q) = \sum_{s=1}^{S} \pi_s v(q \cdot z_s)$$

where $v$ is an increasing strictly concave function.

(A) Show that $U(q)$ is also strictly concave, that is, for any pair of vectors $q^\alpha, q^\beta$:

$$U(\lambda q^\alpha + (1-\lambda) q^\beta) > U(q^\alpha) + (1-\lambda)U(q^\beta) \quad 0 < \lambda < 1$$

(B) Hence confirm that preferences are convex, as depicted in figure 3.3.

ANSWER: $v((\lambda q^\alpha + (1-\lambda) q^\beta) \cdot z_s) = v(\lambda q^\alpha \cdot z_s + (1-\lambda) q^\beta \cdot z_s)$ and, since $v$ is strictly concave:

$$v(\lambda q^\alpha \cdot z_s + (1-\lambda) q^\beta \cdot z_s) > \lambda v(q^\alpha \cdot z_s) + (1-\lambda) v(q^\beta \cdot z_s)$$

Since this holds for each vector $z_s$ it follows that for all $s$:

$$\pi_s v((\lambda q^\alpha + (1-\lambda) q^\beta) \cdot z_s) > \lambda \pi_s v(q^\alpha \cdot z_s) + (1-\lambda) \pi_s v(q^\beta \cdot z_s)$$

Then (A) follows directly by summing over $s$.

To establish (B) we consider two vectors $q^\alpha$ and $q^\beta$ on the same indifference curve. That is $U(q^\alpha) = U(q^\beta) = \bar{U}$. Since $U$ is strictly concave, for any convex combination of these two vectors we have:

$$U(\lambda q^\alpha + (1-\lambda) q^\beta) > \lambda U(q^\alpha) + (1-\lambda) U(q^\beta) = \bar{U}$$

Thus all convex combinations of $q^\alpha$ and $q^\beta$ indeed lie above the indifference curve through $q^\alpha$ and $q^\beta$.

*2 Asset demand with constant absolute risk-aversion*

Suppose $v(c) = \kappa_1 - \kappa_2 e^{-Ac}, \kappa_1, \kappa_2 > 0$. There are $M$ assets, all of which are risky except asset 1.

(A) Write down the individual's optimization problem and then substitute for $q_1$, the demand for the riskless asset, using the wealth constraint.
(B) Write down the necessary conditions for an optimal portfolio and confirm that demands for risky assets are independent of initial wealth $\overline{W}$.

### 3 Demand for a risky asset under increasing relative risk-aversion

Let $\kappa_2$ be the proportion of initial wealth invested in the risky asset in the portfolio problem described in this section.
(A) Obtain an expression for $U(\kappa_2)$, expected utility as a function of $\kappa_2$, and hence show that under constant relative risk-aversion (CRRA) the optimal proportion $\kappa_2^*$ is independent of wealth $(\partial U'(\kappa_2^*)/\partial \overline{W} = 0)$.
(B) Apply methods similar to those used in section 3.2 to establish that, under increasing relative risk-aversion (IRRA), $\kappa_2^*$ declines with wealth.
(C) What occurs under DRRA?

### 4 Demand for a risky asset with different attitudes towards risk (Pratt, 1964)

Suppose that individual J is everywhere more risk-averse than K, so that (in accordance with an earlier exercise) J's preference-scaling function $v_J(c)$ is an increasing concave transformation of $v_K(c)$:

$$v_J(c) = f(v_K(c)) \quad f'(\cdot) > 0, \quad f''(\cdot) < 0$$

(A) Show that, if both individuals face the portfolio-choice problem described in this section, and the prices of the riskless and risky assets are both unity, the optimal holding of the risky asset for J, $q_2^J$, satisfies:

$$\overline{U}_J'(q_2^J) = P_2^A \, E\{(\tilde{R}_2 - R_1) f'(v_k(\tilde{c})) v_k'(\tilde{c})\} = 0$$

where $\tilde{c} = (1 + R_1)\overline{W} + (\tilde{R}_2 - R_1) P_2^A q_2^J$.
(B) Confirm that for each possible realization $R_2$:

$$(R_2 - R_1) f'(v_K(\tilde{c})) < (R_2 - R_1) f'(v_K(\overline{W}))$$

Hence show that $\overline{U}_K'(q_2^J) > 0$ and therefore that:

$$q_2^J < q_2^K$$

## 3.3    Changes in the distribution of asset payoffs

The previous section examined the effects of parametric changes in wealth, or in the prices of state-claims or of assets, upon the risk-bearing optimum of the individual. For example, we showed that, under a regime of Complete Contingent Markets (CCM), if the individual was previously at an interior optimum then an increase in wealth would increase his holdings of each and every state-claim. Owing to this positive wealth effect, the uncompensated demand curve for any contingent claim is negatively sloped in the region where the individual is a net buyer. An analogous conclusion evidently holds for Complete Asset Markets (CAM). But, with incomplete markets, the uncompensated demand for an asset on the part of a net buyer is unambiguously negatively sloped only if the individual is characterized by decreasing or constant absolute risk-aversion (DARA or CARA).

This section represents a shift in point of view. Here the parametric changes impacting upon the individual take the form of shifts in the distribution of the contingent returns or payoffs $z_{as}$ of some particular asset $a$. Let us reconsider the example of the previous section, in which an individual chooses to hold $q_1$ units of the riskless asset with payoff $z_1$ and $q_2$ units of the risky asset with state-$s$ return $z_{2s}$ for $s = 1, ..., S$. For simplicity, assume that the endowment is entirely in units of the riskless asset. Then, with endowed wealth $\bar{W} = P_1^A \bar{q}_1$ the utility-maximizing portfolio choice ($q_1$ and $q_2$) is the solution to:

$$\operatorname*{Max}_{q_1, q_2} \left\{ U(q_1, q_2) \equiv \sum_{s=1}^{S} \pi_s v(q_1 z_1 + q_2 z_{2s}) \mid P_1^A q_1 + P_2^A q_2 = \bar{W} \right\}$$

For simplicity, let $P_1^A = P_2^A = 1$ so that the budget constraint becomes $q_1 + q_2 = \bar{W}$. Then if the individual purchases $q_2$ units of the risky asset his final state-$s$ consumption is:

$$c_s = (\bar{W} - q_2) z_1 + q_2 z_{2s} = \bar{W} z_1 + q_2 (z_{2s} - z_1) \tag{3.3.1}$$

As a first illustration of a parametric change, suppose the return to the risky asset 2 declines in one state of the world but is otherwise unaltered. (In the market as a whole, such a shift would tend to change $P_2^A$ or more generally the entire pattern of asset prices – a topic to be covered in chapter 4. But in this chapter we are continuing to focus upon a single individual so that asset prices are assumed constant.) It is tempting to conclude that the individual would then respond by investing less in the risky asset. However, this intuitively appealing argument is not in general true!

Continuing to assume a single riskless and a single risky asset, suppose there are only two states ($S = 2$) as depicted in figure 3.4. (This is therefore a situation of Complete Asset Markets.) Since the individual's endowment holding consists only of the riskless asset 1, in state-claim space the endowment point is $\bar{C} = (\bar{W} z_1, \bar{W} z_1)$ on the 45° certainty line. If the individual invests everything in the risky asset instead (so that $q_2 = \bar{W}$), his income claims are represented by the point $T = (\bar{W} z_{21}, \bar{W} z_{22})$. Before the postulated parametric change occurs, then, the set of feasible contingent

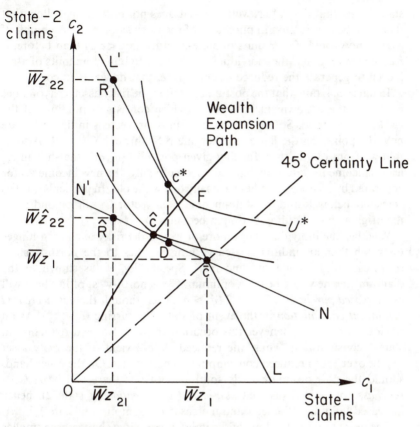

Figure 3.4 Demand for a risky asset

incomes consists of all the weighted averages of $\bar{C}$ and $T$ yielding non-negative consumptions in both states. Geometrically, this is the line LL′ through $\bar{C}$ and T, extending to the axes (since short sales are allowed within the first quadrant). Along this line the optimum position is the tangency at C*.

As depicted, $z_{22} > z_{21}$. That is, the risky asset yields more in state 2 than in state 1. Now suppose that the state-2 yield of the risky asset declines, from $z_{22}$ to $\hat{z}_{22}$. This is equivalent, from the individual's point of view, to a rise in the effective price $P_2$ of state-2 claims. On the basis of the discussion in the preceding section 3.2.1, we know that for a net buyer of the risky asset there will be a *substitution effect* away from state-2 consumption and toward state-1 consumption, together with an *income effect* tending to reduce consumption in both states. So the result is unambiguous that at the new risk-bearing optimum there will be a reduction of consumption in state 2, i.e., that $\hat{c}_2 < c_2^*$. Nevertheless, it does not necessarily follow that there will be a reduction in purchases of the risky asset. Since each unit of asset 2 now yields fewer units of state-2 return ($\hat{z}_{22} < z_{22}$) than before, it *may* be the case that the individual would have to buy more units of asset 2 even to generate the reduced quantity of $c_2$ that he wants to consume.

In figure 3.4, note that the postulated shift in the risky asset's payoff does not affect the endowment position $\bar{C}$ (which consists of holdings of the *riskless* asset only). So the feasible consumption vectors in figure 3.4 are now the points on the flatter market line NN' through $\bar{C}$ and $\hat{R}$. Also, it follows from (3.3.1) that, for any given portfolio $(q_1, q_2)$, the shift in $z_{22}$ leaves income in state 1 unchanged. Geometrically, the new income vector generated by any portfolio lies vertically below the old. In particular, $\hat{R}$ lies vertically below R and the state-income yield vector C* corresponding to the original asset-holding optimum becomes D.

Whether the individual buys more or less of the risky asset then hinges upon whether his indifference-curve tangency lies to the north-west or south-east of D along the line NN'. Specifically, if (as shown in the diagram) the new risk-bearing optimum $\hat{C}$ lies north-west of D, there will be *increased purchases* of asset 2 ($\hat{q}_2 > q_2^*$) even though there is *decreased contingent consumption* in the event of state 2 occurring ($\hat{c}_2 < c_2^*$). As an obvious corollary, whenever this occurs there will also be a reduction in state-1 consumption. Thus, the reduced state-2 yield of the risky asset "spills over" into reduced consumption in both states. On the other hand, should the new optimum $\hat{C}$ lie south-east of C*, there will be *reduced purchases* of asset 2 (as well as *reduced consumption* of state 2), hence increased holdings of asset 1 and increased consumption in state 1.

The more rapidly the slope of the indifference curve changes, the smaller is the substitution effect away from $c_2$-consumption. Hence the more likely it is that the wealth effect of the implicit increase in $P_2$ dominates, so that the individual's purchase of the risky asset increases. Referring back to section 3.1 we see that the curvature of the indifference curve is greater the larger is the individual's aversion to risk. So the seemingly paradoxical result, that demand for the risky asset (after a decline of $z_{22}$ to $\hat{z}_{22}$) can increase, is more likely if an individual exhibits a high degree of risk aversion. (From another point of view, however, this is not paradoxical at all. The shift from $z_{22}$ to $\hat{z}_{22}$ has made the risky asset "less risky" – has reduced the gap between $z_{22}$ and $z_{21}$ – which has to some extent increased its attractiveness for highly risk-averse individuals.)

CONCLUSION: In a simplified regime of two tradable assets (one risky, the other riskless) and two states of the world, a reduction in one of the contingent payoffs $z_{as}$ for the risky asset is equivalent, from the individual's point of view, to an increase in the price $P_s$ of the corresponding state-claim. It follows that at the new optimum the individual will reduce his contingent consumption $c_s$ in that state of the world. But, he will not necessarily reduce his portfolio holding of the risky asset. And, in particular, if $z_{as}$ declines for the higher-yielding state, a highly risk-averse individual's optimal holding of the risky asset may actually increase – since that asset has in effect become "less risky."

Exercise 1 below proves a related proposition, that if $z_{as}$ falls then the demand for the risky asset will decline if the degree of relative risk-aversion, $R$, is not greater than unity.

## EXERCISES AND EXCURSIONS 3.3

### 1 State-returns and relative risk-aversion

Choosing units so that $P_1^A = P_2^A = 1$, a risk-averse individual is endowed with $\overline{W}$ units of a riskless asset 1 returning $z_1$ in each state. He can also make purchases of a risky asset 2 whose payoff is $z_{2s}$ in state $s$. Initially his optimum holding of the risky asset is positive. Show that if the return $z_{2s}$ on asset 2 rises in some state $s$, and if the individual's constant relative aversion to risk CRRA is no greater than unity, then his optimal holding of this asset will rise.

ANSWER: From (3.1.1), expected utility is:

$$U(q_2) = \sum_{s=1}^{S} \pi_s v(\overline{W}z_1 + q_2(z_{2s} - z_1))$$

Differentiating by $q_2$, the optimal holding $q_2^*$ of the risky asset satisfies:

$$U'(q_2^*) = \sum_{s=1}^{S} \pi_s(z_{2s} - z_1) v'(\overline{W}z_1 + q_2^*(z_{2s} - z_1)) = 0$$

Suppose $z_{21}$ rises to $\hat{z}_{21}$. Holding $q_2^*$ constant, only the first term in the summation changes. Then $U'(q_2^*)$ rises when $z_{21}$ rises if:

$$\phi(z_{21}) \equiv (z_{21} - z_1) v'(\overline{W}z_1 + q_2^*(z_{21} - z_1))$$

is an increasing function of $z_{21}$. Differentiating by $z_{21}$ we obtain:

$$\phi'(z_{21}) = v'(\cdot) + q_2^*(z_{21} - z_1) v''(\cdot)$$
$$= v'(\cdot)\left[1 - \frac{q_2^*(z_{21} - z_1)}{\overline{W}z_1 + q_2^*(z_{21} - z_1)} R(\cdot)\right]$$

where $R$ is the degree of relative risk-aversion.

From the first expression for $\phi'$ it follows immediately that, if $z_{21} \leqslant z_1$, $\phi'(z_{21})$ is positive. From the second, if $z_{21} > z_1$ and $R \leqslant 1$, then the bracket is positive and so again $\phi'(z_{21})$ is positive. We have therefore established that $\phi$ rises with $z_{21}$. Thus, for any $\hat{z}_{21} > z_{21}$, $U(q_2)$ is strictly increasing at

$q_2 = q_2^*$. Since, as may readily be confirmed, $U(q_2)$ is a strictly concave function of $q_2$, it follows immediately that the new optimum holding of the risky assets exceeds $q_2^*$.

*Comment*: One feature of this exercise and of the type of parametric change assumed in the text is that the shift in the payoff distribution of the risky asset results in a lower mean return to holding the asset. From this observation it might be conjectured that clearer results would hold for changes in the distribution of consequences that preserve the expected return on the risky asset. In particular, if the expected payoff $E\{\tilde{z}_2\}$ were held constant but the variance $\sigma^2(\tilde{z}_2)$ were to rise, it seems plausible that an individual would reduce his demand for the risky asset. However, as the following exercise indicates, even this conjecture is false. Indeed it is possible for the mean return to rise and for the variance to fall, and yet for the optimal holding of the risky asset to remain unchanged.

## 2 Parametric change lowering mean and raising variance of asset payoff

An individual with an initial wealth of $50 must choose a portfolio of two assets, both of which have a price of $50. The first asset is riskless and pays off $50 in each of the two possible states. The second returns $z_{2s}$ in state $s$, for $s = 1, 2$. The probability of state 1 is $\pi$.

(A) If the individual splits his wealth equally between the two assets, confirm the correctness of the following table, where the risky asset returns may have the form of $\alpha$, $\beta$, or $\gamma$.

(B) Suppose the individual has a preference-scaling function:

$$v(c) = -e^{-Ac}$$

where $A = 1/30 \ln 4$ (and hence $e^{30A} = 4$). Confirm that the individual's preference ranking of the three risky assets is $\gamma > \alpha > \beta$.

| | Risky asset returns $(z_{21}, z_{22})$ | Probability of state 1 | Final consumption $(c_1, c_2)$ | E(c) | $\sigma^2(c)$ |
|---|---|---|---|---|---|
| $\alpha$ | (20,80) | 1/5 | (35,65) | 59 | 144 |
| $\beta$ | (38,98) | 1/2 | (44,74) | 59 | 225 |
| $\gamma$ | (30,90) | 1/3 | (40,70) | 60 | 200 |

(C) With preferences as given in (B) show that in each case the individual's optimal decision is to spend an equal amount on each of the two assets.

ANSWER : (A) and (B) are confirmed by direct computation. To establish (C), suppose that the individual spends a proportion $x$ of his wealth on the risky asset. Then his final consumption in state $s$ is:

$$c_s(x) = xz_{2s} + (1-x)\,50$$
$$= 50 + (z_{2s} - 50)x$$

Since $v(c) = -e^{-Ac}$, expected utility becomes:

$$U(x) = -\pi e^{-Ac_1(x)} - (1-\pi)e^{-Ac_2(x)}$$

Differentiating by $x$ and making use of the expression for $c_s(x)$ we obtain:

$$\frac{dU}{dx} = A\pi\,e^{-Ac_1(x)}\,(z_{21} - 50) + A(1-\pi)e^{-Ac_2(x)}(z_{22} - 50)$$
$$= Ae^{-Ac_2(x)}[\pi(z_{21} - 50)e^{A(c_2(x)-c_1(x))} + (1-\pi)\,(z_{22} - 50)]$$

From the table we know that, in each of the three cases, $c_2(x) - c_1(x) = 30$ at $x = 1/2$. Moreover, by assumption $e^{30A} = 4$. Then, for each of the three cases:

$$\left.\frac{dU}{dx}\right|_{x=1/2} = Ae^{-Ac_2(x)}\,[4\pi(z_{21} - 50) + (1-\pi)\,(z_{22} - 50)]$$

It is then a straightforward matter to confirm that the term in brackets is zero for each of the three cases. That is, even though assets $\alpha$ and $\beta$ have the same mean and $\beta$ has a higher variance, the optimal holding of the risky asset is the same. Moreover asset $\gamma$ has a higher mean and lower variance than asset $\beta$ and yet the optimal holding of the risky asset is still the same.

From these examples it is clear that, to derive strong qualitative predictions as to asset-holdings in response to parametric changes in payoff distributions, we must introduce additional restrictions – either upon probability distributions or upon preferences. In the following section we describe some restrictions that do have general implications.

## 3.4     Stochastic dominance

### 3.4.1    Comparison of different consumption prospects

This section adopts a somewhat different approach to the risk-bearing decision. Instead of considering the specific effects of changes in wealth, in state-claim prices, in asset payoffs, etc., we ask under what general conditions it is possible to assert that one prospect or state-distributed consumption vector is preferred over another. We want to be able to answer this question by comparing the probability distributions of consumption alone, while calling only upon standard properties of individuals' preferences – to wit, positive marginal utility of income

$(v'(c) > 0)$ and risk-aversion $(v''(c) < 0)$. NOTE: in this section it will be more convenient to deal with continuous distributions, equivalent to assuming a continuum rather than a finite or countably infinite number of states of the world.

Let $\tilde{c}_1$ and $\tilde{c}_2$ be two consumption prospects and suppose that an individual with preference-scaling function $v(c)$ prefers the former. That is:

$$E\{v(\tilde{c}_1)\} > E\{v(\tilde{c}_2)\} \tag{3.4.1}$$

We can write the two cumulative distribution functions as:

$$F(c) = \text{Prob}\{\tilde{c}_1 \leqslant c\}$$
$$G(c) = \text{Prob}\{\tilde{c}_2 \leqslant c\}$$

Let us assume that both $\tilde{c}_1$ and $\tilde{c}_2$ lie between the non-negative limits $\alpha$ and $\beta$ and that both $F$ and $G$ are continuously differentiable. Then for the two distributions there are associated density functions, $F'(c)$ and $G'(c)$. We can rewrite (3.4.1) as:

$$\underset{F}{E\{v(c)\}} \equiv \int_\alpha^\beta v(c)F'(c)dc > \int_\alpha^\beta v(c)G'(c)dc \equiv \underset{G}{E\{v(c)\}} \tag{3.4.2}$$

In general, two individuals with different preferences will have different rankings of these two consumption prospects. However, in some cases it is possible to obtain an ordering that holds for all individuals regardless of their preferences (subject only to the standard properties of positive marginal utility and risk-aversion). In other words, we want to see how far we can get looking only at the probability distributions. When a choice between two prospects can be made using this information alone, it will be said that one distribution *stochastically dominates* the other.

DEFINITION 3.1: First-order stochastic dominance
If, for all $c$, $F(c) \leqslant G(c)$ and the inequality is strict over some interval, the distribution $F$ exhibits first-order stochastic dominance over $G$.

This definition leads immediately to:

*Ranking Theorem I*
For all increasing, piecewise differentiable functions $v(c)$, if $F$ exhibits first-order stochastic dominance over $G$ then:

$$\underset{F}{E\{v(c)\}} > \underset{G}{E\{v(c)\}}$$

Consequently, if the prospect or distribution $F$ is first-order stochastically dominant over $G$, then any individual with positive marginal utility of income will prefer $F$ to $G$.

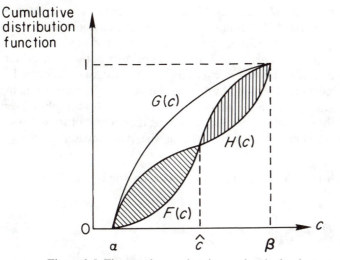

Figure 3.5 First- and second-order stochastic dominance

The property of the distribution functions leading to first-order dominance is evident from inspection of figure 3.5. Here $F$ and $H$ are both first-order stochastically dominant over $G$ but neither $F$ nor $H$ is first-order dominant over the other. Diagrammatically, the $F$ and $H$ curves both lie always below (and so also to the right of) $G$, but the $F$ and $H$ curves cross.

Following our usual practice, we will emphasize the intuitive meaning of this condition. (More rigorous statements are left as exercises.) First, compare the $F$ and $G$ curves. $F$ being always below $G$ means that, for each and every income level $c^\circ$ between $\alpha$ and $\beta$, the cumulative probability that $c$ is smaller than that income, that $c \leqslant c^\circ$, is greater for $G$ than for $F$. Thus, no matter what level of income we look at between these limits, $G$ always has a greater probability mass in the lower tail than does $F$. Alternatively, we could express this in terms of the income associated with any given probability level. For example, a lower-tail cumulative probability of, say, 0·5 occurs at a higher income for $F$ than for $G$. In other words, the distribution $F$ has a higher median (50th percentile) income than $G$. And, similarly, each and every percentile of the $F$ distribution is at a greater income than the corresponding percentile of the $G$ distribution. So we can confidently say (provided only that the marginal utility of income $v'(c)$ is always positive) that $F$ will surely be preferred.[3] We cannot make a similar

[3] We are implicitly assuming here that utility is not state-dependent – that $v(c)$ is unique. Then we can make expected-utility comparisons solely in terms of the probabilities of receiving different levels of income, without attending to *which* states of the world the income is received in. Where the marginal utility of income is not only a function of $c$ but also varies with state of the world, the proposition would not necessarily hold.

comparison of $F$ and $H$, however. Since $F$ and $H$ cross, comparisons of probability masses in the lower tail (or of income levels associated with any percentile of probability) will not always point the same way.

Only under quite stringent conditions will one distribution ever exhibit first-order stochastic dominance over another. So Ranking Theorem I is not very far-reaching. This is not surprising, because only the first standard property of the preference-scaling function, that $v'(c) > 0$, has been exploited. A more powerful theorem, involving the concept of *second-order* stochastic dominance, also makes use of the risk-aversion property – $v''(c) < 0$.

**DEFINITION 3.2**: Second-order stochastic dominance
If for all $c$:

$$\int_{-\infty}^{c} F(r)\, dr \leqslant \int_{-\infty}^{c} H(r)\, dr \tag{3.4.3}$$

with the inequality holding strictly over some part of the range, then the distribution $F$ exhibits second-order stochastic dominance over $H$.

Geometrically, $F$ is second-order dominant over $H$ if, over every interval $[\alpha, c]$, the area under $F(c)$ is never greater (and sometimes smaller) than the corresponding area under $H(c)$. This is equivalent, of course, to the horizontally shaded area in figure 3.5 being greater than the vertically shaded region.

Definition 3.2 leads directly to:

*Ranking Theorem II*
For all *increasing concave* twice-piecewise-differentiable functions $v(c)$, the concavity being strict somewhere, if $F$ exhibits second-order stochastic dominance over $H$ then:

$$\mathop{E}_{F}\{v(c)\} > \mathop{E}_{H}\{v(c)\}$$

The intuitive interpretation of second-order stochastic dominance parallels the interpretation of first-order stochastic dominance. As a first step, it is useful to define $\hat{F}(v)$ to be the cumulative distribution function for *final utility* $v$, when $c$ has the distribution $F(c)$. Note then that:

$$\hat{F}(v(c)) \equiv \text{Prob}\{\tilde{v} \leqslant v(c)\} = \text{Prob}\{v(\tilde{c}) \leqslant v(c)\} = \text{Prob}\{\tilde{c} \leqslant c\} = F(c)$$

That is, at the specific value $c^{\circ}$ located at any given percentile of the distribution of $\tilde{c}$, the corresponding $v(c^{\circ})$ is at the same percentile of the distribution of $v$. Similarly we define $\hat{H}(v)$ to be the cumulative distribution function for $v$ when $c$ has the distribution $H(c)$.

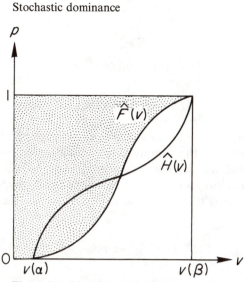

Figure 3.6 Cumulative distribution and expected value

The key point to appreciate is that, as pictured by the dotted region in figure 3.6, the area lying to the left of the cumulative distribution $\hat{F}(v)$ represents the expected value of $v$ – that is, expected utility $U = Ev(c)$ – under the distribution $F$. To see this, define $p = \hat{F}(v)$ to be the cumulative probability, so that:

$$dp = \hat{F}'(v)\, dv$$

The mean of $\hat{F}$ is of course defined by:

$$E\{v\} = \int_{v(\alpha)}^{v(\beta)} v\hat{F}'(v)\, dv = \int_0^1 v\, dp = \int_0^1 \hat{F}^{-1}(p)\, dp$$

Geometrically, this corresponds to finding the dotted area by integrating along the vertical rather than the horizontal axis in figure 3.6. Equivalently, the expected value of $v$ is the area of the rectangle less the area under $\hat{F}(v)$. That is:

$$E\{v\} = v(\beta) - \int_{v(\alpha)}^{v(\beta)} \hat{F}(v)\, dv$$

Then, to compare two distributions $F$ and $H$ we note that:

$$\underset{F}{E\{v(c)\}} - \underset{H}{E\{v(c)\}} = -\int_{v(\alpha)}^{v(\beta)} [\hat{F}(v) - \hat{H}(v)]\, dv$$

That is, the difference in the expected utilities of distributions $F$ and $H$ is just the difference in areas under the implied cumulative distribution functions $\hat{F}$ and $\hat{H}$.

Finally, we can rewrite this integral as:

$$\underset{F}{E\{v(c)\}} - \underset{H}{E\{v(c)\}} = -\int_{\alpha}^{\beta} [\hat{F}(v(c)) - \hat{H}(v(c))]\frac{dv}{dc}\,dc$$

$$= -\int_{\alpha}^{\beta} [F(c) - H(c)]\,v'(c)\,dc$$

Returning now to figure 3.5 and looking at the $F(c)$ and $H(c)$ probability distributions, remember that the condition for second-order stochastic dominance requires that the diagonally shaded area (representing the superiority of $F$ over $H$ at low values of $c$) exceed the vertically shaded area (representing the superiority of $H$ over $F$ at high values of $c$). But, as we have seen:

$$\underset{F}{E\{v(c)\}} - \underset{H}{E\{v(c)\}} = \int_{\alpha}^{\hat{c}} [H(c) - F(c)]\,v'(c)\,dc$$

$$- \int_{\hat{c}}^{\beta} [F(c) - H(c)]\,v'(c)\,dc$$

As long as $v(c)$ is concave so that $v'(c)$ is declining, $v'(c) \geqslant v'(\hat{c})$ for $c \leqslant \hat{c}$ and $v'(c) \leqslant v'(\hat{c})$ for $c > \hat{c}$. It follows that:

$$\underset{F}{E\{v(c)\}} - \underset{H}{E\{v(c)\}} > \int_{\alpha}^{\hat{c}} [H(c) - F(c)]\,v'(\hat{c})\,dc - \int_{\hat{c}}^{\beta} [F(c) - H(c)]\,v'(\hat{c})\,dc$$

$$= v'(\hat{c}) \int_{\alpha}^{\beta} [H(c) - F(c)]\,dc$$

From the definition of second-order stochastic dominance, the last integral is positive and so expected utility is indeed higher under $F$.

With multiple crossings of $F$ and $H$ the argument is only slightly more complicated. Consider the case of three crossings as in figure 3.7. Arguing exactly as above, the concavity of $v(c)$ implies that:

$$\int_{\alpha}^{c_2} (H - F)v'(c)\,dc > v'(c_1)\int_{\alpha}^{c_2} (H - F)\,dc \tag{3.4.4}$$

and

$$\int_{c_2}^{\beta} (H - F)v'(c)\,dc > v'(c_3)\int_{c_2}^{\beta} (H - F)\,dc \tag{3.4.5}$$

Second-order stochastic dominance implies that the integral on the right-hand side of (3.4.4) is positive. Therefore, from the concavity of $v(c)$:

$$\int_{\alpha}^{c_2} (H - F)v'(c)\,dc > v'(c_3)\int_{\alpha}^{c_2} (H - F)\,dc \tag{3.4.6}$$

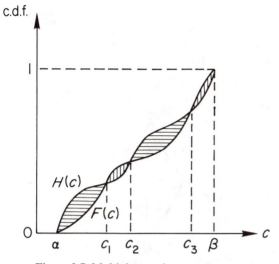

Figure 3.7  Multiple crossings

Adding (3.4.5) and (3.4.6) we have, at last:

$$\underset{F}{\mathrm{E}\{v(c)\}} - \underset{H}{\mathrm{E}\{v(c)\}} = \int_{\alpha}^{\beta} (H-F)\,v'(c)\,dc > v'(c_3)\int_{\alpha}^{\beta} (H-F)\,dc$$

Again, given second-order stochastic dominance, the last integral is positive and so $F$ is the preferred distribution.

The limiting case where the two distributions have the same mean, but $F$ exhibits second-order stochastic dominance over $H$, represents a formalization of the idea that one random variable can be more risky than another. This is illustrated in figure 3.5 where the diagonally shaded region has the same area as the vertically shaded region. Note that the slope of $H$ is greater than the slope of $F$ at both tails of the distribution, while $F$ has a greater slope towards the middle.

From figure 3.5 we can map the density functions $F'(c)$ and $H'(c)$. These are depicted in figure 3.8. As already noted, $H'(c) > F'(c)$ towards the ends of the income distribution while $F'(c) > H'(c)$ towards the middle. Then $H$ must have more probability weight in both tails than $F$. This case, in which probability weight is shifted towards the tails but in such a way that the old and new distributions cross only once, is often referred to as a *simple mean-preserving spread* (Rothschild and Stiglitz, 1971).

As is intuitively clear from figure 3.8, in the special case where the distribution $H$ represents a simple mean-preserving spread of $F$ it must be that $H$ has higher variance. However, a more powerful result (which is not

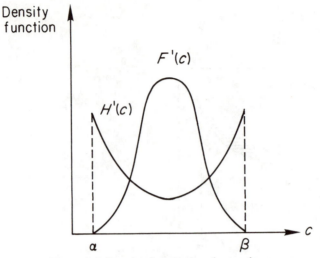

Figure 3.8 Density functions and spread

limited to the single-crossing case) also holds: if $F$ and $H$ have the same mean but $F$ exhibits second-order stochastic dominance over $H$, then $H$ must have higher variance. This is a direct implication of the following proposition which follows directly from Ranking Theorem II:

*Ranking Theorem III*
For all concave functions $v(c)$, the concavity being strict somewhere, if $F$ and $H$ have the same mean and $F$ exhibits second-order stochastic dominance over $H$ then:

$$\mathop{\mathrm{E}}_{F}\{v(c)\} > \mathop{\mathrm{E}}_{H}\{v(c)\}$$

Notice that we need not necessarily interpret $v(c)$ as a preference-scaling function here (or, for that matter, in the preceding Ranking Theorems). Specifically, we can choose here to let $v(c) = -(c-\mu)^2$, which is of course concave in the sense required. Then:

$$-\mathop{\mathrm{E}}_{F}\{(c-\mu)^2\} > -\mathop{\mathrm{E}}_{H}\{(c-\mu)^2\}$$

That is:

$$-\sigma_F^2 > -\sigma_H^2$$

So if $F$ and $H$ have the same mean $\mu$ and $F$ is second-order stochastically dominant, then $F$ has smaller variance.

Thinking now of $v(c)$ as a utility function, we have seen that: (i) if $F$ is second-order stochastically dominant over $H$, then $F$ is strictly preferred; (ii) if in addition $F$ and $H$ have the same mean, then $F$ has smaller variance. But it does not in general follow that, if two distributions $\tilde{c}_1$ and $\tilde{c}_2$ have the same mean and $\tilde{c}_1$ has smaller variance, then $\tilde{c}_1$ is preferred. For, $\tilde{c}_1$ might not be stochastically dominant.

EXAMPLE:

$$\tilde{c}_1 = \begin{cases} 0\cdot4, & \text{with probability } 1/2 \\ 2\cdot1, & \text{with probability } 1/2 \end{cases}$$

$$\tilde{c}_2 = \begin{cases} 0\cdot25, & \text{with probability } 1/9 \\ 1, & \text{with probability } 7/9 \\ 4, & \text{with probability } 1/9 \end{cases}$$

It is readily confirmed that $E\{\tilde{c}_1\} = E\{\tilde{c}_2\}$ and $\operatorname{var}\{\tilde{c}_1\} < \operatorname{var}\{\tilde{c}_2\}$. However, with $v(c) = \ln c$, expected utility is negative in the first case and zero in the second, that is $Ev(\tilde{c}_2) > Ev(\tilde{c}_1)$ so that the second prospect is preferred. It is left to the reader to graph the cumulative distribution functions for $\tilde{c}_1$ and $\tilde{c}_2$ and hence to confirm that neither stochastically dominates the other.

## EXERCISES AND EXCURSIONS 3.4.1

### 1 First-order stochastic dominance

For any pair of distributions $F$ and $G$ and differentiable function $v(c)$, integrate by parts to establish that:

$$\underset{F}{E\{v(c)\}} - \underset{G}{E\{v(c)\}} = \int_\alpha^\beta v(c)\,[F'(c) - H'(c)]dc$$

$$= \int_\alpha^\beta v'(c)\,[H(c) - F(c)]dc$$

Hence establish Ranking Theorem I.

### 2 Second-order stochastic dominance

Appealing to exercise 1, and integrating by parts a second time establish Ranking Theorem II.

### 3 Mean-preserving spreads

Use your answer to question 2 to establish Ranking Theorem III.

### 4 Stochastic dominance as a necessary condition

(A) In the text it was shown that, if $G(c) \geqslant F(c)$, then for any non-decreasing function $v(c)$:

$$\underset{F}{E}\{v(c)\} \geqslant \underset{G}{E}\{v(c)\}$$

By considering the example:

$$v_1(c) = \begin{cases} -1, & c < r \\ 0, & c \geqslant r \end{cases}$$

establish that, if the condition for first-order stochastic dominance does not hold, there are some non-decreasing utility functions for which the ranking is reserved. That is, for the entire class of non-decreasing utility functions to rank $F$ over $G$ (at least weakly), first-order stochastic dominance is a necessary condition.

(B) By considering the example:

$$v_2(c) = \begin{cases} c - r & c < r \\ 0, & c \geqslant r \end{cases}$$

establish the necessity of second-order stochastic dominance if (3.4.3) is to hold for all concave functions.

### *3.4.2    Responding to increased risk

We conclude this chapter by asking how a change in the probability distribution of income that satisfies the conditions of second-order stochastic dominance affects decisions.

Let $c = c(x, \theta)$ be the consequence of taking action $x$ when some exogenous variable takes on the value $\theta$. Moreover, suppose that this exogenous variable is state-dependent. Then, given the underlying beliefs about the likelihood of different states and the way $\theta$ varies across states, there is some derived distribution function for $\theta$, $F_1(\theta)$. For expositional convenience let $\theta$ be distributed continuously. Then, one can write the expected utility of taking action $x$ as:

$$U_1(x) = \int_{-\infty}^{\infty} v(c(x, \theta)) F_1'(\theta)\, d\theta$$

A simple illustration is provided by the portfolio choice problem

---

* Starred sections represent more difficult or specialized materials that can be omitted without significant loss of continuity.

analyzed in section 3.2. Suppose an individual invests $x$ in a risky asset with gross yield of $1+\theta$ per dollar and his remaining wealth $W-x$ in a riskless asset returning 1 per dollar. His final income is:

$$c(x,\theta) = (W-x)1 + x(1+\theta) = W + x\theta \qquad (3.4.7)$$

The question we wish to address is how the individual's portfolio decision is affected by a change in the distribution of the random variable $\theta$.

Returning to the general formulation, suppose that, with distribution function $F_1$, expected utility is maximized by taking action $x_1^*$. That is, the rate at which expected utility changes with $x$:

$$U_1'(x) = \int_{-\infty}^{\infty} \frac{\partial v}{\partial x}(c(x,\theta)) F_1'(\theta) \, d\theta$$

is zero at $x = x_1^*$.

Suppose next that there is a change in the way $\theta$ varies with the underlying state of nature. In particular suppose that the old and new distribution functions for $\theta$, $F_1$ and $F_2$, have the same mean and that $F_1$ exhibits second-order stochastic dominance over $F_2$.

From Ranking Theorem III it follows immediately that, if $\partial v/\partial x$ is a strictly concave function of $\theta$, then:

$$U_1'(x) = \mathop{E}_{F_1}\left\{\frac{\partial v}{\partial x}(c(x,\theta))\right\} > \mathop{E}_{F_2}\left\{\frac{\partial v}{\partial x}(c(x,\theta))\right\} = U_2'(x)$$

In particular this inequality holds at $x_1^*$. Therefore:

$$0 = U_1'(x_1^*) > U_2'(x_1^*)$$

It follows that the individual can increase his expected utility by choosing an action $x_2 < x_1^*$. Thus, assuming $U_2(x)$ has a unique turning point under the new (second-order dominated) probability distribution of returns on the risky asset, the individual will reduce his risky investment.

Note that the requirement that $\partial v/\partial x$ should be concave introduces a restriction on the third derivative of the preference-scaling function $v$. As we shall see in the exercises, this may be satisfied by imposing plausible restrictions on the way absolute and relative risk-aversion vary with wealth.

Developing the arguments above only a little bit more yields the following result:

*Optimal Response Theorem I* (Rothschild and Stiglitz, 1971):
Suppose that the distribution functions $F_1(\theta)$ and $F_2(\theta)$ have the same mean and $F_1$ exhibits second-order stochastic dominance over $F_2$. Let $x_i^*$ be the solution to:

$$\operatorname*{Max}_{x} U_i(x) = \int_{-\infty}^{\infty} v(c(x,\theta)\,F_i'(\theta)\,d\theta, \quad i = 1, 2$$

Suppose further that $x_i^*$ is the unique turning point of $U_i(x)$. Then if $\partial v/\partial x$ is a concave (convex) function of $\theta$, $x_1^*$ is greater than (less than) $x_2^*$.

While this proposition has been widely used in attempts to analyze the effects of mean-preserving increases in risk, results have been somewhat limited. The analysis of section 3.3 suggests the reason. Mean-preserving increases in risk have both income and substitution effects and these are often offsetting.

In an effort to overcome this problem, Diamond and Stiglitz suggested considering the effect of a change to a more risky distribution of returns that keeps expected utility constant. To be precise, suppose that the new distribution leaves expected utility constant at the old optimum $x^*$ but the new distribution of *utility* is more risky in the sense of second-order stochastic dominance. The following theorem provides conditions to sign the effect of such a mean-preserving increase in risk.

*Optimal Response Theorem II* (Diamond and Stiglitz, 1974)
Suppose that $c \in [\alpha, \beta]$ has a continuously differentiable distribution function $F(c)$. Suppose, furthermore, that the solution $x^*$ of the following problem is the unique turning point of $U_F(x)$:

$$\operatorname*{Max}_{x} U_F(x) = \int_{\alpha}^{\beta} v(x,c)\,F'(c)\,dc, \quad \text{where} \quad \frac{\partial v}{\partial c} > 0$$

Then if the distribution shifts from $F$ to $G$ in such a way that, at $x = x^*$, expected utility is unchanged but the new distribution of utility is more risky (in the sense of second-order stochastic dominance), the new optimum $x^{**}$ is less than $x^*$ if:

$$\frac{\partial^2}{\partial c \partial x} \ln \frac{\partial v}{\partial c} < 0$$

Moreover, if the last inequality is reversed $x^{**}$ exceeds $x^*$.

The derivation of this result is only a bit more complicated than that of Optimal Response Theorem I. The interested reader will find a sketch of the proof in the exercises at the end of this section. From these exercises it will become clear that significantly stronger results are possible using Optimal Response Theorem II.

## EXERCISES AND EXCURSIONS 3.4.2

### 1 Optimal responses to a change in risk

(A) In Optimal Response Theorem I, suppose that the assumption that $F_1$ and $F_2$ have the same mean is replaced by the assumption that $\partial v/\partial x$ is an increasing function of $\theta$. Show that the theorem continues to hold.

(B) What conclusions can be drawn if $\partial v/\partial x$ is a *convex* function of $\theta$?

### 2 Life-cycle saving with future income uncertainty (Leland, 1968)

(A) Show that a sufficient condition for $v''(c) > 0$ is that absolute risk-aversion, $A(c) \equiv -v''(c)/v'(c)$, is decreasing with wealth.

(B) An individual with current income $I_0$ and uncertain future income $\tilde{I}_1$ can earn $1 + r$ dollars on each dollar saved. His life-cycle utility is given by the intertemporally additive preference-scaling function:

$$v(c_0, c_1) = v_0(c_0) + v_1(c_1)$$

where $c_0$ is current consumption and $c_1$ is future consumption. Show that, if the distribution of future income becomes less favorable in the sense of second-order stochastic dominance and if $v_1'''(c_1) > 0$, the optimal level of savings increases.

### 3 Portfolio choice

(A) Show that:

$$\mu x \frac{v''(\lambda + \mu x)}{v'(\lambda + \mu x)} = -R(\lambda + \mu x) + \lambda A(\lambda + \mu x)$$

where $A(c) = -v''(c)/v'(c)$ and $R(c) = -cv''(c)/v'(c)$.

(B) An individual with wealth $\bar{W}$ invests $x$ in a risky asset with a return of $\tilde{z}_2$ and the rest of his wealth in a riskless asset with yield $z_1 = 1$.

   If $A(c)$ is decreasing and $R(c)$ is less than unity and non-decreasing, apply Optimal Response Theorem I to establish the impact on $x$ of a change in the distribution of risky returns that is strictly less favorable in the sense of second-order stochastic dominance.

(C) Analyze also the effect of a mean-utility-preserving increase in risk under the assumptions of decreasing absolute and increasing relative risk-aversion.

*4 Mean-utility-preserving increase in risk*

(A) Under the hypothesis of Optimal Response Theorem II, let $c = \phi(x, v)$ be the inverse of the mapping $V = v(x, c)$, that is, $\phi(x, v) = v^{-1}(x, V)$. Furthermore, let $\hat{F}(V)$ be the implied distribution of $V$. Confirm that:

$$U'_F(x) = \int_{V_\alpha}^{V_\beta} \frac{\partial v}{\partial x}(x, \phi(x, V))\hat{F}'(V)dV$$

(B) Let $x^*$ be the optimum under the distribution $F$. Write down the corresponding expression for a new distribution $G$ which has the property that, at $x = x^*$, $\hat{G}'(V)$ is a mean-preserving spread of $\hat{F}(V)$.

(C) Let $x^{**}$ be the optimum under the new distribution $G$. Appeal to Ranking Theorem II to show that $x^{**}$ exceeds $x^*$ if $\partial v(x^*, \phi(x^*, V))/\partial x$ is a concave function of $V$.

(D) Define $y(V) \equiv \partial v(x, \phi(x, V))/\partial x$. That is:

$$y(v(x, c)) = \frac{\partial v}{\partial x}(x, c)$$

Differentiate by $c$ and hence show that $y'(V)$ can be expressed as follows:

$$y'(v(x, c)) = \frac{\partial}{\partial x} \ln \frac{\partial v}{\partial c}(x, c)$$

(E) Differentiate this expression again and hence establish Optimal Response Theorem II.

*5 Owner-operated firms facing demand uncertainty* (Sandmo, 1971)

Each firm in an industry is owned and operated by a single agent whose best alternative is working elsewhere at wage $w$. In the production of $q$ units of output, the cost to firm $i$ of all other inputs, $C(q)$, is an increasing convex function, with $C(0) = 0$. Each owner must choose his output level $q^*$ before knowing the final product price $\tilde{p}$. There is free entry into, and exit from the industry.

(A) If owners are risk-neutral, show that the equilibrium expected price denoted as $\bar{p}_n$ must satisfy:

$$\text{(i) } \bar{p}_n = C'(q^*) \quad \text{(ii) } \bar{p}_n q^* - C(q^*) - w = 0$$

(B) If owners are risk-averse show that the equilibrium expected price $\bar{p}_a$ exceeds $\bar{p}_n$.

(C) Suppose that initially there is no uncertainty so that the equilibrium price is $\bar{p}_n$ and output per firm is $q^*$. If prices become uncertain, apply

Optimal Response Theorem II to establish that the output of firms remaining in the industry will decline if the following expression is a decreasing function of $p$:

$$\phi(q,p) = [pq - qC'(q)] \frac{v''(pq - C(q))}{v'(pq - C(q))}$$

(D) Show that, for all $q > 0$, $qC'(q) > C(q)$. Hence establish that, under the assumptions of decreasing absolute and non-decreasing relative risk aversion, the equilibrium output per firm declines.

HINT: Appeal to Optimal Response Theorem II and (A) of exercise 3.**

REFERENCES AND SELECTED READINGS

Arrow, K. J., "The Theory of Risk Bearing," in *Aspects of the Theory of Risk Bearing*, Helsinki: Yrjö Jahnssonin Säätio, 1965, republished in *Essays in the Theory of Risk Bearing*, Chicago: Markham, 1971.

Diamond, P. A. and Stiglitz, J. E., "Increases in Risk and in Risk Aversion," *Journal of Economic Theory*, 8 (1974), 337–60.

Hart, O. D., "Some Negative Results on the Existence of Comparative Statics Results in Portfolio Theory," *Review of Economic Studies*, 42 (1975), 615–21.

Kihlstrom, R. and Mirman, L. J., "Risk Aversion with Many Commodities," *Journal of Economic Theory*, 8 (1974), 361–88.

Leland, H. E., "Savings and Uncertainty: The Precautionary Demand for Saving," *Quarterly Journal of Economics*, 82 (1968), 465–73.

Machina, M., "A Stronger Characterization of Declining Risk Aversion," *Econometrica*, 50 (1982), 1069–80.

Pratt, J. W., "Risk Aversion in the Small and in the Large," *Econometrica*, 32 (1964), 122–36.

Rothschild, M. and Stiglitz, J. E. "Increasing Risk I: A Definition," *Journal of Economic Theory*, 2 (1970), 225–43 and "Increasing Risk II: Its Economic Consequences," *Journal of Economic Theory*, 3 (1971), 66–84.

Sandmo, A., "On the Theory of the Competitive Firm Under Price Uncertainty," *American Economic Review*, 61 (1971), 65–73.

** End of starred section.

# 4 Market equilibrium under uncertainty

We have so far considered only the decisions of the individual. In this chapter the level of analysis shifts to market interactions and the conditions of equilibrium. The *firm* will be introduced as an agency of individuals engaged in the process of production. We continue to deal only with *event uncertainty* under "perfect markets" – ruling out *market uncertainty* with its characteristic attendant phenomena of search and of trading at non-clearing prices. But account will be taken of possibly incomplete regimes of markets, i.e., we will not always assume that each distinct state-claim is, directly or indirectly, tradable.

## 4.1 Market equilibrium in pure exchange

In the regime of Complete Contingent Markets (CCM), where claims to a generalized consumption good $C$ under each and every state-contingency are separately tradable, as shown in chapter 2 the individual's optimum position can be expressed as the "Fundamental Theorem of Risk-bearing":

$$\frac{\pi_1 v'(c_1)}{P_1} = \frac{\pi_2 v'(c_2)}{P_2} = \ldots = \frac{\pi_S v'(c_S)}{P_S} \tag{4.1.1}$$

(This form of the theorem is valid only for interior solutions.)[1] At this point we call attention to the fact that, in principle at least, all of the following elements may differ among the various individuals $j = 1, \ldots, J$: the probability beliefs $\pi_s^j$, the consumption quantities $c_s^j$, and the preference-scaling functions $v_j(c^j)$. However, the prices $P_s$ will be the same for all market participants.

In moving from individual optimization to market equilibrium under Complete Contingent Markets, equation (4.1.1) must hold for each and

---

[1] Unless otherwise indicated, it will be assumed throughout that interior (and not corner) solutions apply for all economic agents.

every market participant. It follows immediately that, for any two individuals $j$ and $k$, and comparing state 1 with any other state $s$:

$$\frac{\pi_s^j v_j'(c_s^j)}{\pi_1^j v_j'(c_1^j)} = \frac{P_s}{P_1} = \frac{\pi_s^k v_k'(c_s^k)}{\pi_1^k v_k'(c_1^k)} \tag{4.1.2}$$

Thus, for each and every individual (at an interior solution), the price ratio between any two state-claims will equal the ratio of expected marginal utility of incomes in the two states. As an evident corollary, if in addition individuals $j$ and $k$ have the same beliefs, then for all $s$:

$$\frac{v_j'(c_s^j)}{v_k'(c_s^k)} = \xi \quad \text{(a constant)} \tag{4.1.2a}$$

In words: for any individuals $j$ and $k$, the ratio of $j$'s marginal utility of contingent income to $k$'s corresponding marginal utility is the same over all states.

The other conditions required for equilibrium represent market-clearing. In equilibrium under pure exchange, for each and every traded state-claim the sum of the desired holdings (demand quantities) must equal the sum of the endowment amounts (supply quantities):

$$\sum_{j=1}^{J} c_s^j = \sum_{j=1}^{J} \bar{c}_s^j, \quad \text{for} \quad s = 1, \dots, S \tag{4.1.3}$$

EXAMPLE 4.1: In a world of two equally probable states ($\pi_1 = \pi_2 = 1/2$), suppose there are two equally numerous types of individuals: $j$ and $k$. The $j$-types have endowment $\bar{C}^j = (\bar{c}_1^j, \bar{c}_2^j) = (40, 40)$ while the $k$-types have endowment $\bar{C}^k = (20, 140)$. The respective preference-scaling functions are $v_j = \ln c^j$ and $v_k = (c^k)^{1/2}$. Find the equilibrium price ratio and the optimum risky consumption vectors $\hat{C}^j$ and $\hat{C}^k$.

*Answer*: One way of solving the system is to consider the respective demands for $c_2$-claims as a function of the unknown $P_2$. For the type-$j$ individuals, the Fundamental Theorem of Risk-bearing can be expressed as:

$$\frac{0 \cdot 5 \, (1/c_1^j)}{P_1} = \frac{0 \cdot 5 \, (1/c_2^j)}{P_2}$$

or:

$$P_1 c_1^j = P_2 c_2^j$$

And the budget equation is:

$$P_1 c_1^j + P_2 c_2^j = 40 \, P_1 + 40 \, P_2$$

Setting $P_1 = 1$ as numeraire, the type-$j$ demand for state-2 claims becomes:

$$c_2^j = 40(1+P_2)/2P_2$$

An analogous development for the type-$k$ individuals leads to:

$$c_2^k = (20 + 140P_2)/(P_2^2 + P_2)$$

Making use of the clearing condition that $c_2^j + c_2^k = 40 + 140 = 180$, it may be verified that the equilibrium price is $P_2 = 1/2$. The associated optimal consumption vectors are $\hat{C}^j = (30, 60)$ and $\hat{C}^k = (30, 120)$.

Instead of contingent-claims trading, more generally there might be trading of *assets* ($a = 1, ..., A$) at prices $P_a^A$, where a unit of each asset represents a fixed bundle of state-claim payoffs $z_{as}$. The corresponding "Risk-bearing Theorem for Asset Markets" is the individual optimum condition for holdings of assets $q_a$, applicable under regimes of Complete Asset Markets (CAM) and even for incomplete asset-market regimes:[2]

$$\frac{\sum_s \pi_s v'(c_s) z_{1s}}{P_1^A} = \frac{\sum_s \pi_s v'(c_s) z_{2s}}{P_2^A} = ... = \frac{\sum_s \pi_s v'(c_s) z_{As}}{P_A^A}, \quad c_s = \sum_a q_a z_{as}$$

$$(4.1.4)$$

At an interior optimum, this equation will hold in asset-market equilibrium for each and every economic agent. The equilibrium price ratio between asset 1 and asset $a$ will be such that, for any pair of individuals $j$ and $k$:

$$\frac{\sum_s \pi_s^j v_j'(c_s^j) z_{as}}{\sum_s \pi_s^j v_j'(c_s^j) z_{1s}} = \frac{P_a^A}{P_1^A} = \frac{\sum_s \pi_s^k v_k'(c_s^k) z_{as}}{\sum_s \pi_s^k v_k'(c_s^k) z_{1s}} \qquad (4.1.5)$$

Notice once again that not only the asset prices $P_a^A$ are taken as given and thus the same for all individuals, but also the asset state-payoffs $z_{as}$. That is, there is no disagreement among individuals about what each asset will return in each and every state. So the only possible disagreement allowed for in this simple model concerns the *probabilities* of the different states.[3]

Finally, of course, in asset-market equilibrium there must also be market-clearing:

$$\sum_{j=1}^{J} q_a^j = \sum_{j=1}^{J} \bar{q}_a^j, \quad \text{for} \quad a = 1, ..., A \qquad (4.1.6)$$

---

[2] As indicated in chapter 2, an asset-market regime is "complete" if the set of available assets $a = 1, ..., A$ allows each individual to achieve the same contingent consumption vector as under Complete Contingent Markets (CCM). A necessary, though not sufficient, condition for complete asset markets is $A \geq S$.

[3] This is, of course, a very drastic idealization of individuals' portfolio-holding choice situations in the real world.

EXAMPLE 4.2: Under the conditions of the previous example, imagine now that the same endowments are expressed as asset holdings $\bar{q}_a$. Thus, suppose the type-$j$ endowment consists of forty units of asset 1 with state-return vector $(z_{11}, z_{12}) = (1, 1)$ while $k$'s endowment consists of twenty units of asset 2 with return vector $(z_{21}, z_{22}) = (1, 7)$. Find the equilibrium asset price ratio $P_1^A/P_2^A$ and the associated optimum asset holdings $\hat{q}_a$.

*Answer*: This is evidently a regime of Complete Asset Markets (CAM). Using the Risk-bearing Theorem for Asset Markets from section 2.1.2 of chapter 2, and since $c_s = \Sigma_a q_a z_{as}$, following the method of the previous example we could develop the parties' demands for one of the assets as a function of its unknown price. An easier analysis suffices here, however, since we know that under the CAM condition the same consumption vectors can be attained as under the Complete Contingent Markets (CCM) assumption of the previous example. We also know from the development in chapter 2 that the asset prices $P_a^A$ are related to the contingent-claim prices $P_s$ by:

$$P_a^A = \sum_s z_{as} P_s$$

Letting the state-claim price $P_1 = 1$ be the numeraire as before, it follows immediately that $P_1^A = 1(1) + 1(0\cdot5) = 1\cdot5$, while $P_2^A = 1(1) + 7(0\cdot5) = 4\cdot5$. And knowing the optimal $\hat{c}_2$ for each type of individual, the equations $c_s = \Sigma_a q_a z_{as}$ can be inverted leading to the optimum asset holdings $\hat{Q}^j = (\hat{q}_1^j, \hat{q}_2^j) = (25, 5)$ while $\hat{Q}^k = (\hat{q}_1^k, \hat{q}_2^k) = (15, 15)$.

### 4.1.1   Application to share-cropping

In an agricultural situation, assume there are two decision-makers: landlord $l$ owns land but no labor, while worker $w$ owns labor but no land. There are two states of the world: $s = 1$ (loss state, or "bad weather") versus $s = 2$ (non-loss state, or "good weather"). The respective agreed probabilities are $\pi_1$ and $\pi_2 \equiv 1 - \pi_1$. For the sake of the argument, assume that all productive decisions have been made so that the only choices remaining are how to share the contingent outputs and the associated risks.

Figure 4.1 is an Edgeworth box, on axes representing $c_1$ (income in the loss state) and $c_2$ (income in the non-loss state). Because of the difference in the social totals, the box is vertically elongated. The two parties' 45° certainty lines cannot coincide; it is impossible for *both* individuals to attain certainty positions, though either one could do so if the other were to bear all the risk. For individual $h$ (where $h = l, w$), the absolute indifference-curve slope (the Marginal Rate of Substitution $M^h$) at any point in the Edgeworth box is given by $\pi_1 v'_h(c^h_1)/\pi_2 v'_h(c^h_2)$. Along the worker's 45° line, $M^w = \pi_1/\pi_2$ since $c^w_2 = c^w_1$. But at any such point the landlord's $c^l_1 < c^l_2$, hence $v'_l(c^l_1) > v'_l(c^l_2)$, so the landlord's indifference curves must all be steeper than the worker's along the latter's 45° line. Reasoning similarly for the landlord's 45° line, we see that the indifference curves must be shaped as shown in the diagram. It follows that the Contract Curve TT, connecting all the mutual-tangency points where the two parties' indifference-curve slopes are equal, must lie between the two 45° lines. This means that in equilibrium the parties will share the risk.

Assuming price-taking behavior – which would be applicable if there were a large number of competing individuals on both sides of the market – the equilibrium point would depend upon the endowment position. In the diagram, suppose this endowment is $\bar{C}$: the worker is initially receiving a fixed wage while the landlord is bearing all the risk. Under Complete Contingent Markets there will then be trading in state-claims $c_1$ and $c_2$, leading to the CCM equilibrium price ratio $P_1/P_2$. Specifically (4.1.2) takes the form:

$$\frac{\pi_1 v'_w(c^w_1)}{\pi_2 v'_w(c^w_2)} = \frac{P_1}{P_2} = \frac{\pi_1 v'_l(c^l_1)}{\pi_2 v'_l(c^l_2)}$$

The solution point is of course on the Contract Curve, as indicated by point C in the diagram. Note the following properties of the equilibrium position:

1  The parties have shared the risk, and will in fact do so regardless of the endowment position.
2  Since $c_1 < c_2$ for each party at equilibrium, it follows that $v'(c_1) > v'(c_2)$ for both $l$ and $w$, and hence that $P_1/P_2 > \pi_1/\pi_2$. That is, the price of contingent income in the loss state is high *relative* to the corresponding probability. This is of course what we would expect: apart from the probability weighting factor, claims to income in an affluent state of the world should be cheap in comparison with claims to income in an impoverished state.

We digress now to make some remarks on contract structures. If the worker initially receives a contractually fixed wage placing him on his 45° line, we have seen that a certain amount of trading of contingent claims is necessary to achieve an efficient distribution of risk. The same holds if the landlord initially receives a fixed contractual rent placing her on her 45° line. Since such trading is costly, we would expect to observe a tendency to avoid these extreme contractual forms. And, in fact, the worker and landlord functions are very commonly combined in owner-operated farms.

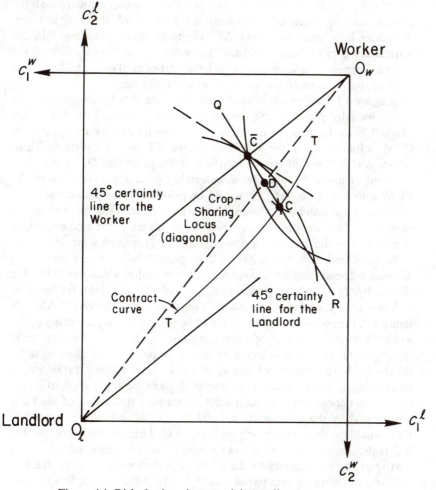

Figure 4.1 Risk-sharing via state-claim trading

An important element affecting the cost of trading is the problem of enforcement of contract – control of "shirking." As it is notoriously easier for labor than for land to shirk its contractual duties, other things being equal we would expect more often to have farm operators leasing land at a fixed rental than farmland owners hiring workers at a fixed wage. (While farmers do sometimes employ hired hands, this is very rarely done on a large scale. Farming typically remains a small-scale, family business.)

In state-claim trading the parties must be able to unambiguously identify which state of the world has occurred in order to distribute the contingent payoffs. The potential for trouble and disagreement on that score is all the greater since in practical situations the number of states $S$ is large. (Consider how many states would have to be distinguished within the general category of "good weather.") One way of reducing the difficulty is a *share-cropping* arrangement in which the parties need only decide in what fixed proportions to divide the crop, whatever its size.

In figure 4.1 the possible proportional divisions of the product would be represented by points along the main diagonal of the Edgeworth box (dashed line). In general, no such division could exactly reproduce the CCM solution along the Contract Curve TT in the diagram. Thus, equation (4.1.2) would not be satisfied. But a point like D, on the main diagonal of figure 4.1, may be a reasonably good approximation of the CCM solution at point C. (It would be possible to reproduce the *exact* state-claim solution by combining share-cropping with side-payments; for example, if there are only two states as in the diagram, the landlord might receive $x$ % of the crop less a side-payment of $\$y$ in each state. However, with more than two states it would in general be necessary to have a different side-payment for each of $S-1$ distinct states, which would involve essentially the same high transaction costs as full state-claim trading.)

Alternatively, consider a regime of Complete Asset Markets (CAM). In figure 4.2, the endowment point $\bar{C}$ could be regarded as representing (i) the worker's initial holding $\bar{q}_a^w$ of a certainty asset $a$, i.e., an asset with payoffs $(z_{a1}, z_{a2}) = (1, 1)$. This is reflected by the 45° slope of the line from $0_w$ to $\bar{C}$; (ii) the landlord's initial holding $\bar{q}_b^l$ of a risky asset $b$, the ratio of whose returns $(z_{b1}, z_{b2})$ is reflected in the steeper slope of the line from $0_l$ to $\bar{C}$. We are free to choose units for each asset, so suppose that a unit of asset $a$ is represented by the unit vector parallel to $0_w\bar{C}$ while a unit of asset $b$ is represented by the unit vector parallel to $0_l\bar{C}$. Then the length of the line $0_l\bar{C}$ is the number of units of asset $b$ initially held by the landlord.

Any exchange of assets by the landlord is a move back along the line $0_l\bar{C}$ and out along a line parallel to $0_w\bar{C}$. By exchanging assets in such quantities as to move to a point on the contract curve such as $C^*$, each party is satisfying the Risk-bearing Theorem for Asset Markets, plus of course the market-clearing guaranteed by the fixed size of the Edgeworth box. Once again, however, for $S > 2$ the ideal CCM solution at $C^*$ cannot in general be attained by trading in only two assets $a$ and $b$.

As an interesting interpretation, we can think of this type of risk-sharing as the exchange of "equity shares" in the two parties' endowments. This interpretation will be developed further later on in the chapter.

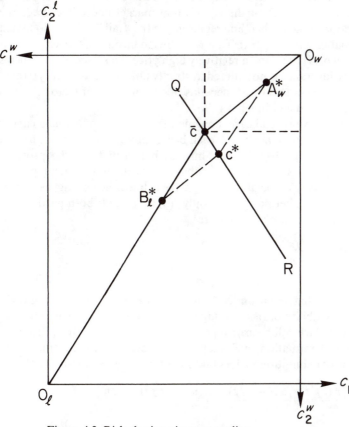

Figure 4.2 Risk-sharing via asset trading

### 4.1.2    Application to insurance

The Edgeworth box of figure 4.1 can be given another interpretation: the risk-sharing that takes place there can be regarded as "mutual insurance." Indeed, all insurance is best thought of as mutual. Insurance companies, since they do not dispose of any resources other than those possessed by their owners, creditors, and policy-holders, are only intermediaries in the risk-sharing process.

Once again, imagine "loss" and "non-loss" states of the world. For example, an earthquake might or might not occur. The Edgeworth box will again be vertically elongated, the social total of income being smaller in the loss state (state 1). From any endowment point like $\bar{C}$ in figure 4.1, price-taking traders under Complete Contingent Markets (CCM) would arrive at a risk-sharing equilibrium like C* on the Contract Curve TT. As before, the absolute slope $P_1/P_2$ of the equilibrium market line QR exceeds the absolute slope of the dashed line representing the "fair" price ratio (equal to the probability ratio $\pi_1/\pi_2$). That is, claims to income in the less affluent state of the world command a relatively high price. This "social risk" helps explain why insurance is not offered at strictly fair (or "actuarial") terms.[4] But the influence of social risk depends upon a number of factors, as will be worked out in detail in what follows.

As an instructive special case, imagine there are two individuals $j$ and $k$ with equal initial gross incomes $\bar{c}$, each being subject to a fixed loss hazard $L$ with the same probability $p$. Thus, each person faces the prospect $(\bar{c}, \bar{c}-L; 1-p, p)$. Here $p$ is the probability of an independent private event. Four possible social states can be defined, according as loss is suffered by: (1) neither party; (2) $j$ only; (3) $k$ only; (4) both parties. The corresponding state-probabilities are:

$$\pi_1 = (1-p)^2$$
$$\pi_2 = p(1-p) = \pi_3$$
$$\pi_4 = p^2$$

It is evident that, even under Complete Contingent Markets (CCM), there is no possibility of risk-sharing in states 1 and 4. So the only trading that can take place will be exchanging state-2 for state-3 claims. From the symmetry of the situation, such exchange will occur in a $1:1$ ratio, so that the equilibrium condition (4.1.1) takes the form, for each individual:

$$\frac{\pi_1 v'(\bar{c})}{P_1} = \frac{\pi_2 v'(\bar{c}-L/2)}{P_2} = \frac{\pi_3 v'(\bar{c}-L/2)}{P_3} = \frac{\pi_4 v'(\bar{c}-L)}{P_4}$$

where, of course, $P_4/\pi_4 > P_3/\pi_3 = P_2/\pi_2 > P_1/\pi_1$.

The equilibrium condition would not take quite so simple a form if inter-individual differences were permitted – as between the losses $L^j$ and $L^k$, the loss-probabilities $p_j$ and $p_k$, initial incomes $\bar{c}^j$ and $\bar{c}^k$, and the preference-scaling functions $v^j(c^j)$ and $v^k(c^k)$. But it nevertheless remains true that, after trading, $c_1 > c_2, c_3 > c_4$ for each individual and that in equilibrium:

$$\frac{P_4}{\pi_4} > \frac{P_3}{\pi_3} \quad \text{and} \quad \frac{P_2}{\pi_2} > \frac{P_1}{\pi_1}$$

Any actual system of contractual insurance arrangements will only approximate the ideal results under CCM. One possible arrangement

---

[4] In actual insurance practice, transaction costs place a "loading" upon the premiums offered purchasers of policies. In accordance with our assumption of perfect markets, transaction costs will be set aside here.

might be a mutual-insurance system with no stated premiums. Instead, policy-holders would be proportionately assessed for the amounts required to match the aggregate of losses experienced. In our fully symmetrical example above, in state 1 there would be no loss and no assessment; in state 2 the assessment would be $L/2$ to each party, summing to the full $L$ required to indemnify individual $j$; similarly in state 3, except that the indemnity would go to individual $k$; in state 4, each party would be assessed $L$ and indemnified $L$, so that no actual transfer of funds would take place. Thus, the assessment system would replicate the results of CCM. More generally, however – allowing for inter-individual differences in loss magnitudes $L$, loss probabilities $p$, endowments, etc. – such an assessment arrangement would diverge from results under CCM. But, if only the loss magnitudes varied among individuals, proportionate assessment would be similar to share-cropping. An individual whose risk is $x\%$ of the total would be assessed $x\%$ of the loss *ex post*, so that the outcome would lie along the main diagonal of an Edgeworth box in four-dimensional space.

Coming closer to conventional insurance arrangements, standard practice would be to quote (say, for individual $j$) a fixed premium $H^j$ to be paid into the pool regardless of which state obtains, while a fixed indemnity $I^j$ will be receivable from the pool in either state 2 or state 4. Inability to provide for differential net payments in these two states, together with the corresponding failure in the case of individual $k$ to distinguish state 3 from state 4, represents a serious incomplete-markets problem. Indeed, under mutual insurance the problem is an impossible one, since owing to social risk the totals of premiums paid in could not always match the totals of indemnities payable. For example, if any premiums at all are collected, should state 1 occur there would be no losses to absorb them. But a zero premium would be absurd, providing no funds for the indemnity payments required in all other states of the world. In practice, this difficulty is avoided by having mutual-insurance pools take on a legal personality, e.g., via the corporate form. Then, premium levels $H^j$ and $H^k$ might be set, for example, to cover indemnities in state 4, the most adverse possibility. Should any other state actually come about, the corporation will show a "profit" that can be rebated back to its owners, the policy-holders. (Alternatively, the corporation might engage in time-averaging, reinvesting profits in good years to accumulate "reserves" to help cover losses in bad years and thus permit a lower level of premiums.) It will be evident that such a system is essentially equivalent to assessable premiums.

Social risk comes about whenever private risks are not perfectly offsetting. It is sometimes thought that the variability of the per-capita social risk is only a result of small numbers. If so, for pools with a sufficiently large membership $N$, mean income could be regarded as effectively constant. It follows that, for large $N$, insurance premiums would become practically actuarial (fair) – apart from transaction costs, of course.

Instead of a fixed loss $L^j$, assume more generally now that each individual faces a loss-probability distribution $f^j(\tilde{L}^j)$, and for simplicity suppose all the distributions are identical. Then the question is whether the per-capita loss $\tilde{\lambda} = (1/N)\Sigma_{j=1}^{N}\tilde{L}^j$ becomes approximately constant over states as $N$ grows large. In accordance with the Law of Large Numbers, as $N$ increases the variance of $\tilde{\lambda}$ does decline, hence the error committed by ignoring social risk does diminish. Nevertheless, this error does *not* tend toward zero as $N$ increases, unless indeed the separate risks are on average uncorrelated.[5]

Suppose that the individual $L^j$ distributions all have the same mean $\mu$ and variance $\sigma^2$ and suppose, also, that the correlations between all pairs of risks equal some common $r$ (which of course can only be possible for $r \geq 0$). That is, for any pair $L^j, L^k$:

$$E\{(L^j - \mu)(L^k - \mu)\} = r\sigma^2$$

The mean average loss $E(\tilde{\lambda})$ is then just $\mu$. The variance of the average loss is:

$$
\begin{aligned}
\sigma_\lambda^2 &= E\{(\tilde{\lambda} - \mu)^2\} \\
&= \frac{1}{J^2} E\left\{\sum_{j=1}^{N}(L^j - \mu)\right\}^2 \\
&= \frac{1}{J^2}\sum_{j=1}^{N} E\left\{\sum_{k=1}^{N}(L^j - \mu)(L^k - \mu)\right\} \\
&= \frac{1}{J^2}\sum_{j=1}^{N}\{\sigma^2 + (N-1)r\sigma^2\} \\
&= \sigma^2\left\{\frac{1 + r(N-1)}{N}\right\}
\end{aligned}
$$

In the limit as $N$ increases, the variance of per-capita loss approaches $r\sigma^2$, and thus always remains positive unless $r = 0$.

We see, therefore, that social risk is not exclusively due to small numbers; it persists even with large numbers if risks are positively correlated. Somewhat offsetting this consideration is the possibility of time-averaging via the accumulation of reserves. Doing so is to employ the Law of Large Numbers in a different dimension: the law tends to operate

[5] See Markowitz (1959), p. 111.

over time as well as over risks at any moment in time. If risks that are correlated at any point in time are serially uncorrelated over time, aggregated over a number of time-periods the variance of per-capita losses will diminish. (The power of the Law of Large Numbers over time will be weakened to the extent that positive serial correlation exists, that is, if high-social-loss states tend to be followed by similar high-loss states.)

Interpreting the main result of this section in terms of the language of portfolio theory, risks have a "diversifiable" element which can be eliminated by purchasing shares in many separate securities (equivalent to mutual insurance among large numbers of individuals), and an "undiversifiable" element due to the average correlation among risks. It follows then that a particular asset will be more valuable the smaller is the correlation of its returns over states of the world with the aggregate returns of all assets together – the variability of which is the source of undiversifiable risk.[6]

Social risk, therefore, provides two reasons why insurance prices may not be fair or actuarial: (i) if the number of risks in the insurance pool is small, the Law of Large Numbers cannot work very fully; (ii) if the separate risks are on average positively correlated, then even with large numbers the variance of the per-capita return does tend to diminish but does not approach zero. In either case there will still be relatively poor social states for which claims to income will command prices that are disproportionately high relative to the corresponding probabilities (with the reverse holding for relatively affluent social states).

In addition, a number of other factors may help bring about non-actuarial terms of insurance: (1) as mentioned in footnote 4, insurance premiums are "loaded" in order to cover transaction costs; (2) state-dependent utility, as discussed in the preceding chapter, may affect the desirability of gambles; (3) *adverse selection* and *moral hazard*, phenomena essentially due to information asymmetries between buyers and sellers, may tend to affect the terms of insurance transactions. (These topics will be considered in detail in chapter 7 below.)

---

[6] In modern investment theory, the correlation of a particular security's return with that of the market as a whole – which represents the returns on all securities together – is measured by a "beta" parameter. Securities with low or, even better, negative betas tend to trade at relatively high prices. That is, investors are satisfied with relatively low expected rates of return on these assets, since they tend to provide generous returns in just those states of the world where aggregate incomes are low (and, therefore, marginal utilities are high). We analyze this topic in detail in section 4.3.

## EXERCISES AND EXCURSIONS 4.1

### 1 Complete versus incomplete asset-market equilibria

(A) In a world of three equally probable states, with equally numerous individuals of types $j$ and $k$, the endowments are $\bar{C}^j = (45, 45, 45)$ and $\bar{C}^k = (15, 67 \cdot 5, 315)$. The preference-scaling functions are $v^j = \ln c^j$ and $v^k = (c^k)^{1/2}$. Verify that under CCM the equilibrium price ratios are $P_1 : P_2 : P_3 = 3 : 2 : 1$. Find the individual optimum positions.

(B) Suppose the same endowment positions are expressed in terms of asset-holdings. Thus, $j$ holds 45 units of asset $a$ with state-returns $(1, 1, 1)$ while $k$ holds 1 unit of asset $b$ with state-returns $(15, 67 \cdot 5, 315)$. Verify that the CCM equilibrium cannot be attained if the parties can exchange only assets $a$ and $b$.

### 2 Efficiency of proportional sharing

In the landlord–worker problem show that, if the two parties have common probability beliefs and identical preference-scaling functions $v(c^w)$ and $v(c^l)$ characterized by constant relative risk-aversion $R$, then – for any finite number of states $S$ – the CCM solution will lie along the main diagonal of the $S$-dimensional Edgeworth box. (Hence simple proportional sharing of the crop will be efficient.)

ANSWER : If $R$ is constant, then preferences are homothetic. That is, for states 1 and $s$ the Marginal Rate of Substitution $M \equiv -dc_s/dc_1$ for either individual is a function only of the probabilities and the state-consumption ratio. Also, $M$ is equal in equilibrium to the price ratio $P_1/P_s$. Thus:

$$M^w \equiv \frac{\pi_1}{\pi_s} f\left(\frac{c_1^w}{c_s^w}\right) = \frac{P_1}{P_s} = \frac{\pi_1}{\pi_s} f\left(\frac{c_1^l}{c_s^l}\right) \equiv M^l$$

Since the equilibrium consumption ratio $c_1/c_s$ between states 1 and $s$ will therefore be the same for each party, the solution must be on the main diagonal of the multi-dimensional Edgeworth box. Hence this main diagonal is the Contract Curve. So any arrangement for proportional sharing of the state-contingent total crop will correspond to an efficient CCM equilibrium attainable from some endowment position in the box.

### 3 Risk-sharing with $\mu$, $\sigma$ preferences

Suppose preferences are given by:

$$U^i = \mu(c^i) - \alpha^i \sigma^2(c^i), \quad i = w, l$$

The aggregate output in state $s$ is $y_s$. The worker, individual $w$, is to be paid a fixed "wage" $\omega$ plus a share $\gamma$ of the residual $y_s - \omega$.

(A) Obtain expressions for $\mu(c^i)$ and $\sigma^2(c^i)$ in terms of $\omega$, $\gamma$, and the mean and variance of $y$.

(B) Write down a first-order condition for the Pareto-efficient choice of $\omega$. Hence show that along the Pareto frontier $dU^w/dU^l = -1$.

(C) Hence, or otherwise, establish that the worker's efficient share of aggregate risk is:

$$\gamma^* = \frac{\alpha^l}{\alpha^l + \alpha^\omega}$$

(D) Is it surprising that this share is constant along the Pareto frontier?

(E) Would a similar result hold if there were $M$ workers and $N$ landlords?

## 4 Insurance with transaction costs

Suppose each individual faces the risk of a loss $L$, the different risks being independent (uncorrelated). Also, there are sufficiently large numbers that the per-capita risk is negligible and so insurance is offered on actuarily fair (i.e., zero profit) terms.

What would be the equilibrium insurance policy if, whenever a loss takes place, the insurance company incurs a transaction cost $c$?

## 5 Complete Contingent Markets (CCM) with constant absolute risk-aversion

Suppose each of $N$ individuals exhibits constant absolute risk-aversion $A$. All have the same probability beliefs. Under a CCM regime, let $P_s$ denote the equilibrium price in state $s$ ($s = 1, ..., S$).

(A) If individual $i$'s degree of absolute risk-aversion is $A_i$ show that his optimum claims in states $s$ and $t$ must satisfy:

$$A_i(c_s^i - c_t^i) = \ln(\pi_s/\pi_t) - \ln(P_s/P_t)$$

(B) Hence obtain an expression for the logarithm of relative prices in terms of the average endowments in states $s$ and $t$, $\bar{c}_s$ and $\bar{c}_t$.

(C) Let $A^*$ be the harmonic mean of the degrees of absolute risk-aversion, that is:

$$A^* = \left[ \sum_{i=1}^{N} \frac{N}{A_i} \right]^{-1}$$

Show that the difference between the price ratio $P_s/P_t$ and the ratio of probabilities $\pi_s/\pi_t$ is positive if and only if $\bar{c}_s > \bar{c}_t$.

(D) Discuss also the effect of changes in the distribution of endowments, and of an increase in $A^*$, upon $P_s/P_t$.

## 6 Insurance premiums with state-dependent utility

Suppose that health risks are independently distributed for all individuals. Suppose, furthermore, that numbers are sufficiently large so that insurance against a deterioration in health is offered on actuarily fair terms.

(A) Suppose an individual has a preference-scaling function $v(c,h) = (ch)^{\frac{1}{2}}$, his health level $h$ being either $h_b$ or $h_g$ (where $h_b < h_g$). Would this individual wish to buy insurance against bad health?

(B) Suppose bad health also reduces income by 50%. Would the individual now wish to buy insurance? If not necessarily, under what conditions would this be the case? Would the individual ever buy enough insurance to completely offset his income loss?

(C) Another individual has a preference-scaling function $\bar{v}(c,h) = \ln(ch)$. Confirm that there is a function $u(\cdot)$ such that:

$$\bar{v}(c,\ h) = u(v(c,h))$$

Hence draw a conclusion as to which individual is more risk-averse.

(D) Repeat (A) and (B) with the new preference-scaling function.

(E) What can you say about an individual who is more risk-averse than both these individuals but again has the same indifference map?

HINT: You might refer back to section 2.2 in chapter 2 before attempting to answer this question.

## 4.2     Production and exchange

The previous section examined regimes of complete and incomplete markets in a pure-exchange economy with a single generalized consumption good $C$. We showed that the analysis of market equilibrium can be interpreted in terms of an S-dimensional Edgeworth box diagram with one axis for each state-claim $c_s$. Just as goods are allocated efficiently in the traditional commodity-market equilibrium under certainty so, under uncertainty, a complete-market equilibrium (i.e., the CCM case where there are markets in all $S$ states, or else the CAM case where an equivalent regime of asset markets exists) distributes social risk efficiently.

We will now generalize this conclusion. In section 4.2.1 we show that, even in a world of production, and allowing for many commodities $G$ as well as any number of states $S$, a complete-market equilibrium allocation is Pareto-efficient. Of course the assumption of complete markets is a strong one. Section 4.2.2 takes up production decisions in a special regime of incomplete markets called a "stockmarket economy." Conditions are derived under which shareholders unanimously agree upon value maximization as the objective of the firm.

### 4.2.1   Equilibrium with production: complete markets

Suppose there is a single commodity (corn), a single firm, and two states of the world (rain or no rain). By varying the production process the firm chooses a state-distributed vector of production levels $y = (y_1, y_2)$. The set of possible production vectors or "production set" $Y$ is illustrated in figure 4.3.[7] We assume that this set is convex.

To illustrate, suppose that when rows of corn are planted close together there will be an especially big harvest *if* the weather is hot. However, if the weather is cool, a better yield is obtained by planting at lower densities. As a special case, let:

$$y_1(x) = 20x, \quad y_2(x) = 100x - 10x^2$$

be the state-dependent outputs associated with a crop density of $x$. Eliminating $x$ yields the production frontier:

$$y_2 - 5y_1 + 1/4\, y_1^2 = 0$$

The production set $Y$ consists of the production vectors $y = (y_1, y_2)$ on or inside the production possibility frontier.

Given state-claim prices $P_1$ and $P_2$, the profit of the firm (since there are no purchased factors of production) is the revenue $P_1 y_1 + P_2 y_2$. Writing the price vector as $P = (P_1, P_2)$, a profit-maximizing price-taking firm chooses $y^*$ and hence profit level $\Pi$ to satisfy:

$$\Pi^* = P \cdot y^* \geqslant P \cdot y, \quad \text{for all} \quad y \in Y$$

(Here and henceforth, we will assume a unique solution exists.) The iso-profit line $P \cdot y = \Pi^*$ is also depicted in figure 4.3 along with the profit-maximizing production vector $y^*$.

We now examine the consumer-shareholders' demands for state-contingent corn. With just two individuals $j$ and $k$, we can illustrate via the Edgeworth box formed in figure 4-3 with corners at the origin and at $y^*$. Suppose the two proportionate shareholdings in the firm are $\bar{q}_f^j$ and $\bar{q}_f^k \equiv 1 - \bar{q}_f^j$.[8] With 0 as the origin for $j$, his budget constraint is:

$$P_1 c_1^j + P_2 c_2^j = \bar{q}_f^j \Pi^* \tag{4.2.1}$$

---

[7] In a more complete model, inputs would be purchased at $t = 1$ and output produced at $t = 2$, as in exercise 3 at the end of this section.

[8] In chapter 2 and elsewhere, $q_a^i$, denoted the *number of units* of asset $a$ held by individual $i$. Here, the total number of shares in firm $f$ is defined as unity, so each individual's shareholding $q_f^i$ will represent a fractional number of units.

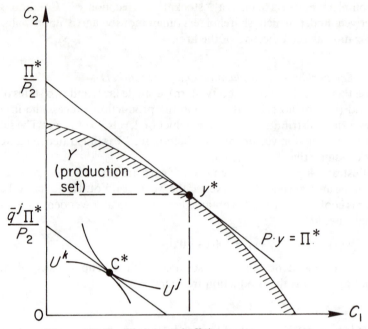

Figure 4.3 Equilibrium and efficiency

This is, as depicted, parallel to $\Pi^* = P \cdot y$ but with vertical intercept $\bar{q}_f^j \Pi^*/P_2$. Then the risk-bearing optimum for individual $j$ is point $C^*$ where $U^j(c_1^j, c_2^j)$ is maximized subject to the budget constraint (4.2.1).

Of course this budget line can also be viewed as the budget line for individual $k$, using the point $y^*$ as her origin. As depicted, the state-claim prices $P_1$ and $P_2$ are such that aggregate consumption equals aggregate production in each state – markets are cleared. Since neither individual can do any better without making the other worse off, the competitive equilibrium is Pareto-efficient. And, specifically, price-taking behavior and profit maximization result in an allocation in which the Marginal Rate of Substitution of state-1 claims for state-2 claims, $M \equiv -dc_2/dc_1$, is, for each individual, equal to his or her marginal rate of productive transformation $-dy_2/dy_1$.

Note that, just as in the pure-exchange case, the analysis is formally equivalent to the traditional certainty model. However, whereas in the standard certainty model $y$ is a vector of outputs of different commodities, $y$ here becomes a state-contingent output vector. This suggests a way of demonstrating the efficiency of a Complete Contingent Markets (CCM) regime in a much more general setting. All we have to do is to show that the description of individual optimization and market clearing is formally equivalent to that in the traditional certainty model, where the efficiency of competitive equilibrium is a standard result.

As a first step let us briefly review the traditional general-equilibrium model. Suppose the economy consists of $I$ individuals indexed by $i$, $F$ firms indexed by $f$, and $G$ commodities indexed by $g$. Firm $f$ chooses a vector of inputs and outputs $y^f = (y_1^f, ..., y_G^f)$ from the set $Y^f$ of feasible vectors. We assume that a firm can always choose not to produce so that the zero vector is in $Y^f$. A positive $y_g^f$ indicates that the firm produces more than it purchases of commodity $g$ while a negative $y_g^f$ indicates that the firm is a net purchaser of the commodity. With commodity prices $P = (P_1, ..., P_G)$ the firm chooses $y_*^f$ to maximize profit.[9] That is:

$$y_*^f \text{ solves } \underset{y^f}{\text{Max}} \{P \cdot y^f \mid y^f \in Y^f\}$$

Since firm $f$ can always choose not to produce, maximized profit $\Pi^f$ is nonnegative.

Each individual $i$, with utility function $U^i(c^i)$ where $c^i \equiv (c_1^i, ..., c_G^i)$, has some initial endowment of commodities $\omega^i \equiv (\omega_1^i, ..., \omega_G^i)$ and owns a proportion $\bar{q}_f^i$ of firm $f$. The individual then chooses $c_*^i$ to maximize utility subject to the constraint that total expenditure on commodities does not exceed the value of his endowment plus profit shares. That is, $c_*^i$ is the solution of:

$$\text{Max} \{U^i(c^i) \mid P \cdot c^i \leqslant P \cdot \omega^i + \sum_f \bar{q}_f^i \Pi^f\}$$

For $P$ to be a market equilibrium price vector, supply must equal demand in every market,[10] that is:

$$\sum_f y_*^f + \sum_i \omega^i = \sum_i c_*^i$$

And on the assumption that each individual, regardless of his consumption vector, always strictly prefers more of some commodity we know also – from the first theorem of welfare economics (Debreu, 1959) – that this market equilibrium is Pareto-efficient.

[9] For example, the production set of the neoclassical firm producing $Q$ units of output with capital and labor according to the production function $Q = \Phi(K, L)$ is:

$$Y^f = \{(Q, -K, -L) \mid Q \leqslant \Phi(K, L), K, L \geqslant 0\}$$

With prices $(P_1, P_2, P_3) = (p, r, w)$ the firm chooses $y^f \in Y^f$ to maximize:

$$P \cdot y^f = pQ + r(-K) + w(-L) = pQ - (rK + wL).$$

[10] As a more general statement (allowing also for corner solutions), supply must at least equal demand, and the price must be zero for any market in which there is excess supply.

We now seek to extend this result to include uncertainty. Instead of just $G$ markets, one for each commodity, we introduce markets for each commodity in each state of the world – $G \times S$ markets in all. The price $P_{gs}$ is then the price of purchasing a unit of commodity $g$ for delivery if and only if state $s$ occurs.

Each firm makes a decision as to its purchases and sales in each state. For example, a firm producing commodity 1 using commodities 2 and 3 as inputs might have a state-dependent production function:

$$y_{1s}^f = \phi_s^f(-y_{2s}^f, -y_{3s}^f)$$

The firm then contracts to purchase contingent inputs and deliver contingent outputs in order to maximize its profit:

$$\Pi^f = (P_{1s} y_{1s}^f + P_{2s} y_{2s}^f + P_{3s} y_{3s}^f) = P \cdot y^f$$

In general, just as in the certainty case, firm $f$ chooses $y_*^f$ so that:

$$\Pi^f = P \cdot y_*^f \geqslant P \cdot y^f, y^f \in Y^f$$

In the same way individual $i$ with endowment $\omega^i$ and preference-scaling function $v^i(c_s^i)$, where $c_s^i = (c_{1s}^i, ..., c_{Gs}^i)$, chooses his final consumption bundle to maximize expected utility:

$$U^i(c^i) = \sum_s \pi_s^i v^i(c_s^i)$$

This maximization is of course subject to the budget constraint:

$$P \cdot c^i \leqslant P \cdot \omega^i + \sum_f \bar{q}_f^i \Pi^f$$

Viewed in this way, it is clear that any conclusions about the certainty model must carry over. In particular the equilibrium allocation must lead to a Pareto-efficient allocation of risk-bearing.

Several aspects of the equilibrium are worthy of note:

1 Under complete markets, the efficient allocation is achieved when firms simply maximize profit (net market value). Profit being deterministic rather than stochastic, there is no need to consider expected profit or to adjust for some concave function of profit representing owner risk-aversion. The point is that, at the time a production decision is made, the firm can also complete all sales of its *contingent* outputs at the ruling state-claim prices. Net earnings or profit can then be handed over to stockholders. Of course, actual input and output levels will be uncertain. However, the market equilibrium state-claim prices already provide the correct adjustments for the risk factor, so owners are best served when the

chosen production vector maximizes net market value. It follows also that stock markets and stock trading have no special role. Indeed, no-one has any incentive to trade his initial asset endowment except to make final consumption purchases.

2 Different consumers need not have the same beliefs about the likelihood of different states. The CCM equilibrium is efficient with respect to beliefs *actually held*.

3 All trading in this economy takes place prior to learning which state $s$ has occurred. This raises the question as to whether any individual might wish to engage in posterior trading after the state of the world is revealed. To answer this question suppose that all prior trading takes place on the anticipation that markets will *not* reopen after the state is revealed. Consumer $i$ will then initially select his state-distributed consumption vector so that his Marginal Rate of Substitution of commodity 1 for commodity $g$ in a particular state is equal to the price ratio:

$$\frac{\dfrac{\partial U^i}{\partial c_{1s}}}{\dfrac{\partial U^i}{\partial c_{gs}}} = \frac{\pi_s^i \dfrac{\partial v^i}{\partial c_{1s}}}{\pi_s^i \dfrac{\partial v^i}{\partial c_{gs}}} = \frac{P_{1s}}{P_{gs}} \tag{4.2.2}$$

Now suppose that the state is revealed to be $s$, and that, unexpectedly, markets do in fact reopen for posterior trading. If the state-$s$ market price *ratios* among the $G$ commodities were to remain unchanged from the prior ratios of (4.2.2), individual $i$, now with utility function $v^i(c_s)$, will wish to trade so that his new Marginal Rate of Substitution of commodity 1 for commodity $j$ will equal the unchanged price ratio, that is:

$$\frac{\dfrac{\partial v^i}{\partial c_{1s}}}{\dfrac{\partial v^i}{\partial c_{gs}}} = \frac{P_{1s}}{P_{gs}} \tag{4.2.3}$$

Comparing (4.2.2) and (4.2.3) it follows immediately that individual $i$ will have no need to trade again. Thus, the prior-trading price ratios for the state-$s$ commodity claims dictate a posterior equilibrium in which no retrading occurs.[11] This proposition will play an important role when we consider the topic of speculation in chapter 6.

---

[11] It is left to the reader to confirm that no firm will wish to change its production plan in state $s$ either.

So far we have considered only the *unanticipated* opportunity for retrading after the state is revealed. If the possibility of posterior trading is indeed *anticipated*, consumers must form beliefs about prices in future states ("future spot prices"). Our argument indicates that, as long as everyone believes that relative future spot prices in the state that actually occurs will be the same as relative prior contingent prices, there will be no gains to multiple rounds of trading. Moreover, such beliefs will be self-fulfilling – the market-clearing future spot price ratios will indeed equal the corresponding contingent price ratio.[12]

4 We have implicitly been assuming that production, consumption, and exchange all occur at a single date in time. This also is an expositional simplification that can easily be generalized. The same equation format for a CCM regime can allow for specifying the commodity, the state, and also the date. The price $P_{gst}$ is then the price paid, in the current period, for commodity $g$ to be delivered at time $t$ in the eventuality that state $s$ occurs. As in the one-period model, firm $f$ chooses $y^f = (y^f_{111}, ..., y^f_{GST})$ from its production set $Y^f$ to maximize $P \cdot y^f$ – which is the net present value of the production plan or, more simply, the *value of the firm* at today's prices. It should be noted that the firm's plan will, in general, be a contingent plan. That is, some farther-future decisions may be contingent upon some still uncertain nearer-future events.

### EXERCISES AND EXCURSIONS 4.2.1

*1 Exchange equilibrium with complete markets*

Consider an economy with two states. Every individual has the same preference-scaling function $v(c) = \ln(c)$ and believes that state 1 will occur with probability $\pi$.

(A) Show that the CCM equilibrium price ratio satisfies:

$$\frac{P_1}{P_2} = \frac{\pi}{1-\pi}\left(\frac{y_2}{y_1}\right)$$

---

[12] Beliefs may then be called "rational," as in the common but confusing term "rational expectations equilibrium" – a more accurate term would be "self-fulfilling beliefs equilibrium." In the absence of such concordant beliefs about future spot prices, those agents whose beliefs were incorrect will wish to re-enter the market. This in turn opens up opportunities for sophisticated traders to "speculate." We shall have more to say on this topic in chapter 6.

where $y_s$ is the aggregate endowment of claims in state $s$.

(B) If the price of a riskless asset yielding 1 unit in each state is 1, show that the state-claim prices are:

$$P_1 = \frac{\pi y_2}{\pi y_2 + (1-\pi) y_1} \quad \text{and} \quad P_2 = \frac{(1-\pi) y_1}{\pi y_2 + (1-\pi) y_1}$$

(C) Suppose there are two types of asset in the economy. A unit of the riskless asset (asset 1) pays off 1 in each state and has market price $P_1^A = 1$. A unit of the risky asset (asset 2) returns $z_{21} = 1/2$ in state 1 and $z_{22} = 2$ in state 2. Aggregate supplies of the two assets are $q_1$ and $q_2$. If the two states are equally likely, show that the price of the risky asset is:

$$P_2^A = \frac{5q_1 + 4q_2}{4q_1 + 5q_2}$$

(D) Suppose initially there are no units of the risky asset. However there is a technology that will create units of the risky asset at the cost of 1 unit of the riskless asset. There is free entry into the industry.

What will be the equilibrium price of the riskless asset? What will be the equilibrium supply of the risky asset, expressed as a proportion of the equilibrium supply of the riskless asset?

## 2 Complete-market equilibrium with production

Consider an economy in which a single firm produces a single commodity. There are two states of the world, state 1 and state 2. The $n^{\text{th}}$ plant in the firm can produce any state-dependent output vector $y = (y_1, y_2)$ lying in the production set $Y^n = \{(y_1, y_2) | y_1^2 + y_2^2 \leq 2\}$. There are two individuals in the economy, each of whom has a 50% share in the firm, and who behave as price-takers.

(A) If there are two plants, confirm that the aggregate production set is $Y = \{(y_1, y_2) | y_1^2 + y_2^2 \leq 8\}$. Hence, or otherwise, show that with state-claim prices $(P_1, P_2) = (1, 1)$ the firm will produce an output vector $(y_1^*, y_2^*) = (2, 2)$.

(B) If individual 1 believes that state 1 will occur with certainty explain why, *at the above prices*, his final consumption vector is $(c_1^1, c_2^1) = (2, 0)$.

(C) If the second individual believes that state 2 will occur with certainty confirm that $P = (1, 1)$ is the complete-market equilibrium price vector.

(D) In the absence of trading possibilities the stockholders are no longer able to place an explicit market value on the firm. They must therefore evaluate the firm directly, in terms of its final output. One possible bargaining agreement would be to split the firm with each stockholder becoming sole owner of one plant. Given such an agreement, would individual 1 produce only output in state 1 and individual 2 only output in state 2?

## 3 Production in a two-period economy with complete markets

In a one-commodity, two-state, two-period economy, a firm can use $-y_1$ units of input at $t = 1$ to produce $y_{2s}$ units of output at $t = 2$ in state $s$, where $(y_1, y_{21}, y_{22})$ is in the production set:

$$Y = \{(y_1, y_{21}, y_{22}) \mid y_1 + (y_{21})^2 + (y_{22})^2 \leqslant 0\}$$

(A)  Depict cross-sections of the production set in $(y_1, y_2)$ space – assuming $y_{21} = y_{22}$ – and in $(y_{21}, y_{22})$ space. Use these to draw the production set in a three-dimensional diagram.

(B)  With prices $(P_1, P_{21}, P_{22})$ assumed to be ruling at date 1, solve for the profit-maximizing production vector.

(C)  If $P_1 = 1$ and $P_{21} + P_{22} = 1 + \theta$ explain why the risk-free real interest rate is $\theta$.

(D)  If $P_{21} = 1/3$ and $P_{22} = 2/3$ show that the firm could issue risk-free bonds in period 1 to cover its input costs. Then in period 1 it could pay off its debt.

(E)  Could the firm still issue risk-free bonds if $P_{12} = 1/4$ and $P_{22} = 3/4$? If not, could it simply issue risky bonds at a higher interest rate?

### *4.2.2    Stockmarket equilibrium

As argued in chapter 2 (section 2.1.2), if the state-contingent returns of the $F$ firms in the economy span the full $S$-dimensional space of contingent claims, then trading in the $F$ "equity" shares suffices for Complete Asset Markets (CAM). In this section we consider trading in equity shares where there may be fewer firms (assets) than states $(F \leqslant S)$. Once again, consider an economy with a single income commodity ("corn"). Before the state is revealed, firm $f$ makes a production decision yielding a state-contingent output vector $y^f = (y_1^f, ..., y_S^f)$, where $y^f$ belongs to the firm's set of feasible output levels $Y^f$. Initial proportionate holdings in firm $f$ are $\bar{q}_f^i$ (for individuals $i = 1, ..., I$), where $\Sigma_{i-1}^I \bar{q}_f^i = 1$. Individual $i$ can trade shares in the stockmarket subject to his portfolio budget constraint:

$$\sum_f P_f^A q_f^i = \sum_f P_f^A \bar{q}_f^i \qquad (4.2.4)$$

---

*  Starred sections represent more difficult or specialized materials that can be omitted without substantial loss of continuity.

where $P_f^A$ is the market price of firm $f$ (asset $f$). After having chosen a portfolio, his final consumption will be:

$$c^i = \sum_f q_f^i y^f, \text{ where } c^i = (c_1^i, ..., c_S^i) \tag{4.2.5}$$

To find the optimal portfolio, the individual solves:

$$\text{Max} \left\{ \sum_s \pi_s^i v_i(c_s^i) \mid c_s^i = \sum_f q_f^i y_s^f \right\} \tag{4.2.6}$$

subject of course to the portfolio budget constraint (4.2.4). These considerations lead, as in chapter 2, to the Risk-bearing Theorem for Asset Markets: the optimal asset holdings equate the expected marginal utility of investing an additional dollar in each asset.

$$\frac{\sum_s \pi_s^i v_i'(c_s^i) y_s^f}{P_f^A} = \lambda_i \quad \text{for } f = 1, ..., F \tag{4.2.7}$$

Here the Lagrange multiplier $\lambda_i$ is his marginal utility of wealth.

EXAMPLE 4.3:
Imagine there are three equally probable states and two firms. Firm 1 produces the certainty output vector $y^1 = (1, 1, 1)$ while firm 2 produces $y^2 = (2, 0, 0)$. There are two individuals $j$ and $k$, each initially endowed with 50% of each firm, and each having the preference-scaling function $v = \ln c$.

The individual's decision problem can be expressed (for $i = j, k$):

$$\text{Max} \, \Sigma_s \, \pi_s \, v(c_s^i) = (1/3) \ln (q_1^i + 2q_2^i) + (1/3) \ln (q_1^i) + (1/3) \ln (q_1^i)$$
$$\text{subject to} \quad P_1^A q_1^i + P_2^A q_2^i = P_1^A \bar{q}_1^i + P_2^A \bar{q}_2^i.$$

But by symmetry we know that the equilibrium solutions for the shareholdings are $q_1^i = q_2^i = 1/2$. Letting the value of asset 1 (firm 1) be the numeraire, so that $P_1^A = 1$, by straightforward steps equation (4.2.7) becomes:

$$\frac{14/9}{1} = \frac{4/9}{P_2^A}$$

So the price of firm 2 is $P_2^A = 2/7$, and the marginal utility of wealth is $\lambda_i = 14/9$ for $i = j, k$.

We now want to consider the conditions under which shareholders will unanimously agree upon *maximization of value* as the criterion for the firm's productive decisions.

From equation (4.2.7), in stockmarket equilibrium we have:

$$P_f^A = \Sigma_s \left[ \frac{\pi_s v_i'(c_s^i)}{\lambda_i} \right] y_s^f \tag{4.2.8}$$

The expression in brackets is the expected marginal utility of consumption in state $s$, divided by the individual's marginal utility of income. This is the consumer's implicit valuation of state-$s$ claims.

Now suppose the production vector for firm $f$ were to change from $y^f$ to $\hat{y}^f + dy^f$, but that *there is only a negligible effect upon the consumers' marginal utilities of income in the various states*. This means that a kind of "large-numbers condition" holds – that no single firm produces such a substantial fraction of the social income in any state as to noticeably affect the consumers' implicit valuations thereof. Then:

$$dP_f^A = \Sigma_s [\pi_s^i v_i'(c_s^i)/\lambda_i] dy_s^f \tag{4.2.9}$$

Turning to the corresponding effect upon shareholders' utility:

$$U^i = \Sigma_s \pi_s^i v_i(c_s^i) = \Sigma_s \pi_s^i v_i(\Sigma_f q_f^i y_s^f) \tag{4.2.10}$$
$$dU^i = q_f^i \Sigma_s \pi_s^i v_i'(c_s^i) dy_s^f \tag{4.2.11}$$

Dividing both sides of the equation by $\lambda_i$ and substituting from (4.2.9) we finally obtain:

$$dU^i/\lambda_i = q_f^i dP_f^A \tag{4.2.12}$$

Thus, since in the absence of any substantial effect upon marginal utilities $\lambda_i$ must remain unchanged, the implication is that any change in firm value $P_f^A$ will shift shareholders' utilities in the same direction.

Following Baron (1979), De Angelo (1981), and Makowski (1983) we call the conjectures of the owners of firm $f$ *competitive* if all believe that a change in the firm's production plan will have negligible effects upon individual agents' shadow prices. We have therefore derived:

PROPOSITION 1: Unanimity over Value Maximization
If all individuals have competitive conjectures with respect to the production decisions of firm $f$, they will unanimously agree on value maximization as the objective function for this firm.

Notice that the condition for "large numbers" or *competitive* behavior is entirely separate from the question of whether or not markets are complete. Even under Complete Contingent Markets, a single firm might be perceived by its owners as having some degree of monopoly power over the aggregate supply of claims in one or more states $s$. Conversely, markets could be seriously incomplete in terms of the number of state-claims explicitly or implicitly traded, and yet there might be so many firms that no single one can substantially affect the supply in any state or set of states.

When asset markets are incomplete (as must happen if there are fewer firms than states), a competitive stockmarket equilibrium cannot in general be Pareto-efficient in the sense of section 4.2.1, even when firms all maximize market values. However, exercise 1 at the end of this section outlines a proof of the following more limited efficiency property of the equilibrium allocation:

### PROPOSITION 2: Constrained Pareto-efficiency

If conjectures by all individuals about all firms are competitive, and denoting $(\hat{q}, \hat{z}, \hat{c})$ as the stockmarket equilibrium allocation of shares $\hat{q}_f^i$, output levels $\hat{z}^f$, and consumption vectors, $\hat{c}^i$, then there is no alternative feasible allocation $(q, z, c)$ that Pareto-dominates $(\hat{q}, \hat{z}, \hat{c})$ when, for all $i$, $c^i = \Sigma_f q_f^i z^f$.

The theorem says that the equilibrium is an optimum, subject to the constraint that the asset returns must be shared using a rule that is independent of the state. This is equivalent to assuming trading in pure equity shares only (see Diamond, 1967).

## EXERCISES AND EXCURSIONS 4.2.2

### 1 Constrained Pareto-optimality

Let $(\hat{c}, \hat{q}, \hat{z}, P^A)$ be a stockmarket equilibrium for the economy described above. If $(\hat{c}, \hat{q}, \hat{z})$ is not Pareto-efficient, then it is Pareto-dominated by some feasible triple $(c, q, z)$.

(A) Explain why, for some $i$:

$$p^i \cdot c^i > p^i \cdot \hat{c}^i$$

where $p_s^i = \pi_s^i v_i'(c_s^i)/\lambda_i$ is the equilibrium marginal valuation of consumption in state $s$ for individual $i$. Explain also why:

$$\sum_i p^i \cdot c^i = \sum_i \sum_a q^{ia} P_a^A > \sum_a P_a^A$$

(B) For a stockmarket equilibrium we must also have, for all $a$:

$$P_a^A = p^i \cdot \hat{z}_a \geqslant p^i \cdot z_a, \quad z_a \in Z^s$$

Use this result to obtain a contradiction of the inequality obtained in (A).

## 2 Stockmarket equilibrium with multiple goods

An economy consists of two firms and two individuals. Firm $f$ produces 1 unit of $x$ in state 1 and 2 units of $x$ in state 2. Firm $g$ produces 1 unit of $y$ in state 1 and 2 units of $y$ in state 2.

Individuals I and II have preference-scaling functions:

$$v^I = \ln x + 3 \ln y \quad \text{and} \quad v^{II} = 3 \ln x + \ln y$$

Individual I assigns a probability of $1/3$ to state 1 while individual II assigns a probability of $2/3$. Each has a 50% share in the two firms.

(A) Confirm that, if the price vector in a complete market regime is $P = (P_{x1}, P_{x2}, P_{y1}, P_{y2}) = (14, 5, 10, 7)$, individual I maximizes expected utility by choosing the consumption vector $(x_1^I, x_2^I, y_1^I, y_2^I) = (1/7, 4/5, 3/5, 12/7)$. Solve also for the optimum for individual II and hence confirm that $P$ is an equilibrium price vector.

(B) Show also that the two stocks have the same equilibrium value.

(C) Suppose that there are no state-contingent markets. However the two individuals can trade initially in the stockmarket and later, after the state is revealed, in commodity markets. Suppose furthermore that the two firms continue to have the same value and that the future spot prices $(\bar{P}_{xs}, \bar{P}_{ys})$ in state $s$ equal the contingent prices $(P_{xs}, P_{ys})$.

Show that, if individual I sells his holdings in firm $f$ and then sells short one-half of firm $f$, his final consumption is exactly as in (A). Establish also that, by entering into such a trade in the asset markets, individual II attains the same consumption in (A).

(D) Explain why, at these prices, there can be no better final consumption vector for either individual. That is:

$$P_a^A = P_b^A, \quad (\bar{P}_{x1}, \bar{P}_{y1}) = (14, 10), \quad (\bar{P}_{x2}, \bar{P}_{y2}) = (5, 7)$$

are equilibrium prices in an economy with a stockmarket and a future spot market.

## 3 Pareto-dominated stockmarket equilibrium (Hart, 1975)

Consider again the stockmarket economy of the previous question. Suppose both individuals believe that the prices in the future spot markets will be:

$$(\bar{P}_{xs}^F, \bar{P}_{ys}^F) = (1, r), \quad s = 1, 2$$

(A) Obtain expressions for the future spot values of the two firms in each state. Hence explain why the price of firm $g$ in the stockmarket will be $r$ times the price of firm $f$.

(B) Explain also why, under such beliefs, there is no gain to trading in the stockmarket.

(C) Assuming individuals do not trade in the stockmarket, show that, if $r = 1$, the final consumption of individual I will be $(x_1^I, x_2^I, y_1^I, y_2^I) = (1/4, 3/4, 1/2, 3/2)$. Solve also for individual II's optimum and hence show that all future spot markets clear. That is:

$$P_a^A = P_{xs}^A, \quad (\bar{P}_{xs}, \bar{P}_{ys}) = (1,1), s = 1,2$$

is a stockmarket equilibrium.

(D) Confirm that both individuals are worse off in this equilibrium than in the stockmarket equilibrium characterized in the previous question. [Note: See Hart (1975) for other illustrations of constrained Pareto-*in*efficient equilibria with multiple goods.]**


*4.2.3 Monopoly power in asset markets*
The analysis above was based on the assumption that all agents are price-takers. In the pure-exchange economy where each agent's wealth is small relative to aggregate wealth, this is a natural assumption. Similarly, if every firm's output is small relative to aggregate output in each state, it seems reasonable to model firms as price-takers also. However, the situation is more complicated if agents spread risk by trading in asset markets rather than contingent-claims markets. For then, even if a firm is small, it will retain monopoly power if it offers a distribution of returns for which there are few close substitutes.

To clarify this result, consider two examples. In the first there are two assets, one of which is riskless, and two states. The asset payoff vectors then span the state-claim space (the regime is CAM) so there is a $1:1$ mapping from state-claim prices to asset prices. In the second example there are again two assets, one of which is riskless, but a continuum of states. In each case we examine the incentive for a monopolist supplier of the risky asset to *underproduce*.

For the first example, suppose there are two individuals $j$ and $k$.[13] Each has the same preference-scaling function $v^h(c) = \ln c$, and each owns half the assets of the economy. That is:

$$(\bar{c}_1^h, \bar{c}_2^h) = (\tfrac{1}{2}\bar{c}_1, \tfrac{1}{2}\bar{c}_2), \quad h = j, k$$

The two individuals differ, however, in their beliefs: individual $j$ assigns a probability of $3/4$ to state 1, and individual $k$ a probability of $1/4$.

** End of starred section.
* Starred sections represent more difficult or specialized materials that can be omitted without substantial loss of continuity.
[13] In an exercise at the end of this section you are asked to show that the results continue to hold for any number of individuals, with possibly differing beliefs and different shares in the aggregate endowment.

We now show that the equilibrium state-claim prices are a function of the ratio of aggregate endowments $(\bar{c}_1, \bar{c}_2)$. Let $(\pi_1^h, \pi_2^h)$ be the probability vector for individual $h$. Since he owns half the aggregate endowment, he chooses a consumption bundle that solves:

$$\max_{c_1, c_2} \{\pi_1^h \ln c_1^h + \pi_2^h \ln c_2^h \mid P_1 c_1^h + P_2 c_2^h = \tfrac{1}{2}(P_1 \bar{c}_1 + P_2 \bar{c}_2)\}$$

Form the Lagrangian, differentiate and then rearrange to obtain the following necessary conditions:

$$\frac{\pi_1^h}{P_1 c_1^h} = \frac{\pi_2^h}{P_2 c_2^h} = \frac{1}{P_1 c_1^h + P_2 c_2^h} = \frac{1}{\tfrac{1}{2}(P_1 \bar{c}_1 + P_2 \bar{c}_2)}$$

Then:

$$P_1 c_1^h = \tfrac{1}{2}\pi_1^h(P_1 \bar{c}_1 + P_2 \bar{c}_2) \tag{4.2.13}$$

Since this is true for both individuals we can sum over $h$ to obtain:

$$P_1 \bar{c}_1 = P_1(c_1^j + c_1^k) = (\tfrac{1}{2}(3/4) + \tfrac{1}{2}(1/4))(P_1 \bar{c}_1 + P_2 \bar{c}_2) \tag{4.2.14}$$

A convenient normalization of the state-claim prices is to set:

$$P_1 + P_2 = 1 \tag{4.2.15}$$

That is, a riskless asset yielding 1 unit in each state has a market value of 1. Solving for $P_1$ and $P_2$ from (4.2.14) and (4.2.15) leads to:

$$P_1 = \frac{1}{1 + \bar{c}_1/\bar{c}_2} \quad \text{and} \quad P_2 = \frac{\bar{c}_1/\bar{c}_2}{1 + \bar{c}_1/\bar{c}_2} \tag{4.2.16}$$

These are the equilibrium state-claim prices.

Suppose that each individual's initial endowment is riskless. Then the aggregate endowment in each state is $\bar{c}_s = \bar{c}$ and so $P_1 = P_2 = 1/2$. If there were markets in state-claims, individual $j$, who believes state 1 is more likely, would purchase state-1 claims from individual $k$. Indeed, from (4.2.13) it can be confirmed that:

$$c_1^j = 3\bar{c}/4 \quad \text{and} \quad c_1^k = \bar{c}/4$$

Now, imagine instead that the riskless endowments consist of holdings of a single riskless asset $a$, with no trading opportunities at all. Each individual is therefore forced to consume his own endowment, that is:

$$\bar{c}_1^j = \bar{c}_1^k = \bar{c}/2$$

It follows that the introduction of any new non-riskless asset generates very significant risk-spreading gains. As long as there are no arbitrary limits on short sales, each individual adjusts his portfolio until his holdings are such that he can achieve his optimal consumption bundle.

Notice that monopoly power here is not derived purely from ability to produce assets that increase risk-spreading opportunities. Suppose someone was able to convert, via a productive transformation, $x$ units of the riskless asset $a$ into $x$ units each of risky assets with state-claim yield vectors $(1, 0)$ and $(0, 1)$. Clearly the state space would now be spanned. However the aggregate endowment ratio $\bar{c}_1/\bar{c}_2$ is unaffected. Hence the value of these two new assets (given by (4.2.16)) would be independent of $x$.

In this limiting case, therefore, the innovator who introduces the new assets has no monopoly power. More generally, however, let $(\bar{c}_1(x), \bar{c}_2(x))$ be the aggregate endowment resulting from the production of $x$ units of a risky asset $b$. Let the payoff per unit of the asset be $(z_1^b, z_2^b)$. Then the price will be:

$$P_b^A = P_1 z_1^b + P_2 z_2^b$$
$$= \frac{z_1^b + \dfrac{\bar{c}_1(x)}{\bar{c}_2(x)} z_2^b}{1 + \dfrac{\bar{c}_1(x)}{\bar{c}_2(x)}}$$

Let $N(x)$ be the number of units of the riskless asset used up in the production of the $x$ units of the risky asset. The new aggregate endowments are therefore:

$$\begin{cases} \bar{c}_1 = \bar{c} - N(x) + x z_1^b \\ \bar{c}_2 = \bar{c} - N(x) + x z_2^b \end{cases} \tag{4.2.17}$$

It is readily confirmed that $P_b^A$ decreases as $x$ increases, as depicted in figure 4.4. Also depicted in the figure is the marginal cost $N'(x)$ of producing additional units of the risky asset.

Thus, if there were only one potential producer of this new asset, we would have a standard monopoly problem. The single producer chooses an output of the risky asset $x_M$ so as to set marginal revenue equal to marginal cost rather than unit price equal to marginal cost. However, the extent of monopoly power hinges upon the sensitivity of the asset price to output changes. From (4.2.17), if the new asset is a close substitute for a riskless asset, that is, if $z_1/z_2 \approx 1$, then the aggregate endowment ratio varies only very slowly with $x$. Monopoly power is therefore negligible if the new asset is sufficiently similar to other tradable assets (or combinations of assets).

Finally, the example suggests that if supply of the new asset is small relative to the aggregate endowment, monopoly power will be small even if the new asset is *not* a close substitute.

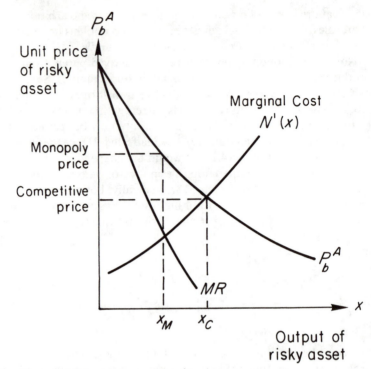

Figure 4.4 Monopoly asset supply

Mathematically, from (4.2.17):

$$\lim_{\bar{c}\to\infty}\left[\frac{\bar{c}_1(x)}{\bar{c}_2(x)}\right] = \lim_{\bar{c}\to\infty}\left[\frac{\bar{c}-N(x)+xz_1}{\bar{c}-N(x)+xz_2}\right] = 1$$

Whether this result holds under much weaker assumptions remains an open question. As the next example shows, the result is certainly not a completely general one.

We now turn from the two-state example to one with a continuum of states. There are $\bar{q}_a$ units of a riskless asset yielding 1 in each state. There is also a single risky asset $b$, each unit of which has a random payoff $\tilde{z}$, where $z$ is distributed according to the exponential density function:

$$f(z) = \frac{1}{\gamma}e^{-\gamma z}$$

And there is a single representative consumer in the economy with preference-scaling function:

$$v(c) = 1 - e^{-\alpha c}$$

Let $(q_a, q_b)$ be the portfolio of a single consumer, where $q_a$ is the number of units of the riskless asset and $q_b$ the number of units of the risky asset held. His expected utility is then:

$$U(q_a, q_b) = \mathrm{E}\{v(c)\} = \frac{1}{\gamma} \int_0^\infty (1 - e^{-\alpha(q_a + q_b z)}) e^{-\gamma z} \, dz$$

$$= 1 - \frac{1}{\gamma} e^{-\alpha q_a} \int_0^\infty e^{-(\alpha q_b + \gamma) z} \, dz \qquad (4.2.18)$$

$$= 1 - \frac{e^{-\alpha q_a}}{\gamma(\alpha q_b + \gamma)}$$

As in the previous example, let the price of the riskless asset be $P_a^A = 1$. Then the consumer solves:

$$\underset{q_a, q_b}{\mathrm{Max}} \{U(q_a, q_b) \mid q_a + P_b^A q_b = W\}$$

From (4.2.18) the first-order condition can be expressed as:

$$\frac{\dfrac{\partial U}{\partial q_b}}{\dfrac{\partial U}{\partial q_a}} = \frac{1}{\alpha q_b + \gamma} = \frac{P_b^A}{1}$$

But, in equilibrium, $q_b = x$. Then the unit price of the risky asset is:

$$P_b^A = \frac{1}{\alpha x + \gamma}$$

Note that demand for the risky asset is independent of aggregate wealth. Therefore, in contrast with the earlier example, monopoly power does not decline as the number of units of the riskless asset grows large.

Of course, this result depends critically upon the nature of the preference-scaling function. The assumed exponential form indicates that the representative individual exhibits constant absolute risk-aversion ($\alpha = $ constant). Together then, the two examples suggest that monopoly power in the production of risky assets will be small as long as (i) the asset is small relative to the total supply of assets in each state and (ii) individuals exhibit approximately constant relative risk-aversion.[14]

As has been seen, where monopoly power in asset markets is non-negligible, firms will have an incentive to underproduce, just as in a world of certainty. However, the choice of a criterion for the firm manager is far

---

[14] We are relying here on the fact that, with concordant beliefs and constant relative risk-aversion, complete-market prices are a function of aggregate endowments.

from clear. If greater production reduces the price of state-$s$ claims, those stockholders who are larger purchasers of such claims will want a higher output than those who believe state $s$ is less likely. This raises the possibility of coalition formation within the firm to buy out other stockholders or to seek a friendly takeover (see Drèze, 1974 and Hart, 1977).

Summing up, this section has provided a theoretical foundation for the value maximization criterion on the part of the firm, and explored the risk-spreading properties of a stockmarket equilibrium. It also indicated how a change in a firm's input decision, and hence in the probability distribution of its output, would affect its equity value.

### EXERCISES AND EXCURSIONS 4.2.3

#### 1 Equilibrium state-claim prices

There are two states and $H$ consumers, each with preference-scaling function $v(c) = \ln c$. Consumer $h$ believes state 1 will occur with probability $\pi_1^h$. His endowment is a fraction $\gamma^h$ of the aggregate endowment $(\bar{c}_1, \bar{c}_2)$.

(A)  If state-claim prices are $P_1$ and $P_2$ show that consumer $h$ will have state-1 consumption:

$$P_1 c_1^h = \pi_1^h \gamma^h (P_1 \bar{c}_1 + P_2 \bar{c}_2)$$

(B)  Summing over $h$, show that in equilibrium:

$$\frac{P_1}{P_2} = \left( \frac{\sum\limits_{h=1}^{H} \pi_1^h \gamma^h}{\sum\limits_{h=1}^{H} \pi_2^h \gamma^h} \right) \frac{\bar{c}_1}{\bar{c}_2}$$

(C)  If all individuals have the same beliefs, show that there will be no trade in this economy.
(D)  Is the converse also true? That is, if beliefs differ there will be trade?
(E)  If individuals can trade two linearly independent *assets* but cannot exchange contingent claims, will the outcome be the same?

#### 2 Equilibrium asset prices

Continuing with the model analyzed in exercise 1, suppose there are two assets in the economy, both risky. Each unit of asset $a$ yields 1 in state 1 and $\alpha$ in state 2. Each unit of asset $b$ yields $\beta$ in state 1 and 1 in state 2, where $0 < \alpha, \beta < 1$.

(A)  Solve for the equilibrium state-claim price ratio $P_1/P_2$ in terms of $\pi, \alpha, \beta$ and the aggregate endowments of the two assets $\bar{q}_a$ and $\bar{q}_b$.

(B) Hence, or otherwise, obtain an expression for the equilibrium asset price ratio $P_a^A/P_b^A$.

(C) Under what conditions is the general-equilibrium asset price ratio insensitive to changes in asset supply?

(D) Suppose $\bar{\pi} = 1/2$, $\alpha = \beta$ and there is a constant-returns-to-scale technology that transforms a unit of asset 1 into a unit of asset 2. With free entry into this industry, what will the equilibrium prices of the two assets be? If initially there are 1,000 units of asset $a$ and no units of asset $b$, what will be the equilibrium number of each type of asset?**

## 4.3 Asset prices in the mean, standard deviation model

We now return to the model introduced in chapter 2 (section 2.3), where individuals are concerned only with the *mean* and *standard deviation* of the final wealth (consumption) generated by their portfolio holdings. Making the additional simplifying assumptions that all individuals have agreed beliefs as to the payoff distributions $\tilde{z}_a$ of each and every asset $a$, and that a riskless asset is available, the "Mutual Fund Theorem" was derived. Suppose we imagine a single mutual fund $F$ holding all the risky assets in the economy. Then, the theorem indicates, each investor can maximize utility by holding a particularly simple portfolio: to wit, he can place a fraction of his wealth in that mutual fund and the remainder in the riskless asset. Thus, whether or not such a fund $F$ is explicitly traded, the implication is that every individual will hold his risky assets in the same proportions as exist economy-wide. (However, individuals will still generally vary in how they divide their wealth between the risky fund and the riskless asset.)

Starting with figure 2.11 of the earlier chapter, we can adjust the scales along the two axes, dividing through by the individual's endowed wealth $\overline{W}$. The result is the very similar-looking diagram shown here as figure 4.5. Using the same notion as in chapter 2, the vertical axis now represents $\mu(c)/\overline{W}$ and the horizontal axis $\sigma(c)/\overline{W}$ – mean portfolio income and standard deviation of portfolio income, both measured per dollar of endowed wealth. The point of this adjustment is that, as explained in the earlier chapter, *in per-dollar units each and every investor has the same market opportunities*. Thus the line N'F that represented the budget line for an individual with specific endowed wealth $\overline{W}$ in figure 2.11 translates, in the per-dollar units of figure 4.5, into the budget line of each and every individual in the economy. We will call it the Portfolio Market Line. (The indifference-curve map is not shown in figure 4.5 because, while the

** End of starred section.

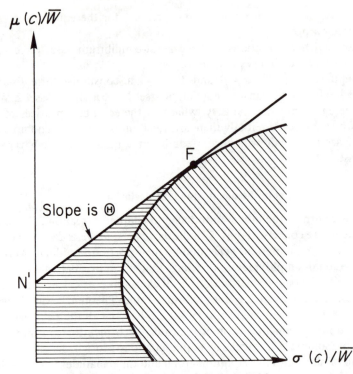

Figure 4.5 Opportunity set per dollar of wealth

*opportunities* can be expressed in terms of trading $\mu$ per dollar for $\sigma$ per dollar, in general an individual's *preferences* cannot be expressed in terms of willingness to substitute $\mu$ per dollar of wealth for $\sigma$ per dollar of wealth, independently of the level of endowed wealth $\overline{W}$.)[15]

Recall that, in the notation of chapter 2, $\mu$ and $\sigma$ represent *portfolio* parameters (functions of the individual's consumption). The underlying *asset* parameters are symbolized:

$$\mu_a \equiv E(\tilde{z}_a) \qquad\qquad \text{Mean of } \tilde{z}_a$$
$$\sigma_a \equiv [E(\tilde{z}_a - \mu_a)^2]^{\frac{1}{2}} \qquad \text{Standard deviation of } \tilde{z}_a \qquad (4.3.1)$$
$$\sigma_{ab} \equiv E(\tilde{z}_a - \mu_a)(\tilde{z}_b - \mu_b) \qquad \text{Covariance of } \tilde{z}_a \text{ and } \tilde{z}_b$$

If the riskless asset is $a = 1$, of course, $\sigma_1 = \sigma_{1b} = 0$.

The individual's portfolio parameters are determined in terms of the asset parameters and his individual asset holdings $q_a$:

[15] For given wealth $\overline{W}$ and utility function $U(\mu, \sigma)$, the individual will have a well-defined utility function in per dollar of wealth terms: $\hat{U}(\mu/\overline{W}, \sigma/\overline{W})$. However, unless his $U$ function is homothetic, the indifference curves of the $\hat{U}$ function will generally change as $\overline{W}$ changes.

$$\mu \equiv \sum_{a=1}^{A} q_a \mu_a \tag{4.3.2}$$

$$\sigma \equiv \left(\sum_{a=1}^{A} \sum_{b=1}^{A} q_a q_b \sigma_{ab}\right)^{1/2}$$

And for the mutual fund $F$ that holds the *economy-wide* quantities $q_a^F$ of the risky assets $a = 2, ..., A$:

$$\mu_F \equiv \sum_{a=2}^{A} q_a^F \mu_a \tag{4.3.3}$$

$$\sigma_F \equiv \left(\sum_{a=2}^{A} \sum_{b=2}^{A} q_a^F q_b^F \sigma_{ab}\right)^{1/2}$$

The covariance between any asset $a$ and the mutual fund $F$ is:

$$\sigma_{aF} \equiv \mathrm{E}(\tilde{z}_a - \mu_a)\left[\sum_{b=2}^{A} q_b^F(\tilde{z}_b - \mu_b)\right] \equiv \sum_{b=2}^{A} q_b^F \sigma_{ab} \tag{4.3.4}$$

The slope of the Portfolio Market Line, the *price of risk reduction* symbolized as $\Theta$, was derived in equation (2.3.18) of the earlier chapter:

$$\Theta \equiv \frac{d(\mu/\overline{W})}{d(\sigma/\overline{W})} \equiv \frac{d\mu}{s\sigma} = \frac{\mu_F/P_F^A - \mu_1/P_1^A}{\sigma_F/P_F^A} = \frac{\mu_F/P_F^A - (1+R_1)}{\sigma_F/P_F^A} \tag{4.3.5}$$

As before, the "rate of return" $\tilde{R}_a$ on any asset $a$ is defined in:

$$\tilde{z}_a/P_a^A \equiv 1 + \tilde{R}_a \tag{4.3.6}$$

The price of risk reduction is the crucial endogenous variable determined in equilibrium, as the separate individuals buy and sell assets with the aim of optimizing their portfolio holdings. And specifically, $\Theta$ is the rate at which the market permits anyone to achieve higher portfolio return per dollar in return for higher standard deviation per dollar. As shown in chapter 2, each individual will be setting his indifference-curve slope or Marginal Rate of Substitution – the rate at which he *is willing to* trade $\mu$ for reduced $\sigma$ – equal to $\Theta$.

Our aim here is to show how the prices $P_a^A$ of the various assets or securities depend upon the price of risk reduction together with the security parameters defined above.

We know that, in equilibrium, the individual simply purchases some quantity $q_F$ of the market fund. Consider then a portfolio that contains the riskless asset, the market fund, and a risky asset $a$:

$$\mu = q_1(1+R_1) + q_a \mu_a + q_F \mu_F$$
$$\sigma^2 = q_a^2 \sigma_a^2 + 2q_a q_F \sigma_{aF} + q_F^2 \sigma_F^2$$

To increase holdings of risky asset $a$ by $dq_a$, the individual can sell $(P_a^A/P_1^A)dq_a$ units of the riskless asset. The net change in mean return is then:

$$d\mu = (q\mu_a - (P_a^A/P_1^A)\mu_1)\, dq_a$$
$$= (\mu_a - P_a^A(1+R_1))\, dq_a$$

This increases the variance of his portfolio according to:

$$d(\sigma^2) = 2\sigma d\sigma = 2(q_a\sigma_a^2 + q_F\sigma_{aF})\, dq_a$$

Also, in equilibrium, $q_a = 0$.

It follows that $\sigma = q_F\sigma_F$. Substituting, we obtain:

$$2q_F\sigma_F\, d\sigma = 2q_F\sigma_{aF}\, dq_a$$

Hence:

$$d\sigma = \sigma_{aF}\, dq_a$$

Combining these results, it follows that the individual's Marginal Rate of Substitution between $\mu$ and $\sigma$ is:

$$\frac{d\mu}{d\sigma} = \frac{\mu_a - (1+R_1)P_a^A}{\sigma_{aF}/\sigma_F} \tag{4.3.7}$$

At his optimum, this must be equal to the steepness of the Portfolio Market Line or *price of risk reduction*, given in equation (4.3.5). Combining these expressions:

### CAPITAL ASSET PRICING RULE*

$$\frac{\mu_a - (1+R_1)\,P_a^A}{\sigma_{aF}} = \Theta = \frac{\mu_F - (1+R_1)\,P_F^A}{\sigma_F^2} \tag{4.3.8}$$

From (4.3.8) the price of any asset is determined by its mean return $\mu_a$, its covariance with the market portfolio $\sigma_{aF}$, and the price of risk reduction $\Theta$.

EXAMPLE 4.4 Suppose each of $J$ individuals has the same utility function:

$$U^j(\mu, \sigma) = \mu - \tfrac{1}{2}\alpha\sigma^\sigma$$

The riskless asset has price $P_1^A = 1$ and yield $1 + R_1$. The market fund has mean $\mu_F$, standard deviation $\sigma_F$, and price $P_F^A$.

If individual $j$ with initial wealth $\overline{W}_j$ purchases $q_F$ units of the riskless asset and holds the rest of his portfolio in riskless bonds, the mean and variance of his final wealth are:

$$\mu = \overline{W}^j(1+R_1) + (\mu_F - P_F^A(1+R_1))\,q_F$$
$$\sigma^2 = q_F^2\sigma_F^2$$

---

* This relationship is known in the finance literature as the Capital Asset Pricing Model (CAPM).

Substituting these into his utility function and maximizing with respect to $q_F$ leads to his optimal fund holding:

$$\hat{q}_{jF} = \frac{\mu_f - (1+R)P_F^A}{\alpha\sigma_F^2}$$

From the Mutual Fund Theorem we know that, in equilibrium, all $J$ individuals will hold the market fund. Also, in equilibrium, demand for the market fund must equal supply:

$$\sum_{j=1}^{J} \hat{q}_{jF} = \left(\frac{J}{\alpha\sigma_F}\right)\left[\frac{\mu_F - (1+R)P_F^A}{\sigma_F}\right] = 1$$

This equation can be solved for the equilibrium price of the market fund. Note also that the bracketed expression is the equilibrium price of risk reduction. Therefore:

$$\Theta = \frac{\alpha\sigma_F}{J}$$

From (4.3.8) the price of asset $a$, $a = 1, ..., A$ satisfies:

$$\mu_a - (1+R_1)P_a^A = \left(\frac{\sigma_{aF}}{\sigma_F}\right)\Theta$$

Then, for this example:

$$P_a^A = \frac{1}{1+R_1}\left(\mu_a - \frac{\alpha}{J}\sigma_{aF}\right)$$

Thus the price of asset $a$ is a decreasing function of the risk-aversion parameter $\alpha$ and of the covariance between $\tilde{z}_a$ and the market fund $\tilde{z}_F$.

In the finance literature it is more common to rewrite (4.3.8) in terms of rates of return. Since $1 + \tilde{R}_a \equiv \tilde{z}_a/P_a^A$ and $\mu(\tilde{R}_a) \equiv \mu_a/P_a^A$, we have:

$$\sigma(\tilde{R}_a) = \sigma_a/P_a^A \quad \text{and} \quad \sigma(\tilde{R}_a, \tilde{R}_b) = \sigma_{ab}/P_a^A P_b^A$$

Substituting these expressions into (4.3-8) and rearranging:

$$\mu(\tilde{R}_a) = R_1 + \Theta\frac{\sigma(\tilde{R}_a, \tilde{R}_F)}{\sigma(\tilde{R}_F)}$$

Hence:

### SECURITY VALUATION LINE (I)

$$\mu(\tilde{R}_a) = R_1 + \Theta\rho(\tilde{R}_a, \tilde{R}_F)\sigma(\tilde{R}_a) \tag{4.3.9}$$

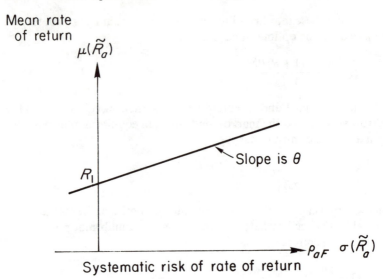

Figure 4.6a Security valuation line (I)

where $\rho(\tilde{R}_a, \tilde{R}_F) \equiv \sigma(\tilde{R}_a, \tilde{R}_F)/\sigma(\tilde{R}_a)\sigma(\tilde{R}_F)$ is the correlation between the rates of return on asset $a$ and the market portfolio.

Figure 4.6a plots Security Valuation Line (I), where the vertical axis is the mean rate of return $\mu(\tilde{R}_a)$ and the horizontal axis is the security's "systematic risk" $\rho_{aF}\,\sigma(\tilde{R}_a)$ – the fraction of the standard deviation of the security's rate of return represented by its correlation with the mutual fund. In this model each and every security in the economy, in equilibrium, will fall on the Security Valuation Line. That is, its price $P_a^A$ must be such as to make the security's mean rate of return and its systematic risk the coordinates of a point on the line. Or, we can say, each security will earn a mean rate of return whose excess over the rate of return on the riskless security represents the degree to which the holder of a security incurs a risk correlated with the overall economy-wide risk of the mutual fund. Putting the emphasis the other way, each security's uncorrelated or idiosyncratic risk *not* associated with the variability of the mutual fund is not reflected in price, because that risk has been diversified away through the Law of Large Numbers.

There is an evident parallel between the individual's portfolio choices of $\mu(c)$ and $\sigma(c)$, as shown in the Portfolio Market Line, and the pricing of securities in terms of their mean rate of return and systematic risk as shown by Security Valuation Line (I). In fact, both lines have the same slope, equal to the price of risk reduction $\Theta$.

However, it has become standard practice to picture the Security

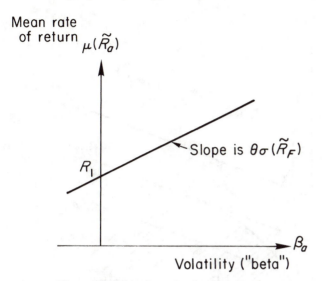

Figure 4.6b Security valuation line (II)

Valuation Line in a slightly different way. On the horizontal axis, instead of the "systematic risk" $\rho_{aF}\,\sigma(\tilde{R}_a)$, a closely related measure is customarily employed: to wit, the security's "volatility" $b_{aF}$. This is a regression coefficient, logically related to the correlation coefficient $\rho_{aF}$ by the standard formula:

$$b_{aF} \equiv \rho_{aF}\,\sigma(\tilde{R}_a)/\sigma(\tilde{R}_F)$$

where $\sigma(\tilde{R}_F) \equiv \sigma_F/P_F^A$ is the standard deviation of the rate of return on the mutual fund. The volatility $b_{aF}$ is commonly called the "beta" $\beta_a$ of risky security $a$. Rewriting (4.3.9), we thus have as a second form of the Security Valuation Line:

SECURITY VALUATION LINE (II)

$$\mu(\tilde{R}_a) = \rho_1 + \Theta\,\sigma(\tilde{R}_F)\beta_a \tag{4.3.10}$$

As indicated in figure 4.6b, with $\beta_a$ on the horizontal axis the slope of the Security Valuation Line becomes $\Theta\,\sigma(\tilde{R}_F)$.

The interpretation is essentially the same, however. The price of each risky security must adjust until its mean rate of return, over and above the rate of return yielded by the riskless security, reflects its additional riskiness as measured here by volatility. The advantage of this formulation is that the volatility $\beta_a$ can readily be statistically estimated, using historical data, by regressing the security's rate of return upon the rate of return on the market portfolio.

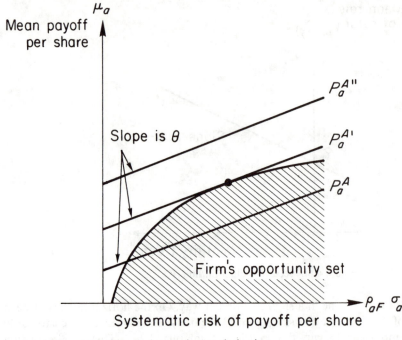

Figure 4.7 Firm's share-price maximization

Finally, the way in which security price is determined by the balance between mean return and systematic risk or volatility has implications for the productive decisions of the firm. In figure 4.7 firm $a$ has an opportunity set showing the combinations of mean payoff $\mu_a$ and correlated standard deviation $\rho_{aF}\sigma_a$ of payoff it can achieve per share. (We are assuming that firm $a$ has a simple financial structure consisting of a fixed number of shares of security $a$.) On these axes, there is a family of "iso-price lines" $P_a^A, P_a^{A'}, \ldots$ as illustrated in the diagram. Thus, the firm can achieve a higher share price, other things equal, by *raising* its mean payoff $\mu_a$ or by *reducing* either its standard deviation of payoff $\sigma_a$ or else the correlation $\rho_{aF}$ between its payoff distribution and that of the mutual fund.

The general equation of the iso-price lines, derived from (4.3.9) above, and using the fact that $P_1^A = 1$, is:

$$\mu_A = \mu_1 P_a^A + \Theta \rho_{aF}\sigma_a \qquad (4.3.11)$$

Evidently, the firm does best (maximizes its share price) at the point of tangency. Thus, we see again that the price of risk reduction $\Theta$ is the crucial endogenous variable of this system. On the one hand each and every individual finds his indifference-curve tangency by setting his Marginal Rate of Substitution $d\mu/d\sigma$, reflecting his degree of risk-aversion, equal to $\Theta$. And on the other hand, each and every firm finds its productive optimum, selecting the characteristics of its payoff distribution $\tilde{z}$, by making the marginal trade-off between its mean payoff and the correlated standard deviation of its payoff also equal to $\Theta$.

## EXERCISES AND EXCURSIONS 4.3

*1 Equilibrium prices in a $\mu$, $\sigma$ model*

Continuing with the numerical example of exercise 4 in E&E 2.3, now suppose that the asset prices are not given but remain to be determined.

(A) Nevertheless, under the stated assumptions that all individuals are alike, it is possible to determine immediately that the price of risk reduction is $\Theta = 3/10$. Why?

(B) Knowing $\Theta$, and since by assumption $P_1^A = 1$, verify that the prices $P_2^A$ and $P_3^A$ are as tabulated in the exercise of chapter 2. Find the corresponding $E(\tilde{R}_a)$ and $\sigma(\tilde{R}_a)$ for each asset.

(C) Find the equation for Security Valuation Line (I), showing $E(\tilde{R}_a)$ as a function of the correlated riskiness $\rho_{aF}\sigma(\tilde{R}_a)$, and locate the points corresponding to each of the three securities.

(D) Do the same for the Security Valuation Line (II), showing $E(\tilde{R}_a)$ as a function of "beta" $\beta_a$.

*2 Unanimity in the $\mu$, $\sigma$ model*

(A) Suppose the owners of firm $f$ take as constant the price of risk reduction $\Theta$ and the prices of all other firms. Since equation (4.3.5) holds for all firms $f$ show that:

$$\sum_{f=1}^{F} \mu_f - (1+R_1)\sum_{f=1}^{F} P_f^A = \sigma_m \Theta$$

(B) Hence confirm that the owners of the firm will unanimously agree upon value maximization as the appropriate goal.

(C) Are the assumptions of (A) plausible?

*3 The effect of large numbers on the price of risk reduction*

(A) Suppose utility is a function of the mean and variance of an individual's portfolio (as is the case with normally distributed returns). Show that $\partial U(\mu, \sigma)/\partial\sigma \to 0$ as $\sigma \to 0$.

(B) Holding fixed the aggregate market risk, suppose the number of individuals in the economy, $N$, becomes large. Given the hypothesis of (A), show that the price of risk reduction declines towards zero.
(C) Suppose each firm produces an independent risk of similar mean and variance. Show that, as the number of firms and individuals rises in proportion, the price of risk reduction again declines towards zero.
(D) What do these results tell us about the ability of insurance companies to offer actuarily fair insurance on independent risks? What about insuring against earthquake losses in Los Angeles?

## 4  Pricing an uncorrelated asset

An individual with utility function $U^j(\mu, \sigma^2) = \mu - \frac{1}{2}\alpha_j \sigma^2$ has current wealth $W_j$. Each dollar invested in the riskless asset yields $1 + R$. There is also a risky asset with price $P_F$ and payoff distribution $\tilde{z}_F$.
(A) If the individual purchases $q$ units of the risky asset, write down an expression for his expected wealth and variance of wealth in terms of $r, P_F^A, \mu_F$, and $\sigma_F^2$.
(B) Hence show that his optimal holding of the risky asset is:

$$q_j = \frac{\mu_F - (1+R)\, P_F^A}{\alpha_j\, \sigma_F^2}$$

(C) If differences in tastes can be represented by differences only in the parameter $\alpha_j$, show that the equilibrium price of the risky asset is:

$$P_F = \frac{1}{1+R}\left(\mu_F - \frac{\bar{\alpha}}{J}\sigma_F^2\right)$$

where $\bar{\alpha} \equiv J/(\Sigma_j 1/\alpha_j)$ is the harmonic mean of the taste parameters.
(D) Show also that the equilibrium price of risk reduction is:

$$\Theta = \frac{\bar{\alpha}}{J}\sigma_F$$

(E) By appealing to the asset pricing equation (4.3.8), show that, if $F$ is the market portfolio, the price of asset $a$ satisfies:

$$\mu_a - (1+R)\, P_a^A = \frac{\sigma_{aF}\,\bar{\alpha}}{J}$$

(F) Suppose asset $a$ is uncorrelated with all the other assets. Show that the equilibrium price of asset $a$ is:

$$P_a^A = \frac{1}{1+R}\left(\mu_a - \frac{\bar{\alpha}}{J}\sigma_a^2\right)$$

## 5 Correlated assets and monopoly power

Suppose the assumptions of exercise 4 are modified as follows. There are $A$ risky assets each with mean return $\mu$ and variance $\sigma^2$. The covariance between pairs of asset returns is $\rho\sigma^2$.

(A) Show that the equilibrium price of asset $a$ is:

$$P_a^A = \frac{1}{1+R}\left(\mu - \frac{\bar{\alpha}}{J}((A-1)\rho+1)\sigma^2\right)$$

(B) Suppose that asset $a$ is replicated $q$ times. That is, there are $q-1$ new assets each with a return identical to asset $a$. Show that the equilibrium price of asset $a$ is:

$$P_a^A = \frac{1}{1+R}\left(\mu - \frac{\bar{\alpha}}{J}((A-1)\rho+q)\sigma^2\right)$$

(C) Hence establish that, if asset $a$ is replicable by the owners at a cost $c(q)$, the profit-maximizing supply will be lower than the efficient supply.

(D) What happens to monopoly power as the number of risky assets $A$ and the number of individuals $N$ grow proportionally large?

REFERENCES AND SELECTED READINGS

Baron, D. P., "Investment Policy: Optimality, and the Mean-Variance Model," *Journal of Finance*, 34 (1979), 207–32.

De Angelo, Harry, "Competition and Unanimity," *American Economic Review*, 71 (1981), 18–27.

Debreu, G., *Theory of Value*, New York: Wiley, 1959.

Diamond, P. A., "The Role of the Stock Market in a General Equilibrium Model with Technological Uncertainty," *American Economic Review*, 57 (1967), 759–76.

Drèze, J., "Investment Under Private Ownership: Optimality, Equilibrium and Stability," chapter 9 in J. Drèze (ed.), *Allocation Under Uncertainty: Equilibrium and Optimality*, London: Macmillan, 1974.

Ekern, S. and Wilson, R., "On the Theory of the Firm in an Economy With Incomplete Markets," *Bell Journal of Economics*, 4 (1974), 171–80.

Hart, O. D., "On the Optimality of Equilibrium When the Market Structure is Incomplete," *Journal of Economic Theory*, 11 (1975), 418–43.

———, "Take-Over Bids and Stock Market Equilibrium," *Journal of Economic Theory*, 16 (1977), 53–83.

———, "On Shareholder Unanimity in Large Stock Market Economies," *Econometrica*, 47 (1979), 1057–84.

Hirshleifer, J., *Investment, Interest, and Capital*, Englewood Cliffs, NJ: Prentice-Hall, 1970.

Makowski, L., "Competition and Unanimity Revisited," *American Economic Review*, 73 (1983), 329–39.

Markowitz, H. M., *Portfolio Selection: Efficient Diversification of Investments*, Cowles Foundation for Research in Economics, Yale University, Monograph 16, New York: Wiley, 1959.

Radner, R., "A Note on Unanimity of Stockholders' Preferences Among Alternative Production Plans: A Reformulation of the Ekern-Wilson Model," *Bell Journal of Economics*, 5 (1974), 181–6.

# Part II

# 5    Information and informational decisions

In part I of this book, covering *the economics of uncertainty*, the key topics addressed were (1) individuals' optimizing "terminal" choices with regard to the bearing of risk, and (2) the market equilibrium determined by the aggregate of such individual decisions. In turning here in part II to *the economics of information*, we will similarly be considering issues on the individual and on the market levels of decision. On the individual level, the cental question is: supposing you could get additional information before having to make a terminal decision, how ought you to decide whether and how much information to collect? On the market level, the main question is: what is the nature of the overall equilibrium that arises when some or all individuals undertake such "informational" actions?

After some introductory discussions, the present chapter first analyzes individuals' decisions as to the acquisition of information. We then consider the informational choices of *groups*, since the necessity to act as a collectivity has significant consequences for the nature and amount of information desired. Later chapters take up the implications for market equilibrium.

## 5.1    Information – some conceptual distinctions

"Information" is a word with many meanings. Some of the distinctions to be brought out here will be useful in what follows.

### Information as knowledge versus information as news

Information is sometimes taken to mean *knowledge* – an accumulated body of data or evidence about the world. From this point of view, information is a stock magnitude. But the word may also denote an increment to this stock of knowledge, in the form of a *message* or an item of *news*.

### Information versus beliefs

Terms like knowledge, information, news, etc. are generally understood to refer to objective evidence about the world. *Belief* is the subjective correlate of knowledge. In this chapter we will be seeing how increments of objective knowledge (news or messages) lead rational individuals to revise their beliefs. Ultimately, however, decisions must be based upon subjective beliefs.

### News and message – messages versus message service

The term "message" is generally taken to mean an intended communication from one to another person. "News" is somewhat more general and may refer to evidence or data arrived at by some process other than interpersonal communication, for example, by observing the weather. (This is receiving a message from Nature, so to speak.) But we will be treating the words "news" and "message" as synonymous. A more essential distinction for our purposes, one that we will be insisting upon, is between a "message" and a "message service" (or between "news" and a "news service"). Rothschild's legendary carrier pigeon, that supposedly brought him early news of the outcome at Waterloo, was a message service; the report of Napoleon's defeat was the message. Since you can never know in advance what you will be learning, you can never purchase a *message* but only a message service – a set of possible alternative messages.

### Communication: intended versus inadvertent, inaccurate versus deceptive

Apart from intended messages, there may of course be unintentional communications of various types: (i) a report intended for one party may be overheard by another (or even intercepted so as never to arrive at its intended destination). More important for our purposes is: (ii) attempting to use your knowledge may inadvertently reveal it. If you purchase stock in Universal Petroleum on the basis of inside information that they have just discovered a new oil field, your action tends to drive up the price of Universal stock, thereby providing a signal to other traders.

As for accuracy, the content of a message may of course be more or less incorrect. Or, even if fully accurate as sent, it may be garbled in transmission before receipt. (It may even be *intentionally* inaccurate as sent, which need not imply a deceptive purpose; the inaccuracy may even be necessary for conveying the truth, as when the laws of visual perspective require that lines be made to converge if they are to be perceived as parallel.)[1]

### Public versus private information

One of the crucial factors affecting the economic value of information is its *scarcity*. At one extreme a particular datum may be possessed by only a single individual (private information); at the other extreme, it may be known to everyone (public information). *Publication* is the conversion of information from private to public status. All dissemination, even confidential communication to a single other person, involves some loss of privacy and thus of any value attaching thereto. (It would be possible to transmit purely private information only if a technology were to emerge whereby *forgetting* could be reliably effectuated. Then, for a price, I might give you some news while arranging to forget it myself!)

Public versus private *possession* of information must not be confused with quite another point, how narrow or widespread is the *relevance* of a bit of news. Whether or not there is oil under my land is of special private relevance to me, but discovery of a cheaper oil-extraction process may affect almost everyone.

### First-order information versus second-order information

First-order information is about events – the outcome of the battle of Waterloo, or the result of tossing a die. In contrast, higher-order information relates to the message or information itself. There are many different aspects of an item of news about which we might like to become informed, quite apart from its content: for example its source (which may be a clue to accuracy), or its privacy (how many people already know it).

We can distinguish an *overt secret* from a *covert secret*. Someone interested in marketing an item of news – or, to state things more carefully, in selling a message service that will emit a not-yet-known news item as its message – of course needs to keep the actual message quite secret in advance of sale. But he will be broadcasting the higher-order information that he has such a secret. In contrast, someone engaged in espionage may be as urgently concerned to conceal the higher-order information (his possession of a secret) as the content of the secret itself.

One special case of higher-order information is the condition called "common knowledge." This is said to exist, say, when two persons both know a certain fact, each knows the other knows it, each knows that the other knows he knows it, and so forth (Aumann, 1976). We will see below that having "concordant beliefs" (agreed estimates of the probabilities of

[1] See Erving Goffman (1969).

different states of the world) does not in general lead to the same economic consequences as having those same beliefs as "common knowledge."

## 5.2     Informational decision analysis

This section analyzes an individual's optimizing choice between the alternatives of: (1) taking immediate terminal action, versus (2) acquiring better information first, with the aim of improving the ultimate terminal decision to be made.

### 5.2.1     The use of evidence to revise beliefs

Table 5.1 is a generalized version of the simple picture of table 1.1 in the opening chapter. For a set of available *terminal* actions $x = (1, ..., X)$ and a set of states of the world $s = (1, ..., S)$, the individual's choice of action and Nature's selection of the state interact to determine the associated consequence $c_{xs}$. The bottom margin of the table shows the distribution of the individual's current probability beliefs, where $\pi_s$ is the probability attached to the occurrence of state $s$, and of course $\Sigma_s \pi_s = 1$.

In taking terminal action, a person will choose whichever act $x$ has the highest expected utility for him:

$$\underset{(x)}{\text{Max}}\ U(x) \equiv \sum_s v(c_{xs}) \tag{5.2.1}$$

Here $v(c)$ is, as before, the elementary-utility or preference-scaling function.

Receipt of any particular message $m$ will generally lead to a revision of probability beliefs, and thus may possibly imply a different choice of best terminal action. We now ask how the individual's probability estimates should be revised in the light of new information, that is, how he should convert his *prior* probabilities into *posterior* probabilities.

In this belief revision process, five different probability measures may be involved:

$\pi_s$ = the unconditional (prior) probability of state $s$

$q_m$ = the unconditional probability of receiving message $m$

$j_{ms}$ = the joint probability of state $s$ and message $m$

$q_{m \cdot s}$ = the conditional probability (or "likelihood") of message $m$, given state $s$

$\pi_{s \cdot m}$ = the conditional (posterior) probability of state $s$, given message $m$

There are a number of ways of displaying the interaction among the various probability distributions involved. The clearest is to start with the *joint probability matrix J* pictured in table 5.2. In the main body of the

Table 5.1 *Consequences of terminal choices*

|  |  | States ($s$) | | | |
|---|---|---|---|---|---|
|  |  | 1 | 2 | ... | $S$ |
| Acts ($x$) | 1 | $c_{11}$ | $c_{12}$ | ... | $c_{1S}$ |
|  | 2 | $c_{21}$ | $c_{22}$ | ... | $c_{2S}$ |
|  | ... | ... | ... | ... | ... |
|  | $X$ | $c_{X1}$ | $c_{X2}$ | ... | $c_{XS}$ |
| Beliefs: |  | $\pi_1$ | $\pi_2$ | ... | $\pi_S$ |

Table 5.2 *Joint probability matrix ($J = [j_{sm}]$)*

|  | $J$ | Messages ($m$) | | | $M$ | Probabilities for states |
|---|---|---|---|---|---|---|
|  |  | 1 | 2 | ... |  |  |
| States ($s$) | 1 | $j_{11}$ | $j_{12}$ | ... | $j_{1M}$ | $\pi_1$ |
|  | 2 | $j_{21}$ | $j_{22}$ | ... | $j_{2M}$ | $\pi_2$ |
|  | ... | ... | ... | ... | ... | ... |
|  | $S$ | $j_{S1}$ | $j_{S2}$ | ... | $j_{SM}$ | $\pi_S$ |
| Probabilities for messages |  | $q_1$ | $q_2$ | ... | $q_M$ | 1·0 |

table, $j_{sm}$ is the joint probability of the state being $s$ and the message being $m$. (For example, the state might be "rain tomorrow" and the message "barometer is falling.")

The sum of all these joint probabilities, taken over all the messages and states, is of course unity: $\Sigma_{s,m} j_{sm} = 1$. For each given state $s$, summing over the messages $m$ (i.e., summing the $j_{sm}$ horizontally in each row of the $J$ matrix) generates the corresponding prior "marginal" state probabilities $\pi_s$ shown in the adjoined column at the right of table 5.2. This corresponds to the probability identity:

$$\sum_m j_{sm} \equiv \pi_s \tag{5.2.2}$$

Similarly of course, summing over the states $s$ (i.e., adding up the $j_{sm}$ vertically in each column) generates the "marginal" message probabilities $q_m$, as shown in the row adjoined at the bottom of table 5.2:

$$\sum_s j_{sm} \equiv q_m \tag{5.2.3}$$

The $q_m$ are the prior probabilities that the individual attaches to receiving the different messages. Since the state probabilities and the message probabilities each comprise a probability distribution, the grand sum – taken either over the $\pi_s$ or over the $q_m$ – must again be 1·0, as indicated in the lower-right corner of the table.

Two other important matrices are readily derived from the underlying joint probability matrix $J$. We will call them the *likelihood matrix $L$* and the *potential posterior matrix* $\Pi$.

The likelihood matrix $L = [l_{sm}]$, table 5.3, shows the *conditional* probability of any message given any state, which will be denoted $q_{m \cdot s}$. Thus:

$$l_{sm} \equiv q_{m \cdot s} \equiv \frac{j_{sm}}{\pi_s} \tag{5.2.4}$$

Numerically, the elements of the $L$ matrix are obtained from the $J$ matrix by dividing the $j_{sm}$ in each row through by the adjoined $\pi_s$. For any row of the $L$ matrix, these conditional probabilities must of course sum to unity, since:

$$\sum_m q_{m \cdot s} \equiv \frac{1}{\pi_s} \sum_m j_{sm} \equiv \frac{1}{\pi_s} \pi_s \equiv 1 \tag{5.2.5}$$

(But note that the *column* sums in the $L$ matrix do not sum to unity, except by accident, and in fact these column sums have no meaning so far as our analysis is concerned.)

The potential posterior matrix $\Pi$, table 5.4, shows the conditional probability of each state given any message $m$, which is denoted $\pi_{s \cdot m}$ and defined in:

$$\pi_{s \cdot m} \equiv \frac{j_{sm}}{q_m} \tag{5.2.6}$$

The elements of the $\Pi$ matrix are obtained numerically from the underlying $J$ matrix by dividing all the $j_{sm}$ in each column through by the adjoined $q_m$ below. The *column* sums must then all be unity, since:

$$\sum_s \pi_{s \cdot m} \equiv \frac{1}{q_m} \sum_s j_{sm} \equiv \frac{1}{q_m} q_m \equiv 1 \tag{5.2.7}$$

(Here the *row* sums do not in general equal unity, and in fact have no relevant meaning for our purposes.) Why we term this the potential posterior matrix should be evident. Each separate column shows the "posterior" probability distribution for states of the world that a person with a given $J$ matrix should logically adopt, after having received the particular message $m$. The entire $\Pi$ matrix therefore gives us an ex-ante picture of *all* the alternative posterior distributions that could come about, depending upon which of the possible messages is received.

Table 5.3 *Likelihood matrix* $(L \equiv [l_{sm}] \equiv [q_{m \cdot s}])$

|  |  | Messages ($m$) |  |  |  |
|---|---|---|---|---|---|
| $L$ | 1 | 2 | ... | $M$ | |
| States ($s$) | | | | | |
| 1 | $q_{1 \cdot 1}$ | $q_{1 \cdot 1}$ | ... | $q_{M \cdot 1}$ | 1·0 |
| 2 | $q_{1 \cdot 2}$ | $q_{2 \cdot 2}$ | ... | $q_{M \cdot 2}$ | 1·0 |
| ... | ... | ... | ... | ... | ... |
| $S$ | $q_{1 \cdot S}$ | $q_{2 \cdot S}$ | ... | $q_{M \cdot S}$ | 1·0 |

Table 5.4 *Potential posterior matrix* $(\Pi \equiv [\pi_{s \cdot m}])$

|  |  | Messages ($m$) |  |  |
|---|---|---|---|---|
| $\Pi$ | 1 | 2 | ... | $M$ |
| States ($s$) | | | | |
| 1 | $\pi_{1 \cdot 1}$ | $\pi_{1 \cdot 2}$ | ... | $\pi_{1 \cdot M}$ |
| 2 | $\pi_{2 \cdot 1}$ | $\pi_{2 \cdot 2}$ | ... | $\pi_{2 \cdot M}$ |
| ... | ... | ... | ... | ... |
| $S$ | $\pi_{S \cdot 1}$ | $\pi_{S \cdot 2}$ | ... | $\pi_{S \cdot M}$ |
| | 1·0 | 1·0 | ... | 1·0 |

Looking at this in a somewhat different way, the prior probability $\pi_s$ of state $s$ is an average, weighted by the message probabilities $q_m$, of the posterior probabilities $\pi_{s \cdot m}$ for state $s$:

$$\pi_s = j_{s1} + \ldots + j_{sM} = q_1 \pi_{s \cdot 1} + \ldots + q_M \pi_{s \cdot M}$$

Or, expressing the relation between the prior state-probability vector $\pi = (\pi_1, \ldots, \pi_S)$ and the message-probability vector $q = (q_1, \ldots, q_M)$ in matrix notation:

$$\pi = \Pi q \tag{5.2.8}$$

And analogously, the message probability $q_m$ is an average of the prior state probabilities weighted by the likelihoods:

$$q_m = j_{1m} + \ldots + j_{Sm} = \pi_1 q_{m \cdot 1} + \ldots + \pi_S q_{m \cdot S}$$

So that, in matrix notation:

$$q = L' \pi \tag{5.2.9}$$

EXAMPLE 5.1: There may be oil under your land. The alternative terminal actions are to undertake a major investment to develop the field or not to do so, and this decision will of course depend upon your estimate of the chance of oil really being there. The underlying "states of the world" are three possible geological configurations: state 1 is very favorable, with 90% chance that oil is there; state 2 is much less favorable, with 30% chance; state 3 is hopeless, with 0% chance.

In order to improve your information before taking terminal action, you have decided to drill a test well. The two possible sample outcomes or messages are that the test well is either "wet" or "dry." On the assumption that the test well is a random sample, then, if the true state is really state 1, there is a 90% chance of the message "wet"; if it is state 2, there is a 30% chance; and if it is state 3, no chance. So the given data specify the likelihood matrix $L \equiv [q_{m \cdot s}]$ shown below.

Suppose that, in addition, you initially attach probabilities $(\pi_1, \pi_2, \pi_3)$ $= (0.1, 0.5, 0.4)$ to the three states. Multiplying each likelihood $q_{m \cdot s}$ in the $L$ matrix by the prior probability $\pi_s$ yields the joint probability matrix $J \equiv [j_{sm}]$. The column sums are then the message probabilities $q_1 = 0.24$ and $q_2 = 0.76$. Using these you can easily compute your potential posterior matrix $\Pi = [\pi_{s \cdot m}]$.

| $L \equiv [q_{m \cdot s}]$ Messages (m) | | | | $J \equiv [j_{sm}]$ Messages (m) | | | | $\Pi \equiv [\pi_{s \cdot m}]$ Messages (m) | | |
|---|---|---|---|---|---|---|---|---|---|---|
| | Wet | Dry | | | Wet | Dry | | | Wet | Dry |
| $L$ | 1 | 2 | | $J$ | 1 | 2 | $\pi_s$ | $\Pi$ | 1 | 2 |
| 1 | 0.9 | 0.1 | 1.0 | 1 | 0.09 | 0.01 | 0.1 | 1 | 0.375 | 0.013 |
| States 2 | 0.3 | 0.7 | 1.0 | 2 | 0.15 | 0.35 | 0.5 | 2 | 0.625 | 0.461 |
| (s) 3 | 0 | 1.0 | 1.0 | 3 | 0 | 0.40 | 0.4 | 3 | 0 | 0.526 |
| | | | | $q_m$: | 0.24 | 0.76 | 1.0 | | 1.0 | 1.0 |

Notice that the message "wet" shifts your prior distribution $(\pi_1, \pi_2, \pi_3)$ $= (0.1, 0.5, 0.4)$ to the much more favorable posterior distribution $(\pi_{1 \cdot 1}, \pi_{2 \cdot 1}, \pi_{3 \cdot 1}) = (0.375, 0.625, 0)$. The message "dry" leads of course to a much less hopeful posterior distribution $(\pi_{1 \cdot 2}, \pi_{2 \cdot 2}, \pi_{3 \cdot 2}) = (0.013, 0.461, 0.526)$.[2]

So far as pure logic is concerned, the relevant data might equally well be presented or summarized in three different ways: (1) by the joint probability matrix $J$; (2) by the prior probability distribution for *states* (the right-hand margin of the $J$ matrix) together with the likelihood matrix $L$;

[2] Random or "unbiased" sampling was assumed here, e.g., in state 1 (defined in terms of a 90% chance of oil being there) the likelihood matrix $L$ indicates a 90% probability $q_{1 \cdot 1}$ of receiving the message "wet." The underlying method is however sufficiently general to allow even for biased sampling. Thus, if state 1 is the true state of the world, conceivably the well (perhaps because it will not be drilled to full depth) could still have only an 80% chance of showing "wet." Whatever the likelihoods are, they can be displayed in the $L$ matrix (and equivalently reflected in the $J$ and $\Pi$ matrices as well).

and, (3) by the prior probability distribution for *messages* (the bottom margin of the $J$ matrix) together with the potential posterior matrix $\Pi$. But from the operational point of view, a decision-maker will usually find it most convenient to use method #2. As in the example above, he is likely to think in terms of having a prior probability distribution for the underlying states together with a likelihood matrix $L$ describing the message service being employed.

Prior beliefs are always *subjective*, while the likelihood matrix summarizing the possible message outcomes may often (though not necessarily) be *objective*. Suppose the message service represents the outcome of two tosses of a coin. For the state of the world that the coin is fair, with unbiased sampling the likelihood of the message "two heads" is objectively calculable from the laws of probability as $1/4$. But someone who is not sure that the sampling is unbiased might subjectively assign a somewhat different likelihood to the message "two heads."

This process of revision of probabilities is called *Bayesian*, after Bayes' Theorem. The derivation is simple. First, the joint probability $j_{sm}$ can be expressed in two ways in terms of the conditional probabilities defined in (5.2.4) and (5.2.6):

$$\pi_s \, q_{m \cdot s} \equiv j_{sm} \equiv q_m \, \pi_{s \cdot m}$$

(Note how these three formulations relate to the information contained in the $L$, $J$, and $\Pi$ matrices respectively.) Solving for the posterior probability $\pi_{s \cdot m}$:

BAYES' THEOREM (I)

$$\pi_{s \cdot m} \equiv \frac{j_{sm}}{q_m} \equiv \pi_s \frac{q_{m \cdot s}}{q_m} \qquad (5.2.10)$$

In words: The posterior probability that an individual should attach to state $s$, after receiving message $m$, is equal to the prior probability $\pi_s$ multiplied by the likelihood $q_{m \cdot s}$ of message $m$, and then divided by a normalizing factor which is the overall probability $q_m$ of receiving message $m$. Since the latter is the "marginal" probability of $m$, we can also write Bayes' Theorem in the alternative forms:

BAYES' THEOREM (II)

$$\pi_{s \cdot m} \equiv \pi_s \frac{q_{m \cdot s}}{\sum_s j_{sm}} \equiv \pi_s \frac{q_{m \cdot s}}{\sum_s \pi_s q_{m \cdot s}} \qquad (5.2.10')$$

The Bayesian belief-revision process is illustrated in figure 5.1. For diagrammatic convenience, the pictorial representation assumes a continuous rather than a discrete state-defining variable, running from a lower

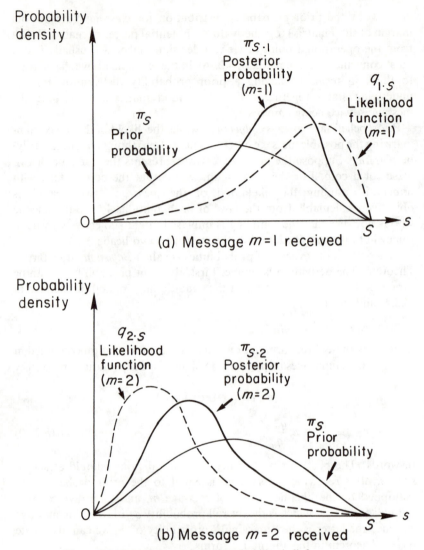

Figure 5.1 Bayesian revision of probability beliefs

limit $s = 0$ to an upper limit $s = S$. The "prior probability" curve in the diagrams is the given initial probability density function $\pi(s)$, where of course $\int_0^S \pi(s)ds \equiv 1$. By assumption here, this density shows some humping toward the middle, i.e., prior beliefs are such that middling values of $s$ are regarded as more likely than extreme ones.

There are two alternative messages: $m = 1$ has much greater likelihood if the true state of the world is toward the high end of the range (upper diagram), while $m = 2$ has greater likelihood if $s$ is small (lower diagram). Although the prior probability distributions are the same in the upper and lower panels, the differing "likelihood function" curves lead to differing "posterior probability" density functions. In each panel the posterior distribution is a kind of compromise or average of the other two curves. More specifically, for any $s$ the height $\pi_{s \cdot m}$ along the posterior probability density curve is the product of the height along the prior density curve ($\pi_s$) times the height along the likelihood function ($q_{m \cdot s}$) – adjusted by a normalization or re-scaling factor to make the new integrated probability equal to unity. (This normalization corresponds to dividing through by the message probability $q_m$, as indicated in equation (5.2.10).)

Three useful propositions are implicit in the Bayesian belief-revision process:

(1) Recall our discussion in the initial chapter about the individual's *confidence* in his beliefs, and how this would affect his decision whether or not to acquire more information. Confidence is indicated in figure 5.1 by the "tightness" of the prior probability distribution – the degree to which a person approaches assigning 100% probability to some single possible value of $s$. The corresponding proposition is: other things equal, the higher the prior confidence the more the posterior distribution will resemble the prior distribution for any given message or weight of evidence. This is intuitively clear if we go to the limit. An individual with "absolute" prior confidence, who attaches 100% probability to some particular value $s = \hat{s}$, can learn nothing from new evidence. From equation (5.2.8), if the prior probabilities $\pi_s$ all equal zero for any $s \neq \hat{s}$, the corresponding posterior probabilities $\pi_{s \cdot m} = 0$ also.

(2) Other things equal, the greater the mass of new evidence the more the posterior distribution will resemble the likelihood function rather than the prior probabilities. A large sample size, for example, will be reflected in a very "tight" likelihood curve in the diagrams. Suppose that, in tossing a coin, $P$ is the unknown true probability of obtaining heads while $p$ is the sample proportion of heads observed in $n$ tosses. Then $p = 0.5$ in a sample of two tosses would be reflected in a "loose" likelihood curve with only a mild peak around $P = 0.5$ – whereas $p = 0.5$ in a sample of 100 tosses would produce a very tight likelihood curve with a sharp peak around $P = 0.5$. As before, the tighter the curve the more pull it has upon the shape of the posterior probability distribution.

(3) Other things equal, the more "surprising" the evidence the bigger the impact upon the posterior probabilities. Intuitively this is obvious:

only when a message is surprising does it call for any drastic change in our beliefs. In terms of equation (5.2.10), a "surprising" message would be one with low message probability $q_m$. Other things equal, the smaller the $q_m$ in the denominator on the right-hand side, the bigger the multiplier causing the posterior probability $\pi_{s \cdot m}$ to diverge from the prior $\pi_s$.

## EXERCISES AND EXCURSIONS 5.2.1

### 1 The game show

A contestant on a television game show may choose any of three curtained booths, one of which contains a valuable prize. Lacking any prior information, she arbitrarily selects one of the booths, say #1. But before the curtain is drawn revealing whether she wins or loses, the Master of Ceremonies says: "Wait, I'll give you a chance to change your mind." He then draws the curtain on one of the *other* booths, say #2, which is revealed to be empty. The M.C. then asks if the contestant cares to change her choice. Should she do so?

ANSWER: Since at least one of booths #2 and #3 *must* be empty (and the M.C. knows which one it is), it might appear that his drawing the curtain conveyed no information, and hence that there is no basis for the contestant to change her choice. But such an inference is incorrect. The tabular form that follows represents a convenient procedure for employing Bayes' Theorem to obtain the *posterior* probabilities implied by any given message $m$ (the message here being "booth #2 is empty").

Computation of posterior probabilities (after message $m$)

| State of the world ($s$) | Prior prob. ($\pi_s$) | Likelihood of message $m$ ($q_{m \cdot s}$) | Joint prob. ($j_{sm}$) | Posterior prob. ($\pi_{s \cdot m}$) |
|---|---|---|---|---|
| Prize is in #1 | 1/3 | 1/2 | 1/6 | 1/3 |
| Prize is in #2 | 1/3 | 0 | 0 | 0 |
| Prize is in #3 | 1/3 | 1 | 1/3 | 2/3 |
| | | | 1/2 | 1.0 |

The next-to-last column represents the column of the joint probability matrix $J$ associated with the particular message received, while the adjoined sum at the bottom of the column is the overall probability $q_m = 1/2$ of that message. (Once the contestant chose booth #1, there were equal prior chances of the M.C. opening the curtain of either booth #2 or #3.) The last column corresponds to the relevant column of the potential posterior matrix $\Pi$. Note how the tabular form makes it easy to compute the posterior probabilities $\pi_{s \cdot m} = j_{sm}/q_m$.

Evidently, the best choice now is booth #3. Intuitively, the M.C.'s action told the contestant nothing about booth #1, her initial choice. But it was a valuable message as to booth #2 versus #3.

### 2 Joint (J), likelihood (L), and potential posterior (Π) matrices

(A) There are two states $s_1$ and $s_2$ and two messages $m_1$ and $m_2$. The prior probability distribution over states is $\pi = (0 \cdot 7, 0 \cdot 3)$. The posterior probabilities $\pi_{s \cdot m}$ include $\pi_{1 \cdot 1} = 0 \cdot 9$ and $\pi_{2 \cdot 2} = 0 \cdot 8$. Calculate the $\Pi$, $L$, and $J$ matrices.

(B) (i)  If you have the $J$ matrix, what additional data (if any) are needed to construct each of the other two matrices?
   (ii) Same question, if you have the $L$ matrix.
   (iii) Ditto, with the $\Pi$ matrix.

(C) For the prior probability distribution $\pi$ above, and still assuming only two possible messages, show (if it is possible to do so):
   (i)  An $L$ matrix representing a *completely conclusive* message service. (That is, a matrix leaving no posterior uncertainty whatsoever.) If it exists, is it *unique*, or are there other such $L$ matrices? Also, does any such matrix depend at all upon $\pi$?
   (ii) An $L$ matrix that is *completely uninformative*. Answer the same questions.
   (iii) An $L$ matrix that (if one message is received) will conclusively establish that one of the states will occur but (if the other message is received) will be completely uninformative. Same questions.

### 5.2.2  Revision of optimal action and the worth of information

If immediate terminal action is to be taken, the individual will choose whichever act has highest expected utility, as indicated in equation (5.2.1). In condensed notation:

$$\underset{(x)}{\text{Max}} \, U(x;\pi) \equiv \sum_s \pi_s v(c_{xs}) \qquad (5.2.11)$$

Denote as $x_0$ the optimal immediate terminal action, which of course must be calculated in terms of the prior probabilities $\pi_s$. What we are concerned with here is the value of an *informational action*, that is, the expected utility gain from using an information service.

After a particular message $m$ has been received from such a service, the decision-maker would use (5.2.11) once again, employing now the *posterior* probabilities $\pi_{s \cdot m}$. This recalculation could well lead to a choice of a different optimal terminal action $x_m$. Then $\omega_m$, the value in utility units of the message $m$, can be defined as:

$$\omega_m \equiv U(x_m; \pi_{s \cdot m}) - U(x_0; \pi_{s \cdot m}) \tag{5.2.12}$$

This is the expected gain from the revision of optimal action, calculated in terms of the individual's *revised* probabilities $\pi_{\cdot m} \equiv (\pi_{1 \cdot m}, \ldots, \pi_{S \cdot m})$. Evidently, the expected utility gain must be non-negative, else $x_m$ could not have been the optimal act using the posterior probabilities. (But message $m$ could lead to *no change* of best action despite the revision of probability beliefs, in which case $\omega_m = 0$ – such a message has zero value.)

However, one cannot purchase a given message but only a *message service*. So it is not the $\omega_m$ associated with some particular message that is relevant but rather the expectation of the utility gain from all possible messages weighted by their respective message probabilities $q_m$. More specifically, for a message service $\mu$ characterized by a particular likelihood matrix $L$ and prior beliefs, $\pi$, the expected value of the information (the worth of the message service) is:

$$\Omega(\mu) = \mathrm{E}\,\omega_m = \sum_m q_m[U(x_m; \pi_{\cdot m}) - U(x_0; \pi_{\cdot m})] \tag{5.2.13}$$

Since each $\omega_m$ is non-negative, we know that a message service can never lower the agent's expected utility (before allowing for the *cost* of the service).

Let $c_{sm}^*$ denote the income in state $s$ associated with the best action $x_m$ after receiving message $m$, and $c_{s0}^*$ the corresponding income for the best uninformed action $x_0$ (that is, the best action in terms of the prior beliefs):

$$\Omega(\mu) = \sum_m q_m \sum_s \pi_{s \cdot m} v(c_{sm}^*) - \sum_m \sum_s \pi_{s \cdot m} q_m v(c_{s0}^*) \tag{5.2.14}$$
$$= \sum_m \sum_s \pi_{s \cdot m} q_m v(c_{sm}^*) - \sum_s \pi_s v(c_{s0}^*)$$

Thus the value of the message service is just the difference between expected utility with and without the service.

For a simplified model with only two states of the world ($s = 1, 2$), figure 5.2 illustrates a situation with three available terminal actions ($x = 1, 2, 3$). In this three-dimensional diagram utility is measured vertically, while the probabilities of the two states are scaled along the two horizontal axes. Each possible assignment of probabilities to states is represented by a point along AB, a line in the base plane whose equation is simply $\pi_1 + \pi_2 = 1$.

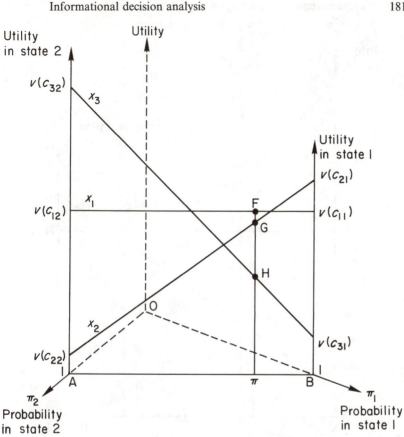

Figure 5.2 Best action in a three-action, two-state world

Suppose state 1 occurs. Then the cardinal preference-scaling values (the elementary utilities) associated with the consequences $c_{x1}$ attaching to the different actions $x$ are indicated by the intercepts labelled $v(c_{11})$, $v(c_{21})$, and $v(c_{31})$ lying vertically above point B in the diagram. Similarly, the elementary utilities of outcomes in state $2 - v(c_{x2})$ for $x = 1, 2, 3$ – are the corresponding intercepts above point A. (Note that $x_1$ is a certainty action, since it yields the same elementary utility in either state.) The expected utility $U(x_i, \pi) = \pi_1 v(c_{i1}) + \pi_2 v(c_{i2})$ of any action $x$, given any probability vector $\pi$, is shown by the vertical distance from the point $\pi = (\pi_1, \pi_2)$ along AB to the line joining $v(c_{x1})$ and $v(c_{x2})$ for that action. In the diagram, if $\pi$ is the prior probability vector then the best immediate *terminal action* is the certainty action $x = 1$ whose expected utility is indicated by the height of point F above the base plane.

In figure 5.2, everything of interest takes place in the vertical plane

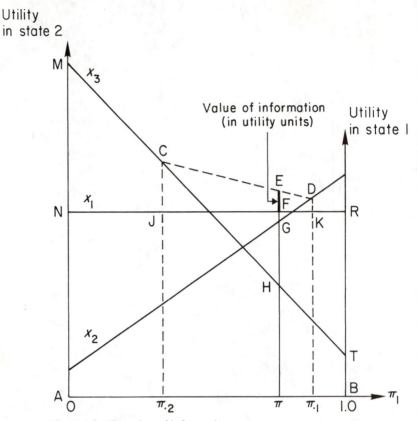

Figure 5.3 The value of information

overlying the line AB. So we can simplify matters by shifting to a 2-dimensional diagram, as in figure 5.3, where the line AB becomes the horizontal axis along which $\pi_1$ varies from zero to unity. In this simplified diagram we see once more the expected utilities of actions $x = 1, 2, 3$ as functions of the prior probability vector $\pi = (\pi_1, \pi_2)$, leading to the choice of $x = 1$ as the best terminal action in terms of the prior probabilities.

We now want to picture the effects of receiving information. Suppose an information service $\mu$ can generate two possible messages $m = 1, 2$. Either message will lead to a revised (posterior) probability vector $\pi_{.m} \equiv (\pi_{1.m}, \pi_{2.m})$. If message $m = 2$ is received, by construction the revised choice of action in terms of the posterior probability vector $\pi_{.2} \equiv (\pi_{1.2}, \pi_{2.2})$ is $x = 3$, with expected utility indicated by the height of point C. The *ex post* expected-utility gain over $x = 1$, $\omega_1$, is therefore equal to the vertical distance CJ (the probability-weighted average of the *gain* MN if state 2 occurs and the *loss* RT if state 1 occurs). If on the other hand the message received is $m = 1$, the best action in the diagram is $x = 2$ (expected utility indicated by point D), so $\omega_2 = DK$. Then $\Omega(\mu)$, the value of the information service in terms of the gain in expected utility, is represented by the vertical distance EF above the point $\pi$ along the line AB.

EXAMPLE 5.2: In an oil-drilling situation suppose there are just two possible states: "wet" (with prior probability $\pi_1 = 0.24$) and "dry" (with prior probability $\pi_2 = 0.76$).[3] If you take action $x = 1$ (drill the well) and it is wet, you gain $1,000,000. If it is dry, you lose $400,000. Action $x = 2$ (not drilling) involves a $50,000 cost in relocating your rig. Suppose your preference-scaling function is simply linear in income (you are risk-neutral), so we can write $v(c) = c$. A message service, taking the form of a geological analysis in advance of drilling, is characterized by the following likelihood matrix $L$. How much should you be willing to pay for it?

|  |  | Message | | |
|---|---|---|---|---|
| $L = [q_{m \cdot s}]$ |  | Wet | Dry | |
| State | Wet | 0·6 | 0·4 | 1·0 |
|  | Dry | 0·2 | 0·8 | 1·0 |

*Answer*: In terms of your prior probabilities, action $x = 1$ involves an expected gain of $0.24$ ($1,000,000) $- 0.76$($400,000) $= -$64,000, whereas action $x = 2$ leads to a loss of only $50,000. So the optimal prior action $x_0$ is $x = 2$. As for the value of the message service, straightforward computations lead to the Potential Posterior Matrix shown below.

|  |  | Message | |
|---|---|---|---|
| $\Pi = [\pi_{s \cdot m}]$ |  | Wet | Dry |
| State | Wet | 0.486 | 0.136 |
|  | Dry | 0.514 | 0.864 |
|  |  | 1.0 | 1.0 |

Using the posterior probabilities, if the message is "dry" the best action remains $x = 2$ (not drilling). But if the message is "wet," the expected gain from drilling (action $x = 1$) becomes $0.486$($1,000,000) $- 0.514$($400,000) $= $140,400. So the expected value of the information is $0.296$ ($140,400 $+ $50,000) $+ 0.704(0) = $56,358. This is the value of the message service, where $0.296$ and $0.704$ are the message probabilities $q_1$ and $q_2$.

[3] These numbers are consistent with those in the previous example. Although in that example there were 3 states, associated with three different possible geological formations, the implied overall probabilities worked out to 0·24 for wet and 0·76 for dry, as shown in the bottom row adjoined to the $J$ matrix.

We have already seen, in discussing Bayes' Theorem, that higher prior confidence implies smaller revision of beliefs from given messages. It follows that higher confidence also implies lower value of information. With more confident prior beliefs, in figure 5.3 the posterior probability vectors $\pi_{.1}$ and $\pi_{.2}$ would both lie closer to the original $\pi$. It is evident that the effect (if any) of greater prior confidence can only be to shrink the distance EF that represents the value of acquiring more evidence.

So far we have discussed the value of information in utility units. The natural next step is to calculate what a message service is worth in income (corn) units – i.e., the maximum fee $\xi$ that someone with preference-scaling function $v(c)$ would be willing to pay for the information.

As follows directly from equation (5.2-14), the fee is determined in:

$$\Sigma_m \Sigma_s \pi_{s \cdot m} q_m v(c_{sm}^* - \xi) = \Sigma_s \pi_s v(c_{s0}^*) \tag{5.2.15}$$

That is, the maximum fee $\xi$ that a person would pay, in advance of receiving the message, is such as to make the expected utility of the best informed action exactly equal to the expected utility of the best uninformed action.

EXAMPLE 5.3: In a 2-state world, suppose the contingent-claim prices for corn in states 1 and 2 are numerically equal to the prior state probabilities: $p_1 = \pi_1$ and $p_2 = \pi_2$, where $\pi_1 + \pi_2 = 1$. (Thus, the prices are "fair.") Specifically, suppose the states are equally probable. Consider an individual with preference-scaling function $v(c) = \sqrt{c}$ and endowment $(\bar{c}_1, \bar{c}_2) = (50, 150)$.

Before acquiring any additional information there are an infinite number of possible actions the individual might take, representing the possible amounts of his endowed $c_1$ he might trade for $c_2$, or vice versa. But, since the prices are fair, in accordance with Fundamental Theorem of Risk-bearing we know that the optimal action will be to trade to the certainty position $(c_{10}^*, c_{20}^*) = (100, 100)$. (The 0-subscript here signifies, as before, the best *uninformed* action.) In terms of a picture like figure 5.3, the "null action" $\bar{x}$ – remaining at the endowment position – would be represented by a line with negative slope, the left intercept being at $\sqrt{150}$ and the right intercept at $\sqrt{50}$. The optimal uninformed action $x_0^*$ would be a horizontal line at $v(100) = \sqrt{100} = 10$. The expected utility of the endowment position is $(\sqrt{150} + \sqrt{50})/2$ or about 9·66, while the expected utility of $x_0^*$ is of course 10. So 0·34 is the utility gain, over the endowment position, of the best action under uncertainty.

Now suppose a message service $\mu$, whose output will be *conclusive* as to which state is going to obtain, becomes available in time for the individual to engage in state-claim trading at the same fair prices. To determine the value of $\mu$ in utility units we first have to find, for each possible message $m$, the individual's best informed action. If message 1 is received, obviously the individual will convert all of his endowed wealth into 200 units of $c_1$, and similarly into 200 units of $c_2$ if message 2 is received. Thus his expected utility will be $\sqrt{200}$ or 14·14 approximately. The value of the information in utility units is $\Omega(\mu) = 4·14$, representing the utility gain of the best informed action over the best uninformed action.

To determine the maximum fee $\xi$ he would be willing to pay, we can use equation (5.2.15) which reduces here to the simple form:

$$v[2(100-\xi)] = v(100)$$

The solution is $\xi = 50$. Thus, the individual here would be willing to pay up to half of his endowed wealth for a conclusive message, arriving in time for market trading, telling him which state is going to obtain.

## EXERCISES AND EXCURSIONS 5.2.2

### 1 Value of information in a simple betting problem

You have an opportunity to gamble on the toss of a coin. If your choice is correct you win \$30, but if it is wrong you lose \$50. Initially, you think it equally likely that the coin is two-headed, two-tailed, or fair. If you are risk-neutral, so that your preference-scaling function can be written $v(c) = c$, how much should you be willing to pay to observe a sample of size 1?

ANSWER: The possible terminal actions are $x_1$ (do not bet), $x_2$ (bet on heads), and $x_3$ (bet on tails). The best action on the basis of your prior information is obviously $x_0 = x_1$. The available message service $\mu$ is a sample of size 1, the possible messages being a head or a tail. Following the tabular method of the first exercise in exercises and excursions 5.2.1 above, we can compute the posterior probabilities given the message $m =$ head as follows:

Computation of posterior probabilities (after message "head")

| State of the world ($s$) | Prior prob. ($\pi_s$) | Likelihood of message $m$ ($q_{m \cdot s}$) | Joint prob. ($j_{sm}$) | Posterior prob. ($\pi_{s \cdot m}$) |
|---|---|---|---|---|
| Coin is two-headed | 1/3 | 1 | 1/3 | 2/3 |
| Coin is fair | 1/3 | 1/2 | 1/6 | 1/3 |
| Coin is two-tailed | 1/3 | 0 | 0 | 0 |
|  |  |  | 1/2 | 1 |

Since the posterior probabilities are 2/3 for "coin is two-headed" and 1/3 for "coin is fair," the overall chance of heads is $(1) \times (2/3) + (0.5) \times (1/3)$ = 5/6. The best posterior terminal action is therefore $x_2$ (bet on heads), with expected gain $U(x_2) - U(x_0) = 30 \times (5/6) - 50 \times (1/6) = 16\frac{2}{3}$. By a corresponding calculation, the message $m$ = tails would lead to exactly the same utility gain from the optimal posterior action $x_3$ (bet on tails). So $16\frac{2}{3}$ is the worth of the message service.

## 2 Value of information in a two-action problem with linear costs

You are the receiving officer of a company that has received a large shipment of ordered goods. You must decide whether to accept (action $x = A$) or reject (action $x = R$) the shipment. Which you will want to do depends upon the unknown proportion defective $P$ in the shipment (population). Your loss function is:

$$L(R, P) = \begin{cases} 0, & \text{for} \quad P \geqslant 0.04 \\ 100(0.04 - P), & \text{for} \quad P < 0.04 \end{cases}$$
$$L(A, P) = \begin{cases} 0, & \text{for} \quad P \leqslant 0.04 \\ 200(P - 0.04), & \text{for} \quad P > 0.04 \end{cases}$$

Your prior probability distribution is defined over four discrete values of $P$ (states of the world):

| Fraction defective $(P)$ | Prior probability $(\pi_s)$ |
| --- | --- |
| 0.02 | 0.7 |
| 0.04 | 0.1 |
| 0.06 | 0.1 |
| 0.08 | 0.1 |
| | 1.0 |

(A) What is your best *prior* decision, in the absence of sample information? Assume that you are risk-neutral, with preference-scaling function $v(c) = c$.

(B) How much should you be willing to pay for a sample of size 1?

## 3 Value of information with logarithmic utility

Two individuals with endowed wealths $W^1$ and $W^2$ have the same preference-scaling function $v = \ln(c)$, the same probability beliefs $\pi_s$, and face the same state-claim prices $P_s$.

(A) Individual #1 will receive no additional information, but individual #2 will be receiving conclusive information revealing the true state before trading takes place. Show that the utility difference between them is given by:

$$U^2 - U^1 = \ln W^2 - \ln W^1 - \sum_s x_s \ln x_s$$

[HINT: Make use of a simple relationship between $W$ and $c_s$ that holds for the logarithmic preference-scaling function.]

(B) Using this result, show that an uninformed individual with this preference-scaling function would be willing to give up a fraction $K^*$ of his wealth to receive conclusive information before trading takes place, where:

$$K^* = 1 - (\pi_1)^{\pi_1}(\pi_2)^{\pi_2}\dots(\pi_S)^{\pi_S}$$

(C) Show that he will pay the most when he initially assigns equal probabilities to all states.

### 4 Value of less-than-conclusive information

Under the conditions of example 5.3 in the text above, suppose the message service $\mu$ does not provide a fully conclusive message as to which state is going to obtain. Instead, suppose message $m_1$ is such as to lead to the posterior distribution $(\pi_{1\cdot1}, \pi_{2\cdot1}) = (0\cdot75, 0\cdot25)$ while message $m_2$ leads to $(\pi_{1\cdot2}, \pi_{2\cdot2}) = (0\cdot25, 0\cdot75)$.

(A) Compute the likelihood matrix $L$ associated with this message service.

(B) Show that the individual with the utility function in the text example, $v(c) = \sqrt{c}$, would be willing to pay a fee $\xi$ equal to 20 units of corn for this information, provided as before that the message arrives in time for market trading.

### *5.2.3 More informative versus less informative message services

In general, the value of a message service for any individual will depend upon: (1) the set of actions available, (2) his preference-scaling function $v(c)$, and (3) his probability beliefs over messages and states. We will be inquiring here into the circumstances in which, regardless of his preference-scaling function and range of available actions, an individual with given prior probability beliefs will be able to rank different message services in terms of their "informativeness." (How the value of a message service also responds to differing utility functions and to different action sets will be taken up in the sections following.)

A message service $\hat{\mu}$ is defined as *more informative* than another service $\mu$, for an individual with given prior probability vector $\pi$, if using $\hat{\mu}$

---

\* Starred sections represent more difficult or specialized materials that can be omitted without significant loss of continuity.

provides him with a greater utility gain regardless of his preference-scaling function $v(c)$ and action set. More specifically, if for some individual $i$ the possible belief revisions brought about by $\hat{\mu}$ will lead him to choose corresponding terminal actions whose expected utility gain $\hat{\Omega}_i$ is higher than the improvement $\Omega_i$ achievable using message service $\mu$.

Figure 5.4 provides an intuitive illustration. The shorter dashed lines represent an information service $\mu$ that generates two possible messages 1 and 2, leading to posterior probability vectors $\pi_{\cdot 1}$ and $\pi_{\cdot 2}$ as in the previous figure 5.3. The alternative information service $\hat{\mu}$, indicated here by the longer dashed lines, also generates two messages 1 and 2. As shown, the additional utility improvement due to using $\hat{\mu}$ rather than $\mu$ is the length KE in the diagram.

Recall that the individual's prior probability vector $x$ can always be expressed as the message-probability-weighted average of the posterior probability vectors $\pi_{\cdot m}$ associated with any message service employed, that is:

$$\pi = q_1 \pi_{\cdot 1} + q_2 \pi_{\cdot 2} = \hat{q}_1 \hat{\pi}_{\cdot 1} + \hat{q}_2 \hat{\pi}_{\cdot 2}$$

In the diagram, $\hat{\pi}_{\cdot 1}$ lies to the right of $\pi_{\cdot 1}$ and $\hat{\pi}_{\cdot 2}$ lies to the left of $\pi_{\cdot 2}$, so the posterior vectors of the alternative service $\hat{\mu}$ are a mean-preserving spread of those of $\mu$. When this holds, so that the posterior vectors associated with $\hat{\mu}$ bracket those of $\mu$ as in the diagram, we can say that message 1 under $\hat{\mu}$ is *more conclusive* than the corresponding message under the original service $\mu$ as to the occurrence of state 1, while message 2 under $\hat{\mu}$ is more conclusive as to state 2. This is the essential interpretation of the "informativeness" property.

One point is worth special note: when the bracketing condition holds as in figure 5.4, *the more informative message service $\hat{\mu}$ leads to higher expected utility even when, as shown, the posterior actions associated with all of the possible messages are unchanged from $\mu$.* The reason is that, both messages being more conclusive, even when the actions are unchanged there is a smaller risk of posterior error (choosing the wrong action) no matter which message is received. Of course, if $\hat{\mu}$ actually implies some change in one or more of the best conditional actions, in comparison with $\mu$, the utility gain will be even larger.

To formalize the argument about the conclusiveness of messages, suppose that for an individual with prior beliefs $\pi$ each possible posterior probability vector $\pi_{\cdot m}$ under the superior message service $\mu$ is a convex combination of the posterior probabilities under message service $\hat{\mu}$, that is:

$$\begin{bmatrix} \pi_{1 \cdot m} \\ \pi_{2 \cdot m} \end{bmatrix} = \begin{bmatrix} \hat{\pi}_{1 \cdot 1} \\ \hat{\pi}_{2 \cdot 1} \end{bmatrix} a_{1 \cdot m} + \begin{bmatrix} \hat{\pi}_{1 \cdot 2} \\ \hat{\pi}_{2 \cdot 2} \end{bmatrix} a_{2 \cdot m}$$

Utility
in state 2

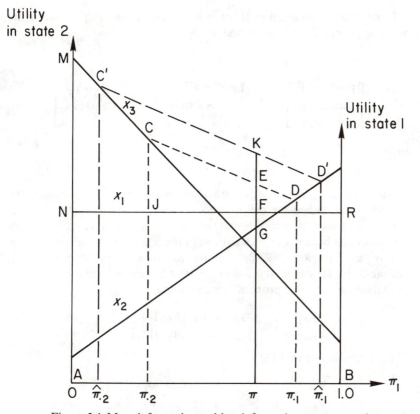

Figure 5.4 More informative and less informative message services

where the $a_{\hat{m} \cdot m}$ are linear weights. In matrix notation:

$$\Pi = \hat{\Pi}A, \quad \text{where } A = [a_{\hat{m} \cdot m}] \qquad (5.2.16)$$

For the columns of $\Pi$ to be convex combinations of the columns of $\hat{\Pi}$, it must be the case that the matrix $A$ is non-negative and has columns summing to 1:

$$\sum_{\hat{m}} a_{\hat{m} \cdot m} = 1, \quad a_{\hat{m} \cdot m} \geqslant 1 \qquad (5.2.17)$$

As Blackwell (1953) first noted, there is a useful interpretation of the elements of $A$. One can think of the message service $\mu$ as representing the result of receiving message $\hat{\mu}$ except that some information has been "garbled" in transmission. To be precise, $a_{\hat{m} \cdot m}$ can be interpreted as the conditional probability that, when message $m$ is received, message $\hat{m}$ was actually sent. Since probabilities must sum to 1, condition (5.2.17) must then hold.

Under this interpretation there is a further relationship between the message probability vectors $q$ and $\hat{q}$:

$$q_{\hat{m}} = \sum_m a_{\hat{m}\cdot m} q_m$$

$$\begin{bmatrix} \text{probability} \\ \text{message } \hat{m} \\ \text{was sent} \end{bmatrix} = \sum_m \begin{bmatrix} \text{probability } \hat{m} \\ \text{was sent if} \\ m \text{ is received} \end{bmatrix} \cdot \begin{bmatrix} \text{probability} \\ \text{message } m \\ \text{was received} \end{bmatrix}$$

In matrix notation:

$$\hat{q} = Aq \qquad\qquad (5.2.18)$$

Returning to figure 5.4, we have argued that the crucial requirement for an individual with prior beliefs $\pi$ to be able to rank the two services, regardless of his preferences, is that the posterior probability vectors $\mu_{\cdot m}$ of service $\mu$ must be convex combinations of the posterior probability vectors $\pi_{\cdot \hat{m}}$ of $\hat{\mu}$. Equation (5.2.18) appears to be a second restriction on probabilities. However, the following relationship between the message probabilities and prior probabilities must hold:

$$\begin{bmatrix} \hat{\pi}_{1\cdot 1} & \hat{\pi}_{1\cdot 2} \\ \hat{\pi}_{2\cdot 1} & \hat{\pi}_{2\cdot 2} \end{bmatrix}\begin{bmatrix} \hat{q}_1 \\ \hat{q}_2 \end{bmatrix} = \begin{bmatrix} \pi_1 \\ \pi_2 \end{bmatrix} = \begin{bmatrix} \pi_{1\cdot 1} & \pi_{1\cdot 2} \\ \pi_{2\cdot 1} & \pi_{2\cdot 2} \end{bmatrix}\begin{bmatrix} q_1 \\ q_2 \end{bmatrix}$$

Then, appealing to (5.2.16):

$$\begin{bmatrix} \hat{\pi}_{1\cdot 1} & \hat{\pi}_{1\cdot 2} \\ \hat{\pi}_{2\cdot 1} & \hat{\pi}_{2\cdot 2} \end{bmatrix}\begin{bmatrix} \hat{q}_1 \\ \hat{q}_2 \end{bmatrix} = \begin{bmatrix} \hat{\pi}_{1\cdot 1} & \hat{\pi}_{1\cdot 2} \\ \hat{\pi}_{2\cdot 1} & \hat{\pi}_{2\cdot 2} \end{bmatrix}\begin{bmatrix} a_{1\cdot 1} & a_{1\cdot 2} \\ a_{2\cdot 1} & a_{2\cdot 2} \end{bmatrix}\begin{bmatrix} q_1 \\ q_2 \end{bmatrix}$$

Since the columns of $\hat{\Pi}$ sum to 1 and differ, the matrix $\hat{\Pi}$ has rank equal to 2. Hence we can premultiply by the inverse $\hat{\Pi}^{-1}$ to obtain:

$$\begin{bmatrix} \hat{q}_1 \\ \hat{q}_2 \end{bmatrix} = \begin{bmatrix} a_{1\cdot 1} & a_{1\cdot 2} \\ a_{2\cdot 1} & a_{2\cdot 2} \end{bmatrix}\begin{bmatrix} q_1 \\ q_2 \end{bmatrix}$$

Thus, in the $2 \times 2$ case equation (5.2.18) is not a separate condition but an implication of equation (5.2.16).

Let us now reinterpret these equations in more general terms. Let $\hat{m}$ be one of $\hat{M}$ messages under message service $\hat{\mu}$ and let $m$ be one of $M$ messages under service $\mu$. As before, condition (5.2.16) indicates that each message under $\mu$ can be interpreted as a "garbling" of the message sent under $\hat{\mu}$. Moreover, arguing as above:

$$\hat{\Pi}\hat{q} = \pi = \Pi q = \hat{\Pi}Aq \qquad\qquad (5.2.19)$$

As long as the columns of $\hat{\Pi}$ are linearly independent, it follows from (5.2.19) that $\hat{q} = Aq$. Thus that condition (5.2.18) is an implication of

(5.2.16) holds not only for the $2 \times 2$ case but quite generally, given linear independence. On the other hand, in the absence of linear independence, there are many possible message probability vectors that are solutions to the system of equations $\hat{\Pi}\hat{q} = \pi$.

As a specific example, consider the following matrices:

$$\hat{\Pi} = \begin{bmatrix} 1 & \frac{1}{2} & 0 \\ 0 & \frac{1}{2} & 1 \end{bmatrix}, \quad \Pi = \begin{bmatrix} \frac{3}{4} & \frac{1}{4} \\ \frac{1}{4} & \frac{3}{4} \end{bmatrix}, \quad A = \begin{bmatrix} \frac{1}{2} & 0 \\ \frac{1}{2} & \frac{1}{2} \\ 0 & \frac{1}{2} \end{bmatrix}, \text{ and } q = \pi = \begin{bmatrix} \frac{1}{2} \\ \frac{1}{2} \end{bmatrix}$$

Here we do not have enough data to uniquely compute the message probabilities $\hat{q}$ from $\hat{\Pi}$, and $\pi$. One possible solution is $\hat{q} = Aq$, so that $\hat{q} = (\frac{1}{4}, \frac{1}{2}, \frac{1}{4})$, which suggests that message service $\mu$ is a garbling of $\hat{\mu}$. On the other hand, an alternative possibility is that $\hat{q} = (0, 1, 0)$. In this case message service $\hat{\mu}$ has no value since neither of the two helpful messages are ever sent. Absent linear independence, therefore, conditions (5.2.16) and (5.2.18) are both needed before one message service can be described as a "garbling" of the other.

Since the posterior beliefs mix prior beliefs and likelihoods, the two conditions may hold for one individual but not for another, unless their beliefs are the same. Indeed, as the following example indicates, two individuals with different priors may rank two information services differently regardless of their preferences.

## EXAMPLE 5.4

Suppose that the message services $\hat{\mu}$ and $\mu$ have the following likelihood matrices:

$$\hat{L} = \begin{bmatrix} \frac{3}{4} & \frac{1}{4} \\ \frac{1}{4} & \frac{3}{4} \\ \frac{1}{4} & \frac{3}{4} \end{bmatrix} \text{ and } L = \begin{bmatrix} \frac{5}{8} & \frac{3}{8} \\ \frac{3}{8} & \frac{5}{8} \\ 1 & 0 \end{bmatrix} \quad \begin{matrix} s = 1 \\ s = 2 \\ s = 3 \end{matrix}$$

If Alex believes that states 1 and 2 each occur with probability $\frac{1}{2}$ while state 3 never occurs, the third row of the likelihood matrices is irrelevant for him. Comparing the first two rows it is intuitively clear that service $\hat{\mu}$ is more valuable to Alex. In fact it is easy to check that the posterior matrices $\hat{\Pi}$ and $\Pi$ are:

$$\hat{\Pi} = \begin{bmatrix} \frac{3}{4} & \frac{1}{4} \\ \frac{1}{4} & \frac{3}{4} \end{bmatrix} \text{ and } \Pi = \begin{bmatrix} \frac{5}{8} & \frac{3}{8} \\ \frac{3}{8} & \frac{5}{8} \end{bmatrix}$$

Thus, for Alex, the posterior probability vectors associated with $\hat{\mu}$ (the columns of the $\hat{\Pi}$ matrix) bracket those associated with $\mu$.

On the other hand, suppose Bev believes that state 1 will never occur while states 2 and 3 are equally likely. For her the top row of each of the likelihood matrices is irrelevant. For likelihood matrix $\hat{L}$ the second and third rows are identical. Receiving a message therefore conveys no information. It follows immediately that Bev will prefer $L$ to $\hat{L}$.

This raises the question as to whether there are circumstances under which different individuals will *always* agree on a ranking of alternative message services, regardless of possibly differing prior beliefs. We now show that there are such conditions.

Suppose it is the case that each service does have an objectively calculable (or, at least, interpersonally agreed) likelihood matrix. Following the terminology of Blackwell, one likelihood matrix $\hat{L}$ is *more informative* than another matrix $L$ if there exists a non-negative $\hat{M} \times M$ matrix $B$, each of whose rows sum to unity, such that:

$$\begin{array}{ccc} (S \times \hat{M}) & (\hat{M} \times M) & (S \times M) \\ \hat{L} & B & = & L \end{array}$$

That is:

$$\sum_{\hat{m}} b_{m \cdot \hat{m}} \hat{l}_{\hat{m} \cdot m} = l_{s \cdot m} \tag{5.2.20}$$

As before we can interpret the relationship between $L$ and $\hat{L}$ in terms of transmission garbling. We can think of $b_{m \cdot \hat{m}}$ as the probability that, if message $m$ is received, it was message $\hat{m}$ that was sent. Equation (5.2.20) can then be understood as the statement that:

$$\begin{bmatrix} \text{the likelihood} \\ \text{of message } m \\ \text{given state is } s \end{bmatrix} = \sum_{\hat{m}} \begin{bmatrix} \text{probability of} \\ \text{receiving message } m \\ \text{when } \hat{m} \text{ was sent} \end{bmatrix} \cdot \begin{bmatrix} \text{the likelihood} \\ \text{of message } \hat{m} \\ \text{given state is } s \end{bmatrix}$$

If condition (5.2.20) holds it follows almost immediately that there must be a matrix $A$ satisfying (5.2.16) and (5.2.18). First, given the definition of $B = [b_{m \cdot \hat{m}}]$, we can compute the corresponding $A$ matrix using Bayes' Theorem:

$$a_{\hat{m} \cdot m} q_m = b_{m \cdot \hat{m}} \hat{q}_{\hat{m}}$$

$$\begin{bmatrix} \text{probability that} \\ \hat{m} \text{ was sent when} \\ m \text{ is received} \end{bmatrix} \begin{bmatrix} \text{probability} \\ \text{that } m \text{ is} \\ \text{received} \end{bmatrix} = \begin{bmatrix} \text{probability that} \\ m \text{ is received} \\ \text{when } \hat{m} \text{ was sent} \end{bmatrix} \begin{bmatrix} \text{probability} \\ \text{that } \hat{m} \\ \text{was sent} \end{bmatrix}$$

Moreover, summing over the messages received:

$$\sum_m a_{\hat{m} \cdot m} q_m = \hat{q}_{\hat{m}}$$

or, in matrix notation:

$$Aq = \hat{q} \tag{5.2.21}$$

Let $U_m$ be maximized expected utility given message $m$ from information service $L$ and let $\hat{U}_{\hat{m}}$ be maximized expected utility given message $\hat{m}$ from information service $\hat{L}$. Then we wish to show that, if $\hat{L}$ is more informative:

$$\sum_m q_m U_m \leqslant \sum_{\hat{m}} \hat{q}_{\hat{m}} \hat{U}_{\hat{m}}$$

If $x_m^*$ is the optimal action, given $m$:

$$U_m = \sum_s \pi_{s \cdot m} V(c_s(x_m^*))$$

From (5.2.20):

$$U_m = \sum_{\hat{m}} a_{\hat{m} \cdot m} (\sum_s \hat{\pi}_{s \cdot \hat{m}} v(c_s(x_m^*)))$$

Since $x_m^*$ is a feasible (but not necessarily optimal) action given message $\hat{m}$, we know that:

$$\sum_s \hat{\pi}_{s \cdot \hat{m}} v(c_s(x_m^*)) \leqslant U_{\hat{m}}$$

Therefore:

$$U_m \leqslant \sum_{\hat{m}} a_{\hat{m} \cdot m} U_{\hat{m}} \qquad\qquad (5.2.22)$$

In words, expected utility given message $m$ of the garbled service $\mu$ is no greater (and generally less) than the probability-weighted expected utility of the best actions associated with the various messages $\hat{m}$ of the ungarbled information service which $m$ garbles together.

This is not, by itself, enough to rank the two services. But multiplying (5.2.22) by $q_m$, summing over $m$ and then appealing to (5.2.20) we obtain:

$$\sum_m q_m U_m \leqslant \sum_m q_m \sum_{\hat{m}} a_{\hat{m} \cdot m} U_{\hat{m}} = \sum_{\hat{m}} [\sum_m a_{\hat{m} \cdot m} q_m] U_{\hat{m}} = \sum_{\hat{m}} \hat{q}_{\hat{m}} U_{\hat{m}}$$

where the expression at the extreme left represents the expected utility under $L$ while the expression at the extreme right represents the expected utility under $\hat{L}$.

EXAMPLE 5-5: A message service $\hat{\mu}$ taking the form of a random sample of size 2 is surely more informative than an alternative message service $\mu$ representing a sample of size 1. To take a specific case, suppose a coin is either fair (state 1) or two-headed (state 2). Suppose Alex attaches prior probability 3/4 to state 1 and 1/4 to state 2, while Bev has the reversed prior probabilities. First, find the $B$ matrix in Blackwell's condition to show, in terms of the likelihood matrices, that $\mu$ is a garbling of $\hat{\mu}$. Then, for both Alex and Bev find the $A$ matrix of equation (5.2.16), and the associated message probabilities, which demonstrate that the posterior probability vectors of $\mu$ are a garbling of those of $\hat{\mu}$. ANSWER: The likelihood matrices $\hat{L}$ and $L$ are:

MESSAGE (# of heads)

| State | $L$ | 0 | 1 | $\hat{L}$ | 0 | 1 | 2 |
|---|---|---|---|---|---|---|---|
| 1 = Fair | 1 | 0·5 | 0·5 | 1 | 0·25 | 0·5 | 0·25 |
| 2 = Two-headed | 2 | 0 | 1 | 2 | 0 | 0 | 1 |

By straightforward computation it can be shown that Blackwell's condition holds in the form:

$$
\begin{array}{ccc}
L & = & \hat{L} \qquad\qquad B \\
\begin{bmatrix} 0·5 & 0·5 \\ 0 & 1 \end{bmatrix} = \begin{bmatrix} 0·25 & 0·5 & 0·25 \\ 0 & 0 & 1 \end{bmatrix} & \begin{bmatrix} 1 & 0 \\ 0·5 & 0·5 \\ 0 & 1 \end{bmatrix}
\end{array}
$$

So $L$ is a garbling of $\hat{L}$.

Alex's joint probability matrices ($J$ and $\hat{J}$) and potential posterior matrices ($\Pi$ and $\hat{\Pi}$) for message service $\mu$ (sample of size 1) and message service $\hat{\mu}$ (sample of size 2) are:

| $J$ | 0 | 1 | |
|---|---|---|---|
| 1 | 0·375 | 0·375 | 0·75 |
| 2 | 0 | 0·25 | 0·25 |
| | 0·375 | 0·625 | |

| $\Pi$ | 0 | 1 |
|---|---|---|
| 1 | 1 | 0·6 |
| 2 | 0 | 0·4 |
| | 1·0 | 1·0 |

| $\hat{J}$ | 0 | 1 | 2 | |
|---|---|---|---|---|
| 1 | 0·1875 | 0·375 | 0·1875 | 0·75 |
| 2 | 0 | 0 | 0·25 | 0·25 |
| $\hat{q}$ | 0·1875 | 0·375 | 0·4375 | |

| $\hat{\Pi}$ | 0 | 1 | 2 |
|---|---|---|---|
| 1 | 1 | 1 | 0·429 |
| 2 | 0 | 0 | 0·571 |
| | 1·0 | 1·0 | 1·0 |

The message probabilities are the column sums of $J$ and $\hat{J}$. The $A$ matrix can then be determined by applying Bayes' Theorem, $a_{\hat{m}\cdot m}\, q_m = b_{m\cdot\hat{m}}\, \hat{q}_{\hat{m}}$.

$$
A = \begin{bmatrix} 0·5 & 1 \\ 0·5 & 0·3 \\ 0 & 0·7 \end{bmatrix}
$$

Straightforward computation reveals that $\hat{\Pi}A = \Pi$ and that $Aq = \hat{A}$. Therefore $\Pi$ is a garbling of $\hat{\Pi}$. Determination of the corresponding $A$ matrix for Bev is left as an exercise for the reader.

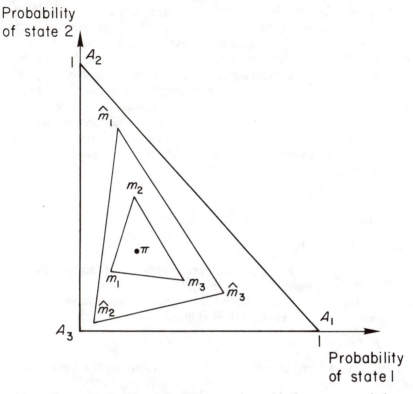

Figure 5.5 Ranking information services with three states and three messages

## EXERCISES AND EXCURSIONS 5.2.3

*1 Generalization of the "bracketing" condition*

(A) Figure 5.4 pictured a situation where, with $S = 2 = M$, message service $\hat{\mu}$ was interpreted as "more informative" than $\mu$ if the posterior probability vectors of $\hat{\mu}$ bracketed those of $\mu$. Show that there is a geometrical interpretation of the bracketing condition if $S = 3 = M$.

(B) What if $S = 2$, $M = 3$?

(C) Explain also why the geometrical analysis of (A) does not generalize to the case of $S = 3$, $M = 4$.

PARTIAL ANSWER

(A) With three states we can represent posterior beliefs as in figure 5.5. At the vertex $A_s$ of the triangle, the probability of state $s$ is 1. Therefore the triple $(A_1, A_2, A_3)$ is the perfect information service. Any other information service with three messages can be represented as a triangle which has the prior probability vector in its interior, since the prior is just the message-weighted average of the posteriors.

In figure 5.5 two information services $\hat{\mu}$ and $\mu$ are depicted. Each vertex of a triangle represents the probability vector associated with a particular message. Note that the triangle for $\mu$ lies inside the triangle for $\hat{\mu}$. (It is not difficult to confirm that the three posterior probability vectors must be linearly independent unless the three points in the figure lie on a line.) It follows that each posterior $\pi_{.m}$ of message service $m$ is a convex combination of the posteriors of message service $\hat{m}$, that is:

$$\Pi = \hat{\Pi}A$$

Also, for consistency we know that:

$$\Pi q = \hat{\Pi}Aq = \pi = \hat{\Pi}\hat{q}$$

where $\hat{q}$ and $q$ are the message probability vectors and $\pi$ is the prior probability vector.

But, since the columns of $\hat{\Pi}$ are linearly independent, there is a unique solution to the system of linear equations:

$$\hat{\Pi}q = \pi$$

It follows immediately that $Aq = \hat{q}$ and so all the conditions for information service $\hat{\mu}$ to be preferred to $\mu$ are satisfied.

(B) With two states and three messages, consider two information services for which the implied posterior beliefs are as follows:

$$\hat{\mu}: \quad \hat{\Pi} = \begin{bmatrix} 1 & \frac{1}{2} & 0 \\ 0 & \frac{1}{2} & 1 \end{bmatrix} \quad \text{and} \quad \hat{q} = (\varepsilon, 1-2\varepsilon, \varepsilon)$$

$$\mu: \quad \Pi = \begin{bmatrix} \frac{5}{6} & \frac{1}{2} & \frac{1}{6} \\ \frac{1}{6} & \frac{1}{2} & \frac{5}{6} \end{bmatrix} \quad \text{and} \quad q = (\tfrac{1}{2}-\varepsilon, 2\varepsilon, \tfrac{1}{2}-\varepsilon)$$

The posterior probability vector $(\frac{5}{6}, \frac{1}{6})$ is a convex combination of $(1, 0)$ and $(\frac{1}{2}, \frac{1}{2})$. Similarly $(\frac{1}{6}, \frac{5}{6})$ is a convex combination of $(\frac{1}{2}, \frac{1}{2})$ and $(0, 1)$. Formally, we have:

$$\Pi = \hat{\Pi}A, \quad \text{where } A = \begin{bmatrix} \frac{2}{3} & 0 & 0 \\ \frac{1}{3} & 1 & \frac{1}{3} \\ 0 & 0 & \frac{2}{3} \end{bmatrix}$$

However, it is no longer possible to draw any conclusion about the relative value of the two information services since many different message probabilities are consistent with prior beliefs of $(\frac{1}{2}, \frac{1}{2})$. In particular, for all $\varepsilon \in [0, \frac{1}{2}]$ the above data are consistent with such prior beliefs, since in each case:

$$\Pi q = \hat{\Pi}\hat{q} = \begin{bmatrix} \frac{1}{2} \\ \frac{1}{2} \end{bmatrix}$$

For $\varepsilon$ sufficiently close to zero the information service $\hat{\mu}$ updates an individual's prior with very low probability while information service $\mu$ updates with probability close to 1. It is therefore necessarily the case that $\mu$ is preferred over $\hat{\mu}$ for $\varepsilon$ sufficiently close to zero. With $\varepsilon$ close to $\frac{1}{2}$, however, the opposite is true. Information service $\hat{\mu}$ is almost perfect while $\mu$ has almost no value.

(C) At the end of the answer to (A) we established that if one information triangle lies inside the other all the conditions for a strict ranking are satisfied. With four messages and one quadrilateral inside the other, this is no longer the case. The answer to (B) should be helpful in proving this.

## 2* Comparison of information matrices

Two information services $\hat{\mu}$ and $\mu$ have potential posterior matrices $\hat{\Pi}$ and $\Pi$ where:

$$\hat{\Pi}A = \Pi$$

and $A$ is an $\hat{M} \times M$ non-negative matrix whose columns sum to unity.

(A) Confirm that each column of $\Pi(\pi._m)$ can be expressed as a convex combination of the $\hat{M}$ columns of $\hat{\Pi}$.

(B) Does it follow that all individuals will prefer $\hat{\Pi}$ to $\Pi$?

HINT: Consider a case in which there are two states. Information service $\hat{\mu}$ sends one of three messages while information service $\mu$ sends one of two messages. For the former let one of the messages be "stay with your prior beliefs."

(C) Suppose that $S \geqslant \hat{M} \geqslant M$. If $\hat{\Pi}A = \Pi$ and $A$ has rank $M$ does it follow that $\hat{\mu}$ is necessarily preferred over $\mu$?

HINT: Show that $\hat{q}$ and $q$ are unique and satisfy $Aq = \hat{q}$.

## 3 Ranking information services

An individual believes that each of two states is equally likely. He has available a message service which will send him one of two messages. If the true state is $s = 1$, the message $m = 1$ is received with probability $\frac{7}{8}$. If the true state is $s = 2$ the message $m = 1$ is received with probability $\frac{5}{8}$.

* Starred questions or portions of questions may be somewhat more difficult.

(A)    Write down the likelihood matrix and the (unconditional) message probabilities. Use these to compute the potential posterior matrix $\Pi$.

(B)    The individual is offered an alternative message service which will also send him one of two messages. If the true state is $s = 1$, the message $\hat{m} = 1$ is received with probability $\frac{3}{4}$. If the true state is $s = 2$ the message $\hat{m} = 1$ is received with probability $\frac{1}{4}$. Intuitively, why is this message service more valuable?

(C)    Write down the likelihood matrix $L$ for this new information service and compute the potential posterior matrix.

(D)    Confirm that the posterior probabilities for the first service are convex combinations of the posterior probabilities for the second service.

(E)*    Show that this conclusion holds regardless of the prior probabilities. That is, all individuals, regardless of preferences and beliefs, will prefer the second service.

(F)    Confirm that the conditions of Blackwell's theorem do not hold. That is, the conditions of Blackwell's theorem are strongly sufficient.

PARTIAL ANSWER

The likelihood matrices are:

$$[l_{m \cdot s}] = \begin{bmatrix} \frac{7}{8} & \frac{1}{8} \\ \frac{5}{8} & \frac{3}{8} \end{bmatrix} \quad \text{and} \quad [\hat{l}_{\hat{m} \cdot s}] = \begin{bmatrix} \frac{3}{4} & \frac{1}{4} \\ \frac{1}{4} & \frac{3}{4} \end{bmatrix}$$

Given prior beliefs $(\frac{1}{2}, \frac{1}{2})$, the message probabilities are:

$$q = (\frac{3}{4}, \frac{1}{4}) \quad \text{and} \quad \hat{q} = (\frac{1}{2}, \frac{1}{2})$$

Since $\pi_{s \cdot m} = l_{m \cdot s} \pi_s / q_m$, we can then compute the potential posterior matrices:

$$\Pi = \begin{bmatrix} \frac{7}{12} & \frac{1}{4} \\ \frac{5}{12} & \frac{3}{4} \end{bmatrix} \quad \text{and} \quad \hat{\Pi} = \begin{bmatrix} \frac{3}{4} & \frac{1}{4} \\ \frac{1}{4} & \frac{3}{4} \end{bmatrix}$$

Since $\hat{\Pi}$ is non-singular, there is a unique matrix $A$ satisfying $\Pi = \hat{\Pi} A$, where:

$$A = \begin{bmatrix} \frac{2}{3} & 0 \\ \frac{1}{3} & 1 \end{bmatrix}$$

It can also be checked immediately that $Aq = \hat{q}$.

Since the likelihood matrix $\hat{L}$ is non-singular, there is a unique matrix $B$ such that $L = \hat{L}B$. It is readily confirmed that the conditions of Blackwell's theorem, $0 \leqslant b_{m \cdot \hat{m}} \leqslant 1$, do not hold.

It remains to consider different priors. Let $\pi$ be the prior probability of state 1. Then:

$$q_1 = (\tfrac{7}{8})\pi + (\tfrac{5}{8})(1-\pi) \quad \text{and} \quad \hat{q}_1 = \tfrac{3}{4}\pi + \tfrac{1}{4}(1-\pi)$$

and so:

$$\pi_{1 \cdot 1} = \frac{l_{1 \cdot 1}\pi}{q_1} = \frac{(\tfrac{7}{8})\pi}{(\tfrac{7}{8})\pi + (\tfrac{5}{8})(1-\pi)} = \frac{\pi}{\pi + (\tfrac{5}{7})(1-\pi)}$$

while:

$$\hat{\pi}_{1 \cdot 1} = \frac{\hat{l}_{1 \cdot 1}\pi}{\hat{q}_1} = \frac{(\tfrac{3}{4})\pi}{(\tfrac{3}{4})\pi + (\tfrac{1}{4})(1-\pi)} = \frac{\pi}{\pi + (\tfrac{1}{3})(1-\pi)}$$

It follows immediately that $\pi_{1 \cdot 1} < \hat{\pi}_{1 \cdot 1}$. It is left to the reader to confirm that $\pi_{2 \cdot 2} = \hat{\pi}_{2 \cdot 2}$, and hence to establish the claim that, for all preferences and beliefs, the second information service is strictly preferred.

### 4 A non-concavity in the value of information (Stiglitz and Radner, 1984)

An individual with initial wealth $\overline{W}$ faces state-claim prices $P_s$, for $s = 1, 2$. His preference-scaling function is $v(c) = \log(c)$.

(A) If he believes that state 1 will occur with probability $\pi$ and state 2 with probability $(1-\pi)$, obtain an expression for his maximized expected utility $U(\pi)$ as a function of $\pi$. Depict this in a diagram for $0 \leqslant \pi \leqslant 1$.

(B) Is $U(\pi)$ convex? Discuss whether your answer holds in general.

(C) Suppose his prior probability of state 1 is $\overline{\pi}$ and that he expects to receive one of two messages that will change his probability of state 1 either to $\overline{\pi} + \theta$ or $\overline{\pi} - \theta$. Explain why the probability of each message must be 0·5, and hence show that the gain in expected utility from having this information prior to trading is:

$$\Omega(\theta) = \tfrac{1}{2}(\overline{\pi} + \theta) \log(\overline{\pi} + \theta) + \tfrac{1}{2}(\overline{\pi} - \theta) \log(\overline{\pi} - \theta) - \overline{\pi} \log \overline{\pi}$$
$$+ \tfrac{1}{2}(1 - \overline{\pi} - \theta) \log(1 - \overline{\pi} - \theta) + \tfrac{1}{2}(1 - \overline{\pi} + \theta) \log(1 - \overline{\pi} + \theta)$$
$$- (1 - \overline{\pi}) \log 1 - \overline{\pi})$$

(D) Hence show that the marginal gain in utility from a "little bit" of information is zero. Also show that for all $\theta > 0$ the marginal value $\Omega'(\theta)$ of $\theta$ is positive and increasing.

(E) Show also that the dollar value of the information, $k(\theta)$, can be expressed as:

$$k(\theta) = \overline{W}(1 - e^{\Omega(\theta)})$$

(F) Using your answers to parts (D) and (E), show that $k(\theta)$ is convex in the neighborhood of $\theta = 0$.**

** End of starred section.

### 5.2.4    *Differences in utility functions and the worth of information*

In the previous section we saw how in some circumstances it is possible to rank information services independently of the individual's preference-scaling function $v(c)$ and action set $x = 1, \ldots, X$. In this and the following sections we will be showing how preferences and the set of actions available affect the worth of information. More specifically, the question examined here is whether or in what circumstances a *more risk-averse* individual is willing to pay more for information.

Intuitively, it might be thought that a more risk-averse individual will always be more anxious to reduce his uncertainty by acquiring more information. But it turns out that this is not valid in general. Whether or not a more risk-averse individual will pay more for a message service depends upon the *comparative riskiness of the decisions that would be made without the information and with the information.*

Consider first a situation in which the optimal prior action $x_0$ for some individual $i$ would generate sure income $c^o$ for him. If he invests in information, each possible message $m$ will be associated with some best terminal action $x_m$. Suppose that $x_m$ is a risky action for at least one possible message $m$, the associated consequence distribution being $(c_{sm}; \pi_{s \cdot m})$. Since there has been some change of optimal action, the information is surely valuable. So there must be some positive maximum fee $\xi$ that the individual would be willing to pay for the information. Thus, as a special case of equation (5.2.15), this maximum fee is determined in:

$$v^i(c^o) = \Sigma_m \Sigma_s \pi_{s \cdot m} q_m v^i(c_{sm} - \xi) \tag{5.2.24}$$

In chapter 3 we saw that, if individual $j$ is everywhere more risk-averse than individual $i$, then $j$'s preference-scaling function $v^j(c)$ could be expressed as a strictly concave function $f(\cdot)$ of $v^i(c)$. So we can write:

$$
\begin{aligned}
v^j(c^o) &= f(v^i(c^o)) = f(\Sigma_m \Sigma_s \pi_{s \cdot m} q_m v^i(c_{sm} - \xi)) \\
&> \Sigma_m \Sigma_s \pi_{s \cdot m} q_m f(v^i(c_{sm} - \xi)), \quad \text{by Jensen's inequality} \\
&= \Sigma_m \Sigma_s \pi_{s \cdot m} q_m v^j(c_{sm} - \xi)
\end{aligned}
$$

Thus the more risk-averse individual $j$ would be strictly worse off purchasing the information at a price of $\xi$. In other words, the information in this case is *less valuable* for the more risk-averse individual.

The key premise here was that the optimal uninformed action was riskless. While the message service was indeed a valuable one, it involved some chance of leading the recipient of the information to choose a risky action. Given that fact, the worth of the service was smaller for the more risk-averse decision-maker. Figure 5.3 illustrated such a situation. The riskless action $x_1$ is the best choice, in the absence of information, for an individual with prior belief vector $\pi$. As illustrated, while acquiring the message service leading to the posterior probability vectors $\pi_{.1}$ or $\pi_{.2}$ (the dashed lines) provides a utility increment EF, it does entail shifting from a riskless action to a risky situation (with conditional utility levels indicated by points D and C). For an individual with the same beliefs but characterized by a more risk-averse preference-scaling function, the vertical scaling would change so that the utility increments CJ and EF both become smaller. (The marginal utility of additional income falls faster as risk-aversion increases.) Thus a more risk-averse individual would not be willing to pay as much for the service.

The opposite case is pictured in figure 5.6. Here $x_0$, the best uninformed choice for individual $i$, is action $x_1$ which is highly risky. To keep matters simple, suppose that the information service reveals the state with certainty. Then, if the information were costless, $i$'s expected utility would rise by the amount AB. As before, let $\xi$ be the maximum that individual $i$ would pay for the message service. That is:

$$\pi_1 v^i(c_1(x_1)) + \pi_2 v^i(c_2(x_1)) \tag{5.2.25}$$
$$= \pi_1 v^i(c_1(x_1) - \xi) + \pi_2 v^i(c_2(x_2) - \xi)$$

(By assumption here, if message 1 is received the optimal action remains $x_1$, but if message 2 is received the new optimal action becomes $x_2$.)

Let $c_{s0}$ and $v^i_{s0}$ be the consumption and the utility in state $s$ with the best uninformed action, and $c_{sI}$ and $v^i_{sI}$ the consumption and utility in state $s$ given the corresponding conclusive message, after deducting the cost $\xi$. (In general, any message $m$ may imply a different best action $x_m$ and so each $c_{sI}$ would be a vector with $m$ elements. But, as defined here, $c_{1I}$ is unique since it is the consumption in state 1 when the message reveals state 1 *with certainty*, and similarly for $c_{2I}$.)

As depicted in figure 5.6, $c_{10} \equiv c_1(x_1) > c_{1I} \equiv c_1(x_1) - \xi$, so that $v^i_{10} > v^i_{1I}$. But $c_{20} \equiv c_2(x_1) < c_{2I} \equiv c_2(x_2) - \xi$, so that $v^i_{20} < v^i_{2I}$. Also, by construction, $c_{1I} > c_{2I}$. It follows that:

$$v^i_{10} > v^i_{1I} > v^i_{2I} > v^i_{20}$$

But the expected utilities of the distributions $(c_{1I}, c_{2I}; \pi_1, 1 - \pi_1)$ and $(c_1(x_1), c_2(x_1); \pi_1, 1 - \pi_1)$ are the same, as indicated in equation (5.2.25) and pictured in figure 5.6 by the intersection at point A. Thus, the no-information distribution of utilities is a *mean-preserving spread* of the full-information distribution attained after paying the maximum fee $\xi$.

From chapter 3 it follows immediately that, for any concave function $f(\cdot)$:

$$\Sigma_s \pi_s f(v^i_{sI}) > \Sigma_s \pi_s f(v^i_{s0})$$

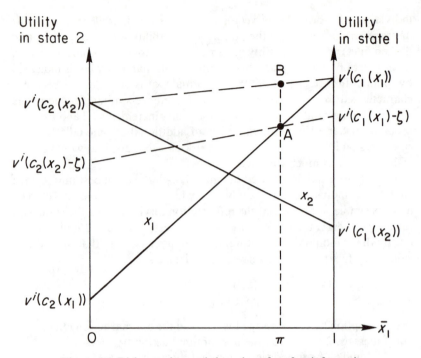

Figure 5.6  Risk-aversion and the value of perfect information

But, as noted above, if individual $j$ is more risk-averse there is some concave function $f(\cdot)$ such that $v^j(c) = f(v^i(c))$. Then:

$$\Sigma_s \pi_s v^i_{sI} = \Sigma_s \pi_s v^i_{s0} \quad \text{implies} \quad \Sigma_s \pi_s v^j_{sI} > \Sigma_s \pi_s v^j_{s0}$$

That is, if a less risk-averse individual $i$ is just indifferent as to receiving information that costs $\xi$, a more risk-averse individual $j$ would strictly prefer to receive the information at that price. Or, $j$ would be willing to pay strictly more for the information.

The key point is that, in this second example, receipt of the information is associated with shifting to a *less risky* consumption prospect. Therefore, the more risk-averse individual is willing to pay more for the message service.

## EXERCISES AND EXCURSIONS 5.2.4

### 1 The value of information

(A) An individual with logarithmic preference-scaling function believes each of two states to be equally likely. He can purchase state-claims at prices $P_1 = P_2 = 1$. Show that he will be willing to pay up to half of his wealth for conclusive information as to which state will occur.

(B) Would a more risk-averse individual be willing to pay as much? [HINT: It might help to draw the individual's budget constraint and indifference curves in state-claim space.]

### 2 The value of risky information

As in the previous exercise, there are two states. However now the price of state-1 claims is higher ($P_1 > P_2$).

(A) If the odds of state 1 satisfy:

$$\frac{\pi_1}{1 - \pi_1} = \frac{P_1}{P_2}$$

confirm that an uninformed individual would take no risk.

(B) Using a diagram, depict his final consumption if he is given conclusive information about the state. Illustrate also the maximum amount that he would be willing to pay for this information.

(C) Hence, or otherwise, show that a more risk-averse individual would not be willing to pay as much for the information.

(D) Suppose the odds of state 1 instead satisfy:

$$1 < \frac{\pi_1}{1 - \pi_1} < \frac{P_1}{P_2}$$

Confirm that an uninformed individual would accept some risk. Confirm also that, if he were to pay his reservation price for conclusive information, the riskiness of his final consumption bundle would be greater.

(E) Hence or otherwise draw a general conclusion regarding the effect of increased risk-aversion upon the value of information.

### 3 Changes in wealth

A risk-averse individual is just on the borderline of being willing to buy an information service. Suppose he becomes wealthier than before, in the sense that he now has a positive riskless endowment $c^o$ in addition to the payoffs of the various terminal actions available to him. Does being richer make him more or less willing to purchase the information service? [HINT: Does the answer have something to do with whether he has increasing, decreasing, or constant absolute risk-aversion (IARA, DARA, or CARA)?]

### 5.2.5    The worth of information: flexibility versus range of actions

In the discussion above we thought of information as being newly generated by an informational action like a sampling experiment or, alternatively, as acquired from others via a transaction like the purchase of expert opinion. But in some cases information may autonomously *emerge* simply with the passage of time, without requiring any direct action by recipients. Tomorrow's weather is uncertain today, but the uncertainty will be reduced as more meteorological data flow in, and will in due course be conclusively resolved when tomorrow arrives. Direct informational actions might still be useful, by providing knowledge *earlier*. So under conditions of emergent information a kind of indirect informational action may become available – adopting a flexible position and *waiting* before taking terminal action.

Suppose a choice must be made now between immediate terminal action and awaiting emergent information. This choice can only be interesting where there is a tradeoff between two costs: (1) a cost of waiting, versus (2) an "irreversible" element in the possible loss suffered from mistaken early commitment. (see Jones and Ostroy, 1984)

The essential idea is pictured in figure 5.7. The individual, if he decides upon immediate terminal action, has a choice among $x_1$, $x_2$, or $x_3$. As the diagram is drawn he would never select $x_1$ as his immediate terminal action, since either $x_2$ or $x_3$ has higher expected utility for any $\pi$. Given his illustrated beliefs $\pi$, the best immediate terminal choice is $x_3$ yielding expected utility F. But suppose that $x_1$ has a "flexibility" property. To wit, *after* receiving emergent information the individual can shift from $x_1$ to $x_2$, at a cost of $\xi_2$, achieving the intermediate overall utility indicated by the dashed line $x_{12}$ – or, should the information point the other way, he can shift from $x_1$ to $x_3$ at a cost of $\xi_3$ with overall utility payoff indicated by the dashed line $x_{13}$. As shown in the diagram, if message 1 is received (leading to the posterior probability vector $\pi_{.1}$) the individual would shift to $x_3$, thus attaining overall utility indicated by point D on line $x_{13}$. Similarly, message 2 would allow him to attain point C on line $x_{12}$. His expected utility is then E, exceeding the utility of the best immediate terminal action $x_3$ by an amount indicated by the distance EF.

The element of "irreversibility" appears here in the fact that line $x_{12}$ lies below $x_2$ in the range where both of these are preferred to $x_1$, and similarly

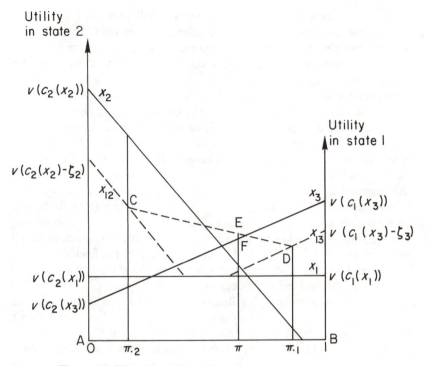

Figure 5.7 The value of flexibility

$x_{13}$ lies below $x_3$ in the corresponding range. One has to pay a price to retain flexibility, the price being that you cannot do as well as if you had made the best choice among the "irreversible" actions in the first place.

After examining the relative advantages of remaining "flexible" (of initially choosing action $x_1$ in figure 5.7) versus higher immediate return (choosing action $x_2$ or $x_3$), natural next questions to ask are: (1) Does the value of remaining flexible tend to increase or decrease as the message service employed becomes more informative? And conversely: (2) Is the value of information greater for someone having taken a flexible position? Intuitively, we would expect the answers to both questions to be affirmative. Remaining flexible is in effect like buying an option as to what later action will be taken. The more informative the message service, or the more flexible the position chosen, the greater is the value of the option. With regard to question 1, in figure 5.7 we can see immediately that a more informative message service – for which $\pi_{.1}$ would be shifted to the right and $\pi_{.2}$ to the left – would increase the height of point E (which represents the expected utility of remaining flexible) while leaving point F (which represents the expected utility of the best immediate action) unaffected. And for the converse question 2 the affirmative answer is trivially true, since having chosen either of the immediately more remunerative but "inflexible" actions $x_2$ or $x_3$ entirely eliminates the option value of later information.

Parallel questions can be asked about the effects of increasing the *range* of possible actions. We might expect the answers to be affirmative once again, since having a greater range of actions is somewhat akin to being in a more flexible position. But, it turns out, the answers as to flexibility and as to range are not at all the same. Consider first the analog of question 2 above: Does increasing the range of possible actions raise the value of information? Intuitively, we might at first think, the greater the range of actions that can be taken, the greater the value of having better information before deciding. But this overlooks a crucial difference between increasing flexibility and increasing range: when flexibility increases, the expected utility of the best "uninformed" decision remains unaffected – but an increase in the range of action can modify the results of the best *uninformed* as well as of the best *informed* decision.

The three panels of figure 5.8 illustrate some of the possibilities. In each case, to begin with there are only actions $x_1$ and $x_2$, the best initial choice being $x_2$ yielding the expected utility indicated by point F. As before, the message service $\mu$ leads to an improved expected utility E, so that the value of information is EF. In the top panel (a), a new action $x_3$ has been introduced that totally dominates the other two actions for any probability beliefs whatsoever. Since $x_3$ would be chosen in any case, this extension of the range of choice reduces the value of any message service to zero! Somewhat less extreme cases are illustrated in the other two panels. Summarizing briefly, the middle panel (b) suggests that, if the new action $x_3$ is very superior toward either boundary (e.g., when one state or the other is initially nearly certain), enlarging the range of action will indeed tend to *increase* the value of information (from EF to GF here). On the other hand, the bottom panel (c) indicates that, if the new action $x_3$ is superior mainly in the interior (i.e., when it remains very uncertain which state will obtain), the enlargement of the range tends to *reduce* the value of information. (The presence of an action that is very rewarding even under uncertainty makes it less essential to acquire information aimed at reducing uncertainty.)

The upshot, therefore, is that the effect upon the value of information of increasing the range of available actions is highly situation-dependent. It will be evident that the same holds also for the analog of question 2: having a more informative message service may either increase or decrease the value of extending the range of available actions.

Utility
in state 2

Utility
in state 1

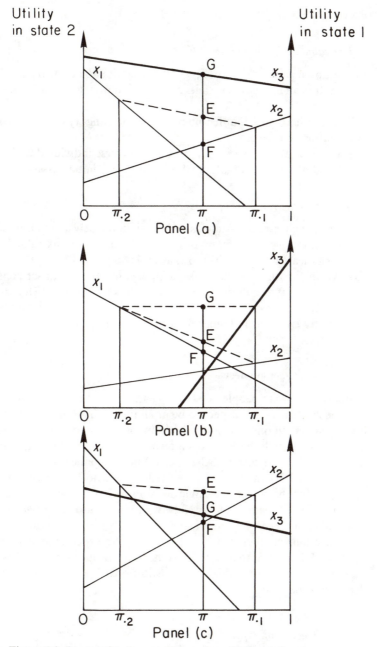

Figure 5.8  Range of actions and the value of information

EXERCISES AND EXCURSIONS 5.2.5

*1 The value of remaining flexible*

In the absence of information, $x_3$ is the optimal action. By waiting for information an individual forfeits action $x_3$ but may still choose between $x_1$ and $x_2$.

Suppose he is just indifferent between choosing $x_3$ or waiting for the information to arrive.

(A) What would an everywhere more risk-averse individual do?

(B) What about an individual who has a higher initial riskless wealth?

*2 Adding to the range of options*

(A) For the general two-state case show that, if a new action is added that is "more risky" than any of the initial feasible set, its value is higher (or at least no lower) if information is better.

(B) Again for the two-state case, suppose that the initial set consists of actions that are all risky. A new action is added that yields the same utility in each state. Is it true that the value of the new action is either strictly *lower* or no higher under superior information?

## 5.3    Multi-person decisions

Suppose a group of people must act together to make a collective decision. For the multi-personal aspect to be at all interesting there has to be some disagreement among the individuals involved as to the best choice of action. As we shall see, such disagreement may stem from (a) conflict of interests, (b) divergence of beliefs, or (c) both together.

In section 5.3.1 the choice to be made (the action to be undertaken) is wholly within the power of a single decision-maker. However, the decision-maker is in a position of possibly wanting to use information at the disposal of an *expert* – a circumstance typically involving both divergence of beliefs and conflict of interest between the expert and his client. In section 5.3.2 we turn to group decisions in the proper sense, that is, where more than one person has some "constitutional" power over the ultimate decision to be made.

*5.3.1    The use of experts*

For concreteness, suppose a decision-maker employs a weather forecaster as expert, where the two relevant states of the world are "rain" (*R*) or "shine" (S). The expert's report may take any of a number of forms, among them:

(i) "My barometer reads 30.52." Here the expert is merely reporting his data or evidence. Assuming there is no reason to doubt the accuracy of the report (more on this below), the client should treat this evidence just as if she had observed the barometer herself. Given her own prior beliefs $(\pi_R, \pi_S)$, where of course $\pi_S \equiv 1 - \pi_R$, and given her likelihood matrix $L$ for the different possible barometer readings (messages) in each possible state of the world, the decision-maker should employ Bayes' Theorem (5.2.10) to obtain her posterior probabilities $(\pi_{R \cdot m}, \pi_{S \cdot m})$. These revised probabilities would then be used in equation (5.2.1) to determine the best (utility-maximizing) terminal action.

(ii) "My probability estimate for rain is 45%." Assuming once again that there is no question about accuracy or sincerity, the expert here is providing a probability distribution which, let us suppose, is *his own* posterior distribution after reading the barometer and applying Bayes' Theorem. Thus: $(\pi_{R \cdot m}^e, \pi_{S \cdot m}^e) = (0.45, 0.55)$. In comparison with (i) above, the client is now getting the benefit of certain additional information in the form of the expert's priors and likelihood function, with which the expert's actual new evidence has been integrated. However, if as indicated here, the expert reports *only* his posterior probabilities, all this information has been confounded together in such a way that the decision-maker cannot in general uniquely infer just what barometer reading occurred. So, something has been lost as well as gained in comparison with the first type of report.

(iii) "My recommendation is, wear a raincoat." Here the expert has taken it upon himself to indicate the *action* with highest expected utility for his client, implying that he knows the decision-maker's consequence matrix $c_{xs}$ and utility function $v(c)$ as well as the appropriate posterior probabilities. Once again, the question of sincerity apart, the client is getting the benefit of additional information – conceivably, the expert might know the decision-maker's consequence matrix and utility function better than the latter does herself. But all this information has now been confounded together into a very bare and stark message, from which the decision-maker cannot in general separately extract either the expert's barometer reading or the expert's posterior probability beliefs.

Thus the expert's report might be a rather modest one, as in (i) above which leaves the decision-maker still in the position of having to do the work of determining her posterior probabilities and ultimately the best action to undertake. Or, the report might be more ambitious and purport to integrate and digest all the information needed to determine the posterior probabilities as in (ii) above or even the best action as in (iii) above.

Nevertheless, ultimately it is the client who must make the decision. If she is rational, and especially since the questions of sincerity and accuracy do always arise, cases (ii) and (iii) above are really not that different from case (i). *Any* report on the part of the expert, whatever its purported content, is really only a "message" which the decision-maker still has to weigh in accordance with her prior beliefs and likelihood matrix.[5] (In the case where an expert is being used, the likelihood matrix can more specifically be termed the client's *credence matrix* for the expert's report.) But it remains true that the actual content of the report is irrelevant for the Bayesian calculation of posterior probabilities – all the useful information that any message can provide is summarized by the likelihood matrix. An example will make this clear.

EXAMPLE 5.6: Suppose the expert will be giving a report that purports to be his posterior estimate $\pi^e_{R \cdot m}$, after consulting his private barometer, for the probability of rain (to the nearest quartile). The decision-maker still would rationally have to construct a credence matrix before she can use such a message. Matrix $L_1$ below is a possible credence matrix. In $L_1$ the client believes that when the true state is shine the expert will never fail to predict it, but that his predictions are somewhat less perfect indicators when the true state is rain. What is the basis for such beliefs? No simple answer can be given. The credence matrix would presumably depend upon the client's opinions as to the expert's character, his possible conflicting interests, prior knowledge, reliability of his barometer, etc. However arrived at, a decision-maker cannot rationally use an expert without implicitly having some such set of beliefs.

|  |  | Message | | | | | |
|---|---|---|---|---|---|---|---|
| $L_1$ |  | 0 | 0·25 | 0·50 | 0·75 | 1·0 | |
| State | $R$ | $\frac{1}{15}$ | $\frac{2}{15}$ | $\frac{3}{15}$ | $\frac{4}{15}$ | $\frac{5}{15}$ | 1·0 |
|  | $S$ | 1·0 | 0 | 0 | 0 | 0 | 1·0 |

Alternatively, suppose the expert will simply be advising the decision-maker to leave her raincoat at home (action $x_1$) or to wear one (action

[5] It might even be the case that the "expert" is producing gibberish noises, as in some of the ancient Greek oracles, or perhaps not intending to convey a message at all. Thus it was once widely believed that the author of the "Maggie and Jiggs" comic strip was providing useful stockmarket up/down predictions, via the tilt of Jiggs' cigar.

$x_2$). While we would expect there to be some correlation, the recommendation $x_2$ is not exactly equivalent to predicting a high probability of rain. What is the significance of such a recommendation for the client's decision? Again, the expert's report is only a *message*. Its weight in the final decision depends upon the client's credence matrix for this type of message, which might take a form like $L_2$ below:

|  | Message | | |
|---|---|---|---|
| $L_2$ | $x = 1$ | $x = 2$ | |
| State    $R$ | 0·4 | 0·6 | 1·0 |
| $S$ | 1·0 | 0 | 1·0 |

Two factors are generally very important in the client's estimate of the evidential significance of an expert's report: (1) the motivation for the expert to be *sincere* (to tell the truth as he sees it) and (2) the expert's motivation to invest the effort necessary to be *accurate*. These factors are, to some extent at least, subject to influence via the contractual reward structure. We will first examine here how such a reward structure can influence the sincerity of the expert's report.

Consider as before a situation where the true states of the world are rain and shine. Adopting a simplified notation for convenience here, let the *expert's belief* (posterior to any evidence he may have collected) as to the probability of rain be $p$. We will suppose that he is asked to report this probability belief; his actual report will be denoted $q$.

Let the reward structure offered to the expert (sometimes called a "scoring rule") take the linear form, where $B > 0$:

$$\begin{cases} \rho_R = A + Bq & \text{Payoff in the event of rain} \\ \rho_S = A + B(1-q) & \text{Payoff in the event of shine} \end{cases} \quad (5.3.1)$$

Assuming risk-neutrality, a self-interested expert will choose the $q$ that maximizes his own mean reward $\bar{\rho}$:

$$\begin{aligned} \underset{(q)}{\text{Max}}\, \bar{\rho} &= p(A + Bq) + (1-p)(A + B(1-q)) \\ &= A + (1-p)B + B(2p-1)q \end{aligned}$$

Since the final term is positive if and only if $p > \frac{1}{2}$, the maximizing strategy for the expert is:

If $p > \frac{1}{2}$, report $q = 1$
If $p < \frac{1}{2}$, report $q = 0$

Thus, this scoring rule does not induce sincerity on the part of a risk-neutral expert.

It has been shown (see Pearl, 1978) that there are three classes of scoring rules that will induce a risk-neutral expert to deliver a sincere report. To wit, if $q_s$ is the reported probability estimate for state $s$:

$$p_s = \ln q_s \qquad \text{Logarithmic}$$

$$p_s = 1 + 2q_s - \sum_s q_s^2 \qquad \text{Quadratic} \qquad (5.3.2)$$

$$p_s = q_s / \left[ \sum_s q_s^2 \right]^{\frac{1}{2}} \qquad \text{Spherical}$$

For example, if the expert is asked to provide a report $q$ for the probability of rain, where his true belief is $p$, the quadratic scoring rule of (5.3.2) reduces to:

$$\begin{cases} p_R = 4q - 2q^2 \\ p_S = 2 - 2q^2 \end{cases}$$

Maximizing $\bar{p}$, it may be verified that this rule leads the expert to report $q = pP$.

As we have seen, the decision-maker will in general not simply *adopt* the expert's probability beliefs. Rather, she will be revising her own probabilities in the light of her credence matrix. But, if the reward structure is such that the client can at least accept the expert's report as sincere, one source of uncertainty will have been eliminated.

The type of scoring rule so far discussed is appropriate for reports of the form (ii) described above, i.e., the expert's message purports to be his posterior probability distribution over states of the world. Alternatively, imagine that the report is to be of type (iii), consisting simply of a recommendation as to the best action $x$. Let us make the following assumptions: (1) client and expert are both risk-neutral, and (2) the expert knows that the client will indeed be adopting his recommendation. Then a very simple reward structure is appropriate:

$$p_s = \alpha c_{xs} (\alpha > 0) \qquad (5.3.3)$$

This amounts to giving the expert a "slice of the action," so that he maximizes his own expected income by recommending the action that maximizes the client's expected income.

Of course, deviations from risk-neutrality would require some revision of the optimal reward structure indicated by (5.3.3). And also, even if she thinks the expert's recommendation is sincere, the decision-maker will not always simply be adopting the recommended action. Hence the expert might be motivated to diverge from the rule in (5.3.3), in order to "fool" his client into taking what the expert believes to be the best action for both of them (in terms of maximizing expected income).

We can also see immediately that, even if the requisite conditions are met for *sincerity*, the expert may not be induced to undertake the ideal investment for achieving *accuracy*. Since the expert's slice $\alpha$ would in general be less than unity, the rule (5.3.3) would give him less than a dollar for each dollar's worth of information provided – measuring the worth to the client in terms of the increase in her expected income $\Delta E(c_{xs})$. An "ideal" effort-inducing reward structure would have to be such that, on the margin, the expert reaps the full value of his final increment of effort.[6]

### 5.3.2   Group choices[7]

A group, for our purposes, is defined by the requirement that the members are required to undertake some *joint action*. How the collective choice emerges from the preferences of the separate members depends upon the group's "constitutional" decision procedure. This might, for example, be a unanimity rule, or simple majority voting, or a weighting system that gives some members more power than others. As already indicated, the possible disagreements that can cause problems for group decision may be due to *differing beliefs* (the members hold different probability distributions for states of the world),[8] to *conflicts of interest* (the individuals derive differing benefits and costs from alternative group actions), or to both of the above. We will be showing in more detail here how the decisions of a group with regard to the acquisition and use of information are affected by disagreements on these scores.

*Conflicts of interest* may stem from differences in payoffs, differences in personal utility functions, or differences in endowments. If the available group actions distribute the payoffs differently over individuals, disagreements are evidently likely. And, even if all the actions at issue involve identical payoffs to each group member under all circumstances, there may still be disagreement owing to divergences in preference-scaling functions $v(c)$. For example, some individuals may be more risk-averse

---

[6] Incentives to induce optimal effort by an expert (or "agent") are discussed in detail in chapter 7.

[7] This section depends substantially upon the discussion in Raiffa (1968), chapter 8.

[8] Consistent with our previous discussions, differences of belief have been defined solely in terms of diverging probability distributions for states of the world. But what of possible variety of opinion among group members as to the *consequences* $c_{xs}$? We need not consider these as a separate category, since any such divergences can be reduced ultimately to assigning differing probability weights to states of the world. Suppose two individuals agree in assigning probability $\pi_s$ to state $s$, but individual $i$ says the state-$s$ consequence for the group is $c'_{xs}$ while individual $j$ says it is $c''_{xs}$. Then we should think in terms of there being two distinct states $s'$ and $s''$. Both members can now agree on describing the respective consequences as $c'_{xs}$ and $c''_{xs}$, the disagreement being that individual $i$ assigns the entire probability $\pi_s$ to the new state $s'$ (and assigns zero probability to $s''$) – while the reverse of course applies for individual $j$.

Table 5.5

| | Individual $j$'s preference-scaling for consequences | | | | | Individual $k$'s preference-scaling for consequences | | |
|---|---|---|---|---|---|---|---|---|
| | | States | | | | | States | | |
| | | (0·8) | (0·2) | | | | (0·2) | (0·8) | |
| | $i$ | $s_1$ | $s_2$ | E($v$) | | $j$ | $s_1$ | $s_2$ | E($v$) |
| Actions | $x_1$ | 10 | 5 | 9* | Actions | $x_1$ | 4 | 8 | 7·2* |
| | $x_2$ | 7 | 9 | 7.4 | | $x_2$ | 8 | 6 | 6.4 |

than others. Furthermore, even with equal division of payoff and the same $v(c)$ functions, members could still differ in utilities assigned to group actions if they possess different amounts of (or different probability distributions of) *endowed income from other sources*. For example, a risky prospect may be valued differently by two equally risk-averse group members, if for one of them the prospect is a risk-widening gamble while for the other it amounts to a risk-offsetting insurance arrangement.

One question that arises is whether there is some way of aggregating or averaging individual beliefs on the one hand, and individual utility assignments on the other hand, so that the best group action may be chosen by a collective analog of the individual expected-utility equation (5.2.1). That is, can we somehow find a *group preference-scaling function* and a *group probability estimate* permitting use of the Expected-utility Rule? The answer to this is generally negative. The following is a simple illustration.[9]

Table 5.5 consists of two matrices, one for individual $j$ and another for $k$. The matrices are in the form of table 1.1 of chapter 1, except that in the body of the matrices the consequences $c_{xs}$ have been replaced by the individual utility evaluations thereof, $v^j(c^j_{xs})$ and $v^k(c^k_{xs})$. This notation indicates that, in a choice among group actions, each self-interested individual will take note only of his own personal consequence $c^i_{xs}$ – which would be some share, though not necessarily a constant proportionate share, of the overall group payoff $\Sigma_i c^i_{xs}$ – in the light of his personal preference-scaling function $v^i(c^i)$. In the specific numerical illustration here, action $x_1$ is preferred in expected-utility terms over action $x_2$ by both individuals, using their respective probability assignments for the two states as indicated in the upper margin.

Table 5.6 is constructed in similar form, but now the body of the matrix indicates the *averaged* utilities (using equal weights) while the similarly *averaged* probability estimates are shown in the upper margin. In terms of these averages, in expected-utility terms the group seemingly prefers action

[9] Based on Dalkey (1972).

## Table 5.6

Average probabilities and utilities from table 5.5

|          |       | States |       |        |
|----------|-------|--------|-------|--------|
|          |       | (0·5)  | (0·5) |        |
|          |       | $s_1$  | $s_2$ | E($v$) |
| Actions  | $x_1$ | 7      | 6·5   | 6·75   |
|          | $x_2$ | 7·5    | 7·5   | 7·5*   |

$x_2$ over action $x_1$! While this is only a numerical instance, a similar example can be constructed to defeat any pre-assigned mode of averaging that purports to generate a group utility and a group probability for use in choosing among actions via the Expected-utility Rule.

Our interest here however is not the general problem of group decision under uncertainty, but rather the analysis of a group's *informational actions*. Can we say whether groups will invest too much or too little in acquiring information? In what follows we will first examine the consequences of differences in beliefs, and afterward turn to conflict of interests.

### Differences of opinion

If differences of opinion are the *only* source of disagreement, there is a clear result that can be stated as follows:

> Suppose states of the world are characterized by a single defining parameter (e.g., a continuous variable like a barometer pressure reading or a discrete one like election of a Republican or Democrat as President), and there are differences of belief but no conflicts of interest involved in the decision to be made. Then groups tend to invest "too much" in information (in a sense to be made explicit below).

The underlying idea is this. Consider any individual who, under the group's constitutional decision rule, is not a sole dictator. In general, then, to influence the collective choice in the direction he thinks best for the group, he will have to persuade some of the others. He might be able to persuade them, to some degree, simply by revealing his own beliefs – as in the case of the expert discussed in the previous section. But we will assume that any such mode of influence (on which, more below) has already been exploited as far as it will go, still leaving some differences of opinion. And in fact, we will assume, the only method of persuasion is through acquiring more evidence. More specifically, the question at issue is a group decision whether or not to postpone terminal action while acquiring more evidence.

Table 5.7

| $\pi_s^j$: | (0·8) | (0·2) | | |
|---|---|---|---|---|
| $\pi_s^k$: | (0·2) | (0·8) | | |
| $C$ | $s_1$ | $s_2$ | $E[v^j(c)]$ | $E[v^k(c)]$ |
| $x_1$ | 100 | −100 | 60* | −60 |
| $x_2$ | −100 | 100 | −60 | 60* |
| $x_3$ | 0 | 0 | 0 | 0 |

In this context we can now indicate the sense in which the group may invest "too much" in acquiring information. Assuming for simplicity a unanimity constitutional rule, the group may unanimously agree to obtain information that each and every member of the group would have thought not worth purchasing if he were the sole dictator, i.e., the information is acquired *solely* because, in the estimate of each and every member, it is needed in order to bring the others around to his own prior views. The key point being, of course, that each member believes that the new evidence will tend to show that his own initial beliefs were correct.

EXAMPLE 5.7: Two identically endowed individuals $j$ and $k$ have the opportunity of making a joint bet of $200 in total ($100 each) either on Seabiscuit (action $x_1$) or on War Admiral (action $x_2$) in their famous match race. The constitutional rule is unanimity, failing which the default action $x_3$ is not to bet at all. Payoffs are to be equally divided, and $j$ and $k$ each have a risk-neutral utility function so there is no conflict of interest. The racetrack is offering even money odds.

The consequence matrix $C$ envisaged by each is shown in table 5.7. If, for example, $j$ and $k$ agree to bid on Seabiscuit ($x = x_1$) and the horse wins ($s = s_1$) the payment is $400 and so each individual nets $100. If the horse loses ($s = s_2$) each individual loses his $100 bet. However, their prior probability estimates diverge as indicated: $j$ has 80% belief in a Seabiscuit victory (state $s_1$) while $k$ assigns 80% probability to War Admiral winning (state $s_2$). Since the two individuals are risk-neutral, we can set $v(c) = c$ for each of them, and thus derive the respective expected utilities of the different actions shown on the right. Since there is no unanimity, the default no-bet action $x_3$ would be the group choice.

Suppose now that a *perfect* information service becomes available, as shown by the likelihood matrix $L$ in table 5.8. Were $j$ and $k$ each in a position to bet $100 independently of one another, each would have been willing to pay only up to $100−$60 = $40 to receive the message. But, if collective bets are the only ones possible, the perfect information is worth a full $100 each. For, it leads to that amount of per-capita profit

Table 5.8

| $L$ | $m_1$ | $m_2$ | |
|-----|-------|-------|------|
| $s_1$ | 1·0 | 0 | 1·0 |
| $s_2$ | 0 | 1·0 | 1·0 |

as against the zero payoff of the default action. Thus, even if the price to the group of the information service were as high as $199, the individuals would unanimously agree to make the purchase.

The tendency toward overinvestment in information may be reversed if uncertainty has more than one dimension (see Raiffa, 1968, p. 231). Suppose for example that individual $j$ is pretty sure that the track will be muddy, *and* also that Seabiscuit does better in mud. Individual $k$ might be equally sure that the track will be dry, and that a dry track is just what Seabiscuit needs. Hence the two members may unanimously agree upon the action $x_1$, bet on Seabiscuit, as a result of compensating disagreements as to the reasons why! Resolving just *one* of the disagreements, as by investing in a message service that would conclusively indicate whether the track will be muddy, will then make it impossible to achieve unanimity as to the bet. So the parties might well unanimously refuse information that would resolve the disagreement in one dimension only, even if such information were fully accurate and free of charge.

We now turn to an issue alluded to earlier, to wit, whether in the absence of conflict of interest there is a way for initial divergences of opinion to be resolved without investing in new evidence. Divergences of beliefs at any moment of time can only result from: (i) differences in prior probability distributions, (ii) differences in the private data in hands of individuals, and/or (iii) differences in the likelihood functions for data observed in common. Suppose there are "objective" grounds for agreed prior beliefs and likelihood functions, so only element (ii) remains as the source of disagreement. Take a coin, for example. In the absence of any knowledge at all there is no basis for choosing heads over tails or vice versa – hence by an "equal ignorance" argument an *agreed prior distribution* (one assigning 50 % probability each to heads and tails) seems warranted. And, if sample evidence is acquired and there is no reason to believe that it is not a random sample from all possible tosses of the coin, an *agreed likelihood function* is required by the laws of probability. It follows then that if members of the group were to disclose all the private evidence each has at his disposal, they should ultimately end up with agreed posterior probability beliefs.

A much stronger proposition has received attention in the recent literature (see Aumann, 1976). The underlying idea is that each member of the group discloses to the others not the *evidence* at his disposal, but rather his own *personal posterior distribution in consequence of having seen his private evidence*. Then assuming that the members' priors are "common knowledge" (which means that the priors are agreed, each individual knows they are agreed, knows that the others know he knows this, etc.), it is in principle possible to work back from the disclosed posteriors to the private evidence incorporated therein.

The process can be illustrated as follows. Two individuals $i$ and $j$ are seeking consensus as to the probability $p$ of head on the next toss of a coin. They have common-knowledge prior distributions over the possible values for $p$, and specifically let the distributions assign equal prior probabilities of $\frac{1}{3}$ each to $p = 0$, $p = \frac{1}{2}$, and $p = 1$. Each person also has private evidence in the form of a single toss of the coin, and the fact that each has such private evidence is also common knowledge. (The private evidence that each possesses is an "overt secret.") Suppose that $i$ has actually observed a head and $j$ a tail. By Bayes' Theorem, $i$'s revised or posterior estimate for the probability of head on the next toss of the coin will equal $\frac{2}{3}$, while $j$'s will equal $\frac{1}{3}$. When they reveal these "first-round" posteriors to one another, each can then immediately infer the content of his partner's private evidence. In this way each comes to know that the combined sample results are one head and one tail. Using that knowledge leads them to an agreed "adjusted" posterior estimate – to wit, a 50% chance of head on the next toss.

What if the respective sample sizes were unknown to the other party? Here each must have a prior probability distribution for the other's sample size as well, which (if these are also "common knowledge") makes for a more complicated but still in principle feasible second-round set of posterior estimates. In general these will not yet be in agreement. However, from the respective weight each person attaches to his own observations in going from the direct Bayesian first-round posteriors to the combined or second-round posterior estimates, each reveals something to the other about the magnitude of his own sample. Eventually, it has been shown, this process leads to agreed final posterior estimates.

Notice, however, that the prior and the posterior distributions do not refer to the same variable. The posterior distributions, either the ones originally revealed by the parties to each other, or the "adjusted" distribution eventually arrived at, both refer to the probabilities of head versus tail. But the common-knowledge prior must refer to the distribution of the parameter $p$ of the coin, or else the process described will not in general work. (This point is often overlooked in discussions based upon Aumann's theorem.)

EXAMPLE 5.8: Individuals $i$ and $j$ have "common knowledge" that, with equal probabilities of $\frac{1}{3}$, a coin is either 2-headed ($p = 1$), fair ($p = \frac{1}{2}$), or 2-tailed ($p = 0$). Also with equal probabilities, either may draw a sample of sizes 0, 1, or 2. Individual $i$ in fact draws a sample of size 1, and observes a head. Individual $j$ draws a sample of size 2, and observes a head and a tail. (a) What first-round posterior distributions do they reveal to one another? (b) What is the agreed final posterior distribution, and how do the individuals' beliefs converge on it?

ANSWER: (a) After making his Bayesian calculation, $i$ will reveal his first-round posterior distribution (head, tail; $\frac{2}{3}, \frac{1}{3}$). And $j$ (who of course now knows for sure that the coin is fair) will reveal hers as (head, tail; $\frac{1}{2}, \frac{1}{2}$). (b) Individual $j$ can infer, with 100 % confidence, that $i$'s sample size must have been 1 (since only a head in a sample of 1 could have led to $i$'s revealed initial posterior distribution). But this hardly matters for $j$, who already knows for sure that the coin is fair. So $j$'s *revised* posterior distribution, on the basis of knowing the merged evidence, remains (head, tail; $\frac{1}{2}, \frac{1}{2}$). As for individual $i$, upon seeing $j$'s initial posterior distribution he cannot be sure whether $j$ has observed nothing at all (sample of size 0) or else has obtained 1 head and 1 tail in a sample of size 2. But upon seeing $j$'s *revised* distribution, and noticing that $j$ has made no change to take account of $i$'s first-round posterior distribution, individual $i$ will also realize that the latter must have been the case. So $i$ will come into agreement with $j$'s revised posterior solution.

There is one puzzling aspect of the process just described. It requires complete sincerity on the part of each member, which could scarcely occur unless their interests are entirely harmonious. But, if so, surely it would have been more efficient and economical for each person simply to disclose his own private sample evidence to his partner! It is only when conflict of interest plays a role that inferring the other party's private evidence from his actions – a process that may be called "information leakage" – really becomes an interesting issue.[10]

*Conflicts of interest*
When conflicts of interest are present, an enormous range of possibilities arise, even if we keep things simple by excluding any initial divergences of belief. Two possibilities will be illustrated here: in the first there is unanimous agreement to reject perfect *public* information, even if free, while in the second, *private* information is similarly rejected.

EXAMPLE 5.9: Suppose a community of 1,000 identical individuals is offered the following deal. Provided there is unanimous agreement to

[10] The problem of "leakage" will be discussed in chapter 7.

the proposal, 999 of them will receive unlimited wealth and glory, but one single member of the group must die. And, no-one can know in advance who the unlucky person will be. This deal *might* (see our discussion of the " value of life " in chapter 2) win unanimous acceptance, and let us suppose that such is the case. But, before that decision is actually effectuated, the members of the community are offered another option: they can now choose to be informed in advance, without charge, as to who the unlucky person would be. Evidently, if the members of the community were unanimously willing to accept the initial gamble, they must now be unanimously *unwilling* to accept the information even if free – since receiving it would destroy the possibility of unanimous agreement upon the gamble.

In the example just given there was no prior difference of opinion, and – the information being perfect and public – there could be no posterior difference of opinion either. The information would be rejected because, while there is a *latent* conflict of interest among the members, that conflict is not relevant for the gamble made in a state of ignorance. Disclosure of the information makes the latent conflict of interest an actual one, thereby (under the group's constitutional rule of unanimity) precluding acceptance of a desired gamble.

EXAMPLE 5.10: Two individuals *i* and *j* are to predict whether the top card of a shuffled deck is black or red. The predictions are made in sequence: *i* guesses first, and then *j* (after hearing *i*'s guess). If they make the same prediction each wins $1, whether their prediction turns out correct or not. If they disagree, the one who is correct wins $3, and the other nothing. Risk-neutrality is assumed.

Since *i* has no basis for preferring one or the other color, he will choose at random. Then *j* will choose the opposite color, so each will have an expected gain of $1.50.

Now suppose someone offers, without charge, an arrangement whereby the first-mover *i* can know the actual color of the top card before he makes his prediction. Evidently, the parties would be unanimous in rejecting that arrangement – even *i* as the "beneficiary." For, with that information individual *i* would choose the correct color, *j* would then make the same choice, and they would each gain only $1 rather than an expectation of $1.50.

In this latter example there was no prior difference of opinion. Furthermore, even though, under the arrangement proposed, the evidence would be privately conveyed only to the first chooser, its content could readily be inferred by the other party. Thus, the second example is not really different from the first. In the absence of information the conflict of interest – the $(3, 0)$ versus $(0, 3)$ payoff possibilities if opposite colors are chosen – remains only latent, since in a state of ignorance each party expects to earn the same $1.50 on average. Supplying the information once again makes the conflict of interest actual, leading to a revised group action in which they both can reap only their second-best payoffs of $1 each.

Finally, let us consider the *interaction* of conflict of interest with differences of belief. Here also a proposition of some generality can be stated, somewhat to the opposite effect of the earlier proposition that applied when *only* differences of opinion are involved:

> In groups characterized by conflicts of interest as well as differences of belief, the acquisition of information tends to be avoided.

This proposition can only be stated in "tends to" form, since the actual choice to avoid acquiring information will depend upon the constitutional decision rule as well as upon the specifics of the situation. The following example will illustrate:

EXAMPLE 5.11: Returning to the match race between Seabiscuit and War Admiral, suppose now that individuals $j$ and $k$ will simply be betting $100 at even money against one another. Since $j$ attaches 80% probability to Seabiscuit winning, and $k$ similarly for War Admiral, each has a $60 expectation of gain. The group decision is whether or not to collectively incur the cost of staging the race, with the cost to be evenly split. Evidently, the decision would be unanimous in favor of doing so at any per-capita cost less than $60. Returning once again to a theme familiar from the examples above, free information in the form of an infallible public forecast (as to which horse will win) would be unanimously rejected.

This example represents an interesting twist in comparison with the preceding. In the earlier examples, despite a latent conflict of interest, under conditions of ignorance the parties were nevertheless able to agree upon a risky action that (in an *ex-ante* sense) was "really" advantageous to all. While in actuality not all would gain – one person out of the 1,000 would lose his life in the "unlimited wealth and glory" example, and there would be a loser as well as a winner if opposite colors were chosen in the card-color example – *viewed in advance* the gain was worth the risk, in everyone's estimate. The twist here is that, while it remains the case that each regards the gain as worth the risk, even viewed in advance the risky action cannot be "really" advantageous to all. In the Seabiscuit/War Admiral match, if anything is paid for information, the group as a whole must lose. In fact, if the true probabilities were known, and assuming some degree of risk-aversion, one or both of them would refuse to bet. Knowing this, the parties would of course unanimously agree not to undertake the cost of staging the race. The upshot then is that, where there are conflicts of interest, each member of a group might prefer not receiving information that would destroy his chance to exploit (what he perceives to be) the erroneous beliefs of others.

Recalling that these examples do not purport to cover all the issues involved, we can nevertheless summarize the indications provided:

1 "Excessive" group investment in information tends to take place (in comparison with what each and every member of the group regards as optimal) when, given differences of belief but no conflicts of interest, each member believes that the additional evidence is likely to convince others of the correctness of his own opinions (as to what is best for the group).

2 "Insufficient" investment in formation tends to take place (as illustrated by our examples in which even perfect and free evidence would be unanimously refused) in a number of cases, among them: (a) in the absence of conflict of interests, where agreements as to the best group action are grounded upon *compensating disagreements* in different dimensions of uncertainty; (b) where, with agreed beliefs as to an uncertain event, resolving the uncertainty makes it impossible for the group to undertake an ex-ante unanimously preferred risky action; (c) where, with differences of opinion and conflicts of interest as well, elimination of the differences of opinion would make it impossible to undertake a group action whereby each expects to profit at the expense of the others.

## REFERENCES AND SELECTED READINGS

Aumann, Robert J., "Agreeing to Disagree," *Annals of Statistics*, 4 (1976), 1236–9.

Blackwell, D., "Equivalent Comparison of Experiments," *Annals of Mathematics and Statistics*, 24 (June 1953), 265–72.

Clark, E. H., "Multipart Pricing of Public Goods," *Public Choice* (1971), 19–33.

Dalkey, Norman, "An Impossibility Theorem for Group Probability Functions," The RAND Corporation Paper, P-4862 (June 1972).

Goffman, E., *Strategic Interaction*, University of Pennsylvania Press, 1969.

Groves, Theodore, "Incentives in Teams," *Econometrica*, 41 (1973), 617–31.

Jones, R. A. and Ostroy, J. M., "Flexibility and Uncertainty," *Review of Economic Studies*, 51 (January 1984), 13–32.

Marschak, J. and Miyasawa, K., "Economic Comparability of Information Systems," *International Economic Review*, 9 (June 1968), 337–74.

Pearl, Judea, "An Economic Basis for Certain Methods of Evaluation Probability Forecasts," *International Journal of Machine Studies*, 10 (1978), 175–83.

Raiffa, Howard, *Decision Analysis*, Reading, MA: Addison-Wesley, 1968.

Stiglitz, J. C. and Radner, R., "A Nonconcavity in the Value of Information", in Marcel Boyer and Richard Kihlstrom (eds.), *Bayesian Models in Economic Theory*, Elsevier Science Publications, 1984, pp. 33–52.

# 6   The economics of emergent public information

In part I, dealing with the *economics of uncertainty*, after covering the "terminal" decisions of the individual in chapters 1 through 3 we moved on in chapter 4 to consider market equilibrium. And similarly here in the realm of the *economics of information*: having examined individuals' "non-terminal" (informational) decisions in chapter 5, we now turn to the analysis of the market equilibrium generated thereby.

A first key distinction is between *public* and *private* information. If an information service provides public information, decision-makers throughout the economy will be attempting to revise their portfolios in the light of their changed beliefs. Consequently, asset prices will adjust. In particular, market values will rise for those assets paying off more handsomely in states of the world now regarded as more likely. If on the other hand the message provided is strictly private, an informed party may be able to profit in various ways without any noticeable effect upon prices. However, as we shall see, almost always there are processes at work tending to "publicize" private information. Sometimes this occurs because the informed individual can gain by intended disclosure of his data, for example if he sells it to others. Or sometimes there may be unintended leakage into the public domain – owing, perhaps, to the fact that the uninformed can monitor the behavior of those who are informed. These more difficult problems are reserved for later chapters; only fully public information will be examined in this chapter.

A second distinction is between *produced* and *emergent* information. Information is produced when, for example, new evidence is generated by a sampling experiment conducted by the agent himself or by an expert on his behalf. Ordinarily, some cost is incurred in producing such data, i.e., in acquiring such a "message service." But it may also be that information emerges costlessly, simply with the passage of time. Tomorrow's weather is uncertain today, but the uncertainty will be reduced as more meteorological data flow in and will in due course be conclusively resolved when tomorrow arrives. Where emergent information is anticipated, an individual might choose a kind of passive informational action – simply waiting before making his terminal move. Just such a choice was examined in chapter 5 under the heading of "flexibility."

This chapter will be devoted to the market consequences of emergent public information. When such information is anticipated, economic agents may have to contemplate market exchanges in two distinct rounds: trading that takes place *prior to* and trading *posterior to* announcement of the news. The equilibria of the two trading rounds will generally be inter-related, but the form of the relationship depends importantly upon the completeness of the prior and the posterior market regimes.

## 6.1 The inter-related equilibria of prior and posterior markets

### 6.1.1 Complete Contingent Markets

In dealing with the *economics of uncertainty* in part I of the book, we mainly considered models with $S$ states of the world and a single consumption good $C$ ("corn"). A regime of Complete Contingent Markets (CCM) was said to exist when all the distinct contingent claims $c_s$ are separately tradable at prices $P_s$. Alternatively, a regime of Complete Asset Markets (CAM) – for which a sufficient condition is that there exist $A = S$ distinct assets characterized by linearly independent state payoff vectors – can of course generate the same results as CCM regimes, but this complication will generally be set aside in the current chapter.

Assuming an interior solution, the familiar optimality condition for the individual (The Fundamental Theorem of Risk-Bearing) and the consequent equilibrium condition for prices take the form:

NON-INFORMATIVE EQUILIBRIUM (single good)

$$\pi_s v'(c_s)/\pi_{\hat{s}} v'(c_{\hat{s}}) = P_s/P_{\hat{s}} \qquad (6.1.1)$$

where $s$ and $\hat{s}$ are any two states and $v'$ is the marginal utility evaluated at the indicated consumption quantity for each state. To achieve this condition, individuals in a world of uncertainty will generally have undertaken both productive transformations and market exchanges, with the effect of modifying the aggregate economy-wide risk and also redistributing it among the various agents.

But now we will be assuming that emergent public information is expected to arrive before the close of trading. Let us call this an 'informative situation." In general, in an informative situation market exchanges may take place both prior to and posterior to receipt of the message. Thus the prospective arrival of public information divides trading into a prior round and a posterior round. In the prior round, the individual makes exchanges toward a "trading portfolio"; in the posterior round, he will be making any other exchanges required to convert his trading portfolio into an optimal "consumption portfolio." We will generally be assuming, however, that the message is not timely enough to permit *productive* adaptations to the changed probability beliefs. For example, a message as to increased flood danger in the rainy season may come in time to affect the market terms of flood-insurance transactions, but not in time to permit construction of dams or dikes.

There is a remarkable theorem about the relationship between the prior-round and the posterior-round equilibria for informative situations in CCM trading, which we will approach in easy stages.

*Model 1* (*single consumption good, conclusive information*): Suppose it is known that the arriving message will be *conclusive* as to which state of the world will obtain, and also *exhaustive* in the sense that to each and every state $s$ corresponds exactly one message $m$. (In what follows the term "conclusive" will be taken to mean "conclusive and exhaustive.") Notice first that, if there really were only a single consumption good $C$, there would be no scope at all for trading in the posterior round. Once it becomes known that some particular state $\hat{s}$ will obtain, income claims $c_s$ for any other state $s \neq \hat{s}$ lose all value. In these circumstances, it is evident, all desired portfolio adjustments must be undertaken in the prior round of trading. In other words, one's trading portfolio will necessarily be his consumption portfolio. Assuming everyone can draw this logical inference, equation (6.1.1) that applied for the economics of uncertainty (i.e., in a non-informative situation) remains applicable here even though now we are dealing with an informative situation.

The symbols $P^O$ and $P^I$ will be used here to distinguish the *prior-round* and *posterior-round* prices determined in informative situations, while $P$ without superscript signifies the price vector associated with a non-informative situation. Then, with a single consumption good $C$ and anticipated arrival of conclusive information, the condition for *prior-round* equilibrium in an informative situation is (where $s$ and $\hat{s}$ are any two states):

INFORMATIVE EQUILIBRIUM (single good)

$$\pi_s v'(c_s)/\pi_{\hat{s}} v'(c_{\hat{s}}) = P_s^O/P_{\hat{s}}^O = P_s/P_{\hat{s}} \tag{6.1.1'}$$

RESULT OF MODEL 1: In an informative situation, given the conditions: (i) Complete Contingent Markets (CCM), (ii) anticipated conclusive information, and (iii) a single consumption good, there can be no posterior-round trading. The equilibrium prior-round state-claim price ratio $P_s^O/P_{\hat{s}}^O$ will therefore be the same as the ratio $P_s/P_{\hat{s}}$ that would have obtained in a non-informative situation where no message at all was expected.[1]

## EXAMPLE 6.1

An economy consists of two equally numerous types of individuals under pure exchange. Everyone has the preference-scaling function $v(c)$ $= \ln c$, where $c$ represents the quantity of a single consumption good $C$ ("corn"). There are just two states ($s = 1, 2$) with probabilities $(\pi_1, \pi_2) =$ $(0.6, 0.4)$. For type-$i$ individuals the state-distributed endowment is $(\bar{c}_1^i, \bar{c}_2^i) = (400, 0)$; for type-$j$ individuals it is $(\bar{c}_1^j, \bar{c}_2^j) = (0, 160)$. In a non-informative situation under pure exchange, equation (6.1.1) becomes:

$$\frac{0.4(1/c_2^i)}{0.6(1/c_1^i)} = \frac{P_2}{P_1} = \frac{0.4(1/c_2^j)}{0.6(1/c_1^j)}$$

Making use also of the budget equations on each side, it is easy to verify that the solution is:

$$(c_1^i, c_2^i) = (200, 80) = (c_1^j, c_2^j)$$
$$P_2/P_1 = 5/3$$

Also, of course, $P_2^O/P_1^O = P_2/P_1$

As indicated in the example, since everyone realizes that no *posterior* exchanges will be possible, in the prior round each person trades to his optimal risk-bearing portfolio.

*Model 2 (G consumption goods, conclusive information)*: Still assuming that the emergent information will be conclusive as to which state of the world is going to obtain, consider now the more general case of multiple consumption goods $g = 1, \dots, G$. In a *non-informative* situation under a CCM regime there would be trading in the $GS$ different claims $c_{gs}$ – entitlements to a unit of good $g$ contingent upon the occurrence of state $s$ – at prices $P_{gs}$. The equilibrium conditions would include ratios of the following two types, where $s$ and $\hat{s}$ are any two states and $g$ and $\hat{g}$ are any two goods:

NON-INFORMATIVE EQUILIBRIUM CONDITIONS ($G$ goods)

$$\frac{\pi_s \, \partial v(c_{1s}, \dots, c_{Gs})/\partial c_{gs}}{\pi_{\hat{s}} \, \partial v(c_{1\hat{s}}, \dots, c_{G\hat{s}})/\partial c_{g\hat{s}}} = \frac{P_{gs}}{P_{g\hat{s}}}$$

$$\frac{\partial v(c_{1s}, \dots, c_{Gs})/\partial c_{gs}}{\partial v(c_{1s}, \dots, c_{Gs})/\partial c_{\hat{g}s}} = \frac{P_{gs}}{P_{\hat{g}s}} \tag{6.1.2}$$

---

[1] We are assuming here that the equilibrium of the equation system is unique. Otherwise, it is conceivable that a non-informative situation would lead to one of the set of possible equilibria, and an informative situation to a different member of the same set. This complication is set aside in our analysis.

Turning to the *informative* situation, a CCM regime in the prior round would again involve trading in the $GS$ different claims $c_{gs}$ – now determining a set of equilibrium prior prices $P^O_{gs}$. After the conclusive message arrives that some particular state $\hat{s}$ will obtain, *posterior* trading among the $G$ commodity claims $c_{g\hat{s}}$ that remain valid could now take place, leading to a set of equilibrium prices $P^I_{g\hat{s}}$. (Whereas in the case of a single consumption good, in contrast, posterior trading was impossible – since only the single claim $c_{\hat{s}}$ remain valid.)

Nevertheless, an analogous two-part result continues to hold for the equilibrium of the informative situation: (1) The prior-round equilibrium price ratios will be the same as those which would have been arrived at in a non-informative situation, and (2) all the needed portfolio adjustments will occur in the prior round, i.e., there will be no posterior-round trading.[2] Thus at the prior-round equilibrium:

INFORMATIVE EQUILIBRIUM ($G$ goods, prior-round trading)

$$\frac{\pi_s\, \partial v(c_{1s}, \ldots, c_{Gs})/\partial c_{gs}}{\pi_{\hat{s}}\, \partial v(c_{\hat{s}}, \ldots, c_{G\hat{s}})/\partial c_{g\hat{s}}} = \frac{P^O_{gs}}{P^O_{g\hat{s}}} = \frac{P_{gs}}{P_{g\hat{s}}}$$

$$\frac{\partial v(c_{1s}, \ldots, c_{Gs})/\partial c_{gs}}{\partial v(c_{1s}, \ldots, c_{Gs})/\partial c_{\hat{g}s}} = \frac{P^O_{gs}}{P^O_{\hat{g}s}} = \frac{P_{gs}}{P_{\hat{g}s}}$$

$$(6.1.2')$$

These are identical with equations (6.1.2) except for the explicit indication that the price ratios with superscript O (the equilibrium ratios for prior-round trading in an informative situation) are the same as those without superscript (the equilibrium price ratios for a non-informative situation).

To get at the intuition underlying these results, let us first step back a moment. Imagine that the parties had all calculated and traded in the belief that the situation was a *non-informative* one, and thus had arrived at the equilibrium indicated by conditions (6.1.2) above. Now, quite unexpectedly, new conclusive information that some particular state $s$ is going to obtain is in fact publicly revealed. At this point it would be possible for any or all of the parties to engage in re-trading, on the basis of their changed probability beliefs in the light of the information received. But the equilibrium condition represented by the lower equation of (6.1.2) evidently continues to hold *if* the price ratios $P_{gs}/P_{\hat{g}s}$ all remain unchanged and the parties engage in no further trading.

Looking at this in more detail, the upper row of equations (6.1.2) represents, for some single good $g$, the conditions for optimal balance between contingent claims valid under different states of the world. Evidently, all these claims will now have become worthless except for those

---

[2] As indicated in the preceding footnote, we are setting aside the possibility that the equilibrium may not be unique. Henceforth, this qualification will be taken as understood without further repetition.

involving the specific state $s$. Hence, $c_{g\hat{s}}$ claims for any $\hat{s} \neq s$ will be non-tradable; anyone stuck with them will be unable to get anything valuable in exchange. As for the lower row, those equations represent the balance between any two goods $g$ and $\hat{g}$, given the particular state $s$. The point to notice is that in these equations no probabilities appear. Hence, if the initial trading satisfied the conditions in the lower equations, knowing now that the probability of the specific state $s$ has become unity in no way calls for additional trading.

We have seen that the *unanticipated* arrival of conclusive information, no matter what its content, cannot lead to any posterior trading. It then follows that, even when the arrival of such public information is *anticipated in advance*, rational individuals would not expect to be able to make advantageous use of it for posterior trading. The equations in the lower row of (6.1.2′) represent how each person would balance in advance between holdings of different goods, *contingent upon* some state $s$ having obtained. Knowing afterward that state $s$ had in fact obtained leaves the situation unchanged since all individuals had already contemplated and allowed for that contingency in their prior-round trading.

Thus, if all individuals have chosen their prior-round trading portfolios in accordance with (6.1.2′), these conditions remain satisfied without anyone revising his portfolio in the posterior round of trading. So:

$$\frac{P_{gs}^{\mathrm{I}}}{P_{\hat{g}s}^{\mathrm{I}}} = \frac{P_{gs}^{\mathrm{O}}}{P_{\hat{g}s}^{\mathrm{O}}} = \frac{P_{gs}}{P_{\hat{g}s}} \tag{6.1.3}$$

RESULT OF MODEL 2: Given the conditions: (i) CCM, (ii) anticipated conclusive information, and (iii) $G$ consumption goods, once again there will be no posterior-round trading. Also, the posterior-round price ratios and the prior-round price ratios will again be the same as the price ratios that would have held in a non-informative situation.

However, this conclusion is based on a crucial implicit assumption: that all the traders in their prior-round decisions *correctly forecast* what the equilibrium posterior price ratio will be. Such forecasts will be termed "self-fulfilling predictions" (SFP). SFP forecasts are easy to make here, since equation (6.1.3) tells us that the price *ratio* between any pair of goods $g$ and $\hat{g}$ contingent upon state $s$ will remain unchanged after receipt of the message that state $s$ will obtain. However, if traders mistakenly thought that posterior price ratios would diverge from those in the prior round, they would be led to make "erroneous" prior-round transactions, affecting the prior-round market equilibrium and thus requiring corrective posterior-round trading. In short, the price ratios will remain unchanged in posterior-round trading *if* in the prior round everyone believed that would be the case. The SFP forecast will be correct, provided that everybody joined in making it. (This corresponds to one of the meanings of the mysterious phrase "rational expectations" to be discussed below.)

### EXAMPLE 6.2

There are two consumption goods: a risky commodity $F$ ("fruit") and a non-risky commodity $N$ ("nuts"). Let everyone have the preference-scaling function $v(c_n, c_f) = \ln (c_n c_f)$ or, in more compact notation, $v(n, f) = \ln (nf)$. And all agree on the state-probabilities $(\pi_1, \pi_2) = (0{\cdot}6, 0{\cdot}4)$.

Once again assume there are two equally numerous types of individuals. Individuals of type $i$ have only a non-risky "nuts" endowment that is constant over states: $\bar{n}_1^i = \bar{n}_2^i = 200$. And those of type $j$ have only a risky "fruit" endowment, varying over states: $\bar{f}_1^j = 400$, $\bar{f}_2^j = 160$. Equations (6.1.2) become:

$$\frac{\pi_1 \dfrac{\partial v^k}{\partial n_1^k}}{P_{n1}} = \frac{\pi_2 \dfrac{\partial v^k}{\partial n_2^k}}{P_{n2}} = \frac{\pi_1 \dfrac{\partial v^k}{\partial f_1^k}}{P_{f1}} = \frac{\pi_2 \dfrac{\partial v^k}{\partial f_2^k}}{P_{f2}}, \quad \text{for } k = i, j$$

For our example with logarithmic preferences:

$$\frac{0{\cdot}6}{P_{n1} n_1^k} = \frac{0{\cdot}4}{P_{n2} n_2^k} = \frac{0{\cdot}6}{P_{f1} f_1^k} = \frac{0{\cdot}4}{P_{f2} f_2^k}, \quad \text{for } k = i, j \tag{6.1.4}$$

These equations are satisfied, and supply and demand equated, if each and every individual trades to the consumption portfolio $(n_1^k, n_2^k, f_1^k, f_2^k) = (100, 100, 200, 80)$. Substituting in the preceding equation, and inverting:

$$\frac{P_{n1} 100}{0{\cdot}6} = \frac{P_{n2} 100}{0{\cdot}4} = \frac{P_{f1} 200}{0{\cdot}6} = \frac{P_{f2} 80}{0{\cdot}4}$$

Choosing the normalization $P_{n1} + P_{n2} = 1$, so that the numeraire is a certainty claim to good $N$, the equilibrium contingent-claims price vector for non-informative trading is $P = (P_{n1}, P_{n2}, P_{f1}, P_{f2}) = (0{\cdot}6, 0{\cdot}4, 0{\cdot}3, 0{\cdot}5)$.

Now consider an *informative* situation, where a conclusive message is anticipated as to which state will obtain, and let us assume all traders make the correct "self-fulfilling predictions" SFP as to the posterior prices. If the prior-round informative price vector $P^O$ is exactly the same as the non-informative price vector $P$, then everyone can achieve in prior-round trading the same portfolios as in the non-informative situation. Thus: $P^O \equiv (P_{n1}^O, P_{n2}^O, P_{f1}^O, P_{f2}^O) = (0{\cdot}6, 0{\cdot}4, 0{\cdot}3, 0{\cdot}5) = P$.

As for the *posterior* price ratios under each of the two contingencies, the equilibrium solutions are:

*In the event that state 1 obtains:*

$$\frac{\partial v(n_1,f_1)/\partial f}{\partial v(n_1,f_1)/\partial n} = \frac{1/200}{1/100} = 0\cdot5 = \frac{P^I_{f1}}{P^I_{n1}} = \frac{P^O_{f1}}{P^O_{n1}}$$

*In the event that state 2 obtains:*

$$\frac{\partial v(n_2,f_2)/\partial f}{\partial v(n_2,f_2)/\partial n} = \frac{1/80}{1/100} = 1\cdot25 = \frac{P^I_{f2}}{P^I_{n2}} = \frac{P^O_{f2}}{P^O_{n2}}$$

One or the other of these conditions would be applicable in posterior trading. Since under the SFP assumption *these posterior price ratios are correctly forecast when the parties make their prior-round trading decisions*, no utility-improving portfolio revision will be needed or possible in the posterior round.

Suppose now that the above equilibrium fails to hold, owing to individuals not making the correct self-fulfilling predictions SFP. Would that imply a loss of Pareto-efficiency? In a world of pure exchange, there can be no change in the social aggregates. So, to the extent that "erroneous" transactions take place in the prior round, such trading will lead only to wealth redistributions. In that case the availability of posterior markets, among the G claims $c_{gs}$ still valid after state s is known to obtain, suffices to ensure that efficient portfolio revision will still occur. But if *production* could be taking place before the message arrives, the erroneous prior-round prices caused by the failure of individuals to make the correct SFP would also imply mistaken prior-round productive decisions, and thus a real efficiency loss. In light of this, we shall at times refer to the equilibrium attained under CCM, given self-fulfilling predictions, as the "efficient" equilibrium. (Recall, however, that we are ruling out productive adaptations *after* the message arrives, such as building a dam upon learning that a flood will occur.)

We can now state the theorem proper, which holds also in the much more general case of messages that are not "conclusive."

PROPOSITION 6.1: Under conditions of emergent public information, with a CCM regime in the prior round of trading and assuming self-fulfilling predictions SFP, after arrival of the message all the still-relevant price ratios will remain unchanged, so that no posterior-round trading need take place. Furthermore, these prior-round prices provide the correct guidance for efficient prior-round productive decisions.

The generalization to the case of non-conclusive messages follows very easily from the above, except that we must now redefine prior-round

Complete Contingent Markets to mean trading in the *GSM* distinct claims $c_{gsm}$ – each being an entitlement to a particular good $g$ in state $s$ provided that message $m$ was received. After the close of prior-round trading some particular message $\hat{m}$ will have arrived, so that only the *GS* claims of type $c_{gs\hat{m}}$ retain any value. It is not difficult to verify, once again assuming that traders correctly forecast that all the relevant posterior-round price ratios will remain unchanged, that no-one will be able to engage in any advantageous posterior revision of the portfolios chosen in prior-round trading.

The practical implications of this proposition may seem disturbing. Can it really be the case that, in an informative situation, a posterior round of trading is never necessary? Such a conclusion would be unwarranted, because the results obtained to this point have been conditioned upon the assumption of a regime of Complete Contingent Markets in both prior and posterior rounds of trading. This assumption will be relaxed in the sections following.

### 6.1.2   Incomplete regimes of markets

Admittedly, it was rather unrealistic of us to keep multiplying the number of tradable commodities, as required by the CCM assumption. Starting with the "natural" case of markets in $G$ goods (that is, markets for certainty claims only), we then allowed $GS$ markets for goods × states and finally $GSM$ markets for goods × states × messages. Issues of great practical importance arise when we consider less complete regimes of markets. However, to maintain simplicity, when we examine different market regimes in what follows we will limit the discussion to the special case of fully *conclusive* information. Then the set of $M$ messages collapses into the set of $S$ states, so that a complete market regime would require trading only in the $GS$ claims $c_{gs}$.

Several possible patterns of market incompleteness will be discussed here:

### Numeraire Contingent Markets (NCM)

Suppose that, with $G$ goods and $S$ states, prior-round trading can take place but only in contingent claims to the single good $g = 1$, which we can select to be the numeraire good. Thus in the prior round there are $S$ tradable $c_{1s}$ entitlements. After receipt of a conclusive message that some particular state $s$ will obtain, in the posterior round everyone will be choosing a preferred consumption basket by trading among the $G$ remaining valid entitlements $c_{gs}$.

PROPOSITION 6.2: Under conditions of emergent conclusive information, in an NCM regime of trading the same efficient allocation as under CCM can be achieved, provided that self-fulfilling predictions SFP may be assumed (Arrow,1964). However, in general, posterior as well as prior trading will be required.

Since the NCM regime has only $S$ tradable claims in the prior round and $G$ in the posterior round, while the CCM regime had (assuming conclusive information) $GS$ claims in the prior round and $G$ again in the posterior round, this proposition correctly suggests that the CCM regime provided more than the minimally necessary trading opportunities for efficiency.

To understand proposition 6.2, consider the budget constraints in the NCM regime. In the prior round each individual can trade only numeraire (commodity 1) claims. Let $\hat{c}^i_{gs}$ denote the typical element of individual $i$'s *trading portfolio*: his holdings at the end of the prior round. If the prior-round price vector is $P^O_1 = (P^O_{11}, \ldots, P^O_{1S})$, his prior-round budget constraint is:

$$\sum_s P^O_{1s} \hat{c}^i_{1s} = \sum_s P^O_{1s} \bar{c}_{1s}, \text{ for } g = 1 \tag{6.1.5}$$

$$\hat{c}^i_{gs} = \bar{c}^i_{gs}, \text{ for } g \neq 1.$$

In the posterior round, when the state is revealed, each individual can then retrade between his claims to commodity 1 and his claims to other commodities. If the posterior price vector in any state $s$ is $P^I_s = (P^I_{1s}, \ldots, P^I_{gs})$, then if state $s$ obtains individual $i$ has the posterior budget constraint (where $c^i_{gs}$ denotes the typical element of his *consumption portfolio*):

$$\sum_{g=1}^G P^I_{gs} c^i_{gs} = \sum_{g=1}^G P^I_{gs} \hat{c}^i_{gs}, \ s = 1, \ldots, S \tag{6.1.6}$$

Whatever state of the world $s$ obtains, in the posterior market prices can be normalized by setting the price of numeraire (good 1) claims equal to the prior-round price, that is:

$$P^O_{1s} = P^I_{1s}, \ s = 1, \ldots, S$$

Under this normalization, $P^I_{1s}$ can be substituted for $P^O_{1s}$ in the prior-round budget constraint (6.1.5). Then, summing (6.1.6) over $s$:

$$\sum_g \sum_s P^I_{gs} c^i_{gs} = \sum_g \sum_s P^I_{gs} \bar{c}^i_{gs}$$

This is the budget constraint for the CCM regime where, for each $s$, the state-claim price vector $P^O_s$ has been replaced by the relevant $P^I_s$. Thus the CCM regime can indeed be replicated by a NCM regime in which $P^I = P$. (That is, where the posterior-round prices, in those markets that remain active, are the CCM equilibrium prices.)

The intuition behind proposition 6.2 should now be clear. In the prior round each individual is able to transfer wealth across states. As long as prices in the prior round equal the CCM prices for the numeraire good in a non-informative situation, the exchange rates across states are the same in the two regimes. Then, in the posterior market, if prices are once again equal to the contingent-claim prices, each individual can purchase the same final consumption bundle as in the CCM regime.

Two separate factors mainly affect the parties' trading portfolios, i.e., their desired holdings of $\mathring{c}_{1s}$ claims, and thereby motivate prior-round trading in the NCM regime: (1) *belief disparities*: an individual attaching a relatively high probability to any particular state $\hat{s}$ will of course want to end up holding a relatively large amount of $\mathring{c}_{1\hat{s}}$ claims; (2) *endowment disparities*: an individual whose endowment of goods in general is disproportionately weighted toward some $\hat{s}$ will attempt to balance his contingent posterior wealths by selling off some of his $\bar{c}_{1\hat{s}}$ claims, i.e., by trading to make $\mathring{c}_{1\hat{s}} < \bar{c}_{1\hat{s}}$. He may even find it optimal to set $\mathring{c}_{1\hat{s}} < 0$, that is, he can take a short position in good 1.

In what follows, it will be convenient to concentrate attention upon an illuminating special case in which: (i) all beliefs are agreed, (ii) the numeraire (good 1) is riskless (that is, each and every person holds a numeraire endowment that is uniform over states), and (iii) there is a common preference-scaling function that is additively separable in the numeraire and non-numeraire goods. The last assumption implies that the marginal utility of each good in any state will depend only upon its own quantity in the consumption portfolio, i.e., there is no complementarity in preference among goods.

The following example illustrates a case where, absent either belief or endowment value disproportionalities, no *prior-round* trading at all takes place under an NCM regime.

## EXAMPLE 6.3
Return to the conditions of example 6.2, with type-$i$ individuals possessing a non-risky endowment $(\bar{n}_1, \bar{n}_2) = (200, 200)$ of good $N$ ("nuts"), where $N$ is the numeraire (so that $P_{n1} + P_{n2} = 1$), while type-$j$ individuals have a risky endowment $(\bar{f}_1, \bar{f}_2) = (400, 160)$ of good $F$ ("fruit"). Each person has utility function $v = \ln(nf)$ and probability beliefs $(\pi_1, \pi_2) = (0.6, 0.4)$ as before.

From proposition 6.2 we know that the NCM regime can replicate the CCM regime. But, assuming self-fulfilling predictions, what trading if any will occur in the prior round?

*Answer*: From example 6.2, the equilibrium CCM prices are:

$$(P_{n1}, P_{n2}, P_{f1}, P_{f2}) = (0.6, 0.4, 0.3, 0.5)$$

In addition, we saw there that the first-order conditions for expected-utility maximization by any individual $k$ can be written:

$$\frac{0\cdot6}{P_{n1}n_1^k} = \frac{0\cdot4}{P_{n2}n_2^k} = \frac{0\cdot6}{P_{f1}f_1^k} = \frac{0\cdot4}{P_{f2}f_2^k}, \quad \text{for } k = i,j$$

It follows that expenditure on each commodity in state 1 is $(0\cdot6)/(0\cdot4) = 1\cdot5$ times expenditure on each commodity in state 2. So total wealth allocated to state-1 expenditure is 1.5 times wealth allocated to state-2 expenditure.

Suppose that prices are the same in the active markets of the NCM regime – the prior-round markets for good-1 claims in all states and the posterior-round markets for all goods in whatever state $\hat{s}$ obtains. Suppose that there is no trading in the prior round. A type-$i$ individual with endowment $(\bar{n}_1^i, \bar{n}_2^i, \bar{f}_1^i, \bar{f}_2^i) = (200, 200, 0, 0)$ then has a state-1 wealth of $P_{n1}\bar{n}_1^i = 120$ and a state-2 wealth of $P_{n2}\bar{n}_2^i = 80$. Similarly, a type-$j$ individual with endowment $(\bar{n}_1^j, \bar{n}_2^j, \bar{f}_1^j, \bar{f}_2^j) = (0, 0, 400, 160)$ has a state-1 wealth of $P_{f1}\bar{f}_1^j = 120$ and a state-2 wealth of $P_{f2}\bar{f}_2^j = 80$. So, in the absence of any prior-round trading, each individual would be allocating his wealth over states exactly as in the CCM regime. It follows that under the conditions of this example no prior-round trading is necessary to achieve the equilibrium of the NCM regime, which in turn replicates the equilibrium of the CCM regime.

More generally, however, under the constrained NCM regime individuals will need to trade in both rounds. The next example will illustrate.

EXAMPLE 6.4
Holding to the other conditions of example 6.3, assume now the following endowment distributions:

Type $i$:   $(\bar{n}_1, \bar{n}_2, \bar{f}_1, \bar{f}_2) = (0, 90, 280, 160)$
Type $j$:   $(\bar{n}_1, \bar{n}_2, \bar{f}_1, \bar{f}_2) = (200, 110, 120, 0)$

Note that the individual endowments of commodity $N$ ("nuts") are no longer riskless. However, the social totals of endowed claims are the same as in examples 6.2 and 6.3 – $(\bar{N}_1, \bar{N}_2, \bar{F}_1, \bar{F}_2) = (200, 200, 400, 160)$. So the *aggregate* $N$-endowment remains riskless.

With CCM trading in a *non-informative* situation, the price vector would remain $(P_{n1}, P_{n2}, P_{f1}, P_{f2}) = (0\cdot6, 0\cdot4, 0\cdot3, 0\cdot5)$ as in example 6.2. Moreover, since the overall wealths are the same as in the previous examples, the CCM equilibrium consumption portfolios must be the same. So, in accordance with the earlier examples, the market value of consumption in state 1 is $1\cdot5$ times that in state 2, for both type-$i$ and type-$j$ individuals.

Now consider a NCM regime. Suppose a type-$i$ individual moves in the prior round to a trading portfolio $(\mathring{n}_1, \mathring{n}_2)$ in $N$-claims. (Of course, he cannot modify his endowment of $F$-claims in the prior round.) If the prior-round state-contingent prices of $N$ remain the same as in the CCM regime, then $P_{n1}(\mathring{n}_1 - \bar{n}_1) = P_{n2}(\bar{n}_2 - \mathring{n}_2)$, or $0.6\,\mathring{n}_1 = 0.4\,(90 - \mathring{n}_2)$.

Given such a trade, if a type-$i$ individual is to replicate the CCM outcome his wealth in state 1 must be 1·5 times his wealth in state 2. Thus:

$$\frac{0.6\,\mathring{n}_1 + 0.3(280)}{0.4\,\mathring{n}_2 + 0.5(160)} = 1.5$$

Solving simultaneously with the preceding equation leads to the type-$i$ individual's trading portfolio:

$$(\mathring{n}_1^i, \mathring{n}_2^i, \mathring{f}_1^i, \mathring{f}_2^i) = (60, 0, 280, 160)$$

For the type-$j$ individual on the other side of this trade, the trading portfolio will be:

$$(\mathring{n}_1^j, \mathring{n}_2^j, \mathring{f}_1^j, \mathring{f}_2^j) = (140, 200, 120, 0)$$

This also meets the condition that wealth in state 1 is 1·5 times wealth in state 2. The NCM therefore once again replicates the results of the CCM regime. However, as this example indicates, if individuals' endowed portfolios differ in such a way that one person's endowment is weighted toward state 1 and the other's toward state 2, prior-round trading under NCM will be required to replicate the CCM equilibrium.

We can now consider the question of what constitutes a minimally sufficient range of markets to achieve efficiency (continuing to assume, for simplicity, that the emergent information is conclusive). With a CCM regime in the prior round, the range of markets ($GS$ tradable claims) is so ample that no *posterior* trading is needed at all. The NCM regime, in contrast, having provided only the minimally necessary $S$ tradable claims in the prior round, must still generally allow for trading among the $G$ surviving claims in the posterior round.

In might seem from this discussion that CCM in the prior round provides a wastefully "excessive" number of markets in comparison with the minimally sufficient NCM: $SG + G$ in comparison with $S + G$. However, such a conclusion is not really warranted when we take into account the plausibility of the SFP assumption in each of the two regimes. Under CCM the SFP forecasts are easy to make, being simply "no change." That is, the prediction for any state $\hat{s}$ is that the posterior price ratios will be the same as the corresponding prior contingent-claim price ratios. But, under NCM, even when probability beliefs are agreed, the correct forecasts *are not in general computable from data available to traders in the prior round* (Radner, 1968). Thus, while technically possible, it is really quite implausible that the NCM regime could reproduce the efficient outcomes achievable under CCM.

Absent self-fulfilling predictions under the NCM regime, what would be the actual outcome for the prior-round and posterior-round equilibrium? In our model, we simply cannot say. In contrast with the CCM regime where there is a theoretical basis for predicting the posterior price ratios, under NCM we do not as yet have a theory for forming the required prior expectations as to posterior prices. (This question will be reconsidered when the topic of "rational expectations" is taken up later in the chapter.)

### No prior-round markets

What if prior-round markets do not even exist? This corresponds to the case where information arrives before any exchanges at all have taken place, i.e., while the parties are all still at their endowment positions. The clearest instance of such a situation is where the arrival of news is totally "unanticipated."[3]

This situation has aroused considerable interest, in view of the surprising implication that incoming public information could be socially disadvantageous, in the sense that everyone in the economy might be willing to pay something *not* to have the message revealed! Think of a group of traders who, in prior-round trading, would have balanced their risks by mutually insuring one another against fire. If they have not yet done so, a message service offering conclusive but "premature" information as to whose houses would burn down might well be rejected by everyone, even if free. In effect, the arrival of the message before the opening of markets would make it impossible for people to diversify their risks. (On the other hand, if the early arrival of the information permitted more effective *productive* adaptations, for example protective measures against fire, this socially valuable consequence of timely information must be weighed against the adverse effect upon individuals' ability to spread risks.)

### Futures and spot markets (F&SM)

The CCM and NCM regimes both allow trading in state-contingent claims. Such trading does take place to some extent in the actual world, directly as in some insurance transactions or indirectly via trading in assets

---

[3] Note that this interpretation does not refer to the *content* of the news or to the message probability $q_m$. "Unanticipated" means that no-one had expected any message at all to arrive.

like corporate shares, which can be regarded as packages of state-claims. But most trading represents exchange of *unconditional* commodity claims – rights to receive one or more units of some good regardless of the state of the world. For such unconditional trading in commodities, the prior-round transactions correspond to dealings in "futures" markets and the posterior exchanges after arrival of the information to dealings in later "spot" markets.

Under such a Futures and Spot Markets (F&SM) regime, it will be assumed, in the prior round futures trading takes place in all the $G$ unconditional claims for the various goods,[4] while the posterior round allows for re-trading of the same claims in spot markets. Since it is reasonable to assume that $G < S$ (there are many more conceivable contingencies than goods), it is evident that the $G + G$ markets in two rounds of trading under F&SM cannot in general achieve the same efficiency as the $S + G$ markets under NCM – not to mention the $GS + G$ markets under CCM.

This negative conclusion is mitigated by two considerations, however. First, since society incurs costs when more markets are provided, the inefficiency due to incompleteness of markets will to some extent be counterbalanced by the savings in transaction costs. And second, our analysis has been oversimplified in assuming just a single prior and a single posterior round, i.e., that message arrival is a one-time event. More generally, less-than-conclusive bits of information will be emerging repeatedly as time progresses, permitting multiple rounds of trading before the final realization of the state of the world. (These two problems – the efficient number of markets to provide, and the degree to which multiple rounds of markets can overcome market incompleteness in any single round – post formidable intellectual difficulties which we will not attempt to address here.)

A number of the important features of the F&SM regime will be clarified in the discussion of *speculation* that follows.

EXERCISES AND EXCURSIONS 6.1

*1 Trading in anticipation of partial information*

Write down the *non-informative* and the *informative* equilibrium conditions if the information provided by the message service is less than conclusive. Can you justify proposition 6.1 for this case?

---

[4] In actuality, effective futures markets exist only for a small subset of the commodities traded in spot markets.

## 2 The value of withholding public information

Given the endowments and other assumptions of example 6.1, would individuals of type $i$ or type $j$ be willing to pay something *not* to have the information as to what state of the world will obtain revealed "prematurely" (before prior-round trading)? What about the circumstances of the other text examples?

## 3 Differences of belief

In examples 6.3 and 6.4 in the text, individuals had diverging endowments but agreed beliefs. Consequently their motivation to engage in prior-round NCM trading was solely to balance endowment risks over states. Holding to the assumption that they share the same preference-scaling function $v(n,f) = \ln(nf)$, suppose now they all have identical nuts–fruit endowments $(\bar{n}_1, \bar{n}_2, \bar{f}_1, \bar{f}_2) = (100, 100, 200, 80)$ but their probability beliefs diverge. In particular, let type-$i$ individuals attach probability 0·5 to state 1 while type-$j$ individuals attach probability 0·6 to that state. So the parties, if they trade at all in the prior round, do so only in order to reflect their differing beliefs as to the likelihood of the two states.

Maintaining the other assumptions of the text examples, would the *posterior*-round prices remain the same as before? What prior-round NCM trading, if any, will take place? Will each individual still be attempting to equalize contingent posterior wealths over states?

## 6.2    Speculation and futures trading

Up to this point we have assumed that individuals merely *adapt* to present and predicted future prices in choosing utility-maximizing consumption portfolios. In some cases, however, individuals can do even better, or at least might believe they can do so, by adopting *speculative* trading positions before emergence of the anticipated public information.

The theory of speculation is still subject to considerable controversy. One of the difficulties is that some authors use the term "speculation" for what is really *arbitrage* – that is, commitments taking advantage of momentary price differentials over space or time, under conditions of market disequilibrium. Consider, for example, the debate over the question "Does speculation tend to stabilize prices?" A premise underlying much of this debate is that prices are initially moving along some arbitrarily specified price path, e.g., a sine curve, before speculators enter. According to one side of the debate, speculators will buy when the price is *low* and sell when it is high, thus tending to smooth out the sine wave. Alternatively, it might be postulated that they buy when the price path is *rising* and sell when it is falling, in which case the effect could be to increase the amplitude of the price fluctuations.[5]

But where does the initial price path, postulated by both sides of the debate, come from? It seems to represent an arbitrary transient pattern without any basis in economic fundamentals. In terms of the comparative-statics *equilibrium* approach employed in our analysis throughout, an initial price path can never come out of thin air. Any time-pattern of prices must be the resultant of underlying economic fundamentals, of supply-demand forces. One possibility might be seasonal variation of supply. If the sine wave represents a continuous moving equilibrium of prices as supply varies over the annual cycle, there is no basis for speculators to enter the market at all – either to smooth or to amplify the price fluctuations. Thus the price path postulated in this debate, a "bubble" that does not reflect any economic fundamentals, may generate *arbitrage* opportunities but these must not be confused with speculative commitments in an equilibrium model.

A second type of error is to confuse speculation with storage over time or carriage over space. Storage and transportation are productive processes, whereas speculation is purely an exchange activity.[6] A party engaged in production might sometimes also want to take a speculative position, but the two activities are not the same.

For our purposes, speculation is purchase with the intention of re-sale or sale with the intent of re-purchase – where the uncertainty of the later spot price is the source of possible gain or loss. A regime of Futures and Spot Markets (F&SM) will be assumed, the two rounds of trading being separated by the anticipated arrival of new public information. Thus speculation is trading in the prior round (in "futures markets"), with a view to re-trading in the posterior round (in subsequent "spot markets"). However, as it turns out, distinguishing the speculative motive proper from other possible reasons for engaging in futures trading raises some subtle issues that are better postponed. Our initial emphasis will therefore be on the broader question of the determinants of *participation in futures markets* generally.[7]

In an F&SM regime, on the basis of their beliefs as to what the incoming message is going to reveal, in the prior round of trading individuals exchange unconditional claims to commodities $g = 1, ..., G$ in order to arrive at optimal *trading portfolios*. This prior trading is associated with

[5] See, for example, Friedman (1960) and Baumol (1957).
[6] In the Soviet Union, newspapers used to report the imposition of jail sentences for the crime of "speculation." In most cases, it appears, these illegal activities were forms of production: carrying goods over time or distance, or breaking bulk, to the advantage of the final consumers.
[7] The analysis that follows is based in part upon J. Hirshleifer (1977).

and determines a set of equilibrium futures prices $P_g^0$. (Notice that, while decision-makers engaging in prior trading necessarily have beliefs about what the later spot prices are going to be, such traders are not envisaging a single arbitrary initial price path. Rather, in an uncertain world they must contemplate *alternative* contingent price paths, each such pattern being the consequence of the supply/demand fundamentals characterizing one of the possible states of the world.) After arrival of the anticipated message, the parties revise their beliefs and then possibly engage in further posterior exchanges in the spot markets in order to arrive at their final *consumption portfolios*. This posterior trading will of course determine the vector of equilibrium posterior-round or spot prices $P_g^1$.

The best-known theory of futures markets is due to Keynes (1930) and Hicks (1946), who emphasized the *price risk* faced by economic agents and their *differential risk-aversion* with regard to bearing that risk. In the prior round (futures trading), they argued, relatively risk-tolerant "speculators" enter to accept the price risk that relatively risk-averse "hedgers" want to divest. For example, a grower of wheat does not know whether the ultimate spot price of wheat will be high or low. So he hedges his price risk by selling his crop today in the futures market, realizing a known futures price from a speculator. Technically, the speculator takes a "long" position in the futures market, while the grower goes "short" in futures (though of course he is "long" the underlying good). Assuming normal risk-aversion, the Keynes–Hicks analysis implies that over time speculators will benefit from a mean positive excess of spot price over futures price – so-called "normal backwardation" – as their reward for bearing the price risk.

Controversy persists as to whether or not the statistical evidence confirms the presence of normal backwardation. Later researchers in the Keynes–Hicks tradition have however brought out that hedgers can in principle be on either side of the futures market. Instead of a grower, consider a miller facing an uncertain purchase price for wheat. To hedge his price risk a miller would *buy* futures (take a long position). Then speculators need bear only the imbalance between the commitments of "short hedgers" and "long hedgers." Since this imbalance could go either way, the risk-compensating average price movement between futures and spot markets could similarly go either way.

On the other hand, in fundamental opposition to the Keynes–Hicks tradition, Holbrook Working (1953, 1962) denied that there need be any systematic difference as to risk-tolerance between so-called speculators and hedgers, or even that these categories could be strictly distinguished at all. In Working's view, *differences of belief* rather than *differences in risk-tolerance* are the primary motivators of futures trading.

To anticipate a bit, we will be demonstrating here that both of these elements, risk-transfer and belief differences, may play a role in futures trading, though sometimes interacting in rather unexpected ways. And, in addition, there are at least two other crucially important factors: *divergences in endowments* and the *elasticity of demand* for the final product.

As a crucial analytical point, the Keynes–Hicks tradition is seriously in error in its sole concentration upon the risk of price fluctuations. For the economy as a whole, the ultimate source of risk is, mainly, the stochastic variability of supply under alternative states of the world. Turning to the individual agents, it follows that their trading decisions will generally be governed by *quantity risk* (the variability of crops in the different states of the world) as well as by *price risk* (the corresponding variability of crop prices) (McKinnon, 1967). Indeed, it is evident, price risk is for the most part only a derivative consequence of the underlying uncertainty as to the actual supply quantity (whether the crop will be good or bad).[8] Furthermore, for the economy as a whole, price and quantity risks always tend to be offsetting. For example, when the crop of a representative wheat-grower is big (good news), the wheat price he receives will be low (bad news). As a result, a grower with an endowed quantity risk might well find it preferable *not* to hedge in the futures market against the offsetting price risk.

Analytically, the crucial differences among the CCM, NCM, and F&SM regimes are reflected in the prior-round individual budget constraints. Letting superscript-O signify prior-round quantities (elements of the "trading portfolio") or prices, the budget equations take the respective forms:

### PRIOR-ROUND BUDGET CONSTRAINTS

$$\sum_g \sum_s P_{gs}^O c_{gs}^O = \sum_g \sum_s P_{gs}^O \bar{c}_{gs} \qquad \text{CCM}$$

$$\sum_s P_{1s}^O c_{1s}^O = \sum_s P_{1s}^O \bar{c}_{1s} \qquad \text{NCM} \,(g = 1 \text{ is numeraire})$$

$$\sum_g P_g^O g^t = 0 \qquad \text{F\&SM}$$

In the F&SM equation, $g^t$ represents the quantity of good $g$ *purchased* in the prior round (or *sold*, if $g^t < 0$), this amount being the same regardless of state of the world. Thus, for each and every state:

$$c_{gs}^O \equiv \bar{c}_{gs} + g^t$$

---

[8] Of course, price risk could also reflect uncertainties on the demand side, e.g., whether or not consumers' tastes are shifting away from wheat bread.

In contrast with (6.1.2) or (6.1.2′) for the CCM regime, the F&SM optimality conditions reduce to the $G-1$ equations:

$$\frac{\Sigma_s \pi_s \, \partial v(c_{1s}, \ldots, c_{Gs})/\partial c^O_{gs}}{\Sigma_s \pi_s \, \partial v(c_{1s}, \ldots, c_{Gs})/\partial c^O_{\hat{g}s}} = \frac{P^O_g}{P^O_{\hat{g}}}$$

## EXAMPLE 6.5

Returning again to the conditions of example 6.3, assume now an F&SM regime. That is, individuals are permitted to exchange only certainty claims to commodities. Given an informative situation in such a world, the individuals of type $i$, with endowment $(\bar{f}_1, \bar{f}_2) = (400, 160)$ – suppliers of "fruit" $F$ – face both quantity risk and price risk. However, since the fruit price will be high when the fruit quantity they have available to sell is small, and vice versa, these risks are more or less offsetting. The type-$j$ individuals with riskless "nuts" endowment $(\bar{n}_1, \bar{n}_2) = (200, 200)$ face no quantity risk but still have price risk, since the posterior price ratio of nuts versus fruit will depend upon which state ultimately obtains.

Just as for the NCM regime of example 6.3, here also the F&SM equilibrium involves zero prior-round trading – in this case, zero trading of certainty commodity claims (futures) rather than of contingent numeraire claims. The logic is very similar. As before, given the homothetic preference-scaling function $v(n,f) = \ln(nf)$, the posterior-round equilibrium price ratios (which are also the correct SFP forecasts for guiding prior-round trading decisions) are $P^I_{f1}/P^I_{n1} = 0.5$ and $P^I_{f2}/P^I_{n2} = 1\cdot25$ for the two possible posterior states of the world. Since the parties already have state-balanced endowment distributions, if they refrain from trading in the prior (futures) round they will, in posterior-round (spot) trading, be able to achieve the same consumption portfolios as under CCM in example 6.2. Specifically, $i$ and $j$ can both achieve $(n_1, n_2, f_1, f_2) = (100, 100, 200, 80)$. Thus, in this case again a restricted trading regime leads everyone to the same efficient final consumption portfolios as the efficient CCM regime.

Of course, for this to come about the prior-round (futures) price ratio between fruit and nuts will have to be such that neither party wants to trade. It turns out that this equilibrium price ratio (where supply and demand are equal at zero trading) is $P^O_f/P^O_n = 0\cdot8$ – or, letting $N$ be the numeraire so that $P^O_n = 1$, then $P^O_f = 0\cdot8$ is the equilibrium futures price of the risky commodity $F$. Why? Recall that, in the CCM regime of example 6.2, the prior-round prices were $(P^O_{n1}, P^O_{n2}, P^O_{f1}, P^O_{f2}) = (0\cdot6, 0\cdot4, 0\cdot3, 0\cdot5)$. Thus a certainty claim to nuts could be bought or sold for $P^O_{n1} + P^O_{n2} = 0\cdot6 + 0\cdot4 = 1\cdot0$ while a certainty claim to fruit could be bought or sold for $P^O_{f1} + P^O_{f2} = 0\cdot3 + 0\cdot5 = 0\cdot8$. Since the prior-round price ratio $(P^O_{f1} + P^O_{f2})/(P^O_{n1} + P^O_{n2}) = 0.8$ supported a no-trading prior-round equilibrium even when the very ample CCM trading regime was available, the same price ratio will also be consistent with zero prior-round ("futures") trading in the less complete F&SM regime.

The possibly puzzling feature of this example, that a no-prior-trading result is achieved even though the F&SM regime is not in general minimally sufficient to replicate the efficient solution of a CCM regime, calls for further comment. Note that, while the F&SM regime provides only $G + G$ markets whereas the minimally sufficient NCM provides $S + G$ markets, in our numerical examples $G = S = 2$. Thus, in the situation of the example (but not in general) even the F&SM regime was minimally complete. Had we considered, say, an example with two goods but three states of the world, then even under the SFP assumption it would not have been generally possible to achieve the efficient CCM portfolios under F&SM.

While example 6.5 is a special case, it demonstrates that the presence of price risks on one or both sides of the market need not dictate futures trading. For the suppliers of the risky commodity $F$ in this example, the price risks and quantity risks are exactly offsetting, the actual revenue (in numeraire units) from sales being the same in either state: $200 \times 0.5 = 100 = 80 \times 1.25$. Put another way, the postulated preference functions implied an aggregate demand curve for "fruit" with unitary elasticity. Thus, there is price risk and quantity risk, but the two offset so as to eliminate all *revenue* risk.

### A more "realistic" model[9]

The general-equilibrium model described above is unrealistic in a number of significant respects. A more realistic model, making use of some strategic simplifications that correspond to known features of actual markets, will cast additional light upon the forces governing futures-market participation. In the actual world, some (in fact, the overwhelming majority) of potential traders are effectively excluded from futures markets by *transaction costs*. In this respect there is a crucial asymmetry between the situations of typical consumers and typical suppliers of goods. Suppliers tend to be specialized in producing some particular commodity, while consumers generally are rather diversified purchasers of a great many commodities. Transaction costs with a substantial fixed component, independent of the size of transaction,[10] will therefore deter the smaller-scale futures trading of consumers more than the larger-scale futures

[9] The analysis here is based mainly upon D. Hirshleifer (1990).
[10] Even if explicit brokerage charges are strictly proportional to volume, the costs of learning and of establishing trading connections will necessarily have a large fixed component.

trading of suppliers. This fact may open up a niche for speculators, to compensate for the absence of consumers on the demand side of futures markets.

Specifically, let us now distinguish among three classes of agents: (1) consumers, (2) "growers" (suppliers of the risky commodity $F$), and (3) speculators. Consumers are endowed only with the non-risky numeraire commodity $N$. Owing to their diversified consumption patterns and the presence of transaction costs, by assumption *the consumers never engage in futures trading*. The suppliers, endowed with a risky distribution of $F$, and the speculators, endowed with a riskless amount of $N$, may trade in futures – but in doing so are only interested in maximizing final wealth measured in units of $N$. Thus, any wealth reshuffling between growers and speculators due to trading gains and losses will have no impact upon the aggregate spot-market demand function for $F$ in any state of the world. In effect, the growers and speculators are sufficiently small in number and/or similar in tastes that any wealth redistributions due to their possible profits and losses do not affect final market prices.

Under these assumptions, it can be shown, when the demand for the risky commodity is *inelastic* (so that the price risk is not fully offset by the countervailing quantity risk) then, as contended in the Keynes–Hicks theory, suppliers will be motivated to take a short position in prior-round trading and the speculators a corresponding long position. And, in these circumstances, there will be "normal backwardation," i.e., the speculators will be rewarded for bearing the price risk. But this conclusion in no way depends upon the speculators being especially risk-tolerant; the endowment disparities alone make it mutually advantageous for the two types of agents to share the underlying risk. If *in addition* the speculators are relatively more risk-tolerant, they will however take an even bigger long position while requiring less reward, thus reducing the normal backwardation of prices.

What if demand is elastic rather than inelastic? Then, paradoxically, the growers will take a long futures-market position while speculators will go short! The suppliers are motivated to increase their exposure to *price* risk, because with elastic demand their endowed price risk is not large enough to offset their endowed *quantity* risk. Where this holds, the reverse of normal backwardation – "contango" – would be expected to hold. Speculators will be rewarded for taking a short rather than a long position in futures.

### EXAMPLE 6.6

There are 1,000 type-$i$ "growers", with endowment $(\bar{f}_1^i = 400, \bar{f}_2^i = 160)$ as in examples 6.2 and 6.3. And similarly there are 1,000 type-$j$

"speculators" with endowment ($\bar{n}_1^j = \bar{n}_2^j = 200$) of the non-risky commodity $N$.

As for the consumers, they begin with an endowment of the riskless numeraire good $N$ and will be trading only in the spot (posterior-round) markets. Denoting the posterior-round price of $F$ as $P_{fs}^{I}$ in numeraire units, suppose the aggregate state-distributed consumer demand for $F$ is:

$$Q_{fs} = 200,000 \, (P_{fs}^{I})^{\eta}$$

where $\eta$ is the price elasticity.[11] All parties agree upon the state-probabilities $\pi_1 = 0\cdot6$ and $\pi_2 = 0\cdot4$.

By hypothesis, growers and speculators are interested only in their final state-distributed consumption vectors of the numeraire good $N$. Specifically, for the suppliers $v^i(n^i) = \ln{(a^i + n^i)}$, while a corresponding equation holds for the speculators. Larger values for the parameters $a^i$ and $a^j$ represent greater risk-tolerance: for the suppliers it will always be assumed that $a^i = 0$ while for the speculators $a^j$ may either equal or exceed zero. The problem is to determine the amount of futures trading and the equilibrium futures price $P_f^O$ for the risky good.

As a first step, this simplified model permits easy direct computation of the spot (posterior round) prices in the two possible states of the world. For example, if the elasticity of demand is $\eta = -1$, aggregate demand for fruit in state $s$ is $200,000/P_{fs}^I$, while aggregate supply is $400,000$ in state 1 and $160,000$ in state 2. The equilibrium spot prices in the posterior round must be $P_{f1}^I = 0\cdot5$ and $P_{f2}^I = 1\cdot25$ – once again, exactly as in examples 6.2 and 6.4.

Assuming that the SFP condition holds, so that all traders correctly forecast these contingent later spot-market prices, a method of solution is to use equation (2.1.10), the Risk-bearing Theorem for Asset Markets. This will determine the respective desired trading portfolio holdings of $F$ and $N$, now regarded as "assets" generating ultimate consumption quantities $n_s$ in the two states of the world. For the type-$i$ suppliers, we can write:

$$\frac{z_{f1}\,\pi_1\,v_i'(a^i + n_1^i) + z_{f2}\,\pi_2\,v_i'(a^i + n_2^i)}{P_f^O} = \frac{z_{n1}\,\pi_1\,v_1'(a^i + n_1^i) + z_{n2}\,\pi_2\,v'(a^i + n_2^i)}{P_n^O}$$

$$(6.2.1)$$

With obvious modifications, a corresponding equation will hold for the individuals of type $j$. Letting $N$ be the numeraire so that $P_n^O = 1$, the $z_{fs}$ on the left-hand side, the contingent "yields" per unit of asset $F$, are

[11] An exercise at the end of this section indicates how such a demand function can be derived from underlying preferences.

Table 6.1. *Speculators' futures trading, futures prices, and mean of spot prices for risky good* (F)

|  |  | Unit-elastic demand $(\eta = -1)$ | Inelastic demand $(\eta = -\frac{1}{2})$ | Elastic demand $(\eta = -2)$ |
|---|---|---|---|---|
| Speculators equally risk-tolerant $(a^j = 0)$ | Speculators' purchases of $F$ in futures market | 0 | 66·03 | −116·28 |
|  | Futures price | 0·8 | 0·6538 | 0·8959 |
|  | Expectation of spot price | 0·8 | 0·775 | 0·871 |
| Speculators more risk-tolerant $(a^j = 50)$ | Speculators' purchases of $F$ in futures market | 0 | 71·84 | −130·20 |
|  | Futures price | 0·8 | 0·6676 | 0·8933 |
|  | Expectation of spot price | 0·8 | 0·775 | 0·871 |

nothing but the posterior prices: $z_{f1} = P^I_{f1}$ and $z_{f2} = P^I_{f2}$. (I.e., in each state the posterior price of $F$ represents the amount of $N$ that a unit of $F$ will buy.) For asset $N$, of course, the "yields" are simply $z_{n1} = 1 = z_{n2}$.

Let $f^t$ be the number of unconditional $F$-claims sold in the futures (prior-round) market by type-$i$ to type-$j$ individuals. With $P^O_n = 1$, type-$i$ individuals purchase $P^O_f f^t$ units of $N$ in the prior round so as to have a portfolio of $(P^O_f f^t, \bar{f}^i_s - f^t)$ if the state is $s$. Since a type-$i$ individual only consumes $N$, he trades in the posterior-round spot market so as to make his final consumption in state $s$ equal to:

$$n^i_s = P^O_f f^t + P^I_{fs}(\bar{f}^i_s - f^t) \qquad s = 1, 2$$

Similarly, type $j$'s final consumption in state $s$ is:

$$n^j_s = \bar{n}^j_s + f^t(P^I_{fs} - P^O_f) \qquad s = 1, 2$$

Substituting into (6.2.1) for the type-$i$ individuals (growers) yields an equation with two unknowns – $P^O_f$ and $f^t$. Substituting into the corresponding first-order condition for type-$j$ (speculators) yields a second equation in these two unknowns. Solutions for particular parameter values are given in table 6.1.

In each panel of the table, the top row represents the variable $f^t$ (the prior-round quantity traded by each grower-speculator pair), the middle

row the variable $P_f^{O}$ (the futures-market price of the risky good), and the
bottom row the mathematical expectation of the posterior prices.

As in example 6.4, when the demand elasticity is unity ($\eta = -1$) there
is no futures-market trading at all at the equilibrium prior-round price
of the risky good, $P_f^{O} = 0.8$. Since this equals the mathematical
expectation of the posterior prices, the "backwardation" is zero. For
inelastic demand ($\eta = -1/2$), where the price risk dominates, speculators take a long position ($f^t > 0$). Of course, the growers are
correspondingly short in the futures market, but they will be making
crop deliveries to meet their short commitments. So to that extent they
have been relieved of price risk. This re-shuffling of the price risk will be
greater, the more risk-tolerant are the speculators and the more risk-
averse the growers. Normal backwardation will correspondingly be
greater or smaller. With elastic demand ($\eta = -2$), on the other hand, the
speculators actually *sell short* the risky commodity. The interpretation is
left as a challenge to the reader.

The "realistic" model of this section has illustrated that risk-transfer
considerations, in association with differential risk-tolerances, may indeed
play a role in futures-market equilibrium as originally contended by
Keynes and Hicks. However, owing to the offsetting nature of the price and
quantity risks, the results are highly sensitive to the distribution of
endowments and to the demand elasticity in the posterior-round spot
markets. In consequence, it is definitely not true that speculators always
step in to bear the price risks, or that backwardation will necessarily be
observed.

Turning now to *differences of beliefs*, instead of providing a full
equilibrium analysis we will illustrate here only the qualitative directions of
effect. Specifically, under the simplified realistic model of this section we
will be asking: Given an initial equilibrium where prices are determined in
accordance with agreed or concordant beliefs as to the state-probabilities
held by almost everyone, how will individual traders with "deviant"
beliefs trade in the futures market and choose consumption portfolios in
the later spot market? It will be convenient to start right off with an
example.

EXAMPLE 6.7
Under the conditions of the previous example, employing the simplified
"realistic" model, consider only the unit-elastic case where the futures
price for the risky commodity $F$ was determined to be $P_f^{O} = 0.8$ while the
later contingent spot prices are $P_{f1}^{I} = 0.5$ and $P_{f2}^{I} = 1.25$ for states 1 and
2, respectively. These prices are dependent upon the agreed prior beliefs
$\pi_1 = 0.6$ and $\pi_2 = 0.4$ as to the state-probabilities. The question concerns

Table 6.2. *Futures market long* ($f^t > 0$) *or short* ($f^t < 0$) *positions as functions of endowments and beliefs*

| Endowment $(\bar{n}_1, \bar{n}_2, \bar{f}_1, \bar{f}_2)$ | Beliefs ($\pi_1$) | | |
|---|---|---|---|
| | "Optimist" (0·7) | Concordant (0·6) | "Pessimist" (0·2) |
| (I)   (100, 100, 200, 80) | −111·11 | 0 | 444·44 |
| (II)   (0, 0, 400, 160) | −111·11 | 0 | 444·44 |
| (III)   (200, 200, 0, 0) | −111·11 | 0 | 444·44 |
| (IV)   (80, 80, 400, 0) | 155·55 | 266·67 | 711·11 |
| (V)   (120, 120, 0, 160) | −377·78 | −266·67 | 177·78 |

the utility-maximizing decisions of traders with "deviant" beliefs. However, it will be assumed, these traders are sufficiently few in number (or else, their choices so offset one another) that their private decisions do not affect equilibrium prices in either the futures or the spot markets. Suppose that the deviant traders do not differ with respect to risk-tolerance, and specifically that for each such trader $k$ the preference-scaling function is of the previous form $v^k = \ln(a^k + n^k)$, where $a^k = 0$.

In these circumstances, as in example 6.6 we can use the Risk-bearing Theorem for Asset Markets to determine the agents' desired trading portfolios and the implied futures-market dealings. Specifically, the table shows the futures purchases or "long" positions $f^t$ (or, if $f^t$ is negative, the futures sales or "short" positions) for individuals with varying *beliefs* and *endowments*.[12] In interpreting table 6.2, note that an "optimist" is someone who assigns a relatively high probability to state 1, representing a large crop of the risky good $F$. (Since price and crop size move in opposite directions, an "optimist" in terms of crop size might be called a "pessimist" in terms of the movement of prices.) For any given endowment, the table shows that as pessimism about crop size increases (as $\pi_1$ falls), long positions get smaller and may be converted to "short" positions. Notice also that, given concordant beliefs, individuals of types I, II, and III do not take any position in futures. (This is of course consistent with the previous two examples.) The underlying reason is that, while these three types of endowments differ from one another, they nevertheless all involve *representative proportions* of the state-claims to the risky good $F$. (However, as also seen in example 6.6,

---

[12] In this example all five endowment categories would have the same wealth under a CCM regime, where the price vector is $(P^O_{n1}, P^O_{n2}, P^O_{f1}, P^O_{f2}) = (0·6, 0·4, 0·3, 0·5)$. But under the F&SM regime, the *tradable* prior-round wealths will differ.

individuals of types II and III would indeed engage in futures trading if the demand elasticity were not unitary.) Types IV and V are included to show that, if individuals are initially holding *non-representative* proportions of state-claims, in an incomplete market regime like F&SM they will generally have to take a futures position regardless of their beliefs – because they need two rounds of trading to achieve their optimal consumption portfolios in either state.

We may close this discussion by asking, finally, what sort of market behavior is "speculative"? Clearly, it cannot be the mere fact of participation in futures trading, which as we have seen may be the result of risk-minimizing (hedging) activities. Nor can speculation be identified always with being on the long, or on the short side, in futures transactions – since taking any such position will again be sensitive to a number of determining elements, and in particular to the endowment position. Individuals with greater-than-average *risk tolerance*, we have seen, may often be more willing to take large futures positions. However, it follows directly from the preceding that, since futures trading is often risk-reducing, a more risk-tolerant individual in some cases will engage in less of it! And the same holds also for deviant *beliefs*: as the table in the preceding example shows, belief differences will sometimes lead to larger, sometimes to smaller futures positions.

Perhaps the clearest instance, which almost everyone would call speculative behavior, would be a futures position in a commodity taken by an agent who is *neither endowed with nor a consumer of that good*.[13] Example 6.6 illustrated that such an individual may take a position in the futures market on the long side if demand is inelastic (thus relieving growers of some of the price risk), or on the short side if demand is elastic (thus "supplying" price risk to growers who need more of it to offset their endowed quantity risk). And even with unit-elastic demand, example 6.7 illustrates that such an agent will also be entering on the one side or the other of futures markets to the extent that he has deviant beliefs. But apart from such special cases, it does not really seem possible to isolate the speculative element in agents' decisions about futures trading.

[13] Even this is not quite an iron-clad example. Consider *money*. No-one consumes money. Yet an individual not endowed with money may find it advisable to acquire some for his "trading portfolio." This need not mean an intention to speculate that money will increase in value. Rather, money inventories are ordinarily held to facilitate exchange transactions, a need that arises only owing to the incompleteness (or imperfection) of barter markets. An analogous situation can arise in our models if some commodities provide more trading flexibility than others.

EXERCISES AND EXCURSIONS 6.2

*1 Futures trading*

Suppose example 6.5 is modified so that type-$i$ individuals have endowments $(n_1, n_2, f_1, f_2) = (0, 150, 200, 160)$ while type-$j$ individuals have endowments $(n_1, n_2, f_1, f_2) = (200, 50, 200, 0)$.

(A) Confirm that, in a CCM regime, final consumption will be exactly as in examples 6.2 and 6.5.

(B) Suppose that the futures (prior-round) price of fruit is 0·8 in terms of nuts as numeraire ($P_f^O = 0.8$ and $P_n^O = 1$). Confirm that, if a type-$i$ buyer purchases 800/3 units of nuts on the futures market and sells 1000/3 units of fruit, his budget constraints in the spot market after the information is revealed are:

state 1: $0.3f + 0.6n = 120$
state 2: $0.5f + 0.4n = 80$

(C) Hence, or otherwise, confirm that such trades are equilibrium trades.

(D) How can it be feasible for a type-$i$ buyer to sell an amount on the futures market which exceeds his endowment in any state?

*2 The martingale property of prices*

In example 6.5, the prior-round equilibrium price ratio $P_f^O/P_n^O$ is the *mathematical expectation* of the posterior ratios $P_{fs}^I/P_{ns}^I$ – specifically here, $0.8 = 0.6\ (0.5) + 0.4\ (1.25)$. (This is sometimes called the "martingale" property of prices.) Would you expect the martingale property to hold generally? In particular, maintaining the conditions of this example except for letting the utility function take a different form, would the martingale property remain valid? [HINT: see example 6.6.] Also, what would happen if the numerators and denominators were interchanged in the price ratios?

*3 Speculation with elastic demand*

Under the conditions of example 6.6, interpret the results obtained for the case of elastic demand ($\eta = -2$).

*4 Determinants of the volume of futures trading*

It is costly to provide futures markets. Such markets will of course be more viable when the volume of trading tends to be large. Comment upon the role of the following factors in making futures markets viable:

(a) If the possible stochastic fluctuations of crops are large or small.

(b) If the commodity is produced in a number of different regions subject to different supply conditions (e.g., differing climates), rather than concentrated in a single small region.

(c) If the demand is elastic versus inelastic.
(d) If beliefs as to different states of the world vary widely.
Are there other possible factors that also may play a role?

## 5 Costly entry into futures markets

Under the conditions of example 6.6, using the simplified "realistic" model, what would happen if transaction costs not only excluded consumers from participation in futures markets but also excluded half of the suppliers? All of the suppliers?

## 6 Endowment risk and trading in futures markets

Under the conditions of example 6.7, for the unitary elasticity case explain why agents with endowment types I, II, and III (if they have non-deviant beliefs) do not trade (do not take a position) in futures markets. Explain why types IV and V do take a position. If there were more than two possible states of the world, would all five endowment types generally have to take a futures position? Explain.

## 7 Non-speculative trading in a spot market

(A) Suppose each of 2,000 consumers has a positive initial endowment $\bar{n}$ of nuts and zero initial endowment of fruit. The common preference-scaling function is:

$$v(f, n) = n + \frac{(100)^{\alpha} f^{1-\alpha}}{(1-\alpha)}, \quad \text{for } 0 < \alpha < 1$$

If the price of $F$ is $P_f$ in terms of $N$ as numeraire, and if the final consumption bundle contains both fruit and nuts, show that the typical individual's demand for fruit is given by:

$$f = 100(P_f)^{1/\alpha}$$

(B) Obtain also an expression for the individual's net supply of nuts. What happens as the price of nuts gets very high?
(C) Confirm that aggregate demand for fruit satisfies the conditions of example 6.6.

## 6.3    Rational expectations

Given the prospective arrival of new information, we have seen, the prior-round decisions of individuals are generally dependent upon their beliefs – first, concerning what the emergent message is going to reveal as to the occurrence of one or another state of the world, and second, concerning the market consequences of that news. A particular type of assumption about the latter has been termed "rational expectations." However, controversy persists about the exact meaning of the term and therefore about both its descriptive realism and its relevance for economic analysis.

As originally proposed, rational expectations referred to anticipations that "are essentially the same as the predictions of the relevant economic theory" (Muth, 1961, p. 316). The simplest supply-demand model will serve as example. As is well known, in an actual market there may be trading at "false prices": for any given unit of the good, a buyer might pay more or less, and a seller correspondingly receive less or more, than the theoretical equilibrium price which would be established if the market were an ideal frictionless mechanism. It is true that, starting from any disequilibrium price, a transient "cobweb" path might lead eventually toward a final equilibrium where there is no further tendency to change. However, even so, if some trades have already taken place at false prices the final equilibrium of price and quantity will not in general be identical with the theoretical supply-demand intersection.

The rational expectations approach to this problem suggests that each trader in the market will make a guess as to the equilibrium price – on the basis of the private information at his disposal, plus his general knowledge of relationships such as the law of supply and demand – and that these guesses balance out to an average that is not far from correct:

allowing for cross-sectional differences in expectations is a simple matter, because their aggregate effect is negligible as long as the deviation from the rational forecast ... is not strongly correlated with those of the others. (Muth, 1961, p. 321)

One important point to note is that two somewhat different types of analysis are involved, corresponding to the professional skills of the *economist* and of the *econometrician*. The economist predicts that the price will be determined by the intersection of the supply and demand curves, while the econometrician provides the actual specific quantitative forms of those curves. Put another way, the economist makes predictions about the endogenous variables of economic systems, and specifically the prices and quantities exchanged or produced, but only *given* the exogenous data. Estimating the actual determining data is a task for the econometrician. So rational expectations corresponds, in effect, to assuming that ordinary individuals can be taken to be both pretty good economists and pretty good econometricians, at least on average.

When it comes to "visible" markets, those involved in trading current goods here and now, rational expectations is a well-validated hypothesis. Innumerable economic studies have successfully employed the assumption that essentially all such trading takes place at the supply–demand intersection. In addition, economic experimentation has verified that, practically always, prices in simulated markets move very rapidly toward the equilibrium – there is very little trading at false prices.[14]

However, futures trading poses a much more difficult problem. Rational traders have to make conjectures about what prices will be at *later* dates, after the prospective arrival of information. The question is, how reasonable is it to postulate that traders can be good enough economists and econometricians so as to make *self-fulfilling predictions* (SFP) about the results that would be observed in "invisible" markets that have not yet opened, or that (since these are *contingent* markets) will in the great majority of cases never open?

In some situations, we have seen, the correct SFP prediction for posterior prices may be easy to make. Our theoretical development in section 6.1 indicated that, given Complete Contingent Markets (CCM) in the prior round of trading, the correct forecast for the posterior round is simply "no change." More specifically, for any state $\hat{s}$ that might obtain, if all traders forecast that the posterior price ratios among the $c_{g\hat{s}}$ claims to different goods contingent upon state $\hat{s}$ will be equal to the prior price ratios, and have made their prior-round trading decisions accordingly, their anticipations will be borne out. So forming "rational" expectations under CCM does not seem difficult. But realistically, we cannot very well call upon results that hold only under the very idealized condition of CCM. And, in particular, we have seen that with *incomplete* regimes of markets in the prior round, traders do not normally have the information for making correct contingent predictions about the price ratios that would be ruling in the alternative possible future states of the world.

One interesting point brought out by Arrow (1978) is that the rational-expectations assumption in effect stands on its head the famous contention by Hayek (1945) about the informational function of the market system. Hayek's view was that prices are marvelously efficient summary statistics, conveying to traders all that they need to know about the vastly detailed particular circumstances of other economic agents which might impinge upon their own decisions. Absent a price system, Hayek argued, a central planner would require an impossibly elaborate data-gathering and data-analyzing scheme to make intelligent economic choices. But rational expectations seems to imply that the price signals from the "invisible" markets are hardly needed. Private traders supposedly can, at least on average, correctly guess what the price signals would have been!

In attempting to replicate the price signals of missing markets contingent upon future events, there are realistic difficulties for both the economist

---

[14] See, for example, Smith (1982).

and the econometrician. Even were the data known, it may not be a trivial matter to compute the equilibrium of a complex system. And forecasting *exogenous* data – for example, assigning correct probabilities to good versus bad weather, or to war versus peace – would seem to require somewhat more than the talents we usually ascribe to the econometrician. In such contexts rational expectations requires that individuals be actually clairvoyant (once again, at least on average). For example, in some macroeconomic models rational expectations has been taken to mean that, in addition to being able to analyze the effects of any given monetary policy, individuals can also decipher the current and future policies of the monetary authorities.

Knight (1921, p. 227) appears to support this view in asserting that: "We are so built that what seems to us reasonable is likely to be confirmed by experience, or we could not live in the world at all." This Lincolnesque idea that "the people can't be fooled" may be based upon viewing the underlying processes that generate observed world events as *stationary*, so that individuals can gradually learn both about the effects of events upon prices and about the probability distribution of events. However, such a learning evolution does not imply that beliefs would be on average correct except in the limit.

While it is difficult to see what an adequate test of the rational expectations hypothesis may be, a number of patterns in the data seem to have been usefully interpreted in these terms. Indeed, in dealing with regimes of incomplete markets, it is difficult to propose any other assumption to deal with individuals' beliefs about future events. Our main concern has been to analyze the theoretical role of self-fulfilling beliefs (SFP) simply as an assumption, and to warn against casual acceptance of the empirical validity of rational expectations as the real-world analog of SFP.

REFERENCES AND SELECTED READINGS

Arrow, Kenneth J., "The Role of Securities in the Optimal Allocation of Risk-bearing," *Review of Economic Studies*, 31 (April 1964). Reprinted in Kenneth J. Arrow, *Essays in the Theory of Risk-Bearing*, Chicago: Markham, 1971.

———, "The Future and the Present in Economic Life," *Economic Inquiry*, 16 (April 1978).

Baumol, William J., "Speculation, Profitability, and Stability," *Review of Economics and Statistics*, 30 (August 1957).

Friedman, Milton, "In Defense of Destabilizing Speculation," in R. W. Pfouts (ed.), *Essays in Economics and Econometrics*, Chapel Hill, NC: University of North Carolina Press, 1960. Reprinted in Milton Friedman, *The Optimum Quantity of Money and Other Essays*, Chicago: Aldine, 1969.

Hayek, Friedrich A., "The Use of Knowledge in Society," *American Economic Review*, 35 (September 1945).

Hicks, J. R., *Value and Capital*, 2nd edn, London: Oxford University Press, 1946.

Hirshleifer, David, "Hedging Pressure and Futures Price Movements in a General Equilibrium Model," *Econometrica*, 58 (March 1990).

Hirshleifer, J., "The Theory of Speculation Under Alternative Regimes of Markets," *Journal of Finance*, 32 (September 1977).

Keynes, J. M., *A Treatise on Money*, London: Macmillan, 1930.

Knight, Frank H., *Risk, Uncertainty, and Profit*, New York: Houghton Mifflin, 1921.

McKinnon, Ronald I., "Futures Markets, Buffer Stocks, and Income Stability for Primary Producers," *Journal of Political Economy*, 75 (December 1967).

Muth, John F., "Rational Expectations and the Theory of Price Movements," *Econometrica*, 29 (July 1961).

Radner, Roy, "Competitive Equilibrium Under Uncertainty," *Econometrics*, 36 (January 1968).

Smith, Vernon L., "Microeconomic Systems as an Experimental Science," *American Economic Review*, 72 (December 1982).

Working, Holbrook, "Futures Trading and Hedging," *American Economic Review*, 43 (June 1953).

———, "New Concepts Concerning Futures Markets and Prices," *American Economic Review*, 52 (June 1962).

# 7 Research and invention

The previous chapter analyzed individual decisions and market equilibrium in a context of *emergent public information* – where tomorrow's weather, for example, will in due time become freely known to all. In contrast, this chapter deals with information that does not emerge autonomously but instead has to be produced or discovered by costly research.

Two kinds of socially new information can be distinguished. There is pure knowledge, desired for its own sake. Alternatively, information might be wanted only instrumentally, as an intermediate good making it possible to reduce the cost of producing hats or shoes or haircuts. We will be dealing only with the second, more materialistic type of knowledge.

A major incentive for incurring the cost of prying out Nature's secrets is that the discovered information will typically be private, allowing the researcher to improve his situation relative to uninformed parties. On the other hand, as will be seen, there are processes always at work tending to publicize private information. The costly efforts of discoverers may leak out and become costlessly emergent information for potential imitators, though possibly subject to intentional or unintentional garbling. In short, discovery is timely but expensive; imitation or second-hand learning is cheap, though possibly subject to distortion and delay.

The essential problems of the economics of research stem from the tensions between the two inter-related processes of *discovery or invention* versus *dissemination of the information thus obtained*. This chapter begins with the first of these. We then turn to the question of dissemination, in order to examine the market processes that may either hamper or enhance a discoverer's ability to profit from superior knowledge. From a welfare point of view, the issue is how to strike a proper balance between the social goals of (i) inducing the ideal amount of effort aimed at the production of information versus (ii) achieving efficient use of information once produced.

## 7.1     The production of information

According to the traditional analysis,[1] already produced information is a "public good"; it can be made concurrently available to any and all members of the community. If so, it is sometimes said, any barriers to use, for example patents or copyrights or property in trade secrets, are inefficient. On the other hand, if researchers cannot gain property rights in their discoveries there may be inadequate motivation to invest in the production of information.

In principle at least, there is an efficient solution to these two problems. *First*, the motivation to produce new ideas would be optimal if the discoverer could be granted a perfectly enforced, perpetual, and exclusive right to his discovery. And *second*, there would be no hampering of efficient use if the owner of the property right could establish a profit-maximizing perfectly discriminating fee schedule, since on the margin the optimal fee would be zero. But in actuality owners of copyrights or patents cannot impose perfectly discriminating royalty fee structures (or their equivalent in terms of lump-sum charges), hence some loss of efficiency in this regard is bound to occur. On the other side of the picture, property rights in ideas can never be perfectly defined or enforced. So the legal protection of patents and copyrights is inevitably incomplete, and of trade secrets not covered by patents or copyrights is even more deficient.

In practice, there is something of a trade-off: greater legal protection to discoverers will ameliorate the underproduction problem, but tend to aggravate the underutilization problem.[2] Thus, the traditional analysis suggests, current legal arrangements – patents, copyrights, and protection of trade secrets that amount to only imperfect and partially effective property rights in ideas – may constitute a defensible compromise between the two competing goals.

More recent investigations have indicated, however, that this analysis does not capture all the important elements of the picture. In contrast with the "public good effect" that discourages investment in research and invention, there are pressures tending to induce *over*investment in the production of ideas. As indicated in table 7.1, two main forces are involved. First, undiscovered knowledge is a common-property resource;

---

[1] See for example Arrow (1962), Machlup (1968).

[2] There are exceptions to this generalization. Suppose that stronger legal enforcement leads some consumers to shift from unauthorized use (copying) to licensed use. There is likely to be an efficiency gain, since the cost of illegal copying of ideas is generally greater than the social cost of extending licensed use. Note that in this case the *extent* of utilization of the information may be unaffected, but a lower-cost is substituted for a higher-cost *mode* of utilization (see Novos and Waldman, 1987).

Table 7.1 *Forces affecting inventive activity*

| |
|---|
| Tending to induce underinvestment |
|   *Public good effect*: Free riders can reap benefits. |
| Tending to induce overinvestment |
|   *Commons effect*: Entrants receive average product (> marginal product) of inventive activity. |
|   *Speculative effect*: Private benefit of invention is, in part, merely redistributive. |

entry into such a commons tends to continue so long as the *average* yield (rather than, as efficiency dictates, the *marginal* yield) is remunerative.[3] This might be called the "commons effect." Second, even if the information itself is of little or no socially productive significance, it may have private value as a means of transferring wealth from uninformed to informed traders. This will be called the "speculative effect."[4]

### 7.1.1    The scale of research: overinvestment or underinvestment?

A property right is the legally enforced power to exclude others from access to some good or activity. For present purposes it is essential to distinguish two kinds of property rights: *rights in the product* versus *rights to engage in the activity of producing it*.[5] The latter may equivalently be interpreted as the right to exclude others from access to the resource from which the product is extracted.

*Research as fishing*: Searching for ideas is, in some respects, like angling for fish. A fisherman normally has property rights in his product – fish taken. Less universally though still not infrequently, someone may hold the exclusive right to exploit a particular fishing ground. In the first case we are dealing with rights *in* fish (as a noun), in the second case with rights *to* fish (as a verb). Applied to the world of research, the "public good effect" concerns the fact that rights *in* already caught ideas are imperfect, implying a tendency to underinvest. (If others can confiscate some of your catch, fishing becomes less attractive.) But, on the other hand, absent the ability to exclude others from rights *to* fish for uncaught ideas, there will be a "commons effect" tending to induce overinvestment.

In figure 7.1, panel (a) illustrates the public good effect. The horizontal

---

[3] Barzel (1968).    [4] Fama and Laffer (1971), Hirshleifer (1971).
[5] Cheung (1979).

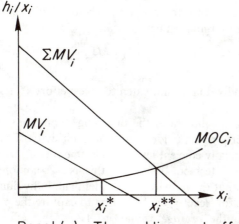

Panel (a) – The public good effect

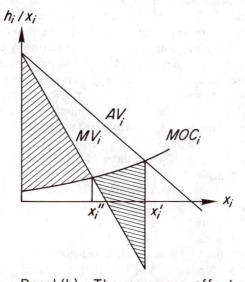

Panel (b) – The commons effect

Figure 7.1 Underinvestment and overinvestment in research: the fishing model

axis scales the research (fishing) effort $x_i$ of an individual $i$ ($i = 1, ..., N$) while the vertical axis measures per-unit product $h_i/x_i$. Each individual will be motivated to invest effort to the point where the marginal opportunity cost ($MOC_i$) equals his own marginal value ($MV_i$) of ideas (fish) produced. However, since the ideas are a public good, the social optimality condition is for each individual to invest to the point where $MOC_i$ equals the aggregate sum of all the marginal values:

$$MOC_1 = MOC_2 = \ldots = MOC_N = MV_1 + MV_2 + \ldots + MV_N \equiv \Sigma MV_i$$
$$(7.1.1)$$

Thus, in panel (a), the individual is motivated to invest effort $x_i^*$, less than the socially efficient $x_i^{**}$.

Panel (b) of the diagram illustrates the opposing "commons effect." Assuming perfect property rights *in* ideas but non-exclusivity of rights *to* (search for) ideas, the socially efficient level of investment is $x_i''$, where the $MOC_i$ and $MV_i$ curves intersect. But, since this is a commons, and assuming for simplicity that the individuals are identical, individual $i$ will be motivated to invest effort level $x_i'$ enabling him to capture the pro-rata share corresponding to the *average* valuation $AV_i$ of his effort. $AV_i$ exceeds $MV_i$ because some fraction of the ideas that individual $i$ captures are not a net social gain; they would have been caught by someone else anyway. At the extreme, if all the $MOC_i$ curves were horizontal, the commons effect under free entry would entirely destroy the social value of the resource – i.e., the average value and the average opportunity cost of effort would be equal. (This is sometimes called "dissipation of rents.") The result is not quite so extreme under the more normal case of rising marginal opportunity cost. As shown in panel (b), here the ideal producer surplus (the lightly shaded area) is only partially counterbalanced by the negative producer surplus (the heavily shaded area) associated with the excessive effort between $x_i'$ and $x_i''$.

A natural next question is how to weigh the public good effect tending toward underinvestment against the commons effect tending toward overinvestment. As indicated by an exercise below, it turns out that there is no clear tendency for the one to overbalance the other.

We have not yet considered the *speculative effect*, however. This drastically revises the outlook.

Consider, for example, the vast amount of effort going into financial research, whether of the "fundamentalist" or the "technical" variety. Fundamentalists attempt to determine whether an oil company's drilling program will be successful, whether a drug company is likely to come up with an effective treatment for cancer, and so forth. Technicians search for patterns in the stockmarket data themselves: whether a rise is more likely than not to be followed by a fall, whether heavy trading volume is a favorable or an unfavorable indicator, and so forth. The successes of individual researchers in either of these directions may possibly confer some small social benefit by improving perfection of the capital markets. But the huge speculative profits sometimes observed – for example, by individuals who learned early on about Texas Gulf's big oil strike in Canada – evidently represent almost equivalent losses to other traders.[6] The process is close to a zero-sum game: the gains to those in the know are balanced by almost equivalent losses to the uninformed investors.[7]

In a sense, the speculative effect is the opposite of the public good effect. The public good effect indicates that information is essentially $N$ times as valuable to the community as it is to the individual; the speculative effect applies where the social value of information is only a small fraction of private value. In terms of panel (a) of figure 7.1, in the extreme case the $\Sigma MV_i$ curve would lie along the horizontal axis. Then, *all* private investment in information would be overinvestment.

Thus the question of over- or underinvestment in information is highly sensitive to the externalities causing discrepancies between private and social valuations. Where these are strongly positive (the public good effect), there will be social underinvestment in information; where negative (the commons and speculative effects), the opposite tends to occur.

*Research as quest for a holy grail*: Under the fishing image of research, the payoff is simply the number of ideas produced. (Just as fish are perhaps more or less alike, so might ideas be.) Such a quantitative metaphor is applicable to lines of investigation generating essentially additive or incremental improvements to existing techniques or products: alloys with greater electrical conductivity, engines with better fuel economy, new rose varieties, etc. But unique great discoveries – the telephone or electric light or airplane – hardly fall in this category. Where the outcome sought is *qualitatively* different from anything previously observed, we have the "holy grail" image. Here, many investigators are competing to capture a single great idea. The individual's goal is to be the first discoverer.[8]

However, the previous analysis remains essentially valid, simply by changing the payoff measure from the *number* of ideas produced ($h$) to the *probability* ($p$) of being the first discoverer. The two panels of figure 7.2 are analogues of those in figure 7.1. Panel (a) of figure 7.2 once more pictures the public good effect. The individual marginal valuation curve $MV_i$ of the previous diagram corresponds here to the marginal expected-valuation

---

[6] Financial information may sometimes be acquired by illegal methods, for example, by bribing a corporate employee to reveal confidential data (the Ivan Boesky case). But even where the knowledge is obtained in entirely lawful ways, as by analyzing publicly reported data, the speculative profit remains almost entirely redistributive in nature.

[7] There are forces, however, tending to limit the extent to which early knowledge can be converted into speculative gains. These will be examined later in the chapter.

[8] Under US law, only the first discoverer of a patentable idea is entitled to the patent. The laws of other countries vary somewhat. For example, in some jurisdictions the right goes not to the discoverer but to the first to apply. The various national laws also differ as to the patentability of ideas discovered or patented elsewhere. See Berle and de Camp (1959).

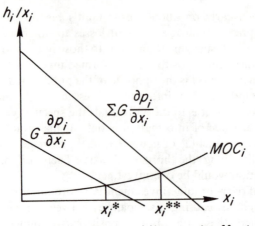

Panel(a) — The public good effect

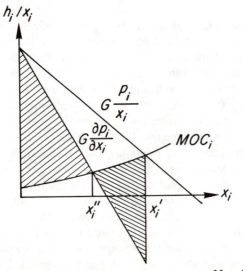

Panel (b) — The commons effect

Figure 7.2 Underinvestment and overinvestment in research: the holy grail model

curve $G\partial p_i/\partial x_i$, where $G$ is the value of the discovery (of the grail) to any single individual while $\partial p_i/\partial x_i$ is the marginal probability of being the successful discoverer.[9] Since by assumption the grail is a public good, the

---

[9] Throughout this chapter risk-neutrality is assumed, so that expected income corresponds to expected utility.

$\Sigma MV_i$ of the previous diagram becomes $\Sigma G\partial p_i/\partial x_i$. As before, the public good effect implies that, in terms of social efficiency, the typical individual will underinvest in information.

Panel (b) illustrates the commons effect under the holy grail model. Let $q_i(x_i)$ represent the $i$-th individual's chance of succeeding, as a function of his effort, *if he were the sole researcher*. Let $p_i(x_1, \ldots, x_N)$ be the probability that he wins the grail (that he is the *first* discoverer). Then, in the simple case where $N = 2$:

$$p_1 = q_1(1-q_2)+0.5\,q_1q_2 = q_1 - 0.5\,q_1q_2 \tag{7.1.2}$$

An analogous equation will of course hold for $p_2$. (The assumption here is that, in the contingency where both would have made the discovery in isolation, each has an equal chance to be declared the discover.) On the other hand, denoting the *social* probability of success as $P$, we evidently must have:

$$P \equiv p_1+p_2 = q_1+q_2-q_1q_2 \tag{7.1.3}$$

Of course, when $q_1 = q_2$ then $P = 2p_1 = 2p_2$.

Individual 1 will invest effort until his marginal opportunity cost equals the average product:

FIRST-ORDER CONDITION FOR PRIVATE OPTIMUM

$$MOC_1 = GP/x_1 = G(q_1+q_2-q_1q_2)/x_1 \tag{7.1.4}$$

But the efficient level of investment involves the marginal effect upon the social probability of success $P$:

FIRST-ORDER CONDITION FOR SOCIAL OPTIMUM

$$MOC_1 = G\partial P/\partial x_1 = G(1-q_2)dq_1/dx_1 \tag{7.1.5}$$

Under the assumption of diminishing marginal impact of effort upon the probability of discovery, $d^2q_i/dx_i^2 < 0$, the second derivative $\partial^2 P/\partial x_i^2$ is also negative. So the latter equation implies an efficient level of investment $x_1''$ which is less than the privately optimal level $x_1'$, as shown in panel (b) of figure 7.2. Just as for the fishing model, then, in the holy grail model also there is a commons effect in the direction of private overinvestment in producing information.

EXERCISES AND EXCURSIONS 7.1.1

*1 Fishing model*

(A) *The commons effect*: In panel (b) of figure 7.1, assuming all individuals are identical let the average valuation curve have the linear form $AV_i = C - Dx_i$, where $x_i$ is individual $i$'s effort. Suppose the corresponding curve of marginal opportunity cost has the form $MOC_i = A + Bx_i$. Show that the ratio of the individual optimum effort $x_i^*$ to the socially efficient effort level $x_i^{**}$ equals:

$$(B+2D)/(B+D) = 1 + D/(B+D)$$

and therefore that the proportionate overinvestment is at most 100%. Comment on the factors tending to increase the scale of overinvestment associated with the commons effect.

(B) *The public good effect*: Under the same assumptions, but assuming for simplicity that the marginal opportunity cost is constant throughout (that is, $MOC_i = A$), show that the equilibrium private investment and socially efficient level of effort will aggregate, respectively, to:

$$x_i^* = \frac{C-A}{2D} \quad \text{and} \quad x_i^{**} = \frac{C-A/N}{2D}$$

What can be said about the ratio $x_i^{**}/x_i^*$ as $N$ increases?

*2 Holy Grail model*

(A) In the case where $N = 2$, if $G = 1,000$ and $MOC_i = 1$ for all $i$, and $q_i = 1 - \exp(-x_i)$, find the solutions corresponding to $x_i'$ and $x_i''$ in panel (b) of figure 7.2.

(B) Show that, for $N = 3$, the equation defining the probability that player 1 will win the grail is:

$$p_1 = q_1 - q_1 q_2/2 - q_1 q_3/2 + q_1 q_2 q_3/3$$

*7.1.2    Timing: is there a rush to invent?*
Using the holy grail image of invention, the previous section examined how an investigator's scale of investment effort determined his probability of being the first discoverer. Although it was recognized that the payoffs typically depend upon who succeeds first, there was no *explicit* analysis of timing. In this section, the timing of effort and of results becomes the central issue.

There are many ways of modelling the race to be the first discoverer.[10] The discussion here deals with a very simple situation where each contender's scale of investment determines a known date at which he will achieve his goal.

Suppose that some particular researcher possesses the exclusive *right to invent*. Figure 7.3 shows his discounted present value functions for total

---

[10] For an authoritative survey see Reinganum (1989).

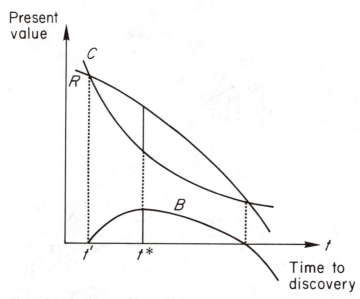

Figure 7.3 The timing of innovation

cost $C$ and for total revenue $R$, both declining with the anticipated date of discovery $t$ (measured from the present, $t = 0$). Discounted revenue declines with $t$ because deferral of the discovery date reduces the present value of the gains from using the invention (or from licensing its use to others). Discounted cost declines with $t$ because advancing the date of discovery is increasingly expensive; indeed, as illustrated here, the cost of discovery with no delay at all (at $t = 0$) may be infinite. Also shown in the diagram is the curve of total net benefit $B \equiv R - C$, the difference between revenue and cost. The optimal invention date for the individual in isolation is evidently $t = t^*$, where the benefit curve reaches a maximum – or, equivalently, where the vertical distance $R - C$ is largest.[11] The amount of the maximum benefit $B^*$ is indicated by the length of the solid vertical line-segments in the diagram.

This outcome will be efficient under two main conditions: (1) If the maximized $B^*$ for this inventor is greater than for any other (if he is the highest-benefit inventor)[12] and (2) if the total revenue received by him represents the full social value of the invention. The first condition would be met if the individual possessed an exclusive marketable right to invent,

[11] This could be interpreted as an equality between the marginal revenue and marginal cost of *advancing* discovery in time.

[12] This discussion in part follows Cheung who speaks of the "lowest-cost" rather than the "highest-benefit" inventor. Since the ranking in terms of cost may vary with $t$, there may be no unambiguously lowest-cost inventor.

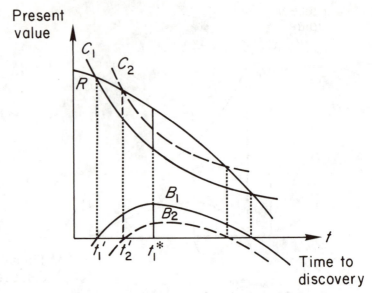

Figure 7.4 The rush to invent: $T_1 = t_2$

since then by the standard Coasian argument the right to invent would be sold to whoever was the highest-benefit inventor. And the second condition would be met if the property right on the invention were exclusive, perpetual, and fully enforceable, and if the inventor could license its use in accordance with a perfectly discriminating fee schedule. In what follows we will usually be making the second assumption but not the first. That is, we will be assuming *there is no way of excluding others from the activity of inventing*.

Now suppose, as indicated in figure 7.4, that the researcher pictured in the previous diagram is an "incumbent" (1) facing potential entry by another investigator (2). While normally only one of the contenders will actually end up making the investment, the threat of competing entry will in general affect the timing chosen by the successful inventor.

Let $t_i^*$ indicate the benefit-maximizing date and let $t_i'$ signify the first zero-profit date for each inventor $i$. By assumption here the total revenue curve is the same for both ($R_1 \equiv R_2 \equiv R$), but the total cost (and so the benefit) curves differ. In particular, here the entrant has higher cost throughout. Then $t_1' < t_2'$. However, by assumption again, the zero-profit point for the entrant, $t_2'$, antedates $t_1^*$. Thus, signifying the outcome in the presence of competition as $T_i$ (where the subscript indicates the *winning* contender) the outcomes will be $T_1 = t_2'$. The incumbent wins the contest, but in order to do so he has to match the zero-profit date of the entrant.

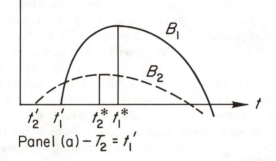

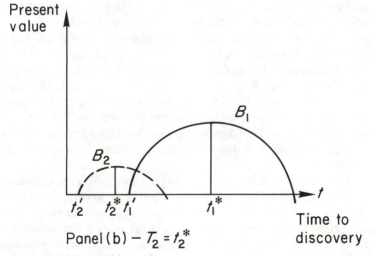

Figure 7.5 More rushing to invent

As can be seen, $T_1 < t_1^*$ – there is a "rush to invent." In addition, the achieved private and social benefit $\bar{B}$ (shown here by the dashed vertical line-segments in the diagram) is less than the $B^*$ achieved (the solid line-segments) when the incumbent had an exclusive property right.

Figure 7.5 illustrates two other possibilities. These are designed to show that the lower-benefit inventor, the one with a smaller maximum $B_i^*$, may win the competition, provided that he is the speedier inventor. (To minimize clutter, only the benefit curves $B_1$ and $B_2$ are shown here.) In panel (a) $t_2' < t_1' < t_2^* < t_1^*$. This means that the entrant, were he alone, would choose a discovery date less than the incumbent's optimum, but not so early a date as the incumbent's zero-profit point. The equilibrium here will be $T_2 = t_1'$: the entrant wins by choosing a date just early enough to deter the incumbent from investing (the incumbent's zero-profit date). In panel (b) the entrant's $t_2'$ optimum is even shorter than the incumbent's zero-profit date, and so the entrant can simply optimize ($T_2 = t_2^* < t_1'$). In either case, of course, the achieved private and social benefit $\bar{B}$ is much less than the $B^*$ achievable by the higher-benefit inventor in isolation.[13]

So threatened entry leads to a "rush to invent" which dissipates large fractions of the potential social benefit. The commons effect not only induces an *excessive scale* of inventive effort (as analyzed in section 7.1.1 above) but also promotes *wastefully early* invention.

As for the public good effect, in figure 7.3 this would reveal itself in a revenue curve $R_i$ that reflects only a portion of the social benefit of the invention. Conceivably, then, the effective or "private" $R_i$ curve for each and every inventor might be so low that the invention would never be made. Assume this is not the case, so that over a portion of its range the private $R_i$ curve would lie above some individual inventor's $C_i$ curve. Such a lower $R_i$ curve of itself has no clear effect upon the location of the $t_i^*$ point – the benefit-maximizing date for the inventor in isolation. But it will tend to *defer* the zero-profit point $t_i'$ for each and every inventor having a range of positive benefit. And, as we saw in the analysis pictured in figure 7.4, in entry competition the $t_i'$ points determine the outcome. Thus once again the analogy holds: the public good effect works in the opposite direction from the commons effect, in this case tending to induce tardy rather than hasty invention.

As for the speculative effect, its logic once again is the opposite of that underlying the public good effect. The public good effect is based upon the premise that private revenue $R_i$ inadequately reflects the social value of the invention. The speculative effect, in contrast, is applicable when the private revenue achievable *exceeds* the social value, which is notably the case when a discovery permits informed traders to profit at the expense of the uninformed. Simply reversing the argument above, then, the speculative effect (like the commons effect but unlike the public good effect) tends to induce a rush to invent.

---

[13] It would therefore be possible, in principle, for the higher-benefit inventor to buy out the other, in which case the efficient outcome would be achieved after all. As indicated in the text, however, the analysis here excludes the possibility of such Coasian negotiations. In defense of this assumption, note that there might be not just one but a great many entrants seeking to be bought out in such negotiations.

A serious flaw of the models considered here is the assumption that a losing contender is simply deterred and so incurs no cost. For one thing, it may not be initially clear just who is going to be the successful inventor, so that more than one contender may end up investing funds on the chance of being the victor. This risk will evidently tend to discourage the inventing process in general. In chapter 10 we will approach such contests in a more general way, distinguishing between two cases: (i) where, as in the standard auctions of commerce, losers do not sacrifice their resource commitments or bids versus (ii) where these commitments are more or less irretrievable (falling into this category are patent races, athletic competitions, political campaigns, and wars).

## EXERCISES AND EXCURSIONS 7.1.2

### 1 The race to innovate (Lowry, 1979)

Two firms each make an investment which will result in an innovation at some future time. The first to achieve the innovation receives a patent. The expected value of the patent, discounted to the date of discovery, is $R$. Suppose that by incurring a date-0 cost $C_i(t)$, where $C_i'(t) < 0$, firm $i$'s probability of successful innovation by time $t$ is $P_i(t)$.

(A) Suppose the patent will yield a revenue flow of $v$ per annum from the discovery date to infinity. Then, if the interest rate is $r$, show that the expected present value (benefit) of the race to firm 1 is:

$$B_1 = -C_1 + R \int_0^\infty e^{-rt}(1 - P_2(t))P_1'(t)dt, \quad \text{where} \quad R = \frac{v}{r}$$

(B) Suppose firm $i$'s probability of making the discovery by date $t$ is:

$$P_i(t) = 1 - e^{-x_i t}, \quad i = 1, 2$$

Confirm that, conditional upon not having made the discovery prior to time $t$, firm $i$'s probability of success in the short time interval $[t, t + \delta t]$ is $x_i \delta t$. That is, $x_i$ is firm $i$'s "discovery rate."

(C) Given such probability functions for the two firms show that:

$$B_1 = -C(x_i) + \frac{Rx_i}{x_1 + x_2 + r}, \quad i = 1, 2$$

(D) In a non-cooperative Nash–Cournot equilibrium, each individual treats the actions of his competitors as parameters. Write down the first-order condition for firm $i$'s optimum. Also write down the first-order conditions for maximizing joint expected benefit $B_1 + B_2$.

Assuming that the social optimum and the non-cooperative equilibrium are both symmetric, show that each firm will invest more if it behaves non-cooperatively.

(E) Suppose firm 2 is prohibited from entering the market. Show that firm 1, acting on its own, will invest more than when both firms were in a race to innovate.

## 2 An R&D race with n firms

Suppose that, as in the previous question, the probability of successful innovation by firm $i$ in the time-interval $[0, t]$ is $P_i(t) = 1 - e^{-x_i t}$. The cost to the firm of a discovery rate $x_i$ is $C(x_i)$, where $C(\cdot)$ is increasing and convex. To further simplify the analysis suppose that the interest rate is zero so that the value of the discovery is a constant $R$ regardless of the time of discovery.

(A) If there are $n$ firms in the race, show that the first-order condition for a symmetric non-cooperative equilibrium is:

$$C'(x_i) = \frac{R(n-1)}{n^2 x_i}, \quad i = 1, \ldots, n$$

(B) Hence, confirm that the larger the number of firms the smaller is the investment by each firm.

(C) If $C(x_i) = \alpha x_i^\beta$, show that the first-order condition can be rewritten as:

$$C(x_i) = \frac{1}{\beta n} R(1 - \frac{1}{n})$$

Hence show that total investment on R&D is an increasing function of the number of firms in the industry.

## 3 An R&D rate with no fixed costs of entry (Lee and Wilde, 1980)

As long as a race among $n$ firms continues, firm $i$ incurs costs at the rate of $c_i$ per period. The interest rate is $r$ and the discovery rate of firm $i$ is $x_i$, $i = 1, \ldots, n$.

(A) If $P(t)$ is the probability of discovery by date $t$, explain why the expected present value of the cost of research by firm $i$ is:

$$c_i \int_0^\infty e^{-rt}(1 - P(t))dt$$

(B) Show that:

$$1 - P(t) = \exp(-\{\sum_{j=1}^n x_j\} t)$$

and hence confirm that the expected present cost of the investment is:

$$\frac{c_i}{\sum\limits_{j=1}^{n} x_j + r}$$

(C) Write down an expression for the firm's expected profit under the assumption that:

$$c_i = \alpha x_i^{\beta}, \quad 1 < \beta < 2$$

(D) From the first-order condition for a symmetric Nash equilibrium, show that the discovery rate (and hence the investment rate) of firm $i$ is an *increasing* function of the number of firms for all $n \geqslant 2$.

(HINT: Write the first-order condition for a symmetric equilibrium in the form $n = f(x)$ and show that the right-hand side is an increasing function.)

## 7.2 Intended dissemination of information

Some of the factors involved in disseminating the products of research and discovery activities have already been touched on. The "public good effect" dealt with in section 7.1 is applicable only if greater or lesser unintended dissemination (*leakage*) is inevitable. The "commons effect" and the "speculative effect," in contrast, can exist only to the extent that property rights in discoveries are enforced – that unintended leakage can be controlled.

This section describes some of the difficulties associated with *intended* dissemination of produced information. The problem of leakage is taken up in the section following.

Two main kinds of intended dissemination of information can be distinguished: *compensated* versus *gratuitous*.

### Compensated disclosure

An inventor, as a specialist in the discovery of ideas, will ordinarily not have a comparative advantage in the actual productive utilization of his ideas. So he will naturally think of marketing his discovery to others better able to make use of it. Apart from the more or less normal transaction costs involved in all market dealings – finding customers, billing them, keeping proper records, and the like – such exchanges may be partially or wholly blocked by difficulties peculiar to the market for information:

(1) In attempting to convince potential buyers of the worth of the information, greater or lesser disclosure may be inevitable. Should the

transaction not ultimately be consummated, the original discoverer has to some extent given his idea away, while the prospective buyer may fear groundless lawsuits. For this reason, many firms refuse to hear unsolicited ideas from outside sources.[14]

(2) Any sale entails some risk of unauthorized *re-disclosure* on the part of the buyer.[15]

(3) Even in the most favorable circumstance, where fully effective legal protection means that the seller is no way inhibited from disclosure, it may still remain difficult to convince buyers of the market value of the idea.

Owing to such problems, discoverers or inventors often are reduced to exploiting their ideas by going into independent production, despite lack of comparative advantage in ordinary business activity. In view of the difficulties either way, it is not surprising that many commercially valuable inventions have failed to be remunerative.[16]

Setting aside these difficulties, the discussion that follows analyzes one additional factor contributing to the "public good effect" (that much of the benefit of new knowledge is often reaped by free riders): inability of sellers to charge users the full value of the information.

Consider a productive innovation where the potential users are firms in a perfectly competitive industry. Suppose the inventor must charge a non-discriminatory royalty $\rho$ per unit of output produced. Also, for simplicity, assume this is a constant-cost industry: as pictured in panel (a) of figure 7.6, marginal cost is horizontal at the level $MC^0 = \kappa^0$. Given the product demand curve $D$, the industry's initial equilibrium output is $q^0$. Finally, imagine that the effect of the invention is to reduce cost uniformly, so that the new marginal cost curve is $MC' = \kappa'$.

As illustrated in the diagram, the industry's demand curve $d$ for use of the invention – let us call it the *royalty demand curve* – can be derived from its product demand function $D$ and the $MC^0$ and $MC'$ curves. Interpreting $\rho$ as the demand price along the $d$ curve, we have:

$$\rho = \begin{cases} \kappa_0 - \kappa' & \text{for } q \leqslant q^0 \\ P - \kappa' & \text{for } q > q^0 \end{cases} \tag{7.2.1}$$

The owner of the information acts as a monopolist with respect to the

[14] See Cheung (1982, pp. 45–6).

[15] E.g., the difficulty of controlling unauthorized copying of software programs.

[16] The cotton gin of Eli Whitney is a famous instance. The invention was instantly successful, and was protected by patent. Whitney attempted at various times both to utilize his invention directly (through his own ginning company) and to license his patent to others in exchange for royalties. Despite his determined and resourceful efforts, it is doubtful whether he ever reaped any substantial profit, net of legal and business costs, from the cotton gin (de Camp, 1961, pp. 29–31).

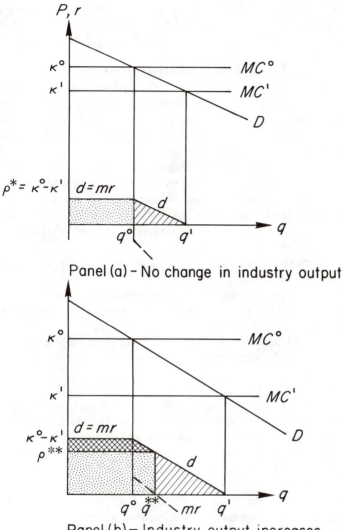

Panel (a) - No change in industry output

Panel (b) - Industry output increases

Figure 7.6 Product demand and royalty demand

royalty demand curve. He will therefore want to set the associated marginal revenue equal to his marginal cost. The latter, by assumption here, is zero. (The patent owner incurs none of the cost of production.) Using the abbreviation *mr* to distinguish the marginal revenue associated with the royalty demand curve from the ordinary marginal revenue *MR* associated with the product demand curve, $mr$ lies along the horizontal leg of the royalty demand curve $d$ curve until $q = q^o$. At that point the kink in $d$ implies a vertical discontinuity in $mr$, after which $mr$ will be falling faster than $d$.

There are two main possibilities. In panel (a) the vertical discontinuity of the $mr$ curve cuts the horizontal axis. Here the profit-maximizing royalty fee $\rho^*$ equals $\kappa^o - \kappa'$, implying no change in the industry output $q^o$. The gain to the patent owner is the dotted rectangle $q^o\rho^*$. In this case neither the consumers nor the firms in the industry derive any benefit from the innovation. Inability to charge discriminatory prices implies a social opportunity loss, indicated by the diagonally shaded triangular area between the $d$ curve and the horizontal axis; ideally, the industry output should be $q'$ where $D(q)$ intersects the new marginal cost curve $MC'$.

The other case is illustrated in panel (b). Here it is the downward sloping branch of the $mr$ curve that intersects the horizontal axis. Without detailed explanation, it can be seen that:

(i) The profit-maximizing royalty is $\rho^{**} < \kappa^o - \kappa'$, and the associated industry output is $q^{**} > q^o$.

(ii) The gain to the patent owner is the dotted rectangle $\rho^{**}q^{**}$.

(iii) The consumers now derive some benefit, indicated by the cross-hatched area lying below $d$ but above $\rho^{**}$.

(iv) A social opportunity loss remains, indicated as before by the diagonally shaded triangle between the $d$ curve and the horizontal axis.

### Gratuitous disclosure

That it may pay someone with valuable private knowledge to gratuitously disclose it, may at first seem surprising. But we see this done every day. Indeed, asymmetrically informed parties often go to considerable expense to "push" their message to others. Advertising is an evident example. Hopeful sellers bombard us with news about products or services offered; somewhat less frequently, potential buyers also try to alert suppliers as to their needs. Or consider the academic profession. Professors volunteer to present their ideas at seminars and conferences, submit their research output to journals for unpaid publication, and eagerly circulate copies of their papers to anyone who might possibly read them.

The explanation is that, in contrast with what we have heretofore been assuming, interpersonal transmission of information is normally a costly and noisy process. Only rarely does mere "disclosure" suffice to convey a message; something more active is typically required of both sender and receiver. Teachers work hard preparing lectures and textbooks; students grind away trying to understand them. In our earlier analysis we treated information as a transparently valuable but fugitive commodity, always liable to escape unless closely guarded. But of at least equal importance are types of information whose nature and value are not transparent, that are hard to transmit even to desirous users, and hard for them to absorb even when offered freely.

In this light let us now reconsider the "speculative effect" – the motive to engage in informational activities for redistributive rather than productive purposes. Speculating upon informational disparities requires both *preventing disclosure* at one stage and then *achieving disclosure* later on. More explicitly: (i) The individual must be able initially to move to a trading position (make a speculative commitment) without thereby revealing his secret. (ii) After having taken a speculative position, however, the underlying information must become public in order for him to profit from the price adjustments he believes are going to occur. Chapter 6 covered the case where, it was anticipated, public information would costlessly emerge in time to influence posterior-round prices. But supposing as in this chapter that only private information is involved, it will be up to the informed individuals to bring about the needed disclosure.

It is this phenomenon that underlies the willingness of informed individuals to disseminate their information gratuitously, or even to incur costs in doing so. In the case of advertising, each seller has made a speculative commitment to his or her own product, which will be validated if demand turns out to be high. The problem is that consumers have only limited time and capacity for analyzing the manifestly biased claims made on behalf of so many competing products, so advertisers have to push their message through a congested and noisy channel. Professors seeking advancement are in essentially the same situation. Each professor has made a speculative commitment by investing in his own human capital. This will turn out to be profitable only if potential employers are convinced of his high worth; once again, the problem is to push the message through the noise generated by other professors trying to do the same thing.

Advertising, it has been in effect argued by Nelson (1974, 1975), is a "signal."[17] Sellers offering higher-quality products want to convey that fact to consumers, but of course any seller can make such a claim. Signaling as a solution to this difficulty takes place when sellers of truly higher-quality products engage in some activity *that would not be as profitable for those selling low-quality products*. Since a high-quality firm will be acquiring a pool of satisfied repeat customers, whereas a low-quality firm can only count on one-time sales, willingness to advertise can serve as a signal. Even if the ad itself has zero information content, a message is still being conveyed: that the product is worth promoting. (On

[17] Signaling will be analyzed in a more general context in chapters 8 and 11.

the other hand, a low-quality firm typically has lower costs of production, and so may find it profitable to advertise even without hope of repeat sales.)

Of course, the content of advertising *might* actually be informative. Ads may call attention to relevant facts and draw valid inferences from them. To the extent that consumers have some ability to distinguish sound from unsound claims, once again the truly higher-quality firms will reap some differential advantage from advertising. In freely disseminating their intellectual products, professors, let us hope, are relying upon this feature more than upon the signal conveyed by sheer willingness to commit effort to the self-promotion process.

### 7.3    Unintended dissemination: the leakage problem

Let us now shift attention to unintended dissemination – the problem of leakage. There are two main ways in which information, produced or acquired at some cost, may leak out. "Direct leakage" occurs if, for example, the valuable secret is disclosed by mistake or, alternatively, is uncovered through industrial espionage. "Market leakage" occurs when the very attempt to exploit a discovery, through dealings with other parties, necessarily entails some degree of disclosure. As soon as a new product embodying a discovery is offered to consumers, for example, competitors may start trying to uncover the secret through reverse engineering.[18] Quite a different form of market leakage will be the center of attention here, however: the possibility that attempting to profit from a discovery may allow free-riders to infer the content of the message *from the impact upon price itself.*

In the previous chapter it was assumed that individuals in general have divergent beliefs as to the likelihood of the possible states of the world, but the *sources* of divergent beliefs were left unexplained. In contrast, here we will be assuming that, while everyone has identical prior beliefs, some parties may have invested in a message service allowing Bayesian updating – for example, a private weather-forecasting service. The informed individuals thus gain an advantage, though of course generally at some cost. (We will also initially assume that everyone knows that this is the case, a "common knowledge" assumption to be reconsidered later on.) Suppose purchasers of information attempt to profit therefrom by taking a long or short position in crop futures. Then the other parties might to a greater or lesser extent be able to infer the content of the hidden message by observing the movement of futures prices.[19] (This is one more instance of the

---

[18] Copyright and patent laws aim at controlling unauthorized use of such disclosures, but of course can never do so perfectly.    [19] Grossman and Stiglitz (1976, 1980).

"public good effect" that tends to reduce the incentive to acquire private information. Conversely, to the extent that such leakage occurs, the "speculative effect" that operates to induce overinvestment in information will be weakened or even eliminated.)

In the interests of simplicity, let us rule out possible monopoly power over price. All traders, informed and uninformed, treat price as parametric. Thus, we can assume, everyone will be submitting a personal excess-demand schedule to a hypothetical auctioneer whose function is to aggregate these and thereby determine the market-clearing equilibrium price.

To illustrate, suppose all individuals have the same preference-scaling function $v(c_s) = \ln c_s$. There are two states of the world, 1 and 2 (say, no rain versus rain). Each individual initially believes that the probability of state 1 is $\pi$. Individual $j$ may be uninformed ($j = U$) or informed ($j = I$).

Initially, suppose the situation is non-informative (as defined in chapter 6), so that all individuals are uninformed. Assuming a regime of Complete Contingent Markets (CCM), each trader will be choosing a portfolio to satisfy the Fundamental Theorem of Risk-bearing:

$$\frac{\pi v'(c_1^j)}{\bar{P}_1} = \frac{(1-\pi)v'(c_2^j)}{\bar{P}_2} \tag{7.3.1}$$

where $\bar{P}_1$ and $\bar{P}_2$ signify the state-claim prices for the non-informative situation.

Given the assumed form of the $v(c)$ function, the marginal utilities are:

$$v'(c_i^j) = 1/c_1^j \quad \text{and} \quad v'(c_2^j) = 1/c_2^j$$

So the Fundamental Theorem implies that:

$$\frac{\pi}{\bar{P}_1 c_1^j} = \frac{1-\pi}{\bar{P}_1 c_2^j} = \frac{1}{W^j} \tag{7.3.2}$$

where the individual's wealth $W^j$ is the value of his endowment:

$$W^j \equiv \bar{P}_1 \bar{c}_1 + \bar{P}_2 \bar{c}_1$$

Therefore the individual state-contingent demands can be written:

$$c_i^j = \frac{\pi}{\bar{P}_1} W^j \quad \text{and} \quad c_2^j = \frac{1-\pi}{\bar{P}_2} W^j \tag{7.3.3}$$

Summing over all individuals, the aggregate demands are:

$$C_1 = \frac{\pi}{\bar{P}_1}(\bar{P}_1 \bar{C}_1 + P_2 \bar{C}_2) \quad \text{and} \quad C_2 = \frac{1-\pi}{\bar{P}_2}(\bar{P}_1 \bar{C}_1 + P_2 \bar{C}_2) \tag{7.3.4}$$

where $\bar{C}_1$ and $\bar{C}_2$ are the aggregate endowments. These are the supply-demand conditions determining the price ratio $\bar{P}_2/\bar{P}_1$ *for the non-informative case.*[20]

### Aggregate demand of informed traders (speculative behavior excluded)

Now we want to consider an informative situation. Specifically, suppose that at a cost (in utility units) of $\Delta$ in each state,[21] an individual may purchase a message service whose output will change $\bar{\pi}$, his prior assessment of the probability of state 1, to some posterior assessment $\pi$. Defining $f(\pi)$ to the probability density of the message $\pi$, we require:

$$E\{\pi\} = \int_0^1 \pi f(\pi)d\pi = \bar{\pi} \tag{7.3.5}$$

An informed individual then has expected utility:

$$U^I(c^I) = \pi \ln c_1^I + (1-\pi)\ln c_2^I - \Delta \tag{7.3.6}$$

Given the output of his message service, an informed individual can use his superior information simply to choose an improved final consumption portfolio in the light of his changed beliefs and the existing market prices. Alternatively, as explained in chapter 6, in some circumstances an informed individual may be in a position to *speculate*, that is, to hold a trading portfolio (or futures position) so as to profit from the prospective changes in market prices when his private information becomes public later on. For simplicity here, we exclude speculative behavior.

Then, by the same reasoning as before, the informed individuals' demands are:

$$c_1^I = \frac{\pi}{P_1}\left(P_1\bar{c}_1^I + P_2\bar{c}_2^I\right) \quad \text{and} \quad c_2^I = \frac{1-\pi}{P_2}\left(P_1\bar{c}_1^I + P_2\bar{c}_2^I\right) \tag{7.3.7}$$

Of course, the price ratio $P_2/P_1$ will now in general diverge from the $\bar{P}_2/\bar{P}_1$ of the non-informative situation.

Suppose that the informed individuals begin with a given fraction $f$ of

[20] Actually, an even simpler result holds here:

$$\frac{\bar{P}_2}{\bar{P}_1} = \frac{\pi}{1-\pi}\frac{\bar{C}_1}{\bar{C}_2}$$

However, the more general form of (7.3.4) is needed later on to determine the composite effect of informed and uninformed groups upon the price ratio $P_2/P_1$.

[21] A fixed cost in utility units is actually a rather unreasonable assumption. Given different consumption levels in different states, a fixed cost in corn units would imply cost in utility units varying from state to state. The assumption is adopted here solely for reasons of tractability.

each of the aggregate state-endowments $(\bar{C}_1, \bar{C}_2)$. (Ultimately $f$ will be an endogenous variable to be determined, but for the moment let us take it as given.) Then, summing over the informed individuals' demands:

$$C_1^I = \frac{\pi}{P_1} f\left(P_1 \bar{C}_1 + P_2 \bar{C}_2\right) \quad \text{and} \quad C_2^I = \frac{1-\pi}{P_2} f\left(P_1 \bar{C}_1 + P_2 \bar{C}_2\right) \quad (7.3.8)$$

### Aggregate demands of uninformed traders (naive behavior assumed)

Exactly the same argument can be applied to the uninformed traders, with endowment equal to the fraction $1 - f$ of the aggregate endowment, on the supposition that these individuals behave "naively." That is, they simply adapt to the ruling market prices in the light of their prior beliefs $\bar{\pi}$ and do *not* attempt to infer the true $\pi$ from the movement of price itself. By a parallel argument, the aggregate demands $C_1^U$ of naive uninformed traders in an informative situation will be:

$$C_1^U = \frac{\bar{\pi}}{P_1}(1-f)\left(P_1 \bar{C}_1 + P_2 \bar{C}_2\right) \quad \text{and}$$

$$C_2^U = \frac{1-\bar{\pi}}{P_2}(1-f)\left(P_1 \bar{C}_2 + P_2 \bar{C}_2\right) \quad (7.3.9)$$

Summing over the two groups:

$$C_1 = \frac{\pi f + \bar{\pi}(1-f)}{P_1}\left(P_1 \bar{C}_1 + P_2 \bar{C}_2\right) \quad \text{and}$$

$$C_2 = \frac{(1-\pi)f + (1-\bar{\pi})(1-f)}{P_2}\left(P_1 \bar{C}_1 + P_2 \bar{C}_2\right) \quad (7.3.10)$$

In equilibrium, supply equals demand. Then setting $C_s = \bar{C}_s (s = 1, 2)$ in (7.3.10) we obtain at last:

$$\frac{P_2}{P_1} = \frac{\bar{C}_1}{\bar{C}_2} \frac{(1-\pi)f + (1-\bar{\pi})(1-f)}{\pi f + \bar{\pi}(1-f)} \quad (7.3.11)$$

Notice that, for all $f > 0$, as $\pi$ increases the numerator on the right-hand side falls while the denominator increases. So, as depicted in figure 7.7, the equilibrium price ratio $P_2/P_1$ is a decreasing function of $\pi$, the informed individuals' posterior belief that state 1 will occur. This is of course what we would expect. The higher is the $\pi$ implied by the message received by the informed individuals, the greater will be their demands (at any given price ratio) for state-1 claims. (For naive uninformed individuals, of course, the demands remain unaffected.) Thus, a high $\pi$ implies a low ratio $P_2/P_1$.

In addition, the equation indicates that $P_2/P_1$ is increasing in $f$ if and

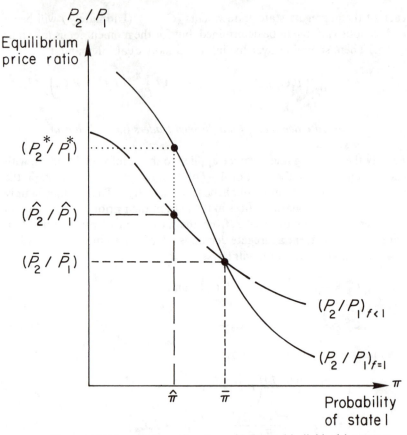

Figure 7.7 Price ratio as a function of informed individuals' message

only if $\pi < \bar{\pi}$. More generally, the larger is $f$, the steeper will be the curve relating $P_2/P_1$ to $\pi$. In other words, the larger the fraction informed, the more sensitive will be the equilibrium price ratio to any divergence of the message $\pi$ from the prior belief $\bar{\pi}$.

*Uninformed traders – from naive to sophisticated behavior*
In the absence of any information gathering (when $f = 0$), the equilibrium price ratio would be $\bar{P}_2/\bar{P}_1$. But, when others are informed about the true probabilities, the uninformed find themselves using the "wrong" beliefs and so at a disadvantage in trading. Ideally, if it were possible to identify the informed individuals, the uninformed should refuse to trade with them; the uninformed group should open a separate market and engage in risk-balancing by trading only amongst themselves, at the equilibrium price

ratio $\bar{P}_2/\bar{P}_1$. However, this is generally infeasible. It is difficult or impossible to know whether your trading partner is informed or uninformed, nor can the uninformed parties know *ex ante* what the $\bar{P}_2/\bar{P}_1$ price ratio would have been in the absence of information-gathering activity. So an uninformed individual who engages in trade at all must expect, to some extent, to be dealing at a disadvantage with informed individuals. This disadvantage could be so great that it would be strictly better to withdraw from the market entirely, even though doing so means foregoing the opportunity to balance risks via market trading. Consider the extreme case in which the uninformed all have identical endowments and preferences. Then, in the absence of the informed parties, no trading would take place; the equilibrium prices would be such as to sustain the initial endowment positions. Knowing this, in the presence of informed parties the uninformed would indeed do better by refusing to trade.

But the uninformed parties have another recourse: they do not have to behave naively. Suppose that the revised state-1 probability for the informed individuals is $\hat{\pi}$. If the fraction informed is some $f < 1$, and the uninformed behave naively as before (use their prior beliefs to trade), the equilibrium price ratio would be some $\hat{P}_2/\hat{P}_1$ as depicted in figure 7.7. However, if the uninformed understand the model and if they also know $f$, they might *be able to infer the message $\hat{\pi}$ from the price ratio $\hat{P}_2/\hat{P}_1$.*[22] Given such an inference, the fraction informed will rise to unity and so the equilibrium price ratio rises to $P_2^*/P_1^*$. But then the uninformed are better off than the informed, not having incurred the utility cost $\Delta$ of gaining access to the information!

It is tempting to think that this result follows from the simplicity of the example. However, as Radner (1979) has shown, even if individuals have differing preferences and endowments and there are an arbitrarily large but finite number of states of nature, the information of the informed agents can be inferred from market prices almost certainly.

Radner's argument can be illustrated by a small modification of the example. Suppose that the aggregate endowment in the rainy state $\bar{C}_2$ is itself uncertain. Initially, suppose that all but a negligible fraction of the individuals have become informed and have the posterior probability $\pi$. The equilibrium price ratio is then given by (7.3.1), with $f = 1$:

$$\frac{P_2}{P_1} = \frac{\bar{C}_1}{\bar{C}_2}\frac{(1-\pi)}{\pi}$$

Note that this is decreasing in both $\pi$ and $\bar{C}_2$. Equilibrium price-ratio

---

[22] This would be true only under rather extreme assumptions, however. Such computations require knowledge not only of the market-clearing price ratio but of the entire function $(P_2/P_1)_{f<1}$. We comment on this further below.

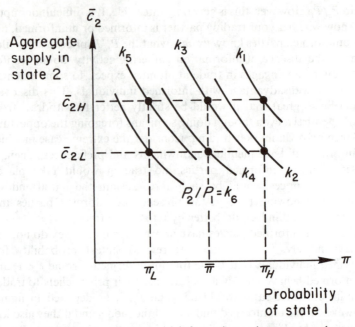

Figure 7.8 Iso-price contours with information and aggregate endowment uncertain

contours as functions of $\bar{C}_2$ and $\pi$ are drawn in figure 7.8. Suppose, as depicted, that $\pi$ can take on three possible values $\pi_L$, $\bar{\pi}$, and $\pi_H$ while $\bar{C}_2$ can take on two possible values $\bar{C}_{2L}$ and $\bar{C}_{2H}$. These generate six possible equilibrium price ratios $k_1, \ldots, k_6$ depicted in figure 7.8. While it would be possible for one of the iso-price contours to go through more than one of the six points, this is an event with zero probability if the parameters are drawn from some underlying continuous distribution. Thus, any of the few uninformed individuals can correctly infer $\pi$.

Next suppose that only a fraction $f$ of the population are informed and that they have learned that $\pi = \pi_H$. Suppose, furthermore, that the auctioneer starts out with a price ratio of $P_2/P_1 = k_4$; that is, a ratio consistent with the beliefs of the uninformed. Finally, suppose that the actual aggregate supply is $\bar{C}_{2H}$. In each round of the Walrasian auction an informed individual submits his true demand, conditional upon the information that he receives. An uninformed individual always bases his beliefs on the hypothesis that the auctioneer has called out the equilibrium price. It follows that in the initial round the informed will generate an excess supply of state-2 claims, since $\pi = \pi_H$. In response, the auctioneer lowers the price ratio to $P_2/P_1 = k_2$. The uninformed then conclude that $\pi$

$= \pi_H$. However again there is excess supply of state-2 claims. The auctioneer then lowers the relative price again to $P_2/P_1 = k_1$ and both markets clear. It follows that all information is revealed via the Walrasian auctioneer.

While we have only examined an example, the underlying conclusion is quite general. Let $m_j$ be the message received by individual $j$ from his information service and let $P(m) = P(m_1, \ldots, m_n)$ be the equilibrium price vector if *every* individual in the economy is provided with all the available information $(m_1, \ldots, m_n)$. If there is a finite number of states and messages, then with probability 1:

$$m' \neq m'' \Rightarrow P(m') \neq P(m'')$$

It follows that, just as in the example, all information is revealed in a Walrasian equilibrium with perfect inference by every agent.

The "generic" existence of a fully revealing equilibrium price raises a disturbing puzzle, as has been seen. If the uninformed behave in a sophisticated rather than naive manner, they can infer messages without incurring the cost of purchasing an information service. As a result, no-one has an incentive to become informed.

But the puzzle is really an artifact of the assumption that uninformed individuals can make essentially perfect inferences from market prices. Consider instead the limiting case of a continuous distribution of aggregate endowment in state 2 (rain) and a continuous distribution of information states. Then all the points on an iso-price contour are feasible and so any inference by an uninformed individual would remain incomplete. He could update his beliefs by observing prices but would not be able to perfectly infer the message $\pi$. Information leakage is therefore only *partial*; the incentive to invest in information is reduced but not eliminated.

What should be made of the difference between the strong leakage result for the discrete case and the more reasonable partial leakage result for the continuous case? The answer is that, with a large finite set of unpriced states (a large number of dots in figure 7.8), the price contour through any one pair $(\pi, \bar{C}_2)$ will pass very close to other pairs. Then, unless the uninformed outsider has access to a high-speed computer, a perfectly accurate model of the economy, and an enormous amount of data, he will be unable to infer the insiders' information with any great accuracy. And, in fact, some of the data required are essentially unknowable, being the demand functions of other individuals at price ratios other than those visible in current market trading.

In view of all these limitations, the leakage effect is, realistically speaking, normally rather less important than might initially have appeared.

## EXERCISES AND EXCURSIONS 7.3

*1 Fully revealing contingent-claim prices*

Consider an economy in which all individuals have the same preference-scaling function $v(c) = \ln c$. There are two states, $s = 1, 2$. Individuals in group $\omega$ believe that the probability of state 1 is $\pi^\omega$. The aggregate endowment of the group is $(\bar{C}_1^\omega, \bar{C}_2^\omega)$.

(A) Show that, if the price of state-$s$ claims is $P_s$, the group's total demand for state-1 claims is:

$$C_1^\omega = \pi^\omega[\bar{C}_1^\omega + (P_2/P_1)\bar{C}_2^\omega]$$

(B) Suppose that there are two groups, $\omega = U, I$. Show that the equilibrium price ratio is:

$$\frac{P_2}{P_1} = \frac{(1-\pi^U)\bar{C}_1^U + (1-\pi^I)\bar{C}_1^I}{\pi^U\bar{C}_2^U + \pi^I\bar{C}_2^I}$$

(C) Suppose group $I$ is the informed group; members of this group receive a message that results in the revised state-1 probability $\pi^I$. Confirm that, if the uninformed group behave naively, the information of the informed is fully reflected in the equilibrium price ratio.

(D) Suppose each member of the informed group sacrifices $\delta_1$ units of state-1 claims and $\delta_2$ units of state-2 claims to obtain the information. Is it still the case that information is fully reflected in the equilibrium price ratio?

*2 Fully revealing asset prices*

Using the date of the previous exercise, suppose that individuals trade in asset markets rather than in state-claim markets. Asset 1, the riskless asset, yields 1 unit of income in each state. Asset 2 yields $z_{2s}$ units in state $s$, for $s = 1, 2$.

(A) Obtain an expression for the equilibrium ratio of asset prices.

(B) Hence, or otherwise, confirm that again the informed traders' information is fully revealed by the price ratio.

*3 Information leakage with more than one informed group*

Using the data of question 1, suppose that there are two informed groups. Group $A$ receives a message that results in the revised state-1 probability $\pi^A$, while group $B$'s message leads to $\pi^B$.

(A) Obtain an expression for the equilibrium ratio of state-claim prices $P_2/P_1$.

(B) If there are a finite number of messages and hence a finite number of pairs $(\pi^A, \pi^B)$, explain why, with probability 1, the beliefs of both informed groups will be fully reflected in market prices.

(C) Taking the rational expectations argument to its logical limit, does this result imply that all individuals will end up with the same beliefs in a "rational expectations equilibrium"?

(D) Explain why your conclusion is not dependent upon the specific assumptions of the model *except* that the number of messages is finite.

### *7.3.1 Partial leakage with constant absolute risk-aversion

Without making very strong assumptions, it is extremely difficult to model partial leakage of information from informed to uninformed individuals. However, there is one special case in which strong results are obtainable.

Suppose each of $n$ individuals exhibits constant absolute risk-aversion (CARA). These individuals have initial endowments of a riskless asset, each unit of which yields one unit of consumption, and also a risky asset with gross yield $\tilde{R}$ which is normally distributed. Let individual $i$'s endowment of the two assets be $(\bar{q}_{1i}, \bar{q}_{2i})$ and his final portfolio be $(q_{1i}, q_{2i})$. If the price of the unit of the risky asset is $P$ and the price of the riskless asset is normalized to be 1, individual $i$'s budget constraints and final consumption are:

$$q_{1i} + Pq_{2i} = \bar{q}_{1i} + P\bar{q}_{2i} \quad \text{and} \quad \tilde{c}_i = q_{1i} + q_{2i}\tilde{R}$$

Substituting for $q_{1i}$, final consumption can be rewritten as:

$$\tilde{c}_i = \bar{q}_{1i} + P\bar{q}_{2i} + q_{2i}(\tilde{R} - P) \tag{7.3.12}$$

Given the assumptions of normality and constant absolute risk-aversion, expected utility is proportional to:

$$U_i = E\{\tilde{c}_i\} - \tfrac{1}{2}A_i \operatorname{Var}\{\tilde{c}_i\}$$

where $A_i$ is individual $i$'s degree of absolute risk-aversion. (See exercise 2 at the end of section 2.3 in chapter 2 for a derivation of this result.)

Substituting from (7.3.12) we obtain:

$$U_i = \bar{q}_{1i} + P\bar{q}_{2i} + q_{2i}[E\{\tilde{R}\,|\,m_i\} - P] - \tfrac{1}{2}A_i q_{2i}^2 \operatorname{Var}\{\tilde{R}\,|\,m_i\}$$

Note that the mean and variance of the risky return are dependent upon some message $m_i$ received by individual $i$ from an information service. Differentiating by $q_{1i}$ and rearranging, individual $i$'s demand for the risky asset is:

$$q_{1i}^* = \left(\frac{1}{A_i \operatorname{Var}\{\tilde{R}\,|\,m_i\}}\right)\left(E\{\tilde{R}\,|\,m_i\} - P\right)$$

---

\* Starred sections represent more difficult or specialized materials that can be omitted without significant loss of continuity.

Let $Q_2$ be the aggregate supply of the risky asset. Summing over $i$ and setting supply equal to demand, leads to the pricing rule:

$$\sum_{i=1}^{n} \left( \frac{1}{A_i \operatorname{Var}\{\tilde{R} \mid m_i\}} \right) \left( \operatorname{E}\{\tilde{R} \mid m_i\} - P \right) = Q_2 \tag{7.3.13}$$

As an illustration, suppose that a subset $I$ of the population all obtain the same message $m$ which is an unbiased but noisy estimate of the unknown yield $\tilde{R}$:

$$\tilde{m}_i = \tilde{m} = \tilde{R} + \tilde{\varepsilon}$$

We assume that $\tilde{\varepsilon}$ is independent of $\tilde{R}$ and normally distributed with mean 0 and variance $\sigma_\varepsilon^2$. Let $\sigma_R^2$ be the variance of $\tilde{R}$. Then, from normal distribution theory, the conditional expectation and variance of $\tilde{R}$ can be expressed as:

$$\operatorname{E}\{\tilde{R} \mid m\} = (1 - \alpha_I)\mu + \alpha_I m,$$
$$\operatorname{Var}\{\tilde{R} \mid m\} = \sigma_I^2$$

The important point to note is that both $\alpha_I$ and $\sigma_I^2$ are functions only of the underlying variances $\sigma_R^2$ and $\sigma_\varepsilon^2$ and *not* of the message $m$.

Following Grossman and Stiglitz (1980) we shall refer to individuals in $I$ as insiders. The remaining individuals or outsiders receive no message. As a final simplification, suppose all individuals have the same degree of absolute risk aversion, that is, $A_i = A$, for $i = 1, \ldots, n$. Then (7.3.13) can be rewritten as follows:

$$\left( \sum_{i \in I} \frac{1}{A\sigma_I^2} \right) \left( (1 - \alpha_I)\mu + \alpha_I m - P \right) + \left( \sum_{i \in 0} \frac{1}{A\sigma_R^2} \right) (\mu - P) = Q_2$$

Collecting terms:

$$\theta_0 \mu + \theta_1 m - \theta_2 P = Q_2 \tag{7.3.14}$$

where $\theta \equiv (\theta_0, \theta_1, \theta_2)$ is a factor of parameters dependent only on the underlying variances.

It follows that, if the aggregate supply of the risky asset is fixed, the equilibrium price increases linearly with the message $m$. Therefore, as Grossman and Stiglitz (1980) point out, the equilibrium price becomes a perfect predictor of the message received by the informed. Just as in the finite-state example above, complete information leakage is possible. Then, if information is costly and outsiders do make the correct inference, they are better off than insiders. It follows that no individual has an incentive to become informed.

To generate *partial* leakage, and hence to restore the incentive for information gathering, a second source of uncertainty must be introduced.

One possibility is aggregate supply uncertainty. Suppose then that $Q_2$ is independently and normally distributed[23] with mean $\bar{Q}_2$ and variance $\sigma_Q^2$. From (7.3.14) the equilibrium price is now an increasing function of the message $m$ and a decreasing function of aggregate supply $Q_2$. It follows that outsiders are no longer able to infer $m$ solely by observing $P$.

Suppose, however, that they *conjecture* a linear equilibrium relationship of the form given by (7.3.14), that is, for some vector of parameters $\gamma = (\gamma_0, \gamma_1, \gamma_2)$:

$$\gamma_0 \mu + \gamma_1 m - \gamma_2 P = Q_2 \qquad (7.3.15)$$

Given such a conjecture, it follows that the equilibrium price $P$ is a linear function of two independently distributed normal random variables and is thus normally distributed as well. From normal distribution theory, the expectation and variance of $\tilde{R}$ conditional upon observing $P$ can be written as:

$$E\{\tilde{R} \mid P\} = (1 - \alpha_0)\mu_R + \alpha_0 P$$
$$\text{Var}\{\tilde{R} \mid P\} = \sigma_0^2$$

where $\alpha_0$ and $\sigma_0^2$ are functions of the underlying variances and the vector $\gamma$. Continuing with the assumption that all individuals have the same degree of absolute risk-aversion, and substituting these expressions into (7.1.12) leads to the revised pricing rule:

$$\left(\sum_{i \in I} \frac{1}{A_i \sigma_{I}^2}\right)((1 - \alpha_I)\mu_R - \alpha_I m - P) + \left[\sum_{i \in 0} \frac{1}{A_0 \sigma_0^2}\right]((1 - \alpha_0)\mu_R - \alpha_0 P - P) = Q_2$$

Collecting terms, it follows that there is some vector $\gamma^* = (\gamma_0^*, \gamma_1^*, \gamma_2^*)$ such that:

$$\alpha_0^* \mu + \alpha_1^* m - \alpha_2^* P = Q_2 \qquad (7.3.16)$$

Comparing (7.3.15) and (7.3.16) it follows that the form of the pricing rule is the one conjectured. That is, for any linear conjecture with parameter vector $\gamma$, there exists an equilibrium pricing rule which is linear with parameters:

$$\gamma^* = f(\gamma; \sigma_R^2, \sigma_\varepsilon^2, \sigma_Q^2)$$

What Grossman and Stiglitz were able to show is that there is a unique fixed point of this mapping. That is, there exists a unique linear conjecture which is correct or "rational." They then established that the difference between the expected utility of the insiders and outsiders declines as the

[23] As formally modelled, each individual's endowment of the risky asset is independently distributed. Therefore, as long as the population is sufficiently large, the fact that an individual knows his own endowment yields essentially no information about aggregate supply.

proportion of insiders rises. It follows that, if information is costly, the number of individuals purchasing information rises until the expected utility of insiders and outsiders is equated.

Hellwig (1980) considers a model in which each individual receives a different message:

$$\tilde{m}_i = \tilde{R} + \tilde{\varepsilon}_i, \quad i = 1, \ldots, n$$

and $\tilde{\varepsilon}_i$ is independently and normally distributed with mean $\sigma_i^2$. Suppose first of all that individuals make no use of information contained in market prices. The pricing rule (7.3.13) then becomes:

$$\sum_{i=1}^{n} \frac{1}{A_i \operatorname{Var}(\tilde{R} \mid m_i)} ((1 - \alpha_i)\mu + \alpha_i(\tilde{R} + \tilde{\varepsilon}_i) - P) = Q_2 \qquad (7.3.17)$$

Suppose the economy is replicated so that there are $T$ individuals of each type and the aggregate endowment is $TQ_2$. Each individual of type $i$ receives an independent message $\tilde{m}_{it} = \tilde{R}_t + \tilde{\varepsilon}_{it}, t = 1, \ldots, T$, with mean zero and variance $\sigma_i^2$. From (7.3.17) it follows that the new equilibrium pricing rule is:

$$\sum_{i=1}^{n} \frac{1}{A_i \operatorname{Var}(\tilde{R} \mid m_{it})} \left( (1 - \alpha_i)T\mu + \alpha_i \left( T\tilde{R} + \sum_{t=1}^{T} \tilde{\varepsilon}_{it} \right) - TP \right) = TQ_2$$

Dividing by $T$:

$$\sum_{i=1}^{n} \frac{1}{A_i \operatorname{Var}(\tilde{R} \mid m_{it})} \left( (1 - \alpha)\mu + \alpha_i \tilde{R} + \left[ \frac{1}{T} \sum_{t=1}^{T} \tilde{\varepsilon}_{it} \right] - P \right) = Q_2$$

In the limit as $T$ becomes large, the variance of the average of the $T$ independent random variables approaches zero. That is, the expression inside the square brackets approaches zero with probability 1. Then, in the limit with probability 1:

$$\sum_{i=1}^{n} \frac{1}{A_i \operatorname{Var}(\tilde{R} \mid m_{it})} ((1 - \alpha_i)\mu + \alpha_i \tilde{R} - P) = Q_2$$

The equilibrium price is then a linear function of the actual return $\tilde{R}$ and the random aggregate supply $\tilde{Q}_2$ and is *independent* of each individual's own message.

Now suppose individuals try to incorporate the information contained in market prices into their own decisions. As in the case considered by Grossman and Stiglitz, suppose individuals all make the same linear conjecture:

$$\gamma_0 \mu + \gamma_1 \tilde{R} - \gamma_2 P = \tilde{Q}_2$$

Individual $i, i = 1, \ldots, n$, then computes a conditional mean and variance. From normal distribution theory the conditional mean is again a linear function of the private signal $m_{it}$ and the price $P$. The analysis then proceeds exactly as before, and it can be confirmed that the linear conjecture implies a limiting relationship (as $T \to \infty$) of the form:

$$\gamma_0^* \mu + \gamma_1^* \tilde{R} - \gamma_2^* P = \tilde{Q}_2$$

That is, once again, for any linear conjecture with parameter vector $\gamma$ there is an equilibrium pricing rule that is linear with parameter vector $\gamma^* = g(\gamma)$. From Hellwig's analysis we know that there is a unique fixed point of this mapping, leading once again to a rational expectations equilibrium with partial leakage. While the algebra is tedious, it is also possible to solve for the equilibrium value of $\gamma$.

This relationship has been exploited successfully in recent contributions to the finance literature. Diamond (1985), for example, characterizes the value of optimal release of public information by firms. Intuitively, the more information released by firms, the lower is the incentive for each individual to obtain private information. Thus, total expenditures on information acquisition are thereby reduced. Verrecchia (1982) focuses on the level of private information acquisition. In his extension of the basic model, the noisiness of individual $i$'s message service, represented by the variance $\sigma_i^2$, is a decreasing function of some costly input. Each individual then chooses his optimal message service. He shows, for example, that if two individuals differ only in their degree of risk-aversion, the less risk averse individual will spend more on information acquisition in the "rational expectations" equilibrium. This is intuitively sensible. A less risk-averse individual takes more risky positions based on his information and the return to more accurate information is therefore greater.

We conclude this chapter with some cautionary remarks. First, the constant absolute risk-aversion/normal distribution model is very special. Second, even within the confines of this model, analytical solutions with partial leakage all hinge on the assumption that the aggregate supply of the risky asset is a random variable. This is hard to justify in many contexts, for example, in a stockmarket.[24]

More fundamentally, recall that we have been excluding speculative behavior on the part of the informed individuals. While the uninformed are assumed to be enormously competent and well-equipped economists and statisticians, the *informed* are supposed to behave rather simplistically – simply presenting their true demands to the auctioneer. In a more realistic model, an informed individual would have a pretty good idea which way

---

[24] An alternative approach is to introduce "noise traders." These are individuals who make trades that are exogenous to the formal model.

prices will move when his private information becomes public knowledge. So he has an incentive to take an initial speculative position in the market and then wait for prices to adjust before moving to his final consumption bundle, in accordance with the analysis in chapter 6. This means that the payoff to becoming informed may become quite large after all.

The speculation option available to the informed traders has two different kinds of effects upon the leakage problem. First, it increases the sensitivity of price to the message received. Suppose the message $m$ indicates that state 1 is more probable than was previously believed. Then informed traders who speculate will initially purchase state-1 claims more heavily than if they were merely adapting their consumption portfolios to their revised beliefs. It follows that state-1 claims will be bid up more sharply in the market, thus providing a more visible clue to the uninformed – at least as to the direction of change signaled by the unknown message. On the other hand, as an analytical matter, the speculation option adds another complication to the already difficult problem that uninformed parties face in trying to infer the missing message on the basis of a still more general economic model and the associated econometric calculations.

The equilibrium of such a generalized model will not be addressed here, but it will involve: (i) speculative as well as adaptive behavior on the part of the informed; (ii) sophisticated behavior on the part of the uninformed, as they attempt with partial success to infer the message generated by the information service; and (iii) an equilibrium fraction $f$ of traders who choose to become informed at cost $\Delta$. An even more general model would provide for an information-supplying industry, so that $\Delta$ itself would be determined endogenously.

## EXERCISES AND EXCURSIONS 7.3.1

### 1 Aggregation of insiders' information

There are $N_I$ insiders who each pay \$$\delta$ and receive a signal correlated with the true return on a risky asset. The signal received by insider $i$ is $m_i = R + \varepsilon_i$, where $R$ and $\varepsilon_i$ ($i = 1, \ldots, N_I$) are $N_I + 1$ independently and normally distributed random variables with means $\mu$ and 0 and variances $\sigma^2$ and $\sigma_\varepsilon^2$. There are $N_O$ outsiders who receive no information. All individuals exhibit constant absolute risk-aversion.

(A) Show that the expectation of $R$ given the observations $m_1, m_2, \ldots, m_{N_I}$ can be expressed in the form:

$$\alpha\mu + (1-\alpha)\left(\frac{m_1 + m_2 + \ldots m_{N_I}}{N_I}\right)$$

(B) In a world in which there is a riskless asset and a single risky asset, suppose that in bidding for the risky asset insiders and outsiders simply use their own endowed or acquired information (i.e., they do not draw inferences from market prices). If all insiders have the same degree of absolute risk-aversion, obtain an expression for the market-clearing price. Confirm that it is a function of the sum of the $N_I$ messages received. Compare this price with the price that would clear markets if the $N_I$ insiders were all to receive all $N_I$ messages.

(C) Suppose outsiders are not smart enough to draw inferences from market prices. However insiders do have this capacity. If inside information is costly to purchase, what incentive is there for any of the insiders to obtain it? Is there an equilibrium number of insiders who purchase the information?

(D) Would your answer to (C) differ significantly if insiders have differing degrees of risk-aversion? (Discuss only.)**

** End of starred section.

## REFERENCES AND SELECTED READINGS

Arrow, Kenneth J., "Economic Welfare and the Allocation of Resources for Invention," in *The Rate and Direction of Inventive Activity: Economic and Social Factors*, Universities-NBER Conference Series, Princeton, NJ: Princeton University Press, 1962.

Barzel, Yoram, "Optimal Timing of Innovations," *Review of Economic Statistics*, 50 (August 1968), 348–55.

Berle, Alf K. and de Camp, L. Sprague, *Inventions, Patents, and their Management*, Princeton, NJ: Van Nostrand, 1959.

Cheung, Steven N. S., "Property Rights and Inventions," University of Washington Institute for Economic Research, Discussion Paper No. 79–11, 1979.

———, "Property Rights in Trade Secrets," *Economic Inquiry*, 20 (January 1982), 40–53.

de Camp, L. Sprague, *The Heroic Age of American Invention*, Garden City, NY: Doubleday, 1961.

Diamond, Douglas W., "Optimal Release of Information by Firms," *Journal of Finance*, 40 (September 1985), 1071–94.

Fama, Eugene F. and Laffer, Arthur B., "Information and Capital Markets," *Journal of Business*, 44 (July 1971), 289–98.

Grossman, Sanford J. and Stiglitz, Joseph E., "Information and Competitive Price Systems," *American Economic Review*, 66 (May 1976), 246–53.

———, "On the Impossibility of Informationally Efficient Markets," *American Economic Review*, 70 (June 1980), 393–408.

Hellwig, Martin F., "On the Aggregation of Information in Competitive Markets," *Journal of Economic Theory* (1980), 477–98.

Hirshleifer, J., "The Private and Social Value of Information and the Reward to Inventive Activity," *American Economic Review*, 61 (September 1971), 561–74.

Lee, T. and Wilde, L. L., "Market Structure and Innovation: A Reformulation," *Quarterly Journal of Economics*, 94 (1980), 429–36.

Lowry, G. C., "Market Structure and Innovation," *Quarterly Journal of Economics*, 93 (1979), 395–410.

Machlup, Fritz, "Patents," in *International Encyclopedia of the Social Sciences*, New York: Macmillan, Free Press, 1968.

Nelson, Phillip, "Advertising as Information," *Journal of Political Economy*, 82 (July/August 1974), 729–54.

———, "The Economic Consequences of Advertising," *Journal of Business*, 48 (April 1975), 213–41.

Novos, Ian E. and Waldman, Michael, "The Emergence of Copying Technologies: What Have We Learned?", *Contemporary Policy Issues*, 5 (July 1987), 34–43.

Radner, Roy, "Rational Expectations Equilibrium: Generic Existence and the Information Revealed by Prices," *Econometrica*, 47 (May 1979), 655–78.

Reinganum, Jennifer F., "The Timing of Innovation: Research, Development, and Diffusion," chapter 14 in Richard Schmalansee and Robert Willig (eds.), *Handbook of Industrial Organization*. Amsterdam; New York, NY: North-Holland, 1989, vol I, pp. 849–908.

Verrecchia, Robert E., "Information Acquisition in a Noisy Rational Expectations Economy," *Econometrica*, 50 (November 1982), 1415–30.

# 8 Informational asymmetry and contract design

The theme of this chapter is *informational asymmetry*, which is not the same as the *differences of beliefs* considered at various points in earlier chapters. Beliefs may differ without there being a consensus that any single person's opinions are intrinsically superior to anyone else's. In some situations, however, it will be clear to all parties involved that some of them are better informed than others. When a principal employs an agent to carry out actions whose outcomes are uncertain – for example, when an absentee landlord engages a farm manager – the latter will evidently be in a better position to know about any shirking or opportunistic behavior he chooses to engage in. As another example, an expert jeweller will evidently be more familiar with the quality of the diamonds he offers for sale than will an ordinary prospective purchaser. We will be considering the first type of situation in section 8.1 under the heading of *hidden actions*. Sections 8.2 and 8.3 explore aspects of the second type of situation, the problem of *hidden knowledge*. In each case the challenge facing the lesser-informed party is to design an incentive scheme (a contract) aimed at mitigating the effects of informational asymmetry.[1]

The primary focus in this chapter will be on the choices made (the contracts designed) by a less well-informed decision-maker or principal who has monopoly power. In the case of hidden actions, introducing competition among principals affects the analysis in only a minor way. On the other hand, in the case of hidden knowledge, when a number of less-informed transactors compete with one another, subtle issues arise regarding the nature of equilibrium. For this reason we defer a discussion of competition and hidden knowledge until chapter 11.

---

[1] In chapter 5 we considered the situation of a decision-maker who employs an expert. That discussion addressed only the problem of sincerity, how to induce the expert to accurately reveal his hidden knowledge.

## 8.1    Hidden actions ("moral hazard") and contract design[2]

Suppose an absentee landlord (the principal) hires a farm manager as his *agent*. The agent's preference-scaling function is $v^A(c, x)$, where her action is $x$ (which we may think of as her *effort*) and her income is $c$. As a result of the agent's choice of action, the gross gain to the principal is the random variable $\tilde{y}(x)$ out of which he must pay the agent the amount $r$. If the principal is risk-neutral, his preference-scaling function can be written:

$$v^P = y(x) - r$$

For simplicity, assume there are just two possible outcomes $y_1$ and $y_2$, with $y_2 > y_1$. By choosing a higher level of $x$, the agent increases the probability $\pi(x)$ of the favorable outcome or event:[3]

$$d\pi(x)/dx > 0$$

Both principal and agent have the same knowledge of the underlying technology, so there is no disagreement about this probability function. Effort enters negatively into the agent's preference-scaling function:

$$\partial v^A(c, x)/\partial x < 0$$

With $x$ not observable, the principal must choose a payment scheme contingent upon the observed outcome or event. Let $r_i$ be the payment if the outcome is $y_i$, for $i = 1, 2$. Then, if the agent takes action $x$, the expected utilities of principal and agent are, respectively:

$$U^P = (1 - \pi(x))(y_1 - r_1) + \pi(x)(y_2 - r_2) \tag{8.1.1}$$
$$U^A = (1 - \pi(x))v^A(r_1, x) + \pi(x)v^A(r_2, x) \tag{8.1.2}$$

where, by assumption, the agent has no source of income apart from the contingent payments $r_1$ and $r_2$.

For any payment scheme $r = (r_1, r_2)$, the agent will respond by choosing the action $x^*(r)$ that maximizes her expected utility. Substituting this optimal action into (8.1.1) and (8.1.2) yields the derived utility levels $U_*^P(r)$ and $U_*^A(r)$, both explicitly dependent upon the payment scheme $r$ and, implicitly, upon the agent's underlying optimal response function $x^*(r)$.

We now examine the nature of the *efficient contract*, one which, holding constant the expected gain of the agent, maximizes the principal's expected gain.

---

[2] This section relies heavily on Grossman and Hart (1983).

[3] Note that the probabilities of the two possible outcomes $y_1$ and $y_2$ are not determined solely by the state of the world, but rather by the interaction between Nature's choice of state and the agent's choice of effort.

First, suppose that the agent also is risk-neutral so that her preference-scaling function can be written as:

$$v^A(r, x) = r - K(x) \tag{8.1.3}$$

Here $K(x)$ is the agent's "cost of effort" which, by assumption here, is commensurate with the payment $r$. Thus, $r - K(x)$ is the agent's net income, and she is neutral towards income risk. Equation (8.1.2) can then be rewritten as:

$$U^A = (1 - \pi(x))r_1 + \pi(x)r_2 - K(x) \tag{8.1.2'}$$

Adding (8.1.1) and (8.1.2') and rearranging:

$$U^P = (1 - \pi(x))y_1 + \pi(x)y_2 - K(x) - U^A$$
$$\equiv E\{\tilde{y}(x)\} - K(x) - U^A$$

So, maximizing $U^P$ for given $U^A$, we see that an efficient contract induces the agent to maximize the expected value of output less her own cost of effort.

We now show that, when both principal and agent are risk-neutral, there is a payment scheme such that the efficient action can be achieved even where $x$ is not directly observed. Suppose the principal (landlord) pays the agent (manager) the value of output, retaining only a fixed rent $t$:

$$r_i = y_i - t, \quad i = 1, 2$$

From (8.1.2'), the agent's expected utility becomes:

$$U^A = (1 - \pi(x))y_1(x) + \pi(x)y_2(x) - t - K(x)$$
$$= E\{\tilde{y}(x)\} - K(x) - t$$

In maximizing this $U^A$ the agent will also be maximizing $E\{\tilde{y}(x)\} - K(x)$, and thus choosing the efficient action. The economic interpretation is that, on the margin, the agent receives the full expected social benefit of her action.

This solution is no longer optimal, however, if the agent is risk-averse. For then even if the agent is induced to take the action that maximizes expected net output, there is an efficiency loss due to the absence of risk-sharing.

Suppose there are just two possible actions $x \in \{L, H\}$, where $L$ indicates that the agent chooses to be lazy and $H$ indicates that she works hard. If she is lazy her cost is lower, that is:

$$K(L) \equiv K(H) - \Delta K$$

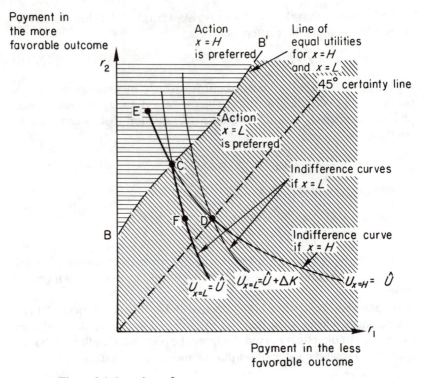

Figure 8.1 Agent's preference map

where $\Delta K$ is the reduction in her cost of effort. We continue to assume that the agent's $v^A(r, x)$ is still separable so it can be written as:

$$v^A(r, x) \equiv V(r) - K(x) \tag{8.1.4}$$

where $V(r)$ is the elementary utility associated with the separable income alone. But note here that $V(r) \neq r$, which means also that while $K(x)$ is commensurate with utility it need not be commensurate with the income payment $r$.

The agent's expected utility can be written:

$$U_x^A = (1 - \pi(x))V(r_1) + \pi(x)V(r_2) - K(x) \tag{8.1.5}$$

Indifference curves for the two effort levels are depicted in figure 8.1. For any payment schedule $(r_1, r_2)$, the agent's Marginal Rate of Substitution is:

$$-\frac{dr_2}{dr_1}\bigg|_{U_x} = \frac{1 - \pi(x)}{\pi(x)} \frac{V'(r_1)}{V'(r_2)}$$

Since effort raises $\pi(x)$, the indifference curve for a hard-working agent is flatter at each $(r_1, r_2)$ point. Moreover, along the 45° certainty line the utility of working hard is lower than the utility of being lazy, since cost is higher and the same fixed payment is received. Thus, for example at D, utility is $\hat{U}$ if the agent works hard and $\hat{U} + \Delta K$ if she is lazy. It follows that the steeper $x = L$ indifference curve with utility equal to $\hat{U}$ must meet the $x = H$ indifference curve with utility equal to $\hat{U}$ to the left of the 45° line, or specifically, in the figure, at C. (At first glance it might appear that, at any given point like C in the diagram, utility would surely be greater along the low-effort indifference curve $x = L$ – since the vector of payments received is the same. This is incorrect; what the diagram does not show is that greater effort raises the probability $\pi$ of the more favorable outcome.)

The set of intersection points like C, for different levels of utility, is the "boundary curve" labelled BB′ in the figure. Consider a point E to the left of BB′. If the agent works hard her utility is $\hat{U}$. If she is lazy her utility is lower since E lies below the indifference curve $U_{x=L} = \hat{U}$. As a utility maximizer, the agent therefore chooses to work hard. Conversely, at a point like F to the right of BB′ her utility is lower if she works hard and so the agent chooses to be lazy. Thus the agent will choose to work hard if and only if the contract is to the left of BB′, that is if the differential between the payments $r_2$ and $r_1$ is sufficiently great.

The kinked curve ECF represents payment schemes which, given optimizing behavior on the part of the agent, yield her a utility of $\hat{U}$. That is, the information-constrained indifference curve has a kink as it crosses the boundary curve BB′. Or, we could say, the *effective* indifference curves (allowing for the optimal $H$ or $L$ action) are kinked as shown.

For a risk-neutral agent, as seen above, the efficient contract implies that $r_2 - r_1 = y_2 - y_1$, i.e., the agent receives the full output increment between the favorable and the unfavorable outcomes. For a risk-averse agent, the contingent payment scheme can be interpreted as follows. In the event of a favorable outcome the agent received a maximum payment $R$. For the unfavorable outcome, the payment is reduced by an amount $Z$. That is:

$$(r_1, r_2) = (R - Z, R)$$

The agent thus accepts a certain absolute share of the reduction in output, $y_2 - y_1$, associated with the less favorable outcome. From (8.1.5) the agent's expected utility at effort level $x$ can be written as:

$$U_x^A(Z, R) = (1 - \pi(x))V(R - Z) + \pi(x)V(R) - K(x) \qquad (8.1.6)$$

Figure 8.2 depicts the risk-averse agent's indifference curves once again, for $x = L$ and $x = H$, but now on $Z, R$ axes. Note, first, that along the

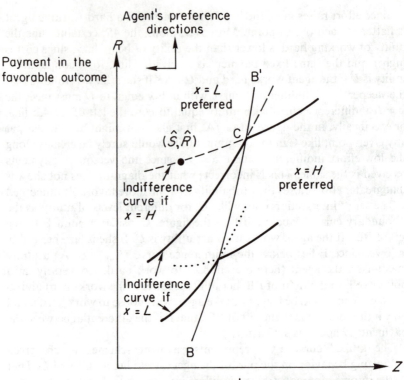

Figure 8.2 Kinked preference map of the agent

vertical axis (where $Z = 0$ so that the agent is not sharing in the reduction in output):

$$U_L^A(0, R) > U_H^A(0, R)$$

Second, since $\pi(H) > \pi(L)$, if the agent chooses to work hard she is more willing to give up income when the outcome is bad in return for a higher income when the outcome is good (since the bad outcome has become less likely). Formally:

$$\left.\frac{dR}{dZ}\right|_{U^A} = \frac{-\partial U^A/\partial Z}{\partial U^A/\partial R} = \frac{(1-\pi(x)V'(R-Z)}{(1-\pi(x))V'(R-Z)+\pi(x)V'(R)} \qquad (8.1.7)$$

$$= \frac{V'(R-Z)}{V'(R-Z)+\dfrac{\pi(x)}{1-\pi(x)}V'(R)}$$

For $x = H$ the denominator on the right-hand side is larger and so the Marginal Rate of Substitution of $R$ for $Z$ is lower:

$$MRS_H(R, Z) < MRS_L(R, Z) \qquad (8.1.8)$$

Third, rearranging (8.1.7) again:

$$\frac{dR}{dZ}\bigg|_{U^A} = \frac{1 - \pi(x)}{1 - \pi(x) + \pi(x)\dfrac{V'(R)}{V'(R-Z)}}$$

Given risk-aversion, $V'(R) < V'(R-Z)$ for all $Z > 0$. Hence the denominator is less than unity and so:

$$MRS_x(R, Z) > 1 - \pi(x) \qquad (8.1.9)$$

In figure 8.2 we see once again the boundary curve BB', but now on $Z, R$ axes. From figure 8.1, when the agent's share in the shortfall is sufficiently great she prefers to work hard, and the reverse for a small shortfall. The *effective* branches of her indifference curves are shown as solid, so that again the preference map can be represented as set of kinked indifference curves, the kinks all occurring along BB'.

Continuing with the assumption that the principal is risk-neutral:

$$U_x^P = (1 - \pi(x))(y_1 - R + Z) + \pi(x)(y_2 - R)$$

So on these axes his indifference curves are linear with slope equal to the probability of the unfavorable outcome, as shown in figure 8.3:

$$\frac{dR}{dZ}\bigg|_{U^P} = \frac{-\partial U^P/\partial Z}{\partial U^P/\partial R} = 1 - \pi(x)$$

Note, furthermore, that if the agent suffers the entire output reduction $(Z = y_2 - y_1)$ the principal is indifferent as to the agent's action. That is:

$$U_x^P = y_2 - R, \quad \text{for } x = L, H$$

Therefore the principal's indifference lines for $x = H$ and $x = L$, for any given level of satisfaction, intersect along the vertical line $Z = y_2 - y_1$ in figure 8.3.

For a given $Z$ (the agent's share of the shortfall), the principal can achieve the same expected profit with a higher payment in the favorable outcome if $x = H$, since the probability of the favorable event is higher. But, as it is the agent who chooses the action, only $x = L$ is relevant to the

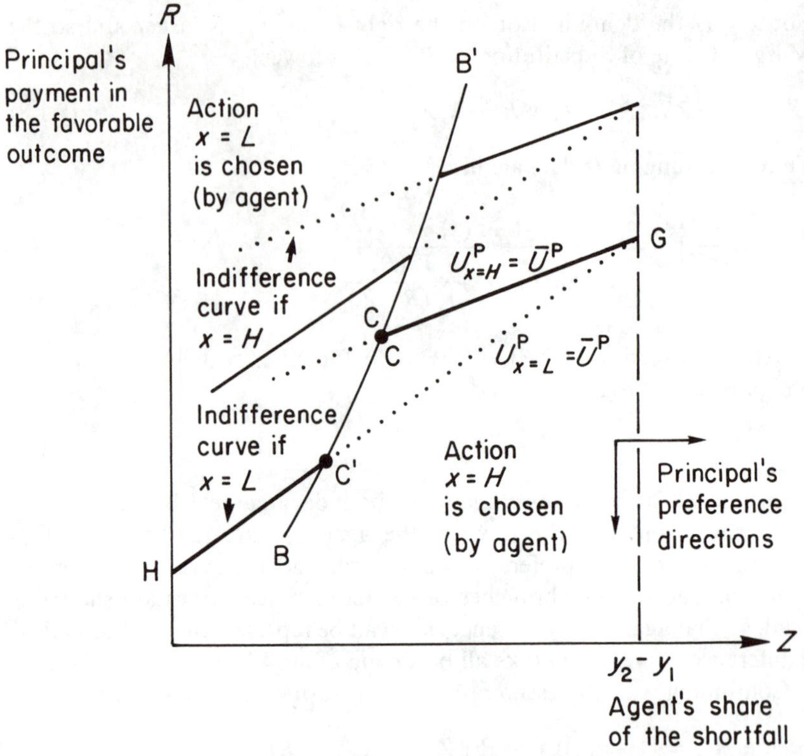

Figure 8.3 Discontinuous preference map of the principal

left of BB′ and $x = H$ to the right of BB′. The relevant parts of the indifference contours through G are therefore the line segments GC and C′H. It follows that the principal's indifference curves also have a *discontinuity* at BB′.

From (8.1.9) we know that the agent's indifference curve is everywhere steeper than the principal's indifference contour, except along the $R$ axis where $Z = 0$. Then the optimal contract can take on one of two forms.

The first possibility is depicted in figure 8.4a. The principal chooses the point $E^* = (Z^*, R^*)$ on the boundary curve BB′ that maximizes his expected gain, subject to the constraint that the agent achieves some reservation level of expected utility. That is, the principal designs a contract which offers just enough of an incentive to induce hard work.[4] If,

[4] Technically, at $(Z^*, R^*)$ the agent is indifferent between the two actions. In such cases the standard convention is to assume that the agent selects the action preferred by the principal. Alternatively, one can view $(Z^*, R^*)$ as the limit of a sequence of contracts in which the agent would strictly prefer $x = H$.

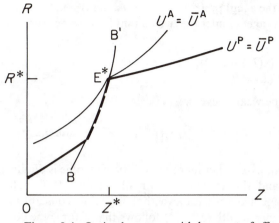

Figure 8.4a Optimal contract with low cost of effort

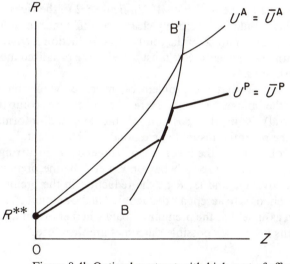

Figure 8.4b Optimal contract with high cost of effort

however, the utility cost of effort is sufficiently high, the optimal contract calls for a low work effort on the part of the agent – in which case she is paid a fixed wage. This is the point $(0, R^{**})$ depicted in figure 8.4b.

In the exercises below you are asked to consider how the optimal contract varies under a variety of parametric changes. We conclude here by asking what happens as the wealth of the agent is increased. To answer this we must determine the effect of higher wealth on the boundary of the set of contracts for which the agent prefers action $H$. Along $BB'$ in figure 8.2 the expected utility of the agent under the two actions is the same. Substituting from (8.1.6):

$$U_H^A - U_L^A = (\pi(H) - \pi(L))[V(w+R) - V(w+R-Z)]$$
$$- K(H) + K(L) = 0$$

Differentiating by the wealth level $w$:

$$\frac{\partial}{\partial w} U_H^A - \frac{\partial}{\partial w} U_L^A = (\pi(H) - \pi(L))[V'(w+R) - V'(w+R-Z)]$$

Since the agent is risk-averse, her marginal utility of income is diminishing and so the right-hand side is negative for all positive $Z$. Therefore if $U_H^A - U_L^A = 0$ for some given wealth level, holding effort constant implies $U_H^A - U_L^A < 0$ for higher wealth levels. It follows that if for some contract $(Z, R)$ the agent is indifferent between the two actions, then with an increase in endowed wealth she would strictly prefer action $L$. An increase in wealth thus shifts the boundary curve $BB'$ in figure 8.2 to the right.

The reason for this should be intuitively clear. The difference in utility associated with the agent's share $Z$ of the total output reduction is smaller for an individual with higher wealth. She must therefore be penalized more to be willing to work hard.

We conclude by noting that the problem of insurance with "moral hazard" parallels the above analysis. Here the insurance company (assumed risk-neutral) is in the position of the less well-informed "principal" while the potential insured corresponds to the "agent."

Let $\pi(x)$ be the probability of the favorable outcome, of *not* incurring a loss $L$, as a function of the insured's behavior $x$. Let $F$ be the premium required under full coverage and let $R$ be the reduction in the premium when the individual chooses to accept a "deductible" in the amount $Z$. For convenience we can assume that the premium is paid whether or not a loss occurs. Final wealths in the two possible outcomes are therefore:

$$c_{NL} = w - (F - R)$$
$$c_L = w - Z - (F - R)$$

The preference-scaling function for an individual with final wealth $c$ who takes action $x$ can be written as $v(c, x)$. Then if this individual has initial wealth $w$ and chooses the insurance policy $(Z, R)$, her expected utility is:

$$U_x(Z, R) = \pi(x)v(w - F + R, x) + (1 - \pi(x))v(w - F + R - Z, x)$$

Comparing this expression with (8.1.6) it is clear that the insurance application is indeed a special case of our basic model. We shall consider insurance in more detail in the following section.

EXERCISES AND EXCURSIONS 8.1

*1 Effect of a change in the agent's costs*

In comparison with the agent whose circumstances are pictured in figures 8.1 and 8.2, consider another agent identical in every respect except that $\hat{K}(H)$, her cost of taking action $H$, exceeds the first agent's $K(H)$.
(A) How will the optimal contract for this agent differ?
(B) What happens when $\hat{K}(H)$ becomes large?
[HINT: How is the curve BB′ affected by the increase in cost?]

*2 Competition among principals and agents*

(A) Characterize the optimal incentive contract when principals compete for the services of an agent and so drive expected profit to zero.
(B) Contrast this with the outcome when there is a single principal and a perfectly elastic supply of agents at some reservation utility level $\bar{V}$.
(C) Modify the model, if necessary, to describe the outcome when there are many principals and many agents.
[HINT: In each case one party or the other is on his or her reservation indifference curve.]

*3 Costless incentive schemes*

Suppose output is $\tilde{y} = \tilde{\varepsilon}\phi(x)$, where $x$ is the agent's effort level and $\tilde{\varepsilon}$ is a random variable taking on the values $\varepsilon_1$ and $\varepsilon_2$ ($\varepsilon_2 > \varepsilon_1$) with equal probabilities. Suppose that the principal is risk-neutral. The agent is risk-averse, and her utility is unbounded from below as her income declines to zero. While output is observable, the principal cannot observe either $x$ or $\varepsilon$.
(A) Let $x^*$ be the optimal action under full information. Suppose that the principal offers to pay a fixed wage $h$ as long as $y$ does not fall below $\varepsilon_1\phi(x^*)$. If $y$ is below this level the agent must pay a penalty $\beta$. Show that, with the appropriate choice of $h$ and $\beta$, the full-information optimum is achievable.
(B) Will the same conclusion hold if $\tilde{\varepsilon}$ is continuously distributed on the interval $[\varepsilon_1, \varepsilon_2]$?
(C) Explain why the incentive scheme breaks down if $\varepsilon_1$ is zero.
(D) If $\varepsilon_1$ is strictly positive, it appears as though the problem of hidden actions is readily solvable in practice. Do you agree? Explain.

PARTIAL ANSWER TO PART (B)

As long as $\phi(x)$ is strictly increasing, the lower support of the output distribution $y_1 = \varepsilon_1\phi(x)$ is strictly increasing in $x$. So if the agent takes the action $x^*$, she will not be penalized by an incentive scheme that pays $h$ for all $y \geqslant \varepsilon_1\phi(x^*)$. On the other hand, if she chooses $x < x^*$ the probability of an output $y < \varepsilon_1\phi(x^*)$ is strictly positive. By making the penalty sufficiently large, the agent will be discouraged from any finite deviation $x < x^*$.

If $\varepsilon_1$ is zero the lower support of the output distribution is zero. Any penalty scheme must then punish, with positive probability, even an agent who takes the correct action.

In practice it would be difficult for the principal to convince the agent about the lower support of the distribution. Any doubts of this kind would make the agent unwilling to accept a contract that involves even a very small chance of unbounded losses.

Of course, in actuality unbounded losses cannot be imposed on an agent, owing to the privilege of declaring bankruptcy and the prohibition of slavery.

### 4 Optimal linear contracting between principal and agent

The owner of a firm (the principal) hires a manager (the agent). If the agent chooses effort level $x$, the profit of the firm is:

$$\tilde{y} = y(x) + \tilde{\varepsilon}$$

The principal offer to pay the agent a percent share $s$ of profit and a wage $h$. That is, the owner offers a payment schedule $h + s\tilde{y}$ which is a linear function of profit. The owner would like to choose the pair of parameters $\langle s, h \rangle$ that maximizes his expected utility, subject to the constraint that the manager's expected utility is at least equal to her reservation utility level $\bar{U}^A$. The owner's income is:

$$\tilde{y}_P = (1 - s)(y(\mathrm{x}) + \tilde{\varepsilon}) - h$$

Finally, suppose $\tilde{\varepsilon}$ is normally distributed with zero mean and variance $\sigma^2$ and that both individuals exhibit constant absolute risk-aversion (CARA). The expected utility of each individual can be written as:

$$U_i = \mathrm{E}(y_i) - \frac{1}{2}\alpha_i \, Var(y_i), \quad i = A, P$$

where $\alpha_i$ is the coefficient of absolute risk-aversion.

(A) Obtain an expression for the owner's expected utility in terms of $s$, $x$, and $\bar{U}_A$. Assume the opportunity cost of effort is $K(x)$.

(B) Explain why it is that $s^*$ and $x^*$, the optimal levels of $s$ and $x$, are independent of $\bar{U}_A$. What does vary as $\bar{U}_A$ varies?

(C) If the manager's effort level is observable, show that $x^*$ and $s^*$ satisfy the following conditions:

(i) $\bar{y}'(x^*) = K'(x^*)$

(ii) $s^* = \dfrac{\alpha_P}{\alpha_A + \alpha_P}$

(D) Suppose next that the principal is unable to observe the effort level. Explain why the agent will respond to a linear contract $\langle s, h \rangle$ by choosing $x(s)$ satisfying:

(iii) $s\bar{y}'(x(s)) - K'(x(s)) = 0$

(E) What conditions guarantee that $x(s)$ is an increasing function?

(F) Assuming that the above conditions are satisfied, prove that for $s \leqslant s^*$:

$$\left. \frac{dU_P}{ds} \right|_{U_A = \bar{U}_A} > 0$$

Show also that this inequality is reversed at $s = 1$.

(G) Draw a conclusion about the new optimal sharing rate relative to $s^*$ and provide an intuitive explanation.

## 8.2 Hidden knowledge

The preceding section explored the implications of the informational asymmetry associated with difficulty of monitoring *actions* of other parties. We now turn to the issues that arise when the private *knowledge* of one individual is hidden from another.[5]

Consider the case where a less well-informed monopolist or monopsonist on one side of the market faces a number of heterogeneous transactors on the other side, each of whom is well-informed about his own situation. Examples include: (i) a company offering life insurance to individuals who know more about their own health prospects than the insurance company does; (ii) an auto dealer purchasing used cars from sellers with better knowledge of their own cars' condition.

Taking up the insurance market as an example, in section 8.2.1 we focus on "adverse selection." There are two central points. First, if the price associated with some contract reflects the *average* quality of the potential

---

[5] In chapter 5 we explored ways in which an "expert" can be provided an incentive to truthfully reveal hidden knowledge. There, however, the expert's knowledge did not directly affect his utility. (Therefore, it is only because the expert is unable to provide *verifiable* information that the efficient contract is not a lump-sum payment.) In this chapter the hidden knowledge is typically some characteristic of the informed individual and is therefore directly payoff-relevant.

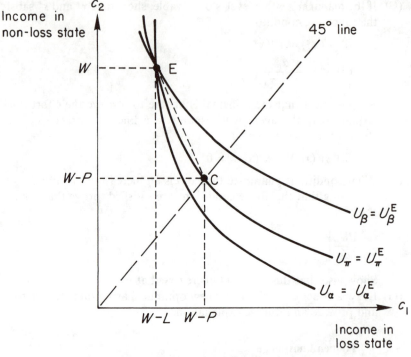

Figure 8.5 Indifference curves for different risk classes

applicants for insurance, there will typically be a tendency for the highest-quality applicants to self-select out of the market. Second, while the adverse selection may be severe, it is only in special cases that the market breaks down completely so that only the lowest-quality applicants (the "lemons") are present in equilibrium.

In section 8.2.2. we show that the insurance company has an incentive to offer a schedule of contracts that at least partially separates the different types of insured. That is, the insurer designs contracts to act as a *screening* device.

Finally, section 8.2.3 shows that monopolistic price discrimination is logically quite similar to the insurance problem considered previously.

### 8.2.1 Adverse selection
In a simple insurance example, consider risk-averse individuals each of whom faces a possible loss $L$, the losses being equal in amount but independently distributed. While preferences and endowments are identical, the individuals differ in probability of suffering loss $L$. But we here

assume that these loss-probabilities are not subject to influence by the individuals' actions. In insurance parlance, we are dealing with "adverse selection" rather than "moral hazard."

Someone whose probability of *avoiding* a loss is $\pi$ may be termed a type-$\pi$ individual. Let $\alpha$ be the lowest level of $\pi$ and $\beta$ be the highest. That is, type $\alpha$ are the worst risks (the "lemons" of the insurance industry) and type $\beta$ are the best (the "peaches"). It is helpful also to define $A(\pi)$ as the average non-loss probability over the interval $[\alpha, \pi]$. Assume that, within these limits, the risk types are distributed continuously with density function $f(\pi)$. So the average is:

$$A(\pi) \equiv \int_\alpha^\pi if(i)di / \int_\alpha^\pi f(i)di$$

Indifference curves through an endowment position E are depicted in figure 8.5 for three types of individuals: $\alpha$, $\beta$, and an intermediate type $\pi$. For any individual, the Marginal Rate of Substitution between income $c_1$ in his private loss state and income $c_2$ in his private non-loss state is:

$$-\frac{dc_2}{dc_1}\bigg|_{\bar{U}} = \frac{\partial U/\partial c_1}{\partial U/\partial c_2} = \frac{1-\pi}{\pi} \frac{v'(c_1)}{v'(c_2)}$$

Since this *MRS* is decreasing in $\pi$, the higher the non-loss probability (the better the risk), the flatter is this indifference curve.

Consider a risk-neutral monopolist insurance company[6] offering *full coverage* insurance policies at a price $P$, where the premium (to be paid regardless of whether or not a loss occurs) is the same for everyone participating. If an individual of type $i$ purchases the policy his state-contingent consumption bundle becomes $(w-P, w-P)$ at point $C$ in the diagram. Note that, as depicted, type $\pi$ is just indifferent between purchasing insurance and remaining out of the market.[7] (Of course, for this to be the case the insurance has to be an adverse gamble; at fair odds, any risk-averse individual will want to fully insure.) Moreover, at the state-claim price ratio represented by the slope of EC all those individuals who represent more favorable risks are strictly better off out of the market, while all individuals who represent worse risks are strictly better off

---

[6] As pointed out in chapter 4, ultimately all insurance is mutual. Despite the working of the Law of Large Numbers, the risk-averse individuals who comprise a mutual insurance pool cannot ordinarily insure one another on a risk-neutral basis – even ruling out transaction costs. The main reason is that the Law of Large Numbers cannot fully cancel out variance of losses from the positively correlated risks ("social risks") that typically characterize actual insurance pools. However, since we are assuming independently distributed risks, the assumption of a risk-neutral insurer is acceptable here.

[7] Remaining out of the market is sometimes called "self-insuring," an oxymoronic term since what is involved is *not* insuring.

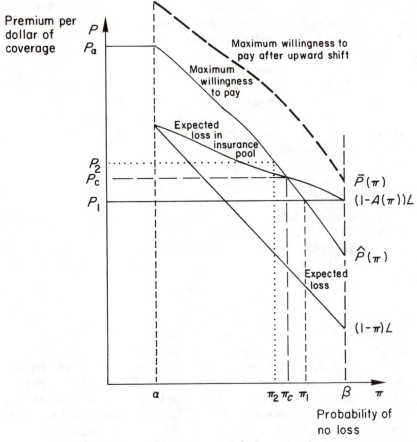

Figure 8.6 Adverse selection – yes and no

purchasing insurance. Thus the insurance company faces adverse selection: at any premium it offers, the poorer risks will be disproportionately represented among the customers who actually choose to insure.

Let $\hat{P}(\pi)$ be the maximum premium that an individual of type $\pi$ is willing to pay for full coverage. In figure 8.6 this is depicted by the curve $\hat{P}(\pi)$ over the range of individuals $\alpha \leqslant \pi \leqslant \beta$. The curve $(1-\pi)L$ similarly shows the expected loss for each type. Note that $\hat{P}(\pi)$ is everywhere greater than $(1-\pi)L$, meaning that each potential insured, being risk-averse, is willing to pay more than his expected total loss. The third curve, $(1-A(\pi))L$, is the expected loss averaged over the risks between $\alpha$ and $\pi$.

Now consider the insurance pool. If anyone purchases insurance at all, the pool would always contain the worst risks $\alpha$ up through some borderline participant $\pi$, where $\pi$ is a function of the premium. Then, on the assumption that in equilibrium there must be a non-negative expected profit for the insurance company, the premium $P$ associated with participation from $\alpha$ up to $\pi$ would have to at least equal the height of the curve $(1 - A(\pi))L$ that shows the average loss for that participation level.

There are two possible cases.

(i) Suppose that the insurance company, in the hope of inducing 100% participation, sets the premium for total coverage $P_1 = (1 - A(\beta))L$. As drawn in figure 8.6, however, this premium exceeds the maximum willingness to pay of the favorable risks between $\pi_1$ and $\beta$ – that is, the $\hat{P}(\pi)$ curve falls below $P_1$ in this range. But if only customers in the range from $\alpha$ through $\pi_1$ participate, $(1 - A(\pi_1))L$ will exceed $P_1$, so the insurance company will incur losses. At the other extreme, if the insurance company sets the premium above $\hat{P}(\alpha)$, the reservation price of the worst risks, there will be no takers. However, by setting an intermediate premium such as $P_2$, the insurance company would attract customers in the range from $\alpha$ through $\pi_2$. Since $(1 - A(\pi_2))L$ is less than $P_2$, such a contract is profitable.

At the premium $P_c$ the expected loss of all those accepting the offer, $(1 - A(\pi_c))L$, is exactly equal to the premium. Therefore, unless the insurance company is willing to incur losses, the premium must lie between $P_c$ and $P_\alpha$. Given the $\hat{P}(\pi)$ curve as depicted here (the distribution of insureds' willingness to pay), even in the most favorable case, where the insurance company sets a premium just high enough to cover the average loss[8] there is adverse selection. Those in the best risk classes (those with sufficiently low probabilities of loss) have dropped out of the market.

On the other hand, a monopolist insurer will never charge so high a price as to eliminate all but the worst risks from the market. Given risk aversion, the willingness to pay $\hat{P}(\pi)$ strictly exceeds the lemons' expected loss $(1 - \alpha)L$ over some interval $[\alpha, \pi]$. Therefore the expected profit of the insurer increases as it lowers the price below $P_\alpha$.

(ii) Thus far we have considered a case in which the curve $\hat{P}(\pi)$ intersects $(1 - A(\pi))L$ in the range between $\alpha$ and $\beta$. Alternatively, if the population were much more risk-averse, maximum willingness to pay for insurance might be considerably higher at all levels of participation. The $\hat{P}(\pi)$ curve would then shift upward, as illustrated by the heavy dashed $\bar{P}(\pi)$ curve in the diagram. Since $\bar{P}(\beta)$ now exceeds $(1 - A(\beta))L$ over the entire population range between $\alpha$ and $\beta$, it is possible to avoid adverse selection. In this situation $P_1$ would be the zero-profit premium, and there would be 100%

---

[8] This may be reinterpreted as the "competitive" case in which premiums are bid down until expected profit is zero.

participation in the insurance pool unless the insurer were to choose a sufficiently higher premium.[9]

Thus, adverse selection tends to come about when (a) the insurance pool contains a relatively wide range of risks (all of whom must be charged the same premium per unit of coverage, owing to the insurer's inability to distinguish among them), and (b) risk-aversion is relatively mild. Conversely, a narrow range of risks and a high degree of risk-aversion tend to retain the better risks in the insurance pool and therefore to prevent adverse selection.

## EXERCISES AND EXCURSIONS 8.2.1

### 1 Adverse selection in a used-car market (Akerlof, 1970)

Suppose cars last for two periods. Cars have different qualities, such that the dollar value of a car per period is uniformly distributed on the interval $[\alpha, \beta]$. After one period of ownership, a consumer knows the quality of his car.

(A) Suppose the price of used cars is $p$. Which owners will wish to sell? Show that the average value of cars on the market will be $\frac{1}{2}(\alpha + p)$.

(B) Assuming free entry into the used-car market, what will be the equilibrium price of used cars and how many cars will be traded?

(C) How does this second-period price affect the price of new cars? (You may ignore time-discounting.)

(D) Are there any efficiency losses associated with the adverse selection in the example?

(E) How would your answer change if old cars can be polished up and sold as new?

### 2 Adverse selection in a labor market

A worker with a marginal value product of $\theta$ can earn $w_r = (1 - d)\theta$ in self-employment. Marginal value products vary across the population according to the uniform distribution:

$$F(\theta) = \begin{cases} 0, & \theta < \alpha \\ \theta - \alpha & \theta \in [\alpha, 1 + \alpha] \\ 1, & \theta > 1 + \alpha \end{cases}$$

Firms cannot measure individual productivity, so all workers are paid a wage equal to the average of the marginal value products of those employed.

---

[9] Whether or not it pays to do so would depend upon the elasticity of demand for insurance, which would reflect (among other things) the distribution of risk classes in the population.

(A) Show that for any $d < \frac{1}{2}(1+\alpha)$, those with the highest marginal value products choose self-employment.

(B) Obtain an expression for the proportion of those self-employed as a function of $d$ and $\alpha$.

(C) Hence show that, as $d$ becomes small, adverse selection becomes severe. In this limiting case is adverse selection economically important?

(D) More generally, let $w_r = (1-\mu)\lambda + \mu\theta$. Show that, for $w_r$ to be less than $\theta$ over $[\alpha, 1+\alpha]$, $\lambda$ must be no greater than $\alpha$. Show also that adverse selection will never occur unless $\mu > \frac{1}{2}$. Under these assumptions, show that adverse selection will be complete in one limiting case. That is, only the "lemons" are actually traded.

## 3 Adverse selection in credit markets (Stiglitz and Weiss, 1981)

By borrowing an amount $D$, an entrepreneur (with no other source of funds) can undertake a risky project. The gross return $\tilde{y}$ is a non-negative random variable with cumulative distribution function $F(y)$. If the project's return $y$ is sufficiently large to permit this, the entrepreneur must repay his loan at the interest rate $r$; otherwise, the bank takes *all* the return $y$.

(A) Depict the return $\tilde{y}_B$ to the bank and the return $\tilde{y}_E$ to the entrepreneur for all non-negative values of $y$. Hence confirm that the former is a concave and the latter a convex function of $y$.

Suppose that both bank and entrepreneur are risk-neutral. Projects A, B, and C have the same expected return but B is more risky than A and C is more risky than B. Suppose also that, at the interest rate $r$, project B just breaks even.

(B) If banks cannot distinguish among the three projects, and all three are offered, which will they end up funding? Which would they prefer to fund?

(C) Would your answer change if all borrowers were required to put up collateral $\gamma$, where $\gamma < D$?

## 4 Gambling at the Golden Kiwi

For a small entry fee, visitors arriving in Kiwiland have an opportunity to compete with a genuine native at the airport casino. The native randomly selects a ball from an urn containing balls numbered from 0 to 99. The number $N$ on the ball is observed by the native only.

The visitor may make some bid $B$ in dollars. The native observes the ball drawn from the urn and then decides whether or not to compete by matching this bid. If the native does not match, the visitor pays $B$ and receives $N$ dollars. If the native matches he pays $B$ but only receives $(\frac{2}{3})N$.

(A) What is the visitor's optimal bid, given that he has decided to play?
(B) What is the expected payoff to visitor and native?
(C) Extend your analysis to the case in which the native's payout is a fraction $k$ of the number $N$ on the ball, where $0 < k < \frac{2}{3}$.
[HINT: If the visitor bids $B$ the native will not match when $B < (\frac{2}{3})N$, that is, when $N > (\frac{3}{2})B$. Use this to compute the expected payoff to the visitor for all $B$.]

### 8.2.2  Screening

When hidden knowledge results in adverse selection, those sellers with a product or service of above-average quality suffer from inability to secure a suitable price. In the insurance context, better-quality insureds may remain out of the market, which means they are unable to spread their risks. As a result they have an incentive to seek alternative, indirect ways of *signaling* product quality. On the other side of the market, buyers seek some way of *screening* products of differing qualities. Intuitively, an action taken or an offer made by a seller of a higher-quality product can only be a signal if it is sufficiently more costly for sellers of lower-quality products to do the same. In this section we show that, for the insurance case, such opportunities may exist and that, as a result, risk classes can sometimes be sorted *ex post*.

At the end of section 8.2.1 we showed that, if insurers offer only full coverage, in a wide range of circumstances adverse selection will occur. However, the set of feasible insurance policies is much richer. In particular, an insurance company or mutual insurance pool can exploit the fact that high-quality risk-classes are more willing to buy partial coverage (insurance with a "deductible").

Consider the willingness of different risk-classes to accept partial insurance in exchange for a reduction $R$ in the insurance premium. As before, all individuals face the same possible loss $L$, where $\pi$ is the non-loss probability. A higher $\pi$ thus represents a higher-quality risk. Let $G$ be the greatest total premium some individual would be willing to pay for full coverage. And let $R$ be the reduction from this maximum offered for accepting a deductible of $Z$, so that $G-R$ is the actual premium. In the non-loss and loss states the final wealths are:

$$c_{NL} = w - (G - R) = (w - G) + R$$
$$c_L = w - (G - R) - Z = (w - G) + R - Z$$

Expected utility is therefore:

$$U_\pi(Z, R) = \pi v(w - G + R) + (1 - \pi)v(w - G + R - Z) \qquad (8.2.1)$$

Indifference curves in $(Z, R)$ space are depicted in figure 8.7. From

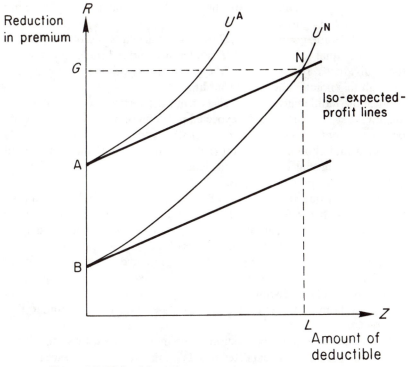

Figure 8.7 Optimal insurance contract

(8.2.1), the individual's marginal willingness to accept further reductions in the premium, in return for accepting a larger deductible, is:

$$\frac{dR}{dZ}\bigg|_U = -\frac{\partial U}{\partial Z}\bigg/\frac{\partial U}{\partial R} = \frac{(1-\pi)v'(w-G+R-Z)}{(1-\pi)v'(w-G+R-Z)+\pi v'(w-G+R)}$$

(8.2.2)

The right-hand side is equal to $1-\pi$, the loss probability, when $Z$ is zero; for all positive $Z$, it will be greater than $1-\pi$. Thus the slope of the indifference curves exceeds the loss probability except along the vertical axis.

For simplicity, assume that the insurer is risk-neutral and thus interested only in expected profit on the contract $(Z, R)$:

$$H_\pi(Z, R) = premium - \left\{\begin{matrix} loss \\ probability \end{matrix}\right\}\left\{\begin{matrix} payout\ in \\ event\ of\ loss \end{matrix}\right\}$$
$$= G - R - (1-\pi)(L-Z)$$
$$= (1-\pi)Z - R + (G - (1-\pi)L)$$

Iso-expected profit contours are therefore lines of slope $1 - \pi$. These are also depicted in figure 8.7.

In the diagram, point N $= (L, G)$ corresponds to absence of insurance (a deductible equal to the loss). The indifference curve through this point is the individual's reservation indifference curve and the iso-profit line through this point is the zero-profit line.

Since the indifference curves, away from the vertical axis where $Z = 0$, are always steeper than the iso-expected profit lines, the profit-maximizing policy is to offer full coverage. A perfectly discriminating monopoly insurer would choose a premium such that the insured is just indifferent between purchasing the policy and going without insurance. This is the policy shown at point B in figure 8.7.

We now introduce asymmetry of information. For simplicity, suppose there are just two risk-classes. If the insurance company can distinguish these risk classes *ex ante*, it maximizes expected profit by offering each risk class full coverage at a cost that extracts all consumer surplus. The two profit-maximizing insurance policies are represented in figure 8.8 by point A for the low-risk and point B for the high-risk group. But suppose the insurer is unable to distinguish the two groups. If it continues to offer policy A, both risk-classes would purchase full coverage under that contract.

We now show that the insurance company can always do better. Specifically, to maximize expected profits it can offer two insurance policies $(Z_i^*, R_i^*)$, $i = 1, 2$, with the following characteristics:

*Characterization of the profit-maximizing insurance policies*
  (i)   The policy accepted by each individual in the good risk-class extracts his entire surplus.
  (ii)  The policy accepted by each individual in the poor risk-class involves full coverage.
  (iii) The deductible level accepted by the good risk-class is strictly positive. The higher the proportion of poor risks in the market, the greater is the deductible.
  (iv)  When there is a sufficiently high proportion of poor risks in the pool, there is no insurance coverage for the good risks. That is, adverse selection occurs.

To explain these results, suppose the insurer offers the single policy C depicted in figure 8.8. Since point C lies to the north-west of both the reservation indifference curves through the no-insurance point N, both risk-classes will find contract C preferable to no insurance. But C is not profit-maximizing for the insurer, since it can raise the premium (reduce R) by shifting the offered contract down to point $C_2^*$ along the reservation indifference curve of the good risk-class.

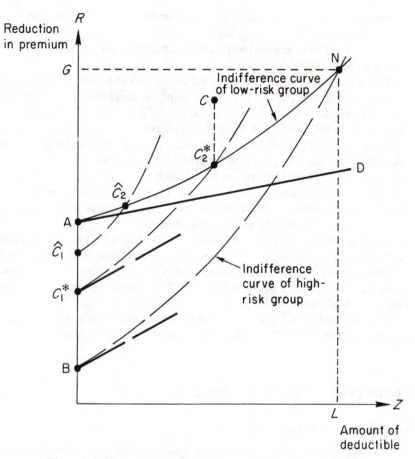

Figure 8.8 Characterizing the profit-maximizing insurance policy

Next, consider the indifference curve of the poor risk-class through $C_2^*$. Since this has a slope exceeding the slope of the iso-profit lines for this risk class, the insurance company increases its profits by offering the second policy $C_1^*$.

$(C_1^*, C_2^*)$ is just one of an entire family of policy pairs that satisfy parts (i) and (ii) of the proposition. Another such pair is $(\hat{C}_1, \hat{C}_2)$. If the insurance company changes its offered pair of policies from $(\hat{C}_1, \hat{C}_2)$ to $(C_1^*, C_2^*)$, its profit on poor risks will be greater and on good risks will be less. Therefore the higher the proportion of poor risks in the population, the more profitable (or less unprofitable) such a move becomes. This is point (iii) above. When essentially all individuals in the population are poor risks, it is optimal to extract the entire surplus from this class and offer the pair of policies (N, B). That is, when the proportion of poor risks gets sufficiently high, the good risks are no longer offered insurance on favorable enough terms to be accepted by them.

When the proportion of poor risks is sufficiently low, the pair of policies $(\hat{C}_1, \hat{C}_2)$ dominates $(C_1^*, C_2^*)$. It is tempting to conclude that, when the proportion gets very small, the optimal pair of policies will collapse to the single "pooling" policy A in figure 8.8. However, this is not the case. Note that the indifference curve NA and the iso-profit line AD are tangential at A. Therefore, the marginal gain in profit from the good risks in moving around the indifference curve towards A declines to zero as $\hat{C}_2$ approaches A. On the other hand the marginal loss in profit from the bad risks is positive and bounded away from zero. Because of this it is always optimal for the insurer to separate the two risk-classes.

More generally, with $n$ risk-classes, it will always be optimal to offer full coverage to the lemons and less than full coverage to all other risk-classes. However, as the next section makes clear, it is not necessarily the case that the insurer's profit is maximized by separating out each of the types. Instead, subsets of types may, in general, be pooled.

Also omitted from the analysis here are the effects of competition among insurance companies. We address these issues further in chapter 11.

## EXERCISES AND EXCURSIONS 8.2.2

### 1 Insurance with three risk-classes

(A) Extend the analysis of section 8.3 to the case of three risk-classes. Depict the insurance contracts $C_1^*$, $C_2^*$, $C_3^*$ in a diagram.

(B) Suppose the proportion of the intermediate risk-class is small relative to the other two classes. Explain why the profit-maximizing strategy is to offer only two policies. Which risk-classes are pooled?

(C) To what extent can the proposition of section 8.3 be generalized to the case of three risk-classes?

### 2 Insurance with different levels of loss

Suppose that an individual of type $t$ incurs a loss of $L_s$ with probability $\pi_s^t$, for $s = 1, \ldots, S$ and $t = 1, 2$. An insurance policy is an offer to pay the entire loss, less some deductible $Z$, to any individual who pays a premium $\phi(Z)$.

(A) Suppose that $\pi_s^1 < \pi_s^2$ for all $S$. Show that the analysis above can be readily extended to this case.

(B) Does it really matter that $\pi_s^1 < \pi_s^2$ for all $s$ or is it only the overall probability of a claim that is critical?

(C) Discuss what the insurer might do if $\Sigma_{s=1}^S \pi_s^1 = \Sigma_{s=1}^S \pi_s^2$ but the first type has higher probabilities of large losses.

### *8.2.3 Monopoly price discrimination with hidden knowledge

In this section we examine the selling strategy of a monopolist seller who cannot distinguish among different types of buyers. From past experience he does, however, have information about the distribution of buyers' demand curves. We also assume that the product cannot be readily resold. Then, rather than sell all units at a single price, the monopolist might offer bundles of different numbers of items at various quantity discounts (one for $50, two for $95, etc.) We shall show that this problem of monopolistic price discrimination is essentially equivalent to the insurance problem analyzed above. In particular, the optimal schedule of quantity discounts is analogous to the schedule offering insureds a lower premium for accepting a bigger deductible.

We assume here that each buyer-type $t$ has a demand curve $p_t(q)$ that is independent of income. Then, if $q$ units are purchased for total outlay of $R$ dollars, the type-$t$ "buyer's surplus" is:

$$U_t(q, R) = \int_0^q p_t(x)dx \qquad - R \qquad (8.2.3)$$

$$\underbrace{\phantom{\int_0^q p_t(x)dx}}_{\substack{\text{area under} \\ \text{demand curve}}} \qquad \underbrace{\phantom{R}}_{\substack{\text{total} \\ \text{outlay}}}$$

What makes this pricing problem simple is that buyers' preferences are linear in income.

For concreteness, suppose that there are $T$ different types of buyers, where $p_1(q) < p_2(q) < \ldots < p_T(q)$. Suppose also that the proportion of type-$t$ buyers is $f_t$, where $\Sigma_{t=1}^T f_t = 1$. Finally, to keep the analysis as simple as possible, we assume that the monopolist has an unlimited supply of the commodity available without cost.[10]

In figure 8.9 the upper diagram depicts the demand curve of a type-$t$ buyer while the lower diagram shows the corresponding preference map in $(q, R)$ space. Differentiating (8.2.3):

$$\left.\frac{dR}{dq}\right|_{U_t} = \frac{-\partial U}{\partial q} \bigg/ \frac{\partial U}{\partial R} = p_t(q) \qquad (8.2.4)$$

---

* Starred sections represent more difficult or specialized materials that can be omitted without substantial loss of continuity.

[10] In an exercise below, you are asked to show that the analysis holds for general cost functions.

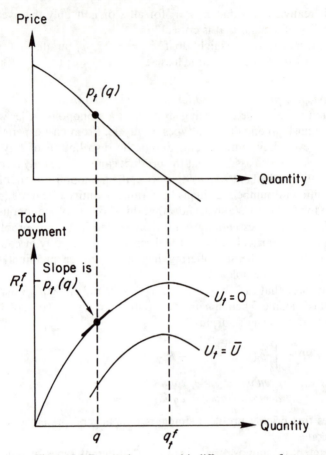

Figure 8.9 Demand curve and indifference curve for a type-$t$ buyer

That is, the steepness of the indifference curve is the buyer's demand price (marginal willingness to pay). Note also that, because of the linearity of $U_t(q, R)$ in $R$, the indifference curves are vertically parallel.

If the monopolist has full information and can engage in perfect discrimination, the solution is straightforward. Each buyer is forced onto her reservation indifference curve, where she is indifferent between the transaction $(q_t^f, R_t^f)$ and purchasing nothing at all. Since the seller wants to maximize the buyer's outlay, in figure 8.9, $(q_t^f, R_t^f)$ is at the peak of the indifference curve through the origin. Thus:

$$U_t(q_t^f, R_t^f) = \int_0^{q_t^f} p_t(x)dx - R_t^f = U_t(0,0) = 0$$

In terms of figure 8.9, the monopolist makes a take-it-or-leave-it offer of $q_t^f$ units for a total payment of $R_t^f$, equal to the integrated area under the demand curve between $q = 0$ and $q = q_t^f$.

With complete information about types, the monopolist can then make $T$ different offers $(q_1^f, R_1^f), \ldots, (q_T^f, R_T^f)$, each of which extracts all of the surplus from a buyer. However, if the monopolist cannot distinguish the different types, he cannot do this well. It is helpful, in what follows, to introduce a fictional buyer who places a large negative value on the product. This fictional "type 0" buyer will always choose to make zero purchases, so her presence or absence has no effect on the monopolist's opportunities. Suppose the monopolist makes $T$ offers. (Certainly he gains nothing by making more than $T$ offers when there are only $T$ types.) For any such set of offers, let $\{(q_0, R_0), (q_1, R_1), \ldots, (q_t, R_t)\}$ signify the best responses by each type, including type 0 who chooses $(q_0, R_0) = (0, 0)$. These need not be distinct. For example, if the monopolist makes just a single offer $(\bar{q}, \bar{R})$, each best response is either to accept this offer or to stay out of the market (equivalently, to choose $(q_0, R_0)$).

While each buyer's type is private information, the monopolist is assumed to know the demand curve for each type. He can therefore compute the best response to his initial set of offers. Therefore, instead of announcing the initial set, the monopolist could equivalently provide a list of types and the optimal choice for each, as shown in table 8.1. The monopolist could then ask each buyer to announce her type. As long as the right-hand column is a set of best responses, each buyer has an incentive to announce her actual type.

Table 8.1 *Direct revelation*

| Buyer type | Best responses |
|---|---|
| 0 | $(q_0, R_0) = (0, 0)$ |
| 1 | $(q_1, R_1)$ |
| 2 | $(q_2, R_2)$ |
| . | . |
| . | . |
| . | . |
| T | $(q_T, R_T)$ |

The key point is that the original "game" between the monopolist and buyers has been converted into an equivalent game of *direct revelation* in which each informed party is asked to reveal her private information. As long as the monopolist has correctly analyzed the incentive constraints so

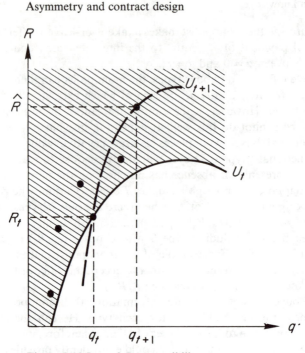

Figure 8.10 Incentive compatibility

that the schedule of offers is *incentive compatible*, no individual can do any better than reveal her true type.

It should now be apparent why we introduced the fictional type 0 who always chooses $(q_0, R_0) = (0, 0)$. Each agent always retains the option of a zero purchase as well as the $T$ offers made by the monopolist. Adding type 0 is thus equivalent to introducing a *participation* constraint for each type of buyer.

Converting a game into the equivalent *direct revelation game* often makes analysis considerably easier,[11] as is indeed the case here. The monopolist can be viewed as designing a table or schedule such that each buyer will choose the row corresponding to her true type.

Figure 8.10 displays an indifference curve for a type $t$ individual (solid) and for a type $t + 1$ individual (dashed). If $(q_t, R_t)$ *is* $t$'s best response, all the other feasible contracts for her must be in the shaded region, on or above the indifference curve:

$$U_t(q, R) = U_t(q_t, R_t)$$

By assumption, type $t + 1$ has a higher demand curve and hence, from

[11] When authors appeal to the *revelation principle* they are simply referring to the point made here that any game can be rephrased as an equivalent direct revelation game.

equation (8.2.4), her indifference curve through $(q_t, R_t)$ is strictly steeper. Then, from the figure, type $t+1$ will prefer $(q_t, R_t)$ to any other offer $(q_i, R_i)$ such that $q_i < q_t$. It follows that, for the offer $(q_{t+1}, R_{t+1})$ to be incentive compatible, it is necessary that:

$$q_t \leqslant q_{t+1} \quad t = 1, \ldots, T \tag{8.2.5}$$

Consider any vector of quantities $(q_1, q_2, \ldots, q_T)$ satisfying (8.2.5). We shall now show that the corresponding revenue-maximizing incentive-compatible vector of payments $(R_1, R_2, \ldots, R_T)$ satisfies:

$$U_t(q_t, R_t) = U_t(q_{t-1}, R_{t-1}), \quad t = 2, \ldots, T \tag{8.2.6}$$
$$U_1(q_1, R_1) = U_1(q_0, R_0) = U_1(0, 0) = 0 \tag{8.2.7}$$

That is, each buyer type is just indifferent between his or her best response $(q_t, R_t)$ and the best response of buyers with the most similar demand among those with lower demands. Moreover, the type with the smallest demand is just indifferent between her allocation and staying out of the market.

It should be noted that this last condition ensures that all types are willing to participate. For, the higher an individual's demand curve, the greater the willingness to pay for a given quantity. Hence:

$$U_t(q_1, R_1) > U_1(q_1, R_1) = 0, \quad t = 2, \ldots, T$$

Ignoring all types but the first, it is clear that revenue from type 1 buyers is maximized by choosing $R_1$ to satisfy (8.2.7). Suppose next that $\{(q_1, R_1), \ldots, (q_t, R_t)\}$ are incentive compatible for types $1, 2, \ldots, t$. Just taking into account the local constraint depicted in figure 8.10, the best that the seller can do is to choose $(q_{t+1}, R_{t+1})$ so that (8.2.6) holds. But all buyers with lower demands have flatter indifference curves than type $t$. Therefore, since $q_{t+1} \geqslant q_t$:

$$U_{t+1}(q_{t+1}, R_{t+1}) = U_{t+1}(q_t, R_t)$$
$$\Rightarrow U_i(q_{t+1}, R_{t+1}) < U_i(q_t, R_t), \quad i < t+1$$

Therefore the set of offers $\{(q_1, R_1), \ldots, (q_{t+1}, R_{t+1})\}$ satisfy (8.2.6) and (8.2.7) and so is incentive compatible for types $1, 2, \ldots, t+1$. Since this argument can be repeated for each $t$ it follows that conditions (8.2.5)–(8.2.7) are together sufficient for incentive compatibility.

These offers are also revenue-maximizing for the given set of quantities. The final step is to choose the profit-maximizing quantities. Define:

$$B_t(q) = \int_0^q p_t(x)\, dx$$

Then (8.2.6) and (8.2.7) can be rewritten as:

$$R_t - R_{t-1} = B_t(q_t) - B_t(q_{t-1}), \quad t = 1, \ldots, T, \quad \text{with } (q_0, R_0) = 0 \tag{8.2.8}$$

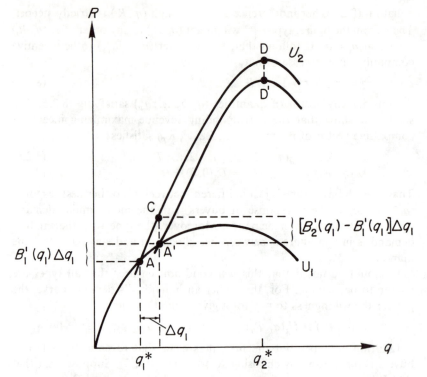

Figure 8.11 Benefit and cost of increasing $q_1$

The monopolist's total revenue $R_M = \Sigma_{t=1}^{T} f_t R_t$ can be expressed as a function of the quantity vector $(q_1, \ldots, q_T)$.

If there are just two buyer types we have, from (8.2.8):

$$R_M = f_1 R_1 + f_2 R_2 \tag{8.2.9}$$
$$= (f_1 + f_2)R_1 + f_2[R_2 - R_1]$$
$$= (f_1 + f_2)B_1(q_1) + f_2[B_2(q_2) - B_2(q_1)]$$
$$= f_1 B_1(q_1) - f_2[B_2(q_1) - B_1(q_1)] + f_2 B_2(q_2)$$

Revenue is therefore maximized by choosing $q_1$ and $q_2$ to maximize $R_m$ subject to the constraint that $q_1 \leqslant q_2$. Actually, with just two types, this constraint is never binding. Differentiating (8.2.9):

$$\frac{\partial R_M}{\partial q_1} = f_1 B_1'(q_1) - f_2[B_2'(q_1) - B_1'(q_1)]$$
$$= f_1 p_1(q_1) - f_2[p_2(q_1) - p_1(q_1)]$$
$$\frac{\partial R_M}{\partial q_2} = f_2 B_2'(q_2) = f_2 p_2(q_2)$$

The optimum is therefore to choose $q_2^*$ where a type-2 buyer's marginal willingness to pay is zero. On the other hand, $q_1^*$ is chosen where a type-2 buyer's marginal willingness to pay is strictly positive.

This is illustrated in figure 8.11. Suppose $A$ and $D$ are the optimal offers. Consider increasing the quantity supplied to type-1 buyers by $\Delta q_1$. Revenue from these buyers rises by an amount $B_1'(q_1)\Delta q_1$ as the offer moves from $A$ to $A'$. This reduces revenue from type-2 buyers, however, by an amount $DD'$. Since the indifference curves are vertically parallel, this revenue loss is equal to the distance $A'C$. But $A'C$ is readily computed. It is just the difference in the slopes of the indifference curves of the two types times the change in quantity. Since these slopes are demand prices, it is profitable to increase $q_1$ if and only if:

$$f_1 p_1(q_1) - f_2[p_2(q_1) - p_1(q_1)] > 0 \qquad (8.2.10)$$

Note that, if either the proportion of type-1 buyers is sufficiently small, or the type-1 demand price is sufficiently low relative to type 2, this inequality is never satisfied and so $q_1^* = 0$.

This result holds quite generally. When the demand prices of some types are sufficiently small relative to others, the monopolist will make offers that exclude these types completely.

Finally, the analysis above can readily be extended to consider more than two types. Suppose there are three. The additional issue is then whether it pays the monopolist to separate all three types. With three types, it is profitable to increase $q_1$ if and only if the additional revenue from type-1 buyers is not offset by the loss in revenue from both of the higher types. Condition (8.2.10) therefore becomes:

$$f_1 p_1(q_1) - (f_2 + f_3)[p_2(q_1) - p_1(q_1)] > 0$$

Similarly, it is profitable to increase $q_2$ if and only if:

$$f_2 p_2(q_2) - f_3[p_3(q_2) - p_2(q_2)] > 0$$

It is left as an exercise to confirm that, as long as $f_2$ is sufficiently large, then $0 \leqslant q_1^* < q_2^* < q_3^*$. Conversely, if $f_2$ is sufficiently small, then $q_1^* = q_2^*$. That is, it is more profitable for the monopolist to pool types 1 and 2 and make only two offers rather than three.

## EXERCISES AND EXCURSIONS 8.2.3

*1 Monopoly pricing with costly production*

(A) Suppose that the aggregate supply of the commodity is fixed and equal to $Q$. Starting with the two-type case, show that the first-order conditions need only be modified by the introduction of a shadow price $\lambda$.

(B)  What is the interpretation of this shadow price?

(C)  Hence, or otherwise, explain why, with a cost function $C(Q)$, the aggregate quantity supplied will be chosen so that $\lambda = C'(Q)$.

## 2 Monopoly and product quality (Mussa and Rosen, 1978)

There are two types of buyers. Type-2 buyers value increases in quality more highly than type-1 buyers. That is, for each quality level $z$, a type-2 buyer's marginal willingness to pay $B_2'(z)$ exceeds $B_1'(z)$, where $B_1(0) = B_2(0) = 0$.

Each buyer wishes to purchase a single unit. The unit cost of production of a unit of quality level $z$ is $C(z)$. The price $p$ that the monopolist charges can then be separated into two parts, the unit cost and profit $\Pi$, that is:

$$p = C(z) + \Pi$$

We can therefore write the net gain to a buyer from type $i$ as:

$$U_i(z, \pi) = B_i(z) - C(z) - \Pi$$

(A)  Assuming $B_i(z) - C(z)$ is concave with a maximum at $z_i^*$, depict the indifference curves of the two buyer types.

(B)  In particular, show the reservation indifferences curves, below which each buyer type would choose not to purchase.

(C)  If the two types are distinguishable, characterize the profit-maximizing quality levels and prices.

(D)  If the two types are not distinguishable, explain why:
   (i)  buyers who value quality less will not gain any consumer surplus
   (ii) it is always profitable to separate out the two types.

(E)  Explain also why one (and only one) of the two types will be offered ·a lower quality level when the two types are not distinguishable *ex ante* than when the seller has full information.

(F)  From a mathematical perspective, does this model differ from the insurance model of section 8.2.2? What are the essential common characteristics of the two models?

## 3 Non-linear pricing and quantity discounts

There are two types of buyers. Type 2 have a demand price $p_2(q)$ exceeding that of type 1. The marginal cost of production is constant and equal to $c$.

(A)  If a buyer of type $i$ accepts quantity $q$ and pays a total of $\$T$ her gain is:

$$U_i = \int_0^q p_i(x)\, dx - T$$

By separating the total payment into cost and profit, show that the buyer's gain can also be expressed as:

$$U_i(q, \Pi) = \int_0^q (p_i(x) - c)\, dx - \Pi$$

(B) Using your answer to exercise 2 as a guide, or otherwise, characterize the optimal selling scheme if it is not possible to distinguish the two types *ex ante*.

(C) Suppose that $p_i(x) = a - x/b_i$, so that individuals with a higher parameter $b_i$ have larger demands. If $a = 10$, $b_1 = 1$, $b_2 = 2$, $c = 2$ and one half of the population are of type 1, solve explicitly for the optimal selling scheme.

HINT: Show that $\Pi_1 = 8q_1 - \frac{1}{2}q_1^2$ and $q_2 = 16$. Then use the latter to establish that:

$$\Pi_2 = 64 + \Pi_1 - (8q_1 - \tfrac{1}{4}q_1^2)$$

(D) Does the optimal selling scheme involve quantity discounting, that is, a lower price per unit for those buying more units?

(E) Is there quantity discounting for all possible proportions of type 1 in the population?

(F) For what market is this model most applicable?

ANSWER

(A) If the monopolist receives $T$ when he sells $q$ units his profit is:

$$\Pi = T - cq$$

Therefore, for any schedule of $(q, T)$ pairs, there is a schedule of $(q, \Pi)$ pairs. A type $i$ buyer has a consumer surplus of:

$$U_i = \int_0^q p_i(x)\, dx - T = \int_0^q p_i(x)\, dx - cq - \Pi$$

$$= \int_0^q (p_i(x) - c)\, dx - \Pi$$

(C) For the numerical example:

$$U_1 = \int_0^q (8 - x)\, dx = 8q - q^2/2 - \Pi$$

$$U_2 = \int_0^q (8 - x/2)\, dx = 8q - q^2/4 - \Pi$$

Type-1 must be indifferent between $(q_1, \Pi_1)$ and not purchasing, that is, $(0, 0)$. Therefore $U_1 = 0$ and so:

$$\Pi_1 = 8q_1 - q_1^2/2$$

Type-2 indifference curves can be written as:

$$\Pi_2 = 8q - q^2/4 - U_2$$

$\Pi_2$ is therefore maximized at $q_2$ satisfying:

$$\Pi_2' = 8 - q/2 = 0 \Rightarrow q_2^* = 16$$

Type-2 must also be indifferent between $(q_1, \Pi_1) = (q_1, 8q_1 - q_1^2/2)$ and $(16, \Pi_2)$. Therefore:

$$8q_1 - q_1^2/4 - (8q_1 - q_1^2/2) = 8(16) - (16)^2/4 - \Pi_2$$

Rearranging, we obtain:

$$\Pi_2 = 64 - q_1^2/4$$

(D) If the proportion of type 1 is $f$, average profit is:

$$\begin{aligned}
\bar{\Pi} &= f(8q_1 - q_1^2/2) + (1-f)(64 - q_1^2/4) \\
&= f(8q_1 - q_1^2/2) - q_1^2(1-f)/4 + (1-f)64
\end{aligned}$$

Average profit is therefore maximized by choosing $q_1^*$ so that:

$$f(8 - q_1^*) - (1-f)q_1^*/2 = 0$$

With $f = 0.5$, $q_1^* = \frac{16}{3} > 4$.

(E) More generally, $q_1 < 8$ for all $f < 1$, and so:

$$\frac{T_1}{q_1} = 10 - q_1/2 > 6$$

On the other hand:

$$\frac{T_2}{q_2} = \frac{64 - q_1^2/4 + 2q_1}{16} = \frac{64 - (8 - q_1)q_1/4}{16} < 4 \quad \text{for all } q_1 < 8$$

Therefore, quantity discounting prevails for all $f$.

(F) It is most applicable for commodities where resale is costly, either because of the nature of the product (e.g., electricity) or because the seller has legal protection.

## 4 Partial separating and partial pooling

There are three types of demand curves:

$$p_t(q) = t + 10 - q, \quad t = 1, 2, 3$$

Output can be supplied at zero cost.

(A) Show that $q_1^*$ is strictly positive if and only if the proportion of type 1 satisfies a constraint of the form $f_1 > \alpha$.

(B)  Assuming this constraint is satisfied, obtain a necessary and sufficient
condition for the monopolist to offer three separating contracts.**

** End of starred section.

## REFERENCES AND SELECTED READINGS

Akerlof, George A., "The Market for 'Lemons': Qualitative Uncertainty and the
Market Mechanism," *Quarterly Journal of Economics*, 84 (1970), 488–500.

Arrow, Kenneth J., "Insurance Risk, and Resource Allocation," *Essays in the
Theory of Risk Bearing*, Chicago: Markham, 1971.

Grossman, Sanford and Hart, Oliver, "An Analysis of the Principal Agent
Problem," *Econometrica*, 52 (1983), 1–45.

Holmstrom, Bengt, "Moral Hazard and Observability," *Bell Journal of Economics*,
10 (1979), 74–91.

Kihlstrom, Richard and Matthews, Steven, "Managerial Incentives in Publicly
Traded Firms," mimeo (1985).

Maskin, Eric S. and Riley, John G., "Monopoly With Incomplete Information,"
*RAND Journal of Economics*, 15 (1984), 171–96.

Mirrlees, James A., "The Optimal Structure of Incentives and Authority Within an
Organization," *Bell Journal of Economics*, 7 (1976), 105–31.

Mussa, Michael and Rosen, Sherwin, "Monopoly and Indirect Quality," *Journal
of Economic Theory*, 18 (1978), 301–17.

Ross, S., "The Economic Theory of Agency: The Principal's Problem," *American
Economic Review*, 63 (1973), 134–9.

Shavell, S., "On Moral Hazard and Insurance," *Quarterly Journal of Economics*, 93
(1979), 541–62.

Spence, Michael and Zeckhauser, Richard, "Insurance, Information and Individual Actions," *American Economic Review*, 61 (1971), 380–7.

Stiglitz, Joseph E., "Incentives and Risk Sharing in Share Cropping," *Review of
Economic Studies*, 61 (1974), 219–56.

Stiglitz, Joseph E. and Weiss, Andrew, "Credit Rationing in Markets with
Imperfect Information," *American Economic Review*, 71 (1981), 393–410.

# 9 Strategic uncertainty and equilibrium concepts

For the most part, the analysis to this point has dealt with *event uncertainty*. Individuals were mainly uncertain about Nature's choice of state of the world. In the following chapters the focus shifts to *strategic uncertainty*, where what is best for individual A to do depends upon individual B's choice, and vice versa. So the main risks that a person has to deal with concern the actions and reactions of others. A first step is the choice of an equilibrium concept for such an environment, which turns out to be a subtle and still controversial issue. As usual, our discussion will not attempt to address formal issues of existence or uniqueness of equilibrium. Our aim instead is to provide an intuitive interpretation of the key ideas.

## 9.1 Nash equilibrium

In a *coordination game* the parties' interests are completely parallel. A specific example known as "Tender Trap" (Hirshleifer, 1982) is illustrated in table 9.1. Here the two parties both gain by coordinating their activities, but they do better by agreeing upon one of the options rather than the other. An example: The Dvorak typewriter keyboard is, it has been claimed, ergonomically superior to the currently standard "Qwerty" arrangement. But having settled on the current standard keyboard, largely by historical accident, now manufacturers are supposedly reluctant to produce Dvorak keyboards so long as almost all typists are trained on Qwerty, while typists don't want to train on Dvorak when almost all keyboards are Qwerty.[1] Even the inferior keyboard as a matched choice is superior to failing to coordinate at all.

Tender Trap illustrates the binding force of convention (of having an agreed rule) even allowing for the possibility that the convention is not

---

[1] In terms of historical fact, this oft-repeated story appears to be mythical. There is no convincing evidence that the Dvorak keyboard is actually superior (Liebowitz and Margolis, 1990).

Table 9.1 *Tender Trap*

|                              |              | Player $k$ (typist) | |
|                              |              | Dvorak $x_1^k$ | Qwerty $x_2^k$ |
| --- | --- | --- | --- |
|                              | Dvorak $x_1^j$ | 10, 10 | 4, 4 |
| Player $j$ (manufacturer) |              |        |      |
|                              | Qwerty $x_2^j$ | 4, 4   | 6, 6 |

ideal. We tacitly agree upon many conventions to order our daily lives – rules of the road, rules of language, rules of courtesy. Although better rules might well have been arrived at, it is hard to change a settled convention.

Approaching this problem in terms of game theory, suppose the players must move one at a time in a pre-specified order. We can depict this situation using a decision tree, as in figure 9.1. Suppose it is player $j$, the manufacturer, who moves first, as indicated by the box at the root or initial node of the tree. A play of the game is a sequence of choices, starting at the initial node and ending with one of the possible final outcomes at the terminal nodes of the tree.

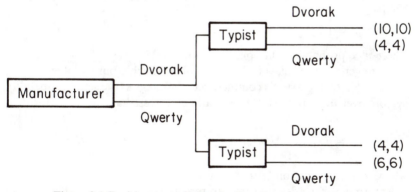

Figure 9.1 Decision tree of "Tender Trap"

The most frequently used solution concept for games is called the Nash non-cooperative solution, or Nash equilibrium (NE) for short.[2] The key idea is that there is an equilibrium when, given the strategies of all the other players, each single participant finds that his own strategy is (at least weakly) a best response to their choices. Thus the NE is a "no regret" equilibrium.

---

[2] Nash (1951). The Nash equilibrium is a generalization of a solution to the oligopoly problem that goes back to Cournot (1838).

For our simple example, the typist's best response is always to match the action of the manufacturer. Moreover, if the manufacturer believes that the typist will match, his best initial choice is Dvorak. The strategy-pair $(x_1^j = x_1^k = \text{Dvorak})$ is therefore a Nash equilibrium. In this equilibrium the parties achieve the mutually preferred outcome (10, 10).

However, suppose the manufacturer believes that the typist will always (perhaps irrationally) choose Qwerty. His best response is then to choose Qwerty also. And given that the manufacturer chooses Qwerty, the strategy of the typist is also a best response. Thus there is a second Nash equilibrium $(x_2^j = x_2^k = \text{Qwerty})$ in which the parties achieve the inferior or "trap" outcome (6, 6).[3]

Next suppose that, instead of moving sequentially, each player must move without knowing the other's decision. In the absence of pre-play communication it is not so clear now what they should do. A fruitful approach to this problem is to extend the range of choice beyond the simple actions or *pure strategies* $X = (x_1, x_2)$ available to each player so as to consider *mixed strategies* as well, that is, the set of probabilistic combinations of the available pure strategies. If there are only two pure strategies, the complete set of pure and mixed strategies available to player $i$ can be expressed (in analogy with the "prospect notation" of chapter 1) as:

$$\bar{X} = \{(x_1^i, x_2^i; \pi^i, 1 - \pi^i) \mid 0 \leqslant \pi^i \leqslant 1\}$$

where $\pi^i$ = probability that player $i$ chooses $x_1^i$.

More generally, if player $i$ has a set of $A^i$ feasible pure strategies $X^i = \{x_1^i, \ldots, x_{A^i}^i\}$, then player $i$'s complete set of strategies (the set of probability vectors over these pure strategies) can be expressed as:

$$\bar{X}^i = \{(x_1^i, \ldots, x_{A^i}^i; \pi_1^i, \ldots, \pi_{A^i}^i) \mid 0 \leqslant \pi_a^i \leqslant 1 \quad \text{and} \quad \sum_{a=1}^{A^i} \pi_a^i = 1\}$$

where $\pi_a^i$ is the probability that player $i$ chooses strategy $x_a^i$.

Returning to the decision tree, to represent simultaneous play one can think of the manufacturer as still having the first move but now the typist must make a decision without knowing the manufacturer's choice.

Figure 9.2, the modified decision tree, differs from figure 9.1 only by a dashed line joining the two nodes of the typist. The typist knows that it is time to make a move but does not know which of the connected nodes in her so-called "information set" has been reached.

With simultaneous play, each player is assumed to have made a hypothesis about the strategies of his opponents. His own strategy is then

---

[3] In section 9.3 we shall argue that this is a less plausible equilibrium.

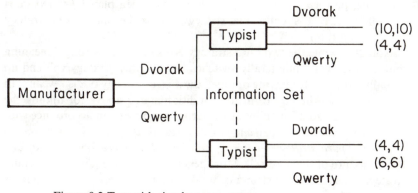

Figure 9.2 Tree with simultaneous moves

a best response to the others' hypothesized strategies. If, for each player, the chosen action coincides with what the other players have hypothesized about his strategy, a Nash equilibrium exists.[4]

In our Qwerty example, for simultaneous play there are once again the same two NE's in pure strategies. Either the players coordinate on strategy 1 (Dvorak) or on strategy 2 (Qwerty). In each case, either party acting alone can only lose by changing to a different action. But now there is also an equilibrium in mixed strategies. The following condition provides a technique for locating mixed-strategy NE's:

> Suppose each player $i = 1, \ldots, I$ has chosen a mixed strategy. For such a set of mixed strategies to be a Nash equilibrium, each player $i$ must then be indifferent – given the chosen mixed strategies of the other players – among all of the pure strategies entering with non-zero probability into his own mixed strategy.

In the Tender Trap game, suppose the players have chosen respective mixed strategies $(\pi^i, 1 - \pi^i)$, $i = j, k$. We now ask when player $j$ will be indifferent between the pure strategies 1 (Dvorak) and 2 (Qwerty). If he chooses Dvorak, his expected payoff is:

$$\pi^k(10) + (1 - \pi^k)(4) = 4 + 6\pi^k$$

If he chooses Qwerty, his gain is:

$$\pi^k(4) + (1 - \pi^k)(6) = 6 - 2\pi^k$$

Player $j$ will be indifferent between Dvorak and Qwerty if and only if player $k$'s probability mixture is $(\pi^k, 1 - \pi^k) = (0.25, 0.75)$. Given the symmetry of

---

[4] Note that the Nash equilibrium is *not* justified by appealing to some plausible dynamic process. Rather, it is a state of affairs in which, if it were somehow to come about, no party would unilaterally want to revise his action.

the game, player $k$'s expected gains are equal when player $j$'s mixture is (0·25, 0·75) also. Evidently, this strategy-pair is the only mixed-strategy Nash equilibrium.

Note that while the two pure-strategy NE's here are "strong," meaning that a player who unilaterally switches to any other strategy will end up actually worse off for having done so, the mixed-strategy NE is "weak." In fact, as follows directly from the condition stated above for finding the mixed-strategy solution, if all other parties are playing in accordance with the mixed-strategy NE then *any single player could equally well have chosen any of the pure strategies entering into his NE mixture* – or, indeed, any other mixture of them as well. More generally, a Nash equilibrium in pure strategies may be either strong or weak, but an NE in mixed strategies is always weak.

Another possibly puzzling feature of the mixed-strategy NE here is that each player assigns the smaller probability weight to the strategy associated with the more profitable of the two pure-strategy equilibria, e.g., in this case less weight is placed on Dvorak and more weight on Qwerty. (It is only in this way that the two pure-strategy elements of the mixture can end up being equally advantageous, as required by the condition above.) Notice also that, comparing the payoffs in our example: (i) when the players both choose Dvorak, they each receive 10; (ii) when they both choose Qwerty, they each receive 6; (iii) when they arrive at the mixed-strategy NE, they each receive only $5\frac{1}{2}$. And, in fact, in all Tender Trap games the mixed-strategy NE will yield a smaller return than the pure-strategy equilibria, for two main reasons: (1) because with some positive probability a mismatch will occur, so that the parties fail to coordinate at all, and (2) because, as just indicated, the more profitable strategy is chosen with lower probability.

We now consider an alternative payoff environment, the famous game of Chicken[5] (table 9.2), again under the assumption of simultaneous play. Here, since the parties' interests no longer fully coincide, even the availability of pre-play communication might not serve to resolve the conflict.

In the Chicken game there are once again two pure-strategy Nash equilibria, but in this case they are asymmetrical – at the off-diagonal cells $(x_1^j, x_2^k)$ and $(x_2^j, x_1^k)$. Again, there is a mixed-strategy NE as well. Given the specific payoffs of table 9.2, the equilibrium mixed strategy is symmetrical: each player chooses strategy 1 (Coward) and strategy 2 (Hero) with probabilities 0·6 and 0·4 respectively. At the mixed-strategy NE each player's expected return is 2·4, intermediate between the Hero payoff of 8 and the Coward payoff of 0 at each of the pure-strategy NE's.

---

[5] In the biological literature, the game of Chicken is known as Hawk-Dove (Maynard Smith, 1976).

Table 9.2 *Chicken*

|              |       | Player $k$            |                    |
|--------------|-------|-----------------------|--------------------|
|              |       | Coward $x_1^k$        | Hero $x_2^k$       |
| Player $j$ | Coward $x_1^j$ | 4, 4            | 0, 8               |
|              | Hero $x_2^j$   | 8, 0            | $-6, -6$           |

We have spoken of Tender Trap and Chicken as two games, but more precisely the "normal form" matrices of tables 9.1 and 9.2 only describe two *payoff environments*. We do not actually have a sufficient description of a game until we specify also the *procedural rules* (for example, whether the players move simultaneously or in sequence, and if in sequence who moves first) and the *information or beliefs* that the different parties possess. These other elements are pictured in the decision tree. In later sections of the chapter we will be describing how these procedural and informational aspects of the problem affect possible solutions of a game. And, in particular, we will be exploring how they provide possible ways of separating more plausible Nash equilibria from those that are less plausible.

## 9.2 Evolutionary equilibrium

The discussion to this point leaves open the question as to what equilibrium is actually likely to emerge. One way of resolving this problem is to introduce evolutionary or natural-selection considerations, as proposed by the biologist John Maynard Smith (1976, 1982). Imagine a large uniform population of organisms who randomly encounter one another in pairwise interactions, with payoffs for each single encounter given by some game matrix. Then, owing to the force of natural selection, over the generations a strategy yielding above-average return will gradually come to be used by larger and larger fractions of the population while strategies with below-average returns will shrink in representation. Among economic players, *imitation* may replace or supplement natural selection, with somewhat similar results (Alchian, 1950; Winter, 1964). If the dynamic evolutionary process leads to a population whose members are fractionally distributed over a set of strategies – or, as a special case, all of whom are following some single strategy – then that distribution is called an *evolutionary equilibrium* (EE), provided that the evolutionary process works to maintain and restore the distribution in the face of all sufficiently small arbitrary displacements of the population proportions ("shocks").

To begin with, consider only pure strategies. Let us assume a symmetrical game (so that the row and column players could be interchanged without affecting the matrix of payoffs).[6] Denote as $V(x_a | x_b)$ the payoff to an organism playing $x_a$ in an environment where everyone else in the population is playing $x_b$. Maynard Smith defined what he termed an "evolutionarily stable strategy" (ESS) as follows:

(i) Strategy $x_a$ is an ESS if $V(x_a | x_a) > V(x_b | x_a)$, for any $b \neq a$.

(ii) Or, even if this condition does not hold, $x_a$ is still an ESS if
$V(x_a | x_a) = V(x_b | x_a)$   and   $V(x_a | x_b) > V(x_b | x_b)$.

The first condition corresponds essentially to the strategy-pair $(x_a, x_a)$ being a *strong* Nash equilibrium. If when everyone else is playing $x_a$, any single player finds that $x_a$ is strictly better for him than any other strategy, then $x_a$ is an ESS. The second condition says that, even if $(x_a, x_a)$ is only a *weak* NE, that strategy-pair can still be an ESS provided that $x_a$ can defeat any other strategy $x_b$ when the population consists almost entirely of players of $x_b$. In effect, the first condition says that the home team prevails when it can beat any intruder. The second says that the home team can still win out even if it only ties some intruders, provided it can beat any such intruder on the latter's own home field.

Satisfying the conditions for an ESS does not necessarily suffice for evolutionary equilibrium, however. In the first place the ESS definition above was pitched in terms of a single evolutionarily stable *strategy* – whereas, more generally, evolutionary stability is a characteristic of a population distribution over a set of strategies. If strategies $a$, $b$, and $c$ are being played within a certain population in proportions $p_a$, $p_b$, and $p_c$ respectively, that distribution may or may not be evolutionarily stable – with no implications one way or the other as to whether any of the three component strategies is an ESS standing alone.

It is important not to confuse a *mixed population* with a *uniform population playing a mixed strategy*. A population distribution in the proportions $p_a, p_b, p_c$ over the pure strategies $a$, $b$, and $c$ does not in general have the same stability properties as a population uniformly playing the corresponding probability mixture of the same three strategies. (Except that when there are only two pure strategies, the stability properties are indeed equivalent.)[7]

Second and more fundamentally, since an evolutionary equilibrium EE is the stable terminus of a natural-selection process over the generations, it is characterized not only by the payoff elements entering into the definition of the ESS but also by the dynamic formula governing the change in population proportions in response to yield differentials in any generation

---

[6] This amounts to assuming a homogeneous population in which everyone is of one single type.

[7] Maynard Smith (1982), pp. 184–6.

(Taylor and Jonker, 1978; Zeeman, 1981; Friedman, 1987; Hirshleifer and Martinez Coll, 1988). It may be, for example, that, even if the payoffs remain unchanged, increasing the sensitivity of the dynamic response formula can lead to explosive cycling instead of the damped behavior of a system consistent with ultimate stability.[8]

In what follows we will generally be employing the evolutionary equilibrium (EE) terminology, although in most of the simple cases dealt with the ESS definition originally proposed by Maynard Smith suffices to locate the equilibrium.

Along the lines of the analysis in Hirshleifer (1982), the essentials of the relation between Nash equilibrium (NE) and evolutionary equilibrium (EE) are pictured in figure 9.3. On the horizontal axis is plotted $p$, the proportion of the population playing the first or "more cooperative" strategy in each of the games just considered. On the assumption that each individual will be randomly encountering other members of the population in a one-in-one interaction, let $\bar{V}_1$ denote the average payoff, as a function of $p$, to an individual choosing the more cooperative strategy 1. Similarly, let $\bar{V}_2$ be the expected payoff to the less cooperative strategy 2 as a function of $p$. Thus:

$$\bar{V}_1 \equiv pV(x_1 \mid x_1) + (1-p)V(x_1 \mid x_2)$$
$$\bar{V}_2 \equiv pV(x_2 \mid x_1) + (1-p)V(x_2 \mid x_2)$$

(9.2.1)

Evidently, the second strategy will be more successful, and thus over the generations will be naturally selected over strategy 2, whenever $\bar{V}_1 - \bar{V}_2 < 0$. From (9.2.1):

$$\bar{V}_1 - \bar{V}_2 = p[V(x_1 \mid x_1) - V(x_2 \mid x_1)] + (1-p)[V(x_1 \mid x_2) - V(x_2 \mid x_2)]$$

If strategy $x_1$ is a strong Nash equilibrium so that the first bracketed term is strictly positive, then $\bar{V}_1 - \bar{V}_2$ is necessarily positive when $p$ approaches unity. Moreover, even if the payoffs were such that the first bracket is zero, $\bar{V}_1 - \bar{V}_2$ is still positive if the second bracket is positive. Hence sufficient conditions for an evolutionary equilibrium are indeed those given by (i) and (ii) above.

Figure 9.3 indicates that two qualitatively different types of situations associated with the payoff environments of Tender Trap (line I) and

[8] Consider the discrete-generation dynamic formula:

$$\Delta p_a = \kappa p_a(\bar{V}_a - V), \text{ for all strategies } a = 1, \dots, A$$

Here $p_a$ is the proportion of the population playing strategy $a$ (where of course $\Sigma_a p_a = 1$), $\bar{V}_a$ is the mean payoff received by a player of strategy $a$, $V$ is the average mean yield for the population as a whole, and finally $\kappa$ is a parameter representing the sensitivity of the dynamic process. Then, if there is an interior NE consisting of a population distributed over a set of pure strategies, whether or not that NE is also an EE depends upon $\kappa$ being sufficiently small (Hirshleifer and Martinez Coll, 1988, pp. 387–90).

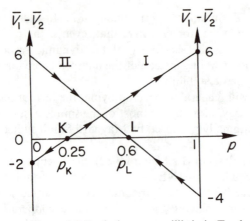

Figure 9.3 Evolutionary equilibria in Tender Trap and Chicken

Chicken (line II). Line I is positively sloped, owing to the fact that in Tender Trap it is more profitable always to conform to what the great majority of the other players are doing; line II is negatively sloped since in the environment summarized by the Chicken payoff matrix it is more advantageous to do the contrary.

For the Tender Trap example of table 9.1, $p = 0$ corresponds to the mutually less profitable "Qwerty" NE at $(x_2, x_2)$; $p = 1$ similarly corresponds to the more profitable "Dvorak" NE at $(x_1, x_1)$; and finally the crossover point K at the population proportions $(p_K, 1 - p_K) = (0.25, 0.75)$ corresponds to the mixed NE. As can be seen, for $p > p_K$ the difference $\bar{V}_1 - \bar{V}_2$ is positive. Then, as indicated by the arrows, the proportion adopting the first strategy will grow over the generations, eventually achieving the extreme at $p = 1$. For any initial proportion $p < p_K$, on the other hand, the evolutionary process over time will go the other way, terminating at $p = 0$. Thus, the mixed-strategy NE[9] represented by point K is not an EE (is not "evolutionarily stable"); only the pure-strategy NE's at $p = 0$ and at $p = 1$ are EE's.

For the Chicken payoff matrix of table 9.2, there is a mixed NE at the crossover point L, where $(p_L, 1 - p_L) = (0.6, 0.4)$. Since in Chicken it is the *less* prevalent strategy that has the advantage, as indicated by the arrows along line II, the evolutionary progression is always away from the extremes and toward the interior solution at point L. Thus, for Chicken only the mixed NE is an EE.

---

[9] Since in both Tender Trap and Chicken only two pure strategies are involved, for purposes of analyzing evolutionary stability we can, as indicated above, deal with a uniform population playing a mixed strategy as if it were a mixed population playing the corresponding distribution of pure strategies.

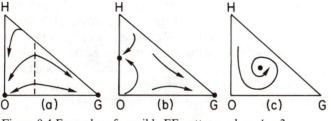

Figure 9.4 Examples of possible EE patterns when $A = 3$

A number of new possibilities emerge when we consider strategy sets where the number of pure strategies, $A$, exceeds 2.[10] Figure 9.4 is a suggestive illustration for $A = 3$. Any point within each triangle represents a distribution of the population over the three strategy options. The horizontal coordinate represents the proportion $p_1$ playing strategy 1, the vertical coordinate the proportion $p_2$ playing strategy 2, while the remaining proportion $p_3$ is measured by the horizontal (or, equivalently the vertical) distance from the hypotenuse. Thus, the origin is the point where $p_3 = 1$. The arrows show convergence possibilities for a number of different possible cases. Without going into the specific conditions here,[11] it is evident that there may be EE's (as indicated by the heavy dots in the diagrams) at various combinations of: (i) one or more vertices; (ii) an edge and a vertex; or, (iii) in the interior.[12] A vertex EE corresponds to the situation where only a single strategy is represented in equilibrium; an edge EE corresponds to more than one, but not all, strategies being represented; an interior EE indicates that all strategies are represented. Or, finally, there may be no EE at all.

For $A \geqslant 3$ there are several other interesting implications. First, it may be that each of two or more strategies can defeat all others, but are tied as against one another. In such cases no single one of the winning strategies will meet the conditions for an EE, since it is not stable with regard to displacements shifting its proportionate representation as against other members of the winning group. Yet, the group as a whole represents a kind of *evolutionary equilibrium region*, since any given starting point of the evolutionary progression will always be attracted to some terminus along the edge connecting those strategies. Second, it is also possible to have a different kind of attractive region: a closed "limit cycle" toward which the population proportions spiral from within or without – but where, along the curve itself, the proportions cycle perpetually.

[10] Here we will always be thinking of *mixed populations*, each member of which plays some pure strategy, rather than *uniform populations playing a mixed strategy*.
[11] On this see Hirshleifer and Martinez Coll (1988, pp. 379–80).
[12] Some of the possibilities are illustrated in the exercises below.

One objection to both the Nash equilibrium (NE) and evolutionary equilibrium (EE) concepts is that the players are imagined as behaving in a very mechanistic way. Presumably, economic decision-makers would be able to bring more sophisticated thought processes to bear upon the choice of strategy. For further progress, what is needed is an explicit model of how players' beliefs are formed. The remaining sections of this chapter examine additional strategic equilibrium concepts in this light.

EXERCISES AND EXCURSIONS 9.2

*1 Nash equilibrium (NE) and evolutionary equilibrium (EE)*

Identify the pure-strategy and mixed-strategy NE's, and the EE's as well, of the following payoff matrices. Show that 1 has EE's at all three vertices; 2 has an EE only along an edge; 3 has only an interior EE; and 4 has no EE at all.

| 1 | a | b | c |   | 2 | a | b | c |
|---|---|---|---|---|---|---|---|---|
| a | 8,8 | 3,2 | 1,7 |   | a | 3,3 | 4,4 | 2,2 |
| b | 2,3 | 5,5 | 4,0 |   | b | 4,4 | 3,3 | 2,2 |
| c | 7,1 | 0,4 | 5,5 |   | c | 2,2 | 2,2 | 1,1 |

| 3 | a | b | c |   | 4 | a | b | c |
|---|---|---|---|---|---|---|---|---|
| a | 1,1 | 2,2 | 3,3 |   | a | 3,3 | 3,3 | 2,1 |
| b | 2,2 | 1,1 | 2,3 |   | b | 3,3 | 3,3 | 2,2 |
| c | 3,3 | 3,2 | 1,1 |   | c | 1,2 | 2,2 | 1,1 |

ANSWER

1 All three payoff combinations along the main diagonal represent strong Nash equilibrium (NE) points, so the corresponding vertices in figure 9.4 are all EE's.

2 Here the only NE is a 50:50 mixture of strategies *a* and *b*, suggesting a possible EE at the corresponding population distribution over these pure strategies. (Strategy *c*, since its payoffs are dominated by those of both *a* and *b* at all population proportions, becomes extinct in the EE.) Since each of *a* and *b* does better the larger the proportion of the other strategy in the population (compare payoff pattern II in figure 9.1), the population is "repelled" from the *a* and *b* vertices and does indeed evolve toward the 50:50 distribution along the *a-b* edge.

3 The only NE is a 1/3:1/3:1/3 mixture. As indicated by the low payoff-pairs along the main diagonal of the matrix, here each strategy does worst

of all at its own vertex. So the population is repelled from all three vertices and evolves toward the corresponding interior distribution.

4 Here there are weak pure-strategy NE's at all four upper-left cells of the matrix. Strategy $c$, being dominated throughout, must become extinct in the EE. But this having occurred, $a$ and $b$ have equal payoffs as do all mixtures of them as well. So there is no determinate evolutionary trend toward any particular point along the $a$-$b$ edge, though the edge as a whole is an evolutionary equilibrium region.

## 2 Evolutionary dynamics

This exercise is designed to illustrate the dynamics corresponding to the two vertex EE's shown in the first diagram of figure 9.4. For the payoff matrix below, let $(p_1, p_2, p_3)$ be the population proportions using strategies $a$, $b$, and $c$ respectively.

|     | $a$   | $b$   | $c$   |
|-----|-------|-------|-------|
| $a$ | 2,2   | 0,0   | 0,0   |
| $b$ | 0,0   | 1,1   | 0,2   |
| $c$ | 0,0   | 2,0   | 1,1   |

(A)  Using the discrete-generation dynamic formula given in footnote 8 above, show that the population proportions evolve according to:

$$\Delta p_1 = \kappa p_1 (2p_1 - V)$$
$$\Delta p_2 = \kappa p_2 (p_2 - V)$$
$$\Delta p_3 = \kappa p_3 (2p_2 + p_3 - V)$$

(B)  Since these changes sum to zero, show that:

$$V = 2p_1^2 + p_2^2 + p_3(2p_2 + p_3^2) = 2p_1^2 + (p_2 + p_3)^2 = 2p_1^2 + (1 - p_1)^2$$

(C)  Hence show that $\Delta p_1 > 0$ if and only if $p_1 > \frac{1}{3}$.
(D)  Show that $V$ exceeds $\frac{2}{3}$ for all $p_1$. Hence explain why $\Delta p_2 < 0$ for all $p_2 < \frac{2}{3}$.
(E)  Show that if $p_1 < \frac{1}{3}$ and $p_3 \approx 0$, $\Delta p_2$ is strictly positive.
(F)  Use these results to explain why the population proportions will evolve as depicted in figure 9.4a (as long as $\kappa$ is sufficiently small).

## 3 NE versus EE, and evolutionary equilibrium region

(A)  For the payoff matrix below, show that there is a weak NE at the $c, c$ strategy-pair along the main diagonal (corresponding to the $c$-vertex of the triangle). However, show that this NE cannot be an EE. (HINT: If $p_c = 1 - \varepsilon$, are there any $p_a, p_b$ population fractions, summing to $\varepsilon$, for which strategy $a$ and/or strategy $b$ has higher payoff than strategy $c$?)

|   | $a$ | $b$ | $c$ |
|---|-----|-----|-----|
| $a$ | 3,3 | 3,3 | 1,4 |
| $b$ | 3,3 | 3,3 | 2,2 |
| $c$ | 4,1 | 2,2 | 2,2 |

(B)  Show that strategy $c$ will be dominated, even as $\varepsilon$ approaches unity, by mixtures of $a$ and $b$ in which the latter has more than 50% representation. Accordingly identify a range along the $a$-$b$ edge of the triangle that represents an evolutionary equilibrium region.

### 4 Interacting populations

The analysis in the text postulated interactions within a single homogeneous population. But sometimes we want to consider interactions between members of two distinct populations: e.g., males versus females, buyers versus sellers, predators versus prey.

(A)  The payoff matrix below is associated with the game known as Battle of the Sexes. What are the three Nash equilibria of this game?

(B)  In considering evolutionary equilibria of games with interacting populations, we seek stable vectors of population proportions $(p_1, p_2, \ldots, p_A; q_1, q_2, \ldots, q_A)$ – where the $p$'s represent the proportions of the first population and the $q$'s are proportions of the second population, both distributed over the $A$ available pure strategies. Find the EE's of the Battle of the Sexes game, if any.

Player $k$

|  | $x_1^k$ | $x_2^k$ |
|---|---------|---------|
| $x_1^j$ | 10, 8 | 4, 4 |
| $x_2^j$ | 4, 4 | 8, 10 |

Player $j$

(C)  In the Chicken game, described earlier in the chapter as taking place within a single homogeneous population, there were three NE's of which only the single "interior" NE (representing a mixed-strategy or mixed-proportions solution) was an EE. Suppose now that the interacting players come from different populations. Do the results differ?

### 5 The "war of attrition" (Maynard Smith, 1976; Riley, 1979)

Two animals are competing for a single prize (item of food). As long as they engage in a merely ritualistic (non-damaging) struggle, neither wins the prize and each incurs an opportunity cost of $c$ per unit of time. If player 2 withdraws at time $t$, the payoffs are:

$$U_1 = V - ct$$
$$U_2 = -ct$$

(A)  Explain why no player will, in equilibrium, choose any particular stopping time $\hat{t}$ with positive probability.

(B)  Suppose player 2 adopts the continuously mixed strategy of dropping out by time $t$ with cumulative probability $G(t)$. Write down the expected payoff to player 1.

(C)  Hence, or otherwise, show that the Nash equilibrium strategy of this game is:

$$G(t) = 1 - e^{-ct/V}$$

(D)  Explain why it is only a matter of notational convenience to choose a unit of measurement so that $c = V$.

(E)*  Under this assumption, show that the expected payoff to playing the Nash equilibrium strategy against a mutant strategy $H(t)$ can be expressed as:

$$V(v\,|\,\mu) = \int_0^\infty G'(t)\,[H(t) - t + \int_0^t H(x)\,dx]\,dt$$
$$= \int_0^\infty [G'(t)\,(H(t) - t) + H(t)\,(1 - G(t))]\,dt$$

[HINT: Integrate $\int_0^\infty G'(t) \int_0^t H(x)\,dx\,dt$ by parts, using the fact that $G'(t) = -d(1 - G(t))/dt$.]

(F)*  Show that $V(\mu\,|\,\mu) - V(v\,|\,\mu)$ reaches a maximum at $\mu = v$, that is, the Nash equilibrium is also an evolutionary equilibrium. [HINT: Write down the Euler condition and then use the fact that $G'(t) + G(t) - 1 = 0$.]

## 9.3    Subgame-perfect equilibrium

While the evolutionary approach can be useful in exploring the long-run equilibria of certain systems, it has nothing to say about games that are not played repeatedly in large populations subject to natural selection. In such cases how should players make decisions, and what can be said about the outcome?

While the Nash equilibrium concept remains at least a preliminary guide, frequently there are multiple NE's. Not only do multiple NE's create difficulties when it comes to prediction, they also pose problems for the theory itself. A condition of equilibrium is that each player's choice be a

* Starred questions or portions of questions may be somewhat more difficult.

Table 9.3 *Entry game*

|  |  | Player 2 (entrant) | |
|  |  | Enter | Out |
| --- | --- | --- | --- |
| Player 1 (incumbent) | Match | 2, 2* | 6, 0 |
|  | Undercut | 0, −1 | 6, 0* |

best response to the strategy of his opponents. But, if the NE in a simultaneous-move game is not unique, how will a player know whether a given strategy choice on his part is a best reply when the opponents may be choosing among several different NE strategies? Owing to such problems, much effort has gone into "refining" the Nash equilibrium concept (Selten, 1975; Myerson, 1978; Kreps and Wilson, 1982; Kohlberg and Mertens, 1986; Cho and Kreps, 1987). Two widely accepted refinements of Nash equilibrium will be examined in this and the next section.

Consider the following game. One firm, the "entrant," moves first by deciding whether or not to invade a market now occupied solely by an "incumbent" firm. If she chooses to enter, the entrant will quote a price lower than that previously ruling. The incumbent must respond in one of two ways. He can (i) match the entrant's price and hence share the market, or (ii) he can quote a price still lower than hers so as to drive out the new competitor. In the latter case the incumbent's profits are further reduced while the entrant suffers a loss.

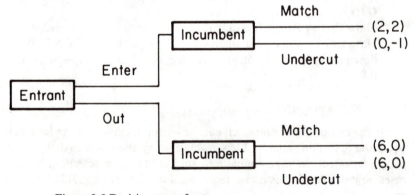

Figure 9.5 Decision tree of entry game

Figure 9.5 depicts the decision tree or "extensive form" of the game; table 9.3 depicts the same game in tabular or "normal" form. Looking at the table, there are two Nash equilibria in pure strategies,[13] indicated by

[13] Since this is a sequential-move game, we need not consider mixed strategies.

the asterisks. (1) If the incumbent is going to choose Undercut, the entrant's best response is to choose Out. And if she chooses Out the incumbent loses nothing by being prepared to Undercut. (2) On the other hand, if the entrant chooses Enter the incumbent's best response is Match. And, given the choice Match, the entrant is indeed better off choosing Enter.

But is the first equilibrium really plausible? In other words, once entry has taken place, will the incumbent carry out this threat or intention to Undercut her price? In terms of the decision sequence or tree, the entrant might reason as follows: "Once I have chosen Enter, the incumbent will be better off choosing Match. Undercut is an empty threat. I therefore am better off choosing Enter."

Formally, the entry game has the simple *subgame* depicted in figure 9.6.[14] Given that fact, instead of requiring only that strategies be best replies for the original game, it seems reasonable to impose the additional condition that the relevant parts of each player's overall strategy be a best response in any subgame as well. In other words, the chosen strategy should not only be rational in the NE "best response" sense but in addition should not involve the player in an irrational choice among available options at any later decision point. Whenever this property holds the equilibrium is said to be *perfect*, or, more precisely, *subgame perfect* (Selten, 1975).

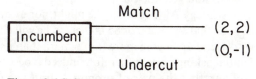

Figure 9.6 Subgame for incumbent

As another illustration, consider an auction conducted under the following rules. The auctioneer starts the bidding at $1,000 and will make raises in steps of $1,000. The $n$ bidders draw numbers out of a hat. The buyer drawing number 1 has the first opportunity to accept or reject the initial asking price. If buyer 1 rejects, he is out of the auction and buyer 2 has a chance to bid $1,000. If buyer 1 accepts, the asking price is raised by $1,000 and the auctioneer moves to buyer 2 who then must decide whether to accept at $2,000 or reject (and hence exit). The auction continues until the asking price is rejected by all buyers, in which case the last acceptance becomes the actual sale.

Suppose there are only two buyers bidding for a diamond tiara. Alex, who drew the number 1, values the tiara at $3,500. Bev, who drew the

---

[14] There is a second degenerate subgame in which each branch leads to the same outcome (6, 0).

number 2, values the tiara at $2,500.[15] The "sensible" solution is for Alex to accept the opening price of $1,000 while Bev accepts the next asking price of $2,000. Alex then bids $3,000 and wins the tiara. However, this is not the unique Nash equilibrium. Consider the following alternative strategy-pair as a solution:

Alex's strategy: Reject the initial price.

Bev's strategy: Accept an asking price if and only if it is less than $5,000.

The strategy described for Bev seems rather weird, since it raises the possibility that she could end up paying for the tiara more than her valuation of $2,500. But let us follow the logic of the proposed solution. Given that Alex does reject immediately, Bev will take the tiara for $1,000, getting her maximum net payoff of $2,500 − $1,000 = $1,500. So this strategy for Bev is indeed a best response to Alex. Now consider whether Alex's strategy is a best response to Bev's. If Alex rejects he ends up with nothing. But if he accepts, that is, if he follows some strategy *other* than the one considered here, for example bidding up to his own valuation, the bidding sequence might go as follows:

Alex bids $1,000

Bev bids $2,000

Alex bids $3,000

Bev bids $4,000 (!) and gets the tiara.

No matter what specific strategy Alex chooses (he might, for example, set himself an upper limit of $1,000 or $3,000 or $5,000 or ...) he will either end up with nothing or, worse, end up paying more for the tiara than it is worth to him. To reject the initial asking price is therefore indeed a best response to Bev's strategy. It follows that the pair of proposed strategies is also a Nash equilibrium.

Just as in the entry game, we can eliminate this "implausible" NE by requiring that the equilibrium be subgame perfect. The tree or extensive form of the game is depicted in figure 9.7, with initial node $A_1$. There are four subgames beginning at $B_1$, $A_2$, $B_2$, and $A_3$. Each is easily analyzed. Starting with the last subgame beginning at $A_3$, Alex loses $1,500 by accepting once Bev has bid $4,000, so his best response is to reject. This is denoted by the arrow pointing down from $A_3$.

Next consider the subgame originating at $B_2$. If Alex had bid $3,000, Bev's payoff from accepting at $4,000 would be −$1,500 (= $2,500 − $4,000) since, as we have just argued, Alex will reject at his next opportunity. Her optimal move at $B_2$ is therefore to reject, which would

---

[15] We are implicitly assuming that the seller does not have full knowledge of the buyers' reservation prices. For, if he did, rather than hold an auction he would simply announce an asking price of close to $3,500.

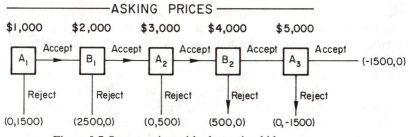

Figure 9.7 Open auction with alternating bids

violate the strategy under consideration. It follows that the implausible Nash equilibrium associated with that strategy-pair is not subgame perfect.

To confirm that the "sensible" intuitive Nash equilibrium is subgame perfect, consider the subgame with initial node $A_2$. From our previous argument, if Alex accepts the asking price of \$3,000, Bev will reject the asking price of \$4,000 and so Alex's net payoff is \$500 ($= \$3,500 - 3,000$). It follows that his optimal strategy is to accept. This is depicted by an arrow pointing across from the node $A_2$.

Now consider the subgame with initial node $B_1$. Bev is outbid if she accepts and gets nothing if she rejects. Therefore to accept the asking price of \$2,000 is a best response. Given this, Alex's optimal strategy in the opening round is to accept also. We conclude therefore that the "sensible" Nash equilibrium (in which Alex will bid up to \$3,000 and Bev up to \$2,000) is subgame perfect.

Unfortunately, this is not the end of the story. From node $B_1$, Bev is indifferent between accepting and rejecting. Rejecting \$2,000 is therefore also a best response. It follows that there is a second subgame-perfect equilibrium in which Alex accepts the starting offer of \$1,000 and Bev then drops out of the bidding. Nor is this an entirely implausible outcome. Intuitively, Bev may note that Alex always has an incentive to outbid her and so she may well decide not to bother going through the exercise of pushing up the price on the seller's behalf. However, if there is any chance at all that Alex will not continue bidding, Bev is strictly better off staying in and accepting the asking price of \$2,000.

This suggests a further approach to "refining" the Nash equilibrium concept. Starting with some game $G$, one might perturb the payoffs and consider what happens as the perturbation approaches zero. A Nash equilibrium for the original game $G$ that is the limit of Nash equilibria in the perturbed game is surely more credible than if this were not the case. For example, in the previous bidding game suppose that Alex's valuation is \$3,500 with probability $1 - \pi_A$ and \$1,500 with probability $\pi_A$ while Bev's valuation is \$2,500 with probability $1 - \pi_B$ and \$500 with probability $\pi_B$.

(Here each person's probability distribution is known to the opponent, but only the individual knows his or her own actual realization.) If Alex accepts the initial price of $1,000 he will take the tiara at that price with probability $\beta_B$, since Bev will not bid if her valuation is $500. If Bev has a valuation of $2,500 she will accept at $2,000 and win with probability $\pi_A$, since Alex will bid $3,000 only if his valuation is $3,500. Of the two subgame-perfect equilibria for the bidding game, the equilibrium in which the price is bid up to $3,000 is therefore more credible than the one in which Alex rejects the original asking price.

A second approach, also due to Selten (1975), introduces "noisy" strategies. Suppose an individual who intends to select some strategy $x_a$ from his set of feasible pure strategies $(x_1, x_2, \ldots, x_A)$ unintentionally plays some other strategy $x_b$ with probability $\pi_b > 0$, where $\Sigma_{b \neq a} \pi_b = \varepsilon$ and $\varepsilon$ is small. Then an opponent may want to choose her strategy in the light of this "tremble" possibility.

For our alternating-bid auction, the possibility of such trembles may induce each buyer to stay in the bidding until the asking price exceeds his or her reservation price. Again the reason should be clear. As long as there is a chance that an opponent will make a mistake and drop out, a buyer is better off accepting any asking price below his or her reservation price, since there is a positive probability of winning.

We explore this idea more systematically in the next section.

### EXERCISES AND EXCURSIONS 9.3

#### 1 Entry game with two types of entrant

Suppose that with probability $\pi$ the entrant, if she decides to enter, signs a short-term contract with a supplier. If so the payoffs in the game are exactly as in table 9.3. With probability $1 - \pi$ the entrant, if she decides to enter, signs a long-term contract. In that case payoffs are:

ENTRY GAME WITH A LONG-TERM CONTRACT

|  |  | Player 2 (entrant) | |
|---|---|---|---|
|  |  | Enter | Out |
| Player 1 (incumbent) | Match | 3, 1 | 6, 0 |
|  | Undercut | −1, −2 | 6, 0 |

(A) If $\pi = 1$ we have seen that there are two Nash equilibrium, one of which is subgame perfect. Show that the conclusion is the same if $\pi = 0$.

(B)  There are two subgame-perfect Nash equilibria if $0 < \pi < 1$. Explain.

(C)  Suppose that the entrant "trembles" as she chooses her strategy so that there is a small probability that she will stray from her pure Nash equilibrium strategy. What will be the outcome of such a game?

(D)  Does your answer change if the incumbent also "trembles" with small probability?

### 2 Sealed second-price auction

Alex has a valuation of \$3,500, Bev a valuation of \$2,500. Bids must be submitted in thousands of dollars. Valuations are common knowledge to the two buyers but are unknown to the seller.

Each buyer makes a sealed bid. The high bidder is the winner and pays the *second* bid.

(A)  Explain why bids by Alex and Bev of \$3,500 and \$2,500, respectively, are Nash equilibrium bids. (Since there are no subgames the solution is also subgame perfect.)

(B)  Explain why bids by Alex and Bev of \$0 and \$10,000 are also Nash equilibrium bids. Are there other equilibria as well?

(C)  Appeal to arguments along the line of those at the end of the section to conclude that the NE of (A) is more credible than any other equilibrium.

## 9.4     Further refinements

As has been seen, the additional requirement of subgame perfectness can reduce the number of Nash equilibria. But subgame perfectness is applicable only to games in which players move one at a time (and where these moves are public information). And, even when there is a strong subgame structure, there may be multiple subgame-perfect equilibria, some of which seem more credible than others. It would be desirable therefore to find other criteria for ruling out certain of the implausible Nash equilibria.

Consider the following modification of the entry game analyzed in the previous section. The rules are as before except that now the entrant as first-mover can enter in two different ways. These affect the outcome if the seller tries to Match. If the entry is Mild, the entrant accepts a price match by the incumbent whereas, if the entry is Tough, the entrant fights with a further price cut. The incumbent must choose his strategy knowing whether entry has occurred but without knowing whether the entrant has chosen Mild or Tough.

Payoffs in this game are given in table 9.4 (note that if the entrant

Table 9.4

|  | | Player 2 (entrant) | | |
|---|---|---|---|---|
|  | | Mild entry | Tough entry | Out |
| Player 1 (incumbent) | Match | 2, 2 | 1, 1 | 6, 0 |
|  | Undercut | 0, −1 | 0, 0 | 6, 0 |

chooses Mild the payoffs are exactly as in the example of table 9.3). The tree or extensive form of the game is depicted in figure 9.8. As before, the nodes connected by the dashed line (the information set) indicate that the player at that point must choose without knowing which branch of the tree he or she is on.

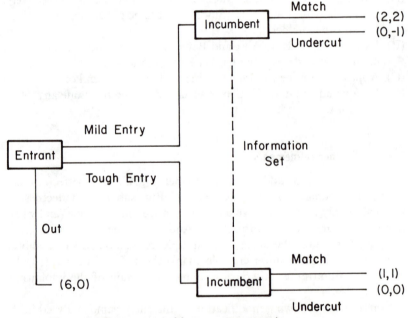

Figure 9.8 Entry game with two entry strategies

There are two Nash equilibria in pure strategies: (1) the entrant stays Out and the incumbent chooses Undercut; (2) the entrant chooses Mild Entry and the incumbent chooses Match.

Since there are no subgames of this game, we need to employ some other refinement of NE to rule out one of these equilibria. Consider how the incumbent fares against each possible entry strategy. With Mild entry the incumbent has a payoff of 2 if he matches and 0 if he undercuts. If the entry strategy is Tough, again the incumbent is strictly better off choosing Match. Therefore, regardless of the type of entry, the incumbent is strictly better off choosing Match.

In the language of game theory, Undercut is a *dominated strategy* once entry has occurred. (And of course, if the entrant remains Out it makes no difference what the incumbent would have done.) It thus seems reasonable to conclude that the incumbent will respond to entry with Match. This eliminates the Nash equilibrium in which the entrant stays out because of the (empty) threat of undercutting.

Another very similar example is given in table 9.5. Here the payoffs in the second column of table 9.4 (when the entrant chooses Tough) have been changed. Now it is no longer the case that Undercut is a dominated strategy. However, consider the choices of the entrant. If the incumbent matches, the entrant's payoff is higher if she chooses Mild. If the incumbent undercuts, the entrant's payoff is the same whether she chooses Mild or Tough. Tough entry is therefore a *weakly* dominated strategy. By eliminating such a strategy the game is reduced to the original entry game analyzed in the previous section.

Eliminating (weakly) dominated strategies[16] is a relatively uncontroversial further refinement. However, only in relatively special cases is the dominance criterion applicable. Consider next the three-player game depicted in tree form in figure 9.9. Each player chooses either Up or Down. The two nodes for player 3 are connected, indicating that this is an information set. That is, player 3 must select his action without knowing whether it was player 1 or player 2 who made the previous move.

If player 1 chooses Up, player 3's best response is Down. Player 1 then ends up with a payoff of 3. Since player 1 is certain to have a lower payoff if he chooses Down, this is a Nash equilibrium.

But what if player 1 and player 2 both choose Down? This will occur if player 1 is a pessimist and thinks that player 3 will choose Up. Player 1 therefore chooses Down. If player 2 is also a pessimist he too will choose Down rather than Up, out of fear that player 3 will choose Down.

Note that this outcome occurs because player 1 thinks that player 3 will choose Up while player 2 thinks that player 3 will choose Down. That is, the players have mutually inconsistent beliefs.

One way of overcoming this problem has been suggested by Kreps and Wilson (1982). Take any strategy vector $s = (s_1, \ldots, s_n)$ for the $n$ players. Consider, for each agent, a completely mixed strategy that is close to $s$. Since all nodes are reached with completely mixed strategies, Bayes'

---

[16] A somewhat stronger refinement is the *successive* elimination of weakly dominated strategies.

Table 9.5

|  | | Player 2 (entrant) | | |
| --- | --- | --- | --- | --- |
|  | | Mild entry | Tough entry | Out |
| Player 1 (incumbent) | Match | 2, 2 | −1, 1 | 6, 0 |
| | Undercut | 0, −1 | 0, −1 | 6, 0 |

Theorem can be applied in a straightforward manner to compute beliefs of each information set. Beliefs are then *consistent* if they are the limiting beliefs as the mixed strategies approach *s*.

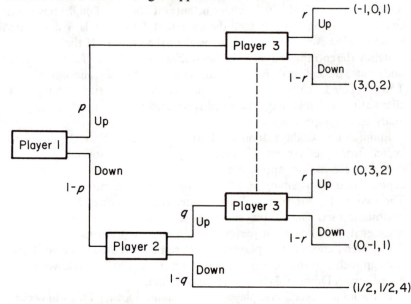

Figure 9.9 Playing against an unknown opponent

For our example, suppose players 1 and 2 choose Down. Then consider this as the limit of mixed strategies in which player 1 chooses Up with small probability $p$, player 2 chooses Up with small probability $q$, and player 3 chooses Up with probability $r$. The probability that player 3 is then called on to play is $p + (1-p)q$ and the conditional probability that it was player 1 who chose Up is:

Prob(1 chose Up | 3's information set is reached)

$$= \frac{p}{p+(1-p)q} = \frac{(p/q)}{(p/q)+1-p} \qquad (9.4.1)$$

In the limit, as $p \to 0$ this approaches:

$$\frac{p/q}{1+p/q}$$

If $q$ goes toward zero faster than $p$, this ratio approaches 1 in the limit. On the other hand, if $p$ goes to zero more quickly than $q$, this ratio approaches zero. Indeed any conditional belief is consistent. To see this, set $p/q = \pi/(1-\pi)$ where $0 < \pi < 1$. Substituting into (9.4.1) and taking the limit we obtain:

$$\lim_{p,\,q \to 0} \text{Prob(1 chose Up} \mid 3\text{'s information set is reached)} = \pi$$

Thus, for this example, consistency imposes no restrictions upon the beliefs of agent 3. However, it still has predictive power since it imposes the restriction that players 1 and 2 must agree about agent 3's beliefs.

For the tree in figure 9.9 the payoffs of players 1 and 2 for the top pair of terminal nodes are just the mirror image of those for the second pair of terminal nodes. If $\pi > \frac{1}{2}$ so that player 3 is more likely to be at the upper node, his best response is Down. If $\pi < \frac{1}{2}$ player 3's best response is Up. Finally, if $\pi = \frac{1}{2}$ then player 3 is indifferent and so willing to play a mixed strategy.

We can now establish that, for any consistent beliefs, the terminal node $(\frac{1}{2}, \frac{1}{2}, 4)$ will not be reached in equilibrium. For if $\pi > \frac{1}{2}$ player 3 chooses Down and so player 1's best response is Up. And if $\pi < \frac{1}{2}$ player 3's best response is Up, in which case player 2's best response is Up. Finally, if $\pi = \frac{1}{2}$ and player 3 adopts the mixed strategy of choosing Up with probability $r$, the payoff of player 1 is $3 - 4r$ if he chooses Up. Moreover, if player 1 chooses Down and player 2 chooses Up, player 2 has an expected payoff of $4r - 1$.

For all possible values of $r$, the larger of these two payoffs is at least 1. It follows that, for all $r$, either player 1 or player 2 or both have a best response of Up. The terminal node of $(\frac{1}{2}, \frac{1}{2}, 4)$ is therefore never reached if beliefs are consistent.

We now formalize the concept of consistency.

DEFINITION: Consistent beliefs
Let $\{(s_t^1, \ldots, s_t^n) \mid t = 1, 2 \ldots\}$ be a sequence of completely mixed strategies which converges to $(\bar{s}^1, \ldots, \bar{s}^n)$. Let $\{(H_t^1, \ldots, H_t^n) \mid t = 1, 2 \ldots\}$ be the corresponding beliefs of the $n$ agents at each node of the tree induced by the completely mixed strategies (via Bayes' Theorem). If $(\bar{H}^1, \ldots, \bar{H}^n)$ is the limit of this sequence then these beliefs are consistent with strategy $(\bar{s}^1, \ldots, \bar{s}^n)$.

Having characterized consistent beliefs at every node and information set in the tree, it is then a straightforward matter to work backwards through the tree and determine whether strategies are best responses. If so, the strategies are said to be sequential (that is, sequentially consistent).

DEFINITION: Sequential (Nash) equilibrium
Let $(\bar{H}^1, \ldots, \bar{H}^n)$ be beliefs that are consistent with the Nash equilibrium strategy $(\bar{s}^1, \ldots, \bar{s}^n)$. If, moving sequentially through the tree, the Nash equilibrium strategies are best responses under these beliefs, then the equilibrium is sequential.

The sequential equilibrium concept is a modification of an earlier approach due to Selten (1975). He too begins by considering a sequence of completely mixed strategies that converges to a Nash equilibrium. However, in contrast with the definition of a sequential equilibrium, the beliefs induced by the completely mixed strategies and not just the limit of these beliefs are a part of the definition.

The basic idea is to start with a Nash equilibrium strategy for the $n$ players $(\bar{s}_1, \ldots, \bar{s}_n)$ and then ask whether, for each $i$, $\bar{s}_i$ is still a best response if each opponent trembles when he tries to play his equilibrium strategy and instead plays each of his other feasible strategies with a small positive probability.

If such a set of trembles can be found, then the equilibrium is said to be trembling-hand perfect. Formalizing our earlier intuitive discussion, we have the following definition:

DEFINITION: Trembling-hand perfect equilibrium
Let $\{(s_t^1, \ldots, s_t^n) \mid t = 1, 2 \ldots\}$ be a sequence of completely mixed strategies converging to $(\bar{s}^1, \ldots, \bar{s}^n)$ and let $\{(H_t^1, \ldots, H_t^n) \mid t = 1, 2 \ldots\}$ be the beliefs of the $n$ agents induced by the completely mixed strategies. If for each $i$ and all $t$ sufficiently large, the best response by agent $i$, given beliefs $H_t^i$, is $\bar{s}^i$, then $(\bar{s}^1, \ldots, \bar{s}^n)$ is trembling-hand perfect.

While the requirements of a trembling-hand perfect equilibrium are mildly stronger, it is only in rather special cases that a sequential equilibrium is not also trembling-hand perfect.

One of these is the simple open bidding game examined at the end of section 9.3. There Alex had a valuation of $3,500 and Bev a valuation of $2,500. It is a dominant strategy for Alex to remain in the bidding as long as the asking price is less than $3,500. Therefore the belief that Alex will be willing to stay in the bidding beyond Bev's valuation is sequentially rational. Thus it is a sequential equilibrium for Bev to reject the initial asking price of $1,000 and drop out of the bidding. However, if there is a positive probability that Alex will tremble and drop out of the bidding at a price below $2,500, Bev is strictly better off staying in the bidding. So dropping out immediately is not a trembling-hand perfect equilibrium strategy for Bev.

At a conceptual level, most people find the trembling-hand analogy quite straightforward. In contrast, consistency as a limit of beliefs seems abstract and difficult to grasp. Given this, it is natural to employ the trembling-hand perfect equilibrium when this proves to be relatively uncomplicated. However, for sophisticated applications it can be significantly easier to check whether there exist sequentially consistent beliefs for a Nash equilibrium.

## EXERCISES AND EXCURSIONS 9.4

### 1 Sequential equilibria

Consider the game depicted in figure 9.9.

(A) Show that (Up, Down, Down) is a sequential equilibrium of this game.
(B) Is (Down, Up, Up) also a sequential equilibrium?
(C) Are there any sequential equilibria in which player 3 adopts a mixed strategy?

### 2 Elimination of a family of Nash equilibria

Suppose that the payoffs for the game depicted in figure 9.9 are modified as follows:

|  | Payoff vector |
|---|---|
| If player 1 chooses Up and 3 chooses Up | (3, 3, 2) |
| If player 1 chooses Up and 3 chooses Down | (0, 0, 0) |
| If player 1 chooses Down, 2 chooses Up and 3 Up | (4, 4, 0) |
| If player 1 chooses Down, 2 chooses Up and 3 Down | (0, 0, 1) |
| If players 1 and 2 both choose Down | (1, 2, 1) |

Let $p$ be the probability that player 1 chooses Up, $q$ be the probability that player 2 chooses Up, and $r$ be the probability that player 3 chooses Up.

(A) Show that for $q \leqslant 2/3$ and $r \leqslant 1/3$, two Nash equilibria are (Up, $q$, Up) and (Down, Down, $r$).
(B) Show that only one of these two classes of equilibria meets the condition for sequential equilibrium.

### 3 Trembling-hand perfect equilibrium

(A) Explain why a trembling-hand perfect equilibrium is a sequential equilibrium.
(B) If the payoff matrix of a simultaneous-move game is as shown below, draw the tree of the corresponding sequential-move game, in which

player 1 moves first and player 2 must respond without knowing what player 1 has chosen.

$$
\begin{array}{c|cc}
 & \multicolumn{2}{c}{\textit{Player 2}} \\
(\alpha \geqslant 1) & l & r \\
\hline
L & 1,1 & 1,\alpha \\
R & 2,0 & -1,-1 \\
\end{array}
$$

*Player 1*

(C) Confirm that there are two Nash equilibria. Then let $\varepsilon_1$ be the probability that player 1 takes an out-of-equilibrium action. For each equilibrium confirm that, as long as $\varepsilon_1$ is small, player 2's best response is unaffected, that is, the equilibrium is sequential.

(D) Suppose, in addition, that player 2 makes an out-of-equilibrium move with probability $\varepsilon_2$. Show that neither player's best response is affected as long as $\varepsilon_1$ and $\varepsilon_2$ are sufficiently small and $\alpha > 1$ in the payoff matrix. That is, the equilibria are trembling-hand perfect.

(E) With $\alpha = 1$ show that there is only one trembling-hand perfect equilibrium (Kreps and Wilson, 1982).

COMMENT: This example illustrates two points. First, it is typically easier to check the requirements of sequentiality than to show that an equilibrium is trembling-hand perfect. Second, it is only for very specific parameter values of the payoff matrix that a sequential equilibrium is not also trembling-hand perfect.

## 4 Open bidding with different valuations

Section 9.3 took up an example in which Alex and Bev made sequential bids for a tiara. For this game there are two subgame-perfect Nash equilibria.

(A) Explain why both are sequential equilibria.

(B) Show that only one is trembling-hand perfect.

(C) Would any small change in the parameters of the model change your answer to (B)?

(D) Try to reconcile your answer with the comment at the end of the previous question.

## 9.5     Games with private information

While the "refinements" discussed in the previous sections succeed in excluding some of the implausible Nash equilibria, important difficulties remain. This is especially the case when players have private information

Table 9.6 *To fight or not to fight*

|  $v^a, v^b \in \{1, -4\}$ | Player $b$ (Bev) Aggressive | Passive |
|---|---|---|
| **Player $a$ (Alex)** Aggressive | $v^a, v^b$ | 6, 0 |
| Passive | 0, 6 | 3, 3 |

but *their actions may signal their type*. Further refinements can be sensibly applied in such games of private information.

Consider the following example. Each of two players simultaneously chooses Aggressive or Passive. If both choose Aggressive so that a fight ensues, for either player the payoff is 1 if he is naturally mean and $-4$ if he is naturally kind. A player knows whether or not he is himself a mean type of individual but this information is private.

The payoff matrix or "normal form" of the game is depicted in table 9.6. If player $a$ (Alex) thinks that player $b$ (Bev) is likely to play aggressively, his best response is to choose Aggressive if $v^a = 1$ and Passive if $v^a = -4$. Since the game is symmetric, the same is true for Bev. On the other hand, if Alex thinks that Bev is likely to choose Passive, then his best response is Aggressive, regardless of his private information.

But what will Alex think about Bev? And what will Alex think Bev will think about Alex? And what will Alex think that Bev will think Alex will think about Bev? ...

Economic theorists have, almost exclusively, chosen to rely on a resolution of this puzzle proposed by Harsanyi (1967). Suppose that the uncertain payoffs $v^a$ and $v^b$ are draws from some joint distribution. Moreover, and this is critical, suppose that this joint distribution is *common knowledge*. Then each player is able to utilize this information to compute a best response.

For our example, there are four possible payoff-pairs when both players choose to be aggressive. Suppose the probability of each payoff-pair is $\frac{1}{4}$. With private information, a complete description of a player's strategy is a description of his strategy (possibly mixed) for each possible private message. We now confirm that it is a Nash equilibrium for each player to choose Aggressive if his or her parameter value is positive and to choose Passive if it is negative.

Suppose Bev behaves in this manner. Given our assumption that each payoff vector is equally likely, there is a probability of 0·5 that Bev will choose Aggressive. If Alex's valuation is $v^a$, his expected payoff to Aggressive is $(\frac{1}{2})v^a + (\frac{1}{2})6$ while his expected payoff to Passive is $(\frac{1}{2})0 + (\frac{1}{2})3$. The net advantage of Aggressive is therefore $\frac{1}{2}(v^a + 3)$. This is positive if $v^a$

$= 1$ and is negative if $v^a = -4$. Therefore Alex's best response is to behave as proposed. Given the symmetry of the example, it follows that the proposed strategy is a Nash equilibrium.

To reiterate, in a game with private information, a strategy is a description of a player's action (or probabilistic mix of actions) for each possible private information state. As long as the underlying distribution of private informational messages is *common knowledge*, each player can compute his expected payoff against a particular strategy of his opponent. Equilibrium strategies are then strategies that are best responses, just as in the earlier discussion of Nash equilibrium with no private information. Because of the importance of the common-knowledge assumption, economists sometimes acknowledge the distinction by referring to the equilibrium as a Bayes–Nash or Bayesian equilibrium.

As a second example, let us consider an advertising game with private information. In this game there is an equilibrium in which a seller of high-quality products can signal that fact by costly advertising.

Suppose that a manufacturer is about to introduce a new product which will either be of superior or mediocre quality. These define two "types" of firm. If the product is superior, optimal use by consumers is High. If it is mediocre, optimal use is Low. High rates of consumption generate high revenue and profit for the firm. Before distribution of the new product the firm chooses either Zero advertising, Radio advertising, or more expensive TV advertising.

It is common knowledge that the odds of a superior product are only 1 to 4. Consumers are not able to observe product quality until it has been used for some time. They do, however, observe the advertising decision of the firm.

The payoff matrix for this game is given in table 9.7. Note that, in switching from Zero advertising to Radio advertising, the manufacturer's payoff declines by 5. This reflects the cost of the advertising. TV advertising costs 7 so there is a further decline of 2 in the manufacturer's payoff if he switches from Radio to TV.

One Nash equilibrium of this game is for consumers to choose a Low rate of consumption and for both types of manufacturers to choose Zero advertising. This is readily confirmed from table 9.7. With consumers choosing Low, there is no incentive for a manufacturer to incur any advertising costs.

This equilibrium is also sequential (and trembling-hand perfect). To see this, consider the mixed strategies of the two types given by the final column in table 9.7. Since both types choose Radio advertising with probability $\varepsilon$, the conditional probability that an advertiser is mediocre is equal to the prior probability, that is, 0·8. The expected payoff to

Table 9.7 *Advertising game*

|  |  | | Consumers' choice | | |
|---|---|---|---|---|---|
|  |  | | Low | High | |
|  | Mediocre | T | −3, 1 | 1, 0 | ε |
|  | | R | −1, 1 | 3, 0 | ε |
|  | (prob. = 0·8) | | | | |
| Type of manufacturer | | Z | 4, 1 | 8, 0 | 1−2ε |
|  | Superior | T | −3, 2 | 5, 4 | ε |
|  | | R | −1, 2 | 7, 4 | ε |
|  | (prob. = 0·2) | | | | |
|  | | Z | 4, 2 | 12, 4 | 1−2ε |

consuming at a high rate is therefore $(0·8)(0) + (0·2)(4) = 0·8$ while the expected payoff to consuming at a low rate is $(0·8)(1) + (0·2)(2) = 1·2$. Given such beliefs, consumers will choose the low rate.

Exactly the same argument holds for TV advertising. Therefore the belief that both types of manufacturers will choose Zero advertising is consistent. This "pooling" equilibrium in which the different types are not differentiated is not the only equilibrium, however. There is a second "separating" equilibrium in which a superior manufacturer signals his product's quality via advertising.

Suppose consumers believe that superior manufacturers will choose TV while mediocre advertisers will choose Radio or Zero advertising. From table 9.7, given such beliefs, the best response to TV is a high rate of use and the best response to Radio or Zero advertising is a low rate of use. Finally, given such choices by consumers, a superior manufacturer has a payoff of 5 if he chooses TV, a payoff of −1 if he chooses Radio, and a payoff of 4 if he chooses Zero advertising. His best response is therefore to advertise on TV. On the other hand, a mediocre manufacturer has a payoff of 4 without advertising and a payoff of 1 if he advertises on TV. It follows that the proposed strategies are Nash equilibrium strategies. Arguing almost exactly as above, it may be confirmed that the consumers' beliefs are consistent. Therefore the Nash equilibrium is also sequential.

But this is far from the end of the story. Suppose consumer beliefs are different, and instead they believe that any manufacturer who advertises on either Radio or TV is of high quality while a manufacturer who does no advertising is of mediocre quality. From table 9.7, a mediocre manufacturer is still better off not advertising while a superior manufacturer will

Table 9.8 *Equilibrium payoffs in the advertising game*

|  |  | Mediocre manufacturer | Superior manufacturer | Consumer |
|---|---|---|---|---|
| $E_1$: | Neither type advertises | 4 | 4 | 1·2 |
| $E_2$: | Superior chooses TV | 4 | 5 | 1·6 |
| $E_3$: | Superior chooses Radio | 4 | 7 | 1·6 |

choose Radio advertising. We therefore have a third Nash (and sequential) equilibrium.

It is instructive to compare the payoffs in the different equilibria, as summarized in table 9.8. Note that no player is made worse off and at least one is made better off in moving from the first to the second and then to the third equilibrium. In particular, a superior manufacturer has a strong incentive to try to convince players to play the third equilibrium. We shall now argue that such a player, if he is allowed to communicate, can plausibly talk his way out of the other two equilibria. More precisely, we begin by proposing a (sequential) Nash equilibrium and then ask whether the equilibrium beliefs are likely to survive if players can communicate.

Suppose, for example, that the proposed equilibrium has the superior-quality manufacturer choosing TV and the mediocre manufacturer choosing Zero advertising.

The superior firm might send the following message to consumers: "I am a superior firm but I am going to advertise on Radio rather than Television. You should believe me and choose a high rate of usage since a mediocre firm would be worse off if it were to choose Radio and you were to make the same response."

Looking at table 9.7, we see that this message is correct. With a high rate of usage, the short-run gains for a mediocre firm are offset by the cost of advertising and so profit is 3 – which is less than the equilibrium profit of 4. However, the superior firm is clearly better off. Therefore if consumers recognize that the argument is correct, the Nash equilibrium with TV advertising fails the communication test.

More formally, let $\Theta = \{\theta_1, \ldots, \theta_n\}$ be the set of possible types of player. We will describe an equilibrium as being *weakly communication proof* if no message of the following type is credible:[17]

> I am taking an out-of-equilibrium action and sending you the true message that my type is $\theta_i \in \Theta$, and you should believe me. For if

[17] This is what Cho and Kreps (1987) refer to rather obliquely as the "intuitive criterion."

you do and respond optimally, I will be better off while any other type of player mimicking me would end up worse off.

This communication test hinges upon the availability of an out-of-equilibrium action that would be in the interests of only one type of player. The following stronger test allows for an out-of-equilibrium action that would be in the interests of a subset of the possible types of player. We describe an equilibrium as being *strongly communication proof* if no message of the following type is credible:

> I am taking an out-of-equilibrium action and sending you the true message that my type is in B, a subset of $\Theta$, and you should believe me. For if you do so and respond optimally (using prior beliefs about types), any type in B would be better off while any other type of seller attempting to do the same would end up worse off.

It may be that none of the NE's survive this strong communication test. Thus, at least so far as we now can tell, game-theoretic methodology will sometimes fail to generate a credible equilibrium. While perhaps regrettable this is, we believe, hardly surprising. In general, games with private information have informational externalities. One player's return yields information about his type and, by inference, information about other players who choose different actions. In the presence of such externalities it would be much more surprising if there were a universal existence theorem for credible equilibria.

Nevertheless, even without equilibrium explanations for every imaginable situation, the Nash equilibrium concept with its refinements has proved to be fruitful for analyzing a wide range of strategic interactions, as will be illustrated further in the chapters to come.

## EXERCISES AND EXCURSIONS 9.5

### 1 Bayesian equilibrium with correlated beliefs

In the first example considered in section 9.5, the probability that an opponent has a positive payoff when both are aggressive is $1/4$ regardless of a player's type. That is, types are independent. Suppose instead that both players have $v_a = 1$ with probability $\frac{1}{4}$ while the probability that Alex has $v_a = 1$ and Bev has $v_a = -4$ is $\beta$. Assume also that the joint probability matrix is symmetric.

(A) Show that types are positively correlated if and only if $\beta > \frac{1}{4}$.

(B) If this inequality holds, show that it is a Bayesian equilibrium for a player to choose Aggressive when $v_a$ is positive and Passive when $v_a$ is negative.

(C) Show also that if $\beta$ is sufficiently small, this is no longer a Bayesian equilibrium.

(D) What is the Bayesian equilibrium in this case?

## 9.6     Non-cooperative bargaining: a cautionary tale

Previous sections have attempted to explain the motivation behind several of the most important refinements of Nash equilibrium. Using a variety of examples, we showed how such refinements can justify the elimination of "implausible" Nash equilibria. However, it remains true that these refinements can at best help to guide, rather than conclusively establish, which Nash equilibrium is the right one.

On some occasions the problem is that the common refinements still leave multiple Nash equilibria. On other occasions, as seen in the previous section, there may be no NE satisfying plausible refinements. This section illustrates a third problem. Using a simple model of non-cooperative bargaining with a continuum of Nash equilibria, we show that, while a unique subgame-perfect equilibrium of the game exists *this unique equilibrium is itself highly implausible* under some conditions.

Consider the following bargaining game. The reservation or demand price $P_D$ of the buyer (Bev) is higher than the reservation or supply price $P_S$ of the seller (Alex), and these two reservation prices are common knowledge. Starting with the seller, the two individuals alternate in proposing a transaction price $P$. Once a proposal is accepted, the exchange takes place. After a rejection, there is a (possibly short) delay and then the rejecting individual makes the next proposal. Let $t$ be the number of delays, so that the initial proposal is at $t = 0$. The game continues until either agreement occurs or an exogenously determined terminal round $T$ is reached in which the buyer makes the final proposal. If this is rejected, the seller gets an exogenously predetermined price $P^*$ where $P_S \leqslant P^* \leqslant P_D$.[18] Finally, let $\delta = 1/(1+\rho)$ be the discount factor per bargaining round for each individual, where $\rho$ is the discount rate per bargaining round.

Consider possible Nash equilibria of this game. Suppose $\rho$ and $T$ are sufficiently large so that the present value of the payoffs to each player, if the game goes beyond round $T$, is less than some small value $\varepsilon$. One strategy for Alex as the seller is to ask for a price $P = P_D - \varepsilon$ in each and every period and reject any offers below this price. With such a stand by the seller, for Bev as buyer the gain, if the game ends in round $t$, is:

$$k(P_D - P)\delta^{t-1} = \varepsilon\delta^{t-1} \quad \text{for } t = 1, \ldots, T$$

---

[18] In an exercise at the end of this section you are asked to show that it does not matter whether the object is sold to the buyer after round $T$ or to a third party (in which case the buyer gets nothing).

She can do no better, therefore, than to accept any asking price of $P_D - \varepsilon$ or less in the first and subsequent rounds. By so doing she gains at least $\varepsilon$. Given the buyer's strategy of accepting any price of $P_D - \varepsilon$ or less, the seller can do no better than this fixed-price offer. Each strategy is therefore a best response to the other and so we have a Nash equilibrium.

Consider now an alternative strategy-pair defined as follows. For any specific $P$ whatsoever, provided that $P_S + \varepsilon \leqslant P \leqslant P_D - \varepsilon$, the strategies are:

Seller:   Ask for a price $P$ in rounds $0, 2, \ldots, T$. Reject any price offer less than $P$ in rounds $1, 3, \ldots, T-1$.

Buyer:   Reject any price greater than $P$ in rounds $0, 2, \ldots, T$. Ask for a price $P$ in rounds $1, 3, \ldots, T-1$.

To take a polar case, suppose $P = P_S + \varepsilon$. That is, the buyer is holding to a price just greater than the seller's reservation price. By waiting until the $T$ rounds are over, Alex as the seller gets less than $\varepsilon$. His maximum payoff in round $t$ is:

$$(P - P_S)\delta^t = \varepsilon\delta^t$$

Therefore his best response is to sell immediately at the price $P = P_S + \varepsilon$.

Thus there is a continuum of NE solutions, one at each and every price $P$ between $P_S + \varepsilon$ and $P_D - \varepsilon$. Of course, some of these are highly asymmetrical in favoring one player over the other.

To most people,[19] the highly asymmetric Nash equilibria of this game seem implausible. Rubinstein (1982) was the first to provide dramatic theoretical support for this intuition. While he considered an infinite-horizon game, his results can be illustrated beginning with the simpler finite-horizon game and letting the number of rounds grow very large.

Suppose initially there are just two rounds. Each individual then gets one chance to name the terms of exchange. Normalizing, let the seller's reservation price be 0 and the buyer's be 1. Then if the items are exchanged at the price $P$ at time $t$, the seller, Alex, gets a *share* $P$ of the item's value and his discounted payoff is $P\delta^t$. The buyer, Bev, thus has a discounted payoff of $(1 - P)\delta^t$. Once again, if there is no agreement the price will be some predetermined $P^*$ between $P_S$ and $P_D$. The extensive form of the game is depicted in figure 9.10.

Consider the subgame that starts at B's decision node. Bev knows that, if her price proposal is rejected, Alex will end up with $\delta^2 P^*$. If Bev offers a price $P_1$ in period 1, Alex gets a present value of $\delta P_1$ if he accepts. Alex will therefore have an incentive to reject only if $\delta P_1 < \delta^2 P^*$. Bev's best strategy is then to ask for a price $P_1$ such that:

$$\delta P_1 = \delta^2 P^* \Rightarrow P_1 = \delta P^*$$

[19] Economic theorists and everyone else!

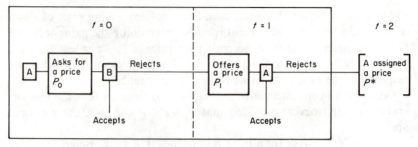

Figure 9.10 A two-round bargaining game

The present value of the subgame to Bev is therefore:

$$\delta - \delta P_1 = \delta - \delta^2 P^*$$

A similar argument can now be applied at the initial node of the game. Alex reasons that any price $P_0$ such that Bev's payoff, $1 - P_0$, is less than $\delta - \delta^2 P^*$ will be rejected. Alex then maximizes by setting $P_0$ to equate these and so:

$$P_0 = 1 - \delta + \delta^2 P^* \tag{9.6.1}$$

This is the unique subgame-perfect equilibrium of the two-period game.

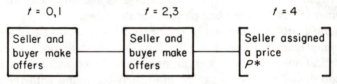

Figure 9.11 A four-round bargaining game

Next consider a four-period game in which the seller and buyer each make two price proposals. The extensive form of this new game is depicted in figure 9.11. If $P^*$ is the price paid the seller when all offers are rejected, the final two rounds are exactly the same as in the two-round game. Alex will therefore ask for a price in period 2 of:

$$P_2 = 1 - \delta + \delta^2 P^* \tag{9.6.2}$$

The extensive form of the four-period game is then reduced to the extensive form of the two-period game except that the end-price $P^*$ is replaced by $P_2$. It follows from (9.6.1) that Alex's subgame-perfect equilibrium strategy is to open with a price of:

$$P_0 = 1 - \delta + \delta^2 P_2$$

Substituting for $P_2$ from (9.6.2):

$$P_0 = 1 - \delta + \delta^2 - \delta^3 + \delta^4 P^* \tag{9.6.3}$$

Comparing (9.6.1) and (9.6.3) it is easy to infer what the initial asking price will be if there are further rounds of bargaining. If $T-1$ is the period in which the final offer is made (by Bev), the unique subgame-perfect initial asking price is:

$$P_0 = 1 - \delta + \delta^2 - \ldots - \delta^{T-1} + \delta^T P^* \qquad (9.6.4)$$
$$= \frac{1 - \delta^T}{1 + \delta} + \delta^T P^*$$

As $T \to \infty$ the equilibrium approaches that for the infinite game with discounting. From (9.6.4):

$$\lim_{T \to \infty} P_0 = \frac{1}{1+\delta} \Rightarrow \lim_{T \to \infty}(1 - P_0) = \frac{\delta}{1+\delta} \qquad (9.6.5)$$

Thus, in the limit, Alex and Bev end up by sharing the surplus in the ratio $1:\delta$. This, of course, is because the game assigned the first move to Alex. Allowing the buyer, Bev, to make the first offer would give her the same proportional advantage in the limit as $T \to \infty$.

In the usual interpretation of this game it is then argued that, if the time between rounds is brief, the discount factor $\delta$ is approximately 1 and so total surplus is shared approximately in the ratio $1:1$. Subgame perfection, typically regarded as the least controversial of all refinements, therefore eliminates all but a very plausible Nash equilibrium in which the surplus is split almost equally.

However, as we shall see, this conclusion hinges critically upon the assumption of an infinite horizon. Suppose that the buyer and seller are trying to negotiate their share of the profit from an invention. Currently there is only one possible producer (the buyer). If the inventor (the seller) and buyer agree, they can patent the invention and earn a profit of 1, discounted to the date of patent. However, at the end of $T$ periods a competing innovation will be introduced that will make the patent worthless.[20] The analysis proceeds exactly as before except that now the price received by the seller, in the absence of agreement, is $P^* = 0$. From (9.6.4):

$$P_0 = \frac{1 - \delta^T}{1 + \delta} \qquad (9.6.6)$$

Suppose we choose $\delta$ and $T$ such that:

$$\delta^T = 0 \cdot 5 \qquad (9.6.7)$$

---

[20] A more plausible model would have the value of the patent decline as period 2 approaches. In an exercise at the end of this section you are asked to show that this does not alter the main conclusions.

For example, if the annual interest rate is 5% so that the annual discount factor is 0·95, the number of years before the competing innovation occurs is approximately fourteen. Now let the number of rounds get large and the discount factor per round approach 1 so that (9.6.7) continues to be satisfied. From (9.6.6):

$$\lim_{\delta \to 1} P_0 = \lim_{\delta \to 1} \frac{0\cdot 5}{1+\delta} = \tfrac{1}{4}$$

The seller of the innovation therefore gets a $\tfrac{1}{4}$ share leaving the buyer with a $\tfrac{3}{4}$ share.

While we will not derive it formally, an almost identical analysis establishes that, if it is the buyer rather than the seller who makes the first proposal, the shares are reversed. That is, as $\delta \to 1$ the buyer's share approaches $\tfrac{1}{4}$ and the seller's $\tfrac{3}{4}$. Subgame perfectness thus yields two puzzling implications. First, even though bargaining might take place frequently each day and could go on for as many as fourteen years, the shares do not approach equality. Second, despite the arbitrarily large number of potential rounds of bargaining and a very small delay between rounds, there remains a very great disadvantage to moving first!

We have analyzed this example in detail in order to make the point that refinements cannot be applied to Nash equilibrium without regard to the context. Expressing this in the most positive way, applied theorists must be willing to combine data (experimental or otherwise) and introspection to justify any refinement they choose to apply. To help them, theorists must do more to explore the weaknesses of NE refinements.

In the bargaining game examined above, the conclusions hinge very critically upon whether or not bargaining must cease after some arbitrarily large number of rounds. That is, decisions made in the short run hinge critically upon events that are due to take place well in the future. Putting this a bit differently, the inferences made by the two bargainers require computations of great complexity and accuracy, despite the seeming simplicity of the results. Wherever such complexity is called for in formal analysis, the explanatory power of the theory is likely to be relatively low.

## EXERCISES AND EXCURSIONS 9.6

### 1 The finite bargaining game

(A) Consider the two-period bargaining game analyzed above. If neither offer is accepted, the seller gets $P^*$. Suppose the buyer gets $V^* \leqslant 1 - P^*$. That is, some or all of the surplus goes to a "mediator" if bargaining fails. Show that the subgame-perfect equilibrium is independent of $V^*$.

(B) Suppose the buyer makes the first price proposal. Solve for the subgame-perfect equilibrium price in round 0 and show that it is independent of $P^*$.

(C) Extend your conclusion to $T$-period bargaining games.

*2 Bargaining with a disappearing surplus*

Suppose that, if agreement is reached in period $t$, the date-$t$ value of the surplus is $V_t$ where:

$$V_0 > V_1 > V_2 \dots > V_T = 0$$

For simplicity, assume that there is no discounting.

(A) Solve for the subgame-perfect equilibrium of the game assuming that the seller moves first and buyer moves last.

(B) What if $T$ is odd so that it is the seller who moves both first and last?

(C) Compare your answers with the subgame equilibrium when:

$$V_0 = V_1 \dots = V_{T-1} > V_T = 0$$

*3 Last-mover advantage in the finite bargaining game*

Two individuals take turns proposing how to share a pie. The pie shrinks with each period so that, after $t$ periods, it is a fraction $f(t)$ of its original size, where $f(t) = \delta^t$, $t \leqslant T$ and $f(t) = 0$, for $t > T$.

(A) Explain why, if agreement is not reached prior to period $T$, the last mover has the bargaining advantage.

(B) Let $\alpha$ be the fraction of the original pie that the last mover will claim if agreement is not reached earlier. Suppose that $\delta$ is close to 1. Show that the subgame-perfect equilibrium is for the last mover to receive a fraction $\alpha$ of the pie plus an (approximately) equal share of the remaining $1 - \alpha$.

## REFERENCES AND SELECTED READINGS

Alchian, Armen A., "Uncertainty, Evolution, and Economic Theory," *Journal of Political Economy*, 58 (1950).

Cho, In-Koo and Kreps, David M., "Signalling Games and Stable Equilibria," *Quarterly Journal of Economics*, 102 (1987), 179–221.

Cournot, Augustin, *Recherches sur les Principes Mathématiques de la Théorie des Richesses*, Paris: Hachette, 1838.

Friedman, Daniel, "Evolutionary Economic Games," UC Santa Cruz Economics Discussion Paper 156 (August 1987).

Friedman, James W., *Game Theory with Applications to Economics*, New York: Oxford University Press, 1986.

Grossman, Sanford and Perry, M., "Perfect Sequential Equilibrium," *Journal of Economic Theory*, 39 (1986), 120–54.

Harsanyi, John G., "Games with Incomplete Information Played by 'Bayesian' Players," *Management Science*, 14 (1967–8) (November), 159–89 (January) 330–4 (March), 486–502.

Hirshleifer, Jack, "Evolutionary Models in Economics and Law: Cooperation Versus Conflict Strategies," *Research in Law and Economics*, 4 (1982), 1–60.

Hirshleifer, Jack and Coll, Juan Carlos Martinez, "What Strategies can Support the Evolutionary Emergence of Cooperation?" *Journal of Conflict Resolution*, 32 (June 1988), 367–98.

Kohlberg, Elon and Mertens, Jean-François, "On the Strategic Stability of Equilibria," *Econometrica*, 54 (1986), 1003–38.

Kreps, David M. and Wilson, Robert, "Sequential Equilibrium," *Econometrica*, 50 (1982), 863–94.

Liebowitz, S. J. and Margolis, Stephen E., "The Fable of the Keys," *Journal of Political Economy*, 33 (April 1990), 1–25.

Maynard Smith, John, "Evolution and the Theory of Games," *American Scientist*, 64 (1976), 41–5.

——, *Evolution and the Theory of Games*, Cambridge University Press, 1982.

Myerson, Roger, "Refinements of the Nash Equilibrium Concept," *International Journal of Game Theory*, 7 (1978), 73–80.

Nash, John F. Jr., "Non-Cooperative Games," *Annals of Mathematics*, 54 (1951), 286–95.

Riley, John G., "Evolutionary Equilibrium Strategies," *Journal of Theoretical Biology*, 76 (1979), 109–23.

Rubinstein, Ariel, "Perfect Equilibrium in a Bargaining Model," *Econometrica*, 50 (1982), 97–109.

Selten, Reinhard, "A Reexamination of the Perfectness Concept for Equilibrium Concepts in Extensive Games," *International Journal of Game Theory*, 4 (1975), 25–55.

Taylor, P. D. and Jonker, L. B., "Evolutionarily Stable Strategies and Game Dynamics," *Mathematical Biosciences*, 40 (1978), 145–56.

Winter, S. G., "Economic 'Natural Selection' and the Theory of the Firm," *Yale Economic Essays*, 4 (1964).

Zeeman, E. C., "Dynamics of the Evolution of Animal Conflicts," *Journal of Theoretical Biology*, 89 (1981), 249–70.

# 10    The economics of contests

In this chapter we consider a class of social struggles commonly referred to as *contests*. A contest, for our purposes, is a rivalrous situation in which a single prize, or a small number of prizes, are awarded to the "high bidders" – the contestants willing to sacrifice the most in terms of some specified input variable. (A special rule is necessary if ties are possible; in that event, it will always be assumed here, the winner is selected at random from the tying high bidders.) Among such contests are auctions, whether conducted by means of sealed or open bidding. Other examples include athletic races, election campaigns, and wars – each of which represents a kind of competition where prizes are won by the high bidders in terms of resource commitment.[1]

What distinguishes a contest from other forms of economic competition is that reward is in no way proportionate to the quantitative resource commitment – total, average, or marginal. Rather, winning or losing depends solely on how one's commitment *ranks* in the distribution of such offerings. In general a contest may have multiple prizes, not necessarily all equal in value. But, unless otherwise indicated, single-prize contests will be assumed here.

To proceed further it is necessary to describe the rules of the contest. As indicated in table 10.1, the rules considered here vary according to a two-fold dichotomy: the first dichotomy, *Discriminatory/Non-discriminatory*, refers to the pricing rule imposed on the winning bidder; the second, *Refundable/Non-refundable*, refers to the disposition of unsuccessful bids (the resource commitments).

*Discriminatory/Non-discriminatory*: In a Discriminatory contest the high bidder is required to pay the amount of his actual bid in return for the prize. In a Non-discriminatory contest, in contrast, the high bidder would

---

[1] Chance-determined lotteries, while sometimes loosely called "contests," do not fall under the definition here adopted. However, an exercise below illustrates a contest that does have a lottery-like interpretation.

Table 10.1 *Equilibrium bidding strategies*

Symmetrical information and unequal valuations ($V_1 < V_2$)

| Pricing rule | Disposition of bids | |
|---|---|---|
| | Refundable | Non-refundable |
| Non-discriminatory | $b_1 = V_1$<br>$b_2 = V_2$ | $G_1(b) = k_1(1 - e^{-b/V_1})$<br>$G_2(b) = k_2(1 - e^{-b/V_2})$<br>$0 < \min\{k_1, k_2\}$<br>$\quad < \max(k_1, k_2) = 1$ |
| | EXAMPLES:<br>English Auction,<br>Sealed Second-price<br>Auction | EXAMPLE:<br>War of<br>Attrition |

|  | BIDDING SET | | |
|---|---|---|---|
| | Discrete | Continuous | |
| Discriminatory | $b_1 = \beta^{m-1} < V_1$ | $G_1(b) < \dfrac{V_2 - V_1}{V_2 - b}$<br><br>and<br><br>$\lim_{b \to 1} G_1(b) = 1$ | $G_1(b) = \dfrac{b}{V_1}$<br><br><br>$G_2(b) = 1 - \dfrac{V_1}{V_2} + \dfrac{V_1}{V_2}\dfrac{b}{V_1}$ |
| | $b_2 = \beta^m = V_1$<br>EXAMPLES:<br>Sealed First-price<br>Auction, Dutch Auction | $b_2 = V_1$ | EXAMPLE:<br>Secret Arms Race |

take the prize after *paying no more than the amount offered by the second-highest bidder.* (Such competitions are therefore sometimes termed "second-price auctions," though this term is strictly applicable only to a contest with a single prize.)[2] Under Discriminatory conditions the winner always pays his full bid, so it might be thought that a Discriminatory contest always extracts higher outlays from bidders. But this does not necessarily follow, since under Non-discriminatory rules the contestants *might be motivated to bid higher.*

In terms of the ordinary auctions of commerce, those conducted under sealed-bid provisions are commonly Discriminatory (though a Non-

---

[2] More generally, in a contest with $k$ prizes, the winning $k$ contenders would each have to pay only the amount of the $(k+1)^{\text{th}}$ highest bid.

discriminatory sealed-bid arrangement would be entirely feasible).[3] As for visible auctions, the so-called "Dutch" auction (in which prices are called from high to low, with the *first* bidder taking the prize) is also Discriminatory. But the ordinary ascending-bid "English" auction approximates Non-discriminatory conditions, since the winner need pay only a little more than the second highest bid.

*Refundable/Non-refundable*: In a Refundable contest the losing bidders do not pay anything. If a contest is Non-refundable, in contrast, *the losing players also pay*, that is, they do not recover their bids! (Again, intermediate cases are possible.) Any contest in which a losing participant must nevertheless sacrifice resources, particularly if the sacrifice is an increasing function of the amount bid, has Non-refundable aspects. Even in an ordinary commercial auction, *deciding* upon the amount to bid is in some degree costly (exhausts resources). So the auctions of commerce have some Non-refundable elements.[4] Nevertheless, the term "auction" will generally refer in this chapter to a contest meeting the Refundable condition, i.e., the losers' bids are returned. For athletic races or wars, on the other hand, the actual situation is usually quite close to strict Non-refundable conditions. In these contests one generally "bids" by the actual irrevocable input of resources and efforts.

Section 10.1 focuses on the purely strategic aspects of competition where contestants have full information about each other's preferences. That is, any differences among contestants are known to all. More specifically, it is assumed that:

1 The prize is in the same commodity units as the resource variable in which bids are stated – or, we might as well say, the prize and bids are both in money units.
2 Each contestant seeks to maximize the expected value of his net money gain. This rules out any effects due to differing risk-tolerances (tastes for risk-bearing).
3 All contestants seek their private advantage; they are neither altruistic nor malevolent with regard to their competitors.
4 Individuals are not necessarily identical in terms of resources available or desire for the prize. However, all contestants have complete information about their opponents' capabilities and preferences, and

---

[3] U.S. Treasury bills have been auctioned from time to time under both Discriminatory and Non-discriminatory rules (Baker, 1976). Under the Discriminatory rule winners pay the Treasury the amounts they actually bid. Under the Non-discriminatory rule, all winners pay the price offered by the highest-ranking losing bidder. (These are of course multi-prize auctions, since a large number of Treasury bills are being marketed.)

[4] To counteract the discouraging effects of these costs, agencies that call for competitive bids sometimes provide a fixed compensation for all bids submitted in proper form.

in particular about others' valuations of the prize. Any residual uncertainty is due to strategic behavior within the contest itself.

These assumptions are maintained in section 10.2, except that individuals are allowed also to have private information. In the simplest interpretation, each contestant's valuation of the prize can be regarded as drawn from some known distribution, whose characteristics are "common knowledge" in the sense defined in previous chapters, but no-one knows the specific values that others have drawn. Equilibrium bidding behavior is then analyzed as a function of the individual's private valuation.

In this chapter we will generally be using the Nash equilibrium concept with possible "refinements" (such as trembling-hand perfect), as discussed in chapter 9. Thus, in equilibrium each bidder's action is a best reply to the choices of the other contenders, taken as given. A player's strategy will typically take the form of a choice of bid or, for a mixed strategy, a probability distribution of bids. We will not attempt here to justify use of the Nash solution concept by specifying any plausible dynamic process leading to such an outcome. In actual sealed-bid auctions, for example, the contestants are very likely to choose a set of bids not meeting the Nash condition. While some or all of the bidders will then be regretting the choices made, under the rules of the auction there is nothing they can do about it. So the Nash equilibrium condition is not to be regarded as a very confident prediction of what will actually happen. It is, instead, a state of affairs that, if it were somehow to come about, would not lead any party to unilaterally want to revise his chosen course of action.

## 10.1    Contests with full information

In the simplest case, suppose there is a single prize and two contestants. Individual 1 (Alex) values the prize at $V_1$ and individual 2 (Bev) at $V_2$, where $V_2 > V_1$. These valuations are common knowledge.

In the course of the contest, resources are spent by one or both contestants. Assuming risk-neutrality, we need only consider the expectation of this spending. Let $c_i$ be individual $i$'s expected spending and let $p_i$ be the corresponding probability of winning. Then $i$'s expected return is:

$$U_i = p_i V_i - c_i, \quad i = 1, 2 \tag{10.1.1}$$

Also, since no-one is compelled to participate, in equilibrium both individuals have non-negative expected return.

In what follows we first consider equilibrium bidding strategies under Refundable rules (where no costs are imposed upon losing bidders). The analytically rather less tractable Non-refundable rules are taken up in the following subsection.

### 10.1.1   Refundable bids

Under this heading fall the two most common types of commercial auctions: (1) the sealed high-bid auction (Discriminatory) and (2) the "English" or open ascending-bid auction (Non-discriminatory).

*First-price auctions* (*Discriminatory*): We can think in terms of the standard sealed-bid auction of commerce. This is Discriminatory since the high bidder must pay the full amount he bids. For analytical convenience, to begin with suppose there is a *discrete* set of feasible bids $0, \beta^1, \beta^2, \ldots, \beta^T$ which includes the two valuations $V_1$ and $V_2$. Thus, there is some $m < n$ such that $\beta^m = V_1 < \beta^n = V_2$.

Suppose the lower-valuing individual 1 (Alex) bids $b_1 = \beta^j < V_1$. If he wins, his gain would be $V_1 - \beta^j$. The best reply for individual 2 (Bev) is to bid a minimally higher amount, that is, $b_2 = \beta^{j+1}$. She then gains $V_2 - \beta^{j+1}$. But individual 1 can respond with a bid of $\beta^{j+2} < V_1$, and so on.[5]

The only resting-place is where the lower-valuing party, Alex, no longer can profitably raise his bid. In particular, when Alex's $b_1 = \beta^{m-1}$, Bev's best reply is the smallest higher bid $b_2 = \beta^m = V_1$. Since Alex cannot profitably overbid this, as shown in the lower left portion of the table an equilibrium of any Refundable Discriminatory (first-price) contest under symmetrical information, as exemplified by the standard sealed-bid auction of ordinary commerce, is the pair of bids:

$$b_1 = \beta^{m-1}, \quad b_2 = \beta^m \equiv V_1 \tag{10.1.2}$$

Note that the equilibrium requires Alex to make a bid very close to his full value $V_1$, even knowing he will be outbid. This may seem somewhat implausible. As justification, suppose there is some chance that Bev will "underbid," that is, she "trembles" (as discussed in the previous chapter) and bids $\beta^j$ with a small probability $\pi^j$ for all $j = 0, 1, \ldots, m-1$ and $\beta^m = V_1$ with probability $1 - \Sigma_{j=0}^{m-1} \pi_j$. Of course in the limit, as all the small probabilities approach zero, this completely mixed strategy approaches the Nash equilibrium strategy.

Consider Alex's best response to the mixed strategy. By bidding less than $V_1$ he has a strictly positive expected return. Which of the bids is optimal then depends upon the *relative* probability weights. Intuitively, if Bev's probability weight on $\beta^{m-1}$ is large relative to the weight on lower bids, i.e., she is much more likely to make the smallest possible "tremble," Alex's best response will be to bid $\beta^{m-1}$. (You are asked to confirm this in an exercise at the end of this section.)

---

[5] As indicated earlier in the text, we are not describing here a *dynamic process* of sequential response, which might not be feasible under the auction rules. We are only looking for a "best reply" equilibrium.

An almost identical argument holds for Bev. It is possible to choose arbitrarily small probability weights on out-of-equilibrium actions by Alex such that Bev's Nash equilibrium action remains a best reply. In the terminology of chapter 9, the equilibrium is trembling-hand perfect.[6]

We now remove the limitation to discrete strategies and suppose instead that any non-negative real number is an acceptable bid. By analogy with the equilibrium strategy-pair shown above for the discrete case, it might appear that the equilibrium for the continuous strategy space will be $b_1 = V_1 = b_2$. However this is not correct. With these strategies Bev has a 50% chance of winning, whereas by raising her bid just slightly she wins for sure. But what bid will Bev make? Since in the continuum there is no minimum bid above $V_1$, there is no *best* reply by Bev.

Despite this difficulty, the intuition gleaned from the discrete case continues to be essentially correct. Even though the lower-valuing Alex does not bid $V_1$, Bev will continue to do so as long as Alex bids sufficiently aggressively. Define $G_1(b) \equiv$ probability $\{\tilde{b}_1 \leqslant b\}$. Of course Alex will never bid $V_1$ or more with positive probability. Therefore $G_1(V_1) = 1$. Alex bidding aggressively means that $G_1(b)$ is small for small $b$ and rises rapidly for $b$ close to 1, that is he almost always bids close to $V_1$.

We shall now show that any mixed strategy for Alex will be an equilibrium mixed strategy if it is sufficiently aggressive, that is, if it satisfies the following two conditions:

$$\lim_{b \to V_1} G_1(b) = 1 \tag{10.1.3}$$

$$G_1(b) < \frac{V_2 - V_1}{V_2 - b}, \quad b < V_1 \tag{10.1.4}$$

To confirm that this is the case, note first of all that if (10.1.3) holds then Alex bids $V_1$ with zero probability. So by bidding $b_2 = V_1$, player 2, the higher-valuing contender, wins with probability 1. Can Bev do still better by setting $b_2 < V_1$? For any such bid $b_2 = b$ she wins with probability $G_1(b)$. Then her expected gain would be, from (10.1.4):

$$U_2(b) = G_1(b)(V_2 - b) < V_2 - V_1$$

Since her gain is $V_2 - V_1$ by bidding $V_1$, any lower bid $b_2 = b$ is less profitable.

The "Dutch auction" is an open-auction equivalent of this sealed high-bid auction. In the Dutch auction a bid-value clock is started at some number known to be higher than any of the buyers' valuations. As the possible bid-values tick down toward zero, the first player to bid wins the prize. As before, in equilibrium the higher-valuing individual 2 will jump in at $b_2 = V_1$.

It is tempting to think that such an open auction conveys information not available in the sealed high-bid auction. However, the only information available to anyone is that no opponent has bid. Therefore, prior to the start of the auction, a buyer can ask himself whether he should raise his hand if the clock reaches any particular level. Having answered this question, he can then write down on a piece of paper the price at which he will jump in. By looking at all these pieces of paper, the auctioneer can determine the outcome without actually introducing the clock at all. Instead, the paper bearing the highest stated price wins, exactly as in the sealed high-bid auction.

*Second-price auctions* (*Non-discriminatory*): Returning to the sealed-bid auction, now suppose instead that the pricing rule is Non-discriminatory, i.e., the high bidder need pay only the amount bid by the runner-up. (These conditions correspond to the upper-left portion of table 10.1.) Then, regardless of whether the bidding set is discrete or continuous, each individual's *dominant* strategy is to bid his full valuation $V_1$. Thus, as shown in the table: $b_1 = V_1$, $b_2 = V_2$.

The reasoning is almost self-evident. If Alex (say) were to bid higher than his valuation, there would be some risk of the bidding pattern being $V_1 < b_2 < b_1$. In this case he wins the prize, but must pay an amount $b_2$ that exceeds his valuation $V_1$. Alternatively, if Alex were to bid less than his valuation, there would be some risk of the ultimate bidding pattern being $b_1 < b_2 < V_1$. Here he loses a prize that he could have won while paying less than his valuation $V_1$. It is easy to verify that, in all other cases as well, Alex loses nothing by bidding his full valuation: for example, if the pattern is $b_2 < b_1 = V_1$, Alex wins the prize while paying no more than the amount $b_2$.

Now let us turn to the familiar "English auction," where ascending bids are called until all but one participant stops bidding. The English auction is essentially equivalent to the sealed-bid second-price auction.[7] To explain this, we must distinguish between an actual bid and a *bidding strategy*. (Note that table 10.1 shows the equilibrium bidding strategies, not the actual bids.) Think of a participant as working through an agent, in which case the bidding strategy consists of instructions left with the agent. By the same reasoning as above, individual $i$ should instruct his agent to bid, if necessary, up to his full valuation $V_i$. The agent would of course not initially bid this full valuation, but instead only the minimal permissible increment over any other player's bid – up to the $V_i$ limit. The upshot is

---

[7] Vickrey, 1961.

that the equilibrium *bidding strategies* remain $b_1 = V_1$, $b_2 = V_2$ as shown in the table. But, supposing that Bev has the higher valuation, her actual *winning bid* $b_2$ would exceed $V_1$ only by a minimal finite amount (if the bidding set is discrete) or an infinitesimal amount (if the bidding set is continuous). Thus, as contended above, the English auction is essentially equivalent to a second-price sealed-bid auction – i.e., it is Non-discriminatory.

## EXERCISES AND EXCURSIONS 10.1.1

### 1 Trembling-hand perfect equilibrium in the sealed high-bid auction

In the sealed high-bid auction examined above, the strategy-pair $b_1 = \beta^{m-1} < V_1$ and $b_2 = \beta^m = V_1$ was a Nash equilibrium.

(A) Suppose individual 2 (Bev) bids $\beta^j$, $j = 0, \dots, m-2$, with probability $\lambda p$ and $\beta^{m-1}$ with probability $p$, so that $\beta^m$ is bid with probability $1 - p - \lambda(m-1)p$, both $\lambda$ and $p$ being small. Explain why the expected return to individual 1 (Alex) is $((m-1)p\lambda + p/2)(V_1 - \beta^{m-1})$ if he bids $\beta^{m-1}$.

(B) Obtain also an expression for his expected return if he bids $\beta^j < \beta^{m-1}$.

(C) Show that, if $\lambda$ is sufficiently small, then bidding $\beta^{m-1}$ is a best reply for Alex.

(D) Use a similar argument to establish that there is a completely mixed strategy for individual 1 such that bidding $\beta^m = V_1$ remains a best reply for individual 2. Hence confirm that the Nash equilibrium is trembling-hand perfect.

### 2 Auctions with equal valuations

(A) If there are $n$ bidders, each with the same valuation $V$, show that, in both the sealed high-bid auction and open ascending-bid auction, it is an equilibrium for each bidder to bid his full valuation.

(B) In the open ascending-bid auction another equilibrium is for one buyer to bid $V$ and the others to bid zero. Is this a less plausible equilibrium?

(C) Are there other Nash equilibria in the sealed high-bid auction? If so, are all the equilibria equivalent from the seller's viewpoint?

### 3 Equilibrium bidding in the open ascending-bid auction

Individual $i$ has valuation $V_i = i$, $i = 1, 2$.

(A) Show that there are many Nash equilibria for the open ascending-bid auction.

(B)  Show that bidding one's reservation value is a trembling-hand perfect equilibrium strategy.

(C)  Are other Nash equilibria trembling-hand perfect?

### 10.1.2   Non-refundable Discriminatory contests

The Non-refundable heading covers a wide range of contests from athletic competitions to wars, the key point being that non-winners' investments are lost beyond recall.

Consider "rent-seeking." Almost any government decision leads to wealth transfers. Evidently, individuals and firms will be motivated to influence the outcome of the political process by spending resources to generate political pressure. Winners stand to gain, but the losers' efforts ("bids") are irretrievably lost. Similarly in a marathon race, the first runner to cross the finish line gains the prize while losers sacrifice their entire "bids" – their commitments of effort.

Marathons are typically conducted under "visible" conditions. Since each contender can see how well opponents are doing and can adjust his effort level accordingly, the winner need only do infinitesimally better than the runner-up. Thus the victor in effect pays only the amount of the second-highest bid; i.e., this is the analog of a second-price or Non-discriminatory auction. Such "visible" contests correspond to the conditions in the upper-right portion of table 10.1. Now consider instead the race to build an atomic bomb during the Second World War. This was a contest conducted under conditions of utmost secrecy – an "invisible" contest. A crucial factor in the Allied calculations was uncertainty about how far along the Germans might be toward building an atomic bomb themselves. As it happened, Germany had largely abandoned the effort early on. But that fact not being known to the Allies, they could not take advantage of it to slacken their efforts. More generally, *secret arms races* typify the Non-refundable Discriminatory condition, as indicated in the lower-right portion of table 10.1.

Turning to the formal analysis, consider again a simple situation with two potential bidders for the prize (Alex and Bev). As above, it will be assumed that their valuations are mutually known and that Bev is the strictly higher-value player: $V_1 < V_2$.[8] We will also assume that the strategy set is a continuum of bid levels from zero to infinity.

It can be shown that the equilibrium bidding strategies must have the following properties.

(i)  The equilibrium expected return of the higher-valuing player is positive.

---

[8]  Where valuations are equal, the equilibrium is the limit of the equilibrium with asymmetric valuations.

(ii) Bidding strategies are mixed for both players, with no mass points for all $b_i > 0$.

(iii) The maximum bids of the two individuals are the same.

(iv) The probability of winning is strictly increasing in the size of an individual's bid.

(v) The minimum bid of each individual is zero.

(vi) The higher-valuing player bids higher than zero with probability one.

To understand why these conditions hold, first note that, since bids are Non-refundable, no individual will ever commit more than his valuation. Then any bid strictly between $V_1$ and $V_2$ by the higher-valuing Bev guarantees her a positive return. Thus Bev can guarantee herself a return of almost $V_2 - V_1$ by bidding just higher than $V_1$. We have therefore established (i).

If Bev does bid $V_1$ or higher, Alex's best reply is to bid zero. But then Bev could have won with any small positive bid. We conclude, therefore, that in equilibrium Bev's bid must be sufficiently less than $V_1$ so as to encourage positive bids by Alex.

To understand (ii), assuming for concreteness that $V_1 > 2$, suppose Alex were to bid 2 with probability 0·5 (where $V_1 > 2$). In that case Bev's best reply cannot include a bid between 1·9 and 2. For, by increasing her bid to just above 2, her win probability would rise by at least 0·5 at a cost of no more than 0·1, and so her expected payoff would rise by at least $0·5V_1$.

But, with Bev never bidding between 1·9 and 2, Alex can lower his bid to 1·9 without changing his win probability, thus increasing his expected payoff. This contradicts the initial hypothesis that Alex bids 2 with probability 0·5.

Similar arguments can be used to derive properties (iii) through (v).[9]

Finally, suppose Bev bids zero with probability $p$. Then, by bidding zero Alex achieves a probability of winning of $p/2$, since the winner is selected at random in the case of a tie. And, by making an extremely small positive bid, Alex's win probability rises discontinuously to $p$ and so leaves him strictly better off. It follows that Bev's best reply is to bid greater than zero with probability 1. We have therefore established (vi).

Let us define the equilibrium cumulative distribution functions (c.d.f.):

$$G_i(b) \equiv \text{Probability \{individual } i \text{ bids } b \text{ or less\}}, \quad i = 1, 2$$

Conditions (i)–(vi) imply that $G_i(b)$ is strictly increasing and continuous over some interval $(0, \bar{b})$ where $G_i(\bar{b}) = 1$, $i = 1, 2$. Therefore Alex's expected return, if he bids $b$, is:

$$U_1 = \text{Prob\{2 bids } b \text{ or less\} Valuation} - \text{bid}$$
$$= G_2(b)V_1 - b$$

[9] See exercise 1 at the end of this section.

Similarly, Bev's expected return is:

$$U_2 = G_1(b)V_2 - b$$

It is readily confirmed by substitution that the following are equilibrium distribution functions:

$$G_1(b) = 1 - V_1/V_2 + b/V_2$$
$$G_2(b) = b/V_1 \tag{10.1.5}$$

Thus, for the higher-valuing Bev, the mixed strategy is a uniform distribution from $b_2 = 0$ to $\bar{b}_2 = V_1$. For the lower-valuing Alex, there is a positive probability $G_1(0) = (V_2 - V_1)/V_2$ of bidding zero and thereafter a uniform distribution over the range from $b_1 = 0$ to $\bar{b}_1 = V_1$.

So far $G_1(0) > 0$ has been interpreted as a positive probability that individual 1 bids zero. Alternatively, we can think of Alex as first deciding whether or not to compete. With probability $V_1/V_2$ he does compete. Conditional upon having chosen to do so, he adopts the same uniform distribution as Bev. That is, he bids $b$ or less with probability $b/V_1$.

On this interpretation, the bids conditional upon entry are independent of Bev's valuation. However, the smaller the ratio $V_1/V_2$, the lower is the equilibrium probability of entry by Alex.

With each individual bidding according to a uniform distribution on $[0, V_1]$, the expected bid conditional upon entry is $V_1/2$. Since Alex enters with probability $V_1/V_2$, expected total resources committed to the contest are equal to:

$$\bar{R} = V_1/2 + (V_1/V_2)(V_1/2) = V_1\left(\frac{V_1 + V_2}{2V_2}\right)$$

Note that this is strictly less than $V_1$, the lower of the two valuations. In the limit as $V_2$ becomes large, $\bar{R}$ approaches $V_1/2$. So expected total spending approaches one half of total spending in either of the common auctions, when bids are Non-refundable.

Recall now that, in the common auctions under the Refundable-bid condition studied in section 10.1.1 (sealed high-bid and open ascending-bid), while the losing bidder paid nothing, the cost to the winner was $V_1$ – the value attached to the prize by the lower-valuing player. But under the Non-refundable rule here the winner and loser *together* expend a lesser amount. It follows that, surprisingly perhaps, the Non-refundable condition is in total less costly to bidders! So, even apart from the fact that the seller may not capture all the costs incurred by the bidders,[10] someone auctioning off an item would surely be ill-advised to choose Non-refundable Discriminatory rules for the bidding.

[10] The bids irretrievably lost by the bidders might or might not be forfeited *to the seller*.

EXERCISES AND EXCURSIONS 10.1.2

*1 Characterizing the equilibrium*

The text above sketched a proof of conditions (i), (ii), and (vi).

(A)  Use condition (ii) to argue that, if Alex has a maximum bid of $\bar{b}$, Bev wins with probability 1 by bidding $\bar{b}$. Hence establish (iii).

(B)  Suppose that Bev bids in the interval [2, 3] with zero probability. Let $\hat{b}$ be her smallest bid above 3. Explain why Alex is better off bidding 2 than in the interval $(2, \hat{b}]$. Hence argue that bidding $\hat{b}$ cannot be a best reply for Bev and use this to establish (iv).

(C)  Extend this argument to show that there can be an interval $[0, \hat{b}]$ over which Bev does not bid, hence establishing (v).

(D)  Confirm that the pair of c.d.f.'s defined in (9.1.5) are an equilibrium of the Non-refundable Discriminatory contest.

(E)  Use conditions (i)–(vi) to establish that this is the unique equilibrium.

*2 Non-refundable Discriminatory contests with more than two contestants*

Suppose there are three contestants and that $V_2 > V_1 > V_0$. You may assume that the conditions correspond to a Non-refundable Discriminatory contest.

(A)  If individuals 1 and 2 bid according to their equilibrium strategies as if there were no third player, what is the latter's best reply?

(B)  Hence or otherwise show that an equilibrium of this contest is for the third contestant to stay out of the bidding entirely.

(C)  Is this result still true for the limiting case of equal valuations?

(D)  In the latter case, show that there is a symmetric equilibrium. That is, each contestant bids according to the same mixed strategy.

REMARK: As Hillman and Riley (1989) establish, when individuals have different valuations the equilibrium described in (B) is unique.

*3 Non-refundable Discriminatory competition with exogenous uncertainty*

In a political contest where each candidate $i$ spends $x_i$ dollars, the winner will be the one for whom $x_i \tilde{\theta}_i$ is largest, where $\tilde{\theta}_i$ is an independent draw from an exponential distribution with c.d.f.:

$$F(\theta_i) = 1 - e^{-a\theta_i}$$

(A)  Show that, if there are two contestants and the first has a realization $\hat{\theta}_1$, then his conditional probability of winning is:

$$\exp\{-a(x_1/x_2)\hat{\theta}_1\}$$

(B) Integrate by parts to show that contestant 1's unconditional probability of winning is $x_1/(x_1+x_2)$.

(C) With such a win probability explain why the expected gain to contestant $i$, if his valuation is $V_i$, is:

$$U_i = \frac{V_i x_i}{x_1 + x_2} - x_i, \quad i = 1, 2$$

(D) Show that there is a pure-strategy equilibrium in which contestants spend the same fraction of their own valuations.

(E) Show that total spending will be $V_1 V_2/(V_1 + V_2)$. Hence confirm that, if $V_1 \leqslant V_2$, equilibrium spending is between $V_1/2$ and $V_1$, depending on the relative size of $V_1$ and $V_2$.

REMARK: Since the probability of winning is the contestant's own spending divided by total spending (as in a lottery), this is sometimes referred to as a lottery contest.

### 10.1.3   Non-refundable Non-discriminatory contests

In the standard rent-seeking model, each contestant decides on a bid and is then committed to spend that amount regardless of what opponents do. In practice, political competition takes place over time so that individuals have an opportunity to reconsider after noting how much others have already spent and whether they are still actively competing. Similarly in a marathon or an arms race under open rather than secret conditions,[11] contestants can observe how well opponents are doing and adjust their effort levels accordingly.

To model this type of interaction, suppose that a number of contestants all spend at the same constant rate per period. Without loss of generality, define units of time so that spending per period is at a rate of 1. Each contestant "bids" by deciding upon a maximum number of periods over which to compete. If after $b$ periods (after spending $b$ units) a contestant finds that his last remaining opponent has dropped out, he becomes the winner without necessarily having to pay his full bid. Thus, assuming he can perfectly observe opponents' actions and immediately respond to them, the winner's cost equals the bid of the second-highest contender. So this type of test fits our fourth category: the pricing is Non-discriminatory, while the resource disposition is Non-refundable.

In the sociobiological literature, contests of this type are known as "wars of attrition" (Maynard Smith, 1976). Animals compete for food, territory, or mates. Typically such contests involve ritualistic combat or

---

[11] Battleships being too big to hide, the battleship races among the naval powers that began in the mid-nineteenth century were essentially non-secret contests.

displays rather than all-out battle. Eventually one contestant concedes and leaves the other to enjoy the prize. In economics, the "war of attrition" model has been applied to the exit decisions of firms in a declining industry (Fudenberg and Tirole, 1986); R&D races can be similarly analyzed (see chapter 7 above).

Consider again the simple case of two contestants, Alex and Bev, the latter being now a weakly higher-valuing player so that $V_1 \leqslant V_2$.

The Non-refundable Non-discriminatory analysis here closely parallels the previous discussion of the Non-refundable Discriminatory contest. As in that case, no positive bid $\hat{b} > 0$ can enter into the equilibrium strategy with positive probability. Thus each individual's strategy can be represented by a continuous distribution function $G_i(b)$, $i = 1, 2$.

The simplest way to solve for the equilibrium is to consider a contest in which the price has already been bid up to some level $b$. Each individual must compare the relative merits of dropping out immediately or staying in and bidding a further amount $\Delta b$. In equilibrium each player must be indifferent between the two alternatives, if both are part of his mixed strategy. Consider individual 1. If he drops out immediately, his loss is $b$. The additional cost of staying in is $\Delta b$. Offsetting this is the possibility that his opponent will drop out.

Conditional upon individual 2 having stayed in the contest until the price is $b$, 1's probability of dropping out is:

$$\frac{G_2(b+\Delta b) - G_2(b)}{1 - G_2(b)} \approx \frac{G_2'(b)\Delta b}{1 - G_2(b)}$$

For small $\Delta b$, the net expected gain to remain in the bidding is:

$$\left[\frac{G_2'(b)\Delta b}{1 - G_2(b)}\right] V_1 - \Delta b$$

Since this must be zero in equilibrium:

$$\frac{G_2'(b)}{1 - G_2(b)} = \frac{1}{V_1}$$

Integrating:

$$G_2(b) = 1 - (1 - G_2(0)) e^{-b/V_1} \tag{10.1.6}$$

Applying an identical argument for individual 2:

$$G_1(b) = 1 - (1 - G_1(0)) e^{-b/V_2} \tag{10.1.7}$$

As a remarkable fact, note that the equilibrium mixed strategies involve a positive probability of "bidding more than a dollar for a dollar"!

It remains to determine each individual's probability of bidding zero (or, equivalently, of refusing to compete at all). We shall now argue that:

$$\text{Min}\{G_1(0), G_2(0)\} = 0 \qquad (10.1.8)$$

That is, at least one individual makes a strictly positive bid with probability 1.

To demonstrate this, suppose to the contrary that $G_1(0)$ and $G_2(0)$ are both positive. Then each individual would have a strictly positive expected return when he or she bids zero. Since in the case of a tie the winner is selected at random, individual 1's expected return to bidding zero is $\frac{1}{2}G_2(0)V_1$. On the other hand, if he bids $b_1 = b > 0$ his win probability is at least $G_2(0)$ so that his expected return is at least $G_2(0)(V_1 - b)$. For sufficiently small $b$, therefore, $G_2(b)(V_1 - b) > \frac{1}{2}G_2(0)V_1$. So individual 1's best reply is to make a positive bid with probability one, contradicting the original supposition.

In fact condition (10.1.8) is all that can be said about each individual's probability of bidding zero. So there is a continuum of alternative equilibria, each associated with a different mass point at $b = 0$.

One possibility is that neither contestant bids zero with positive probability. Then, from (10.1.6) and (10.1.7):

$$G_1(b) = 1 - e^{-b/V_2} \quad \text{and} \quad G_2(b) = 1 - e^{-b/V_1} \qquad (10.1.9)$$

With the two individuals bidding according to (10.1.9), the expected total resources committed to the contest can readily be computed. The probability that the bidding stops in the interval $[b, b + \Delta b]$ is:

$$(1 - G_1(b))G_2'(b)\Delta b + (1 - G_2(b))G_1'(b)\Delta b$$
$$= Ae^{-Ab}\Delta b, \quad \text{where} \quad A \equiv \frac{1}{V_1} + \frac{1}{V_2}$$

In that case the expenditure of the two individuals is $2b$. Expected total expenditure is therefore:

$$\bar{R} = 2A \int_0^\infty be^{-Ab}\, db = \frac{2V_1 V_2}{V_1 + V_2}$$

It is straightforward to confirm that, if $V_2$ strictly exceeds $V_1$, $\bar{R}$ also strictly exceeds $V_1$. Therefore expected total expenditure is higher in this Non-refundable Non-discriminatory case than in any of the other contests.

However, this is not the only equilibrium. Suppose we set $G_1(0) = 0$ but allow $G_2(0)$ to be positive. From (10.1.6) note that $G_2(b)$ is everywhere strictly increasing in $G_2(0)$. Therefore, the higher the probability of a zero bid, the higher is the probability that individual 2's bid will be less than any arbitrary level $b$. That is, individual 2's bid distribution becomes more conservative. Since changes in $G_2(0)$ have no effect upon individual 1's equilibrium bid distribution, it follows that expected total expenditure strictly decreases as $G_2(0)$ increases. Indeed, in the limit as $G_2(0)$ approaches 1, expected total expenditure approaches zero.

Given this continuum of Nash equilibria, we must conclude that theory, at least as developed here, is unable to provide much guidance about how contestants are likely to play.

This criticism cannot, however, be leveled at the simple sociobiological application of the model to the "wars of attrition" (Maynard Smith, 1976). In the latter, two contestants for a prize are assumed to be drawn at random from a population of identical individuals. The fact that they are identical does not change the conclusion that there is a continuum of Nash equilibria. The essential difference is the way equilibrium is modeled. An evolutionary equilibrium strategy for a uniform population is a (pure or mixed) strategy that cannot be successfully invaded by any mutant.[12] Writing the equilibrium strategy as $v$ and a mutant strategy as $\mu$, a necessary condition for such an evolutionary equilibrium is that:

$$U(v|v) \geqslant U(\mu|v), \quad \text{for all } \mu \tag{10.1.10}$$

That is, $v$ is a symmetric Nash equilibrium strategy.

From $(10.1.6)-(10.1.8)$, the symmetric Nash equilibrium of the war of attrition is:

$$G_v(b) = 1 - e^{-b/V}, \quad \text{where } V_1 = V_2 = V$$

Since $v$ is a completely mixed strategy, an individual playing against $v$ has the same expected payoff regardless of his strategy. Then, from chapter 9, a sufficient condition for the symmetric Nash equilibrium $v$ to be an evolutionary equilibrium is:

$$U(v|\mu) > U(\mu|\mu)$$

for all possible mutant strategies $\mu$. Rather than dwell here on technicalities, let us consider only pure-strategy mutations. (An exercise at the end of this section covers the mixed-strategy case.)

Consider the mutant strategy of always bidding $\hat{b}$. An individual playing the exponential mixed strategy $v$ then wins at a cost of $\hat{b}$ with probability $1 - G(\hat{b}) = e^{-\hat{b}/V}$. His expected payoff is

$$\begin{aligned} U(v|\mu) &= e^{-\hat{b}/V}(V-\hat{b}) - \int_0^{\hat{b}} b dG_v(b) \\ &= V(2e^{-\hat{b}/V} - 1) \end{aligned}$$

[12] We are speaking here of the equilibrium of a population all members of which are playing a single common pure or mixed strategy. More generally, as developed in chapter 9, there may be equilibria in which different *proportions* of the population play different strategies. The analysis here is not applicable to that case.

Two mutants competing against one another both spend $\hat{b}$ and the winner is then chosen at random. Therefore:

$$U(\mu\,|\,\mu) = V/2 - \hat{b}$$

Subtracting this from the previous expression:

$$U(\nu\,|\,\mu) - U(\mu\,|\,\mu) = \hat{b} + 2Ve^{-\hat{b}/V} - 3V/2$$

It is readily confirmed that this expression is strictly positive for all $\hat{b} \geqslant 0$.[13] The symmetric Nash equilibrium mixed strategy is therefore secure from invasion by any pure strategy.


## EXERCISES AND EXCURSIONS 10.1.3

*1 The war of attrition with different valuations $(V_1 < V_2)$*

(A) Suppose individual 1 bids zero with probability $\pi$. Show that the equilibrium expected payoffs are $U_1 = 0$ and $U_2 = (1-\pi)V_2$.
(B) Show also that expected total spending is $(1-\pi)\,2V_1V_2/(V_1+V_2)$.
(C) Are there also equilibria in which individual 1 has a strictly positive expected gain?


*2 Evolutionarily stable strategy (ESS) in the war of attrition*

At the end of the above section, the Nash equilibrium strategy $\nu$ in the war of attrition was compared with the alternative strategy $\mu$ of choosing to bid $b$. It was shown that:

$$U(\nu\,|\,\mu) - U(\mu\,|\,\mu) = \hat{b} + 2Ve^{-\hat{b}/V} - 3V/2$$

(A) Differentiate twice by $b$ and hence confirm that this expression takes on its minimum at $b = b^*$ satisfying $e^{b^*/V} = 2$.
(B) Hence confirm that:

$$U(\nu\,|\,\mu) - U(\mu\,|\,\mu) = b^* - V/2$$

(C) Use the fact that $\ln 2 \geqslant \frac{1}{2}$ to establish that the right-hand side of this last equality is strictly positive.


*3 The war of attrition with discounting*

Two firms, with the same fixed cost $a$ per period, initially engage in Bertrand price competition, bidding the price down to the constant marginal cost $c$. Both discount the future at the rate $\rho$. The present value

---

[13] An exercise below provides a guide to the proof of this assertion.

of selling indefinitely at the monopoly price is $V$. Then, if firm 2 exits at time $t$, the present value to firm 1 is:

$$U_1 = e^{-pt}V - C(t), \quad \text{where} \quad C(t) \equiv \int_0^t ae^{-px}\,dx$$

while the present value to firm 2 is:

$$U_2 = -C(t)$$

(A) Suppose firm 2 adopts a continuous mixed strategy $G_2(t)$. Suppose also that both are still in the contest at time $t$. Compare firm 1's payoff if it drops out immediately or stays in a further period $\Delta t$.

(B) Hence, or otherwise, show that if $G(t)$ is an equilibrium strategy:

$$\frac{G_2'(t)}{1 - G_2(t)} = \frac{a}{V}$$

(C) Solve for the evolutionary equilibrium strategy.

(D) Is it surprising that this strategy is independent of the discount rate?

## 10.2     Contests with private information

In the contests of the previous section, there were two levels of uncertainty. First, each individual had to make his or her choice without knowing the strategy of the opponent. Second, even in equilibrium, there was uncertainty if at least one of the contestants played according to a mixed strategy. We now introduce a third level of uncertainty which arises when contenders are unsure about other players' valuations (preferences).

Assume that each individual knows his own valuation of the prize. With regard to any opponent, he knows only that the valuation must come from some set $(V_0, V_1, \ldots, V_T)$ where:

$$0 = V_0 < V_1 < \ldots < V_T \qquad (10.2.1)$$

In addition, assume he can assign a likelihood to each possible valuation of the opponent. Furthermore, everyone shares the *same beliefs* about the valuation of each contestant $i$ and these beliefs are *common knowledge*. Thus, let $\pi_t^i$ denote the commonly believed probability that individual $i$'s valuation is $V_t$.

The previous section assumed, in effect, that all the probability was placed on one single valuation. Here we allow for private information, but require that beliefs about *opponents'* valuations are identical. That is:

$$\pi_t^i = \pi_t, \quad t = 0, \ldots, T \qquad (10.2.2)$$

This "symmetric belief" assumption rules out cases in which buyer 2 thinks buyer 1 is likely to have a high valuation while buyer 1 thinks buyer 2 is likely to have a low valuation.[14]

### 10.2.1  Revenue equivalence in identical-belief contests

A focus of much of the research on auctions and contests has been the comparison of the expected expenditures made by the participants. One very striking result is that, if beliefs are identical (so that equation (10.2.2) holds) and individuals are risk-neutral, then the double dichotomy of contests described in section 10.1 all generate the same expected expenditure. This result is termed the *Revenue Equivalence Theorem*.

In those discussions, however, one important distinction has often been overlooked. Under the Non-refundable condition, two types of contests can be distinguished: dissipative and non-dissipative. Suppose an auctioneer announces bidding conditions such that all losing bids are forfeited *to him*. If the auctioneer is counted as a member of the community, this would be a non-dissipative contest. More usually, however, we think of the Non-refundable condition as exemplified by political campaigns, marathon races, wars of attrition, and so forth. In all of these cases the losing bids are of no benefit to anyone – they are simply dissipated. In this discussion we make explicit what the current analysis has implicitly assumed, to wit, that we are dealing with non-dissipative contests so that *expenditures and revenues are equivalent amounts*.

Consider a simple example in which there are just three possible valuations, the lowest being zero, and two bidders Alex and Bev. (Recall that, in contrast with most of the illustrative discussions in section 10.1, here Alex and Bev's valuations are drawn from the same probability distribution.) We begin by considering the open ascending-bid auction and then examine a family of seemingly very different sealed-bid auctions. In the equilibria of all these auctions, expected revenue of the seller turns out to be the same.

For the open ascending-bid (English) auction, as indicated in table 10.1, each individual's dominant strategy is to bid his or her full valuation. Suppose that both Alex and Bev follow this strategy. If Alex has valuation $V_1$ he then has a positive payoff if and only if Bev has a valuation of $V_0 = 0$, in which case he wins by bidding essentially zero. His expected payoff is therefore:

$$U_1 = \pi_0 V_1 \tag{10.2.3}$$

If Alex has a valuation $V_2$, the bidding stops at 0 with probability $\pi_0$, at $V_1$

---

[14] See an exercise at the end of section 10.2.2 for an example of a contest with private information and asymmetric beliefs.

with probability $\pi_1$, and at $V_2$ with probability $(1 - \pi_0 - \pi_1)$. Alex's expected payoff is therefore:

$$U_2 = \pi_0 V_2 + \pi_1 (V_2 - V_1) = (\pi_0 + \pi_1)(V_2 - V_1) + \pi_0 V_1 \qquad (10.2.4)$$

Now consider a sealed-bid auction in which the high bidder wins and pays a convex combination of his own bid and the second bid. Formally, writing the $r^{th}$ ranked bid as $b_{(r)}$, the higher bidder pays:

$$\lambda b_{(1)} + (1 - \lambda) b_{(2)}, \quad 0 < \lambda \leqslant 1$$

Note that in the polar case with $\lambda = 1$ this is just the usual sealed high-bid auction. Moreover, at the other extreme, as $\lambda \to 0$ this approaches the sealed second-bid auction. As has already been seen, the latter is equivalent to the open ascending-bid auction.

In this sealed-bid auction, the equilibrium bidding strategies of buyers with positive valuations are continuous mixed strategies. A buyer with valuation $V_1$ bids over some interval $[0, \bar{b}_1]$ while a buyer with valuation $V_2$ bids over some adjoining interval $[\bar{b}_1, \bar{b}_2]$.[15]

Let $G_i(b)$ be the cumulative distribution function for a buyer's mixed strategy if his valuation is $V_i$, that is:

$$G_i(b) = \text{Prob}\{\text{Buyer with valuation } V_i \text{ bids } b \text{ or less}\}$$

It is intuitively plausible that a higher-valuing player will necessarily bid higher. We can begin by assuming this is the case and later confirm that this is consistent with equilibrium bidding.[16]

After these preliminaries, it will be possible to solve for the equilibrium expected payoffs. If Alex has a valuation of $V_1$ and bids $b \in [0, \bar{b}_1]$, he wins if Bev has a zero valuation. He also wins if Bev's valuation is $V_1$ and the realization of her mixed strategy is less than $b$. His expected gain is therefore:

$$U_1(b_1) = \pi_0(V_1 - \lambda b) + \pi_1 G_1(b)\left[ V_1 - \lambda b - (1 - \lambda) \int_0^b \frac{G_1'(b_2)}{G_1(b)} db_2 \right]$$
$$(10.2.5)$$

In equilibrium, Alex must be indifferent as to all bids in the support of his bid distribution $[0, \bar{b}_1]$. Setting $b_1$ first equal to zero and then equal to $\bar{b}_1$ in (10.2.5) we therefore require that:

$$U_1 = \pi_0 V_1 \qquad (10.2.6)$$

[15] While we do not go through the argument here, it is not difficult to prove that, in equilibrium, a strictly positive bid is never made with strictly positive probability. The proof is almost identical to that for Non-refundable Discriminatory contests (see section 10.1.2).

[16] In an exercise at the end of this section you are asked to show that equilibrium bids necessarily increase with valuations.

and

$$U_1 = (\pi_0 + \pi_1)(V_1 - \lambda\bar{b}_1) - \pi_1(1-\lambda)\int_0^{\bar{b}_1} b_2 G_1'(b_2)db_2 \qquad (10.2.7)$$

Next consider a buyer with valuation $V_2$. By hypothesis, he bids according to a mixed strategy over the interval $[\bar{b}_1, \bar{b}_2]$. In particular, if he bids $\bar{b}_1$ he only wins with positive probability against an opponent with a lower valuation. Arguing exactly as above for any $b \leqslant \bar{b}_1$:

$$U_2(b) = \pi_0(V_2 - \lambda b) + \pi_1 G_1(b)\left[V_2 - \lambda b - (1-\lambda)\int_0^b b_2 \frac{G_1'(b_2)}{G_1(b)}db_2\right]$$

Substituting from (10.2.4):

$$U_2(b) = U_1(b) + (V_2 - V_1)(\pi_0 + \pi_1 G_1(b)), \quad b \in [0, \bar{b}_1]$$

Since $U_1(b)$ is constant over $[0, \bar{b}_1]$ and $G_1(b)$ is increasing, it follows that $U_2(b)$ is increasing over this interval. Hence a buyer with valuation $V_2$ strictly prefers to bid $\bar{b}_1$ rather than make any lower bid. This confirms that bidding is indeed monotonic. Finally, setting $b = \bar{b}_1$ and substituting from (10.2.6):

$$U_2 = (V_2 - V_1)(\pi_0 + \pi_1) + \pi_0 V_1 \qquad (10.2.8)$$

Equations (10.2.6) and (10.2.8) characterize equilibrium payoffs in the family of sealed-bid auctions. Since $U_1$ and $U_2$ are independent of $\lambda$, it follows that expected payoffs to buyers are the same in all auctions. Also comparing (10.2.6) with (10.2.3) and (10.2.8) with (10.2.4) it follows immediately that the open ascending-bid auction generates the same expected payoffs as well.

Moreover, since the winner is always the buyer with the high valuation, the gross social benefit is the same in all the auctions. Since expected revenue is the difference between expected gross surplus and the expected payoff of the buyers, it follows that there is *revenue equivalence*.

Finally, the above argument can easily be extended to the two contests with Non-refundable bids (provided, as noted, that the contest is non-dissipative). Indeed expected total spending is the same in any type of contest in which the buyer with the highest valuation wins with probability 1.

Recall again, however, that this result hinges critically upon the assumptions of risk-neutrality, symmetrical beliefs,[17] and non-dissipative contests. In the next two sections we will relax the first two of these assumptions.

[17] In contrast, section 10.1 dealt with an extreme example of asymmetric beliefs. We assumed there that each agent had a *different* valuation and that this was common knowledge.

EXERCISES AND EXCURSIONS 10.2.1

*1 Monotonicity of bids*

Consider the class of sealed-bid auctions analyzed above. Suppose there are $n$ buyers. Let $p(b)$ be the probability that a buyer wins with a bid of $b$ and let $c(b)$ be his expected payment. Then, if his valuation is $V$, his expected payoff is:

$$U(b; V) = Vp(b) - c(b)$$

(A) Consider any pair of bids $b$ and $b'$ where $b' > b$. Show that:

$$U(b'; V_2) - U(b; V_2) = U(b'; V_1) - U(b; V_1)$$
$$+ (V_2 - V_1)(\pi(b') - \pi(b))$$

(B) Noting that $p(b)$ must be non-decreasing, use this to establish that, if a buyer with valuation $V$ is at least as well off if he chooses $b'$ rather than $b$, any buyer with a higher valuation is strictly better off choosing $b'$ rather than $b$.

(C) Hence establish monotonicity.

*2 The sealed high-bid auction with continuous distributions*

Suppose each of two buyers believes that his opponent's valuation is $V$ or less with probability $F(V)$ where $F(0) = 0$, $F(1) = 1$, and $F(\cdot)$ is strictly increasing and continuously differentiable on $[0, 1]$.

Suppose also that buyer $\beta$ adopts the strategy:

$$b_\beta = B(V_\beta)$$

where $B(\cdot)$ is strictly increasing and continuously differentiable.

(A) Explain why buyer $\alpha$'s reply can be written as $b_\alpha = B(x)$ for some $x \in [0, 1]$. HINT: What is buyer 1's probability of winning if he bids $B(1)$?

(B) Show that buyer $\alpha$'s expected payoff is:

$$U_\alpha = F(x)(V_\alpha - B(x))$$

Hence show that buyer $\alpha$'s best reply $b_\alpha^* = B(x^*)$ satisfies:

$$F'(x^*)V_\alpha = \frac{d}{dx}[F(x^*)B(x^*)]$$

(C) In a symmetric equilibrium both buyers must bid according to the same bidding strategy $b = B(V)$. Use (B) to explain why $B(V)$ must satisfy the differential equation:

$$\frac{d}{dV}[B(V)F(V)] = VF'(V)$$

(D) Integrate and show that:

$$B(V) = \int_0^V \frac{x F'(x) dx}{F(v)}$$

(E) Extend this analysis to solve for the equilibrium bid function if there are $n$ buyers.

## 3 Sealed tendering

A firm solicits sealed bids from $n$ potential contractors for the construction of a new plant. The contractor submitting the lowest successful bid will be awarded the contract. Each contractor knows his own cost $c_i$ and believes that others' costs are independently drawn from the c.d.f. $G(c)$. Solve for the equilibrium bidding strategy.

## 4 Minimum bids

Suppose there are two buyers. Each buyer's valuation is an independent draw from the distribution $F(V)$ where $F(\underline{V}) = 0$, $F(\bar{V}) = 1$, and $F(\cdot)$ is continuously differentiable and strictly increasing on $[\underline{V}, \bar{V}]$. If the seller introduces a minimum or "reserve" price he stands to gain when there is just one bidder with a high valuation. On the other hand, he loses if no-one has a valuation above the announced minimum.

(A) In the open ascending-bid auction, suppose the seller raises the minimum acceptable bid from $b_0$ to $b_0 + \Delta b$. Show that, as $\Delta b$ approaches zero, the net expected gain approaches:

$$[2(1 - F(b_0)) F(b_0) - 2 F(b_0) F'(b_0 b_0)] \Delta b$$

(B) Hence show that, if $\underline{V}$ is sufficiently close to zero, the seller can increase expected revenue by announcing a positive minimum price.

(C) Extend the argument of this section to show that expected seller revenue will be the same in the sealed high-bid auction and open ascending-bid auction if the seller imposes the same minimum price $b_0$.

## 5 Risk-aversion in auctions

(A) Explain why equilibrium bidding in the open ascending-bid auction is the same when buyers are risk-averse or risk-neutral.

(B) Explain why the sealed high-bid auction continues to be formally equivalent to the open descending-bid ("Dutch") auction if buyers are risk-averse.

(C) In a Dutch auction, what effect will risk-aversion have on a bidder's willingness to let the price drop below his valuation?

(D) From your answer to (C) or otherwise explain why expected revenue will be higher in the sealed high-bid auction than in the open ascending-bid auction when buyers are risk-averse. [NOTE: The answer to this question does not require a single equation.]

## 6 Equilibrium bidding with risk-averse buyers

Suppose preferences are normalized so that the utility of losing is 0 and the utility of winning at a price of $b$ is $U(V-b) = (V-b)^{\alpha}$, $0 < \alpha \leqslant 1$. There are two buyers and each has a valuation $V$ drawn from the uniform distribution.

(A) Suppose buyer 2 bids according to $b_2 = B(V_2)$ where $V_2$ is his valuation, and $B(\cdot)$ is a strictly increasing continuously differentiable function. Show that if buyer 1 bids $b_1 = B(x)$ his expected utility is:

$$U_1 = x(V_1 - B(x))^{\alpha}$$

(B) Explain why buyer 1's best reply is to choose $b_1 = B(x_1)$ so as to maximize:

$$x^{1/\alpha}V_1 - x^{1/\alpha}B(x)$$

[HINT: For any increasing function $f$, $U_1$ and $f(U_1)$ have turning points at the same values of $x$.]

(C) Hence or otherwise explain why, if $B(V)$ is the symmetric equilibrium bidding strategy, it must satisfy:

$$\frac{1}{\alpha}V^{1/\alpha} = \frac{d}{dV}[V^{1/\alpha}B(V)]$$

(D) Integrate and hence show that the equilibrium bid function is linear. Show also that the greater the individual's aversion to risk, the less he will shade his bid below his valuation.

## *10.2.2 Correlated beliefs

Central to the Revenue Equivalence Theorem of section 10.2.1 is the assumption that all buyers have given and identical beliefs about opponents' valuations. A person obtaining private information does not change his beliefs about *other* parties' valuations. While this is a natural first approximation, it is often the case that beliefs are positively related. Consider oil-field leases. A bidder who obtains favorable information via seismic testing will realize that his competitors are likely to have obtained favorable information as well. Conversely, a bidder who obtains unfavorable information will believe it more likely that his opponents' information is also unfavorable.

---

\* Starred sections represent more difficult or specialized materials that can be omitted without significant loss of continuity.

Consider once again an example with two buyers and three possible valuations $0 = V_0 < V_1 < V_2$. If a buyer has a valuation of $V_0 = 0$, beliefs are immaterial since he has no incentive to bid. Suppose that, if his own valuation is $V_1$, he believes his opponent's valuation is 0 with probability $\pi_0$, $V_1$ with probability of $\pi_1$, and $V_2$ with probability $1 - \pi_0 - \pi_1$. A buyer with the high valuation $V_2$, however, assigns different probabilities $\hat{\pi}_0$, $\hat{\pi}_1$, and $1 - \hat{\pi}_0 - \hat{\pi}_1$ to the opponent's valuations. The correlation of beliefs can be expressed by the following assumptions:

$$\frac{\hat{\pi}_0}{\hat{\pi}_0 + \hat{\pi}_1} < \frac{\pi_0}{\pi_0 + \pi_1}, \quad \hat{\pi}_0 + \hat{\pi}_1 < \pi_0 + \pi_1 \qquad (10.2.9)$$

The first inequality requires that, upon learning that his opponent has a valuation of $V_0$ or $V_1$, a buyer with a high valuation will believe it less likely that the opponent's valuation is $V_0$. The second inequality requires that, if a buyer has a high valuation, he thinks it is more likely that his opponent has a high valuation as well.[18]

We begin the analysis by comparing the open ascending-bid and sealed high-bid auctions if beliefs satisfy (10.2.9) but buyers are unaware of this. That is, each buyer thinks that his opponent's beliefs are the same as his and independent of valuations. First consider the open ascending-bid auction. If a buyer has a valuation of $V_1$ his expected payoff is just as before. From (10.2.3):

$$U_1 = \pi_0 V_1$$

If he has a valuation of $V_2$ his expected payoff is, from (10.2.4):

$$\hat{U}_2 = (\hat{\pi}_0 + \hat{\pi}_1)(V_2 - V_1) + \hat{\pi}_0 V_1$$

For the sealed high-bid auction, the expected payoff to a buyer with valuation $V_1$ is, from (10.2.5):

$$U_1(b) = \pi_0(V_1 - b) + \pi_1 G_1(b)(V_1 - b) \qquad (10.2.10)$$

Similarly, the expected payoff to a buyer with valuation $V_2$ is:

$$\hat{U}_2(b) = \hat{\pi}_0(V_2 - b) + \hat{\pi}_1 G_1(b)(V_2 - b) \qquad (10.2.11)$$

Again the arguments proceed exactly as before so that:

$$U_1 = \pi_0 V_1 \quad \text{and} \quad \hat{U}_2 = (\hat{\pi}_0 + \hat{\pi}_1)(V_2 - V_1) + \hat{\pi}_0 V_1$$

Thus if beliefs differ but buyers are unaware of this, the Revenue Equivalence Theorem continues to hold.

[18] More generally, the crucial assumption is that beliefs satisfy a conditional first-order stochastic dominance property (see Riley, 1989). While mildly weaker, this is the essence of what has been called "affiliation" (Milgrom and Weber, 1982).

There is one important point to be noted about the equilibrium in the sealed high-bid auction. Let $\bar{b}_1$ be the maximum bid of a buyer with valuation $V_1$. From (10.2.10), setting $b = 0$ and then $b = \bar{b}_1$ and noting that the buyer must be indifferent between these bids:

$$\pi_0 V_1 = (\pi_0 + \pi_1)(V_1 - \bar{b}_1)$$

Hence:

$$V_1 - \bar{b}_1 = \left(\frac{\pi_0}{\pi_0 + \pi_1}\right) V_1$$

Next let $\hat{b}_1$ be the maximum bid by a buyer with valuation $V_1$ if he has the beliefs of a buyer with valuation $V_2$. From (10.2.11):

$$\hat{\pi}_0 V_1 = (\hat{\pi}_0 + \hat{\pi}_1)(V_2 - \hat{b}_1)$$

Hence:

$$V_1 - \hat{b}_1 = \left(\frac{\hat{\pi}_0}{\hat{\pi}_0 + \hat{\pi}_1}\right) V_1$$

Given assumption (10.2.9), it follows that:

$$\hat{b}_1 > \bar{b}_1$$

The minimum bid by a buyer with valuation $V_2$ is $\hat{b}_1$ and the maximum bid by a buyer with valuation $V_1$ is $\bar{b}_1$. So there is a gap between these bids if buyers ignore the correlation of beliefs.

From this observation it is a simple matter to see what must happen if buyers take the correlation into account. In the sealed high-bid auction a high-valuation buyer realizes that he need not be so aggressive. In particular, he can reduce his minimum bid from $\hat{b}_1$ to $\bar{b}_1$. It follows that high-valuation buyers have a strictly greater expected payoff when they take the correlation of beliefs into account. On the other hand, equilibrium bidding behavior is unaffected in the open ascending-bid auction, so expected buyer payoffs are also unaffected.

Thus, expected payoffs to buyers are never higher and sometimes lower in the open ascending-bid auction as compared with the sealed high-bid auction. Since expected gross surplus is the same in the two auctions, it follows immediately that expected seller revenue must be greater in the open ascending-bid auction.

It is the linkage between the bids of higher-valuing bidders and the more conservative beliefs of lower-valuing bidders that leads to lower seller revenue under sealed bidding. This linkage is reinforced if each individual's valuation is at least partly a function of some common imperfectly observed parameter, as when bidders for an offshore oil tract independently engage in seismic testing.

How much should a buyer be willing to bid in such circumstances? Consider the sealed high-bid auction. If the true value is great it is likely there are several buyers who estimate a high probability of success. The probability that any one buyer will be the winner is therefore relatively small. On the other hand, if a buyer has an estimate of a high probability of success and the true value is small, he is much more likely to end up the winner. Winning is therefore, very often, the consequence of having overestimated the expected value of the prize.

This phenomenon is known as the "winner's curse." The name, however, is somewhat misleading. It is not really a curse to win. Rather, a careful bidder should take into account the fact that he is more likely to win the bidding if he mistakenly overestimates.

To make all this more precise, suppose the oil field is equally likely to be of high or low value. Without loss of generality, let the low value be zero and the high value $V$. In the absence of further information, a risk-neutral buyer would bid the expected value, $b = V/2$. But if seismic testing is employed suppose the likelihood matrix (see chapter 5) is such that if the true value is $V$ the chance of correctly estimating it to be high is $\frac{3}{4}$, while if the true value is zero the chance of correctly estimating the value as low is also $\frac{3}{4}$.

The equilibrium pattern of bidding parallels the independent case. A buyer with a low estimate has an equilibrium bid $b_L$, which yields an expected payoff of zero. A buyer with a high estimate bids according to a mixed strategy over some interval $[b_L, \bar{b}]$. Since a buyer with a low estimate wins only against another with a low estimate, in equilibrium:

$$U_L = \tfrac{1}{2}[V\pi(V\,|\,L,L) - b_L]\pi(L\,|\,L) = 0$$

Applying Bayes' Theorem, the probability of the true value being high when both buyers have a low estimate is:

$$\pi(V\,|\,L,L) = \frac{\pi(L,L\,|\,V)\pi(V)}{\pi(L,L\,|\,V)\pi(V) + \pi(L,L\,|\,0)\pi(0)}$$

$$= \frac{\frac{1}{16}\cdot\frac{1}{2}}{\frac{1}{16}\cdot\frac{1}{2} + \frac{9}{16}\cdot\frac{1}{2}} = \frac{1}{10}$$

Therefore $b_L = 0{\cdot}1V$. If a buyer with a high estimate bids just higher than $b_L$, he wins if and only if his opponent has a low estimate. His expected payoff is therefore:

$$
\begin{aligned}
U_H &= [V\pi(V\,|\,L,H) - b_L]\pi(L\,|\,H)\\
&= [0{\cdot}5V - b_L](0{\cdot}375), \quad \text{by Bayes' Theorem}\\
&= 0{\cdot}15V, \quad \text{since } b_L = 0{\cdot}1V
\end{aligned}
$$

At the maximum bid, a buyer with a high estimate wins for sure. His expected payoff is therefore:

$$U_H = V\pi(V\,|\,H) - \bar{b} = 0.75V - \bar{b}$$

Since a high-estimate buyer must be indifferent between each of the bids entering into his mixed strategy, it follows that $\bar{b} = 0.6V$.

It is left as an exercise to compute the equilibrium mixed strategy. Two points are worth noting. First, the equilibrium bids by a buyer with a high estimate are all strictly less than his own estimate of the value of the oil field prior to the bidding. (This prior estimate is $V\pi(V\,|\,H) + 0\pi(0\,|\,H) = 0.75V$.) Second, because there is a strictly positive expected payoff to a buyer with a high valuation, there is an equilibrium expected return to purchase of the message service – investing in seismic testing.

Under the assumptions here that rule out *productive* adaptations to information, the auction process is purely redistributive. So there is no social gain to seismic testing.[19] This is another example illustrating that the private return to information acquisition may be excessive (as discussed in chapter 7).

EXERCISES AND EXCURSIONS 10.2.2

*1 Correlated beliefs and revenue equivalence*

There are two buyers, each of whom has three possible valuations $(\alpha_0, \alpha_1, \alpha_2)$. Let $\pi_{ij}$ be the probability of the compound event that individual 1 has valuation $V_1 = \alpha_i$ and individual 2 has valuation $V_2 = \alpha_j$, where $i, j = 0, 1, 2$. Suppose this joint probability distribution is:

$$[\pi_{ij}] = \begin{bmatrix} 0.58 & 0.08 & 0.04 \\ 0.08 & 0.08 & 0.04 \\ 0.04 & 0.04 & 0.02 \end{bmatrix}$$

(A)  Show that, for $i = 0, 1$ and $j = 1, 2$:

$$\text{Prob}\{V_2 \leqslant \alpha_i\,|\,V_1 = \alpha_j\} \geqslant \text{Prob}\{V_2 \leqslant \alpha_i\,|\,V_1 = \alpha_{j+1}\}$$

(B)  Suppose $\alpha_0 = 0$, $\alpha_1 = 1$, and $\alpha_2 = 2$. Show that equilibrium expected buyer payoffs in the open ascending-bid auction are:

$$U(\alpha_0) = 0, \quad U(\alpha_1) = 0.4, \quad U(\alpha_2) = 1.2$$

(C)  In the sealed high-bid auction show that a buyer with a valuation $\alpha_1 = 1$ will bid according to the mixed strategy $G_1(b) = b/(1-b)$, $b \in [0, \frac{1}{2}]$.

---

[19] This would not be the case if buyers were risk-averse rather than risk-neutral.

(D) Hence or otherwise show that equilibrium expected buyer payoffs are the same as in the open auction.

(E) Explain why it follows directly that expected seller revenue is the same in the two auctions.

(F) Suppose $\pi_{00}$ declines to 0·44 and that $\pi_{21}$, $\pi_{12}$, and $\pi_{22}$ all rise to 0·08. Show that the conditional stochastic dominance inequalities of (A) are all now strict.

(G) Confirm that the expected payoff to a buyer with valuation $\alpha_1 = 1$ will be unaffected.

(H) Show finally that a buyer with valuation $\alpha_2 = 2$ has a higher equilibrium expected payoff in the sealed high-bid auction and hence that the latter auction generates lower expected revenue.

## 2 Sealed high-bid and second-bid auctions with correlated valuations

In the oilfield example it was shown that, for the sealed high-bid auction, a buyer with a high estimate has an equilibrium mixed strategy over the interval $[b_L, \bar{b}] = [0·1V, 0·6V]$.

(A) Show that, if the c.d.f. for the symmetric equilibrium mixed strategy is $G(b)$, then:

$$U_H(b) = [V\pi(V\,|\,L, H) - b]\pi(L\,|\,H) + G(b)\,[V\pi(V\,|\,H, H) - b]\pi(H\,|\,H)$$

(B) Hence solve for $G(b)$.

(C) In the sealed second-price (Non-discriminatory) auction, explain why it is an equilibrium for a low-estimate buyer to bid $b_L = V\pi(V\,|\,L, L)$ and for a high-estimate buyer to bid $b_H = V\pi(V\,|\,H, H)$.

(D) Compare expected seller revenues from the two auctions.

## 3 Auctions with negatively correlated beliefs

Suppose that each buyer's valuation $\theta_i$ is either 0, 1, or 2. Suppose, furthermore, that the joint probability distribution is:

|             |   | $\theta_2$ |   |   |
|-------------|---|---|---|---|
| $f(\theta_1, \theta_2)$ |   | 0 | 1 | 2 |
|             | 0 | 0 | 0 | 1 |
| $\theta_1$  | 1 | 0 | 1 | 0 |
|             | 2 | 1 | 0 | 0 |

Solve for the equilibrium bidding strategy in the sealed high-bid auction. REMARK: This exercise illustrates the point that, without some restrictions on the joint distribution of beliefs, a buyer with higher valuation will not necessarily bid higher.

### 4 Auctions with differing beliefs

Suppose individual 1's valuation is equally likely to be 0 or 1 while individual 2's valuation is $V_2 = 1$. Assume that if individual 1 has a zero valuation he will not submit a bid, so the item will go to individual 2 at a price of 0.

(A) Explain why, for the sealed high-bid auction, the equilibrium strategies of both individuals must be mixed strategies.

(B) Explain also why individual 1 will never bid more than $\frac{1}{2}$ in the sealed high-bid auction.

(C) Solve for the equilibrium mixed strategies.

(D) Appealing to (B), show that expected revenue will be lower in the sealed high-bid auction than in the open ascending-bid auction.**

### 10.2.3    Designing an optimal contest

A central conclusion of section 10.2.1 was that – under the assumptions of independent and symmetrical beliefs, risk-neutrality, and non-dissipation of outlays – many seemingly different contests elicit the same aggregate receipts from bidders, at least on average.[20] From this it is perhaps tempting to believe that a seller in such auctions would be indifferent as to the bidding rules. As we shall see, this is not correct. In particular, it is often in the interest of the seller to set a minimum price that excludes individuals with low valuations. If the buyers' valuations are discretely distributed, it may also be in the seller's interest to restrict bids to some finite set.

The key assumption underlying the analysis is that the seller knows as much about each buyer as the buyers themselves do. That is, he knows the underlying distribution of all the buyers' valuations. The question is how to make use of this information.

Let us continue to assume that buyers are risk-neutral, that contests are non-dissipative, and that beliefs are independent and identical. That is, regardless of buyer $i$'s own valuation, he believes buyer $j$ has valuation $V_t$ with probability $\pi_t$. In addition, these beliefs are common knowledge. So from section 10.2.1, the equilibria of contests under all four paired conditions generate the same expected revenue. Then we need only compare any alternative contest with the open ascending-bid auction (Refundable Non-discriminatory case).

Two examples will illustrate the central points. First, suppose there are

---

** End of starred section.

[20] In sections 10.1.2 and 10.1.3 we saw that the Non-refundable Discriminatory rule generated less revenue and the Non-refundable Non-discriminatory rule more revenue than contests conducted under Refundable rules. However, there the analysis ran in terms of non-identical beliefs about the opponent. Typically, one party had a higher valuation than the other, and both sides knew this.

two buyers Alex and Bev, and that each is equally likely to have a valuation of 2 or 16. With 0·75 probability, therefore, the lower of the buyer valuations is 2. Since in the open ascending-bid auction the selling price is the second-highest valuation, expected revenue is $(0·75)2 + (0·25)16 = 5·5$. Alternatively, suppose the seller were to announce a minimum price of 16 (or just less than this). In doing so he runs the risk of not selling the item at all, but stands to gain if there is at least one buyer with a high valuation. Since this probability is 0·75, expected revenue becomes $(0·75)16 + (0·25)0 = 12$. Evidently, the seller may wish to announce a minimum or "reserve" price despite the risk of failure to sell.[21]

This is not always the case, however. Intuitively, if the minimum valuation is sufficiently high relative to the maximum valuation, the loss associated with no sale will be the dominant effect. For example, if the valuations are 12 and 16 rather than 2 and 16, expected revenue from the open ascending-bid auction is $(0·75)12 + (0·25)16 = 13$. Since setting a minimum price at 16 resulted in an expected return of only 12, here the unrestricted auction is superior.

Introducing a minimum price is not the only way of possibly increasing expected revenue. Continuing with the assumption that valuations of 12 and 16 are equally likely, suppose the seller indicates that he will only accept bids of 11 or 14. (If there is a tie, the winner will be selected at random.) Clearly, a buyer with a valuation of 12 will never bid 14. Suppose Alex bids 14 if his valuation is 16. If Bev has a high valuation and bids 11, she ties Alex with probability 0·5 and therefore wins with probability 0·25. Her expected gain is therefore $(0·25)(16 - 11) = 1·25$. If Bev bids 14 she beats Alex with probability 0·5 and otherwise ties. Her expected gain then becomes $(0·75)(16 - 14) = 1·5$.

Consequently it is an equilibrium for high-valuation buyers to bid 14 and low-valuation buyers to bid 11. Expected revenue is then $(0·25)11 + (0·75)14 = 13·25$, which exceeds revenue in the open ascending-bid auction.

This second result indicates that a seller can gain by forcing buyers to select from a finite number of alternatives, rather than allow any non-negative bid. Let us now examine this, and the minimum-bid effect, more closely.

The analysis is similar to that in section 8.2.3 ("Monopoly Price Discrimination with Hidden Knowledge"), except that here the seller is constrained to sell exactly one unit. Then, with just two valuations and two bidders, a high-valuation bidder wins when his opponent has a low

---

[21] In the event of no sale, why would the seller not simply turn around and auction the item off again, this time without a minimum price? The answer is that if buyers anticipated such behavior, their equilibrium response would be to adjust their bidding in the first auction. This would completely offset the effect of the minimum price (Riley and Samuelson, 1981).

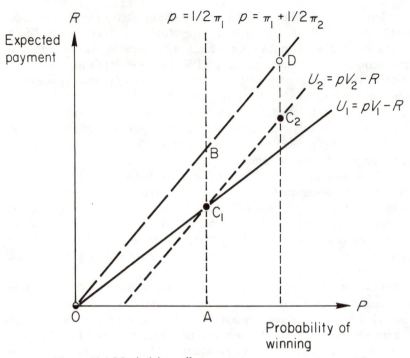

Figure 10.1 Maximizing seller revenue

valuation and ties for the win when his opponent has a high valuation. His probability of winning is then $\pi_1 + \frac{1}{2}\pi_2$. If a buyer has a low valuation, she ties if her opponent also has a low valuation. Her probability of winning is therefore $\frac{1}{2}\pi_1$.

We can now analyze the contest graphically. In figure 10.1, an indifference contour for a lower-valuation buyer $(V = V_1)$ is drawn as a solid line with slope $V_1$ and indifference contours for a high-valuation buyer $(V = V_2)$ are drawn as dashed lines with slope $V_2$. With the two types separated and participating, win probabilities must be on the vertical lines:

$$p = \tfrac{1}{2}\pi_1 \quad \text{and} \quad p = \pi_1 + \tfrac{1}{2}\pi_2$$

Since buyers have the option of not participating, the seller cannot force a low-valuation buyer onto a higher indifference contour than that through the origin. The maximum expected payment by a low-valuation buyer is therefore the vertical coordinate of the point $C_1$.

Similarly, given that $C_1$ is a feasible alternative, a high-valuation buyer cannot be forced onto an indifference curve to the north-west of $C_1$. His maximum expected payment is therefore the vertical coordinate of the point $C_2$.

It is easy to see how the sealed high-bid auction can be modified to achieve this outcome. The seller announces that he will accept only sealed bids of $b_1^* = V_1$ and $b_2^* > V_1$. In the event of a tie, the winner is to be selected at random. Note that a high-valuation buyer is indifferent between his optimal point $C_2$ and $C_1$, that is:

$$U_2(C_2) = (\pi_1 + \tfrac{1}{2}\pi_2)(V_2 - b_2^*) = \tfrac{1}{2}\pi_1(V_2 - V_1) = U_2(C_1)$$

Rearranging:

$$b_2^* = V_1 + \frac{\tfrac{1}{2}(\pi_1 + \pi_2)}{\pi_1 + \tfrac{1}{2}\pi_2}(V_2 - V_1)$$

Does the seller gain by the introduction of a minimum price? Consider figure 10.1 once more. By announcing a minimum price of $V_2$, the low-valuation buyer is forced out of the contest. A high-valuation buyer is forced onto his indifference curve through the origin. The decline in expected payment by a low-valuation buyer is therefore equal to:

$$\overline{AC_1} = V_1\overline{OA}$$

since the slope of a low-valuation indifference curve is $V_1$. Similarly, the increase in expected payment by a high-valuation buyer is:

$$\overline{DC_2} = \overline{BC_1} = \overline{BA} - \overline{AC_1} = (V_2 - V_1) \times \overline{OA}$$

Since the probability that a buyer has a low valuation is $\pi_1$, the expected increase in expected revenue is:

$$\Delta \bar{R} = [-V_1\pi_1 + (V_2 - V_1)(1 - \pi_1)]\overline{OA} \qquad (10.2.12)$$

While we have considered only the two-valuation, two-buyer case, the analysis is essentially unchanged when there are more than two valuations and more than two buyers. Therefore the intuition gleaned from the numerical example is quite general. If the minimum valuation is sufficiently low, it pays the seller to introduce a minimum price that exceeds the minimum valuation. Conversely, if the minimum valuation is sufficiently high, the seller loses by introducing such a minimum price.

It is easy to see that the effect of a reserve price upon expected revenue can be very significant, especially when the number of buyers is small. In contrast, as will now be shown, the gains from restricting bidders to a finite number of bids are generally small.

As explained above, expected seller revenue is maximized by making a buyer with valuation $V_t$ indifferent between his optimal $(p, R)$ pair and that of a buyer with the next lowest valuation. That is:

$$
\begin{aligned}
U_t^* &= p_t^* V_t - R_t^* = p_{t-1}^* V_t - R_{t-1}^* \\
&= p_{t-1}^* V_{t-1} - R_{t-1}^* + p_{t-1}^*(V_t - V_{t-1}) \\
&= U_{t-1}^* + p_{t-1}^*(V_t - V_{t-1})
\end{aligned}
\qquad (10.2.13)
$$

Also, returning to the two-buyer case, if buyers are separated:

$$p^*_{t-1} = \pi_1 + \pi_2 + \ldots + \pi_{t-2} + \tfrac{1}{2}\pi_{t-1} = F_{t-1} - \tfrac{1}{2}\pi_{t-1}$$

Substituting this equation into (10.2.13) and rearranging:

$$\frac{U^*_t - U^*_{t-1}}{V_t - V_{t-1}} = F_{t-1} - \tfrac{1}{2}p_{t-1} \tag{10.2.14}$$

Now compare this difference equation with that for the two common auctions. From equation (10.2.4), in the open ascending-bid auction the buyers' expected payoffs satisfy:

$$\frac{U_t - U_{t-1}}{V_t - V_{t-1}} = F_{t-1} \tag{10.2.15}$$

Since $U_1 = U^*_1 = 0$, it follows that for all $t > 1$, buyers' expected payoffs are strictly lower in the revenue-maximizing auction. That is, the seller extracts strictly higher expected revenue from buyers of every valuation greater than $V_1$.

However, in the limit, as the discrete distribution approaches some continuous distribution $F(V)$, (10.2.14) and (10.2.15) both reduce to the same differential equation:

$$\frac{dU}{dV} = F(V)$$

Therefore, as long as the discrete distribution can be approximated by a continuous distribution, the gains to announcing a finite set of feasible bids – one for each type – are small.

Finally, we have not addressed the question of whether an optimal auction might pool buyers with different valuations. This is too complex a matter to be analyzed here. However, as Myerson (1981) has shown, such pooling can increase revenue only under rather special assumptions about the underlying distribution function.


EXERCISES AND EXCURSIONS 10.2.3

*1 Setting minimum prices to increase expected revenue*

(A) Explain why, even with $n$ buyers, raising the minimum price to $V_2$ increases expected revenue if and only if:

$$-V_1\pi_1 + (V_2 - V_1)(1 - \pi_1) > 0$$

[HINT: In figure 10.1 the horizontal distance $\overline{OA}$ declines but the slopes of the indifference contours remain constant.]

(B) Either by a direct argument, or by carefully iterating the above argument and then taking a limit, show that, if valuations are continuously distributed on $[\alpha, \gamma]$ with c.d.f. $F(V)$, the expected revenue-maximizing reserve price satisfies:

$$-VF'(V)+1-F(V) = 0$$

(C) Solve for the seller's optimal reserve price if $V$ is uniformly distributed on $[\alpha, \gamma]$

## 2 Maximizing expected revenue with correlated beliefs

Each of two agents has a valuation $V_1$ or $V_2$, where $V_2 - V_1 = 1$. The joint probability matrix $[\pi_{ij}]$ is:

$$[\pi_{ij}] = \begin{bmatrix} \frac{1}{2} & \frac{1}{6} \\ \frac{1}{6} & \frac{1}{6} \end{bmatrix}$$

(A) Show that the conditional probability that one agent has a valuation $V_i$ when the other has a valuation $V_j$ is:

$$[\pi_{i \cdot j}] = \begin{bmatrix} \frac{3}{4} & \frac{1}{2} \\ \frac{1}{4} & \frac{1}{2} \end{bmatrix}$$

(B) If the two agents bid in an open auction, what is the expected consumer surplus for a low-value bidder? A high-value bidder?

(C) Suppose that each agent must bid either $V_1$ or $V_2$. The high bid wins and the winner pays the second bid. In the case of a tie the winner is selected randomly. In addition, the bidders enter a lottery. If agent $i$'s opponent bids $V_2$, agent $i$ must pay $\frac{3}{2}$ to the seller. However, if agent $i$'s opponent bids $V_1$, $i$ receives $\frac{1}{2}$ from the seller. Show that truth-telling is a Nash equilibrium of this game and confirm that, in equilibrium, consumer surplus is zero for both low- and high-value bidders.

(D) Is the equilibrium also a dominant-strategy equilibrium?

(E) Generalize your analysis to show that if the joint probability matrix is:

$$[\pi_{ij}] = \begin{bmatrix} 1-3\alpha & \alpha \\ \alpha & \alpha \end{bmatrix}, \quad \alpha \leq \frac{1}{4}$$

there again exists a lottery that extracts all the expected buyers' surplus.

(F) What happens to the lottery payments as $\alpha$ approaches $\frac{1}{4}$?

(G) In the light of your answer to (F), or otherwise, comment on the feasibility of this scheme.

## REFERENCES AND SELECTED READINGS

Baker, Charles C., "Auctioning Coupon-Bearing Securities: A Review of Treasury Experiences," in Y. Amihud, *Bidding and Auctioning for Procurement and Allocation*, New York: New York University Press, 1976.

Fudenberg, Drew and Tirole, Jean, "A Theory of Exit in Duopoly," *Econometrica*, 54 (1986), 943–960.

Hillman, Arye L. and Riley, John G., "Politically Contestable Rents and Transfers," *Economics and Politics*, 1 (1989), 17–40.

Hirshleifer, J. and Riley, John G., "Elements of the Theory of Auctions and Contests," UCLA Economics Dept., Working Paper 118B (1978).

Maynard Smith, John, "Evolution and the Theory of Games," *American Scientist*, 64 (January–February 1976).

Milgrom, Paul and Weber, Robert J., "A Theory of Auctions and Competitive Bidding," *Econometrica*, 50 (November 1982), 1089–122.

———, "Auctions and Bidding: A Primer," *Journal of Economic Perspectives*, 3 (Summer 1989), 3–22.

Myerson, Roger, "Optimal Auction Design," *Mathematics of Operations Research*, 5 (1981), 58–73.

Nalebuff, B. and Riley, John G., "Asymmetric Equilibrium in the War of Attrition," *Journal of Theoretical Biology*, 113 (1985), 517–27.

Riley, John G., "Expected Revenue From Open and Sealed Bid Auctions," *Journal of Economic Perspectives*, 3 (Summer 1989), 41–50.

Riley, John G. and Samuelson, William F., "Optimal Auctions," *American Economic Review*, 71 (June 1981), 381–92.

Selten, R., "Reexamination of the Perfectness Concept for Equilibrium Points in Extensive Games," *International Journal of Game Theory*, 4 (1975), 25–55.

Tullock, Gordon, "Efficient Rent Seeking," in J. M. Buchanan, R. Tollison, and G. Tullock (eds.), *Toward a Theory of the Rent Seeking Society*, Texas A&M Press, 1980, 267–92.

Vickrey, W., "Counterspeculation, Auctions and Competitive Sealed Tenders," *Journal of Finance*, 16 (March 1961), 8–37.

# 11 Competition and hidden knowledge

In preceding chapters we modeled situations with a large number of *informed* individuals on one side of the market, for example, potential purchasers of insurance who are aware of their individual likelihoods of suffering loss, or potential bidders in an auction aware of their own reservation prices. On the other side of the market we assumed a relatively *uninformed* trader possessing some degree of monopoly power – the insurance company, or the seller at auction. The main issue addressed was contract design: a schedule of options whereby the monopolist might induce the different types of traders on the other side of the market to reveal themselves. An insurance deductible option will tend to separate the better from poorer risks, and any auction structure will similarly tend to separate the more desirous from the less desirous purchasers.

This chapter relaxes the assumption that the uninformed transactor has no close competitors. Instead, in each market a number of decision-makers compete with one another in the design of contracts intended to separate the different types of trading partners they might be dealing with.

In section 11.1 we consider situations where the traders on the uninformed side of the market move first, offering contracts aimed at *screening* their possible trading partners. Later on, section 11.3 takes up the opposite case in which the parties on the informed side of the market take the initiative, *signaling* their respective types by some choice of action. Interpolated between these two analyses is a discussion in section 11.2 of "reactive equilibrium" in information-revealing situations.

## 11.1 Screening

Consider an industry in which workers have productivities of either $\theta_0$ or $\theta_1$, where $\theta_0 < \theta_1$. The proportions of type-0 and type-1 workers are $f_0$ and $f_1$. Firms hire workers without knowing which type they are. In the absence of outside opportunities, and assuming risk-neutrality, competition among firms pushes the wage offer up to the average productivity:

$$w = \bar{\theta}_{01} \equiv f_0 \theta_0 + f_1 \theta_1$$

Suppose, however, that workers also have available an outside opportunity which, without requiring any educational credential, pays a wage $w_0$ that exceeds the average productivity $\bar{\theta}_{01}$. Since all workers will take up this offer rather than accept a wage of $\bar{\theta}_{01}$, the industry cannot operate without some screening mechanism. What is going on here is akin to adverse selection in the insurance market studied in chapter 8. Just as adverse selection may rule out the possible social gains that risk-averse insureds could achieve from risk-sharing, here the impossibility of screening makes it unfeasible for firms to achieve the potential social gains from employing high-productivity workers.

### 11.1.1   Screening by means of a non-productive action

Following the argument in Spence (1974), suppose there is some available action that is not productive of itself but (i) is observable and (ii) can be engaged in at lower marginal cost by higher-productivity workers. Specifically, consider educational credentials. Let $C(z, \theta)$ be the total cost of an education level $z$ to a worker of type $\theta$. Then, if paid a wage of $w$, the payoff of type $\theta$ (assuming risk-neutrality) is:

$$U(z, w, \theta) = w - C(z, \theta)$$

In figure 11.1 indifference curves of the two types are depicted. The type-1 workers' (dashed) indifference curves are flatter than the type-0 (solid) curve, reflecting the lower marginal opportunity cost of the credential for type-1 workers: $MC(z, \theta_1) < MC(z, \theta_0)$, where $MC(z, \theta) \equiv \partial C / \partial z$. Or, equivalently, $dw/dz \,|_U$ is a declining function of $\theta$.

Firms compete by associating a wage offer with a particular level of education. Consider the two indifference curves through the point $\langle 0, w_0 \rangle$. These are the reservation indifference curves of the two types of workers. Since the dashed curve for type 1 is flatter, any offer acceptable to the inferior type 0 will also be acceptable to the superior type 1. However the converse is certainly not true. The shaded region in the diagram represents the offers that (i) only type-1 workers strictly prefer over the outside opportunity and (ii) are profitable to the firm ($w < \theta_1$).

One such offer is $\langle \hat{z}, \hat{w} \rangle$. This offer does separate the two types and therefore overcomes the adverse-selection problem. But, being strictly profitable, it is not viable in equilibrium. Another firm has an incentive to offer a higher wage for workers of education level $\hat{z}$ and thereby bid away the high-quality workers. In fact, competition will then bid the wage up to the zero-profit level $w = \theta_1$ at the point $\langle \hat{z}, \theta_1 \rangle$.

But this is still not the end of the story. If all other firms are offering the contract $\langle \hat{z}, \theta_1 \rangle$, any single firm can make an alternative offer such as

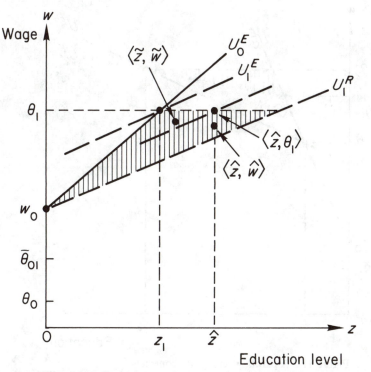

Figure 11.1 Screening out low-productivity workers

$\langle \tilde{z}, \tilde{w} \rangle$ that is strictly preferred by high-productivity workers and is also strictly profitable. Indeed, such an alternative exists for all points in the shaded region, except for the offer $\langle z_1, \theta_1 \rangle$ at the north-west corner. This last is therefore the unique Nash equilibrium: all firms offer a wage $\theta_1$ equal to the marginal product of high-quality workers, while screening out low-productivity workers by an educational requirement $z_1$ just tough enough to deter the entry of these workers.

Low-productivity workers are deterred because the benefit of satisfying the educational screen, in terms of the wage differential $\theta_1 - w_0$, is just offset by the total cost of the education $C(z_1, \theta_0)$. High-productivity workers are paid their marginal product but incur the screening cost $C(z_1, \theta_1)$. The presence of the low-productivity workers thus imposes a *negative externality* of $C(z_1, \theta_1)$ upon the high-productivity workers.

Note that the size of this externality depends critically on the relative cost of education. As just argued, the cost of education level $z_1$ to the low-productivity workers is $C(z_1, \theta_0) = \theta_1 - w_0$. Then, if the difference in the cost of education is small, the negative externality has a cost almost equal

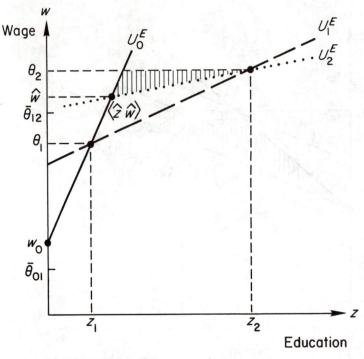

Figure 11.2 Separating zero-profit contracts

to the wage differential. At the other extreme, if the cost of education for high-quality workers is very small, the negative externality has a negligible cost.

So far the only issue has been sorting out those workers who should enter a particular industry from those who should work elsewhere. More generally, there will be more than one type of worker who is best employed in the industry. Suppose there were another type of worker with productivity level $\theta_2$ in the industry, where $\theta_0 < w_0 < \theta_1 < \theta_2$. As before let $f_i$ be the proportion of type-$i$ workers in the overall population.

Suppose that, if types 0 and 1 cannot be distinguished, their average productivity is $\bar{\theta}_{01} < w_0$. Finally, continue to assume that the marginal cost of education is lower for higher-quality workers, that is, $MC(z, \theta_0) > MC(z, \theta_1) > MC(z, \theta_2)$. Arguing exactly as above, the offer $\langle z_1, \theta_1 \rangle$ separates the type-0 and type-1 workers. This is depicted in figure 11.2. Also depicted is the (dotted) type-2 indifference curve through point $\langle z_2, \theta_2 \rangle$. If type-2 workers are to be separated from type-1 and competition bids type-2 workers' wages up to $\theta_2$, the only potentially viable contract is $\langle z_2, \theta_2 \rangle$.

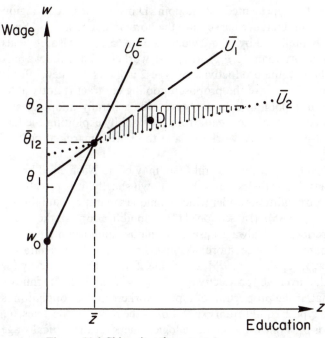

Figure 11.3 Skimming the cream

But this is far from the end of the analysis. The shaded area in figure 11.2 represents offers preferred by type-1 workers over $\langle z_1, \theta_1 \rangle$ and by type-2 workers over $\langle z_2, \theta_2 \rangle$. In particular, consider $\langle \hat{z}, \hat{w} \rangle$ at the south-west corner of the shaded region. For any wage in excess of $\hat{w}$, there are offers that are strictly preferred by types 1 and 2. Therefore if, contrary to the case depicted, the average productivity $\bar{\theta}_{12}$ of these workers exceeds $\hat{w}$, a firm can always enter with a contract close to $\langle \hat{z}, \hat{w} \rangle$ and make a strictly positive profit. So these separating contracts are not equilibrium contracts.

Thus, the $\langle z_2, \theta_2 \rangle$ contract is a separating equilibrium when $\bar{\theta}_{12} < \hat{w}$. But, if this is not the case, the alternative possible equilibrium involves pooling of different types as depicted in figure 11.3. If types 1 and 2 are pooled, competition forces up the wage until it is equal to the average productivity:

$$\bar{\theta}_{12} = \left(\frac{f_1}{f_1 + f_2}\right)\theta_1 + \left(\frac{f_2}{f_1 + f_2}\right)\theta_2$$

As before, since a type-2 worker has a lower marginal cost of production, his (dotted) indifference curve through $(\bar{z}, \bar{\theta}_{12})$ is flatter than the corresponding (dashed) indifference curve for a type-1 worker.

Consider the offer represented by the point D inside the shaded region bounded by these indifference curves and the horizontal line $w = \theta_2$. Such an offer is strictly preferred by type-2 workers over $\langle \bar{z}, \bar{\theta}_{12} \rangle$. Also, it yields a strictly lower utility than $\langle \bar{z}, \bar{\theta}_{12} \rangle$ to type-1 workers. Since the wage is strictly lower than $\theta_2$, the productivity of type-2 workers, the new offer is strictly profitable. Therefore the proposed pooling contract is not viable. To summarize, if a pooling contract were ever generally adopted, any individual firm could skim the cream from the pool by exploiting the fact that the highest-productivity workers have the lowest marginal cost of education.

It follows, therefore, that in general there may be no Nash equilibrium in pure strategies. Nevertheless, as will be shown shortly, it is possible to characterize those conditions under which a unique separating equilibrium does exist (Riley, 1985). (In section 11.2 a modification of the game structure is described that always ensures a unique equilibrium.)

Consider figure 11.2 once more. As has been seen, the separating contracts $\{\langle 0, w_0 \rangle, \langle z_1, \theta_1 \rangle, \langle z_2, \theta_2 \rangle\}$ are viable if and only if the wage $\hat{w}$ exceeds $\bar{\theta}_{12}$, the average productivity of types 1 and 2. It follows immediately that, if the proportion of type-1 workers in the population is large relative to type 2, equilibrium exists. For as the ratio $f_2/f_1$ declines, $\bar{\theta}_{12}$ declines towards $\theta_1$. Following the same logic, whenever the critical wage $\hat{w}$ is sufficiently large, equilibrium again exists. Consider then a parametric change reducing the marginal cost of education for type 2. This flattens the (dotted) indifference curve through the contract $\langle z_2, \theta_2 \rangle$ and leaves the rest of figure 11.2 unchanged. The lower edge of the shaded region therefore shifts up and so $\hat{w}$ increases.

It is only slightly more difficult to show that a *ceteris paribus* increase in the marginal cost of education for type 1 also increases $\hat{w}$. The dashed indifference curve becomes steeper and so lowers $z_2$. This again results in an upward shift in the lower edge of the shaded region. Since the other two edges are unaffected, $\hat{w}$ must rise.

The conclusion, therefore, is that the relative marginal costs of signaling, for the different types, determine the viability of a separating equilibrium. An activity is potentially useful as a screening device if higher-quality workers can undertake it at lower marginal cost, but this is only a necessary condition for a Nash equilibrium. For sufficiency, marginal cost must decline rapidly enough as worker quality increases.

We will not extend the argument here, but it should be intuitively clear that additional types can be introduced without greatly complicating the analysis. As long as $f_{i+1}/f_i$ or $MC(z, \theta_{i+1})/MC(z, \theta_i)$ is sufficiently small, for all $i$, the set of separating zero-profit contracts is the unique Nash equilibrium.

EXERCISES AND EXCURSIONS 11.1.1

*1 Screening by a monopsonist*

There are two types of workers. Type 0 has a marginal product of 1 and an outside opportunity of $w_0(\theta_0) = 2$. Type 1 has a marginal product of 4 and an outside opportunity $w_0(\theta_1) = 3$. The cost of education, $z$, is given by $C(z, \theta) = z/\theta$.

(A) In the absence of any educational screening, show that the monopsonist will face adverse selection unless the proportion of high-quality workers is at least 2/3.

(B) Assuming that this proportion is less than 2/3, establish that the monopsonist profits from screening. What contract will he offer?

(C) Contrast this with the competitive (Nash) equilibrium.

(D) Returning to the case of the monopsonist, for what range of outside opportunities $w_0(\theta_1)$ is it possible to screen for the high-productivity workers?

(E) Suppose the cost of education doubles to $C^*(z, \theta) = 2z/\theta$. Is anyone made worse off in either the monopsonistic or competitive allocations?

*2 Screening and the opportunity cost of time*

Traditionally, labor economists have viewed time costs as the single most important part of the cost of education. Suppose that time costs are the only opportunity cost of education. To simplify matters, assume every individual works the same number of years, regardless of his time in school. The type-$\theta$ individual has a lifetime marginal product (discounted to his initial date of employment) of $\theta$. Types are distributed continuously on the interval $[\beta, \gamma]$. To achieve an education level of $z$, a person must spend $T(z, \theta) = \alpha z/\theta$ years in school.

(A) Let $W(z)$ be the present value of lifetime earnings offered to an individual with education level $z$ (discounted to the initial date of employment). Write down an expression for an individual's present value of lifetime income, discounted to birth. If $z = Z(\theta)$ is the choice of a type-$\theta$ worker, explain carefully why the following two conditions must hold in a separating equilibrium:

$$\text{(i)} \quad \frac{W'(Z(\theta))}{W(Z(\theta))} = \frac{r\alpha}{\theta} \qquad \text{(ii)} \quad W(Z(\theta)) = \theta$$

(B) Hence obtain an expression for $W(z)$ in terms of $z$ and the parameters $r$, $\alpha$, and $\beta$.

(C) Substituting for $z$, show that the equilibrium mapping from time in school into discounted earnings is:

$$W^*(t) = \frac{\beta}{1-rt}$$

ANSWER
(A) An individual who spends $T(z, \theta)$ years in school can earn an income stream from time $T$ with present discounted value $W(z)$. Then, discounting to time $t = 0$ the individual's wealth is:

$$U(z, W(z); \theta) = e^{-rT(z, \theta)} W(z)$$

Taking logarithms and noting that $T = \alpha z/\theta$:

$$u(z, W(z); \theta) \equiv \ln U = \ln W(z) - r\alpha z/\theta$$

Assuming $W(z)$ is differentiable, a type-$\theta$ worker chooses $z = Z(\theta)$ satisfying the first-order condition:

(i)    $$\frac{W'(z)}{W(z)} = \frac{r\alpha}{\theta}$$

Also, the present value of the profit on such work is:

$$\Pi = \theta - W(z)$$

Therefore, in a competitive equilibrium with separation, it must be the case that:

(ii)    $\theta = W(z).$

(B) Combining (i) and (ii):

$$W'(z) = r\alpha$$

Also, since education has no effect on productivity, the least able (type $\beta$) will have $z = 0$. Integrating the above expression:

$$W(z) = r\alpha z + \beta$$

(C) Note that $T = \alpha z/\theta$ and $\theta = W(z(\theta))$, and substitute into the above expression.


*11.1.2   Screening with productive actions*
The analysis of section 11.1.1 focused exclusively on the screening role of education and ignored its possible direct effect upon productivity. This section shows how the earlier model can be extended to allow for

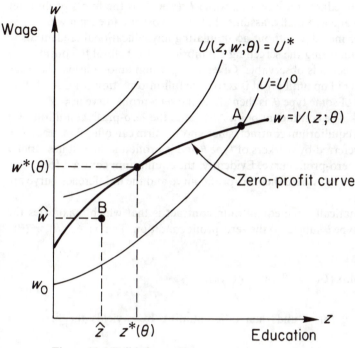

Figure 11.4 Full-information contract

productivity effects. We will also see that the generalized model can be used to analyze competitive screening in quite different applications.

As before, assume that an individual of type $\theta$ has a utility function $U(z, w; \theta)$ over education-wage contracts $\langle z, w \rangle$. And, once again, an individual with higher $\theta$ requires a smaller increment in income to be willing to increase his education level. That is, the marginal opportunity cost of education, $MC(z, \theta)$, declines with $\theta$.

In the earlier analysis, education did not actually contribute to the productivity of the worker, but only served to signal his quality to employers. In this section, in contrast, the value to a firm of a specific worker's contract $\langle z, w \rangle$ is a function not only of the individual's type but of his education level. To be precise, let the net value of the contract to the firm be:

$$U^f(z, w; \theta) = V(z; \theta) - w$$

Here $V$ is increasing in both $z$ and $\theta$, where $\theta$ can be thought of as the individual's innate ability. $V(z; \theta)$ is then his marginal product after receiving an education level of $z$ while $U^f(z, w; \theta)$ is the firm's profit after paying a wage $w$. Finally, assume that each worker can earn a wage $w_0$ in some other industry without accumulating any educational credentials.

Before analyzing the screening equilibrium, it is helpful to consider the outcome when $\theta$ is observable. Given competition among firms, the wage of type $\theta$ is bid up until profit is zero. The full-information contract, for an individual of some type $\theta$, is then along the zero-profit curve $w = V(z; \theta)$ in figure 11.4. The contract at point A satisfies the zero-profit condition. But it is not an equilibrium contract, since another firm can offer B instead. The latter is preferred by workers of type $\theta$ and is profitable since it lies strictly below the zero-profit curve. Evidently, the equilibrium contract for type $\theta$ is $\langle z^*(\theta), w^*(\theta) \rangle$ where the zero-profit curve and the indifference curve are tangential.

Mathematically, the equilibrium contract is that which maximizes the payoff of type $\theta$ subject to the zero-profit condition. That is, $\langle z^*(\theta), w^*(\theta) \rangle$ solves:

$$\underset{z, w}{\text{Max}} \{U(z, w; \theta) \mid w = V(z; \theta)\}$$

Substituting for $w$ and then differentiating by $z$ yields the first-order condition:

$$\frac{dU}{dz} = \frac{\partial U}{\partial z} + \frac{\partial U}{\partial w}\frac{\partial V}{\partial z} = 0$$

Rearranging, leads to the tangency condition:

$$\left.\frac{dw}{dz}\right|_U = -\frac{\partial U/\partial z}{\partial U/\partial w} = \frac{\partial V}{\partial z}(z; \theta)$$

That is, the opportunity cost of education is equal to its marginal product.

Figure 11.5 depicts the full-information equilibrium when there are two types, $\theta_1$ and $\theta_2$. If the types are observably distinct, their equilibrium contracts are $\langle z_1^*, w_1^* \rangle$ and $\langle z_2^*, w_2^* \rangle$. But, if the two types cannot be distinguished, workers of type 1 would strictly prefer the contract of type 2. Therefore, just as in the previous analysis, there is a further incentive for type-2 workers to accumulate education.

Consider the shaded region. It is bounded from above by the lower envelope of the zero-profit curve for type 2 and the indifference curve for type 1 through point $\langle z_1^*, w_1^* \rangle$. Therefore any new offer in the region will screen out the low-productivity workers and generate profits on high-

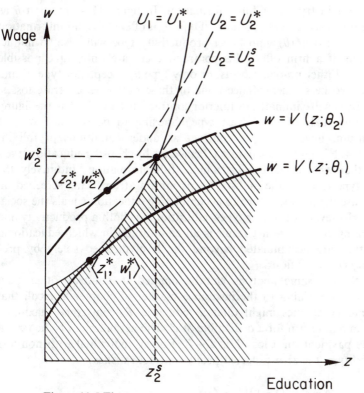

Figure 11.5 The two-type case

productivity workers. Given competition among firms, the only potentially viable contract is $\langle z_2^s, w_2^s \rangle$ where the return to high-quality workers is maximized.

The analysis, therefore, proceeds exactly as in the previous section. Assuming an equilibrium is viable, it must separate out the different types in such a way that (i) there is zero profit on each contract, and (ii) workers of each type are just indifferent between their own contract and the contract of individuals of the immediately superior type.

Given these conditions, once the contract of the lowest type is known the other contracts can, in principle, be computed.

Since in equilibrium types are separated and yield zero profit, no individual can be better off than in the full-information equilibrium. It follows that any type $\theta$ choosing the reservation wage $w_0$ in the full-information equilibrium will also choose it in the screening equilibrium. Let $\theta_*$ signify the lowest-productivity worker type who would prefer to enter the industry under full information. In figure 11.4, interpret $\theta$ as representing this $\theta_*$. By hypothesis, if type $\theta_*$ is offered the full-information contract $\langle z^*(\theta), w^*(\theta) \rangle$, no lower-productivity type will wish to mimic. Therefore, if a firm offers this contract, there are only three possible outcomes. Either no-one accepts, or only type $\theta_*$ accepts, or type $\theta_*$ and superior workers accept. Since none of these outcomes generate losses, competition will eliminate any inferior contract such as $\langle \hat{z}, \hat{w} \rangle$ in the figure.

So individuals of the lowest type choosing to be screened will, in equilibrium, have the same contract as under conditions of full information. Higher types separated themselves by choosing education levels higher than what would be chosen under full information.[1] Intuitively, the lowest type to enter the industry gains nothing from being screened, in which case the private return to accumulating education equals the social return. However, for higher types, education has both a productivity and a screening effect. The net result is an equilibrium in which educational credentials are accumulated beyond the level dictated solely by productivity considerations.

Exactly the same analysis can be applied in contexts other than education. Returning to the insurance market of chapter 8, recall that insurance companies might offer a reduction $R$ from some maximum premium $\alpha$ in return for a deductible of $Z$. The net premium is then $\alpha - R$ and the payment on a loss $L$ is $L - Z$. For an individual with non-loss probability $\pi$, the zero-expected-profit contract satisfies:

$$\alpha - R = (1 - \pi)(L - Z)$$
Premium = probability of loss × payout in the event of a loss

Rearranging:

$$R = \alpha + (1 - \pi)(Z - L)$$

In figure 11.6, the zero-expected-profit contract therefore has slope $1 - \pi$ through the point $(Z, R) = (L, \alpha)$. At such a contract an individual's premium and coverage are both zero, i.e., this is the no-insurance point.

The zero-expected-profit lines are depicted in figure 11.6 for two risk classes. The solid and dashed lines through $(L, \alpha)$ are the zero-expected-profit lines for the high-risk type $\pi_1$ and the low-risk type $\pi_2$, respectively.

---

[1] In the two-type case it is possible that the full-information equilibrium separates, in which case it is also the screening equilibrium. However, if differences between types are sufficiently small, this possibility is eliminated (as shown in an exercise at the end of this section).

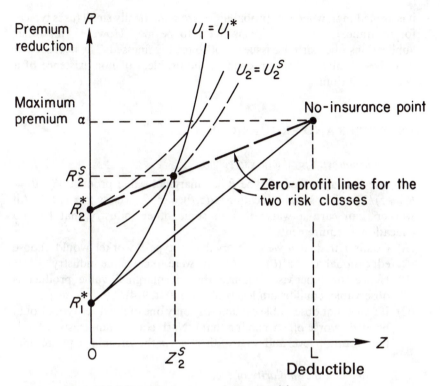

Figure 11.6 Screening out poor insurance risks

As argued in chapter 8, the better risks have flatter indifference curves. Because the probability of a loss is lower, they are willing to accept a smaller reduction in premium in exchange for taking on a larger deductible. Under full information (and ignoring moral hazard), all individuals receive full coverage. The full-information equilibrium contract for risk-class $\pi_i$ is therefore the point $(0, R_i^*)$ on the vertical axis.

In the absence of information about type of risk, competitive screening in the insurance context operates exactly as in the educational example. The bad risks, type $\pi_1$, continue to receive full coverage. The good risks, type $\pi_2$, are offered a deductible just big enough to separate them from type $\pi_1$ while continuing to generate zero-expected profits. In figure 11.6 this new contract is the point $(Z_2^s, R_2^s)$.

Once again, however, the separating equilibrium may not be a Nash equilibrium. As explained earlier, the crucial condition for existence of a Nash equilibrium is the rate at which the marginal opportunity cost of the screening activity declines with improvement of "quality." In Riley (1985) it is argued that, when loss probabilities are numerically small (as is typical for insurance), this condition is likely to be met. However, for other applications, the existence issue is not so readily finessed. The next section describes an alternative approach to the problem of non-existence of a Nash equilibrium.

### EXERCISES AND EXCURSIONS 11.1.2

#### 1 Equilibrium with productive screening

Suppose that a worker of type $\theta$ has marginal value product $V(z;\theta) = \theta(1+z)/2$ and cost of education $C(z,\theta) = z^2/\theta$, where $\theta = 1, 2, 3$. All workers can earn a wage of 1 in some other industry that has no educational requirements.
(A) Confirm that, if $\theta$ were observable, a type-$\theta$ worker would choose educational level $z^*(\theta) = \theta^2/4$ if he were to enter the industry.
(B) Hence, or otherwise, confirm that, if marginal value product is observable, equilibrium levels of $z$ are $(0, 1, 9/4)$.
(C) If $\theta$ were not observable explain why only one of the three types would be made worse off. Assuming that a Nash equilibrium exists, what is the education level and wage of this type in the screening equilibrium?

#### 2 Screening and the similarity of types

An individual of type $\theta$ has marginal value product $V(z;\theta) = \theta + z$ and cost of education $C(z,\theta) = z^2/2\theta$.
(A) With full information show that type $\theta$ chooses an education level $Z^*(\theta) = \theta$ and earns a wage $W(Z^*(\theta)) = 2Z^*(\theta)$.
(B) Suppose that there are just two types, $\theta = 1$ and $\theta = \hat{\theta}$. If $\hat{\theta} = 4$ show that the full-information equilibrium is also a screening equilibrium. Show next that $\hat{\theta} = 3$ is a borderline case. That is, for all $\hat{\theta}$ between 1 and 3, the full-information equilibrium is not a screening equilibrium. HINT: In a diagram depict the full-information earnings function $W(Z)$ and also the indifference curve for type 1 through his equilibrium contract $(1, 1)$. Where do these two "curves" intersect?

#### 3 Screening in financial markets

By raising outside equity $z$, an entrepreneur with a product of quality $\theta$ can produce next period an output of value $f(z,\theta)\tilde{\varepsilon}$, where $\tilde{\varepsilon}$ is a random variable with a mean of unity. Suppose $f$ is increasing in $\theta$, concave in $z$, and that the elasticity of output with respect to equity input, $e \equiv (\partial f/\partial z)/(f/z)$, is higher for higher-quality projects.

Let $P$ be the market price of the firm so that outsider shareholding is $z/P$. The remaining "promoter stock" held by the entrepreneur is non-tradable.

(A) Explain why the present value of entrepreneurial profit is:

$$U(z, P; \theta) = \left(1 - \frac{z}{P}\right) \frac{f(z, \theta)}{1+r}$$

(B) If outside investors can observe $z$, and all individuals are risk-neutral, show that the level of investment $z^*$ will satisfy:

$$\frac{1}{1+r} \frac{\partial f}{\partial z} = 1$$

(C) Confirm that the increase in share price that the entrepreneur is just willing to accept, in exchange for additional dilution of his ownership due to an increment of outside equity, can be expressed as:

$$\frac{dP}{dz}\bigg|_U = \frac{-\dfrac{\partial U}{\partial z}}{\dfrac{\partial U}{\partial P}} = \frac{P}{z} - \frac{P^2}{z^2}\left(1 - \frac{z}{P}\right)\frac{z}{f}\frac{\partial f}{\partial z}$$

(D) Hence confirm that the level of outside equity can be used by outsiders to screen out projects of lower quality. Illustrate graphically for the case of just two quality levels.

ANSWER

(A) The entrepreneur needs to raise $z$ dollars. To do so he must offer outside investors a share in the present value of the firm so that the risk-neutral shareholders achieve the riskless market return $r$. That is:

$$sf(z, \theta) = z(1+r)$$

He sells shares with a value of $z$ and retains insider "promoter stock" with a value of $z^*$. The value of the firm is then:

$$P = z + z^*$$

The outsider share $s$ is therefore $z/P$ and so the entrepreneur's expected return is:

$$U(z, P; \theta) = \left(\frac{z^*}{P}\right)\frac{f(z, \theta)}{1+r} = \left(1 - \frac{z}{P}\right)\frac{f(z, \theta)}{1+r} \tag{1}$$

(B) If $\theta$ is observable, the value of the firm is $P(z, \theta) = f(z, \theta)/(1+r)$. Therefore, substituting into expression (1):

$$U(z, P, \theta) = \frac{f(z, \theta)}{1+r} - z$$

(C)     $\ln U = \ln\left(1 - \dfrac{z}{P}\right) + \ln f(z, \theta) - \ln(1+r)$

$$\frac{1}{U}\frac{\partial U}{\partial P} = \frac{\dfrac{z}{P^2}}{\left(1 - \dfrac{z}{P}\right)}$$

$$\frac{1}{U}\frac{\partial U}{\partial z} = \frac{-\dfrac{1}{P}}{\left(1 - \dfrac{z}{P}\right)} + \frac{\dfrac{\partial f}{\partial z}}{f}$$

Consequently:

$$\left.\frac{dP}{dz}\right|_U = \frac{-\dfrac{\partial U}{\partial z}}{\dfrac{\partial U}{\partial P}} = \frac{P}{z} - \frac{P^2}{z^2}\left(1 - \frac{z}{P}\right)\frac{z}{f}\frac{\partial f}{\partial z}$$

(D)  By hypothesis, output elasticity is increasing in $\theta$. Therefore:

$$\frac{\partial}{\partial \theta}\left(\left.\frac{dP}{dZ}\right|_U\right) < 0$$

## 11.2     Reactive equilibrium

Section 11.1 showed that, unless certain sufficient conditions hold, there is no Nash equilibrium in pure strategies that separates the different types. Moreover, there is no Nash equilibrium in which different types are pooled. (While there are always mixed-strategy Nash equilibria (Dasgupta and Maskin, 1982), these seem implausible empirically, at least for the applications considered here.) In this section it is shown that if an additional stability property holds, the outcome will be a set of contracts that separates out the different types. Since this property is an assumption about the reactions of other agents to defection, the associated outcome is called a Reactive equilibrium.

To illustrate, return to the pure screening model of section 11.1.1. Let there be three types, where type 0 is better off accepting the outside

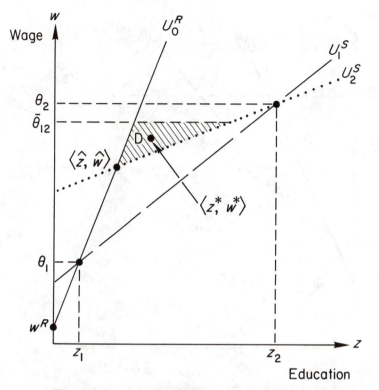

Figure 11.7 A profitable defection

reservation wage while types 1 and 2 are better off choosing $z > 0$ and being employed in the industry. The separate zero-profit contracts must of course involve wage rates of $\theta_1$ and $\theta_2$ for these two groups.

The efficient separating contracts are depicted in figure 11.7. This is essentially the same as figure 11.2 except that the point $\langle \hat{z}, \hat{w} \rangle$ now lies below the average productivity $\bar{\theta}_{12}$. All contracts in the interior of the shaded region are below the reservation indifference curve for type 0 and above the indifference curves for types 1 and 2 through the efficient separating contracts $\langle z_1, \theta_1 \rangle$, and $\langle z_2, \theta_2 \rangle$. Since any wage in the interior of the shaded region is less than $\bar{\theta}_{12}$, all such offers are strictly profitable. Therefore, starting with the separating contracts $\{\langle 0, w_0 \rangle, \langle z_1, \theta_1 \rangle, \langle z_2, \theta_2 \rangle\}$, any firm can enter and make a profit with a "pooled" contract such as $\langle z^*, w^* \rangle$. Thus, it appears, the separating equilibrium is not viable.

However, if a firm in fact exploits this opportunity, it exposes itself to risk. Figure 11.8 shows the indifference curves of the two types through the "defect" contract $\langle z^*, w^* \rangle$. Since the highest-quality workers have the

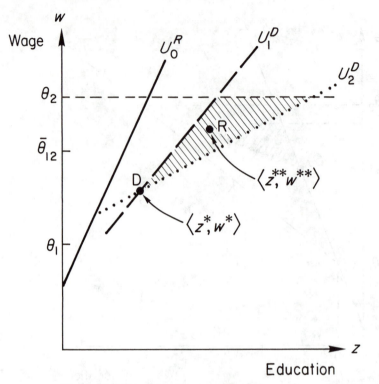

Figure 11.8 Skimming the cream from the pool

flattest (dotted) indifference curve through $\langle z^*, w^* \rangle$, there is always a reaction $\langle z^{**}, w^{**} \rangle$ which can skim the cream from the defecting firm's pool. Since $w^{**} < \theta_2$, such a reaction is profitable and, since $w^* > \theta_1$, the reaction results in losses for the initial defector. Note, moreover (and this is crucial), that the reactor runs no risk from his reaction. That is, unlike the initial defector, he has no risk of being undercut and ending up with losses. The reason is that the reactor attracts only workers for whom $\theta_2 < w^{**}$, and employing them is strictly profitable. Therefore, the worst that can happen to a reactor is that other reactors outbid him, in which case he ends up with zero profit.

More generally, a reactive equilibrium is defined as follows:

DEFINITION: Reactive equilibrium

A set of offers (contracts) $E$ is a Reactive equilibrium if, for any addition to this set $D$ that one of the uninformed agents (the defector) prefers, there is a further addition $R$ that another uninformed agent (the reactor) might offer such that:

(i)   When the informed agents can choose from $E$, $D$, and $R$, the defector is strictly worse off and the reactor is strictly better off than under the initial set of offers $E$.

(ii)  No further additions to the set of offers leave the reactor worse off than under $E$.[2]

In Engers and Fernandez (1987) it is shown that, under the assumptions of the screening model outlined in this chapter, there is a unique Reactive equilibrium. This is the set of efficient, separating, zero-profit contracts. For finite sets of offers, the arguments are essentially those made above. That is, it is possible to show that, for any finite number of new offers made by a defector, there is a corresponding reaction that skims the cream and produces losses for the defector.

The key idea is that an offer announced and promoted by a firm cannot be quickly and costlessly withdrawn. Potential defectors cannot simply hit and run, announcing a new offer with the intent of withdrawing it as soon as other firms react. Instead, defectors must consider the possibility of incurring losses once these reactions occur. If the reaction time is short relative to the length of time over which a defector is committed to his new offering, all defectors from the efficient, separating, zero-profit set do suffer losses.

## EXERCISES AND EXCURSIONS 11.2

### 1 Ice cream vendors

There are $n$ vendors selling ice cream on a beach represented by the interval $[0, 1]$. Sunbathers are distributed uniformly along the beach. Vendor $i$ must choose a location $x_i$, $i = 1, \ldots, n$ somewhere on $[0, 1]$. Without loss of generality, assume that $x_1 \leqslant x_2 \leqslant \ldots \leqslant x_n$. Sunbathers purchase exclusively from the nearest vendor (there is no price competition). If two vendors choose the same location, they share their market equally.

(A)  As Hotelling first noted, when $n = 2$ each ice cream vendor will locate at $x = \frac{1}{2}$ although the efficient location vector is $(x_1, x_2) = (\frac{1}{4}, \frac{3}{4})$. Show that the latter is also the unique Reactive equilibrium.
      [HINT: For any other initial location consider a defection to $x = \frac{1}{2}$.]

(B)  When $n = 3$, there is no Nash equilibrium. Explain why not. Show that there exists a Reactive equilibrium with $x_1 = \frac{1}{4}$ and $x_3 = \frac{3}{4}$. Show

---

[2] Note that any Nash equilibrium is automatically a Reactive equilibrium since, for a Nash contract set, the set of strictly preferable defections is empty. See Wilson (1977) for the related concept of "anticipatory equilibrium."

also that $x_2$ may take on any value between $x_1$ and $x_3$. Are any of the
Reactive equilibria efficient?

(C) What happens when $n = 4$?

## 11.3     Signaling

Up to now the analysis has had transactors on the uninformed side of the
market designing contracts in an attempt to screen for quality. The
informed individuals were supposed to respond in an essentially passive
way, simply choosing among the offered contracts. This section asks what
happens when it is the informed transactors who move first.

An individual trying to sell an item or service that he knows to be
valuable may attempt to convince buyers by undertaking some *signaling*
activity. Just as with screening, an activity is a potential signal if engaging
in it is less costly for someone offering a higher-quality product. Returning
to the basic model of section 11.1.1, now suppose workers can first choose
their level of education. The employer firms observe the distribution of
educational achievements and only then make offers.

What makes the signaling game more complicated is the need to specify
the beliefs of the uninformed transactors (firms). As will be seen, the
hypotheses about how these beliefs are formed are critical for characterizing the equilibrium.

The key issues can be illustrated when workers are of two types. As
before, let $\theta_i$ be the marginal value product of type $i$, for $i = 0, 1$. Let $w_0$ be
the alternative reservation wage for both types, where $\theta_0 < w_0 < \theta_1$. Type
$i$ can achieve an education level $z$ at a cost $C(z, \theta_i)$. As in section 11.1.1, the
cost of education is assumed linear in $z$ and lower for the higher-quality
workers (type 1).

In figure 11.9, suppose the only two education levels observed are 0 and
$z^A$. What wages should firms offer? One possible belief is indicated by the
thick step function. That is, anyone choosing an education level less than
$z^A$ is believed to be of type 0, while anyone with an education level of $z^A$ or
more is believed to be of type 1. Given such beliefs, the most that any firm
will offer an individual choosing $z = 0$ is $\theta_0$. For those choosing $z = z^A$,
competition among firms bids the wage up to $\theta_1$ where expected profit is
zero.

Now consider the educational choice of the two types of workers. Since
competition bids the wage up to the expected marginal value product, each
individual can attain any point on the thick step function. A type-0 worker
is clearly better off remaining out of the industry and taking the reservation
wage $w_0$. Type-1 workers, however, maximize their return by choosing the

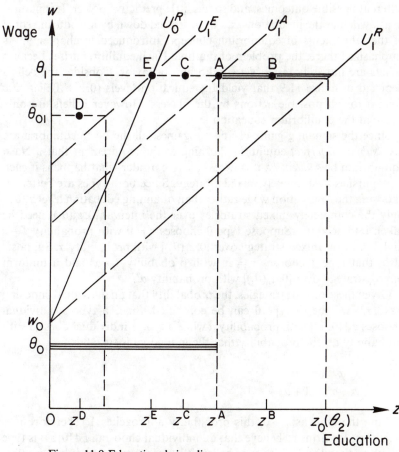

Figure 11.9 Educational signaling

education level $z^A$. It follows that the assumed initial beliefs are consistent with optimal responses and so the outcome is a Nash signaling equilibrium.

But these proposed beliefs are just one of a continuum of possibilities. Suppose instead that firms believe that only individuals with an education level of at least $z^B$ are of type 1. Using exactly the same argument, it can be seen that the pair of education levels $(0, z^B)$ is also an equilibrium.

A rather different alternative belief is that education and productivity are uncorrelated. Expected marginal value product at each level of $z$ is then the population average $\bar{\theta}_{01}$. With such beliefs no-one has an incentive to be educated. The resulting outcome is that both types are hired at the wage $w = \bar{\theta}_{01}$.

The Nash equilibrium concept therefore leads to a wide range of different possible outcomes, and so has little predictive power. It is natural to ask whether the predictions can be narrowed down by introducing some of the refinements of equilibrium concepts introduced in chapter 9. As emphasized there, the problem of multiple Nash equilibria arises because beliefs are not fully tested via equilibrium behavior. Consider the beliefs depicted in figure 11.9 that yield the education levels $(0, z^A)$. Beliefs are *defined* for all possible actions by the players. However beliefs are only *tested* at the equilibrium education level $z = z^A$.

Since the signaling game has no subgames, all the Nash equilibria are also *subgame-perfect* equilibria. Turning to the requirement that a Nash equilibrium be *sequential*, it is necessary to consider what happens if each type pursues a completely mixed strategy. Since both types are better off choosing the reservation wage rather than obtaining education level $z_0(\theta_2)$, only the completely mixed strategies over the interval $[0, z_0(\theta_2)]$ need be taken into account. Suppose type 0 chooses $z = 0$ with probability $1 - \alpha$ and a uniform mixed strategy over $[0, z_0(\theta_2)]$ with probability $\alpha$. Suppose, also, that type 1 chooses $z = z^A$ with probability $1 - \alpha^2$ and a uniform mixed strategy over $[0, z_0(\theta_2)]$ with probability $\alpha^2$.

Given these mixed strategies, the probability that an individual choosing $z \notin \{0, z^A\}$ will be of type 0 can be computed. Since a type-0 individual chooses $z \notin \{0, z^A\}$ with probability $\alpha$ while a type-1 individual does so with probability $\alpha^2$, the probability that the individual is type 0 is:

$$\frac{\alpha}{\alpha + \alpha^2} = \frac{1}{1 + \alpha}$$

Taking the limit as $\alpha \to 0$, this probability approaches 1. Therefore it is *consistent* for firms to believe that an individual choosing $z \notin \{0, z^A\}$ is type 0 with probability 1. With such beliefs it is clear that the equilibrium offers by the firms $\langle 0, \theta_0 \rangle$, $\langle z^A, \theta_1 \rangle$ are best replies. That is, the Nash equilibrium is sequential.

Since exactly the same argument holds for any educational level between $z^E$ and $z_0(\theta_2)$, it follows that the sequential refinement adds little or nothing in this context. Despite this, the educational level $z = z^A$ seems implausible. Why would firms believe that anyone with an educational level lower than $z^A$ was of type 0? Consider figure 11.9 once more. Suppose someone were to choose education level $z^C$. The most that a firm would pay is $\theta_1$, the high marginal product. Even if offered this, a type-0 individual would be strictly better off choosing the reservation wage. So it is surely more plausible that the worker choosing $z^C$ will be judged to be of high quality. The worker will then succeed in earning the high wage $w = \theta_1$. In the face of such logic, the sequential Nash equilibrium beliefs collapse.

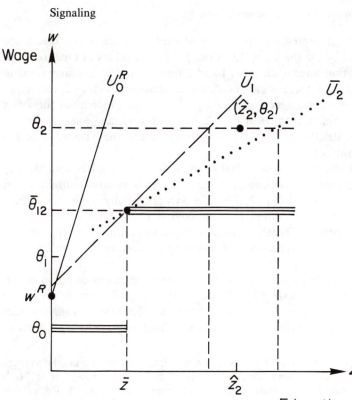

Figure 11.10 Non-credible pooling equilibria

In chapter 9 the idea of logically testing a Nash equilibrium was made precise in two *communication tests*. The above argument is, in essence, a demonstration that the education level $z = z^A$ is not "weakly communication proof." Recall that an equilibrium is weakly communication proof if no message of the following class is credible:

> I am sending you the message that my type is $\theta_i$ and you should believe me. For if you do and respond optimally, I will be better off while any other type who mimicks me will be made worse off.

As has been seen, if a worker chooses $z = z^C$ and sends a message that he is of type 1, he should be believed. For, if he is and his wage is bid up to $w = \theta_1$, the reservation wage $w_0$ is still strictly preferred by type 0.

Such arguments rule out all separating Nash equilibria that are not Pareto-efficient. In terms of figure 11.9, any separating equilibrium with $z_1 > z^E$ is not weakly communication proof. As for the pooling equilibrium, the argument as to why it cannot be weakly communication proof proceeds almost exactly as in section 11.2.

Figure 11.10 represents three types of workers. Once again, beliefs are represented by the thick step function. Suppose workers of type 0 choose the reservation wage while types 1 and 2 are pooled. For any such pooling contact, $\langle \bar{z}, \bar{\theta}_{12} \rangle$, there is always a level of education such as $\hat{z}_2$ that type-2 workers can choose as a credible signal. For, if an individual chooses $z = \hat{z}_2$ and is believed to be of type 2, he earns a wage $w = \theta_2$. While this makes him strictly better off, type 1 strictly prefers the Nash equilibrium pooling contract.

From all this the conclusion is that, of the family of Nash equilibria, only the efficient, separating, zero-profit equilibrium is weakly communication proof. As seen in section 11.1, this is the only potentially viable equilibrium when it is the uninformed (the employing firms) who move first by screening workers. Therefore, once a communication test is applied, the differences between signaling and screening turn out to be more apparent than real.

An even closer parallel can be drawn when the *strong* communication test is applied. Suppose, as in figure 11.9, that type 1 strictly prefers to receive the average product $\bar{\theta}_{01}$ rather than the efficient separating contract $\langle z^E, \theta_1 \rangle$. Then a worker can choose $z = z^D$ and communicate to firms as follows:

> Type 0 and type 1 are both strictly better off being paid the average product $\bar{\theta}_{01}$ with education level $z^D$ rather than accept their Nash equilibrium contracts. Therefore you should use the population weights in estimating my value and so bid my wage up to $\bar{\theta}_{01}$.

The absence of such a credible message is precisely the requirement for an equilibrium to pass the strong communication test. Therefore, if this test is imposed there is, in general, no viable Nash equilibrium.

Evidently, the conditions under which no Nash signaling equilibrium satisfies the strong communication test are exactly the conditions under which there is no Nash screening equilibrium. This result is quite general. That is, the sufficient conditions for existence of a Nash screening equilibrium, described in section 11.1.2, are sufficient for the existence of a signaling equilibrium that satisfies the strong communication test. On the other hand, the assumptions that lead to non-existence of a screening equilibrium also result in a signaling equilibrium that fails the strong communication test.

To conclude, when plausible restrictions are imposed upon beliefs, the question of existence and the nature of the equilibrium when it exists are essentially the same for screening and signaling models. Thus the order of the moves in the game does not matter. Very often, economic interactions are ongoing so that it is not clear who moves first. A theory in which the order of moves is immaterial is particularly applicable in such contexts.

## EXERCISES AND EXCURSIONS 11.3

*1 Educational signaling – a discrete example*

There are two types of worker. Type 0 has marginal value product $\theta_0 = 2$. Type 1 has marginal value product $\theta_1 = 6$. The cost of educational level $z$ for type $\theta$ is $C(z, \theta) = 4z^2/\theta$. Workers signal by choosing education levels from the set $Z = \{0, 1, 2\}$. Firms compete for workers by making a wage offer from the set $W = \{1, 3, 5\}$. For both types, the reservation wage is zero.

(A) If a worker of type $i$ chooses an education level $z$ and is offered a wage $w$, what are the expected payoffs to worker and firm?

(B) Compute the payoffs for worker and firm along each branch of the game tree. Depict this in a neat figure.

(C) If the proportion of type 0 is 0·8, show that there exists a Nash equilibrium. Are there multiple equilibria? [HINT: Competition by firms bids wages up.]

(D) Does the Nash equilibrium satisfy both the weak and strong communication tests?

(E) Suppose the proportion of type 0 is 0·5. Confirm that there are at least two Nash equilibria in which the types are pooled, as well as a separating equilibrium.

(F) Which of these equilibria satisfy the weak communication test?

(G) Which satisfy the strong communication test?

*2\* Divine equilibria*

Banks and Sobel (1987) have argued that the strong communication test is unreasonably strong. Essentially, their point is that an informed decision-maker taking an out-of-equilibrium action will not be sure about the response to his action. Banks and Sobel describe an equilibrium as being "divine" if, whenever the set of responses that would benefit one type is contained in the set of responses that would benefit another type, the uninformed party believes that the latter type is more likely to take an out-of-equilibrium action.

To illustrate, consider a simple signaling model with three types as in figure 11.7.

(A) Confirm that, for all $z \in [z_1, z_2]$, the set of wages that would make type 1 better off contains the set of wages that would benefit type 2.

(B) Consider offers $\langle z, w \rangle$, with $z \in [z_1, z_2]$, such that only types 1 and 2 would be better off. Banks and Sobel then require that the wage offered, given such an out-of-equilibrium signal, should be based

---

\* Starred questions may be somewhat more difficult.

upon posterior beliefs in which the relative weight of type 2 is no greater than under the prior beliefs. That is, they would impose only the restriction that the firm's belief about expected productivity lies somewhere between $w_1$ and the average productivity under the prior beliefs. Confirm that, for all prior beliefs, this implies that the best separating set of contracts is a "divine" equilibrium. (You must also apply the "divinity criterion" over the interval $(0, z_1)$.)

(C) If the proportions of the three types in the population are, respectively, 0·001, 0·010, and 0·989, does the line of reasoning by Banks and Sobel seem adequate?**

## REFERENCES AND SELECTED READINGS

Banks, Jeffrey S. and Sobel, Joel, "Equilibrium Selection in Signaling Games," *Econometrica*, 55 (1987), 647–61.

Cho, In-Koo and Kreps, David M., "Signaling Games and Stable Equilibria," *Quarterly Journal of Economics*, 102 (1987), 179–222.

Dasgupta, Partha and Maskin, Eric S., "The Existence of Equilibrium in Discontinuous Economic Games: 1: Theory, 2: Applications," London School of Economics Discussion Papers (1982).

Engers, Maxim and Fernandez, Luis, "On the Existence and Uniqueness of Signalling Equilibria," *Econometrica*, 55 (1987), 425–40.

Grossman, Sanford and Perry, M., "Perfect Sequential Equilibrium," *Journal of Economic Theory*, 39 (1986), 97–119.

Riley, John G., "Informational Equilibrium," *Econometrica*, 47 (1979), 331–59.

———, "Competition with Hidden Knowledge," *Journal of Political Economy*, 93 (1985), 958–76.

Rothschild, Michael and Stiglitz, Joseph E., "Equilibrium in Competitive Insurance Markets: An Essay in the Economics of Imperfect Information," *Quarterly Journal of Economics*, 90 (1976), 629–49.

Spence, A. Michael, *Market Signaling*, Cambridge, MA: Harvard University Press, 1974.

Wilson, Charles A., "A Model of Insurance Markets With Incomplete Information," *Journal of Economic Theory*, 16 (1977), 167–207.

** End of starred section.

# 12 Long-run relationships and the credibility of threats and promises[1]

The previous chapter showed that individuals may be willing to undertake otherwise wasteful "signaling" activities in order to make favorable information about themselves credible to other parties. However, that analysis presumed a one-time interaction among players. This chapter inquires into the further information transmission opportunities that are introduced when individuals interact with one another *repeatedly*.

In some cases at least, an individual should be able to make favorable information about himself (information that he is a high-quality or otherwise desirable trading partner) credible by actions taken in the early periods of a long-run relationship. That is, an individual should be able to develop a *reputation*. As we shall see, however, reputation-building may be unprofitable even when the distant future is only very mildly discounted.

## 12.1   The multi-period Prisoners' Dilemma

Let us begin by examining the Prisoners' Dilemma. In table 12.1 below, each individual $i$ ($i = 1, 2$) may choose to play either "Defect" (strategy $x_1$) or "Cooperate" (strategy $x_2$). The Prisoners' Dilemma environment is *defined* by the ranked payoffs in table 12.1 if $e > f > g > h$. Table 12.2 is a numerical example.

When the Prisoners' Dilemma is played just once, it is evident that the Defect strategy $x_1$ is strictly dominant for each player. The unique Nash equilibrium is therefore for both individuals to choose $x_1$. In the illustrative example of table 12.2, each player's payoff would be zero.

When the Prisoners' Dilemma (or any other game) is played repeatedly so that the parties will be interacting in an ongoing long-run relationship, the menu of possible strategies is widened. It would be possible, for example, for a player to choose Defect in each odd-numbered round and

---

[1] This chapter relies heavily upon the discussions in Fudenberg, Levine and Maskin (1986) and Fudenberg and Levine (1989).

Table 12.1 *Prisoners' Dilemma*

$(e > f > g > h)$

|  |  | Defect $x_1^2$ | Cooperate $x_2^2$ |
|---|---|---|---|
| Defect | $x_1^1$ | $g, g$ | $e, h$ |
| Cooperate | $x_2^1$ | $h, e$ | $f, f$ |

Table 12.2 *Prisoners' Dilemma*

(numerical example)

|  |  | Defect $x_1^2$ | Cooperate $x_2^2$ |
|---|---|---|---|
| Defect | $x_1^1$ | $0, 0$ | $6, -4$ |
| Cooperate | $x_2^1$ | $-4, 6$ | $2, 2$ |

Cooperate in each even-numbered round. More interesting is the possibility of selecting a reactive or *contingent* strategy. That is, a player's choice of Cooperate or Defect in any particular round could be a function of the opponent's moves in previous rounds.

The issue here is whether, if the Prisoners' Dilemma game is repeated a large (but finite) number of times, some more cooperative strategy might be superior to playing Defect in every round. One possible alternative is the contingent strategy known as Tit for Tat. A Tit for Tat player chooses Cooperate in the opening round, and thereafter mirrors his opponent's previous move. Thus a Tit for Tat player "punishes" an opponent who defects in any round, but in a measured way that leaves open the possibility of mutual return to a cooperative relationship.

We now ask whether Tit for Tat is a Nash equilibrium (NE) strategy. (More precisely, whether the symmetrical strategy-pair in which both players choose Tit for Tat is an NE.) Suppose that, while player 1 adopts Tit for Tat, player 2 has chosen another strategy in which he plays Cooperate until round $t$ and then switches to Defect for one round only. Using the numbers of table 12.2 we see that such a switch yields player 2 a net gain of 4 in period $t$ (he receives 6 instead of 2) but a net loss of 6 in period $t+1$ (he receives $-4$ instead of 2). Therefore, as long as the future is only mildly discounted, player 2 is worse off for his defection. And if he were to defect for more than one period, while the very adverse payoff of $-4$ would be deferred, this would be at the cost of receiving payoffs of zero instead of 2 in the interim. Thus once again, so long as the future is only mildly discounted, player 2 does not gain by his defection.

One qualification: For this to hold, it must be the case that $2f > e+h$ in terms of the generalized payoffs of table 12.1. The explanation is that the payoff from the mutual cooperation achievable via Tit for Tat must exceed the average payoffs of alternately playing Defect against Cooperate and Cooperate against Defect.

This argument suggests, therefore, that mutual adoption of Tit for Tat may be a Nash equilibrium. However, there is a problem when we take account of the final rounds of the game. Suppose the game is played a finite number of times $T$. In period $T$, no matter what his opponent is doing, any player does best choosing his dominant strategy $x_1 = $ Defect. So in the final round it will always be more profitable to switch away from Tit for Tat. But then there is no way of rewarding cooperative play in round $T-1$, so the players should switch away from Tit for Tat in that round as well. Arguing iteratively back through the periods, it follows that Tit for Tat is not an equilibrium strategy for any number of rounds.

In fact we have proved more than this. The iterative argument against Tit for Tat applies to *any* alternative strategy that might be selected by either player. It follows that the unique Nash equilibrium strategy of the finitely repeated game is, after all, always to play Defect. What we have established, therefore, is that the Nash equilibrium admits of no reputation-building in the finitely repeated Prisoners' Dilemma game.

But what if the game is infinite, i.e., if there is no final round? If so, a Tit for Tat player will always be able to reward an opponent's cooperation, or punish defection, on the next round. Then the original argument holds and Tit for Tat is indeed an NE strategy – provided that discount of the future is sufficiently mild.

How mild must the discount be? Let $c_t^i$ be the round-$t$ payoff to individual $i$. Let $\rho$ be the annual discount rate, and define the future-valuation factor $\delta$ as:

$$\delta \equiv \frac{1}{1+\rho} \tag{12.1.1}$$

Then, letting each player's utility $U^i$ simply be the discounted sum of the payoffs:[2]

$$U^i = \sum_{t=1}^{\infty} \delta^{t-1} c_t^i \tag{12.1.2}$$

---

[2] The form of equation (12.1.2) implies additive separability over time, and – since implicitly the preference-scaling function is $v_t(c_t) = c_t$ – risk-neutrality at each moment of time as well. The second condition could be relaxed, however, simply by writing $v_t(c_t)$ in place of $c_t$ on the right-hand side, so as to allow for the possibility of the individual being characterized by risk-aversion or risk-preference.

Another way of thinking of this is to define the *effective* number of rounds, $M$, as:

$$M \equiv \frac{1}{1-\delta} = 1+\delta+\delta^2+\ldots \tag{12.1.3}$$

Then the utility associated with mutual cooperation through Tit for Tat, in terms of the magnitudes in table 12.1, is:

$$U^i = f+\delta f+\delta^2 f+\delta^3 f\ldots = f/(1-\delta) = Mf$$

We need only look at player 2's incentive to defect in the first round. If he chooses $x_1$ in the first round only, reverting to cooperation thereafter, in terms of the magnitudes in table 12.1 his utility will be:

$$U^i = e+\delta h+\delta^2 f+\delta^3 f+\ldots$$
$$= e+\delta h+\delta^2 f/(1-\delta)$$

Thus the utility gain from defection is:

$$\Delta U_i = e+\delta h-(f+\delta f)$$

Evidently, $\Delta U_i$ will be negative if:

$$\delta > (e-f)/(f-h) \tag{12.1.4}$$

For the payoffs in the example of table 12.2, $(e-f)/(f-h)$ is $(6-2)/(2+4)$ $= \frac{2}{3}$. A future-valuation factor $\delta$ greater than $\frac{2}{3}$, which means the effective number of rounds is $M > 3$, corresponds to a discount rate $\rho$ less than $\frac{1}{2}$. Thus, if the discount rate is no greater than 50%, Tit for Tat will be a Nash equilibrium for the infinitely repeated game with payoffs as in table 12.2.

But one might well be hesitant about drawing practical conclusions from games that are (hypothetically) replayed an infinite number of rounds. A more believable situation, probably, is a game where in each round there is a fixed probability $\omega$ of continuation to another round of play. Then, evidently, all the results above will continue to hold, allowing, for both *time-discount* and *probability-discount*. The letter adjustment involves replacing $\delta$ everywhere above with $\delta\omega$. Thus, the effective number of rounds would be redefined as:

$$M \equiv \frac{1}{1-\delta\omega} = 1+\delta\omega+(\delta\omega)^2+\ldots \tag{12.1.5}$$

Condition (12.1.4) for Tit for Tat to be an NE then becomes:

$$\delta\omega > (e-f)/(f-h) \tag{12.1.6}$$

In the numerical illustration, this means that the product of the future-valuation and probability-discount factors would have to exceed $\frac{2}{3}$ for Tit for Tat to be a Nash equilibrium strategy.

Tit for Tat is just one of an infinity of possible schemes for penalizing an opponent who deviates from cooperative play. Another such, the "Grim" strategy, consists of initially playing Cooperate but punishing an opponent's defection by thereafter playing Defect forever (Friedman, 1971).[3] Then the infinite stream of lower payoffs forevermore will outweigh any one-period gain from defection (from choosing $x_1$) if the future-valuation factor is sufficiently close to unity. Moreover, once one individual is playing Grim, for the opponent Grim is a best response. So mutual choice of Grim is a Nash equilibrium.

Of course, the Tit for Tat strategy is an equally good response to Grim, as is Grim to Tit for Tat. (In either case, the actual behavioral or payoff-relevant *moves* will be cooperation forever.) Thus not only are Tit for Tat and Grim both symmetrical NE's, but also there are asymmetrical NE's involving each of them played against the other. On the other hand, while the simple Cooperate strategy is also a best response to either Tit for Tat or Grim, it cannot form part of an asymmetrical NE when Defect is an available strategy. The reason is that Defect is strictly dominant against an opponent playing simple Cooperate.

One way of selecting among possible Nash equilibria in the repeated-play game is to bring to bear the stability considerations summarized by the *evolutionary equilibrium* (EE) concept described in chapter 8. When more profitable strategies tend to increase in representation in the population over the generations, while strategies yielding lesser return gradually become less prevalent, some of the NE's may be possible termini of the dynamic evolutionary process while others are not.[4]

---

[3] The ancestral motto of one of the authors is "Never forget a friend, never forgive an enemy." No wonder the Grahams thrived! In contrast, Tit for Tat corresponds to the Old Testament "eye for an eye." Alas, there is little hope, on this earth, for those choosing the unconditional Cooperate strategy "turn the other cheek."

[4] Heretofore in the chapter we have thought of games as being repeated via multiple rounds of play between a given pair of participants (implying a long-term relationship between the parties). Evolutionary games involve a different kind of repetition in which it is the overall situation – random encounters among members of a population distributed over a set of possible strategies – rather than any single interaction that is replicated in each and every generation. These two types of repetition are quite independent of one another. Chapter 8 considered an evolutionary process involving many generations but *single-round* play in

Table 12.3 *Repeated-play Prisoners' Dilemma with Tit for Tat* ($M = 4$)

|     | D       | C        | T      |
| --- | ------- | -------- | ------ |
| D   | 0, 0    | 24, −16  | 6, −4  |
| C   | −16, 24 | 8, 8     | 8, 8   |
| T   | −4, 6   | 8, 8     | 8, 8   |

The analysis in chapter 8 showed that a *strong* NE is always an EE (in geometrical terms, it is a vertex solution). It follows immediately from the above that in a $2 \times 2$ situation involving Tit for Tat and simple Defect, or Grim and simple Defect, the more cooperative strategy is indeed an EE as well as an NE when $M \equiv 1/(1 - \delta\omega)$ is sufficiently large. In $3 \times 3$ situations involving simple Defect and simple Cooperate with Tit for Tat as the third strategy, the symmetrical Tit for Tat strategy-pair remains an NE. And the same holds when it is Grim that is the third strategy. However, it is not immediately evident whether either of these NE's is evolutionary stable. For, while either Tit for Tat or Grim at its own vertex is strongly optimal against Defect, it is only weakly optimal there against simple Cooperate. In effect, strategies that maintain cooperation through the threat of retaliation can be invaded and thus possibly subverted by the presence of unconditional "Golden Rule" cooperators.

Cooperate and Defect are the two archetype strategies of Prisoners' Dilemma. Since Tit for Tat and Grim are evidently equivalent to one another as against these archetype strategies, the discussion can be limited to Tit for Tat. As an example based upon the one-time $2 \times 2$ payoffs of table 12.2, table 12.3 shows the discounted payoffs for the $3 \times 3$ game when the effective number of rounds is $M = 4$.[5] It is immediately evident that Defect is a strong NE, and hence is also an EE. But since Tit for Tat and Cooperate are tied with one another at both the Tit for Tat vertex and the Cooperate vertex, neither of these is an EE.

However, it turns out that a range of combinations of Tit for Tat and Cooperate meet the criterion for an *evolutionary equilibrium region* as defined in chapter 8. As sketched in figure 12.1 (based on the specific payoffs of table 12.3), from initial population distributions where the proportion of Defect is sufficiently small, the evolutionary progression will be toward some proportionate mixture ($p_D, p_C, p_T$) of Defect, Cooperate,

each generation; here the evolutionary process involves *multi-round* play in every one-to-one encounter in each generation as well as many generations.

[5] In the Defect–Tit for Tat interaction, in the first round the former obtains payoff of 6 while the latter (playing its opening Cooperate move) suffers −4. Thereafter, however, Tit for Tat plays like Defect, so both parties obtain zero in succeeding rounds for a total of 6 each.

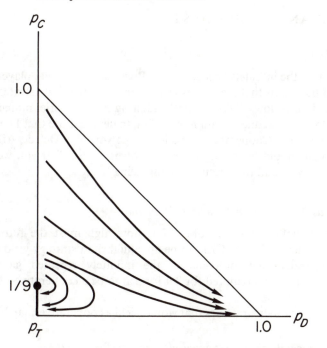

Figure 12.1 Repeated-play Prisoners' Dilemma with Tit for Tat: vertex
EE plus evolutionary equilibrium region

and Tit for Tat such that $p_D = 0$ and $0 \leqslant p_C < \frac{1}{9}$. Otherwise, however, the
dynamic process will always lead to the vertex EE at $p_D = 1$.

In interpreting these solutions, it is important to appreciate that they
deal with *population distributions over pure strategies*. As pointed out in
chapter 9, in general the evolutionary equilibria of such a population need
not coincide with those of a *uniform population* each member of which is
playing the corresponding mixed strategy.

While our discussion has concentrated upon a numerical example, it
should be intuitively clear that corresponding arguments will hold
generally for the Prisoners' Dilemma game. The remainder of the chapter
does not consider evolutionary equilibrium further. However, the next
section shows that, as regards the Nash equilibrium concept, similar results
hold for all infinitely repeated games.

EXERCISES AND EXCURSIONS 12.1

*1 Talk is cheap*

Suppose that, in the infinitely repeated $2 \times 2$ Prisoners' Dilemma, player 1 defaults and then finds that player 2 is responding with the Grim strategy. Player 1 pleads as follows. "We are both suffering from my brief moment of greed and your cussedness. I am now willing to demonstrate that I have reformed by playing Cooperate this period while you play Defect. After that surely you should be willing to play Cooperate also?" If you were player 2 would you find this argument convincing?

*2 Grim versus Tit for Tat in Prisoners' Dilemma*

(A)  For the payoffs shown in table 12.1, how high must the future-valuation factor $\delta$ be for Grim to be an equilibrium strategy yielding the cooperative-play outcome in the infinitely repeated game? Compare with the $\delta$ required for Tit for Tat to be a cooperative-play NE.

(B)  Suggest some other strategies that would yield a cooperative-play NE.

*3 Evolutionary equilibria for repeated-play games* (Boyd and Lorberbaum, 1987)

In the Prisoners' Dilemma game, Tit for Tat (TFT) is a "nicer" strategy than Grim (G). Even nicer is Tit for 2 Tats (TF2T), which does not respond with a non-cooperative move until the opponent has failed to cooperate twice in a row. Somewhat less nice is Suspicious Tit for Tat (STFT), which opens with a non-cooperative move and thereafter responds in kind to the opponent's prior move.

(A)  With Prisoners' Dilemma payoffs, show that, when more than one of the available strategies involves a "nice" opening move, then none of these can be an EE. If several such nice strategies can be played while simple Defect is the only non-nice strategy, can Defect ever fail to be an EE?

(B)  On the other hand, when more than one strategy on the menu of possible strategies involves a "non-nice" opening move, for example Defect and STFT, can any one of these be an EE? If a number of such non-nice strategies are played against simple Cooperate as the only nice strategy, can Cooperate be an EE, for $M$ sufficiently large? What if Tit for Tat is the only nice strategy?

(C)  If the menu of strategy possibilities consists only of TFT, STFT, and TF2T show that, for $M$ sufficiently large, the only EE is a combination of the rather tolerant strategy TF2T and the somewhat exploitative strategy STFT.

*4 Cooperation in a finitely repeated game* (Benoit and Krishna, 1985)

Consider the following payoff matrix:

<table>
<tr><td></td><td></td><td colspan="3" align="center">Player 2</td></tr>
<tr><td></td><td></td><td>$x_1^2$</td><td>$x_2^2$</td><td>$x_3^2$</td></tr>
<tr><td></td><td>$x_1^1$</td><td>5, 5</td><td>0, 0</td><td>0, 0</td></tr>
<tr><td>Player 1</td><td>$x_2^1$</td><td>10, 0</td><td>4, 4</td><td>0, 0</td></tr>
<tr><td></td><td>$x_3^1$</td><td>0, 0</td><td>0, 0</td><td>2, 2</td></tr>
</table>

(A) Confirm that there are two Nash equilibria of the one-shot game.

(B) In the absence of any discounting, show that, if the game is played $t$ times, where $t$ is greater than 4, there is a Nash equilibrium of the repeated game in which cooperation takes place except during the last three rounds.

(HINT: Suppose players begin playing the Pareto-superior Nash equilibrium of the one-shot game. Player 2 has an incentive to propose "cooperation" with payoffs of (5, 5) even though player 1 has an incentive to cheat and play $x_2^1$. The reason is that player 2 can credibly threaten to switch forever to $x_3^2$ – leading, after player 1's best reply, to the Pareto-inferior Nash equilibrium with payoffs (2, 2). This will act as a disincentive as long as there are enough rounds of the game left to play.)

## 12.2    The folk theorem for infinitely repeated games[6]

This section generalizes Prisoners' Dilemma by allowing for a continuum of strategies.

Consider a simple Cournot duopoly model. Two firms, each with constant marginal cost $c$, face a linear demand curve for their common product:

$$p = a - q_1 - q_2$$

Firm $i$'s profit is therefore:

$$U_i = (b - q_1 - q_2) q_i \quad \text{where } b \equiv a - c$$

In the single-round game, the unique Nash equilibrium (the "Nash–

---

[6] The analysis here follows Fudenberg, Levine and Maskin (1986). The expression "folk theorem" is used since it is not clear who proved what first.

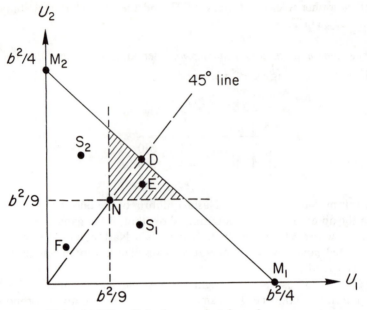

Figure 12.2 Payoffs in the one-shot duopoly game

Cournot solution") is for each player to choose $q_i = b/3$. The resulting profits are:

$$U_1^N = U_2^N = b^2/9$$

Firm $i$'s profit is maximized when the opponent does not produce at all. The profit-maximizing output is $b/2$ and the resulting monopoly profit is $U_i^M = b^2/4$. Finally, if firm 1 is a Stackelberg leader and firm 2 chooses its best response given $q_1$, the profit levels are:

$$(U_1^S, U_2^S) = (b^2/8, b^2/16)$$

Profit levels of the two firms under monopoly ($M_i$), Nash–Cournot ($N$), and Stackelberg play ($S_i$) are depicted in figure 12.2. The entire set of feasible profit levels is the region bounded by the axes and the line $M_1 M_2$. To see why this must be the case, note that joint profit can be written:

$$U_1 + U_2 = (b - q_1 - q_2)(q_1 + q_2)$$

Then joint profit is maximized with total output equal to the monopoly output $q^M = b/2$. Profit shares are then equal to output shares.

Consider point D on the 45° line. Output for each firm is $q^M/2 = b/4$ and profit is $b^2/8$. D is one possible outcome of "cooperative" play, to wit, where the firms split the monopoly output and profit equally. Arguing just as in the previous section, D can be attained under a number of different symmetrical or asymmetrical pairs of strategies – Nash equilibria of the infinitely repeated game when the future-valuation factor is sufficiently close to unity. One such is again the Grim strategy: switching to non-cooperative play (e.g., producing an output larger than $b/4$) *forever*, if an opponent ever deviates from his cooperative output level.

Once again, it turns out that cooperative outcomes can be supported by readiness to engage in non-cooperative behavior. But this does not tell us what the outcome will be. First of all, the single-round Nash–Cournot solution is also a Nash equilibrium of the infinitely repeated game. But, more important, *any* outcome that is Pareto-superior to the single-round Cournot solution can be supported by Nash equilibrium strategy-pairs in the infinitely repeated game. Consider point E to the north-east of N in figure 12.2, with associated output levels $q_1^E$ and $q_2^E$. Arguing just as above, if each player adopts the Grim strategy of responding to any deviation by switching to the Nash–Cournot strategy, then neither player will want to deviate.

All the points in the shaded region of figure 12.2 are therefore Nash equilibria of the infinitely repeated game, as long as the future-valuation factor is sufficiently close to unity. However, it will now be shown, the complete set of such equilibria will generally be much larger.

The intuition is fairly straightforward. Suppose that players 1 and 2 are currently playing $q_1$ and $q_2$. Suppose also that player 1 has available an alternative strategy $q_1^*$ which would make his opponent strictly worse off, regardless of her response. Then player 1 can threaten to switch for a long time to $q_1^*$ if player 2 deviates from $q_2$. As long as the future is discounted sufficiently mildly, carrying out such a threat would make agent 2 strictly worse off. Therefore it effectively deters player 2 from any deviation. If player 2 also has an effective threat, $q_1$ and $q_2$ are equilibrium strategies of the infinitely repeated game.

Let $q_i^*$ be the minimax strategy of player $i$. For player 1, this is the strategy that minimizes 2's payoff, given that player 2 is choosing her payoff-maximizing response. Formally $q_1^*$ solves:

$$\text{Min Max } U_2(q_1, q_2)$$
$$\;\; q_1 \quad q_2$$

Similarly, $q_2^*$ solves:

$$\text{Min Max } U_1(q_1, q_2)$$
$$\;\; q_2 \quad q_1$$

Let $U_i^*$ be the payoff of player $i$, given that his opponent has adopted her minimax strategy. It turns out that any payoff vector $(U_1, U_2)$ that is strictly preferred over $(U_1^*, U_2^*)$ is a subgame-perfect Nash equilibrium when the future-valuation factor is sufficiently large.

For the duopoly example, firm 1's minimax strategy is to "saturate the market" – choosing an output $q_1^*$ such that $p = a - q_1^* = c$. That is, price is driven down to marginal cost, even in the absence of sales by firm 2. Then firm 2's best response is to choose $q_2 = 0$, with resulting profit of zero for each of them. Since the same holds for firm 2, $(U_1^*, U_2^*) = (0, 0)$. So all the points in figure 12.2 north-east of the origin and within the region bounded by $M_1 M_2$ can be equilibria of the infinitely repeated game. This therefore includes the Stackelberg outcomes as well as outcomes such as F that are Pareto-inferior to the single-round Nash–Cournot outcome N.

Consider some output-pair $(q_1, q_2)$ and associated profit levels $(U_1, U_2)$ $> (U_1^*, U_2^*)$. That is, an output-pair such that both $U_1$ and $U_2$ are strictly positive. Let $U_i^0$ be the profit to firm $i$ if *both* firms choose their minimax strategies. Since price is equal to marginal cost when one firm produces $q_1^* = b$ units, the profit $U_i^0$ when both firms produce $b$ units is strictly less than zero.

We now sketch a proof of the following result.

Folk Theorem
Let $(U_1, U_2)$ be any feasible payoff vector strictly preferred over the minimax payoff vector $(U_1^*, U_2^*)$. Let $x^1$ and $x^2$ be the strategies in the single-round game that generate the payoffs $U_1$ and $U_2$. Then, if discounting is sufficiently mild, there exists a number $\tau$ such that the following strategy, when played by both players, is a subgame-perfect Nash equilibrium.
(A) Player $i$ plays $x^i$ as long as $(x^1, x^2)$ was played last period.
(B) In the event of any deviation from (A), both play the minimax strategy for $\tau$ periods and then starts again with (A).
(C) If there are any deviations while in phase (B), player $i$ begins phase (B) again.

To understand this result, first note that, with both firms playing their minimax strategies, payoffs are negative. Phase (B) therefore imposes a punishment upon any player who deviates. The basic idea is to design a scheme with a punishment phase sufficiently long to deter any deviations but not so long as to yield either player a negative present value. The present value of (B) to firm $i$ is:

$$PV_i(B) = \sum_{t=0}^{\tau-1} \delta^t U_i^0 + \sum_{t=\tau}^{\infty} \delta^t U_i = \frac{1-\delta^\tau}{1-\delta} U_i^0 + \frac{\delta^\tau}{1-\delta} U_i \qquad (12.2.1)$$

Now define:

$$\hat{U}_i = (1-\delta^\tau) U_i^0 + \delta^\tau U_i \qquad (12.2.2)$$

From (12.2.1):

$$\frac{\hat{U}_i}{1-\delta} = PV_i(B)$$

$$\sum_{t=0}^{\infty} \delta^t = \frac{1}{1-\delta}$$

And so, combining these expressions:

$$PV_i(B) = \sum_{t=0}^{\infty} \delta^t \, \hat{U}_i$$

That is, $\hat{U}_i$ is the steady-state equivalent of the punishment phase. From (12.2.2), for each $\delta$ sufficiently close to unity, $\tau$ can be chosen so that $\hat{U}_i$ satisfies $0 < \hat{U}_i < U_i/2$, $i = 1, 2$.

Suppose, then, that a player has deviated and the punishment phase is underway. For this phase of the strategy to be a Nash equilibrium of the associated subgame, any deviation must make the deviator no better off. Since his opponent is playing her minimax strategy, the most that agent $i$ can obtain immediately, if he deviates, is zero. But then his opponent begins phase $(B)$ again and the best response to phase $(B)$ yields $\hat{U}_i/(1-\delta)$. The net present value of any further deviation is therefore at most $\delta \hat{U}_i/(1-\delta)$. But, by not deviating, agent $i$ achieves a present value of $\hat{U}_i(1-\delta)$. It follows that the punishment phase strategies are best responses to one another.

It remains to show that neither agent has an incentive to make an initial deviation. Let $\bar{U}_i$ be the maximum possible one-period payoff from a deviation by agent $i$. The present value of any deviation is therefore bounded from above by:

$$\bar{U}_i + \frac{\delta}{1-\delta} \hat{U}_i = \frac{1}{1-\delta}[(1-\delta) \bar{U}_i + \delta \hat{U}_i]$$

But, by construction $\hat{U}_i < U_i/2$. Therefore, for $\delta$ sufficiently large the expression in brackets is strictly less than $U_i$. It follows that:

$$\bar{U}_i + \frac{\delta}{1-\delta} \hat{U}_i < \frac{U_i}{1-\delta}$$

The deviation therefore leaves agent $i$ strictly worse off.

With more than two players, the strategies required to sustain outcomes other than the Cournot solution of the single-period game are slightly more complicated. But essentially the same conclusion continues to hold. As long as the future-valuation factor is sufficiently close to unity, any outcome vector in the interior of the set of outcomes that Pareto-dominates the minimax outcome vector can be achieved as a subgame-perfect Nash equilibrium. In addition, while only symmetric games have been discussed, the analysis extends immediately to asymmetric games as well.

EXERCISES AND EXCURSIONS 12.2

*1 Large numbers in the infinitely repeated game*

In the formal theory, cooperative outcomes can be achieved via a Nash equilibrium no matter how many players participate. What assumptions, if any, make the model and such equilibria less plausible for large $n$?

*2 Cournot duopoly*

(A) For the example discussed above, suppose $a = 14$ and $c = 2$. Each firm has a capacity of 12 units per period. For what future-valuation factors $\delta$ is the symmetric efficient outcome achievable as a Nash equilibrium?

(B) Suppose $\delta$ is the smallest future-valuation factor for which the efficient symmetric outcome is achievable. What other efficient outcomes are achievable?

(C) What does your answer to (B) suggest about the effect of a lower $\delta$ upon the set of achievable outcomes?

*3 Cournot oligopoly*

Suppose there are $N$ firms with constant marginal costs $c_1, c_2, \ldots, c_N$ such that $c_1 \leqslant c_2 \leqslant \ldots \leqslant c_N$. They face a demand curve:

$$p = p\left(\sum_{i=1}^{N} q_i\right) = a - \sum_{i=1}^{N} q_i$$

(A) Show that, with $N = 2$, the strategies characterized in section 12.2 continue to be Nash equilibria.

(B) In the symmetric case with $c_1 = c_2 = \ldots = c_N$ the analysis of section 12.2 is easily generalized. Confirm that this is so.

(C) Can the analysis be extended to $N$ firms whose costs are different?

## 12.3    The role of chivalry

The results of the previous section suggest that cooperative outcomes are much more difficult to achieve for finitely as opposed to infinitely repeated games. However, up till now in this chapter it has been assumed that all players know the payoffs of their opponents and also know that all players

Table 12.4 *Prisoners' Dilemma* ($\alpha > \gamma > 0 > \beta$)

|          |         | Player 2 | |
|----------|---------|----------|---------|
|          |         | $x_1^2$  | $x_2^2$ |
|          | $x_1^1$ | $0, 0$   | $\alpha, \beta$ |
| Player 1 |         |          |         |
|          | $x_2^1$ | $\beta, \alpha$ | $\gamma, \gamma$ |

adopt individually rational strategies. It turns out that cooperation can be promoted if there is some uncertainty, to wit, a small possibility that an opponent is chivalrous and will always cooperate.[7]

Consider the Prisoners' Dilemma example once more, with payoffs as indicated in table 12.4.

As before, the unique single-round Nash equilibrium is for each player to choose Defect ($x_1$). And, once again, the sole NE is where $x_1$ is played in each round. However, suppose that a fraction $\varepsilon$ of the underlying population are chivalrous (or perhaps, stupid) and will irrationally play the cooperative strategy $x_2$ up to and including the final round $T$, so long as the opponent also plays Cooperate. However, if a chivalrous individual finds that his opponent has deviated in some period, he responds as in Grim, playing $x_1$ thereafter.

In these circumstances, it will be shown, for any $\varepsilon$ there exists a $\tau$ such that it is an equilibrium for all players to cooperate as long as there are more than $\tau$ periods left to play.

With imperfect information, it is necessary to take account of the players' beliefs about types if a deviation occurs early in the game (that is, if an out-of-equilibrium strategy is played). Suppose that no individual believes that a chivalrous player would ever deviate, without provocation, from the cooperative equilibrium.

Assume first that player 1 is fully rational. Once he comes to believe that his opponent is not chivalrous, the argument of section 12.1 applies. That is, his best reply is to play $x_1$ (Defect) thereafter. Moreover, by hypothesis, a chivalrous player responds to deviation from Cooperate in this way also. Suppose there has been cooperation for the first $T - \tau$ periods. If player 1 deviates with $\tau$ periods remaining, an upper bound to his payoff over the $\tau$ periods is just the immediate-period payoff $\alpha$. In all future periods his opponent plays $x_1$ and so the payoff is zero.

Next suppose that player 1, although not himself irrational, in effect mimics the chivalrous strategy. That is, with $\tau$ periods remaining he plays

[7] For our purposes it does not matter whether "chivalry" is pursued through stupidity, or because it is believed to be morally superior, or because the chivalrous player has payoffs for which cooperation is a dominant strategy.

$x_2$ and continues to do so until a deviation occurs, in which case he shifts irrevocably to $x_1$. With probability $\varepsilon$ his opponent is chivalrous. In this case, if player 1 always plays $x_2$ then so does his chivalrous opponent.[8] The present value of player 1's payoff over the last $\tau$ periods would then be:

$$\gamma(1+\delta+\ldots+\delta^{\tau-1})$$

But with probability $(1-\varepsilon)$, player 1's opponent is not chivalrous. If so, for player 1 the worst possible situation is for his opponent to play $x_1$ in all future rounds. Then player 1 has an immediate payoff of $\beta < 0$ and zero thereafter. It follows that player 1's expected payoff from mimicking the chivalrous strategy is bounded from below by:

$$\varepsilon\gamma(1+\delta+\delta^2+\ldots+\delta^{\tau-1})+(1-\varepsilon)\beta$$

Since the payoff to deviating is $\alpha$, cooperation is optimal as long as:

$$\varepsilon\gamma[1+\delta+\ldots+\delta^{\tau-1}]+(1-\varepsilon)\beta > \alpha$$

Rearranging, cooperation is optimal as long as:

$$1+\delta+\delta^2\ldots+\delta^{\tau-1} = \frac{1-\delta^\tau}{1-\delta} > \frac{\alpha-\beta}{\gamma\varepsilon}+\frac{\beta}{\gamma} \tag{12.3.1}$$

As $\tau$ becomes large, the left-hand side approaches $1/(1-\delta)$. Therefore, inequality (12.3.1) necessarily holds, for sufficiently large $\tau$, if:

$$\frac{1}{1-\delta} > \frac{\alpha-\beta}{\gamma\varepsilon}+\frac{\beta}{\gamma}$$

So cooperation is individually rational for non-chivalrous players during the early rounds of a game, as long as the future is discounted sufficiently mildly and the number of rounds is sufficiently great.

If the overall time period involved is short enough so that discounting can be ignored, condition (12.3.1) reduces to:

$$\tau > \frac{\alpha-\beta}{\gamma\varepsilon}+\frac{\beta}{\gamma} \tag{12.3.2}$$

It then follows that, no matter how small the proportion of chivalrous players in the underlying population, cooperation is achievable as an equilibrium outcome in all but a fixed number of rounds at the end of the game. Therefore, as $T$ becomes large, the *proportion* of periods in which cooperation is achievable approaches unity.

While only a simple example has been examined, the point is quite general. That is, for any game in which there are outcomes that strictly

---

[8] This is a feasible rather than an optimal strategy for player 1 since he can always do better by deviating in the final round.

Pareto-dominate single-period Nash equilibria, such outcomes are achievable except near the end of a finitely repeated game as long as some players are chivalrous. A striking point is the potentially large social payoff for a small amount of chivalrous (altruistic) behavior. While we cannot pursue the idea further here, this raises intriguing questions about the evolution of altruism.

## EXERCISES AND EXCURSIONS 12.3

### 1 Cooperation with N players

(A) For the finitely repeated Prisoners' Dilemma, extend the analysis to the $N$-person case.

(B) Holding other parameters fixed, does adding players lengthen or shorten the initial period of cooperation?

### 2 Cournot duopoly in a finitely repeated game

For the duopoly model of section 12.2, assume there is no discounting and that the game will be played a finite number of times. Show that any payoff vector that Pareto-dominates the payoffs in the single-period Nash equilibrium is achievable except near the end of the game, if there is a positive probability that one of the participants is "chivalrous" in an appropriately defined sense.

## 12.4    Building a reputation[9]

The previous sections considered long-term or repeated interactions among two or more decision-makers. Here we examine situations in which one party is a long-run player while the identity of the opponent or opponents changes. An example might be a retail store (the long-run player) dealing with transient customers (short-run players). Another example, much analyzed in the literature, is the interaction between a firm operating in a large number of markets (the long-run player) and potential entrants, each in one specific market (short-run player).

In each case the crucial distinction is that a short-run player makes a single decision while the long-run player makes a sequence of decisions. The issue addressed is how decisions by the long-run player influence the beliefs of short-run players in later rounds and thus affect the outcome of the game.

What follows is a variant of the "chain store" game (Selten, 1977),

[9] The initial papers on this topic are Kreps and Wilson (1982) and Milgrom and Roberts (1982). Fudenberg and Levine (1989) have simplified and generalized the early results.

Table 12.5 *Chain store game*

|  |  | Potential entrant | |
|  |  | Enter | Out |
|  |  | --- | --- |
| Chain store | Match | 1, 2 | 4, 0 |
|  | Undercut | 0, −1 | 3, 0 |

which is an extension of the entry game of chapter 9. The chain store operates in *n* markets. In each of *n* periods there is an entry threat in one of these markets. The potential entrant must choose whether to enter or stay out. Simultaneously, the chain store prepares a pricing response in case entry occurs, the choices being to acquiesce, matching the entrant's price, or to fight by undercutting.

Suppose payoffs are as in table 12.5.[10] The chain store's best response, if the potential entrant chooses Enter, is Match. Moreover, given that the chain store chooses Match the potential entrant's best response is Enter. The pair (Match, Enter) is therefore a Nash equilibrium (NE) when the game is played only once. Indeed it is the unique Nash equilibrium.[11]

Now consider the game from the point of view of the chain store. If it could establish a reputation for toughness by fighting early entrants, later ones might be discouraged. If so, a payoff higher than the NE payoff of 1 would be possible. However, just as in section 12.1, the argument breaks down in the final stage. Since there are no future entrants following her, the last entrant need not fear that the chain store will play tough to build a reputation. That is, the threat of choosing Undercut is no longer credible. As a result the last-stage equilibrium strategy-pair is (Match, Enter).

But then the same argument can be applied to the penultimate stage and so on. This is the "chain store paradox." Despite a potentially large long-run payoff, the chain store is unable to build a reputation for toughness.

But this negative conclusion is not robust with respect to small changes in the model. In particular, dramatically different results can emerge if there is imperfect information about the payoffs of the long-run player. Specifically, suppose that with positive probability the long-run player has a payoff matrix for which Undercut is his dominant strategy (in the

[10] While not numerically identical, these payoffs are qualitatively similar to those in table 8.3 except in one respect. Where the earlier chapter had the incumbent's payoff remain the same as between (Match, Out) and (Undercut, Out), here the chain store is better off under (Match, Out) than (Undercut, Out). The explanation is that we are assuming here that *preparing* to fight a potential entrant is costly even if entry does not actually take place.

[11] Recall that in chapter 9 the alternative Nash equilibrium (Undercut, Out) was not a sequential equilibrium. That alternative non-credible NE has been eliminated here by adjusting the payoffs (see previous footnote).

Table 12.6 *Payoff matrix with a "strong" long-run player*

|  |  | Potential entrant | |
|  |  | Enter | Out |
|---|---|---|---|
| Chain store | Match | 1, 2 | 4, 0 |
|  | Undercut | 2, −1 | 4, 0 |

repeated game).[12] Given that entrants are uncertain about his payoffs, the long-run player, regardless of his actual payoffs should choose the strategy Undercut. For then, with each round of play, short-run players will apply Bayes' Theorem and revise upward their assessment of the probability that the long-run players does have Undercut as his dominant strategy. As will be seen, this probability rises at least geometrically each time there is an entry. From this it follows that the probability reaches unity after the number of entries has reached some bound $\bar{m}$, independent of the length of the game. For most of a sufficiently long game, therefore, the mimicking strategy deters entry.

Specifically, suppose there is a positive probability that the chain store's technology yields the payoff matrix of table 12.6:

For this "strong" chain store, Undercut is the dominant strategy of the $n$-period game. Clearly, if a potential entrant knows for sure that she is up against a strong chain store, her best reply is to choose Out. Moreover, as long as the probability that the chain store is strong is sufficiently high, Out remains the best reply.

Let $\varepsilon$ be the entrants' prior probability that the chain store is strong (with the payoffs just shown) and $1 - \varepsilon$ the probability that it is weak (with the payoffs of table 12.5). For $\varepsilon$ sufficiently close to 1, a potential entrant will always choose Out since she is almost sure to find the chain store playing Undercut. Let $\bar{\pi}$ be the borderline probability such that, for all $\varepsilon > \bar{\pi}$, a potential entrant will choose Out regardless of the strategy chosen by a "weak" chain store.

In terms of our numerical example, if a weak chain store also were to choose Undercut, a potential entrant will always choose Out. If the weak chain store chooses Match but the probability of a strong chain store is $\bar{\pi}$, the expected payoff to Enter is:

$$\bar{\pi}(-1) + (1 - \bar{\pi})(2) = 2 - 3\bar{\pi}$$

Since the payoff to Out is zero, in our example the potential entrant's best choice is Out for all $\varepsilon > \bar{\pi} = \frac{2}{3}$.

---

[12] Actually, all we require is that Undercut be the unique sequential equilibrium strategy of the repeated game.

Now, if the first potential entrant's prior probability that the chain store is strong exceeds $\frac{2}{3}$, she will choose Out rather than Enter. If so, lacking information for updating his prior beliefs, the second potential entrant will choose Out also, and so on.

Alternatively, now suppose that the prior probability belief of potential entrants is that $\varepsilon$ is less than $\frac{2}{3}$, so there could be at least one initial entrant. We know that a weak chain store's short-run equilibrium strategy is to choose Match. However, suppose that it chooses to disguise this fact and chooses Undercut over $t$ initial periods. Then potential entrants will employ Bayes' Theorem to update their estimate of the probability that the chain store is strong.

Let $x_{2t}$ be the action taken by the entrant in round $t$ and let the vector $x_{1t}$ be the chain store's planned responses to each of the entrant's possible actions. Then $x_t = (x_{1t}, x_{2t})$ completely describes the play of the game in round $t$. Also let $X^{t-1} = (x_1, x_2, ..., x_{t-1})$ be the complete history of the play of the game up to round $t$. Since it will simplify the discussion, it will be assumed that $X^{t-1}$ is observable in round $t$. That is, the chain store's planned responses – even if not actually executed – are observable immediately after a round is played.[13] (Thus, even if entry did not occur, the chain store's *intention* to undercut in response to entry might have involved some visible preparation, for example printing new price lists.)

As Fudenberg and Levine (1989) have observed, there is a simple rule for updating entrants' beliefs about the chain store's type. First of all, if the history $X^{t-1}$ contains a match, $\Pr(S \mid X^{t-1}) = 0$, since the strong chain store always chooses Undercut ($x_{1t} = U$ for all $t$). Consider then a history $X^{t-1}$ that contains no matches, that is, $x_{1\tau} = U$, $\tau = 1, ..., t-1$. Applying Bayes' Theorem:

$$\Pr(S \mid x_{1t} = U, x_{2t}, X^{t-1}) = \frac{\Pr(S, x_{1t} = U \mid x_{2t}, X^{t-1})}{\Pr(x_{1t} = U \mid x_{2t}, X^{t-1})} \tag{12.4.1}$$

Since $x_{1t} = U$ for a strong chain store:

$$\Pr(S, x_{1t} = U \mid x_{2t}, X^{t-1}) = \Pr(S \mid x_{2t}, X^{t-1}) \tag{12.4.2}$$

Moreover, since the entrant knows the history of the game but not the chain store type, the entrant's strategy can be expressed as:

$$x_{2t} = f(X^{t-1}) \tag{12.4.3}$$

Substituting (12.4.2) and (12.4.3) into (12.4.1):

$$\Pr(S \mid x_{1t} = U, x_{2t}, X^{t-1}) = \frac{\Pr(S \mid X^{t-1})}{\Pr(x_{1t} = U \mid X^{t-1})}$$

---

[13] An exercise at the end of this section extends the analysis to the case where the chain store's planned action is only observable if entry takes place. The analysis is essentially identical.

Therefore, for any history $X^t$ that contains no matches:

$$\Pr(S|X^t) = \frac{\Pr(S|X^{t-1})}{\Pr(x_{1t} = U|X^{t-1})} \tag{12.4.4}$$

It is this relationship that drives the results. First of all, since the denominator is a probability:

$$\Pr(S|X^t) \geqslant \Pr(S|X^{t-1})$$

Second, as already argued, there is some $\bar{\pi} > 1$ such that entry will only take place if:

$$\Pr(x_{1t} = U|X^{t-1}) \leqslant \bar{\pi}$$

Therefore, for any round in which there is entry:

$$\Pr(S|X^t) \geqslant \left(\frac{1}{\bar{\pi}}\right) \Pr(S|X^{t-1})$$

Since the initial probability of a strong chain store is $\varepsilon$, if there are $m$ periods of entry then, in any subsequent round $t$:

$$\Pr(S|X^t) = \frac{\Pr(S|X^t)}{\Pr(S|X^{t-1})} \frac{\Pr(S|X^{t-1})}{\Pr(S|X^{t-2})} \cdots \frac{\Pr(S|X^1)}{\Pr(S|X^0)} \varepsilon \tag{12.4.5}$$

$$\geqslant \left(\frac{1}{\bar{\pi}}\right)^m \varepsilon$$

Let $\bar{m}$ be the largest integer such that $(1/\bar{\pi})^m \varepsilon \leqslant 1$, that is, $\bar{m}$ satisfies:

$$\frac{\ln \varepsilon}{\ln \bar{\pi}} - 1 < \bar{m} \leqslant \frac{\ln \varepsilon}{\ln \bar{\pi}} \tag{12.4.6}$$

Then, if there were more than $\bar{m}$ entries in the first $t$ rounds:

$$\Pr(S|X^t) > 1$$

which is impossible. Therefore, there will be at most $\bar{m}$ rounds in which beliefs by the potential entrant will be such as to stimulate entry.

What has been established is that a weak chain store prepared to fight over the early phase of the game will face at most $\bar{m}$ actual entrants. Such a chain store therefore has, in the numerical example, payoff 0 in at most $\bar{m}$ periods and payoff 3 in the remaining $n - \bar{m}$ periods. Taking the worst-case scenario in which entry occurs in the first $\bar{m}$ rounds, the present value for a weak chain store of mimicking a strong one is bounded from below by:

$$PV^0 = (1 + \delta + \ldots + \delta^{\bar{m}-1})(0) + (\delta^{\bar{m}} + \delta^{\bar{m}+1} + \ldots + \delta^{n-1})(3)$$

$$\equiv \hat{\alpha}\left(\frac{1-\delta^n}{1-\delta}\right)$$

Table 12.7 *Lower bound to mimicking*

| Number of periods $n$ | Single-period bound $\hat{\alpha}_n$ |
|---|---|
| 48 | 0·9 |
| 54 | 1·0 |
| 60 | 1·1 |
| 120 | 1·6 |
| $\infty$ | 2·8 |

where:

$$\hat{\alpha} \equiv 3\delta^{\bar{m}} \frac{1-\delta^{n-\bar{m}}}{1-\delta^n} \tag{12.4.7}$$

Note that a payoff of $\hat{\alpha}$ for $n$ periods has a present value of:

$$\left(\frac{1-\delta^n}{1-\delta}\right)\hat{\alpha}$$

Therefore, $\hat{\alpha}$ is the steady-state equivalent single-period payoff.

It is plausible to assume that if a chain store chooses Match all future potential entrants will be certain that they are up against a weak opponent. Then, if there is entry in the first round and the chain store chooses Match, there will be entry in every round. If so, the chain store would achieve a payoff of 1 per period, that is, a present value of:

$$(1+\delta+\dots+\delta^{n-1})(1) = \frac{1-\delta^n}{1-\delta}$$

Since $\bar{m}$ is independent of $\delta$, $3\delta^{\bar{m}}$ exceeds 1 for all sufficiently large $\delta$. Moreover, as $n$ becomes large $\delta^{n-\bar{m}}$ approaches zero.

Therefore, from (12.4.7), as long as the future-valuation factor $\delta$ is sufficiently small and the number of time periods is sufficiently long, $\hat{\alpha}$ exceeds unity and the strategy of mimicking is indeed the equilibrium strategy.

To get an idea of the strength of this result, suppose that the chain store game is played monthly. An *annual* discount rate of 12% corresponds to a *monthly* discount rate of about 0·95%, so that the *monthly* future-valuation factor is $\delta \approx 0.99$. From (12.4.6), if there is a 0·04 prior probability that the chain store is strong, the number of entries is bounded above by:

$$\bar{m} = \ln(0.04)/\ln(\tfrac{2}{3}) \approx 8$$

Under the mimicking strategy the steady-state equivalent one-period payoff is bounded from below by $\hat{\alpha}$. From (12.4.7), $\hat{\alpha}$ is readily computed.

It follows from table 12.7 that, as long as the number of periods (months) exceeds 54, mimicking is the equilibrium strategy for the weak chain store. Of course, with a longer time horizon, the gain to mimicking is greater. In the limit, as $n$ goes to infinity the bound approaches 2·8. That is, the payoff to mimicking is close to the payoff of 3 that would ensue if the chain store were able to *commit* itself to always fight an entrant. It should also be noted that the actual payoff to mimicking is greater than the bound established above. The reason is that the "worst case" scenario used to compute the bound assumes that entry occurs in the first $m$ rounds. In fact, however, there will be no entry until late in the game. Early in the game, when both a strong and a weak chain store play Undercut, the potential entrant's best choice is Out.[14]

While we have focused on an example in which the long-run player is one of only two possible types, the analysis is exactly the same with any number of types. The only factors affecting the bound are (i) the prior probability $\varepsilon$ that one or more types will be strong (will always choose Undercut), and (ii) the critical probability $\pi$ (that the long-run player is strong) above which short-run players will always choose Out. As one of the exercises shows, the analysis also extends to the case in which there are different types of short-run players as well. The key, once again, is that there is a long-run player who will always choose Undercut regardless of the type of opponent he faces.

## EXERCISES AND EXCURSIONS 12.4

### 1 Building a reputation for toughness with more than two strategies

Suppose that a chain store can choose mild fighting or hard fighting. The complete payoff matrix is as follows:

|             |            | Potential entrant | |
|-------------|------------|---------|--------|
|             |            | Enter   | Out    |
| Chain store | Match      | 1,  2   | 4, 0   |
|             | Mild fight | $\frac{1}{2}, -\frac{1}{2}$ | 3, 0 |
|             | Hard fight | 0, $-1$ | 0, 0   |

Suppose that there are two other types of chain store. Type $M$, for which the prior probability is $\varepsilon_M$, has a dominant strategy of fighting mildly. Type

---

[14] Near the end of the game the weak chain store switches to the matching strategy with probability 1. Moreover, as Kreps and Wilson (1982) show, it is quite possible for there to be a middle phase in which both players adopt mixed strategies.

$H$, for which the prior probability is $\varepsilon_H$, has a dominant strategy of fighting hard. The future-valuation factor is $\delta < 1$ and the number of periods is $n = \infty$. You should assume that the chain store's strategy is observable, ex post, even if the entrant stays out.

(A) Let $m^*$ be the maximum number of entries if the chain store chooses Mild Fight and let $m^{**}$ be the maximum number of entries if the chain store chooses Hard Fight. Show that, if $\varepsilon_H = \varepsilon_m$:

$$m^* \approx 2m^{**}$$

(B) If the chain store matches it earns a return per period of 1. Define $v^* = (1-\delta)PV^*$ and $v^{**} = (1-\delta)PV^{**}$ where $PV^*$ is the present value of fighting mildly in the early rounds and $PV^{**}$ is the present value of fighting hard. (You should assume the worst-case scenario so that all entry takes place in the initial rounds.) Depict $v^*$ and $v^{**}$ in a neat figure as functions of $\delta$. By examining the derivatives at $\delta = 1$ confirm that, for all $\delta$ sufficiently close to 1:

$$v^{**}(\delta) > v^*(\delta) > 1$$

Mimicking the hard fighter is then the chain store's best strategy.

(C) Show also that, for the parameter values in the problem, the strategy of fighting mildly is never optimal.

(D) If the payoff to the chain store when it matches is $1-\theta$, confirm that, for $\theta$ sufficiently close to $\frac{1}{2}$, there are values of $\delta$ for which fighting mildly is optimal. Is it still the case that the chain store will fight hard for $\delta$ sufficiently close to 1?

(E) How would your answer to (B) change if $\varepsilon_M > \varepsilon_H$?

## 2 Building a reputation with two types of entrant

For a type-1 entrant, payoffs are as in table 12.5. For a type-2 entrant the payoff matrix is as follows:

|                  |          | Type-2 entrant | |
|                  |          | Enter | Out |
| --- | --- | --- | --- |
|                  | Match    | $\frac{1}{2}, 3$ | 4, 0 |
| Weak chain store |          | | |
|                  | Undercut | 0, 1 | 3, 0 |

With prior probability $\varepsilon$ the chain store is strong and has a dominant strategy of choosing to fight. The number of rounds $n$ is finite and the future-valuation factor $\delta$ is strictly less than unity.

(A) Explain why the chain store will choose to acquiesce if the prior probability of a type-2 entrant is sufficiently high.

(B) Suppose instead that the prior probability of a type-2 entrant is low. Does it necessarily follow that a weak chain store's optimal strategy is to mimic and fight any entrant in the early rounds?

(C) Will it fight forever?

## 3 Reputation-building with different types of long-run player

With probability $\varepsilon$ the chain store is strong and always fights. With probability $\beta(1-\varepsilon)$ the chain store is weak with payoffs given by table 12.5. With probability $(1-\beta)(1-\varepsilon)$ the chain store is less weak with payoffs as follows:

|  |  | Enter | Out |
|---|---|---|---|
|  | Match | 2, 0 | 4, 0 |
| Less weak | Undercut | 0, $-1$ | 3, 0 |
| chain store |  |  |  |

(A) Obtain conditions under which both the weak and less weak chain stores will choose to build a reputation by mimicking the strong chain store and undercutting any entrant.

(B) If these conditions do not hold, is it possible that one type of chain store would choose to mimic while the other would not? Explain.

## 4 Sequential versus Stackelberg equilibrium strategies

What is wrong with the following argument?

> Each entrant knows that there is a small probability that the chain store is tough. She knows also that a soft chain store has an incentive to mimic the tough chain store and fight any entrant. Given this, no potential entrant will ever wish to fight. Therefore the bound discussed in the text greatly overstates the cost of establishing a reputation.

## 5* Building a reputation when the chain store's action is unobservable unless entry takes place

Consider the chain store game summarized in tables 12.5 and 12.6 but suppose that the chain store's action is observable only if entry takes place. Then after round $t$ one of three possible outcomes will be observed: Out, In/Match and In/Undercut. Symbolize this as: $h_t \in \{O, (U, I), (M, I)\}$.

(A) Explain why $\Pr(S \mid h_t = O, H^{t-1}) = \Pr(S \mid H^{t-1})$.

(B) Appeal to the argument of the section above to show that:

$$\Pr(S \mid x_{1t} = U, x_{2t} = I, H^{t-1}) = \frac{\Pr(S \mid H^{t-1})}{\Pr(x_{1t} = U \mid H^{t-1})}$$

* Starred questions may be somewhat more difficult.

(C) Hence show that, for any observable history $H^t$ that contains no matches:

$$\Pr(S\,|\,H^\tau) \geqslant \Pr(S\,|\,H^{\tau-1}), \quad \tau = 1, \ldots, t$$

(D) Suppose the chain store always chooses $x_{1\tau} = U$ over the first $t$ periods. Show that the maximum number of times that entry takes place is the same as if the chain store's actions were observable ex post.

(E) Explain why the equilibrium in this game will be for the weak chain store to adopt a mixed strategy except in the final rounds when it always chooses Match.

## 6 The "chain-store paradox" paradox

An entrant may stay out and get nothing (0), or may enter. If she enters, the incumbent may fight or acquiesce. The entrant gets $b$ if the incumbent acquiesces, and $b-1$ if he fights, where $0 < b < 1$. There are two types of incumbent, both receiving $a > 1$ if there is no entry. If there is a fight, the strong incumbent gets 0 and the weak incumbent gets $-1$; if a strong incumbent acquiesces he gets $-1$, a weak incumbent 0.

Only the incumbent knows whether he is weak or strong; it is common knowledge that the entrant *a priori* believes she has a $\pi_0$ chance of facing a strong incumbent. Define:

$$\gamma = \frac{\pi_0}{1-\pi_0} \frac{1-b}{b}$$

(A) Sketch the extensive form of this game.

(B) Define a sequential equilibrium of this game.

(C) Show that if $\gamma \neq 1$ there is a unique sequential equilibrium, and that if $\gamma > 1$ entry never occurs while if $\gamma < 1$ entry always occurs.

Now suppose that the incumbent plays a second round against a different entrant who knows the result of the first round. The incumbent's goal is to maximize the sum of his payoffs in the two rounds.

(D) If $\gamma > 1$, show there is a sequential equilibrium with no entry in either round.

(E) If $\gamma < 1$, show that the following scenario involves Nash equilibrium strategies for the three players. There is entry on the first round. The second entrant comes in if there is a fight in the first round and stays out if there is no fighting. Both types of incumbent acquiesce in the first round.

(F) Explain carefully why this is also a sequential equilibrium.

(G) Does the weak communication test (see chapter 9) rule out either of the equilibria in (D) and (E) above?

## REFERENCES AND SELECTED READINGS

Aumann, Robert and Shapley, Lloyd, "Long Term Competition: A Game Theoretic Analysis," mimeo, Hebrew University of Jerusalem, 1976.

Benoit, J. P. and Krishna, Vijay, "Finitely Repeated Games," *Econometrica*, 53 (1985), 905–22.

Boyd, Robert and Lorberbaum, Jeffrey P., "No Pure Strategy is Evolutionarily Stable in the Repeated Prisoner's Dilemma Game," *Nature*, 327 (7 May 1987), 58–9.

Friedman, J., "A Noncooperative Equilibrium for Supergames," *Econometrica*, 38 (1971), 1–12.

Fudenberg, D. and Levine, D., "Reputation and Equilibrium Selection in Games with a Patient Player," *Econometrica*, 47 (1989), 759–78.

Fudenberg, D., Levine, D., and Maskin, E. S., "The Folk Theorem in Repeated Games with Discounting and with Incomplete Information," *Econometrica*, 54 (May 1986), 533–54.

Kreps, D. and Wilson, R., "Reputation and Imperfect Information," *Journal of Economic Theory*, 27 (1982), 253–79.

Milgrom, Paul and Roberts, John, "Limit Pricing and Entry Under Incomplete Information," *Econometrica*, 50 (1982), 443–60.

Rubinstein, Ariel, "Equilibrium in Supergames with the Overtaking Criterion," *Journal of Economic Theory*, 21 (1979), 1–9.

Selten, R., "The Chain Store Paradox," *Theory and Decision*, 9 (1977), 127–59.

# Index of topics

# Index of names